HART'S POSTS

HART'S POSTSCRIPT

Essays on the Postscript to
The Concept of Law

Edited by
JULES COLEMAN

OXFORD
UNIVERSITY PRESS

OXFORD
UNIVERSITY PRESS

Great Clarendon Street, Oxford OX2 6DP

Oxford University Press is a department of the University of Oxford.
It furthers the University's objective of excellence in research, scholarship,
and education by publishing worldwide in

Oxford New York

Athens Auckland Bangkok Bogotá Buenos Aires
Cape Town Chennai Dar es Salaam Delhi Florence Hong Kong Istanbul
Karachi Kolkata Kuala Lumpur Madrid Melbourne Mexico City Mumbai
Nairobi Paris São Paulo Shanghai Singapore Taipei Tokyo Toronto Warsaw
and associated companies in Berlin Ibadan

Oxford is a registered trade mark of Oxford University Press
in the UK and in certain other countries

Published in the United States
by Oxford University Press Inc., New York

British Library Cataloguing in Publication Data

Data available

Library of Congress Cataloging in Publication Data

Hart's postscript: essays on the postscript to The concept of law/edited by Jules
L. Coleman.
p. cm.
Includes bibliographical references and index.
1. Hart, H. L. A. (Herbert Lionel Adolphus), 1907—Concept of law.
2. Jurisprudence—Methodology. 3. Semantics (Law) 4. Law—Philosophy.
I. Coleman, Jules L.   II. Hart, H. L. A. (Herbert Lionel Adolphus), 1907—Concept of law.
K237.H315 2001   340'.1—dc21   2001021840
ISBN 0–19–829908–7
ISBN 0–19–924362–X (pbk.)

1 3 5 7 9 10 8 6 4 2

Typeset by Cambrian Typesetters, Frimley, Surrey
Printed in Great Britain
on acid-free paper by
T.J. International Ltd, Padstow, Cornwall

Preface

The Concept of Law is the most influential and important book in the analytic tradition of jurisprudence written in the second half of the twentieth century. The quality of the work it has spawned—from Joseph Raz's *Authority of Law* to Ronald Dworkin's *Law's Empire*—is testimony to its genius. That a field of inquiry that was once nearly barren is now talent-laden is its lasting legacy. Unfortunately, Hart did not pursue many of the themes that he brought to attention in the book; subjecting them to critical inquiry, and further developing and extending the argument, was left to others. None of Hart's critics has been more influential than Ronald Dworkin. Early in his career Dworkin focused his critical energies on some of the claims most central to Hart's theory, for example the rule of recognition, judicial discretion, and the separability of law and morality. Even in these critical reflections, Dworkin was laying the foundation for his own general jurisprudence: a jurisprudence that builds on the perceived shortcomings in Hart's view in much the same way that Hart's theory builds by filling in the gaps he located in Austin's account.

Over the last ten years of his life, Hart undertook to produce a response to Dworkin's objections and to explore some of the more recent developments in jurisprudence in the years since the publication of the book. By the time of his death, only his response to Dworkin was sufficiently well developed to see the light of day. Consequently, the book's editors, Joseph Raz and Penelope Bullock, published an edited and revised version of Hart's response as the Postscript to the second edition. The Postscript represents Hart's final reflections on his substantive and methodological commitments as well as on Dworkin's objections to both. The Postscript is important not just because it sets out Hart's response to Dworkin but also because it provides us with a tool for interpreting the original text.

Hart pursued several themes in the Postscript. Among the most important of these are: (1) the extent to which his theory of the concept of law has a semantic basis—whether Hart's positivism is rooted in a criterial semantics; (2) whether Hart sees himself as an exclusive or an inclusive legal positivist; (3) whether his analysis of the concept of law is descriptive or normative; that is, whether jurisprudence—or his particular version of it—is in the first instance an activity of moral/political philosophy.

The essays collected here, written by some of the world's leading legal theorists, address these issues. Joseph Raz, Timothy Endicott, and Nicos Stavropoulos explore the alleged semantic foundations and commitments of Hart's jurisprudence. Jules Coleman, Scott Shapiro, Andrei Marmor,

Ben Zipursky, and Kenneth Himma explore the nature of Hart's commitment to the conventionality of law and the compatibility of that commitment with other of his commitments—especially his claim that the function of law is to guide conduct. Stephen Perry, Brian Leiter, Liam Murphy, and Jeremy Waldron discuss aspects of Hart's methodological approach to jurisprudence, especially its nature and limits. These essays are not only essential reading for anyone working in contemporary analytic jurisprudence. They represent the efforts of the contributors fittingly to honour Hart's memory as well as his contribution to their scholarship.

J. L. C.
New Haven, Connecticut

Contents

CONTENTS

Notes on Contributors

Jules Coleman is a Wesley Newcomb Hohfeld Professor of Jurisprudence at Yale Law School and Professor of Philosophy at Yale University.

Timothy A. O. Endicott is a Fellow of St Catherine's College, Oxford.

Kenneth Einar Himma is a Lecturer in Philosophy at the University of Washington.

Brian Leiter is Charles I. Francis Professor in Law, Professor of Philosophy, and Director of the Law and Philosophy Program, The University of Texas at Austin.

Andrei Marmor is a Professor in the Faculty of Law, Tel Aviv University.

Liam Murphy is Professor of Law and Professor of Philosophy, New York University.

Stephen R. Perry is John J. O'Brien Professor of Law and Professor of Philosophy, University of Pennsylvania.

Joseph Raz is Professor of Philosophy of Law at the University of Oxford.

Scott J. Shapiro is Professor of Law, Benjamin N. Cardozo School of Law, Yeshiva University.

Nicos Stavropoulos is University Lecturer in Legal Theory, University of Oxford, and Fellow of Mansfield College, Oxford.

Jeremy Waldron is Maurice and Hilda Friedman Professor of Law and Director of the Center for Law and Philosophy at Columbia University.

Benjamin C. Zipursky is an Associate Professor at Fordham University School of Law.

1

Two Views of the Nature of the Theory of Law
A Partial Comparison

JOSEPH RAZ

In *Law's Empire*, Ronald Dworkin has advanced a new theory of law, complex and intriguing. He calls it law as integrity. But in some ways the more radical and surprising claim he makes is that not only were previous legal philosophers mistaken about the nature of law, they were also mistaken about the nature of the philosophy of law or jurisprudence. Perhaps it is possible to summarize his main contentions on the nature of jurisprudence in three theses. First, jurisprudence is interpretive: 'General theories of law . . . aim to interpret the main point and structure of legal practice' (*LE*, 90).[1] Second, legal philosophy cannot be a semantic account of the word 'law'. Legal philosophers 'cannot produce useful semantic theories of law' (*id.*). Third, legal philosophy or jurisprudence 'is the general part of adjudication, silent prologue to any decision at law' (*id.*).

Of these, the only surprising aspect of the first thesis is that it should be thought new and different from what many contemporary legal philosophers took themselves to be doing. An interpretation of something is an explanation[2] of its meaning. Many if not all legal philosophers think of themselves as explaining the essential features of legal practices, and explaining the relations between them and related phenomena such as other forms of social organization, other social practices, and morality. H. L. A. Hart explained in the Postscript to *The Concept of Law* that his aim was 'to give an explanatory and clarifying account of law as a complex social and political institution with a rule-governed (and in that sense "normative") aspect'.[3] In other words, he was seeking to interpret the complex social institution the law is. If Hart and others did not make as extensive a use of 'interpretation' as Dworkin does, this is in part because fashions dictate the use of terms, and because they may well have wished

I am grateful to Andrei Marmor, Grant Lamond, Penelope Bulloch, and Timothy Endicott for very helpful comments on a draft of this article.

[1] *LE* refers to Ronald Dworkin, *Law's Empire* (1986). Page numbers in parentheses are from this 1986 edition.

[2] Except that interpretations through performance (of music, a play, etc.) display rather than explain the meaning of what they interpret.

[3] H. L. A. Hart, Postcript, *The Concept of Law* (1994), 239.

to avoid being associated with theories that, in their eyes, misconstrued the nature of interpretation.[4]

Dworkin's conception of legal philosophy surprises not in regarding its task as interpretive, but in the arguments he deploys to support it, in particular the argument he dubbed the 'semantic sting'.[5] The argument purports to establish the second thesis, that is, a theory of law cannot be an explanation of the meaning of the word 'law'. Until Dworkin published his semantic sting argument, many, including myself, took this second thesis to be as firm and as uncontroversial as anything in legal philosophy at the time. It was, therefore, surprising that Dworkin saw a need to argue for it, and even more surprising that he thought that in doing so he was rebutting the conceptions of legal philosophy endorsed by many philosophers who did not think of themselves as in the business of explaining the meaning of the word 'law'.[6]

It seemed that no one need pay much attention to the semantic sting. It may be a sting, but an idle one. It stings no one. Thus, Hart starts his reply by simply denying that the argument applies to his theory:

Though in the first chapter *of Law's Empire* I am classed with Austin as a semantic theorist and so as deriving a plain-fact positivist theory of law from the meaning of the word 'law', and suffering from the semantic sting, in fact nothing in my book or in anything else I have written supports such an account of my theory. Thus, my doctrine that developed municipal legal systems contain a rule of recognition specifying the criteria for the identification of the laws which courts have to apply may be mistaken, but I nowhere base this doctrine on the mistaken idea that it is part of the meaning of the word 'law' that there should be such a rule of recognition in all legal systems.[7]

But one must wonder why Dworkin did not take this answer, of which, as I pointed out, he was aware, as sufficient. Hart himself must have puzzled over this, and, as the rest of his reply in the Postscript shows, he realized that the matter is not that straightforward.

---

[4] In one of the best studies of Hart's work, D. N. MacCormick has described Hart's internal point of view, reliance on which was central to his methodological innovation, as 'hermeneutic'. See *H. L. A. Hart* (1981), 37–40. I remember a conversation with Hart in which it was clear that he saw nothing wrong with the description. He was more ambiguous about the attractiveness of the word.

[5] His other argument, consisting in a new and challenging account of the nature of interpretation, shows not that other theorists did not see their accounts as explanations of the meaning of—i.e. as interpretations of—social practices, but that they did not share his understanding of interpretation. I will not discuss Dworkin's own account of interpretation in the present essay.

[6] By the time the book was published, Dworkin was aware of the fact that Hart and others did not think of themselves as explaining the meaning of 'law'. Nevertheless, he persisted in thinking that that was exactly what Hart was doing. Cf. Dworkin, *Law's Empire*, *supra* n. 1, at 418 n. 29.

[7] Hart, *The Concept of Law*, *supra* n. 3, at 246.

In this essay my aim is to explain (1) why Dworkin was wrong to think that Hart and others were concerned with the meaning of the word 'law'; (2) why nevertheless if the semantic sting is a good argument against explanations of the meaning of the word 'law' it is also a good argument against any explanation of the concept of law, including that which Hart provides; and (3) why it is a bad argument. My reason for this last conclusion will be different from Hart's. Hart's response is to deflect the argument: it may sting, but I (Hart) am not its target. I agree with Dworkin (though not entirely for his reasons) that if the argument is good then Hart's explanation of law is stung by it. I do not think, however, that the argument is valid. I will then (4) explain some mistakes that may have led Dworkin to endorse his third thesis about the nature of legal philosophy, namely the thesis that jurisprudence is a silent prologue to any legal decision.

I. PHILOSOPHY OF LANGUAGE IN THE SERVICE OF LEGAL PHILOSOPHY

At its most fundamental, legal philosophy is an inquiry into the nature of law, and the fundamental features of legal institutions and practices. Yet some writers think that it is, at least in part, an inquiry into the semantic meaning of words, or of some words, such as 'law' or 'rights'. Why do they think so and to what extent are they right?

The first point to emphasize is that our question is about the relevance and role of questions about the meaning of words in legal philosophy, not about the relevance of all questions of meaning. 'Meaning' is sometimes used to mean point or value. 'What is the meaning of law?' can mean 'What is the point or value of law?' This is what 'meaning' means in 'the meaning of life'. Alternatively, meaning is often used to refer to content. 'What did he mean?' means something like: 'What did he say?' 'What was the content of his utterance?' 'What is the meaning of this law?' can mean 'What is the content of this law? Or what is its significance, its aims or likely consequences?'[8] When referring to semantics I will use the term narrowly to refer to the study of the meaning of words, phrases, sentences, and other linguistic elements.[9]

---

[8] When I remarked that interpretation is the explanation of the meaning of its object, I used 'meaning' broadly to include non-semantic meaning. Explaining the meaning of words ('bachelor' means an unmarried male, etc.) is never an interpretation, and explaining the literal meaning of sentences only given some special circumstances.

[9] In that narrow sense of 'semantics', one needs more than semantics to answer questions of content. That when he said 'I wish I were dead' he meant that he is very unhappy, and cannot see a way out, is not something we can learn from the meaning of the words or the sentence uttered (by itself) nor from rules for its use (alone).

How, then, did Hart see the relevance of semantics, and philosophy of language generally, to legal philosophy? He thought of it as central to his investigation. His philosophical outlook was formed at the time when many regarded Russell's theory of descriptions as a paradigm of philosophical explanation. The theory of descriptions 'solved' the problem of the reference of definite descriptions while avoiding the need to postulate fictional or other non-existing objects. The statement 'The present king of France is bald' is not *about* a non-existing king (and how can we tell whether the non-existing king is or is not bald?). It is simply the false statement that there is one and only one person who is both king of France and bald.

Eventually, Russell's account was challenged by Strawson, and later by others. The truth of Russell's account does not matter. What matters is that it showed how logical analysis can solve an ontological mystery. Moreover, the mystery was deemed highly relevant to the philosophy of law, for law is overpopulated by mysterious objects such as rights and duties, corporations and states, and many more. This was the point at which, for Hart, Russell's theory touched base with Bentham's account of fictions, and of rights, etc. In short, the motivation was an endorsement of naturalism (though not under that name) according to which the only things there are (or the only things whose existence has duration) are things located in space, knowledge about which is gained from the natural sciences, or at any rate is subject to correction by them. Naturalism created the problem of how to understand legal notions such as rights, duties, and corporations. Logic provided the answer, or more precisely it provided the programme—that is, the faith—that the answers will be found in that way. The same motivation and the same hope dominated the work of many legal philosophers in the middle of the twentieth century.

But logic is not semantics, nor is it the philosophy of language, you may say. However, soon after Russell's important work the emphasis shifted from logic to language and to the philosophy of language. The notorious linguistic turn in twentieth-century philosophy led to a reinterpretation of logic, which to a degree came to be absorbed in either mathematics or the theories of language. We can see how the theory of descriptions is part of the theory of language; in Chomskyan terminology it shows that the surface structure of sentences including definite descriptions is not their deep structure.

In the early years of his career, Hart sought to find help particularly in the then brand-new theory of speech acts, developed by J. L. Austin.[10]

---

[10] In part the same approach was supported by Wittgenstein's reflections on the variety of language games. For Hart's comment on those years, see *Essays in Jurisprudence and Philosophy* (1983), 2–3.

Hart believed that various problems with explaining responsibility would be dissolved once we allowed for non-assertoric use of language.[11] He also believed that the problems about the ontological standing of legal 'things' such as law, rights, and corporations, which troubled Bentham and many others, can be dissolved with the judicious application of speech-act theory.[12] By the time Hart published *The Concept of Law* many of these hopes had receded. But his faith in the benefits for legal analysis of learning the lessons of speech-act theory is manifested in his way of understanding legal statements as statements from what he called the internal point of view.

His view on this point derives as much from the attempts by Stevenson, and later R. M. Hare, to apply linguistic analysis to moral utterances as from the persisting influence of J. L. Austin. Both Stevenson and Hare made their respectively emotivist and prescriptivist accounts of moral utterances more plausible by allowing that, apart from pure assertions and pure expressions of emotions (in Stevenson's case), or prescriptions (in Hare's case), there are utterances that combine both. Hart's legal statements from an internal point of view are one such case of a hybrid statement: stating how things are under the law, while endorsing or expressing an endorsement of the law at the same time. The problem Hart sought to solve in this way was the problem of the relations between law and morality in the face of two philosophical beliefs: first, his doubts about the objectivity of ethics and of all evaluative judgments, and second, his belief in the objectivity of law. The objectivity of the law is accounted for by his social-practice-based explanation of the existence of the law and its content. The non-objectivity of morality and of all evaluative judgments is compatible with the fact that the evaluative component of legal judgments (which according to Hart need not be a moral evaluation) is their (as it were 'subjective') expression of an endorsement of (rather than assertion of the value of) the law.[13] This enables Hart to remain true to a naturalist view of the world, and to an empiricist epistemology, and yet to reject the reductive accounts of legal statements advocated by Bentham and his followers, including both American and Scandinavian realists, who regarded statements of law as factual statements about commands, or sanctions, and so on.

There are probably no general lessons to learn from the story I have

[11] 'The Ascription of Responsibility and Rights', 49 Proc. Aristotelian Soc. 171 (1948/9), later disavowed by him.

[12] 'Definition and Theory in Jurisprudence', repr. in *Essays, supra* n. 10.

[13] My claim is not that Hart's analysis of legal statements and utterances is incompatible with belief in the objectivity of value and of morality. It is that the plausibility of the analysis depends on the rejection of the objectivity of value and morality. Once their objectivity is admitted there is no reason for accepting Hart's analysis rather than the view that legal statements and utterances are just like all other statements.

told, but it strikes me as a sad one. Very little seems to have been gained in all of Hart's forays into philosophy of language. The problems with the explanation of responsibility, legal agents such as corporations, the nature of rights and duties, the relations between law and morality—none of them was solved nor their solution significantly advanced by the ideas borrowed from philosophy of language. Moreover, the reason for that was not that Hart borrowed bad ideas from the philosophy of language, nor that he did not understand properly the ideas he borrowed. Essentially the fault was in the philosophical analysis of the problems which speech-act theory and other ideas from the philosophy of language were meant to solve. Hart's failure on all the points I mentioned resulted from his adherence to naturalism and to empiricist epistemology, and his rejection of evaluative objectivity.

You may feel that I have been disingenuous in overlooking, or disregarding, the most obvious source of the dependence of jurisprudence on philosophy of language, namely the web of issues to do with interpretation. Interpretation, however, is a bigger subject, belonging to the theory of understanding of action, of cultures, and of their products. It is not a topic that philosophy of language by itself can explain. Still, interpretation gives rise to problems with which philosophy of language can help, notably the problems arising out of vagueness.

None of this means that legal philosophers can avoid philosophy of language, or that they cannot be led into error by supporting misguided views in semantics. But possibly philosophy of language and semantics can help primarily by providing clarifications where misunderstanding of language or its use may lead to an error. By and large, as long as in one's deliberation about the nature of law and its central institutions one uses language without mistake, there is little that philosophy of language can do to advance one's understanding.

II. IS THE QUESTION OF THE NATURE OF LAW A QUESTION OF THE MEANING OF LAW?

It is time to turn to our first topic: does the question about the nature of law itself—that is, when taken in its most general form—call for significant help from semantics? As mentioned, until recently many writers, myself included, assumed that it does not. Hart and Dworkin were among the clearest in repudiating the idea that it does. However, recently Stavropoulous[14] has offered a revisionist interpretation of Dworkin, argu-

[14] See N. Stavropoulos, *Objectivity in Law* (1996), 129–36. For a conflicting view, see K. Kress, 'The Interpretive Turn' 97 Ethics 834, 855 ff. (1987).

ing that his theory can be understood as an explanation of the meaning of 'law', and Dworkin may have come to accept the same or a similar view.[15] That view is not without initial plausibility. After all, a theory about the nature of law attempts to elucidate a concept, the concept of law, and what is the elucidation of a concept if not an explanation of its meaning? And what could that be if not the explanation of the meaning of the concept-word?[16]

But what is the word the meaning of which is explained by the explanation of the concept of law? It is not an explanation of the meaning of the word 'law', which applies to many things, scientific laws, mathematical laws, divine laws, and others to which the concept of law, the one the explanation of which legal philosophy is after, does not apply. But, it may be claimed, the explanation of that concept of law is *part* of the explanation of the meaning of the word 'law' or 'the law'. Perhaps the explanation of the meaning of the word 'law' consists in a list of all the different kinds of law to which the word applies, the laws studied by jurisprudence being among them, and jurisprudence studies that part of the meaning of the word. Alternatively, perhaps the word has different, albeit cognate, meanings, and jurisprudence explains one of them. Perhaps. Though it is interesting to note that it may be otherwise. It may be that the word is univocal, and is susceptible of a general explanation: 'laws', let us say, being general rules of some permanence, or general rules giving rise to a degree of necessity ('given the law, it must be thus and thus'). 'The law' may refer to the situation obtaining under some system of laws. If so, then the law studied by jurisprudence is just one instance of law, a species of law, and does not merit special mention in the explanation of the meaning of the word 'law'. In the definition of a genus we do not refer to its species.

Perhaps concepts need not be associated that closely with words after all. The following is a 1985 example of the use of the word 'concept' I found in the *OED*: 'We aim to sell a total furnishing concept based on the "one pair of eyes" principle.' This illustrates a contemporary use of the word to mean something like 'a general notion or idea, esp. in the context of marketing and design; a "theme", a set of matching or coordinated items, of e.g. furniture, designed to be sold together. Chiefly advertisers' jargon.' Plainly, we are not interested in this use of the notion. But the chief meaning of 'concept' is not unrelated. It is, in its logical and philosophical use, 'an idea of a class of objects, a general notion or idea'—or so the *OED* tells us. There is nothing here about necessarily having a distinctive word,

---

[15] To judge from conversations with him, and from a draft of an unpublished reply to Hart's Postscript.

[16] I should make it clear that this is not Dworkin's reason for regarding the question as a semantic one. I will come to his reason later.

which in at least one of its meanings expresses that concept and nothing else. The context, rather than the use of a word, may be part of what indicates that the concept of law being talked about is the one we are interested in. The context, rather than any special linguistic device may—or may not—indicate whether the law talked about is that of a state rather than a moral law, etc. While we can do little with language without words, we can express in words concepts and ideas for which we have no specific words or phrases.[17]

We may suspend the question whether the explanation of the concept of law explains the meaning of any word. Possibly in explaining concepts we encounter many of the problems we face in explaining semantic meanings. What, then, counts as an explanation of a concept? It consists in setting out some of its necessary features, and some of the essential features of whatever it is a concept of. In our case, it sets out some of the necessary or essential features of the law.

Broadly speaking, the explanation of a concept is the explanation of that which it is a concept of. But this statement has to be qualified, and clarified. Different concepts can apply to the same object or to the same property: equilateral triangles are also equiangular triangles, and the property of being an equilateral triangle is necessarily such that whatever possesses it also has the property of being an equiangular triangle. Each concept picks out its object or property via a different aspect of it. An explanation of a concept involves explaining the feature through which it applies to its object or property, but also explaining more broadly the nature of the object or property that it is a concept of. This does not mean providing a comprehensive explanation of the nature of that of which it is a concept—explanations are context-sensitive. An explanation is a good one if it consists of true propositions that meet the concerns and the puzzles that led to it, and that are within the grasp of the people to whom it is (implicitly or explicitly) addressed.

You may say that, taken in that sense, explanations of concepts, inasmuch as they include explanations of (the puzzling aspects of) what the concept is a concept of, are more than just explanations of the concepts involved, narrowly conceived. However, Hart and others, when they offered explanations of the concept of law, or the concept of mind, or others, understood conceptual explanations in that wider sense; and therefore, to understand and evaluate their methodology I will use the notion as they did.

It is essential to remember, however, that *having a concept* can fall well short of a thorough knowledge of the nature of the thing it is a concept of.

---

[17] Even when we count words with several meanings as several words, one for each meaning.

People have a concept if they can use it correctly in normal circumstances.[18] Having a concept in that sense is compatible with a shallow and defective understanding of its essential features, and of the nature of what it is a concept of. Hence, while some ordinary explanations of a concept may aim at making people competent users of it, a philosophical explanation has different aims. It assumes that they are competent users, and it aims at improving their understanding of the concept in one respect or another.[19]

Should explanations of concepts set out necessary and sufficient conditions for their application? Sometimes this stronger condition is objected to on the ground that one can rarely state necessary and sufficient conditions for the application of interesting concepts. This objection seems to me to spring from exaggerated expectations of what necessary and sufficient conditions can provide, leading to unjustified pessimism about their availability. They can, for example, be very vague. Possibly it is a necessary and sufficient condition of being a good person that one is like Jesus. But this explanation of the concept, even if true, is not necessarily instructive and helpful. Possibly, in order to know in what ways Jesus was a good person, one needs an understanding of the concept in the first place. Explanations can more often than is sometimes supposed provide necessary and sufficient conditions for the application of the concept. Nevertheless, it is a mistake to believe that all good explanations must do so.

First, some essential characteristics of some concepts are neither necessary nor sufficient conditions for their application. They may be defeasible conditions for their application. Second, to insist that conceptual explanations provide necessary and sufficient conditions is to concentrate excessively on the distinctive features of concepts, overlooking the importance of other features. An explanation of 'a human being' as 'a rational animal (i.e. one belonging to a species of rational animals)' may well provide necessary and sufficient conditions for the application of the concept. But it is false to conclude that human beings' rational nature is 'more important' or more crucial to their understanding than the fact that they are sexual animals, for example, even though they are not unique in their sexuality as they are in their rationality.

---

[18] Perfect command of a concept implies being able to use it correctly in all possible circumstances. But not only is that a condition which in fact few achieve, it gives rise to theoretical difficulties. One who has perfect command of a concept can make mistakes in its application or use. But the boundary between a mistake about the concept and a mistake about its application is vague, as is its theoretical nature.

[19] These remarks about the difference between philosophical explanations of concepts and the conditions for having concepts are consistent with and parallel C. Peacocke's distinction between possession and attribution conditions for concepts: *A Study of Concepts* (1992), 27–33.

A third doubt about the suitability of the necessary-and-sufficient-condition requirement for good explanations is that it misses out on an important part of the explanatory task. Conceptual explanations not only explain the conditions for correct application of a concept ('an act of torture is an infliction of pain or suffering for its own sake or to obtain some benefit or advantage') but also its connections with others ('torture is worse than murder'). We explain concepts in part by locating them in a conceptual web. These aspects of conceptual explanations can be said to be statements of conditions for the application of the concept only by stretching the idea of a condition for application.

Finally, the fourth objection to the necessary-and-sufficient-condition view of conceptual explanation is that it results from a false picture of what explanations seek to achieve. In particular, it is associated with the view that, while one can partially explain a concept through necessary or through sufficient conditions for its application, only a list of necessary and sufficient conditions will provide a complete explanation. But concepts can have more than one set of necessary and sufficient conditions for their application, and they may have many other conditions that do not readily fall into place as part of sets of necessary and sufficient conditions. If there were a complete explanation it would consist of the minimal finite list of essential features of the concept, possession of which entails possession of all its essential features. There need not be such explanations regarding all concepts. There is certainly no reason to aspire to provide them. They may resemble telephone directories in being long lists devoid of interest. Explanations are of puzzling or troubling aspects of concepts, and they are therefore almost always 'incomplete'.

One important point reinforces the previous one. There is no uniquely correct explanation of a concept, nothing which could qualify as *the* explanation of the concept of law. There can be a large number of correct alternative explanations of a concept. Not all of them will be equally appropriate for all occasions. Appropriateness is a matter of relevance to the interests of the expected or intended public, appropriateness to the questions which trouble it, to the puzzles which confuse it. These vary, and with them the appropriateness of various explanations. The appropriateness, aptness, or success of explanations presupposes their truth. But the truth of an explanation is not enough to make it a good explanation. To be good it has also to be appropriate, that is (a) responding to the interests of its public and (b) capable of being understood for what it is by its public (should they be minded to understand it).

The relativity of good explanations to the interests and the capacities of their public makes them ephemeral and explains why philosophy has a never-ending task. It also helps explain away the impression that philosophy is forever engaged in a fruitless debate on unsolvable questions. The shifting kaleidoscope of explanations, which is the history of philosophy, has that character, at least in part, because of the shifting interests of its public. It is important to emphasize that there is nothing in the relativity of good explanations to their public to threaten the non-relativity of truth.

John Austin thought that, necessarily, the legal institutions of every legal system are not subject to—that is, do not recognize—the jurisdiction of legal institutions outside their system over them. (I am somewhat rein-terpreting his claim here.[20]) Kelsen believed that necessarily constitu-tional continuity[21] is both necessary and sufficient for the identity of a legal system. We know that both claims are false. The countries of the European Union recognize, and for a time the independent countries of the British Empire recognized, the jurisdiction of outside legal institutions over them, thus refuting Austin's theory. And the law of most countries provides counterexamples to Kelsen's claim.[22] I mention these examples not to illustrate that legal philosophers can make mistakes, but to point to the susceptibility of philosophy to the winds of time. So far as I know, Austin's and Kelsen's failures were not made good. That is, no successful alternative explanations were offered. In spite of this there is no great flurry of philosophical activity to plug the gap. Rather, the problem that their mistaken doctrines were meant to explain, namely the problem of the identity and continuity of legal systems, lost its appeal to legal philosophers, who do not mind leaving it unsolved. Interest has shifted elsewhere.

III. THE SEMANTIC STING

Dworkin's semantic sting argument is meant to show that certain concepts cannot be given a semantic account.[23] In particular, Dworkin

---

[20] To be precise, his claim was that they do not habitually obey the commands, i.e. laws, of such institutions. That condition, strictly understood, would mean that they are not disposed to obey, do not have a habit of obeying.

[21] Two laws are constitutionally continuous if either they derive their validity from the same authorizing norm (directly or indirectly) or one of them is a basic norm and the other derives from it.

[22] Most of the countries that gained their independence from Britain and France after the Second World War became independent without a break in constitutional continuity. On the other hand, most countries absorb breaches in constitutional continuity without much effect on their identity. In Britain the loss of the Great Seal in 1688 and the House of Lords' Practice Statement of 1966 are sometimes mentioned as examples.

[23] Strictly speaking, this sentence is false. Dworkin says (*LE*, 45), 'I shall call the semantic sting the argument I have just described', and that is 'the argument that unless lawyers and judges share factual criteria about the grounds of law there can be no significant thought or debate about what the law is' (*LE*, 44). I believe that I follow most readers of Dworkin in taking the sting to refer not to the argument which he finds mistaken, but to his own argu-ment, which is meant to refute the mistaken argument, and exhibit its absurdity. In any case,

concludes that legal theory cannot provide a semantic account of 'law' (*LE*, 45–6). I argued before that the conclusion is right, for an account of the concept of law is not an account of the meaning of the word 'law'. However, this is not Dworkin's reason for the conclusion, and as expressed his conclusion seems to rest on a verbal misunderstanding. To say of an account that it is a semantic account or explanation does not characterize the type of explanation it gives, except by identifying its object: it is an explanation of the meaning of a word, or some other linguistic component. There is no reason to think that Dworkin believes that the meaning of the word 'law' cannot be explained. If so, then the conclusion of his argument should be not that there is no semantic explanation of 'law', but that a particular type of semantic explanation is misguided. As I mentioned, Dworkin may have come to the view that his conclusion should be rephrased. He seems willing to regard his own theory as a semantic account of the word 'law': it is an interpretive explanation of the meaning of the word. As revised, the semantic sting argument claims that certain words, including the word 'law', cannot be explained by criterial semantics.

What is criterial semantics? It claims that 'we follow shared rules . . . in using any word: these rules set out criteria that supply the word's meaning' (*LE*, 31). Later we learn by implication that the criteria set conditions for the correct application of the words the meaning of which they define.[24] As I argued, an explanation of the concept of law is not a semantic account of anything, but that does not show that the semantic sting argument does not apply to it. Arguably, it applies to explanations of many concepts, whether or not they are associated with concept-words. To make the argument apply to the law we need to reformulate it to apply beyond the explanation of the meanings of words. 'A criterial explanation' of a concept, let us say, (1) states a rule setting out conditions for the (correct) use of a concept; and (2) is a true explanation by virtue of the fact that it is a correct statement of the conditions for the correct use of the concept actually used by those who use it.[25]

---

the quotation above cannot refer to the issue of how to explain the meanings of words or of concepts, since it incorporates the claim that the law is identified by factual criteria, which is not part of that dispute.

[24] e.g. 'Semantic theories suppose that lawyers and judges use mainly the same criteria . . . in deciding when propositions of law are true or false; they suppose that lawyers actually agree about the grounds of law' (*LE*, 33). Dworkin nowhere limits the rules to conditions of application in the narrow sense, i.e. conditions under which statements of the form 'it is the law that . . .' are true. Even though his discussion gravitates in that direction, we should remember that it is meant to apply to an explanation by reference to shared rules that provide criteria for the meaning of the word. Like all explanations, criterial explanations are successful to the degree that they respond to the interests that prompted them.

[25] The circularity in this characterization can be easily eliminated by making clear that the identity of the concept is determined by the existence of a population that uses a concept with criteria for correct use that are correctly described by the explanation.

Dworkin's conclusion that certain concepts, the concept of law among them, cannot be given a criterial explanation rests on the claim that the application of criterially explained concepts cannot be subject to dispute regarding what he calls 'pivotal cases'. Therefore, where, as in the case of the law, the application of a concept can be disputed in pivotal cases, the concept is not susceptible to criterial explanation.

What are pivotal cases? We have to distinguish, Dworkin explains,

two kinds of disagreements, the distinction between borderline cases and testing or pivotal cases. People sometimes do speak at cross-purposes in the way the borderline defense describes. They agree about the correct tests for applying some word in what they consider normal cases but use the word somewhat differently in what they all recognize to be marginal cases. . . . Sometimes, however, they argue about the appropriateness of some word or description because they disagree about the correct tests for using the word or phrase on any occasion. We can see the difference by imagining two arguments among art critics about whether photography should be considered a form or branch of art. They might agree about exactly the ways in which photography is like and unlike activities they all recognize as 'standard' uncontroversial examples of art like painting and sculpture. They might agree that photography is not fully or centrally an art form in the way these other activities are; they might agree, that is, that photography is at most a borderline case of an art. Then they would probably also agree that the decision whether to place photography within or outside that category is finally arbitrary, that it should be taken one way or another for convenience or ease of exposition, but that there is otherwise no genuine issue to debate whether photography is 'really' an art. Now consider an entirely different kind of debate. One group argues that (whatever others think) photography is a central example of an art form, that any other view would show a deep misunderstanding of the essential nature of art. The other takes the contrary position that any sound understanding of the character of art shows photography to fall wholly outside it, that photographic techniques are deeply alien to the aims of art. It would be quite wrong in these circumstances to describe the argument as one over where some borderline should be drawn. The argument would be about what art, properly understood, really is; it would reveal that the two groups had very different ideas about why even standard art forms they both recognize—painting and sculpture—can claim that title. (*LE*, 41–2)

I had to provide this long quotation, for Dworkin does not offer an abstract characterization of pivotal cases, and their difference from borderline cases. The metaphorical analogy with spatial location—at the border or in the middle of an area—is useful in dramatizing the contrast, but it provides little guidance in trying to classify cases. The text provides one crucial guide: disputes regarding pivotal cases involve, as disputes about borderline cases do not (never? one wonders), a disagreement about the criteria for the correct use of the concept, and not merely (as in borderline cases (always?)) about their application to the instant case. As this is far from a clear criterion, it is important to bear the example in mind when evaluating Dworkin's argument.

Criterial explanations cannot explain concepts regarding which pivotal disputes are possible. Why so? Nothing in the definition of criterial explanations makes the conclusion obvious. Dworkin may be assuming that all competent users of a concept, which can be explained criterially, agree on its explanation, i.e. on the criteria for its correct application. Were this the case, then they could not disagree on pivotal cases. On this assumption, when two people converse using a concept that can be criterially explained, then each of them uses the concept according to a set of criteria for its correct use, and each knows or can easily find out the criteria used by the other; and if they match they are using the same concept and cannot disagree regarding the criteria for its correct use, whereas if they do not match then they are using two different concepts and there is no disagreement between them. If they do not realize that, then they are talking at cross-purposes. Is that Dworkin's argument? It seems to be. The following is as explicit a statement of the argument as I can find:

Notice the following argument. If two lawyers are actually following *different* rules in using the word 'law', using different factual criteria to decide when a proposition of law is true or false, then each must mean something different than the other when he says what the law is. . . . [here I omit Dworkin's example] So the two judges are not really disagreeing about anything when one denies and the other asserts this proposition. They are only talking past one another. (*LE*, 43–4)

There is nothing wrong with this passage. But why should Dworkin think that it describes the situation which must obtain when people disagree about a criterion for the use of a concept that can be criterially explained? Dworkin never explains why he believes that concepts capable of being explained criterially land one in this situation. I will explain how once one avoids three possible mistakes it becomes plain that the argument fails. First, it is not the case that believing of a concept that it is susceptible to a criterial explanation commits one to an individualistic explanation of it. Second, one needs to be aware of the diversity of criteria for the correct use of concepts and of their possible opacity. And finally, one needs to remember that criterial philosophical explanations of concepts differ somewhat from other criterial explanations.

IV. CRITERIAL EXPLANATIONS AND THE REJECTION OF INDIVIDUALISM

The argument of the semantic sting inhabits a territory much discussed over the last fifty years, namely the question of the relation between agreement and understanding. Disagreement, we are often told, presupposes a degree of agreement. Why? Because disagreement means endorsement of inconsistent propositions. It therefore presupposes the common use of the same concepts, the concepts that feature in the inconsistent propositions. This is not democratic, you say. Oh yes it is, say I. We disagree. A precondition of our disagreement is that we both use the same concept of democracy. Agreement in concepts, however, implies agreement in judgment. Where concepts can be explained by criterial explanations, it means agreement over the criteria for application of the concept.

The argument I have just rehearsed trades on an ambiguity in the notion of disagreement. In one sense it means, as I said, the endorsement of inconsistent propositions. In another sense it means a conversation, discussion, or some other encounter in which people communicate but disagree (in the first sense). Disagreement in the first sense does not presuppose sharing concepts because it does not presuppose communication. Jesus and Genghis Khan disagreed on many issues, and this is so even if there are few concepts which they shared. To bring out their disagreement it may be necessary to deploy concepts that neither of them possessed or understood. This does not mean that there are no limits to possible disagreement, no sharing in judgments which is presupposed by it. Possibly the very possession of a faculty of judgment, of a power to have opinions, presupposes certain beliefs, which will therefore be shared by all believers. But the argument we are interested in is not of that kind. It is about the limits on disagreement imposed by the sharing of the same concepts. What are they? They are in the knowledge one must have to possess the concepts. If, for example, one cannot understand the concept of a cheque without knowing that banks are financial institutions in which people can deposit their own money, then anyone who possesses the concept of a cheque shares the knowledge that banks are financial institutions.

Criterial explanations presuppose that the possession of concepts consists in knowing how to use them in normal circumstances, namely in the possession of rules setting criteria for their correct use. It would seem to follow that those who share a concept share the criteria for its correct use and cannot disagree about them. The question is: what are these criteria and what does sharing them consist *in*? We can approach the matter through the second issue.

The individualistic picture regards each person as holding to a set of criteria that he or she follows when applying the concept. In principle each person may be the only person using that concept, i.e. the only one using these criteria. Those who have the concept may make mistakes in application (due to misperception, miscalculation, etc.) but cannot make mistakes about the criteria. Each person's criteria define the concept for that person. If others follow different criteria, that cannot show that either of them made a mistake. It only shows that they are following different concepts. You will recognize that Dworkin's articulation of the semantic sting contains echoes of this view.

A series of arguments, deriving from the work of Wittgenstein, Putnam, and Burge,[26] shows that the individualistic picture is mistaken, but its rejection does not require rejecting criterial explanations of concepts. Here is one way to approach the matter. By the criterial approach to explanation, according to both the individualistic and the non-individualistic versions of it, when one speaks, one is uttering sentences and using terms, relying on a rule that sets the criteria for their correct use. This does not mean that speakers always consider the rule for the use of the terms before using them. It means that they take themselves to be using the terms according to the rule and the criteria it embodies. They hold themselves responsible to the criteria set by their rule. For example, they are committed to admitting (at least to themselves) that their statements are mistaken if, when understood by these criteria, they are mistaken. If other people make the same utterance, holding themselves responsible to a different rule, i.e. one that sets different criteria, then they are using the words with different meanings, and there is no disagreement between them.

So far so good. Where the individualistic approach goes wrong is in thinking that the criteria set by each person's personal rule for the correct use of terms and concepts are fully specified. In fact, their personal rules are not specified. Each person takes his use of terms and concepts to be governed by the common criteria for their use. That is all their personal rule says. The criteria that govern people's use of language are simply the criteria generally relied on in their language community for the use of those terms. People who think that they understand a term or a concept think that they have at least some knowledge of what the common criteria are. They may be wrong. They may be partially or completely mistaken about the common criteria. It is part of each person's rule for the use of the term or concept that mistakes can occur, for the rule refers to the criteria as they are, rather than to what that person thinks they are. What they are, however, does depend on what people think they are. The correct criteria are those that people who think they understand the

---

[26] Wittgenstein's rule-following argument in *Philosophical Investigations* (1953), Putnam's twin-earth arguments in *The Meaning of 'Meaning'* and *Is Semantics Possible?*, in H. Putnam, *Mind, Language and Reality* (1975), 215, 139. See also S. Kripke, *Naming and Necessity* (1980). T. Burge, 'Individualism and the Mental', 4 Midwest Stud. Phil. 73 (1979), and 'Other Bodies', in *Thought and Object* (ed. A. Woodfield, 1982), 97. My remarks in the sequel are not meant to relate to all aspects of their arguments. In particular, they do not relate to Putnam's conclusions regarding the 'world-involving' aspects of natural kind words. Nor is there reason to expect my comments to be entirely in line with the arguments of these philosophers.

concept or term generally share, i.e. those that are generally believed to be the correct criteria are the correct criteria.[27] An example will bring out the point.

When I say 'This is a table' I am taking myself to have used 'table' according to the criteria governing its use in English,[28] which I believe to include the condition that any item of furniture up to 4 feet high with a flat top normally used to place things on is a table. Suppose that I am wrong. I call an item a table and am told that I made a mistake. It is a drawing-board. On the individualistic account I should say: 'Do not correct me. I made no mistake. You simply misunderstood what I said. You took me to be using "table" in the meaning you are using it. But I did not. I used it according to a meaning rule by which this object is a table.' As we know that is not how people react on these occasions. They acknowledge that they made a mistake. They meant to use 'table' in its so-called ordinary meaning. They had a view on what this meaning is, and they made a mistake. Note that the same is true not only of what I say, but of what I think. Overhearing a conversation between others, I may realize that whereas I always thought that this object is a table in fact it is not, and my understanding of the rule for the use of 'table', the very same rule which I was using, was mistaken.

I am making this as a point about an important feature of speech, communication, and thought. The example, and others like it, cannot establish that things must be so, only that they are so. Our practices may change, and individualism may be right regarding such changed practices.[29] I share with others the belief that not all concepts and words can be explained in a way consistent with individualism, that fundamentally language and thought are not susceptible to individualistic explanations. But we need not argue that point here. Be that as it may, given how things are, most of our concepts and terms cannot be explained individualistically, and this shows that what we think and what we mean is 'not in the head'. Individualism is mistaken.[30] Two people thinking about the same

---

[27] Note that there is no implication here that a linguistic community can share criteria only if there is someone who knows them completely. The criteria may be shared by the linguistic community even if no single person knows all aspects of them.

[28] Or in British English, or in some dialect, depending on the language I am using at the time. It may be undetermined.

[29] Burge has tried to show how radical and unappealing such a change will have to be. See e.g. his 'Individualism and Psychology', 95 Phil. Rev. 3 (1986).

[30] Burge defines individualism as 'the view that if one fixes those non-intentional physical and functional states and processes of a person's body whose nature is specifiable without reference to conditions beyond the person's bodily surfaces, one has thereby fixed the person's intentional mental states and processes in the sense that they could not be different intentional states and processes from the ones that they are'. See T. Burge, 'Cartesian Error and the Objectivity of Perception', in *Subject, Thought, and Context* (ed. P. Pettit and J. McDowell, 1986), 117.

object 'This is a table' will have different thoughts in mind depending on whether their linguistic community has one or another rule for the correct use of 'table'.

The rejection of individualism does not amount to a rejection of criterial explanations. Criterial explanations are explanations in terms of rules setting criteria for the correct use of concepts, or words—and there is nothing individualistic in that—which are the correct rules if they are shared by the linguistic community. That sharing is precisely what non-individualism insists on. The sharing is established by the fact that all language users hold themselves responsible to the common criteria, whatever they are.

Does Dworkin tacitly assume that supporters of criterial explanations are guilty of individualism? It is a moot point. When he introduces the subject of semantic explanations of 'law', he is careful to add:

It does not follow that all lawyers are aware of these rules [the shared rules for correct use of 'law'] in the sense of being able to state them in some crisp and comprehensive form. For we all follow rules given by our common language of which we are not fully aware. (*LE*, 31)

The penultimate sentence is irrelevant to the issue. One can have perfect knowledge of rules without 'being able to state them in some crisp and comprehensive form'. The question is whether Dworkin is aware that one can use words and concepts in accord with rules with only partial knowledge of their content. Does his reference to not being 'fully aware' of the rules refer to not knowing them all that well, or does it repeat the idea of the previous sentence, referring merely to one's ability to articulate the content of the rules? The context of the passage, and the rest of Dworkin's discussion, suggest the second. On several occasions he repeats that supporters of criterial explanations allow for the fact—indeed, build on the fact—that people may be unable to articulate the rules they know. Nowhere does he seem to allow that supporters of criterial explanations build on the fact that people may not know well the rules governing the use of their words.

The point is of some importance in assessing the force of the semantic sting argument. It stings those whose account denies that one can have disputes about the criteria set by the rules for the correct use of terms. If criterial explanations are committed to the view that people who use concepts that can be explained by them cannot be mistaken about the criteria for their application, then they cannot explain the existence of disputes about these criteria.

As we saw, this argument fails. Criterial explanations of concepts are consistent with the fact that people who use the rules setting out these criteria may make mistakes about which criteria are set by the rules.[31]

---

[31] Naturally, they cannot make just any mistake. To be people who use the rule, they must have some notion of what the criteria are.

This means that there could be disagreements about the criteria for the use of concepts, even if the concepts are susceptible to criterial explanations. But in and of itself this does not explain the possibility of theoretically interesting disputes about such criteria. To do that we have to add other elements to the rejection of individualism.

V. THE COMPLEXITY AND NON-TRANSPARENCY OF CRITERIAL EXPLANATIONS

A. The general case from complexity and non-transparency

Agreement in the actual use of concepts is, of course, neither necessary nor sufficient for agreement on the criteria for their application. It is not necessary, for people may and do make mistakes in applying concepts even when they have a very clear and correct understanding of the criteria for their application. It is not sufficient, for people who agree about the use of a concept in all the cases that they have examined so far, or will examine in the future, may still disagree about the criteria. Their disagreement may reveal itself in disagreement about some hypothetical cases, had such cases come to their attention.

The criteria used in explaining a concept are typically statements about its relation to other concepts, or applications of it to some criterial examples. But which other concepts? And which examples? Talk of criteria may suggest some official definitions, like the mathematical or scientific definitions one learned at school: 'A triangle is an area of the plane enclosed by three straight lines', or 'Water is H_2O'. In such cases there are fixed paradigmatic ways of explaining concepts. They display the criteria by which a concept is to be explained. Explanations in other terms are derivative, and secondary. But such cases are the exception rather than the rule. For the most part there are no canonical explanations for concepts. They can be explained in many ways, using or avoiding various other concepts, or examples. The pragmatic considerations that distinguish a good explanation from a bad one, considerations of what puzzles the addressees of the explanation, what they are or are not interested in, and of their capacities to understand, are among the considerations guiding the choice of concepts to be used, and examples to refer to in good explanations. You may say that there are no criteria for the use of most concepts, only concepts and examples which are used as criteria—that is, used to explain the rules governing the correct use of the concepts on one occasion or another. Moreover, it is virtually always the case that explanations are not exhaustive. They point to one or another essential feature of the concept explained, and leave many others unmentioned (and unentailed).

As we saw, even explanations in terms of necessary and sufficient conditions are not exhaustive.

All this points to endless possibilities of disagreement. Imagine that you are used to explaining a concept one way. I am used to explaining it another way. Do we agree? And if we do not, who is right? These questions are as complex as any questions comparing different concepts or analysing different examples. The suggestion that, because the correctness of the explanation of concepts is judged by their faithfulness to the shared rules governing their use, such explanations are so transparent that they leave little room for doubt about their correctness or accuracy lacks plausibility.

Another result of these considerations is that dispute and disagreement may come apart. People may dispute each other's explanations even when there is no disagreement between them. Their dispute may result from a failure to realize that both offer compatible explanations.

B. Concepts explained by example

Let me illustrate these points with reference to explanations using examples. A common, correct, and effective way to explain what is a table is to say, 'It is an item of furniture like this one' (pointing to a table as one speaks). For most purposes such an explanation would do perfectly. If the rule one learned from needs correcting or supplementing, this could be done when the need arises. But suppose that you have just learned the word by such an explanation, and that I want to find out how good your understanding of the notion is now. It could be a somewhat lengthy process, involving other examples, and various descriptions. Now suppose that instead of this rather simple notion we are discussing the notion 'a good person' and we both agree that a good person is someone who is like Jesus. Not surprisingly, while in a pub conversation we may leave it at that; if we really want to establish whether we understand the notion in the same way, we could spend a productive evening comparing the ways in which being like Jesus shows one to be a good person. The very act of establishing agreement will be prolonged, as may be the process of establishing the location and scope of any disagreement.

Some concepts, including some evaluative concepts, cannot be explained except with the help of examples, with the inevitable elaborate exploration of their reach and direction that any attempt to study systematically such concepts involves. The notion of good looks is such a concept. It is futile to explain what it is to have good looks, to be good-looking, except by pointing to examples.

Focusing on evaluative concepts, an objecter may grant all I wrote so far and reply that it still fails to explain the sort of disagreement which marks disputes about, for example, whether justice requires redistribution to the poor, or whether abortion is murder. We should admit that that is so, and it is hardly surprising. It would be a mistake to think that all evaluative disagreements are of a kind. The fact that the disagreements I gestured toward are not like those about distribution and justice, or about abortion and murder, does not mean that they are not typical examples of common evaluative disagreements.

C. The ethical significance of disputes about criterial explanations

It may seem that disputes that concentrate on identifying what are the criteria for the correct use of concepts cannot be significant evaluative disputes, for they are merely disputes about the content of shared rules, and one can always dissent from them. The first point to note here is that even if this contention is correct it does not vindicate the semantic sting. If the remarks above are correct, then the semantic sting argument does not have a sting. Its conclusion was that there cannot be disputes about the criteria for the application of criterially explainable concepts. That conclusion is mistaken. So far as Hart's own understanding of his own theory goes, this is the end of the matter, for he denied that the explanation of the nature of law is evaluative. For him it was a 'descriptive' enterprise. For reasons explained by John Finnis[32] and others,[33] I believe that Hart is mistaken here, and Dworkin is right in holding that the explanation of the nature of law involves evaluative considerations. In any case, it is of interest to see the place that conceptual disputes about criterially definable concepts can occupy within normative disputes.

Where criterially explainable concepts are concerned, evaluative disputes begin (the objection is) only after conceptual disputes are settled, and at the point at which one raises the question of whether or not the concept under discussion should find its place in the articulation of a correct evaluative theory. It is true, we can say in reply, that the very moral or evaluative legitimacy of concepts can be called into question. I can doubt whether one should use the notion of honour in today's circumstances, on the ground that the value it refers to has its place in a society with an aristocracy, and a valuing of ceremony and of formal standing that has no room, should have no room, in our society. That being said, it remains the case that the clarification of evaluative concepts has an important role in evaluative disputes. Most of the time we neither wish nor are able to jettison the concepts we have. The point is very well

---

[32] *Natural Law and Natural Rights* (1980), ch. 1.
[33] For my own explanation, see e.g. *Ethics in the Public Domain* (rev. edn., 1995), chs. 9 and 10.

known. We need concepts to be able to criticize or jettison other concepts. It does not follow that some specific concepts are immune from change. But change can only be gradual. At any given time we are inescapably committed to most of the concepts we have.

The same goes for our beliefs: we assess some of them while relying on others. We cannot do otherwise. We are committed to our beliefs, and when wondering about issues about which we are not clear, much of the time our process is not so much a process of belief revision as of finding out what are the implications of the beliefs we have for the matters we are undecided about. An important part of such deliberation is a process of clarifying to oneself the contours of one's own concepts. One is committed to them, in the way one is committed to one's beliefs, but one may not understand them all that well, as one is not always clear about the implications of one's beliefs. Trying to make up one's mind on an issue, or trying to sort out whether a view incompatible with one's own has some merit, is primarily a process of examining the implications of one's beliefs, and the contours of one's concepts, an exploration proceeding through a debate about the adequacy of various criterial explanations of them.

One reason the significance of conceptual clarification may be misunderstood is the mistaken belief that if the truth of a statement of criteria for the use of a concept depends on the fact that they pick out the common rule for the use of the concept, then the only possible argument supporting such a statement is that this is how everyone uses the concept. Such statistical claims, this mistaken argument proceeds, are not the stuff that normative disagreements are made of. The argument confuses the presupposition for the sharing of concepts with the reasons used in debates about the contours of concepts. To be sure, on occasion argument becomes pointless. If someone claims to be my blood relation because I donated blood to him before an operation, or if someone says that entrenched constitutions are consistent with democracy because trenches are dug by working people, there is little one can do but point out that the other is talking about a different concept from the one commonly referred to by these words. But such cases are the exception rather than the rule. If you deny that a certain feature is a necessary feature of a concept and I assert that it is, we will proceed by appealing to clear examples, to analogies, or to agreed conceptual connections, and will pursue their implications. When one defines 'a table' as an item of furniture made to put things on, the typical response is not: 'This is not how the term is used' (though this response is true), but: 'By your definition a drawing-board is a table, therefore the definition is mistaken.' The sharing of the rule is assumed. It is not part of the argument.

D. Refuting the sting through the relative independence of interlinked
   concepts

I remarked earlier that different concepts have different shapes, and therefore their explanations relate them to other concepts in a variety of ways.
Let me illustrate the relevance of the point to the possibility of disagreement and dispute, using the examples of the notions of justice and of just
war. Let us assume that a condition of a war being a just war is that the
measures used in its pursuit are proportionate to the harm avoidance of
which makes it necessary to use them. Judgment of proportionality
involves comparing the severity of various harms. Does it follow that a
comprehensive understanding of how to compare the severity of different
harms is part of understanding the concept of a just war? Not according
to the notion of a concept as we have it. We understand the concept if,
among other things, we understand that it includes a condition of proportionality. We can understand that even if we are at a loss as to how to
compare the severity of various harms. Such ignorance means that sometimes we will not know whether this war or that is just. But it does not
mean that we will have a defective or incomplete understanding of the
concept of a just war. The criteria by which we judge the relative severity
of harms are not part of the rules governing the correct use of the concept
of a just war.

The reasons for that are deep-rooted. Given that in explaining concepts
we inevitably use other concepts, but for the fact that the criteria for one
are not necessarily the criteria for any other that it is necessarily connected
with, we would have ended up with a vast array of concepts sharing the
same criteria for understanding such that we either understood all of
them or none of them; and if we understand one of them to a certain
degree only, then we understand all of them to a degree not higher than
that. That is not how concepts are, and they are not like that because of the
relative independence of interrelated concepts.

The relative independence of interrelated concepts is consistent with
the thesis that concepts like just war can be explained criterially. Does
Dworkin ignore the point when he charges supporters of criterial explanations with not being able to account for disagreement about the criteria
for the application of concepts? It seems to me that he does. He charges
supporters of criterial explanations with inability to explain the existence
of what he calls 'theoretical disputes', which he identifies with disagreements about what he terms 'the ground of law' (*LE*, 4–5). As far as I can
tell, these are disagreements about the truth conditions of legal propositions, or of some class of them. Dworkin does not distinguish here
between levels of abstraction in the description of the truth conditions.
Both disagreement about whether proportionality is a condition of just

war and disagreement over whether cost of repair is the exclusive test of proportionality are disagreements about the truth conditions of propositions of the form 'so and so is [was, will be] a just war'. Therefore, in Dworkin's terms they are both disputes about the criteria for the application of the concept of a just war. This amounts to overlooking the relative independence of interrelated concepts. The relative independence of concepts establishes that Dworkin is mistaken in his criticism of criterial explanations.

Assume, for the sake of the argument, that the concept of a just war can be criterially explained, but that the notion of proportionality of harm must be explained by Dworkin's interpretive method. It follows that even according to Dworkin there can be a theoretical dispute over the criteria for application of the proportionality of harm. As we saw, this would constitute a disagreement regarding the truth conditions of statements about just war, which is, by assumption, criterially explainable. Because Dworkin regards all disagreements about the truth conditions of a concept as theoretical, it follows that once the relative independence of concepts is allowed it must be recognized that there can be so-called theoretical disagreements regarding concepts which can be criterially explained.

This refutation of the semantic sting presupposes that some concepts are not capable of being criterially explained. Those who believe that many concepts, including the concept of law, can be criterially explained need not deny this. It is Dworkin who used the semantic sting to deny that concepts like the concept of law or that of justice can be criterially explained. This refutation shows that it fails to do so. Notice that considerations like those which apply to just war apply to justice as well. Suppose, for example, that a just state is a state the basic institutions of which make it highly likely that, given the conditions of life at the place and time, all its inhabitants will have a good life, should they conduct themselves rationally. It follows that to know whether this state or that is just one has to know what a good life is. But one's understanding of the notion of a just state is not defective just because one has mistaken views on that issue. Such mistakes will, most likely, lead to mistakes in judging which states are just, but not to a failure properly to understand the notion of a just state. As before, it follows that, for all that Dworkin's argument shows, the notion of a just state can be explained criterially, whereas those who use it engage in so-called theoretical disputes about the truth conditions of judging states to be just.[34]

---

[34] In the Postscript, *supra* n. 3, at 246, Hart writes that one mistake which led Dworkin to belief in his semantic sting argument is his conflation of meaning with criteria of application. (See also *The Concept of Law*, 160.) I do not know how Hart understood that distinction.

The argument from the relative independence of interlinked concepts refutes the semantic sting argument, and that refutation is independent of its refutation (in the previous section) by the argument from the opacity and complexity of criterial explanations. Two distinctions, between the refutation of the sting which is based on the non-transparency of criterial explanations and that based on the relative independence of interlinked concepts, bring out their differences. The refutation from non-transparency establishes the possibility of disagreements about the rule for the use of a concept, which show that at least one of those who disagree has an incomplete grasp of the concept.[35] The refutation from relative independence does not assume such lack of mastery. It shows that even those who have complete understanding of the concept may disagree about the truth conditions of propositions applying it to concrete cases. The second difference between the refutations is that the one from relative independence shows that the semantic sting does not apply to criterially explainable concepts, which are interlinked to other concepts regarding which there could be so-called theoretical disagreements. The lack of transparency argument shows that there could be such disagreement regarding criterially explainable concepts that are sufficiently complex to lack transparency.

E. Theoretical and other criterial explanations

There is a difference of some importance between 'ordinary' and theoretical criterial explanations. It cannot be adequately discussed here; a few observations will have to do. As has already been noted, ordinary criterial explanations are offered in reply to specific questions reflecting a puzzle or a difficulty which is indicated in the question, or understood from its context. This is true of explanations one gives to oneself as well. If you ask what is a state because you wonder whether Lichtenstein is a state, the answer is likely to be other than if you ask what is a state wishing to know whether the European Union is a state. Theoretical explanations, philosophical explanations among them, are somewhat different. They too relate to a purpose, or purposes, and they too vary with the interests of their public. But their interest is different. They seek a more systematic understanding of the concepts (and we are discussing only explanations of concepts, and not stipulations of new concepts in the

---

Possibly my remarks regarding the relative independence of interlinked concepts is relevant to an elucidation of such a distinction. However, in the absence of an explanation of his distinction it is impossible to evaluate this reply by Hart.

[35] The same is true of Dworkin's interpretive disputes about the meaning of a concept. They too presuppose that at least one of the parties has an incomplete understanding of the concept.

process of theory construction). This means that they are looking for a more comprehensive explanation, and one that will not only guide correct use but will also improve understanding.

It is common for this interest in comprehensiveness and improved understanding to lead to a freer attitude to existing practice. Theorists usually feel free to make their explanations less vague than the concept they explain. Explanations that aim at accuracy should be vague where the concept is vague. 'Ordinary' explanations are vague, partly because they explain vague concepts and partly because they are incomplete. Theoretical explanations also are incomplete, but they aim to be relatively (i.e. relative to the concerns of the theory in question at the time) complete. They tend to be more precise than the contours of the vague concept would allow, were one to be true to them. Their interest in improved understanding facilitates this. Being built around ideas deemed important for our self-understanding, they can and do use these ideas to reduce the vagueness in the concept as we find it in the more chaotic, more fluctuating social life of the linguistic community. In some cases theorists may not only reduce vagueness but also introduce distinctions between different uses or senses of the terms or phrases used to express the concept, distinctions not normally noticed by ordinary speakers, and which redraw somewhat the boundaries of the concept.[36]

Theoretical explanations, while dependent for their success on achieving their theoretical goals, are also criterial. Their truth or adequacy is tested also by their conformity to the rules governing the use of the concept. Had they not been so tested they would fail in their aim to explain the concept as it is, the concept that people use to understand features in their own life and in the world around them. To succeed in explaining our own self-understanding through the explanation of some of our concepts requires explaining them as they are. Therefore, if ordinary explanations of them are criterial, so must their theoretical explanations be, subject to the minor latitude in deviating from common practice that I explained.

This means that the reduction in vagueness can only be limited, or the explanation will not be true to the concept explained. A correct account of the nature of law will be more or less vague in the same way as the concept of law is vague. As a result, there sometimes is no answer to questions of the form: is this a legal system?

---

[36] Do we use one concept of 'promise' or two when saying 'I promise to get you the book by tomorrow', and when saying 'I'll break your bones if you do it again, and that's a promise'? Most philosophers who have written on promises take it for granted that two concepts are involved. I believe that that position is not based on an analysis of the common understanding of the concept(s) of a promise, but on theoretical reasons they have for drawing the boundaries between promises and threats.

In *Law's Empire,* Dworkin deploys what is in effect a second argument against criterial explanations of the concept of law, an argument altogether independent of the semantic sting. He thinks that the nature of adjudication shows that courts always presuppose a correct answer to the question 'How should this case be decided?' and that this question is the same as the question 'What is the law which applies to this case?' As the rules by which people judge correctness of use of the concept of law do not always yield such an answer, they cannot provide the explanation of the concept of law. This shows that the concept cannot be criterially explained.

The major flaw in this second argument is its identification of the two questions. It reflects Dworkin's view that the only norms by which courts are allowed, according to law, to decide cases are the law of that legal system. Or perhaps the right way to express Dworkin's view is that what makes norms into the law of a system is that, by law, the courts are allowed to rely on them in deciding cases. The argument about this claim of Dworkin's has continued since his first major essay.[37] But important as that issue is, it is irrelevant to the debate about the possibility of criterial explanation of the concept of law, for a determination of the content of the law of this legal system or that and the explanation of the concept of law are very different enterprises. This is denied by Dworkin's third thesis about jurisprudence, the thesis that it is a silent prologue to any legal decision. It is time to examine this thesis.

VI. LAW AND ITS THEORY

The semantic sting argument stands on its own and falls on its own. Its demise does not in itself undermine Dworkin's wider view of the nature and role of legal philosophy. Hart disagrees with him about that too, but in the Postscript his disagreement is muted. Having decided to restrict the Postscript to deflecting or refuting Dworkin's criticism of his own views, he is content to point out that Dworkin's theoretical aims are different from his, as if that makes them compatible. To be sure, Hart is right that their understandings of the character of legal philosophy differ. Hart regards his own enterprise as describing those features of the law which are general, i.e. shared by all legal systems.[38] Dworkin takes the task of legal philosophy to be the construction of a theory of adjudication, a theory which if correctly followed yields a uniquely correct answer to any

---

[37] Repr. as 'The Model of Rules: I', in *Taking Rights Seriously* (1977).
[38] Note that that task is wider than the explanation of the nature of law, which is confined to essential features of the law, i.e. features without which it would not be law.

question of American law. But it does not follow that that makes the theories compatible. Dworkin is right to maintain that if his theory is correct
then Hart's is flawed at its foundations. In this section I want to show (a)
how Dworkin's conception of the role of legal philosophy is not affected
by the fault in the semantic sting argument and (b) why that view of
jurisprudence is not merely different from but incompatible with Hart's
conception of descriptive jurisprudence.

We can start again with the semantic sting. At a conference in Jerusalem
Ruth Gavison pointed out to Dworkin that neither Hart nor many others
take Hart to be affected by the semantic sting because Hart was not offering an account of the meaning of 'law'. In reply, Dworkin added a note to
Law's Empire:

It is sometimes said that the goal of the theories I call semantic is not, as that name
suggests, to develop theories about what the word 'law' means, but rather to lay
bare the characteristic and distinctive features of law as a social phenomenon. See,
e.g., Ruth Gavison, 'Comments on Dworkin', in Papers of the Jerusalem
Conference (forthcoming).[39] But this contrast is itself a misunderstanding. The
philosophers I have in mind . . . recognize that the most distinctive aspect of law
as a 'social Phenomenon' is that participants in institutions of law deploy and
debate propositions of law and think it matters, usually decisively, whether these
are accepted or rejected. The classical theories try to explain this central and
pervasive aspect of legal practice by describing the sense of propositions of law—
what these mean to those who use them—and this explanation takes the form
either of definitions of 'law' in the older style or accounts of the 'truth conditions'
of propositions of law—the circumstances in which lawyers accept or reject
them—in the more modern style. (*LE*, 418–19)

Hart replies to this with some puzzlement:

[E]ven if the meaning of . . . propositions of law was determined by . . . their truth
conditions this does not lead to the conclusion that the very meaning of the word
'law' makes law depend on certain specific criteria. This would only be the case if
the criteria provided by a system's rule of recognition and the need for such a rule
were derived from the meaning of the word 'law'. But there is no trace of such a
doctrine in my work.[40]

Granted that Hart was right in what he wrote, is it not the case that
truth conditions of all propositions of law follow from an explanation of
the concept of law, including Hart's own? According to Hart the law is a
normative system combining primary and secondary rules, one of which,
the rule of recognition, exists as a social practice, and its content sets
conditions for the validity of the other rules in that system. Does it not

---

[39] Since published as R. Gavison, *Issues in Jurisprudence: The Influence of H. L. A. Hart*
(1987).
[40] Postcript, *supra* n. 3, at 247.

follow that a proposition of law is true, according to Hart, if there is a social practice, a rule of recognition, setting out criteria for the validity of rules of law, and that the proposition states the content of a rule or rules meeting these criteria (or of the rule of recognition itself), or follows from them? This formulation has to be refined, and hedged, but is essentially correct.

There is, however, one important caveat. Many of the conditions that propositions must meet to be true legal propositions, and all the fundamental conditions of this kind, are that they were made law by content-independent processes or activities. Content-independent conditions are those that can endorse different propositions regardless of their content. Typically, they can endorse both a proposition and its contradictory, though this is not always the case, and there can be degrees of content-independence (make any law, make any law that does not violate human rights, make any law—regulation—necessary to the implementation of a fair rent act, etc.). If a condition of the truth of a legal proposition is that it conforms with the demands of justice, for example, the condition is content-dependent: it depends (not exclusively, but among other things) on the content of the proposition. If the condition of the truth of a legal proposition is that it was endorsed by the legislature, then the condition is content-independent, since while the legislature's endorsement was probably motivated by the content of the proposition, it is itself an act that can give validity to propositions of varying contents.[41] It is the act of endorsing the content of a bill, whatever it may be.

Content-independence is, as I pointed out, a matter of degree. A central feature of Hart's explanation of the nature of law is that it is just about absolutely content-independent at bottom. That is, the fundamental criteria for validity, those whose existence does not presuppose others, are almost entirely content-independent. Jurisprudence stipulates that legal systems are systems with a certain structure (including law-making and law-applying authorities). But beyond that, all is contingent. The content of the law and the specific identity and powers of its institutions are entirely dependent on the relevant practices in the country, i.e. on its rule of recognition. It is an equally central feature of Dworkin's account of the law that it is not entirely content-independent. No general theory of law can hope to succeed unless it is content-independent to some extent. To deny that the criteria which determine the content of the law of this country or that have a content-independent component is to deny that there

---

[41] Legal rules are typically expressed by normative propositions (assigning rights, liabilities, responsibilities, etc.) or propositions setting conditions for the application of normative propositions. While often legislative measures are not formulated in such terms, their meaning is expressed by them, and we can say that the legislation endorses the propositions or makes them into law.

can be law-making authorities. Dworkin's theory no less than Hart's
leaves room for content-independent criteria among those determining
what he calls 'the grounds of legal propositions'. In his most abstract
formulations, this expresses itself in the role of the history of the legal
system as an element contributing to the determination of its content. But
his account of law emphasizes the importance of content-dependent
determinants of its content. It is part of Dworkin's account that the theory
of law makes the truth of legal propositions depend on values like justice,
and an alleged value which he calls integrity.

This difference may explain why Hart is surprised at the suggestion
that his theory provides an account of the truth conditions of legal propositions. An account of the nature of law that regards it as determined
largely by content-dependent factors is much more readily thought of as
providing truth conditions for legal propositions than is one that regards
the law as determined by content-independent processes like legislation.
It has much more of substance to say about the content of the law.
Nevertheless, Dworkin is right in arguing that both stake claims as to
what determines the content of the law, and therefore the truth of propositions about the law.

It does not belong to this article to evaluate the relative claims of Hart's
and Dworkin's theories. Our subject is their different conceptions of legal
philosophy, its tasks and methods, not the relative merits of their different
theories. As far as I can see, the fact that the concept of law can be criterially
explained is consistent both with the view that the explanation is largely
content-dependent and with the view that it is largely content-independent. It appears, however, that Dworkin thinks otherwise. He explains:

Legal philosophers are in the same situation as philosophers of justice and the
philosopher of courtesy we imagined. They cannot produce useful semantic theories of law. They cannot expose the common criteria or ground rules lawyers
follow for pinning legal labels onto facts, for there are no such rules. . . . [T]hey are
constructive interpretations: they try to show legal practice as a whole in its best
light, to achieve equilibrium between legal practice as they find it and the best
justification of that practice. *So no firm line divides jurisprudence from adjudication or
any other aspect of legal practice. Legal philosophers debate about the general part, the
interpretive foundation any legal argument must have. We may turn that coin over. Any
practical legal argument, no matter how detailed and limited, assumes the kind of abstract
foundation jurisprudence offers. . . . So any judge's opinion is itself a piece of legal philosophy.* (*LE*, 90, emphasis added)

To repeat, we can agree with Dworkin that legal philosophers do not
produce semantic explanations of the word 'law'. But they do produce
explanations of the law, and therefore also of the concept of law, the
concept which singles out legal systems from other normative and social
institutions and practices. Dworkin's theory of law, in being an account of

the nature of law, is also an explanation of the concept of law; that is, if true, it improves our understanding of the concept, mastery of which enables us to identify legal systems and to distinguish them from other phenomena, and understanding of which yields understanding of the nature of law. I should make it clear that I am using 'concept' in its normal meaning. Dworkin provides a sketchy discussion of 'concepts' (*LE*, 92–3) from which it appears that his understanding of the term is idiosyncratic. My statement that his theory provides an account of the concept of law is therefore consistent with the claim that he, using his own special notion of concept, does not view it as including an account of the concept of law.

In providing an explanation of the concept of law, legal philosophers aim to improve our understanding of the law-that-is: theirs are interpretive explanations.[42] Interpretive explanations can be criterial explanations. The rejection of the semantic sting argument does not force us to revise our understanding of legal philosophy as an exploration of the meaning of certain social practices and institutions. This is not to say, of course, that all interpretations are criterial explanations of concepts. An interpretation of *Hamlet* (the play) is not an interpretation of the concept of Hamlet, if there is such a concept. Similarly, an interpretation of the French Revolution is not an explanation of the concept of the French Revolution, nor is an interpretation of the Rent Act 1984 an interpretation of any concept.[43]

When in the course of rendering judgment a court interprets the law, it does not interpret the concept of law. It interprets the law as it bears on the issue before it. Is Dworkin denying that? The answer is far from clear. The boundaries of jurisprudence or legal philosophy are not clear. Some who write about the economic principles that, in their view, should govern town planning regulations, or about the proper definition of the offence of rape in English law, regard themselves as writing legal philosophy. Courts certainly engage in reasoning about such issues. It is a little hyperbolic to think that every one of their decisions is a 'piece of legal philosophy' on that account. But that does not matter much. What does is that Dworkin does not seem to have such considerations, or not only them, in mind when he declares all judicial opinions to be 'pieces of legal philosophy'. The crucial question is whether the passage I quoted from Dworkin applies, in his view, to the account of the nature of law—

[42] You may say that not every explanation which improves understanding is an interpretation. But every explanation that improves the understanding of a phenomenon with a meaning, or a content, is an interpretation, for interpretation is an explanation, or display, of the meaning of what is explained. Here what is explained are social practices and institutions that constitute the backbone of legal systems. Their meaning is illuminated by jurisprudential explanations.

[43] Though in all these instances an interpretation of this concept or that may be part of the case for the interpretation of the play, historical events, or law.

that is, whether he believes that every judicial opinion is a piece of legal philosophy because it includes such an account. The textual evidence suggests that he does. The relevant distinctions are not drawn by Dworkin, but that is part of the evidence, for the drift of the passage and of his general argument is to deny the importance, sometimes the possibility, of such distinctions. In what follows I consider the truth of the quotation regarding the account-of-the-nature-of-law part of legal philosophy, the part exemplified by *Law's Empire*.

The quotation drifts from the moderate to the extreme. It starts with a denial of a sharp line between jurisprudence and any part of legal practice. It proceeds to say that any legal argument assumes a basic part which legal philosophy provides, and it concludes by saying that all judicial decisions are 'pieces of legal philosophy'. The three claims are very different from each other. The first, for example, entails that conveyancing is part of a continuum at one end of which is jurisprudence, with no sharp boundary anywhere. I tend to believe that no boundaries worth bothering with are sharp. That does not mean that they lack theoretical or practical importance. It merely means that they are vague, and some questions of their location yield only indeterminate answers. It is best to put Dworkin's first point on one side. It is too vague to have any theoretical bearing in itself. We could also put on one side the third hyperbolic claim that '*any judge's opinion is itself a piece of legal philosophy*'. A 'piece' of legal philosophy they may be, but discussions, arguments, or whatever regarding the nature of law they are not.

There is no denying that questions about the nature of law can arise in courts, and can feature in judicial decisions. But so can just about any other issue, from astrophysics to biology, sociology, and the rest. That does not make judicial decisions into dissertations in any of these areas. In some areas it is easy to overlook this fact. This is because some courts' decisions set precedents. They create law that may be difficult to overturn. As always, where courts' decisions set precedents they do so even when they are mistaken or misguided (though certain mistakes can deny them precedent status or weaken it—it depends on the detailed regulations of the specific country in question). Therefore, if a court makes a mistake in its disquisition on the nature of law, its mistake may nonetheless set the law for that country. There were some intriguing examples of this during the 1960s and 1970s, as various constitutional regimes of the then new states of the British Commonwealth were swept aside by *coups d'état*.[44] Kelsen's theory found favour with various courts. On some occasions the

---

[44] Similar litigation occurred in Rhodesia after it unilaterally declared independence. See discussions of these in J. Eekelaar, 'Principles of Evolutionary Legality' and J. Finnis, 'Revolutions and Continuity of Law', in *Oxford Essays in Jurisprudence* (2nd ser., ed. A. W. B. Simpson, 1973).

courts' misunderstandings of Kelsen's misguided theory became the law of their countries.

Such judicial use of jurisprudential ideas may sometimes be in place, but it is analogous to the judicial use of ideas from biology. Dworkin's claim, as I understand it, does not rely on the fact that jurisprudence is occasionally invoked by the courts. It relies on a claim that jurisprudential theses are among the presuppositions of any decision by the courts, such that if the jurisprudential presuppositions of this or that court's opinion are false the decision is flawed. The chain of reasoning leading to this conclusion seems to be as follows. The court relies on some or other propositions of law. In relying on them it relies on some criteria for their truth according to which, in its opinion, they are true propositions. But the assumption, explicit or implicit in the decision, that these are criteria for the truth of the propositions is a jurisprudential assumption. It is part of, or a consequence of, an account of the nature of law. Hence—as in Dworkin's middle proposition in the quotation earlier (somewhat recast in light of the discussion above)—every judicial decision presupposes the truth of a theory about the nature of law, even when it does not discuss such a theory explicitly.

Persuasive as this argument appears, it is not valid as it stands. The thought that in order to know their own law the courts need to know that it falls under a general concept of law, or, indeed, that they require legal theory in order to have the concept of law, is surprising. But before I explore these concerns I will clarify one crucial point. My discussion is of the argument I spelled out, and not of its conclusion, which may be established by some other arguments. It will become clear that if I am right in the observations that follow, then this is unlikely. Nevertheless, this limitation of my inquiry is of some importance. Assume, as Dworkin claims, that some theory of the nature of law is presupposed by every judicial decision. It may then be possible to establish that that is so by considering the nature of a theory of law (plus some basic knowledge of the nature of judicial opinions). On the other hand, it may be impossible to establish the conclusion without actually establishing the correct theory of law, and showing that it entails that conclusion. Arguably, Dworkin is pursuing both methods toward the same conclusion. Arguably, his theory of law, if true, is presupposed by anyone who reasons cogently about the law. As this essay is about conceptions of legal philosophy I will not explore such avenues here. My interest is in the argument set out in the previous paragraph, which purports not to assume the truth of Dworkin's own theory of law (at that stage of the book we do not know yet what it is).[45] It is

---

[45] Though, importantly, we do know that it has to accommodate the existence of 'theoretical disputes' about the law.

meant to tell us something about the nature of legal philosophy in general, and it is interesting to see why it does not.

The argument (and while it is based on Dworkin's ideas, it is not one advanced in these terms by him) claims that to know the law governing each case one must be making, explicitly or implicitly, assumptions about the nature of law. Why so? American courts are required to decide in accordance with American law, just as Chinese courts are required to decide in accordance with Chinese law. It would follow that in rendering decisions American judges, acting in good faith, as we can assume that they do, presuppose that their decisions are in accordance with American law. They presuppose, perhaps, something about American law. This need not be much. It could be that it contains a particular rule, and that nothing else in it modifies the application of the rule to the facts of this case. Courts usually rely on a much richer set of beliefs, but these are commonly only about a tiny fragment of the law. They invariably rely on the assumption that there is nothing else in the law to upset the conclusion reached on the basis of the rules they relied on.[46] To make such an assumption, even to be justified in making it, one need have little idea of what the rest of the law is, let alone an idea of how exactly it is to be established. An analogy may illustrate the point. To believe that if I move my legs I will walk forward, I need to assume that no natural force will stop me, but I need have no specific ideas about what natural forces there are, and hardly any idea at all how to find out what they are. I am not suggesting, of course, that judges have very little knowledge of the law outside that which is relevant to the case before them. How much knowledge they actually have is a contingent matter that is neither here nor there. The point is that they need not make any specific assumptions about the content of the rest of the law or of the way to establish it when they believe that it makes no difference to the case before them.

These remarks would refute Dworkin's thesis if it is understood to be about what judges presuppose when rendering judgment. But the thesis can be readily adjusted to be about what has to be true if their decisions are to be correct, or justified according to law. It can be read to say that any judicial decision or any legal argument is sound only if the correct theory of the nature of law would bear them up, or at any rate would not contradict their conclusions. I believe that even this modest claim is mistaken. By American law, let me repeat, American judges have to decide cases according to American law (including its conflict of law doctrines). It is a mistake to believe that that duty is discharged in, or in some sense

---

[46] In these comments I wish neither to endorse nor to deny the view that courts' decisions always represent the state of the law at a time just prior to their decision, as the courts believe it to be.

presupposes, two stages, the first establishing what the law is (the answer being provided by legal philosophy) and the second applying these conclusions to establish the content of American law. Judicial decisions in American courts are vulnerable to the charge that they are wrong as a matter of American law. But it is irrelevant to their justification that they conform, if we can make sense of the notion, with the correct theory of the nature of law. Of course, we know well that if some theory of law yields the result that American law is not law, it is a misguided theory of law.

But suppose we are discussing some marginal case. Suppose we are discussing the putative law established by some government in exile over a country which it does not control, or where its control is minimal, and suppose that its judges discover that by the correct legal theory their system is not a legal system, for it lacks the necessary characteristics of control. This may make them decide to resign, or rebel, though I can see little reason why it should.[47] The point is that their duty (under the system in whose courts they sit) is to judge in accordance with the rules of that system, and it matters not at all whether these rules are legal ones.[48] I have argued elsewhere[49] that there could be legal systems in cultures that do not have the concept of law. The concept of law is a historical product, changing over the years, and the concept as we have it is more recent than the institution it is used to single out. If one accepts the point, it helps to illustrate my argument here. A court in a country with law but which does not think of it as such will be concerned to decide cases in accordance with the rules of its system, which are in fact rules of law, but that fact is not one the court is aware of, and *a fortiori* it makes no difference to the court.

There is another reason why the reconstructed argument fails, or is at best misleading. It assumes that legal philosophy creates the concept of law, whereas in fact it merely explains the concept that exists independently of it. To see the point, we must suspend for the sake of argument the previous objection. The argument was that the soundness of legal arguments establishing conclusions according to the law of the United States, let us say, depends on their conformity with the correct theory of law (or even on the correct theory having them among its consequences). But that confuses the theory of law and the concept of law. If we waive the

---

[47] I can see plenty of reasons why they should not penalize people for violation of laws which were not in effect in the country, and so on. Such facts have a moral bearing on the issue of the justice of these courts. The theoretical conclusion that the system they operate is or is not a legal system seems to have little bearing.

[48] Unless, of course, that system refers them to the writings of jurisprudence as setting a test of validity in it.

[49] 'On the Nature of Law' (The Kobe Lectures of 1994), 82 Archiv Rechts und Sozialphilosophie 1–25 (1996).

previous objection, we accept that legal arguments are sound only if they and their conclusions involve, or are consistent with, correct use of the concept of law. But the concept of law is not a product of the theory of law. It is a concept that evolved historically, under the influences of legal practice, and other cultural influences, including the influence of the legal theory of the day. Legal philosophy seeks to understand the nature of law, and that involves improving our understanding of the concept of law. If they acquire such understanding, judges will gain in the same way that they will gain if their understanding of history, economics, and politics is improved. But the soundness of their arguments, even if it depends on correct application of the concept of law, does not depend on their having the understanding which legal philosophy aspires to provide.

VII. CONCLUSION

It will be obvious that the arguments of the preceding section rely on an understanding of the task of explaining the nature of law, which is alien to Dworkin. For example, he writes:

In the heyday of semantic theories, legal philosophers were more troubled by the suggestion that wicked places really had no law. Semantic rules were meant to capture the use of 'law' generally and therefore to cover people's statements not only about their own law but about very different historical and foreign legal systems as well. It was a common argument against strong 'natural law' theories, which claim that a scheme of political organisation must satisfy certain minimal standards of justice in order to count as a legal system at all, that our linguistic practice does not deny the title of law to obviously immoral political systems. . . . if useful theories of law are not semantic theories . . . , however, but are instead interpretive of a particular stage of a historically developing practice, then the problem of immoral legal systems has a different character. Interpretive theories are by their nature addressed to a particular legal culture, generally the culture to which their authors belong. The more abstract conceptions of law that philosophers build are not. . . . But there is no reason to expect even a very abstract conception to fit foreign legal systems developed in and reflecting political ideologies of sharply different character. (*LE*, 102–3)

It is passages like this that prompt Hart to deny that Dworkin's theory competes with his own. Read literally, it seems to say that Dworkin is interested more in some of the law's provinces than in its empire. I suggested that this reconciliation of the two enterprises cannot be sustained because if Dworkin is right even only about the law of the United States then Hart's explanation of law is mistaken. But beyond that is the fact that the book belies the modesty of passages like the above. Time and again, from its beginning to its very last section, it declares itself to be offering an account of law, unqualified, in all its imperial domains.

Hart's claim that 'it is not obvious why there should be or indeed could be any significant conflict between enterprises so different as my own and Dworkin's conceptions of legal theory'[50] denies, by implication, that Dworkin's is a theory of the nature of law, not even of American law. To maintain that his is a theory of law, Dworkin has to show that it is wrong to think that there can be a general theory of the nature of law, even legal systems 'developed in and reflecting political ideologies of sharply different character'. He has to establish that the concept of law does not single out a form of political organization with central features that make it a major factor in understanding all societies in which it is to be found, however much they differ in their political ideology. After all, the fact that some countries differ in one important respect (their political ideologies) does not mean that they differ in all major respects, and therefore that there is no possibility of regarding their different institutions of government and conflict resolution as exemplifying the same type that we have, the law, whose essential features are of great importance to an understanding of forms of social organization.

That is why the semantic sting is so crucial to Dworkin's case for his conception of jurisprudence. It is his main argument to deny that there is a possible alternative to his way of conceiving the tasks of legal philosophy. Without that argument he has little to rely on, and his 'concession' that his theory does not apply to various legal systems is tantamount to conceding that his is not a theory about the nature of law. But if Hart's implied claim that Dworkin does not offer an explanation of the nature of law at all is correct, then the considerations which showed that if he has a correct account of American law then Hart is wrong in his explanation of the nature of law are reversed. It would now seem that Hart may come closer to a correct understanding of the tasks and methods of a central element in legal philosophy: the inquiry into the nature of law. For if Dworkin does not have a method to explain the nature of law in general he cannot explain the nature of American law either (it is the same). His book is not so much an explanation of the law as a sustained argument about how courts, especially American and British courts, should decide cases. It contains a theory of adjudication rather than a theory of (the nature of) law. Dworkin's failure to allow that the two are not the same is one reason for the failure of his conception of the tasks and method of jurisprudence.

---

[50] Hart, Postscript, *supra* n. 3, at 241.

2

Herbert Hart and the Semantic Sting

TIMOTHY A. O. ENDICOTT

Even to disagree, we need to understand each other. If I reject what you say without understanding you, we will only have the illusion of a disagreement. You will be asserting one thing and I will be denying another. Even to disagree, we need some agreement.

Ronald Dworkin has long been concerned with accounting for the agreement we need in order to disagree; in recent lectures he has called it a 'fulcrum of disagreement'. But it is also a fulcrum for any articulate *agreement*, because we need to understand each other in order to agree. If I nod my head without understanding you, we will only have the illusion of an agreement. Whatever the fulcrum of disagreement is, we need it for *any* communication.

The most fundamental challenge that Dworkin has made to H. L. A. Hart's theory of law is that it cannot account for the nature of legal disagreement. This is the interpretivist challenge: (i) that Hart thought that the fulcrum of disagreement is a set of shared criteria for the application of legal concepts, and (ii) that we typically do not share such criteria. The challenge is so basic that, if it succeeds, genuine disagreement about the requirements of the law is impossible in Hart's theory. That itself would be a fatal objection to a theory of law. But the challenge is even more basic: if it succeeds, it shows that Hart's theory of law makes agreement and communication about the law illusory, because the fulcrum of *agreement* that the theory postulates is something that we do *not* share. That means that Hart's theory cannot explain how law accomplishes what Hart considered its basic function: to provide standards that guide behaviour.

Dworkin's *Law's Empire* presents an interpretive theory of law as an alternative to theories that suffer from a 'semantic sting'[1]—theories, that is, that 'insist that lawyers all follow certain linguistic criteria for judging propositions of law' (*LE* 32). Dworkin claims that legal theories like Hart's cannot explain theoretical disagreement in legal practice, because they suffer from this semantic sting: they think that lawyers share uncontroversial tests ('criteria') for the truth of propositions of law. I will use the

---

[1] *Law's Empire* (1986), 45. I will refer to this work as *LE*, with page numbers in parentheses.

term 'criteria' in Dworkin's idiosyncratic way, to refer to tests for the application of an expression that are more or less complete.[2]

If, like Hart, you suffer from the semantic sting, you think that the language of the law can be meaningful only if lawyers share such criteria. And then they cannot disagree about the tests for the truth of propositions of law. They can only disagree about how penumbral cases should be resolved, or about whether the law should be changed. To disagree about the criteria for application of the language of the law would amount to speaking different languages.

If 'semantic' simply means 'concerning meaning' (or even if it means 'concerning truth-conditions'), then Dworkin's argument cannot be that Hart makes semantic claims. Any non-sceptical theory of law needs to treat law as a practice that is carried on using meaningful language. No theory is less sceptical than Dworkin's. The argument must be that Hart's semantic claims are misconceived. So we can redescribe Dworkin's distinction between interpretive theories and semantic theories as a distinction between theories that have an 'interpretive semantics' and theories that have a 'criterial semantics'. Dworkin can accept this clarification and can describe Hart's theory not as a 'semantic theory' but as a theory that misapplies 'criterial semantics' to legal terms. But Dworkin does not claim that we never share criteria for the application of a word. His theory has the apparent virtue of allowing that different semantic theories might give the best account of the meaning of different words: criterial semantics for words like 'book' and interpretive semantics for law (and presumably for most legal terms). We can look at the semantic sting argument, then, as a claim that Hart applies criterial semantics to all legal (and, incidentally, jurisprudential) terms in a way that makes real disagreement about the law impossible.

In the face of this fundamental challenge, readers might expect Hart's Postscript to defend a criterial semantic theory. But instead, Hart simply dismisses out of hand the allegation that he suffered from a semantic sting: 'Nothing in my book or in anything else I have written supports such an account of my theory.'[3] Hart seems mystified by the allegation. He denies that he ever held the 'mistaken idea that if the criteria for the

---

[2] I conclude that criteria (in this special sense) are more or less complete from Dworkin's assumption that there can be no interesting disagreement about the requirements of the law between people who share criteria. That conclusion is also supported by Dworkin's suggestion that a theorist who suffers from the semantic sting will say that, in borderline cases, 'people speak somewhat differently from one another. So lawyers may use the word "law" differently in marginal cases' (*LE*, 39). The suggestion is that two people who share criteria cannot disagree about an application of a word.

[3] H. L. A. Hart, *The Concept of Law* (2nd edn. with Postscript, ed. Penelope A. Bulloch and Joseph Raz, 1994), 246. I will refer to this work as *Concept*, with page numbers in parentheses.

identification of the grounds of law were not uncontroversially fixed, "law" would *mean* different things to different people', and he claims to have drawn 'in effect the same distinction between a concept and differ- ent conceptions of a concept which figures so prominently in Dworkin's later work' (*Concept*, 246). The denial does not explain what Hart had instead of criterial semantics. And it creates a mystery for Dworkin: *Law's Empire* used Hart as the very model of a theorist who suffers from the semantic sting.

I think that we can clear up these mysteries. There are turns of phrase in *The Concept of Law* and aspects of Hart's approach that encourage the notion that Hart had a criterial semantic theory. But it is a misinterpreta- tion. The semantic claims that Hart actually made are simple and remark- ably modest. I will argue that Hart did not have a criterial semantic theory or any semantic theory at all, if a semantic theory is a general explanatory account of what makes an application of an expression correct. I will also argue that his theory *can* make sense of genuine theoretical disagreement. When we identify the claims that Hart makes we will see the answer to Dworkin's basic question about disagreement: to Hart, the fulcrum of disagreement is nothing more than the use of paradigms.

Paradigms also feature prominently in Dworkin's view of the fulcrum of disagreement. I will address the role of paradigms in *The Concept of Law* and *Law's Empire*, for the purpose of clarifying what each theory says about the meaning of words (sections I and II). That discussion identifies a point of contention between Hart and Dworkin: can paradigms be indisputable? (section III). Section IV briefly discusses the important notion of 'pivotal cases' in *Law's Empire* and uses it as a test for the competing claims about paradigms.

I conclude that a sound theory will reject criterial semantics, but I doubt that anyone has ever had a criterial semantics. I also conclude that a sound theory cannot accept two distinctive claims of *Law's Empire*: that no paradigm of an abstract concept is secure from the interpretive process, and that abstract words are not vague.

I. THE MODESTY OF HART'S SEMANTIC CLAIMS

Why is it so tempting to think that Hart has a criterial semantic theory? To some extent, the reasons are atmospheric. He calls his book *The Concept of Law*. He confesses in his Preface to addressing 'questions which may well be said to be about the meaning of words' (p. v), and he twice quotes J. L. Austin's comment about 'using a sharpened awareness of words to sharpen our perception of the phenomena' (pp. v, 14). In cases of the open texture of a general term, he says that 'no firm convention or general agreement dictates its use' (127), suggesting that a firm convention or general agreement *dictates* the use of general terms in other cases. If 'vehicles' are banned from the park, he says that 'the language used in this context fixes necessary conditions which anything must satisfy if it is to be within its scope' (128–9) (and he seems to extend the same claim even to highly contestable legal concepts like 'fair rate' or 'safe systems of work' (131)).

All this would support the claim that Hart thinks that the fulcrum of legal disagreement is a set of shared, uncontroversial criteria for the correct application of the word 'law'. Except that he rejects that notion.

Consider a dilemma that Hart would face if he had a criterial semantic theory. Imagine that an anthropologist returns from a trip to Freedonia and says to Hart, 'You'd be interested in the legal system of Freedonia. Their law consists entirely of primary rules.' Here is the dilemma: *The Concept of Law* finds 'the key to the science of jurisprudence' in the union of primary and secondary rules (*Concept*, 81). It seems that Hart has to say that his friend the anthropologist has made not just a bad mistake, but a *bizarre sort* of mistake: by applying the word 'law' to a regime of primary rules, she is not using the word in accordance with the rules for its use. She is not even speaking English. But whatever her qualities as a legal theorist, it seems absurd to question her grasp of her mother tongue.

In fact, Hart did not believe there was any dilemma here at all. In the situation we have imagined, he would not set out to teach the anthropologist English. Nothing in *The Concept of Law* even gives him a reason to correct her. He thought that he could distinguish between 'elucidating the concepts that constitute the framework of legal thought' (*Concept*, 81) (which he was trying to do) and identifying rules for the use of words (which he was not trying to do):

We shall not indeed claim that wherever the word 'law' is 'properly' used this combination of primary and secondary rules is to be found; for it is clear that the diverse range of cases of which the word 'law' is used are not linked by any such simple uniformity, but by less direct relations—often of analogy of either form or content—to a central case. (*Concept*, 81)

This passage does not make an offhand caveat; it states three features of Hart's approach that are consistently articulated throughout *The Concept of Law*: (1) that he is not giving rules for the correct use of words,[4] (2) that there may be no shared, uniform test for the extension of a concept, and (3) that we can say no more in general terms about the extension of a concept than that its instances are linked by relations to central cases—to

---

[4] Cf. ibid. 17: 'Its [the book's] purpose is not to provide a definition of law, in the sense of a rule by reference to which the correctness of the use of the word can be tested.' See also ibid. 209.

paradigms. Those relations cannot themselves be described in the form of a criterion or set of criteria. They may be relations of analogy, and analogy is not a shared uncontroversial test of application.

The most important statement of this manifesto is Hart's account in Chapter 1 of the limited usefulness of the traditional form of definition *per genus et differentiam*. If that form of definition gave a model for the meaning of an expression, it would yield criterial semantics: to know the meaning of a word would be to know its genus and also the characteristics that speakers use to distinguish its instantiations from instantiations of other species of the same genus. That is the notion that Hart rejects:

The supposition that a general expression can be defined in this way rests on the tacit assumption that all the instances of what is to be defined as triangles and elephants have common characteristics which are signified by the expression defined. Of course, even at a relatively elementary stage, the existence of border-line cases is forced upon our attention, and this shows that the assumption that the several instances of a general term must have the same characteristics may be dogmatic. (*Concept*, 15)

All that Hart is claiming about concepts is that their instances must be linked together by resemblances to 'plain indisputable cases' (131), to 'the clear standard case or paradigm for the use of an expression' (4), to 'paradigm, clear cases' (129). But 'the several instances of a general term are often linked together in quite different ways from that postulated by the simple form of definition' (16).

For Hart, as for Wittgenstein, the fulcrum of disagreement is 'general agreement in judgments in familiar cases' (126).[5] 'General terms would be useless to us as a medium of communication unless there were such familiar, generally unchallenged cases' (126). That claim about meaning is important to Hart, but it is no part of a semantic theory, because it does not support any explanation of what makes an application of a word correct (except the non-theoretical proposition that the word applies to objects that are sufficiently similar to paradigms). It does not claim that we share criteria of applicability. He would view that sort of claim as dogmatic. The fulcrum of agreement and disagreement, in this view, is nothing more than the use that is made of a set of paradigms of the concept in question: their use as standards of comparison.

There are two possible objections to characterizing Hart's semantic claims as modest in this way: (1) that I have made them look more modest than they are, and (2) that they are still too immodest—that Hart

---

[5] Cf. the reference at ibid. 297 to Ludwig Wittgenstein, *Philosophical Investigations* (1953), ss. 208–38. At s. 242 Wittgenstein writes, 'If language is to be a means of communication there must be agreement not only in definitions but also (queer as this may sound) in judgments. . . .'

proposes, as the fulcrum of agreement and of disagreement, a form of agreement that we do not have and do not need. These two objections are discussed below.

(1) The modest characterization of Hart's claims may seem inaccurate, because he *does* discuss 'tests for' and 'characteristics' of the instantiations of concepts. We may ask, aren't those all just *criteria* for the application of concept-words? Take the concept of *law*. The purpose of Hart's book is to elucidate that concept, and he does not stop at pointing to examples. Indeed, he starts by insisting that people in general know examples of laws, and standard cases of legal systems (*Concept*, 4), and he asks whether we should answer the question 'What is law?' by simply appealing to their knowledge and saying, 'Such is the standard case of what is meant by "law" and "legal system" ', and reminding them that there may be borderline cases. He rejects that approach as unhelpful. But Hart's alternative is *not* to give criteria of applicability of 'law' that he claims we share. His alternative is to stop and ask what particular puzzles we face when we ask 'What is law?' and to address those puzzles by pointing out and describing those features of the clear cases that he judges to be salient and useful for resolving the puzzles. The features he proposes are his account of the nature of social rules, and his account of what is distinctive about *legal* rules (the union of primary and secondary rules, and in particular the role of rules of recognition).

But don't those very elements of Hart's theory of law amount to a set of criteria for the application of the word 'law'? *Not* in the sense required by the allegation that he has a criterial semantic theory: he insists that you do not need to follow his theory to use the word correctly, and he never claims that English-speaking people share the view that the features he identifies are criteria for the application of the word 'law'.[6] Hart never claims that his theory of law is true by definition, or that anyone who understands the word 'law' will agree with him in virtue of their understanding. His claims always remain vulnerable to an argument that the characteristics of law that he identifies are not actually features of what goes on in an ordinary sort of municipal legal system, or that he has misdescribed them, or they are not salient in the way he thinks.

There is another feature of Hart's theory of law that might encourage the view that he analyses the meaning of a concept-word as consisting in a set of criteria for its application. His analysis of the concept of law yields the claim that a community with law has a rule of recognition—a social rule which provides *criteria* of legal validity. Those criteria determine the

---

[6] Hart *does* claim that the officials of a legal system share criteria of legal validity (and his theory, though *not* his account of the meaning of the word 'law', is vulnerable if that claim cannot be supported). But those criteria are not semantic; see text below.

law, to the extent that it is determinate (see e.g. *Concept*, 94–5, ch. vi.1, 148). But it would be a misinterpretation of Hart to take him to be proposing that the *meaning of the word 'law'* consists of a set of criteria for identification of laws in a community. His claim is that, in the central case of a legal system, officials follow a social rule that provides such criteria. Those criteria are not criteria for the application of the word 'law', though they do identify *the law* of the community. There is nothing semantic about the criteria of legal validity: rules providing that higher courts' decisions bind lower courts, that legislation binds ministers, and so on, are not semantic rules. Hart claims that Dworkin has misunderstood him in this way—that Dworkin ignores the distinction between statements 'of what "law" is' and statements 'of what *the law* is, *i.e.,* what the law of some system permits or requires or empowers people to do' (*Concept*, 247). To Hart, rules of law are not (and are not derived from) rules for the use of the word 'law'.[7]

Hart believes there are indisputable paradigms, and that is all there is to his semantic claims. Or rather, he makes no claim that we need, or share, *more agreement* than can be captured in the proposition that the instantiations of a concept must be sufficiently similar to paradigms in relevant respects. Not that Hart believes there is anything magical about paradigms: we can explain the meaning of concept-words with or without reference to paradigms. We can explain meaning by giving accounts of the characteristics of instantiations of the word, just as well as we could by pointing to examples. But those accounts will not carry more information than we could convey by explanations that refer to paradigms. They will not report shared criteria of application any more complete than we would provide if we pointed to paradigms.[8]

On this modest view of Hart's claims about the application of a concept-word, he only claims to be pointing out important features of plain indisputable cases of the concept. An apparent counter-example to this view is Hart's talk of two 'necessary and sufficient conditions' for the existence of a legal system: general obedience by citizens and effective acceptance by officials (*Concept*, 116). Acceptance by officials is, he says, 'logically a necessary condition of our ability to speak of the existence of a single legal system'. That certainly reads as if he is giving a rule for the correct use of the phrase 'legal system': he is claiming that nothing less

---

[7] There is a further objection to the view that the notion of a rule of recognition commits Hart to a criterial semantics for the word 'law'. A rule of recognition does not provide 'criteria' in the Dworkinian sense (see *supra* n. 2): the tests for the truth of propositions of law provided by a rule of recognition lack the completeness of 'criteria' (see *Concept* ch. vii, 4).

[8] Here too Hart could agree with Wittgenstein: 'if a person has not yet got the *concepts,* I shall teach him to use the words by means of *examples* and by *practice.*—And when I do this I do not communicate less to him than I know myself.' Wittgenstein, *supra* n. 5, at s. 208.

than his two conditions would suffice for that phrase to apply, and no more can be required. If the modest view of Hart's semantic claims is right, you might say, he should have talked of characteristic features of paradigm cases of legal systems, and not of necessary and sufficient conditions for speaking of a legal system.

I believe a charitable interpretation of Hart will take this passage in the following way. His concern there was to develop an account of acceptance of the rule of recognition. He wanted to insist that acceptance by citizens is not required, because he thought that, if a legal regime were imposed on a populace by force, it would still be relevantly similar to paradigm municipal legal systems. He also wanted to insist that acceptance by officials *is* required, because without it 'the characteristic unity and continuity of a legal system would have disappeared' (*Concept,* 116). Acceptance by officials of a rule of recognition is not a criterion of law required by a rule for the use of the word 'law'; it is a condition for the existence of a characteristic feature of paradigm legal systems. Even if Hart's claim is true, official acceptance is 'logically a necessary condition' just in the sense that, without general official acceptance of a rule of recognition, a characteristic feature of paradigm legal systems would be missing. On this interpretation, the passage is consistent with the modest view of Hart's semantic claims; his desire to contrast acceptance by officials with acceptance by citizens led him to use the misleading phrase 'necessary and sufficient conditions'. A similar approach to the interpretation of Hart could deal with his comment that, in a prohibition on 'vehicles', 'the language used in this context fixes necessary conditions which anything must satisfy if it is to be within its scope' (129). I am proposing that, in Hart's theory, those 'conditions' simply have the same content as a requirement that the thing in question must be similar in relevant respects to paradigm vehicles.

So all that Hart claims that people share concerning a concept like law is the ability to identify 'examples of law', and the idea that there are different legal systems in different countries, and an ability to identify salient points of similarity among legal systems. People can articulate those similarities in something like the following 'skeleton way':

They comprise (i) rules forbidding or enjoining certain types of behaviour under penalty; (ii) rules requiring people to compensate those whom they injure in certain ways; (iii) rules specifying what must be done to make wills, contracts or other arrangements which confer rights and create obligations; (iv) courts to determine what the rules are and when they have been broken, and to fix the punishment or compensation to be paid; (v) a legislature to make new rules and abolish old ones. (*Concept,* 3)

Now, the claim that Hart has a criterial semantics might seem to be borne out by this set of features of a municipal legal system, which appear to amount to a set of criteria for application of the word 'law' or of the phrase 'legal system'. But Hart is not even committed to the claim that English speakers share the understanding that these are features of law (he says that he put this account 'perhaps optimistically . . . into the mouth of an educated man' (*Concept*, 5)). More importantly, look at what the account amounts to. We can cross out the word 'rule', which, since Dworkin wrote 'The Model of Rules',[9] has carried theoretical baggage that Hart did not have in mind. Read Hart's account to say that 'legal systems (i) forbid or enjoin . . . ; (ii) require people . . . ; (iii) specify . . . ; (iv) have courts . . . ; (v) have a legislature . . .'. If that is all that Hart's theory provides in the way of shared criteria for application of 'law', it does not support the claim that he had a criterial semantics for such concepts: *those* features of law are, again, simply the least controversial sorts of statement that can be made about paradigm legal systems. We share the view that these are features of law, but that is no more than to say that we share a set of paradigms, and these are obvious (and obviously important) features of the paradigms. In Hart's view, we can come to understand the concept better by developing a more searching account (an account that is *not* generally shared by English speakers) that addresses and resolves a particular puzzle about the concept. The standard of success for that account will *not* be that it provides 'correct tests for applying some word' (*LE*, 41), or that it is uncontroversial: Hart was all too aware, throughout his career, that his theory of law was controversial. The standard of success will be that it addresses the puzzle in question, and is a faithful account of the paradigms. Such an account will not provide criteria for the application of its theoretical terms, because it will leave ample room for uses of those terms that are analogous. In fact, Hart's approach suggests that the extension of any theoretical term in the social sciences will be determined by principles of analogy.[10]

(2) If the modest interpretation of Hart is right, he still retains the basic, controversial claim that paradigms are indisputable. It may seem that Hart's account as I have characterized it still supposes too much agreement of the wrong sort. That charge calls for a closer look at Dworkin's interpretivist claim that paradigms can be eradicated.

---

[9] In *Taking Rights Seriously* (1977), ch. 2.

[10] In *Natural Law and Natual Rights* (1980), John Finnis gives a valuable elaboration of this aspect of Hart's approach, associating it with Aristotle's notion of '*pros hen* homonymy', and with Joseph Raz's approach to the extension of theoretical terms (at 9–11).

II. DWORKIN ON PARADIGMS

Paradigms anchor interpretations, but no paradigm is secure from challenge by a new interpretation that accounts for other paradigms better and leaves that one isolated as a mistake. (*LE*, 72)

To Dworkin, paradigms are part of the pre-interpretive material on which an interpreter goes to work. That is, they are part of what a successful interpretation (in fact, 'any plausible interpretation'—*LE*, 72) must fit. But no single paradigm is guaranteed to emerge intact from the post-interpretive stage, at which the interpreter 'adjusts his sense of what the practice "really" requires so as better to serve the justification he accepts at the interpretive stage' (*LE*, 66). No eligible interpretation could abandon all the paradigms, but no individual paradigm is safe: for an interpretation to be eligible is for it to fit some proportion of paradigms. And an interpretation that ousts a particular paradigm can only do so by accounting better for other paradigms than any interpretation that retains the ousted paradigm.

Paradigms of interpretive concepts are different from 'cases in which, as philosophers say, a concept holds "by definition", as bachelorhood holds of unmarried men' (*LE*, 72). No paradigm of an interpretive concept is secure.

The same point can be framed in terms of Dworkin's distinction between concepts and conceptions. Dworkin claims that the expressions used to set out fundamental rights in a constitution, such as 'equal' and 'cruel', are not vague, but abstract, and represent appeals to contested concepts that admit of different conceptions. To apply such an expression, it is never enough to be familiar with the concept and the facts. You must also develop a conception of the concept. In Dworkin's theory, no legal indeterminacy arises from the use of such concepts, because there is always a best conception of a contested concept.[11]

Law's Empire uses the concept of courtesy as an example of an abstract concept. Any member of the community will know of paradigms of courtesy. But no paradigm is secure. Picture a paradigm of courtesy: that men should stand when a woman enters a room (*LE*, 72). A new interpretation of the practice of courtesy might oust that paradigm, and conclude that it is *not* courteous for men to stand when a woman enters the room. And such a paradigm-busting interpretation would not be a proposal to

---

[11] More precisely, the best conception will yield a determinate outcome in any case unless there is a tie (which is inconceivable) or unless the pre-interpretive materials which a conception must fit are too meagre (which does not happen in any real legal system). For a recent discussion, see Ronald Dworkin, 'Objectivity and Truth: You'd Better Believe It', 25 Phil. & Pub. Aff. 87, 136–8 (1996).

change the requirements of the practice, but a conclusion as to what those requirements really are. So where Hart might say that possessing a concept entails knowing that it applies to a paradigm case, Dworkin sees no such connection. Dworkin's theory denies that abstract words have any application that is independent of theory-building: every question of the application of an abstract concept-word is an interpretive question.

We have seen that Hart's Postscript associates a concept with the *meaning* of a concept-word, and a conception with its *application*. He claims that Dworkin accused him of confusing 'the *meaning* of a concept with the criteria for its *application*' (*Concept*, 246). Denying that he had suffered from that confusion, he writes, 'I drew in effect the same distinction between a concept and different conceptions of a concept which figures so prominently in Dworkin's later work' (246).[12]

If we are to make sense of Hart's work, it is essential to distinguish between knowing the meaning of a word and being able to apply it correctly in any particular case. *Meaning* is what speakers share (it is the fulcrum of agreement and disagreement). It is something that a philosopher can hope to elucidate or clarify by pointing out what is important about practices with which we are already familiar—though the elucidation itself may be controversial. *Correct application* may be controversial, and we should not expect that philosophers will be much help in resolving controversies about the application of words (those controversies are, after all, just controversies about what is the case). Hart's theory needs some such distinction if it is to give a satisfying account of the role of 'agreement in judgments'.

But it is very hard to see how Hart could have been working with the distinction between concepts and conceptions as Dworkin understood it, despite what Hart says in the Postscript. Dworkin has insisted that his distinction between concept and conception is 'very different' from the distinction between meaning and application ('extension') (*LE*, 71). His distinction is between a 'more abstract idea' and a 'particular substantive theory' (*LE*, 71). Even an uncontroversial statement about the concept of courtesy (Dworkin's example is that courtesy is a matter of respect) is interpretive. In fact, it seems that even such an abstract statement *may not* be conceptual at all: Dworkin is careful not to say that it *is* conceptual, stating that it would be 'natural for people to regard' it as 'in the way of conceptual' (*LE*, 70) and adding significant

---

[12] The distinction Hart refers to is at *Concept*, 160. He discussed the same distinction in an introduction he wrote for Chaim Perelman, *The Idea of Justice and the Problem of Argument* (1963), pp. vii–viii: 'Justice is a concept of complex structure within which we should distinguish a constant formal element and a varying material element. This distinction might be presented in terms used in recent English moral philosophy as one between the constant *definition* of justice and the varying *criteria* for its application.'

quotation marks to the claim that there is 'a "conceptual" connection between courtesy and respect' (71). Similarly, in Dworkin's theory, paradigms of courtesy are not conceptual, but have a 'kind of conceptual flavour' (72). Concepts, for Dworkin, are 'plateaus'. On the plateau, paradigms have a conceptual flavour, and statements that are abstract and uncontroversial enough will *seem* to be conceptual.

Dworkin's agile account of the distinction between concepts and conceptions does not support the association of concepts with meaning and of conceptions with application. In his usage, concepts and conceptions are just different levels at which more abstract and more concrete interpretive statements are made. Dworkin never says what the *meaning* of a word like 'courtesy' is. We could think of the concept of courtesy or the best conception of courtesy as giving the meaning of the word 'courtesy'. But if we think of the meaning of a word as 'linguistic ground rules everyone must follow to make sense' (the notion of meaning that Dworkin ascribes to criterial semantic theories) (*LE*, 71), then neither a Dworkinian concept nor a Dworkinian conception can be equated with the meaning of a word. Perhaps, on Dworkin's understanding of the nature of rules, in the case of abstract concepts there is no such thing as 'linguistic ground rules everyone must follow to make sense'. That does not mean that such words have no meaning, of course. Meaning just *is* the 'fulcrum of disagreement', and Dworkin's account of the interpretive process is itself, in part, an account of the meaning of abstract expressions.

To summarize, in Dworkin's view the fulcrum of disagreement is a shared interpretive attitude toward a shared set of paradigms. In Hart's view, the fulcrum of disagreement is a shared set of paradigms, and a shared understanding that the word applies to those paradigms and to cases that are sufficiently similar in relevant respects.

There are two distinctive differences between these theories: their view of the relation between paradigms and the application of the concept in other cases (to Hart it is a relation—perhaps a variety of relations—of similarity; to Dworkin the relation is interpretive), and their view of the status of paradigms. I will address the second point, and ask whether paradigms can be ousted.

III. CAN PARADIGMS BE INDISPUTABLE?

Some paradigms are not so easily abandoned as men-rising-when-a-woman-enters-the-room was abandoned as a paradigm of courtesy. Some paradigms have a very strong 'conceptual flavour', such as *The Blue Danube* as an example of music, or the *Odyssey* as an example of epic poetry, or the rack as an example of cruel punishment.[13] It seems that no conception of epic poetry could account for other instances of the genre if it excluded the *Odyssey,* and no conception of cruel punishment could account for other paradigms if it claimed that the rack is not cruel. Dworkin's theory has resources to provide an account of such paradigms, but I will argue that no such account can do justice to their persistence.

Dworkin's theory could account for persistent paradigms as being particularly deeply embedded as integrated members of groups of paradigms that are so significant that no acceptable holistic interpretation could 'isolate' them. But that approach would admit that those examples do not simply have a conceptual flavour, but *are* conceptual, so that anyone who knows the meaning of the phrase 'epic poetry' and is familiar with the *Odyssey* knows that the *Odyssey* is an epic poem. If you only need to know the English language, and to be familiar with the rack, in order to know that the rack is a cruel punishment, then it seems that you do not need to interpret anything to arrive at the judgment that the rack is cruel.[14] You do not need to develop a conception of cruelty; you only need to grasp the concept.

So it seems that Dworkin's theory should account for persistent paradigms simply by maintaining the claim that a successful interpretation could conceivably show that any such object is not an instance of the concept in question. Conflicting, intuitively attractive notions militate for and against that claim: (1) After all, *The Blue Danube is* music, and no interpretation can show otherwise. (2) After all, we can understand someone who says that *The Blue Danube* is *not* music. It seems attractive to say that such a person is using the same concept as everyone else, and offering an (eccentric) interpretive claim. If their mistake were conceptual, how could we even understand them? They would not be speaking our language.

A. Crazy claims

To sort out these conflicting notions, consider the following collection of crazy claims, which deny that concept-words of various kinds apply to objects that seem to be paradigms:

- *The Blue Danube* isn't music; it's Muzak.
- The *Odyssey* isn't an epic poem—an epic has a hero who represents a race, or a nation. Odysseus is just one Greek, pitted against some Greeks and some gods.

---

[13] Cf. *Taking Rights Seriously, supra* n. 9, at 136: 'If the Court finds that the death penalty is cruel, it must do so on the basis of some principles or groups of principles that unite the death penalty with the thumbscrew and the rack.'

[14] I do not mean that you can know English, or the meaning of words such as 'epic' or 'cruel', without knowing anything else.

- The rack is not a cruel punishment—for a vicious crime. It's not cruel to do to the offender what the offender did to an innocent person.
- The United States doesn't have a legal system; a legal system has rules and the United States just has lawyers.
- *David Copperfield* isn't a novel; it's an autobiography.
- Pele wasn't a soccer player; he was an artist.
- I'm not bald; I just have removable hair.
- He may not be *married*, but he's no bachelor.
- The sky is not blue. You haven't *seen* blue until you've seen a sapphire.

These crazy claims seem to pose a dilemma for Hart. Consider the claim about *The Blue Danube*. From Hart's point of view, that seems to be a claim that *x* is not F, where the concept of F can be elucidated by pointing out salient features of (e.g.) *x*. So the claim seems to be nonsense. In fact, all the claims in the list seem to be nonsense. But *that* can't be right: nonsense is meaningless, and these claims are all too meaningful. We can understand them perfectly well. They are false (or they combine true claims with false claims), but they are not nonsense.

We can imagine theories that arrive at the crazy claims. That very fact seems to make the case for an interpretivist semantic theory (in fact, it seems to extend the interpretivist claim to *all* words, including words for which Dworkin would adopt a criterial semantics, like 'bachelor' and presumably 'bald'). The fact that we can conceive of theories that reach the conclusions in the list suggests that, if we are to contradict any of the crazy claims, what we need to do is to develop a better theory. Of course, the theories that yield the crazy claims are bad theories—but that is no problem for interpretivism. The interpretivist claim still seems to be made out: we can only conclude that each of the claims is wrong by working out theories that compete with the faulty theories, and that succeed by showing that those theories give unsatisfactory accounts of the concepts in question.

But what is the flaw in, for example, the theory of epic poetry that concludes that the *Odyssey* is not an epic poem? The flaw is that it is not a theory *of epic poetry*. Perhaps the theorist is making a striking claim for rhetorical effect, to draw attention to a feature of some epics that is especially intriguing—perhaps to claim that the *Odyssey* lacks a feature that is distinctive of much of the epic tradition. But there is just no prospect that a better interpretation of that tradition could eject the *Odyssey* from the material that an interpretation of epic poetry must give an account of. That does not mean that people will not start excluding the *Odyssey* from what they call 'epic poetry' tomorrow. It means that, if they do so, they will not be using the concept of epic poetry that we have today.

Dworkin's theory has the equipment to give a rather similar account of the crazy claims—but an account that reaches different conclusions about paradigms. Dworkin distinguishes between eligible and ineligible interpretations (*LE*, 255), between hard and easy cases (255), and between questions on which a statute is clear (so that, we might say, a decision contrary to the clear meaning would not be giving effect to the requirements of the statute) and cases on which it is unclear (351–3). A decision is based on an ineligible interpretation when it does not meet the 'rough threshold requirement' of fit (255) (i.e. when it lacks 'textual integrity') (338–40) or when it does not present 'any competent justification' (339). Dworkin's account portrays people who make the crazy claims as perfectly competent speakers of the English language, whose theories still count *as theories* of the concepts they purport to interpret, but are ineligible because they ignore the interpretive requirements of integrity. The conclusion that they fail to oust the paradigms they attack is an interpretive conclusion.

The issue, it seems, is how to describe what is going on when people make the crazy claims. Are they best described as not giving a theory of music, etc. (as Hart might say)? Or as giving bad theories of music, etc.— so bad that we can call them ineligible (as Dworkin might say)?

There are two related considerations in favour of the first description.

1. The crazy claims *are* nonsense, in a sense. People who make those claims could very well understand the English language. But people who understand English do lots of things with it, and the people who make these claims are using it to talk nonsense. Nonsense is not necessarily meaningless, or self-contradictory—it may only be absurdly false. The crazy claims are all instances of a useful and common rhetorical figure, in which the speaker withholds a term from an object to which it clearly applies. So they can be explained as *parasitic* uses of concepts. If x is clearly an F, then saying that x is not an F can be a usefully hyperbolic way of saying that x is a pre-eminent F (Pele), or a bad F (*The Blue Danube*), or not *just* an F; or not the *only* F . . .[15] When we read each claim, the first half just seems silly, but when we read the second half we see the point. The claims are figurative ways of saying such things as that the concept is too good for the object, or that the object is too good for the concept. It is the indisputability of the paradigms disputed by the crazy claims that gives those claims their ironic or dramatic impact. Such claims would not have the meaning that they have if they were not disputing the indisputable— if the paradigms they attack were not secure from challenge.

---

[15] Note that Hart begins *The Concept of Law* with some crazy claims about law (from Llewellyn, Holmes, Gray, Austin, and Kelsen; *Concept*, 1). He does not dismiss them as senseless, he describes them as seeming 'strange and paradoxical', and says that 'such statements are *both* illuminating and puzzling: they are more like great exaggerations of some truths about law unduly neglected, than cool definitions' (ibid. 2).

2. The interpretivist can describe the people who make the crazy claims as linguistically competent, but so can Hart. We have already seen that *The Concept of Law* does not claim to state rules for the use of words. If Hart does not have a criterial semantic theory, then obviously he does not claim that there are shared rules in the form of criteria—or so I claimed in the discussion of the anthropologist who visited Freedonia.

However, the crazy claims are different from the anthropologist's use of the phrase 'legal system': the anthropologist did not deny, for example, that the United States has a legal system; she only applied the phrase to a social order that does not share the features of paradigm legal systems that Hart identified as salient. So what about the proposition that things like Pele count as soccer players? Doesn't Hart believe *that* is a rule for the use of the term 'soccer player'? If Hart thinks that paradigms are indisputable cases on which there must be general agreement if communication is to be possible, how can the people who make the crazy claims be speaking English?

Perhaps Hart could say that agreement in paradigm cases must be general for communication to be possible but it need not be absolute. If someone made crazy claims about every clear case of the application of every concept, communication with that person would become, if not impossible, rather strained. And if many people did so, there would be no clear cases. But there is plenty of latitude in human communication—more latitude, no doubt, than Hart pointed out. People do not stop talking English, and do not become unintelligible when they start talking nonsense. People are surprisingly intelligible. Lawyers in particular ought to be aware that people are capable of disputing the indisputable. The fact that people can make crazy claims does not mean that those claims are interpretations of the concepts they purport to interpret.

But there is more to say than Hart said. Dworkin has pointed out that objects that appear to be paradigms (understood as clear examples of the application of the expression, which are useful in explaining the meaning of the expression) can sometimes be eradicated. The difficult task is to make claims of the right level of generality. Dworkin's theory overgeneralizes when it claims that no paradigm of an abstract concept is secure from challenge. Perhaps a theory that claims that there are ineradicable paradigms of all genuine concepts would also overgeneralize. Of course, 'paradigm' is only a technical term, and we could define 'paradigm' as an ineradicable instantiation of a concept (so that ostensible paradigms that have to be eradicated are simply not *genuine* paradigms). Contrary to what Dworkin's theory suggests, that is a definition that would make perfect sense, even for concepts that he calls interpretive. But we would not be able to offer criteria for identifying such things, and there may be many items concerning which we would encounter considerable doubt and disagreement as to whether they are paradigms in that sense. 'Paradigm' in that sense would not be meaningless, and it would have genuine application, but it would be vague. Some paradigms (in the sense of examples that people find useful in explaining meaning) can be ousted and some cannot be ousted by a theory of the concept, and the distinction is not sharp.

We can make another important point about how general a claim can be made concerning the ineradicability of paradigms. The concepts of music, cruelty, law, and so on (which Dworkin calls abstract or interpretive concepts) are certainly more interesting, complex, debatable and evaluative than 'bald' or 'bachelor' or 'blue' (words of the sort for which Dworkin proposes a criterial semantics). But they are similar in this respect: there are indisputable paradigms of the application of both sorts of word. The meaning of any of these words can be conveyed by pointing out paradigms and saying 'things *like this* are . . .'. So the claim that there are indisputable paradigms can be made about a very wide variety of expressions.

I propose that the ineligibility of the crazy claims is misdescribed as the outcome of a theory; the conclusion that they are ineligible cannot be the outcome of a theory, if any alternative theory would be a theory *of* something other than (e.g.) music or epic poetry. And by the same token, a claim that *David Copperfield* is a novel, or a claim that the rack is a cruel punishment, is misdescribed as the successful outcome of a theory of the novel or a theory of cruelty.

That view is compatible with a great deal of genuine theoretical disagreement about the requirements of the law. *Law's Empire* shows how disagreement can go deeper than a criterial theory would allow. But disagreement can go deeper than a competition between conceptions. People can have genuine disagreements not just about conceptions, but about the concept of, for example, law. Hart and Dworkin do not simply offer competing conceptions of law—they disagree about the concept.[16] Of course, people can even disagree about the nature of concepts themselves. And the crazy claims can actually be sincere.

---

[16] I think that this claim about their debate is consistent with what Dworkin says about the nature of concepts, since 'the contrast between concept and conception is . . . a contrast between levels of abstraction at which the interpretation of the practice can be studied' (*LE*, 71). 'Political philosophy thrives . . . in spite of our difficulties in finding any adequate statement of the concept of justice' (*LE*, 93). He implies that we could say the same about the concept of law.

IV. 'PIVOTAL CASES': A TEST FOR THE NOTION OF PARADIGMS

To counter what he calls the 'sophisticated' or 'borderline case' defence of legal positivism, Dworkin proposes that genuine legal disputes can arise not only in borderline cases, but also in 'pivotal cases' (*LE*, 39–43). A pivotal case concerning the application of an expression is one that each side in a dispute claims is a clear case. Presumably most legal disputes over the application of an expression are pivotal cases, because litigants do not commonly argue that they have a borderline case.

Dworkin argues that pivotal cases must be something different from (and less trivial than) borderline cases of the application of vague language. But the most mundane vague expressions can yield pivotal cases. You and I might agree that someone is a borderline case, for example, for 'bald' or 'tall', and disagree about how to draw the line. Or you could think someone is clearly tall, or clearly bald, and I could think the person is clearly not tall, or clearly not bald—even though we both speak English. When we engage in either form of dispute, 'borderline' or 'pivotal', we are differing about whether the person in question is sufficiently similar in relevant respects to paradigms of tallness or baldness.[17] And that suggests that Hart need not deny that there are pivotal cases. Consider Dworkin's example of a dispute over a pivotal case—whether photography is an art form:

One group argues that (whatever others think) photography is a central example of an art form, that any other view would show a deep misunderstanding of the essential nature of art. The other takes the contrary position that any sound understanding of the character of art shows photography to fall wholly outside it, that photographic techniques are deeply alien to the aims of art. It would be quite wrong in these circumstances to describe the argument as one over where some borderline should be drawn. The argument would be about what art, properly understood, really is; it would reveal that the two groups had very different ideas about why even standard art forms they both recognize—painting and sculpture—can claim that title. (*LE*, 42)

Perhaps we can view these claims as a potent argument against criterial semantics—against the view that the dispositions of speakers determine the correct application of the word 'art'. But nothing in Dworkin's scenario conflicts with Hart's claims about language. All that Hart claims is what Dworkin suggests—that the debate makes sense because there are standard art forms.

---

[17] So we could *not* have a 'pivotal' dispute about whether someone with no hair is bald, or about whether someone 7 ft. 6 in. high is tall. I could still disagree with you even in a paradigm case, however, by making a crazy claim. There is no sharp distinction between pivotal disputes and disputes in which one party is making a crazy claim.

There are paradigms of art—such as painting and sculpture—and I can elucidate the concept of art by pointing out what is salient about those paradigms. That task of elucidation will require me to make controversial claims about what is salient, and it may require me to make controversial judgments as to whether (for example) photography is art. What the task will *not* require me to do is to conclude whether, in the final analysis, painting and sculpture really are forms of art. It is not just that the conclusion is easy to reach. It is that the propositions that painting is an art form or that sculpture is an art form *are not conclusions*. When people talk about art forms, they are talking about things like painting and sculpture, and there is nothing I can do to change that. Of course, I can deny that painting is an art form. My crazy claim will be intelligible, and it might conceivably be a useful way of getting some point across. Or I can just decide to use the phrase 'art form' to mean something other than *art form*. Those possibilities tell us nothing about the meaning or application of the expression 'art form'. They just remind us of the variety of things that people can do with language.

V. CONCLUSION

An account of the use of language should dissent from two elements of Dworkin's semantic theory: the claim that no paradigm of an abstract concept is secure, and the claim that vagueness is a semantic defect of words like 'bald' and is not a feature of words like 'courtesy or cruel' (see e.g. *LE*, 17).[18] Accepting these claims does not commit anybody to criterial semantics; if I am right, it is very important in understanding Hart to see that he was not offering a criterial semantic theory.

For at least some abstract concepts, we should accept that some paradigms are indisputable instances, just as it is indisputable that a person with no hair is bald.

That does not mean that *The Concept of Law* is the last word on the meaning of language. My argument has partly been that Hart said very little about it. Dworkin has pointed out the important fact that some cases that appear to be paradigms of some concept (even cases that everyone has always treated as paradigms) may not in fact be instances of the concept at all. And there is no sharp distinction between ostensible paradigms that can be ousted in that way and paradigms that cannot be ousted. If people can

---

[18] This claim becomes important in assessing Dworkin's theory if there is no answer to some questions of the application of vague expressions. For an argument to that effect (and a brief discussion of Dworkin's claim that abstract concepts are not vague), see T. A. O. Endicott, 'Vagueness and Legal Theory', 3 Legal Theory 37 (1997).

have pivotal disagreements, it seems that vagueness (which Hart vaguely called 'open texture') is more than a matter of a fringe or periphery. These insights are not inconsistent with Hart's semantic views. But they add important elements.

3

Hart's Semantics

NICOS STAVROPOULOS

I. INTRODUCTION

There is no doubt that H. L. A. Hart thought the study of words important to the study of law. He announces that methodological principle in the Preface to *The Concept of Law*,[1] saying that he has raised in that book 'questions that may well be said to be about the meaning of words', including how 'being obliged' differs from 'having an obligation', and that he has examined the semantics of certain kinds of statements (p. v). He goes on to explain the place of such questions in metaphysical inquiry:

Notwithstanding its concern with analysis the book may also be regarded as an essay in descriptive sociology; for the suggestion that inquiries into the meaning of words merely throw light on words is false. Many important distinctions, which are not immediately obvious, between types of social situation or relationships may best be brought to light by an examination of the standard uses of relevant expressions and of the way in which these depend on social context, itself often left unstated. In this field of study it is particularly true that we may use, as Professor J. L. Austin said, 'a sharpened awareness of words to sharpen our perception of the phenomena'.

It appears, then, that Hart thought that semantic analysis casts light on the nature of the objects to which words apply—in general, not only in the case of law. Further, his semantics was general, not special to the case of law. He explicitly took his semantic insights regarding the relations between instances of general terms, as well as his views on rule-following, from Ludwig Wittgenstein, and his open-texture doctrine from Friedrich Waissmann's gloss on Wittgenstein.[2] He returned to discussion of general semantic issues in a paper published almost ten years after *The Concept of Law*, where, describing to a German audience developments in Anglo-Saxon jurisprudence, he credits Wittgenstein and J. L. Austin with

I am grateful to David Dyzenhaus, Pavlos Elefheriadis, Mark Greenberg, James Penner, Joseph Raz, Richard Tur, and participants at the Oxford–Toronto Jurisprudence Colloquim, held at the University of Toronto Law School in September 2000, for comments on earlier drafts.

[1] 2nd edn., ed. P. Bulloch and J. Raz (Oxford, Clarendon Press, 1994). Herinafter *CL*; simple page references to that book are given in parentheses in the text.
[2] *CL*, 279–80 (n. to p. 15), 297 (n. to p. 125), and 297 (n. to p.128), respectively.

inspiring a whole new 'phase' in analytical jurisprudence.[3] They provided 'the main stimulus'[4] for that new phase, even though they were concerned with language. Hart explains in that paper in no uncertain terms what he thought to be the relation between semantic theory and jurisprudence:

much of what they had to say about the forms of language, the character of general concepts, and of rules determining the structure of language, has important implications for jurisprudence and the philosophy of law.[5]

This passage expresses what I mean by saying that semantics was important to Hart's theory of law. By 'semantics' I mean non-trivial, often controversial, theoretical claims regarding the structure and nature of language and the character of concepts. I mean the subject matter, in other words, of philosophy of language.[6]

After laying out his thesis regarding the relation between semantics and legal theory, Hart proceeds to give his audience 'two examples of the philosophy underlying this newer form of analytical jurisprudence'. First, the 'open texture' of 'most empirical concepts and not merely legal concepts', a notion that Wittgenstein, he said, expressed in words 'which fit the law very closely'. He goes on to quote him: 'I said that the application of a word is not everywhere bounded by rules.' 'We are not equipped with rules for every possible application [of it].' 'The extension of the concept is *not* closed by a frontier. It is not everywhere circumscribed by rules.'[7] The second example involves Austin's claims regarding the performative function of language, a notion that can be understood by recognizing that 'given a background of rules or conventions which provide that if a person says certain words then certain other rules shall be brought into operation, this determines the function or, in a broad sense, the meaning of the words in question.'[8]

---

[3] 'Jhering's Heaven of Concepts and Modern Analytical Jurisprudence', originally published 1970, repr. in Hart's collected *Essays in Jurisprudence and Philosophy* (Oxford, Clarendon Press, 1983), at 271.

[4] Ibid. 274.   [5] Ibid.

[6] Some substantive issues in semantics, under my terminology, are nowadays studied under the rubric of the philosophy of mind: these are issues involving the nature of concepts and more specifically the individuation of thoughts, in which particular concepts figure. I believe I do not do violence to philosophical use by calling such issues semantic. There is no doubt that the study of concepts involves a great number of strictly semantic questions (of correct application, of sense and reference, of extension, and so on) and everyone agrees that thoughts are semantically evaluable. My use does not imply that language is somehow more fundamental to thought, or any other contentious philosophical thesis. Philosophers of mind are divided as to whether language is analytically prior to thought or vice versa, or neither, but they all seem agreed that the two are very intimately related.

[7] I am using the translation of paras. 84, 80, and 68 respectively, of the English edn. of *Philosophical Investigations* (Oxford, Blackwell, 1968).

[8] 'Jhering', 274–6.

Hart's explicitness regarding the relevance and importance of semantics to the theory of law places upon us an intellectual burden: we should try to work out the precise relation between semantics and legal theory in Hart's thought, and identify the substantive semantic views which drive it. We should ask, not whether Hart thought semantics is important— Hart says as much; rather, we should ask *why* he thought so; *which* particular semantic insights he thought were crucial to the study of law; and *how* semantic theory affected his theory of law.

These and other more specific questions regarding Hart's view on the relation between semantics and the metaphysics of law remain hotly contested. Did Hart employ a particular theory of language in the course of seeking semantic insight? What was his method for studying the use of words? How, according to Hart, does the study of words support conclusions as to the nature of law? These questions are important, among other reasons because they bear on the question whether Hart's theory, as well as any theory of law that follows his methodology, is vulnerable to an argument of Ronald Dworkin's against the viability of such theories that has become known as the semantic sting (hereinafter, the sting) argument.[9]

Dworkin attributes to Hart a philosophical prejudice to the effect that sharing concepts amounts to sharing criteria for their correct application. Dworkin argues that the prejudice—the sting—made Hart unable adequately to explain disagreement among lawyers. Lawyers disagree, Dworkin says, because they have competing conceptions of some concepts. They rely upon substantively different understandings of the relevant concept, and they exchange arguments in support of one or the other understanding. Disagreement about whether a certain behaviour is negligent is substantive, theoretical disagreement about what negligence really is. The sting makes such disagreement impossible: to disagree about negligence we must share the concept of negligence; but if sharing the concept amounts to sharing criteria for its correct application, we cannot really disagree at all. We can only disagree insofar as at least one of us does not fully understand the concept, and therefore fails to use the shared criteria; alternatively, if we are both using the same criteria, we can only disagree about borderline cases where the criteria provide inadequate guidance. Dworkin claims that the fact that Hart's theory cannot adequately account for a central feature of legal practice—theoretical disagreement—suggests that his entire project is misguided. Dworkin

---

[9] See *Law's Empire* (Cambridge, Mass., Harvard University Press, 1986), 41–6. There seems to be some confusion as to who stings whom in Dworkin's argument, so some terminological clarification may be necessary. The semantic sting argument is an argument to the effect that Hart suffers from the semantic sting. Dworkin's argument *attributes* the sting to Hart. If Dworkin is right, the sting belongs to Hart, not Dworkin.

says that the sting shows that a descriptively accurate theory of law would have to be *interpretive* in the sense that it would have to fit and justify legal practice; but recasting Hart's views on law in interpretive terms cannot save it either, since as an interpretive theory of law it does not fit and justify legal practice as well as Dworkin's own interpretive project based on the ideals of philosophical and political integrity.

In Parts II and III, I am going to argue that Hart relied on broadly semantic considerations in building his theory of law in at least two ways: first, by engaging in 'conceptual analysis' informed by a set of assumptions about the nature of concepts; second, by embracing a particular doctrine—the doctrine of open texture—regarding the semantics of general terms. Both ways of relying upon semantic considerations are part of an empiricist philosophical outlook.

Hart probably relied on semantics in more ways than the two outlined above. For example, it is plausible that, at least early in his career, he thought that Austin's work on the 'performative' function of language would resolve certain metaphysical difficulties regarding evaluative judgments. I have in mind here the idea that the context of an utterance, specified in terms of certain rules, contributes to the meaning of such utterances. An example would be cases in which a certain *capacity* of the utterer partly determines the meaning of an utterance: when a judge says that a contract is not valid, his having said so entails that the contract does not generate any rights and duties. This is explicable in terms of the rules constituting his judicial capacity, i.e. rules conferring powers to the judge, including the power to pronounce contracts invalid. A further, more complicated way in which semantics plausibly drove or affected Hart's theory involves his thesis that certain evaluative judgments are analysable into two distinct components, one factual and the other evaluative. The factual component underwrites the classification of facts under an evaluative concept or rule; the evaluative component, which consists in an attitude of approval toward the relevant rule or concept, explains the evaluative force of the classification.[10] So, for example, the judgment that a certain behaviour is cruel or tortious can be split into the descriptive part, which consists of the moral or legal rules specifying how the facts must be for behaviour to count as cruel or tortious, and the evaluative part, which consists in the approval or 'acceptance' of these rules by those making the classification.

By leaving such influences to one side, I want to focus on what seem to me more straightforwardly semantic foundations of Hart's theory—the method of conceptual analysis and the doctrine of the open texture of

---

[10] Joseph Raz's 'Two Views of the Nature of the Theory of Law: A Partial Comparison', (this volume) focuses on these semantic influences on Hart.

language. I think that these two elements of Hart's thought are more central to his theory, and more directly relevant to Dworkin's sting argument—an argument virtually all of Hart's defenders want to deflect—than his early commitment to speech-act analysis and his conception of evaluative discourse.

My claim goes against a number of arguments that have been made in Hart's defence vis-à-vis Dworkin's sting argument. In this essay I will discuss defences that claim either that Hart did not have or did not rely upon any semantic doctrine at all or that his reliance on semantics was limited to his views on adjudication without infecting his general theory about the nature of law. These defences reject the intellectual burden I mention above. They say—strictly against, it seems, what Hart himself said—that Hart's views about the nature of law have nothing to do with the nature of language. I will not address in this essay the line of defence that accepts that Hart relied upon some version of criterial semantics, yet argues that this kind of semantics need not entail difficulties with representing disagreement and therefore need not support rejection of Hart's methodology in favour of interpretivism.[11] I believe that the latter type of defence is more to the point, even if it ultimately fails, as I think it does. But we should first get clearer on just what Hart's semantics was, and how it affects his theory.

II. MEANING AND CONCEPTUAL ANALYSIS

A. Definition

Hart begins his analysis by noting that most educated people are capable of identifying standard cases of law or of legal systems, and can easily describe some central features of law or of a legal system, but have difficulty in articulating a definition of 'law'. He says that it would be easy to list the criteria on the basis of which people make these classifications, but that this would leave confusion and puzzlement in place (5). By contrast, the quest for a definition is motivated by a desire for deeper illumination than such a list. What is a definition?

Sometimes . . . a definition of a word . . . may make explicit the latent principle which guides our use of a word, and may exhibit relationships between the type of phenomena to which we apply the word and other phenomena. It is sometimes

---

[11] Jules Coleman adopts such a line of defence, arguing that disagreements are about the application of shared criteria. For a recent formulation of his defence, see 'Incorporationism, Conventionality, and the Practical Difference Thesis' (this volume). In 'Two Views', Raz also argues that disagreement about concepts constituted by shared criteria is possible. I discuss Coleman's and Raz's defences in 'Criteria and Disagreement' (in progress).

said that definition is 'merely verbal' or 'just about words'; but this may be most misleading where the expression defined is one in current use. Even the definition of a triangle as 'three-sided rectilinear figure', or the definition of an elephant as a 'quadruped distinguished from others by its possession of a thick skin, tusks, and trunk', instructs us in a humble way *both to the standard use* of these words *and about the things to which the words apply*. A definition of this familiar type does two things at once. It simultaneously provides *a code or formula* translating the word into other well-understood terms *and locates for us the kind of thing to which the word is used to refer*, by indicating the features which it shares in common with a wider family of things and those which mark it off from others of that same family. In searching for and finding such definitions we 'are looking not merely at words . . . but also at the realities we use words to talk about. (14)[12]

Hart claims in this passage that, at least concerning expressions 'in current use', the quest for definitions is not exclusively about language, but is meant to provide metaphysical knowledge: we want to define 'law', for example, so that we learn what *counts* as legal, and thereby so that we discover certain important properties of things legal—so that we gain insight, that is, into the nature of law. A definition, Hart argues, achieves this by revealing the 'latent principle' that 'guides our use' of a word.

Hart points out, however, that attempts at providing a good definition of 'law' have been frustrated by a number of difficulties. The first is that law is intimately related to other categories themselves fundamental and not well understood, such as rule-governed behaviour; obligation; coercion (6–13, 15). Secondly, even though there are some central cases of application of 'law', there are also borderline cases, whose classification under 'law' is questionable. This difficulty—the open texture of language—is, however, not special to 'law', but infects all general terms (4, 126–8).[13] Finally, instances of law are not related to each other and distinguished from other things, in a single, rigid, uniform way: they do not all share common qualities. Rather, they are related to each other in different ways, such as by way of analogy or on the basis of some other unifying principle relating them to a central case.[14] These three difficulties, Hart claims, reveal that the classical definition *per genus et differentiam* cannot account fully for any such term.[15]

The first of Hart's difficulties is special to the domain of law—it is to do

---

[12] (Emphasis added), Hart quotes again, at the end of this passage, from J. L. Austin's 'A Plea for Excuses', *Proc. Arist. Soc.* 57 (1956–7), 8. See also *CL*, 279 (n. to p. 13), where Hart cites some literature on the function of definition, contrasts the general quest for definitions with the traditional model of definition *per genus et differentiam*, and appeals to Ryle's argument that definition is necessary and serves a clarificatory function, even where no doubts exist in the day-to-day use of terms.

[13] See also the discussion of open texture in Part III below.

[14] *CL*, 15–16, 279–80 (n. to p. 15), where Hart appeals to Wittgenstein's notion of family resemblance.   [15] *CL*, 16.

with the fact that the concept of law is related to the concept of rule-governed behaviour, normativity, and other fundamental notions. The problem this feature of law creates, according to Hart, is that analysing 'law' in terms of rule-governed behaviour, for example, will not explain much because the nature of rule-governed behaviour is itself a puzzle. It follows, then, that a definition of 'law' in those terms would be incomplete, but not impossible or misguided. Absent the other difficulties, we should be able to define law in these terms, although we would further request that the *definiens* be defined itself in order fully to understand what law is all about.

The second and third difficulties, by contrast, follow from general semantic features that Hart attributes to concepts or general terms, and render definitions impossible, not simply incomplete. Hart says that *all* general terms have borderline instances, and that it is true of *every* term that there are multiple relations of similarity among its instances as well as multiple relations of dissimilarity between its instances on the one hand and other things on the other. These difficulties follow from the open texture of language and from the fact that instances bear a family resemblance to each other, two theses about the nature of language, usually attributed to Wittgenstein, to which Hart subscribes. The implication Hart draws from these two features of language is that there are no jointly sufficient and severally necessary conditions for the application of terms. Rather, a new type of semantic analysis is needed.

This new semantics involves the notion of *criteria*, conditions 'normally' necessary and sufficient, yet 'defeasible' in special circumstances, where a term may apply even though some of the criteria are not satisfied, and vice versa. The doctrine of criteria, which I further discuss in connection with Hart's views on discretion, is a genuine semantic doctrine that is intended to replace the old doctrine of severally necessary and jointly sufficient conditions. It is a doctrine about the semantic properties of expressions and concepts including 'law' and the concept of law, not an argument in support of some non-semantic method of inquiry. Hart did not use the technical terminology of criteria in drawing the further implication that a new semantics is necessary from his arguments against classical definitions. What he said, however, in connection with hard cases in law and with borderline cases of the application of general terms suggests that that doctrine is fairly attributed to him. But even if the doctrine of criteria does not fit Hart's semantic views, it remains true that the implication of Hart's argument against definitions is that we should look for a different kind of analysis rather than classical definitions of 'law', not ignore semantic questions altogether.[16]

---

[16] So Timothy Endicott is wrong to argue that, if Hart believed in the availability of criteria for 'law', he would have to believe in necessary and sufficient conditions for 'law'. See

Hart's arguments against definitions are directed against the classical model—*per genus et differentiam*. He says that there exist other types of definition, but doubts that, given the difficulties outlined above, any type of definition will do what is needed. It is plausible to assume that the other types of definition Hart has in mind are also in terms of jointly sufficient and severally necessary conditions. This assumption is plausible, since the implication that Hart draws from his second and third difficulties is that the relevant terms are open-ended and so there is no conjunction or finite disjunction of conditions that define them. The implication therefore militates against definitions based on such sets of conditions.

Hart explicitly says that the *motivation* underlying the quest of definitions is legitimate: it is possible and desirable to identify and explicate by means of analysis a set of features essential to law.[17] The difficulties identified above would set some methodological constraints to the investigation. Since the general categories law is related to are themselves puzzling and fundamental, we must pursue the analysis through to them: we cannot rest content, for example, with explicating law in terms of rules governing behaviour, but must instead provide an explication of such rules too. Furthermore, we should expect that, given the open texture of language, some borderline classifications under 'law' will not be secure. Finally, we should expect to discover complex and multiple relations among instances of law and between them and the key elements he identified. The results of such an investigation would *serve the purpose* of a definition (i.e. the purpose of providing the principles that guide our use of words and exhibit relations among the phenomena to which we apply them) without being a definition that fits the traditional model. The analysis would not provide a concise formula codifying relations among instances in the classical mode (i.e. by explaining the nature of law by way of its relation to a *genus* and explaining what is common among instances in terms of a unique feature or relation) and would not strive fully to resolve all classification questions. It would nevertheless address some borderline cases of the application of 'law' or 'legal system' (17).

The investigation Hart undertakes in lieu of an attempt at strict definition focuses on three concepts or sets of relations that seem intimately connected with law, but which he thinks have proved resistant to clear and consistent explication. In terms of relations, the investigation roughly

---

'Herbert Hart and the Semantic Sting' (this volume), at 43. Criteria are not necessary and sufficient conditions. They are what is supposed to govern the use of words once it is accepted that they have the semantic attributes Hart says they do, viz. they are open-ended and their instances are linked by family resemblance. See further the discussion of criteria in Part III below.

[17] Hart is fully explicit on this point, at *CL*, 16.

focuses on the relation between being obliged and having an obligation; the relation between moral and legal obligation; and the relation between regularity of behaviour and rule-following (6–17).[18] Hart thinks that it is failure to notice the distinctions implied by these relations, or correctly to explicate the notions involved that is chiefly responsible for the frustration of the attempts by theorists' preceding him at providing a good definition of 'law' (17). These failures have engendered conceptual confusion that needs dispelling.

Hart then takes up the definitional project, with the *caveat* that it must be pursued subject to the constraints posed by the difficulties identified in relation to the classical model (the complex and fundamental nature of the categories to which law is related, the open texture of general classificatory terms, and the complexity and multiplicity of law's relations to other things and among its instances), and proposes to carry it out by investigating the three concepts essential to law. The investigation proceeds in part by examining the semantics of imperatives; the meaning of expressions such as 'to order' (18–19) and 'to give an order' (19); 'to address', as applied to commands (22) and to laws (19); 'obedience' (113–15); 'being obliged', 'having an obligation', and 'duty' (82–91); and 'valid' (103). It also results in the truth conditions of propositions such as 'a legal system exists' (117); 'it is the law that X' and 'in England they recognize as law X' (102); 'rule X is valid' (103), or those expressing the existence of obligations (88); and a number of other expressions and propositions. It further employs less obviously linguistic methods, namely the pursuit of philosophical argument as to the true content of the key concepts, by means of the familiar techniques of drawing distinctions and defending them through thought experiments.

One might object, at this point, that the list of expressions that I offer by way of illustration of Hart's preoccupation with questions of meaning chiefly concerns expressions other than 'law'. One could use the claim that Hart did not discuss the meaning of 'law' as part of an argument to the effect that he was not concerned with semantic questions.[19]

---

[18] In terms of concepts or categories, law is intimately related to rule-governed behaviour, coercion, and obligation. If it were analysable in the classical mode, it would be a species of these genera.

[19] Raz makes a related yet different claim in 'Two Views', and in work in progress. He says that Hart was not concerned at all with the meaning of 'law', and offers an explanation why not: explaining the concept of law—Hart's project—is not explaining the meaning of that word, and possibly not of any other word either. Raz says that 'law' is univocal, and designates rules of some permanence and generality that involve some kind of necessity; it thus applies not only to the institution whose nature Hart was investigating, but to scientific, mathematical, and all kinds of other laws. Raz infers that 'law' is not a word that uniquely expresses the concept of law and therefore elucidation of the concept is not explanation of the meaning of that word. He generalizes by saying that perhaps we do not need to explain any word's meaning in explaining a concept. I think that Raz's point establishes, not

It is worth noting that such an argument would not establish that Hart was not concerned with meanings of words in general. It is sufficient for establishing that he did worry about meaning to show that he worried about the meaning of *some* words—which he did, as my examples illustrate—and indeed that he did so because he thought that the questions about the meaning of those words would contribute to the understanding of *law*. He thought that we could learn something about the nature of law by considering whether we would use the word 'obligation' to describe certain facts. Moreover, Hart did consider questions involving the meaning of 'law'. He discussed the truth conditions of propositions containing 'law' ('it is the law that X') (102). He also discussed whether 'unjust law' is contradictory (209); he concluded that it is not, and argued that this did not suffice to *prove* that law is distinct from morality (209); rather, he thought that this could be proven in a more roundabout way, namely by showing that failing to distinguish among law and morality entailed collapsing certain important distinctions and therefore generated confusion (209–12).

Hart also considered 'at various points in the book' borderline cases of the application of 'law' (17). Regarding one such case, that of international law, he said that the issue concerning the legality of international law cannot be settled *simply* by appeal to conventions that govern the application of 'law' to international rules and thereby determine the extension of 'law'; rather, it is to be settled by examining *the principles that guide* the application of the expression to things in the world, which are complex and perhaps variable (215).

So Hart did exercise himself over questions about the meaning of words, including 'law', despite the ambiguities that word plausibly involves. It is important to note, nevertheless, that whenever he discusses the meaning of 'law', he is adamant that the linguistic rules governing that word's use cannot alone settle the important metaphysical questions

---

that 'law' is univocal, but that it is ambiguous. We *may* formulate a rough definition of 'law' in terms that are neutral among all possible meanings, but the word may in fact be used to express several very different concepts—the concept of law that Hart was after, the concept of a scientific law, the concept of a mathematical law, and so on—and therefore has several different meanings. But it does not matter whether I am right on this point. Perhaps 'law' expresses a master concept, and the law that interested Hart is a species of the law to which the master concept refers. Even so, it could still be possible to study the special concept that designates the political institution by studying the meaning, not of 'law' *simpliciter*, but of 'law' as applied to the institution, as I think Hart did. Moreover, nothing hangs on the question whether 'law' or any other particular word uniquely expresses the concept Hart was elucidating. As long as we can express in language thoughts involving the concept of law, there will be *some* expression, perhaps complex, that expresses the concept. The expression would bear the same relation to the concept as that borne by a simple concept-word to the concept it expresses. If you can explain the concept of a chair by explaining the meaning of 'chair', you can also explain the concept of law by explaining the meaning of some expression or other.

about law's nature. There seems to be, therefore, a tension: on the one hand, Hart professes to seek metaphysical insight from the way words are used; on the other, he says that the rules governing use will not take us far enough in the metaphysical inquiry.

Does the fact that Hart goes about analysing law through considering strictly semantic questions imply that he was chiefly concerned with providing rules for correct use of words such as 'law', 'obligation', 'duty', and so on? Not necessarily. He said that even *definitions* do not have that principal purpose.

Hart emphasized that the motivation for definitions, a motivation that he adopts in his project, is not *simply* to report or recommend rules for the correct use of words. This implies that the motivation encompasses more than, but certainly includes, the identification and recommendation of such rules. Hart did not think that use of the expressions is problematic—lawyers know a law when they see one; it is only when more difficult questions, questions concerning the bindingness of law or its relation to morality, or the question whether rules constitute the law or are 'mere' sources of it, and so on, are posed to lawyers that they are puzzled. His analysis is aimed at resolving those deeper puzzles, not at listing the situations in which lawyers apply words to facts (5). He cites Ryle as arguing[20] that we need analysis even where daily use is smooth and unproblematic. So Hart's analysis need not have the sole or main purpose of recommending rules for using those expressions (17)—even though the outcome of his inquiry must have the side effect, at least, of providing such rules.

B. Conceptual analysis

Rather than seeking rules for using the key expressions, or setting out to list the situations in which users apply the expressions, Hart's method was what is usually called conceptual analysis. What conceptual analysis is, however, is not altogether clear. I will not try to give a comprehensive answer to this question here, but only to sketch some aspects. My purpose is to develop, at least roughly, a conception of the tasks of conceptual analysis that I want to attribute to Hart. Given that my primary concern is attribution, I will provide criticism of this conception only where it is useful for sharpening the claims the conception involves.

Conceptual analysis is traditionally supposed to be the prologue to metaphysics. The latter is concerned with the nature of things, and their relations to other things. But discussion about the nature of something presupposes an understanding of what *counts* as that something. If I say

---

[20] *CL* 279, n. to p. 13.

that beliefs are neurochemical episodes, I inevitably rely on some conception of what counts as a belief, as well as a neurochemical episode. Conceptual analysis is traditionally supposed to be the part of the inquiry that addresses that issue: it is supposed to define the subject of inquiry.

It seems natural to suppose that conceptual analysis aims at articulating the existing, *common* understanding of the terms whose extension constitutes the field of inquiry.[21] The argument behind that supposition is that, unless I mean by 'belief' what everyone else does, my substantive claim will miss its target. It is not interesting, and perhaps not even sensible, the argument goes, to say that beliefs as *I* understand the term are neurochemical episodes. Rather, for my claim to have any philosophical importance it must be the case that beliefs in the sense common to all thinkers are what I say they are.[22]

Assuming that substantive claims need to engage wider concerns, conceptual analysis seems committed to elucidating the understanding inherent in the ordinary, day-to-day use of the term and reflection about the things it designates. It seems targeted, as one of the few modern defenders of conceptual analysis suggests, to explication of the ordinary conception of the target concept, the 'folk theory' of the nature of the things that fall under the concept.[23] And this is achieved by means of reflection on possible cases designed to elicit intuitions that reflect that theory. Consider the claim that knowledge is justified true belief. Suppose Mary believes, based on what her husband told her, that he has gone to work. In fact, Mary's husband has gone out to meet his mistress. The mistress has not shown up, however, so he has gone to work instead. Mary's belief that her husband is at work is true and justified, but not knowledge. So-called Gettier examples of justified true belief arrived at by fluke[24] operate as *counter-examples* to the analysis of knowledge as justified true belief by eliciting the intuition that these examples are *not* to be described as knowledge. They are supposed to prove that the 'folk theory' of knowledge would not count flukey justified belief as knowledge.[25]

To say that analysis aims at capturing the 'folk theory' is not to say that analysis is limited by any theories the folk, or a privileged subset of the folk, can articulate, nor is it to say that the folk need explicitly rely upon any theory in order to use the expressions or concepts they do, as opposed to using them unreflectively. The 'folk theory' is not the set of actual

---

[21] In 'Realism and Conceptual Analysis' (in progress), I argue against that supposition.
[22] Cf. Frank Jackson, *From Metaphysics to Ethics: A Defence of Conceptual Analysis* (Oxford, Clarendon Press 1998), 31.
[23] Ibid.
[24] After Edmund Gettier's seminal 'Is Justified True Belief Knowledge?', *Analysis*, 23 (1963), 121–3.
[25] See Jackson, *Metaphysics*, 28, 32, 36.

beliefs about he nature of the things designated by expressions; rather, it is the theory that users, or a subset of them, must have, given how they apply the expression in ordinary contexts and in thought experiments. In this broad sense of 'folk theory', the claim that analysis has that as its target is compatible with many different views. For example, it is compatible with the view that the applications or intuitions of ordinary folk count, or that only those of specialists do. It is also compatible with different views as to how these data constrain analysis, e.g. with the views that the data fully determine the 'folk theory', and the view that the theory must only be such as to explain and justify the data, but not treat them as necessarily correct.

Hart's conception of analysis is a specific and highly controversial version of the claim that analysis aims at the 'folk theory'. Hart's method implies, first, that conceptual analysis is a mode of inquiry that is distinct from and logically prior to substantive theory; and second, that conceptual analysis aims at recovering some, perhaps idealized, common understanding, in the sense that it articulates but can never transcend the understanding already implicit in ordinary use and reflection. The second claim implies that the intuitions elicited by conceptual analysis reflect the ordinary, conventional understanding of the target concept. Conceptual analysis based on these two claims is methodologically *ambitious*. I call it ambitious because it supposes that use alone, in the way that I am going to describe, determines the correct understanding of concepts. Having captured actual understanding *explains* the success of ambitious analysis, in the sense that such analysis is true *in virtue* of its fitting actual usage. Jackson's claim that conceptual analysis aims at revealing the 'folk theory' *may* imply that it is ambitious in this sense.[26] Hart's methodology *does* imply that he is pursuing ambitious analysis, even though it is less obvious that he is aiming at articulating 'folk theory'.[27] Hart would probably restrict his attention to lawyers rather than just any folk. And he would probably be hostile to the idea that the folk must have theories, rather than unreflective mastery of the concepts they use, and perhaps also to the idea that his own theory ought to respect whatever theorizing the folk do engage in. It could then be suggested that Hart was interested in expert understanding, rather than in 'folk theory'. But we saw that such a contrast is not genuine. 'Folk theory' is the theory of certain aspects of the nature of whatever is

[26] Jackson says, however, that analysis has the form of a hypothesis that best fits the data of usage. See ibid. 36. Whether the conception of analysis that I develop here is attributable to Jackson, therefore, turns on the nature of the constraints he would assume such hypotheses are subject to. I shall not pursue this question here.

[27] Joseph Raz assures me that Hart would be hostile to the idea that his theory aimed at articulating 'folk theory'.

denoted by an expression that is determined by the understanding of the expression that is implicit in its use by ordinary users or a subset of them. In that sense, Hart's method aims to articulate 'folk theory' too, and is ambitious in the required sense, since it accepts both crucial assumptions: that analysis is a distinct part of inquiry, and that it is concerned with articulating the understanding implicit in 'ordinary use'.

No one doubts that Hart embraced the first assumption. He said that his jurisprudence is general, and aims at conceptual clarification only. He said that this project is entirely independent of substantive legal investigation. He wanted to elucidate '*law*', not '*the* law', as the slogan goes.[28] So I need not further defend attributing that methodological claim to Hart, but will instead focus on developing and attributing to Hart the second assumption implied by ambitious analysis.

Hart treats ordinary use as a source of theoretical knowledge. He thinks, in other words, that attention to use will sharpen our understanding of the concepts that figure in use, and so provide insight into the nature of the things the concepts designate. Moreover, he seems to suggest that collecting the data of use should not be particularly difficult. He says we can dissolve many persistent problems by *looking* at how words are ordinarily used.[29] The understanding implicit in use must be manifest, for Hart, in the behaviour of users. So the data he has in mind must be widely and easily available, not hidden or requiring substantial theoretical machinery for their retrieval and employment in the service of philosophical explanation. He is after, so to speak, the surface data of ordinary discourse.

What could such data be? Plausibly, the data comprise the *applications* of the target expression which users make or are disposed to make, as well as the *explications* of the meaning of the expression, i.e. the rough rules which users are disposed to offer when required to explain or to teach to novices the sense of an expression, or to defend their applications against challenges. Consistently with the constraint that the data be close to the surface of ordinary use and reflection, they could also include the *explicit procedures* by which users establish that an expression applies to certain situations, their methods for ascertaining that something is an instance, including what they count as evidence that it is. Arguably, the data might also include the *abilities* of users to discriminate instances of a term. In other words, the data plausibly include what the users apply the expression to, the rules they say they are following in applying it, their methods for identifying the instances, and their ability to spot instances

---

[28] See the Postscript to *CL*, at 239–40.
[29] See 'Jhering', 277, where Hart quotes approvingly Wittgenstein's dictum that we must look at concepts when they are 'at work', not when they are 'idling' or 'on holiday'.

and tell them apart from other things. In the conception that I want to attribute to Hart, these data are constitutive of the actual understanding of the expression.

There are many other candidates for inclusion in a database for analysis, which I exclude from Hart's database. For example, his data could not include any deep structural properties, mental or otherwise, that might underlie the explicit data of use, as well as nomological connections between use and aspects of users' environment. By excluding such data, I exclude from consideration accounts of meaning or concepts that rely on such deep structures and laws. I think it is fair to suppose that Hart's project cannot have involved such accounts. In fact, the database that I attribute to Hart, even though restricted to superficial facts of use, may already be too wide. For example, given Hart's conviction that the extant *philosophical* explications of law were confused, and given also his Wittgensteinian programme of elucidating concepts by considering them 'at work', it is plausible to suppose that his database of use would privilege the data of non-philosophical, substantive use of the target concepts—use in the context of legal or other social practice, rather than philosophical reflection about the practice. For the same reason, it is plausible that, even within the domain of usage by practitioners, Hart would privilege the applications of terms and the procedures used for that purpose, over the explications offered by users and their ability to spot instances: applications and procedures are aspects of users' behaviour, whereas explications and abilities belong with what explains the behaviour and therefore cannot be fully manifest. So Hart might disown as unhelpful or irrelevant some of the types of data that I include. But the points that follow in connection with analysis based on the set of data that I do attribute to Hart should equally apply to a more restricted set. Even if he meant, for example, to appeal to the facts of use only in respect of the applications that users make, my points would still stand in respect of such facts alone. By broadening the database, I strengthen Hart's position with respect to the problems that I identify.

Now the raw data of actual usage cannot support analysis on their own. Rather, they stand in need of some sifting and ordering. To start with, ambitious conceptual analysis, as well as theoretical, scientific definition, as opposed to dictionary definition, must go deeper than the rough rules and procedural formulas offered in explication of meaning. These rules for ordinary use are the rules available to ordinary competent users. Such rough definitions, rules, or procedures may exploit connections between the analysandum and other things in the world that *typically* obtain and thus allow for correct application on the whole reliably. They may thus be rules of thumb that 'cheat', in the sense that they rely on some contingent correlations between the occurrence of instances of the relevant term and the occurrence of something else, where the latter is taken as a sign that an instance of the target term obtains. The rules may provide rough guides and need not guarantee correctness of application in all circumstances, nor need they associate the target expression with the essential features of whatever it applies to. Such definitions and procedures, however, may be sufficient for day-to-day use of terms.[30]

Hart says, however, that actual usage of general terms is guided by implicit principles or rationales that need explicit articulation (215). He does not explain what it means to say that a *principle* underlies usage, nor what it means to say that the principles *implicitly guide* practice even though it takes theory to uncover and articulate them. These are important questions. Any theory of concepts that involves the view that a concept's identity and content is fixed by principles, rather than use as it stands, must explain the notion of a principle that is involved, as well as the relation between the principles and use. And a theory such as Hart's, which says that the principles are implicit in use and guide it, must specifically explain the relation of implicit guidance. But we may temporarily leave the latter question open and instead explore the former, broader question with respect to Hart's theory. That question is simpler, and we can begin by noticing that what Hart says seems to imply that use places strict limits on the principles that could underlie it.

The principles Hart is after are supposed to reveal the deeper rationale of rules of conventional use. Dictionary definitions may be thought of as attempts to go somewhat deeper than ordinary conventional rules, in the sense that they seek to order and rationalize ordinary use.

By contrast, conceptual analysis is supposed to go even deeper than that. Ambitious analysis aims at capturing the essential features of the thing to which an expression refers, and so at providing an account of its nature. And it is supposed to achieve this by a process of idealization. Ambitious analysis seeks to articulate a standard to which ordinary use is responsible, which is *drawn* from ordinary use. Such a standard is supposed to be derived from the data of actual usage—the applications of the expression made by ordinary users, the explications of its meaning offered by them, and the procedures and abilities of users.

Ambitious conceptual analysis aims at ordering usage. To do so, it must unify the rules and procedures used by speakers, by identifying the common ground among different personal rules. It must further reconcile the rules and the procedures with applications, and eliminate inconsistencies, and might therefore precisify the formulation of the rules and procedures insofar as other parts of usage justify doing so. That method

---

[30] Raz suggests that such rules and procedures are all users have and need. See 'Two Views', 90.

constitutes an idealization that includes discounting certain applications as mistaken and certain explications of meaning as confused.

It is not clear that the process of idealization that I describe is coherent and workable. But it would be unfair to Hart to attribute to him the view that all the data must be respected. Discounting some of the data is necessary because they will inevitably include mistakes, as a result either of defective understanding of the target concept or of perceptual or other epistemic failures whose character is independent of the concept, but stand in the way of its correct application. For example, users who do not fully understand a concept are bound to misapply the concept word. And even users who fully understand a concept may misapply it in certain adverse conditions—when background noise interferes with their recognition of an instance. Ambitious analysis must have a way to distinguish such mistakes and discount them.

It seems plausible, for example, to attribute mistakes where, on reflection, a user would be prepared to abandon an explication of meaning, or admit that an application is incorrect, or there exist other signs of confusion.[31] It is important to note, however, that ambitious analysis can only appeal to resources within use for determining what counts as such a sign: it can discount some of the data if they conflict with other data of use, rather than on the basis of considerations that are independent of use. For example, a user's being drunk counts as a sign of confusion and gives reasons to discount an application of an expression that he makes while drunk, only insofar as he would withdraw the application when sober, or the application made while drunk does not fit his sober applications. A user's consistent application of a term counts as defective understanding only insofar as it does not fit other data of use, e.g. others' applications. If analysis determines what is a mistake on the basis of considerations independent of use, then use cannot determine correctness but rather may be corrected itself.

Whatever detailed method ambitious analysis uses to sift and select from among individual explications, procedures, and applications of a term, it is subject to an overarching constraint. The judgments on which most agree and the applications most are disposed to make are secure from discounting. Analysis cannot respect actual usage in the required sense, unless it accords the judgments that are firm and widely shared, and the more prevalent applications, defining status. Mistake is defined by reference to such common ground: the applications, procedures, and rules that are discounted are those inconsistent with the common ground.

Ambitious analysis, therefore, uses the common ground as a benchmark of correctness, on the basis of which individual mistake, irrespective

---

[31] See Jackson, *Metaphysics*, 35–6, for an account of the process by which sophisticated analysis selects the data it must respect.

of its source and character—whether the result of incomplete under-standing or general epistemic handicap—is defined as such. Given that the common ground is the standard of correctness, ambitious analysis is committed to there being and to its aiming at articulating, shared criteria, i.e. the procedures and rules shared among users and used for supporting their judgments of application of the term.

There are at least two reasons why ambitious analysis is committed to shared criteria. The first is partly historical: appeal to communal use was thought to be a last resort vis-à-vis Wittgenstein's sceptic. The sceptic is supposed to have helped us see that there is nothing about the facts of *individual* use—rules, dispositions, procedures, etc.—to distinguish between an individual's using a concept incorrectly and his using a differ-ent concept correctly, and therefore to determine a standard for correct use of a concept. Since we cannot construct a standard out of facts about an individual, restricting ourselves to those facts leaves no room for error. Communal use, on the other hand, conceived of as the common ground among the facts of individual usage, is supposed to supply the material for constructing a standard of sorts—a condition of appropriateness, if not correctness. There is nothing else to ground correctness, Wittgenstein was supposed to have proved, but what is done in the community, how the concept is used collectively.[32]

But notwithstanding what Wittgenstein said or meant, ambitious analysis cannot avoid defining correctness in terms of shared criteria for a more general reason. Suppose it did not. Suppose, that is, that it accepted that actual communal use could be at least partly wrong—it could fail to be what it ought to be. That would imply that among the common responses and procedures, some at least are incorrect. For that to be true, it would have to be the case that we had another standard, inde-pendent of actual communal use, by reference to which we could select from among communal responses and procedures the correct ones. But then appeal to use in the first place would be much less decisive than it is supposed to be, if not altogether idle. It seems likely that we could advert to that other standard from the start, and ignore use altogether. But even if it were the case that the extra standard were to work somehow in tandem with use, the explanatory significance of use would be greatly weakened. Moreover, Hart never suggests that use must be restricted by any further standard in order to guide philosophical explication. The

---

[32] The classic discussion of the so-called sceptical solution is Saul Kripke's *Wittgenstein on Rules and Private Language* (Oxford, Blackwell, 1982). Those who appeal to communal use need not accept the sceptical version. They might hold that a fully fledged standard of correctness is reducible to the facts of communal use. See Paul Boghossian's brilliant critical survey 'The Rule-Following Considerations', *Mind*, 98 (1989), 507–49, esp. 520, 534. Bog-hossian develops several powerful arguments against the viability of such a reduction.

explanatory significance of the extra standard would be such that it makes no sense to suppose that, given that Hart never mentioned it, he had such a standard in mind.[33]

Appeal to use sharpens and restricts the requirement that conceptual analysis articulate the 'folk theory' implicit in deployment of concepts. The requirement alone seems, on its face, to imply the shared criteria thesis. To attempt to articulate the 'folk theory' is to assume that a unique determinate theory underlies ordinary use, rather than many conflicting theories. It seems to follow that analysis must articulate the criteria of correct application which are implied by this unique theory.

Appeal to use reinforces this implication by blocking an interpretation of the requirement that may avoid assuming that common criteria constitute a condition of correctness. That is an interpretation according to which 'folk theory' is in fact the *best* theory attributable to users, the theory the folk *ought* explicitly to have, even if no-one's explicit theory actually matches it, and even if the facts of use do not conform to it. On that interpretation, the understanding that analysis articulates may not reducible to the facts of usage. The right theory may be, for example, the theory that best explains and justifies usage, makes best sense of people's responses and procedures in the context of their environment. That interpretation would allow for the possibility of substantial error in usage: nothing guarantees that people will not tactitly rely on substantially mistaken theories and that they will not be massively mistaken in their deployment of the relevant concepts. The standard to which their use would be responsible could be very different from that supposed or implied by ordinary use.[34]

Relations of justification are not legitimate for Hart. Not only does he say that his account is descriptive; moreover, what justifies use is too far away from the surface of use, too deep to be acceptable to him. Inquiry into what justifies use is not limited, in the way Hart's is, to looking at how words are used. Such inquiry may go beyond whatever is manifest in users' behaviour, and the standard it identifies may be such that users' behaviour fails to conform to it. By contrast, Hart's appeal to use is meant to make use itself a standard of correctness. His appeal implies that the standard he seeks to identify must be reducible to the facts of use, that there is one unique 'folk theory' singled out by the facts of use, and that the rules and procedures common among users have defining or criterial status.

---

[33] Cf. ibid. 536. My point also holds for any suggestion that Hart be interpreted to reject 'communitarianism', i.e. the thesis that communal responses, applications, dispositions, etc. are necessarily correct, and be taken instead to appeal to *individual* use under some optimal conditions specified in terms independent of the target concept.

[34] See n. 41.

So far we have established that use places limits on the principle that Hart is after, by supplying a set of common criteria that determine which principle is the one underlying use. But in what sense is the principle whose identity is fixed by the criteria a *principle*, and in what sense does it *guide* use?

Recall that Hart said that he was looking for the principle behind use, as opposed to a *list* of the situations in which speakers apply terms, or a *list* of the conventional rules that specify when they should apply it. The contrast seems to imply that Hart thought that analysis should seek to identify a *pattern* in such lists. He also said that there is a deeper *rationale* behind the lists, a principle that *implicitly guides* users. On the other hand, we have concluded that the principle must be reducible to the facts of use and that this constraint rules out principles that justify use. Furthermore, Hart could not have thought that some principle explains use in a causal sense, or in the sense of inner guidance. Causal or other mechanisms may misfire in such a way that the manifest behaviour would not reflect them. Appeal to use is meant to replace the quest for such hidden mechanisms.

I suggest that Hart's understanding of the idea of a principle that implicitly guides use is as follows. Theory discerns a pattern in the behaviour of users. The pattern is whatever fits the facts after minimal sifting to eliminate inconsistencies. Theory formulates a principle that captures that pattern. The principle's content is fully determined by and is reducible to the criteria common among users. Actual users' usage may be unreflective or else immediately guided by partial sets of criteria for using the relevant expressions. Yet the principle fits their behaviour taken collectively, so the theory treats it as if it guided usage. Therefore the criteria identified by theory are not simply common, but shared in that 'as if' sense. They are what really guides use, not in the sense of users' knowing what they are or explicitly following them, but in the sense of constituting the standard to which their use is responsible.[35]

I could be wrong in attributing to Hart the 'as if' conception of implicit guidance. Moreover, many questions remain regarding the conception that I attribute—e.g., does the fact that users act as if they were guided by the principle means that they would not consider it surprising, or even informative, to be told what the principle is? Hart does not say enough to attribute to him with confidence a precise conception of implicitness. But what he says is sufficient for the purposes of attributing to him the two crucial theses that I do: that the principle is constituted by the set of common criteria; and that the criteria, in some or other implicit sense, truly guide practice, and so are shared by practitioners.

---

[35] Notice that it is questionable whether a projection from the facts of actual usage to a standard is possible. If arguments against the reducibility of meaning to the facts of actual usage are correct, the facts are insufficient uniquely to determine any standard. See Boghossian, 'Rule-Following', for arguments to that effect.

If I am right, then, the use-based model of analysis that I want to attribute to Hart is committed to there being shared criteria, which analysis is trying to identify and articulate, and which constitute the standard of correctness for the analysed expressions. This implication of the appeal to use in the service of analysis has a further implication for understandings, rules, and procedures that diverge from the shared criteria. These recalcitrant data, according to this model of ambitious analysis, must be explicable either as the result of epistemic interference, or else confusion. Suppose I am offering an explication of the meaning of 'obligation' that is inconsistent with the shared ground among the explications offered by everyone else, and insist that 'obligation' applies to a situation even though most other users do not think so. Suppose further that it is reasonable to think that there are no epistemic obstacles independent of my understanding of the term that impair my judgment. Ambitious analysis is committed to treating me as confused, having an imperfect understanding of the concept of obligation. It precludes a further possibility, namely that, instead of suffering from confusion, my understanding of 'obligation' is not defective but different, the result of an unorthodox theory of what obligation really is.

C. Actual usage and conceptual insight

The contrast between conceptual analysis and ordinary linguistic rules and procedures does not entail a contrast between conceptual analysis and semantics. First, conceptual analysis necessarily has implications as to correct use. If Hart is right that having an obligation involves the existence of a practice, complete with a critical reflective attitude toward some convergent behaviour, it follows that 'obligation' is incorrectly applied to a situation where only convergence of behaviour obtains, and may be correctly applied even where a sanction for deviation is not likely. So conceptual analysis has semantic *consequences*.[36]

This kind of connection between conceptual analysis and semantics is implied by a more general point about the relation between metaphysics and language. Whatever we claim about the nature of things, our claims are bound to have consequences in the domain of semantics. If biologists tell us that necessarily fish have gills, their claim entails that the word

[36] Hart seems to accept that: see the passage quoted above, n. 12, where he says that definitions instruct us not *merely* about the standard use of words, but *also* about the things to which words refer. This implies that definitions do instruct us about use too. Recall, moreover, that his case against definitions relies upon some semantic properties of expressions, such that sets or perhaps clusters of criteria are what truly governs expressions' use. Criteria, as much as definitions, serve the same semantic purposes—they reflect understanding and determine correct application of expressions.

'fish' is incorrectly applied to creatures that lack gills. If that connection were the only one between Hart's theory and semantics, then the connection would not be special or distincitve of Hart's philosophical views. Anyone's theory of law has such connections. This point is related to Dworkin's claim that legal theory must necessarily involve an answer to 'the question of sense', i.e. it must include or imply an account of the truth conditions of propositions of law.[37] Any theory, however austere semantically, must at least imply the conditions under which 'the law requires that φ' is true. If law is really, say, a function of the ruling class's interests, then the concept of law refers to that function, and therefore it is not the case that law includes a putative right that does not serve such interests. If for something to be part of the law it must meet the criteria set out in the rule of recognition, and if principles do not meet the criteria, principles are not part of the law.

Ambitious conceptual analysis not only has consequences for use but is also, as we saw, dependent upon it. Hart's version of conceptual analysis is expressly designed to rely upon ordinary use. It aims at revealing the rules users of an expression unreflectively use in applying the expression, even if they are unable to articulate those rules or are only capable of offering incomplete and lame formulations of them, or perhaps just 'cheating' rules of thumb. In Hart's scheme, analysis is designed to tease out of ordinary use distinctions and relations that are essential to the phenomena in which he is interested. He therefore tries to derive his account of obligation, for example, from the ways we describe, or would be disposed to describe, certain situations carefully set up to suggest crucial distinctions and relations (e.g. the situation in which one is subjected to a bald threat, as opposed to a request to conform to a rule). In this indirect way, therefore, Hart's method does consist in *derivation* of theory from the semantics of expressions, even though it does not consist in simple description of rough or dictionary definitions or conventional linguistic rules and procedures.

This second kind of connection between analysis and semantic is driven by a certain controversial conception of the nature of concepts and of language in general. Ambitious conceptual analysis supposes that investigation into actual usage and understanding of terms produces a standard that cannot transcend actual usage.[38] Actual usage is not, as it

---

[37] 'Legal Theory and the Problem of Sense', in R. Gavison (ed.), *Issues in Contemporary Legal Philosophy* (Oxford, Clarendon Press, 1987), 9–10. See also Dworkin's reply to Soper, regarding the question whether Dworkin's theory is conceptual: *Taking Rights Seriously* (London, Duckworth, 1977), 350–2.

[38] I follow Tyler Burge's 'Frege on Sense and Linguistic Meaning', in D. Bell and N. Cooper (eds.), *The Analytic Tradition* (Oxford, Blackwell, 1990), on the conception of meaning as supervening upon and reducible to actual usage, as opposed to transcending such usage.

stands, sufficient for correct explication of meaning, as it is usually too unruly or haphazard, and may rest on incomplete understanding or be affected by general epistemic impediments. Ambitious analysis is supposed to order and rationalize such usage, and to *project* from that to a standard, a norm that guides actual usage—to make explicit, in Hart's words, the latent principle that guides our use of words, the rationale behind a word's extension.[39] But actual usage sets limits to such a projection: the principle cannot fail to fit actual usage, except to the extent that it orders and ensures consistency of such usage. The principle cannot introduce distinctions never made in the course of or entailed by actual usage, nor can it collapse distinctions actually made or entailed. Ambitious analysis, therefore, must track actual understanding.

Under that conception of the tasks of analysis, meaning supervenes upon and is reducible to actual responses, procedures, and abilities of ordinary speakers, which constitute actual understanding. The idealized understanding furnished by analysis subordinates individual understandings that survive the process of idealization and forms their shared foundation. The concepts that figure in cognitive practices are individuated by this conception of actual understanding of practitioners. The distinctions actually drawn and the judgments of classification actually made by lawyers are individuative of the concepts that figure in those judgments: they are defining features of them.

There are alternatives to Hart's view which suggest that correct explication of meaning need not be limited in that way. I will sketch an alternative, simply to suggest that Hart's understanding of the relation between the meaning of expressions and the facts of their use is not without some serious competition.

Concepts may go deeper than actual usage. It may be the case that the standard to which actual usage is responsible is given by a projection *beyond* actual usage itself. Perhaps the meaning of an expression is such that it is possible to come to an understanding that is substantially different from and better than the understanding actually possessed by any current speaker, or even by all current speakers collectively.[40] We may realize that the right standard is the standard that justifies actual usage, which need not be the standard that most accurately reflects it and is reducible to it. We may discover that actual usage is riddled with mistakes, and that even idealized actual understanding misconstrues true meaning. Ambitious conceptual analysis gives too ambitious a role to actual understandings, procedures, dispositions, and abilities, by treating them as setting limits to cognitive practices. By contrast, such practices

---

[39] See n. 35 above.
[40] See ibid. 47. Burge attributes such a view to Frege.

may be subject to norms that transcend those limits. The concepts with which lawyers think may be such that the discriminations lawyers actually make are not defining of them. Even those judgments of application on which all lawyers agree may turn out to be mistaken. Lawyers may discover that a concept requires them not to draw a distinction they are used to drawing, that the standard they are under is not the one that fits their practice of drawing that distinction. Concepts may be deeper than reflection and ordering of actual usage may suggest. Such depth may be revealed by theory, which may discover that what Burge calls the deep rationale behind actual usage is even deeper than ambitious analysis supposes, that the principles that justify usage are not reducible to the applications and procedures that express or constitute actual understanding, and so that the identity of the concepts that figure in actual usage is not fixed by the facts of usage.[41]

A key motivation for doubting that actual understanding of concepts fixes the identity of the concepts that are the objects of understanding comes from the conception of science as capable of improving our understanding of concepts. It is plausible to think that the understanding of the concept of influenza improves as scientific knowledge about the condition that caused the epidemics by that name improves. We learn that the epidemics do not have the occult causes and influences that gave it its name, and we learn to discriminate more finely. Some medieval *influentiae* would not have the viral cause common to most of them and therefore would not be influenza as we understand it today. But we may insist that we and the medievals were deploying the same concept, even though we now have a very different understanding of it. We insist, in other words, that correct understanding of the medieval concept need not be reducible to the beliefs, procedures, and discriminatory abilities of the medievals, and so that the concept used by the medievals is not the concept that is individuated by their applications and procedures.

---

[41] See Burge, 'Frege on Sense and Linguistic Meaning', 53. Burge contrasts the view that correct understanding transcends usage with the view that it supervenes upon usage, and so implies that correct understanding need not supervene upon usage at all. It is an open question whether it is possible to preserve the distinction between actual and correct understanding while accepting that correct understanding supervenes upon, albeit is not reducible to, the data of actual usage. It may further be possible for such a non-reductivist conception of understanding to allow for substantive knowledge to improve our understanding of concepts. Such a conception of analysis may make room for substantial error within the practice. Under such a conception, users' actual procedures and rules may reflect, not the concept but what users think the concept is, their conceptions of it. A further implication would be that science and other theoretical activity may improve our understanding of concepts, and therefore that there is no distinct logical space for conceptual analysis, for inquiry that aims at improving understanding alone, without improving knowledge. I explore this possibility in 'Realism and Conceptual Analysis'. Notice that such a non-reductivist model would appeal, not to the facts of use, but to substantive reasons including evaluations in support of a recommended conception of the concept.

There are examples where it is almost inconceivable that the early thinkers were not deploying the concepts we only now consider well understood. To take a famous example used by Christopher Peacocke, Newton could not, however hard he tried, articulate the definition of the mathematical concept of a limit. His attempts at a definition were not coherent, and it was not until much later that a satisfactory definition was articulated. In the light of the *modern* definition, though of course not in the light of his own, non-coherent one, his calculations of limits were correct. But then the meaning of 'limit' cannot be reduced to the facts of Newton's usage: he was deploying a concept whose correct explication had to wait for substantive advances in mathematics.[42]

These examples suggest that ordinary use and ordinary reflection are in an important way continuous with science or substantive inquiry more generally. Actual procedures and explications of meaning offered in the course of ordinary reflection have cognitive aspirations. The business of applying expressions and of offering explications of the rules and procedures for doing so involves users' effort correctly to describe the examples, to respect metaphysically important distinctions, and to explain aspects of the world around them. It is indeed these explanatory and metaphysical ambitions of ordinary use that conceptual analysis seeks to exploit in constructing its idealized account of the 'folk theory'. But the conviction that the facts of use constitute a standard of correctness and so fix the identity of the concepts used falsifies the ambitions of ordinary reflection. By contrast, thinking of concepts as going deeper than actual usage respects those ambitions. Users do not think they are guaranteed to get it right, and readily draw a distinction between questions about the circumstances under which they apply an expression and the circumstances under which they ought to apply it.[43]

Moreover, we adopt rules for using words, not because these rules are also used by others or by those who correct our use, but because we think that these rules are correct. We do not have the conventionalist motivation to conform with common rules and procedures because they are common, but rather have the cognitive motivation to adopt rules and procedures

---

[42] Peacocke's 'Implicit Conceptions, Understanding, and Rationality', *Philosophical Issues*, 9 (1998), 43–88, is the best attempt to preserve the idea that meaning is explicable in terms of current understanding, by attributing to Newton, in this example, an implicit conception of a limit, specified in terms that were only subsequently articulated explicitly. Notice, however, that Peacocke suggests that this implicit conception was strictly possessed by Newton, and explains why the concept he was using was the concept of a limit. In Peacocke's view, implicit conceptions are deep psychological properties that need not be manifest in but can causally explain use. I cannot discuss Peacocke's defence here. See Georges Rey, 'What Implicit Conceptions Are Unlikely to Do', in the same volume, 92–104.

[43] See Rey, 'Concepts and Stereotypes', in Eric Margolis and Stephen Laurence (eds.), *Concepts* (Cambridge, Mass., MIT Press, 1999), for a discussion of that distinction.

that we think are, or are more likely to be, correct. We therefore stand corrected in our meaning explications.[44] We are under a commitment to defend those explications and procedures if challenged, and to abandon them in the face of counter-examples. When we agree about the correct application of a term we agree for substantive reasons as to the correct characterization of the examples. When corrected, we take the correct explication to capture a standard to which we were antecedently committed.[45] Science corrects us because it merely continues from where ordinary reflection leaves off for lack of time, discipline, or opportunity. Conversely, the cognitive aspirations of ordinary use and reflection explain why concepts can go deeper than ordinary use and understanding seems to permit.

The last few paragraphs are meant only to sketch some elements of an alternative view of the nature of concepts and meaning, and to illustrate points on which the view differs from the one that Hart adopts. Needless to say, there are serious objections to the alternative. Moreover, there exist further alternative views, which explain actual understanding in terms of deeper facts about users' dispositions, capacities, or other psychological states and properties, which need not be manifest in use.[46] The point is that the claim central to Hart's methodology, namely the claim that meaning must be manifest in use, faces strong competition in the philosophy of language and mind by a number of approaches that aim to go deeper than the surface of use.

Hart's methodology does not permit pursuit of such semantic depth. Reflection on ordinary use must yield the criteria which individuate the relevant concepts. The slack between ordinary and theoretical meaning cannot be such as to permit substantial mistake in actual usage. Rather, the distance between actual usage and theoretical explication must be fully explicable, for Hart, in terms of local inconsistencies, or outright confusion owing to conceptual incompetence. Theory cannot reform practice, but only report its shared features. Moreover, such theory is purely conceptual, only clarifying what counts as law. Substantive theory is wholly distinct: it concerns itself with investigation into what-

---

[44] Hart's methodology might accept that users try to get it right, rather than conform to the community. But it cannot accept that they stand corrected even when their use conforms with the community: for that methodology, getting it right and conforming with the community must coincide.

[45] See Burge, 'Intellectual Norms and Foundations of Mind', *J. Phil.*, 83 (1986), 697–720, esp. 704, for an elaboration of the structure of the reasoning involved in correcting meaning explications. See Nicos Stavropoulos, *Objectivity in Law* (Oxford, Clarendon Press, 1996), chs. 2 and 5, for a development of the implications of Burge's discussion for legal theory.

[46] e.g. Peacocke's implicit conception view, outlined in his 'Implicit Conceptions'; or Georges Rey's view, 'The Unavilability of What We Mean: A Reply to Quine, Fodor and Lepore', *Grazer Philosophica* (1993), 61–101.

ever is singled out by the conceptual part, dissecting and describing the objects that fall within the concept's extension, but unable to reform our understanding of which these objects are.

The space, however small, that Hart notices between ordinary use and understanding, on the one hand, and the deeper principles conceptual analysis tries to derive from use, on the other, explains why those deeper principles need not be available to ordinary thinkers.[47] Hart can consistently set out to articulate semantic rules on the one hand and on the other insist that he is not interested in reporting ordinary, conventional rules and rough definitions involved in the day-to-day use of words. His semantic rules are too sophisticated to be tranparent to users. Conversely, actual usage is too flexible for him: actual usage may include applications not supported by his deeper rules, and is content with explications of meaning that are incomplete or relatively confused. For that reason, it is not sufficient to point out that 'unjust law' is not contradictory in order to establish that law is conceptually distinct from morality. Rather, he has to establish that conclusion by divining the true rules governing the use of 'law', those that may be too complex and theoretical for users consciously to possess and employ. Nevertheless, *they are the rules they really share and commonly employ*, whether they realize it or not, since they are the rules that capture the shared ground of usage. Given that the rules Hart was after are criteria, rather than scientific definitions, the result is that he is, after all, trying to articulate shared criteria, notwithstanding the fact that such criteria are not shared in the sense of users being aware of them.[48]

D. Further consequences

Hart's conviction that use manifests a shared, tacitly agreed basis for judgments is apparent throughout his theory. It underwrites his explanation of rule-governed behaviour in terms of practices, his general methodological claims that concern the character of his theory, and his explanation of indeterminacy in the law. In this section I will sketch the role of Hart's conviction in respect of the first two aspects of his theory. In Sections III(A) and (B) I will take up in more detail the question of

---

[47] Hart's discussion of international law in *CL*, 215, includes one of his best characterizations of the distinction he wants to draw between conventional rules and the deeper principle or rationale behind them.

[48] So Endicott is wrong to argue from the premiss that Hart's eschews rules for day-to-day usage, and that he accepts that 'law' could be sensibly used to describe systems that do not exhibit all of the characteristics that his theory presents as necessary, to the conclusion that Hart eschews semantics altogether, and so that his theory is not meant to supply shared criteria. So is Michael Moore, who argues in a similar vein. See Endicott, 'Hart', 42, and Moore, 'Hart's Concluding Scientific Postscript', in *Educating Oneself in Public* (Oxford, Oxford University Press, 2000), at 89–90.

indeterminacy. My purpose is to make a threat plausible, namely that, if the use-based theory of concepts goes, a number of Hart's most distinctive doctrines about law are left with no apparent foundation.

For Hart, rules are defined by a practice conceived of in terms of convergent behaviour and agreement in judgments.[49] This is no coincidence. Hart thought that the explanation of correct application of expressions is very closely related to the explanation of rule-following. Stressing the affinity between the two types of issue has a Wittgensteinian pedigree, as does offering the communitarian explanation that Hart offers for both issues. Consistently with other domains, law's boundaries are defined in Hart's theory by judicial convergent practice, judges treating a set of criteria as conclusive evidence of legality. Hart's conception of rule-governed practices in general and legal practice in particular, as constituted by participants' convergent behaviour and shared criteria, would be mysterious in the absence of the general communitarian semantic doctrine.

It is true that the fact that Hart conceived of legal and moral practices in terms of convergent behaviour and agreement in judgments does not *entail* that he subscribed to a communitarian semantics.[50] But if not from (what is taken to be) Wittgenstein's conception of meaning, where did Hart get this idea? Why could it not be the case that the domain of agreement in judgments as to what a rule requires, and of convergent behaviour in conformity with the rule, is simply *the area of overlap among competing theories* of what the rule requires, rather than definitional of the rule? Such overlap would explain the *appearance* of shared criteria: different practitioners would agree on a large number of judgments as to what the rule requires, albeit for very different reasons. Rather, the fact that Hart subscribed to communitarian semantics *explains* why he thought of rules and of law in this way. The principle that the actual practice sets limits to the concepts engaged by the practice, a principle that comes from some fundamental conception of rules and concepts that Hart found in Wittgenstein, is partly concealed by Hart's insistence that use *alone* is not sufficient for theoretical reflection—by the space between ordinary use and theory. But the space is only small, and Hartian concepts and rules are only skin-deep, relative to practices.

Hart cannot disown the thesis that theory aims at articulating shared criteria. If he did, his project would be distorted both methodologically

---

[49] For simplicity of exposition, I am ignoring here the special attitude toward such behaviour and judgments which Hart said is also necessary. This attitude of acceptance is itself shared and is defined over rules or practices that are individuated by convergence and agreement. It is a shared attitude toward a definite *pattern* whose identity is fixed by convergence and agreement. My point in the text concerns the idea that patterns are fixed by these two elements.

[50] As Endicott sensibly points out. See 'Hart', 44–5.

and in substance. If Hart said that his theory need not reflect any *shared* understanding of law, his theory would not genuinely derive any insight from ordinary use. Suppose he said that his theory is correct, even though it is not shared, not derived from and reducible to lawyers' actual common understanding of law, but is instead an elaboration of one among many understandings of law. Then he would be committed to the belief that his theory's merit is independent of ordinary use, that his theory is correct, not in virtue of reflecting common understanding but perhaps in virtue of some theoretical or other value. The reliance on and derivation of wisdom from ordinary use would become empty rhetoric. He would not be able to say, as he does, that the truth about the nature of law has escaped ordinary lawyers and previous theorists because of conceptual *confusion* that needs dispelling. His theory would be one among many tolerated by the practice, and would have to include appeal to some independent political, moral, or methodological principle.

Moreover, if Hart were prepared to give up the claim that common understanding limits the concepts with which legal theory is concerned, he would be left with no good argument for his claim that rules and normative practices are explicable in terms of convergent behaviour, or that legal practice is individuated by the tests judges share. Two possibilities seem to exist, neither of which is plausible. First, Hart might claim that practices are individuated by convergent behaviour, not in virtue of a conceptually necessary feature of concepts and practices, but in virtue of a contingent feature of (some of) them, which Hart happened to discover. Under this interpretation, many practices just *happen* to consist in patterns of convergent behaviour and a common understanding of what they require of practitioners.[51] But Hart makes no such claims of empirical discovery; and in any event, once it is conceded that practices are not necessarily limited by common understanding, very few practices could plausibly be said to be so limited and thus be suitable for Hart's analysis. All the interesting practices could be plausibly conceived of as

---

[51] Hart's claim in the Postscript that he came to think that his analysis of practices was applicable only to those which are genuinely conventional—in which convergence of behaviour, insofar as it exists, is explicable in terms of convergence of convention, not of conviction—may suggest that he was disposed to take that line. But again, in the absence of any empirical claim to the effect that certain practices are in fact conventional, Hart's concession seems to be, not a reinterpretation of his claim as empirical rather than conceptual, but rather a concession that his claim is a conceptual claim about conventional practices only, if there be any, not just any type of practice. So the claim would still remain conceptual, arrived at through reliance on the thesis about the nature of concepts and rules that I am concerned to attribute to Hart here. Of course, to that restricted claim the objection that follows in the text, viz. that probably no practice, and anyway not law, is conventional, still stands: practices that are characterized by controversy and divergent behaviour do not on their face seem conventional in nature. In any event, I am not concerned to disprove Hart's conceptual claim here, only to trace its origin.

consisting of a great number of *competing* understandings of their requirements and *divergent* patterns of behaviour of practitioners.[52] Alternatively,
Hart might claim that, for independent reasons, even though practices
contain a large number of competing understandings and partially divergent behaviour, we would do better to identify them in terms of the
common ground among those competing understandings and the overlap among diverging patterns of behaviour. Such independent reasons
would provide an argument for treating only the highest common factor
among competing conceptions as genuine parts of the practice. Hart
made no argument for that bizarre claim either, and it is unclear what
such an argument could be.

Ambitious analysis, i.e. the attempt to distil metaphysical wisdom out
of ordinary use, makes no sense without the assumption that ordinary use
is founded on shared, common ground that *defines or individuates* the concepts that figure in use. So the method presupposes the shared-criteria
thesis. Conversely, a theory that claims to find a defining foundation of
shared ground in conceptual practices, as Hart's theory did, makes no
sense without the assumption that practices are *individuated* by shared
criteria. Otherwise, the theory must be interpreted as making some
implausible empirical claim, or alternatively some bizarre theoretical
claim in support of a *restricted* conception of practices that are individuated otherwise.

Instead of selecting either of these alternatives, Hart made some ostensibly conceptual claims about practices in general and law in particular.
He thought he deduced his claims about the nature of practices and
specifically legal practice from the character of concepts—as he had told
his German audience on the occasion of talking to them about Jhering's
Heaven of Concepts.[53] And his pursuit of common understandings led
him to the thesis that practices are underlain by shared criteria.

III. OPEN TEXTURE AND CRITERIA

A. Legal indeterminacy

Hart famously thought that the law is partly indeterminate. Why did he
think so? His explanation is in purely semantic terms. He conceives of the
problem of determinacy in the law as a problem about the application of
expressions—general classificatory terms. And he thinks that that problem is equivalent to the problem of following a rule.

---

[52] Dworkin's unpublished paper on Hart's Postscript develops that line of argument.
[53] See n. 5 above.

Even those who think that there is nothing semantic in Hart's general theory of law—or at least most of them—admit that Hart's view on legal indeterminacy derives from a semantic doctrine.[54] But not everyone agrees on why Hart had that view. Michael Moore, for example, says that, while for his general theory of law Hart did *not* rely on his preferred semantics, i.e. 1950s Oxford-style criterial semantics exemplified in the Paradigm Case Argument tradition, he did rely on it in the context of adjudication *only*.[55] Moore claims that Hart only had to resort to his semantics in connection to questions of interpretation of texts such as statutes, so he did not need to do so in the context of discussing the nature of law, regarding which no authoritative text exists. Moore also employs another distinction to support his claim that Hart used semantics only for questions of adjudication: such questions, Moore says, involve propositions internal to some legal system of the form 'it is the law that φ', or 'the law requires that φ'. By contrast, questions about the nature of law involve propositions external to any system, e.g. 'all legal systems have structure π'.[56]

Moore's contrasts are not true to the structure of Hart's argument. Hart's discussion of legal indeterminacy comes straight after his articulation of 'the foundations of a legal system',[57] i.e. his statement of the central aspects of the nature of law, and is explicitly offered as continuous with it. The discussion of indeterminacy continues the discussion of the metaphysics of law: law is essentially a matter of the union of primary and secondary rules, under the umbrella of the master rule of recognition, Hart says. The fact that the law consists in a set or system of rules implies, Hart thinks, a further metaphysical property: partial indeterminacy (123). The law is in its nature partly indeterminate, because rules are so, including the rule that individuates legal systems. Moreover, Hart thinks that law is indeterminate for a more abstract reason: anything that is designated by general classificatory terms is only partially determinate (4, 123).

Neither of Moore's distinctions fits Hart's project in the part of the book where Hart discusses open texture. That part of Hart's discussion is not exclusively about texts. In fact, he is adamant that indeterminacy is a feature of law, whether or not law is expressed in canonically formulated texts. The difference between precedent and statute makes no difference, Hart says, because of the nature of the problem common to both, namely classifying under general terms (127–8). Hart is not switching from exter-

---

[54] Endicott is an exception. He says that Hart had no semantic theory in support of his doctrine of discretion, and that his open texture thesis is only 'a platitude' to the effect that there are clear and unclear cases. See discussion below.

[55] See his 'Hart's Postscript', at 93.

[56] The examples of the two kinds of proposition are mine.

[57] Ch. 6 of *CL*, with that title.

nal to internal propositions either, in that part of his book. He does not move from talking about law to talking about *the* law; rather, he carries on talking about the nature of law.

Hart does begin his exposition of indeterminacy by discussing cases of application of ordinary law, before moving on to discussion of indeterminacy at the foundations—the rule of recognition. But that shows that he thinks, not that there are two distinct questions to answer, one about the nature of law and one about the nature of *the* law, but that there is only one. Hart says that law is essentially a system of rules individuated by a master rule. He also thinks that any rule, as well as any concept, involves partial indeterminacy. Indeterminacy affects the question of what counts as law as much as the question of what counts as negligence. Hence, some questions, legal as well as jurisprudential, have no answer. Does the prohibition of vehicles in the park apply to toy cars? Is this plaintiff entitled to recovery? Does this society have law? Can an immoral rule be part of the law?[58]

Hart relies on two prima facie different sources of indeterminacy: the one comes from the partial indeterminacy of language in general, the other from the partial indeterminacy in the application of rules. He treats, however, both sources as ultimately identical. In his discussion of indeterminacy he freely switches among difficulties involving instances of rules and difficulties involving instances of general classificatory terms (126–7). He thinks that law is indeterminate, because both the rules law consists in and concepts including the concept of law are indeterminate.[59] Hart treats both sources of indeterminacy as identical because he reduces both to an underlying problem of *classification*. Both rules on the one hand and expressions and concepts on the other have extensions or ranges of application. Indeterminacy consists in there being no fact of the matter as to whether an expression or a rule is applicable to certain things.

---

[58] It is no objection to say that Hart would accept that there is an important distinction between legal and jurisprudential questions. Hart did endorse that distinction in the abstract, as he did in many specific contexts. But he did not base his discussion of indeterminacy on the distinction. He closes his chapter on the foundations of a legal system as follows: '[The duality of a core of certainty and a penumbra of doubt] imparts to all rules a fringe of vagueness or "open texture", and this may affect the rule of recognition specifying the ultimate criteria used in the identification of law as much as a particular statute. This aspect of law is often held to show that any elucidation of the concept of law in terms of rules must be misleading. To insist on it in the face of the realities of the situation is often stigmatised as "conceptualism" or "formalism", and it is to the estimation of this charge that we shall now turn' (123).

[59] 'I certainly did *not* think I was saying something applicable only to the language of *statutes* or *rules* or *statutory* interpretation etc. My view was (and is) that that the uses of *any* language containing empirical classificatory general terms will, in applying them, meet with borderline cases calling for fresh regulation. This is the feature of language called "open texture".' Hart, correspondence to Brian Bix, quoted in *Law, Language, and Legal Determinacy* (Oxford, Clarendon Press, 1993), 24 (emphasis original).

Hart, as much as Waissmann, from whom he takes the doctrine of open texture, treats questions about correct application as equivalent to questions about rule-following. In the Wittgensteinian tradition, the question of what determines the meaning of an expression can be formulated as the question of what constitutes following a certain rule.[60] Moreover, both questions involve the problem of correct application. Correct application of legal rules involves, Hart explicitly says, correct application of the expressions that figure in them; and any rule governing correct application of such expressions is itself expressed in language, and so itself raises issues of correct application of *its* constituent expressions (126).

Hart's method of conceptual analysis yields a specification of the nature of law in terms of the union of two kinds of rule. He expressed that union in terms of a set of conditions necessary and sufficient for the existence of a legal system (116). Had he left it at that, all his early talk about the impossibility of analysis in terms of such conditions would be mysterious. But in the discussion of indeterminacy, Hart cashes the semantic cheque drawn at the beginning of the book. He gives there two constraints for an adequate semantics: instances of a general term are related to each other in multiple ways, such as by way of analogy; and, because of the open texture of language, there exist borderline cases.

In the discussion of indeterminacy, Hart shows how these two constraints operate in the analysis of law. First, law cannot be fully analysed in terms of necessary and sufficient conditions, because the concept of law, as much as any other concept, is vague at the boundaries. Consequently, the concept of law is not reducible to any set of jointly sufficient and severally necessary conditions. So Hart's discussion of indeterminacy restricts and qualifies his analysis of law in terms of the union of primary and secondary rules. In marginal cases, all claims of conceptual necessity about law may fail. Secondly, in the discussion of hard cases in the law, he suggests that relations of similarity to exemplars determine correct application of a rule or a term. In spelling out the semantics that respects the constraints, he confirms and reinforces his understanding of concepts as reducible to the facts of use, the applications of a term that users consistently make, their procedures for establishing that a term applies, or more generally the criteria of application that they use.

B. The nature of hard cases

Hart's argument for indeterminacy is that the application of rules—whether linguistic or substantive—concepts, and expressions is partly

---

[60] See the discussion of the meaning of 'plus' and of following the rule of addition in Kripke's *Wittgenstein*, ch. 2. See also the discussion of convergence of behaviour and agreement in judgments in Hart's account of rules and practices in Part II above.

indeterminate because of an epistemic shortcoming: the possibility of uncertainty about the applicability of a concept, expression, or rule. He draws the contrast between the determinate core of a concept and its indeterminate penumbra in terms of *certainty* and *doubt* (123). He says that certain cases are *clear* or *plain* (126): these constitute the exemplars or paradigms (127, 129) which meet the 'necessary conditions fixed by language which anything must satisfy if it is to be within [a rule's] scope' (129). In such cases there is 'general agreement in judgments as to the applicability of the classifying terms' (126). By contrast, there exist *unclear* cases possessing 'only some of the features of the plain cases' and so producing *uncertainties* (126). Unclear cases are such that there are 'reasons both for and against our use of a general term'. In those cases 'no firm convention or general agreement dictates [a term's] use, or, on the other hand, its rejection'; rather, all we have to go by is the exemplars, against which the case is assessed for defensible similarities, i.e. sufficient resemblance in relevant respects (127). But a judgment of resemblance constitutes a *choice* between open alternatives (127): it is neither true nor false that the term correctly applies to such cases.

In defending this understanding of indeterminacy, Hart is concerned to show that it is inescapable: that no amount of care or precision in the formulation of rules—legal or linguistic—can eradicate the penumbra of doubt in their application.[61] He appeals to the epistemic handicap to which humans are subject: we do not know in advance what the future may bring (128).[62] The possibility of unforeseen circumstances places a limit to what conditions can do. He cites Waissmann's freak possibilities that one-foot tall creatures, otherwise possessing all characteristics of humans, may occur, or that a metal otherwise indistinguishable from gold may fail to emit the right kind of radiation.[63] These cases are not simply epistemically bizarre, Hart suggests; they are semantically indeterminate.

---

[61] Gordon Baker accuses Hart of circularity in this connection. Hart argues, he says, that it is impossible to frame rules in a way that would eradicate the possibility of hard cases because rules must be framed in language and language is open-textured. But Baker says that Waissmann, from whom Hart got the open-texture thesis, premissed the thesis on the impossibility of framing linguistic rules in a way that would eradicate the possibility of hard cases. Hence Hart's argument is circular. See 'Defeasibility and Meaning', in P. M. S. Hacker and J. Raz (eds.), *Law, Morality, and Society* (Oxford, Clarendon Press, 1977), 37. Notice that Baker explicitly takes Hart's discussion to be about hard cases in the application of statutes only, rather than in the application of expressions in general. But I think that Hart needs no convincing that the statutory and the linguistic problems are identical, and so that one cannot explain the other. Rather, he thinks that uncertainty entails indeterminacy in both contexts, and for the same reason, namely that correct application of both expressions and rules consists in shared judgments. See Stavropoulos, *Objectivity*, 65–8 for discussion of the relations among certainty, controversy, and indeterminacy.

[62] See also 'Jhering', 269–70.   [63] Ibid. 275.

Waissmann's doctrine figures prominently in many of Hart's writings. In *CL*, Hart appears to be trying to find a further ground for the inevitability of indeterminacy. Given the epistemic limitation, we suffer from a political limitation: not only do we not know what to say, how to *describe* unforeseen and unforeseeable bizarre cases, but we do not know what we would *want to do* with respect to such cases. Not having anticipated the bizarre cases—e.g. flying saucers in the park—we have never had the opportunity to form determinate aims relative to them. There is no answer to the question whether they *do* come, nor to the question whether we would *want* them to come, under the prohibition of vehicles.

It is important to note that, in Hart's explanation, political indeterminacy is parasitic on semantic indeterminacy. Contrary to what Endicott suggests,[64] Hart clearly says that the open texture of language *alone* renders complete determinacy impossible; the political aspect of indeterminacy shows that the impossible state of affairs in which everything was regulated in advance is not even desirable—that we should not cherish an impossibility, not that we should renounce a real option.

Moreover, the political handicap is parasitic on the semantic because the issues of political indeterminacy arise only in respect of those bizarre cases that are semantically *relevant* yet indeterminate. Flying saucers landing in the park, humanoids one foot tall strolling through it, and goldish metal emitting non-standard radiation found in its soil are all unforeseeable contingencies; yet the question of political aims as to the prohibition of vehicles in the park arises only in respect of the first contingency, which Hart treats as *arguably* an instance of a vehicle, yet *indeterminately* so. Aims, whether fixed in advance or adjusted as we go, are individuated by reference to concepts—of a vehicle (129) or of due care (130–2), in Hart's examples. It is because the *concepts*, he thinks, are partly indeterminate, that the aims are themselves indeterminate.

Both Hart's characterization of easy and hard cases and his attempts to explain why hard cases and thus indeterminacy are inevitable are framed in epistemic terms. Throughout the discussion, he moves from epistemic premises to metaphysical conclusions. Our being certain, or the case's being clear, amounts to there being determinate answers to questions of correct application. Our being uncertain, the case's being unclear, by contrast, entails that such questions have no determinate answer.

It is important to emphasize that Hart is *not* simply saying that there are easy and hard cases. He is not simply reporting the 'platitude' that uncertainties in the application of words are inevitable;[65] rather, he draws from the 'platitude' the *metaphysical* implication that in cases of

---

[64] Book review, *LQR*, 113 (1997), 508–12, at 511.
[65] Contrary to what Endicott suggests, ibid. See also 'Hart', 43.

uncertainty there is no fact of the matter as to how things in the world are arranged, as to whether some metal is gold or a certain sort of behaviour is negligent. Contrary to Endicott's suggestion, indeterminacy is not a further, unconnected thought that Hart mysteriously chooses to report just after he mentions uncertainty. Rather, Hart clearly and forcefully argues *from* uncertainty *to* indeterminacy. He explicitly says that under certain conditions, namely conditions of uncertainty, there is no answer to the question of application of a term. He therefore believes that uncertainty entails indeterminacy.

Why should Hart think that certainty or uncertainty, our ease or difficulty or generally our ability to *tell* when an expression applies, would imply anything at all as to whether the expression *does* apply? Why should he think that what we *know* about the future has any implication as to what counts as what's in it? Arguments that move from our epistemic position in respect of a proposition to metaphysical conclusions that concern the proposition's truth and determinacy seem not, as a general matter, to be valid. We may be uncertain as to whether life ever existed on Mars, but this is no reason to think that there is no answer to the question of whether it did. Rather, such arguments may perhaps be valid only in exceptional contexts. Perhaps I cannot be in pain if I am unsure as to whether I am.[66]

Not only did Hart claim that certainty and uncertainty entail determinacy and indeterminacy, respectively, and so explained one in terms of the other; he had a more general explanation for that entailment, which he set out both in his general methodological remarks and in the discussion of indeterminacy itself.

Unlike life on Mars, an empirical question, Hart wants to move from epistemic premises to metaphysical conclusions regarding conceptual questions. His open-texture argument implies that there is no answer to the question what *counts* as life, where there is uncertainty about it. And it is clearly his conviction that concepts are constituted by epistemic abilities. Consequently, epistemic failure implies conceptual failure. Our not knowing whether something counts as life entails that there is no fact of the matter as to whether it counts. Uncertainty about the application of concepts entails that concepts fail to divide up the world in a determinate way.

At the most abstract level, Hart says that use determines meaning, which as we saw implies that, roughly, whether concepts apply is determined by what speakers say and do on cases of putative application.

---

[66] See Dworkin's 'Objectivity and Truth: You'd Better Believe It', *Philosophy and Public Affairs*, 25 (1996), 88–139, for discussion of the relations among propositions of uncertainty and propositions of indeterminacy.

More precisely, concepts are individuated by the facts of usage. Therefore, the concepts that are so individuated are such that their boundaries are fixed by the applications and procedures involved in actual usage. If actual usage fails to fix definite boundaries, the concept that is individuated by actual usage does not itself have definite boundaries but is instead vague. It follows that where speakers don't know what to say, where they are baffled or divided, there is no fact of the matter as to whether the concept applies or not.

But even if we prescind from Hart's general methodological claims, what he says in connection with indeterminacy is sufficient to attribute to him a specific semantic theory. Hart says that correct application is constituted by exemplars and relations to them. Speakers' ability to recognize something as an exemplary instance of a vehicle, or as very similar to the exemplars, makes application determinate. The cases that strike users as easy are *ipso facto* cases of correct application. These cases supply a set of shared criteria (Hart calls them conditions, as we saw) that determine how the facts must be for a concept to be applicable. Hart seems to suggest that these criteria pertain to respects in which other cases are related to the exemplars, so that cases are instances in virtue of their being similar to the exemplars in this or that respect.

Hart says, however, that it is not the case that the criteria fully determine correct application. It is not the case that criteria are either met, and the expression applies correctly, or they are not met, and the expression does not apply. Rather, there are cases where the criteria fail to provide unequivocal support, in which, as Hart says, there are reasons both for and against application. In such cases, he does not infer that we have the wrong criteria, that the criteria are not in fact the conditions of correct application; rather, he infers that we *choose* to apply or withhold application, based not on criteria but on *arguments* of similarity to the exemplars.

There are, therefore, two kinds of relation of similarity to exemplars. The first is such that something's being similar in *this* way to the exemplars entails that the expression is correctly applied to it. The second is such that something's being similar in *that* way to the exemplars entails, not that the expression is correctly applied to it, but that application constitutes an ad hoc decision, a choice to *extend* the concept beyond its boundaries. What is the difference? Hart says that choice in the latter case is based on *arguments* that defend the case as relevantly and closely similar. *E contrario*, he must think that the relation of similarity in the former case is a matter not of argument but of fiat or convention: such a relation is not to be defended by argument, but is trivially true. This conclusion is reinforced by the other contrast Hart draws between the two types of case. In the former case he says that there exists general agreement as to the applicability of the term; in the latter, no convention or general agreement is available. It follows that Hart thinks there are two distinct bases for judgments of application. The first is criteria shared as a matter of convention; the second is substantive argument. Correct application is determinate only in the first case.

Criteria, we should recall, are an epistemological category: they involve how speakers *tell* that the expression applies. They are the basis on which speakers find cases easy, exemplary, or hard. Also, they are flexible to a degree—not all the criteria have to be met, since cases can be equally easy by virtue of their being similar in this or that respect. Moreover, given that satisfaction of the criteria is not dispositive of questions of application, it follows that satisfaction of all or most of the criteria constitutes *evidence* that the expression applies, albeit *defeasible* evidence.[67] As the jargon goes, they provide conclusive yet not incontrovertible support to judgments of application. The idea behind the jargon is that, in normal circumstances, the criteria's satisfaction makes application certain. Unusual circumstances interfere with evidentiary support and may defeat, i.e. warrant withholding, application despite satisfaction of the criteria. Such circumstances, however, cannot be captured in any finite list of defeating conditions. Correct application of the concept is determinate only in normal circumstances, where as we saw, questions of application are resolved on the basis of the criteria's satisfaction alone.

All this is, of course, substantially more than in outline, the semantic theory of criteria, in the technical sense of the term developed by some Wittgenstein commentators.[68] Moreover, whether or not it is that particular theory, it is a definite theory that explains correct application of concepts in terms of exemplars and relations to them, in the specific way just discussed.

The idea that correctness is constituted by evidentiary relations to exemplars is as problematic as the general inference from epistemic

[67] It is perhaps more accurate to say that the *judgment of application* may turn out to be defeasible, even where the criteria are satisfied. I follow what has become standard philosophical usage in characterizing *evidence* and *criterial support* as defeasible.

[68] See Baker, 'Defeasibility', who suggests that Hart had better adopt the theory of criteria, as it is the only theory available that respects all his semantic constraints. My claim is, in effect, that Hart does adopt it in substance, in virtue of his tying meaning to exemplars, his view on cases where the conditions associated with the exemplars are not smoothly met, and more generally his epistemic conception of determinacy and indeterminacy. See Stavropoulos, *Objectivity*, 62–8, for elaboration and criticism of the theory of criteria as adopted by Hart. Roger Albritton's 'On Wittgenstein's Use of the Term "Criterion" ', in George Pitcher (ed.), *Wittgenstein: The Philosophical Investigations* (London, Macmillan, 1968), was among the works that identified the doctrine of criteria in Wittgenstein. See further Albritton's recanting Postscript to his paper; Baker, 'Criteria: A New Foundation for Semantics', *Ratio*, 16 (1974); Crispin Wright, 'Anti-realist Semantics: The Role of *Criteria*', in Godfrey Vesey (ed.), *Idealism Past and Present* (Cambridge, Cambridge University Press, 1982); 'Second Thoughts about Criteria', *Synthèse*, 58 (1984), 383–405; and John McDowell 'Criteria, Defeasibility, and Meaning', in *Meaning, Knowledge, and Reality* (Cambridge, Mass., Harvard University Press, 1998).

premisses to metaphysical conclusions. Perhaps people consider peaches exemplars of fruit, and they judge whether other things are fruit on the basis of relations of similarity to them. So perhaps apricots are judged as fruit because they look much like small peaches and they are about as sweet if not quite so, and strawberries are fruit because, though they look very different, they are rather sweet themselves and, just like peaches, supremely suitable for dessert. So perhaps something's being sweet, looking like a peach, and being good for dessert (and perhaps coming from trees and plants also) operates as the set of criteria that people in fact use in order to decide whether something is a fruit or not. In certain cases people are baffled. Tomatoes do not look or taste anything like peaches, and you cannot serve them as dessert, but they contain seeds, just as peaches do. Most people will not be confident as to whether they are fruit or not. This goes to show that perhaps taste and looks and typical ordering in a meal is not what defines fruit, not that classifying tomatoes as fruit is an exercise of botanical discretion.

More generally, peaches' exemplary status and similarities to them concern people's *methods* for ascertaining whether something is a fruit, not whether something *is* a fruit. Waissmann's one-foot tall humanoids may *be* humans, notwithstanding our bafflement as to what they are. Metaphysical necessity need not be identical to, nor need it track, epistemic necessity.[69] Hart's doctrine of indeterminacy is implied by a semantics that makes one depend on the other, in virtue of an epistemic understanding of the nature of concepts.

We saw that Hart also says that within a concept's determinate boundaries, instances bear *conventional* relations to exemplars: such relations are specified by criteria, Hart thinks, that are shared as a matter of convention. By contrast, no agreed basis for judgments exists in the penumbra, but only argument. This contrast is among Hart's most explicit statements of the thesis that concepts are individuated by shared criteria, and so that there can be no such thing as genuine theoretical disagreement within a concept's boundaries. Where lawyers have several different views as to what counts as negligence, such that no view is widely shared and all are supported by sensible arguments, Hart is committed to the position that it cannot be the case that one or the other view is true, and the rest false; rather, he is committed to the position that they are all neither true nor false.

[69] See Rey, 'Concepts and Stereotypes', for these and other examples and discussion of the difficulties of 'stereotype' or 'exemplar' and other epistemic theories of concepts; Stavropoulos, *Objectivity*, ch. 2, for discussion of the importance for semantics of the distinction between epistemic and metaphysical necessity; and ch. 5, for discussion of the possibility that exemplars might turn out to be cases of misapplication of the expression with respect to which they are considered exemplars.

I said that Hart's epistemic account of determinacy and indeterminacy amounts to a definite semantic theory, even if we prescind from his general methodology. We can also prescind in the other direction. Hart's general method by itself implies an account of indeterminacy. Even if he had not written anything about hard cases and open texture, his methodology would commit him to a position similar to the one he did in fact spell out. His method seeks to articulate concepts whose identity is fixed by actual usage. To the extent that actual usage, even after it has been ordered and unified by analysis, yields principles that remain imprecise or indefinite, the concepts identified on the basis of usage will themselves be indefinite. Such analysis can only yield 'porous' concepts.

In fact, the account of indeterminacy that Hart did supply spells out the details of that methodological implication. Not surprisingly, his detailed explanation of open texture, as *Porosität* was rendered in English, fully coheres with and reinforces his methodology, his project of analysing the concept of law by investigating how that concept as well as other concepts are used. His detailed explanation of open texture in terms of epistemic failures, and his more abstract methodology of analysis based on use, are parts of a systematic, coherent, controversial, if ultimately unsatisfactory theoretical view on the nature of concepts. I conclude that Hart is deeply in semantic debt, so much so that the success of his overall theory of law turns on the defensibility of the semantics that underwrites it.

IV. THE STING

Dworkin offered the sting argument as a diagnosis of Hart's inability properly to accommodate and draw the correct implication from lawyers' disagreements. Dworkin said that the semantic prejudice to the effect that concepts are shared by virtue of sharing criteria for their correct application explains Hart's failure in this connection. I have tried to provide some detailed reasons why Dworkin's diagnosis is essentially correct, and why the sting stings Hart, despite his protests. If I am right in attributing to Hart the semantic theses that I describe in this essay, those theses set part of the agenda of a successful defence. Defending Hart's theory requires, not disowning the theses, but defending them. A proper defence of Hart would involve showing how the facts of endemic disagreement on which Dworkin relies can be adequately explained by the semantics that drives Hart's theory of law, a semantics that gives the facts of actual usage the role of individuating the concepts used, and identifies determinacy with collective certainty. If that can be shown, the venom will be taken out of the sting. For the record, I think it cannot, but saying why will have to wait for another occasion.

4

Incorporationism, Conventionality, and the Practical Difference Thesis

JULES COLEMAN

H. L. A. Hart's *The Concept of Law*[1] is the most important and influential book in the legal positivist tradition. Though its importance is undisputed, there is a good deal less consensus regarding its core commitments, both methodological and substantive. With the exception of an occasional essay,[2] Hart neither further developed nor revised his position beyond the argument of the book. The burden of shaping the prevailing understanding of his views, therefore, has fallen to others: notably, Joseph Raz among positivists and Ronald Dworkin among positivism's critics. Dworkin in particular has framed, then reframed, the conventional understanding not only of Hart's positivism but of the terms of the debate between positivists and him.[3] While standing on the sidelines, Hart witnessed the unfolding not only of a lively debate between positivists and Dworkin but also of an equally intense one among positivists as to positivism's (and his) core claims. The most important debate has been between so-called inclusive and exclusive positivists: a debate as much about Hart's legacy as about the proper interpretation of legal positivism.

This essay is the first in a series, the first two of which focus on legal positivism; others focus on analogies between methods in epistemology, metaphysics, and philosophy of language, and jurisprudence. These issues are explored in my upcoming Clarendon Lectures. I have benefited from numerous discussions with several people, in particular Joseph Raz, Stephen Perry, Jeremy Waldron, Ben Zipursky, Ruth Chang, and Liam Murphy. I am, however, especially indebted to Scott Shapiro, who has reawakened my interest in the field, and from whom I have gained more than I have given.

Many of the themes first articulated in this essay are more fully expressed and developed in *The Practice of Principle: In Defence of a Pragmatist Approach to Legal Theory* (Oxford University Press, March 2001). The arguments presented here are superceded by those developed in the book.

[1] 2nd edn., ed. P. Bulloch and J. Raz (1994), hereinafter cited as *CL*.

[2] 'American Jurisprudence Through English Eyes: The Nightmare and the Noble Dream', 11 Ga. L. Rev. 969 (1977).

[3] It would not be unfair to say that first Dworkin framed the debate in terms of a disagreement about the nature and scope of judicial discretion; next as a debate about the nature of adjudication generally; then as a debate between competing theories of interpretation, as part of an even more general debate about the methods and projects of jurisprudence. There have been common themes throughout, of course, among the most important, but least appreciated, concerning the relative importance of controversy and disagreement to our understanding of legal practice: the nature and scope of agreement necessary to make sense of controversy in law.

With the posthumous publication of the Postscript to the second edition of *CL*, Hart has recaptured centre stage. The published Postscript is roughly one-half of an extended reply to his critics including observations drawn from thirty years of reflecting on *CL* and its progeny. The portion of Hart's reflections that made it to print contains a point-by-point reply to Dworkin, and only parenthetical allusions to the work of others.[4] Though limited in this way, the Postscript is certain to be at least as carefully studied as the book itself and to be the subject of a substantial body of literature.

That the Postscript focuses so closely on Dworkin's work is both appropriate and unfortunate. It is appropriate because Dworkin is the most influential legal philosopher of the post-Hart era; his sustained and systematic critiques of *CL* have inscribed the book in the conscience of every analytic legal philosopher currently working in the field. In the same way in which many of us have learned our Austin through Hart, many have come to understand Hart through Dworkin. No matter where one's loyalties lie, every theorist has wondered how Hart would have replied to Dworkin's most familiar and penetrating objections. Still, the focus on Dworkin is unfortunate because Razian concerns about the implications for positivism of law's claim to practical authority are at least as worrisome for Hart's positivism as are any of Dworkin's more celebrated and discussed objections. Unfortunately, the Postscript is silent on Raz's concerns.

In the Postscript, Hart explicitly embraces 'soft positivism' (his label for inclusive positivism, or what I call Incorporationism), apparently settling the issue between inclusive and exclusive legal positivists for Hart's legacy.[5] Very roughly, Incorporationism allows that morality can be a condition of legality: that the legality of norms can sometimes depend on their substantive (moral) merits, not just their pedigree or social source. Razians (or exclusive positivists) have argued that in attempting to accommodate Dworkin's views about the way in which moral argument figures in legal discourse, Incorporationism is rendered incompatible

---

[4] The editors determined that Hart's observations beyond his response to Dworkin were not sufficiently well developed to be published.

[5] In the Postscript, Hart embraces the form of legal positivism that I have been developing since 'Negative and Positive Positivism'. This form of positivism has gone under a variety of names. Wil Waluchow refers to it as 'inclusive positivism'; Hart refers to it as 'soft positivism'; Dworkin calls it 'soft conventionalism'. It is most commonly referred to as inclusive legal positivism, which is designed to emphasize the contrast with Raz's exclusive legal positivism. I prefer 'Incorporationism', and that is the label I will employ throughout. Jules L. Coleman, 'Negative and Positive Positivism', 11 J. Legal Stud. 139 (1982), repr. in *Ronald Dworkin and Contemporary Jurisprudence* (ed. M. Cohen, 1984), 28–48; also repr. in *Markets, Morals and the Law* (1988), 3–27. See also Wilfrid Waluchow, *Inclusive Legal Positivism* (1994), 2–3; Hart, Postscript, *supra* n. 1, at 250–4; Ronald Dworkin, *Law's Empire* (1986), 124–30.

with law's claim to authority. Therefore, in embracing Incorporationism, Hart is placed in the unenviable position of having to defend himself against Raz as well as against Dworkin.

There is overwhelming textual and philosophical support for the view that, in addition to Incorporationism, Hart accepts what I call the Conventionality and the Practical Difference Theses.[6] Roughly, the Conventionality Thesis is the claim that law is made possible by an interdependent convergence of behaviour and attitude: what we might think of as an 'agreement' among individuals expressed in a social or conventional rule. For Hart, this is the rule of recognition. Again roughly, the Practical Difference Thesis is the claim that, in order to be law, authoritative pronouncements must in principle be capable of making a practical difference: a difference, that is, in the structure or content of deliberation and action.

The problem is that Incorporationism and the conjunction of the Conventionality and Practical Difference Theses constitute an inconsistent set. No positivist, not even Hart, can simultaneously maintain all three. Adding Incorporationism to the familiar medley of positivism's core commitments appears to render it incoherent. Far from constituting a modest amendment to or development of traditional legal positivism, Incorporationism forces a positivist to rethink and, very likely, to revise one's understanding of its most basic commitments. Like many legal positivists who have embraced Incorporationism as a way of absorbing Dworkin's insights and thereby meeting his objections, Hart did not fully appreciate the implications for his overall position of doing so.

The set's inconsistency is a problem for any Incorporationist, not just Hart. Whereas I believe that Hart is more likely to have abandoned Incorporationism, thus bringing his position considerably closer to Raz's in crucial respects, I propose that we abandon or at least significantly modify the place of the Practical Difference Thesis within positivism.

This paper has two main ambitions: one interpretive, the other substantive. It develops Hart's positivism in terms of the Conventionality and Practical Difference Theses, highlighting the particular versions of each that he embraces. Despite his explicit embrace of Incorporationism, Hart's commitments to the Conventionality and Practical Difference Theses preclude his doing so. We do Hart no service by uncritically accepting his embrace of Incorporationism. Substantively, the present paper outlines the sort of legal positivism that emerges when the place within it of the Practical Difference Thesis is thoroughly revised. Both ambitions require a good bit of argument and staging.

---

[6] These are my ways of characterizing and describing a family of views about the conditions of law's possibility and normativity.

Setting the stage requires a preliminary inquiry into the projects and methods of jurisprudence. Therefore, we begin with a compressed account of the problems of jurisprudence and the methods available to their resolution. This is followed by a detailed discussion of the Conventionality and Practical Difference Theses. Characterizing positivism in terms of the Conventionality and Practical Difference Theses has many advantages, not the least of which is that it enables us to locate precisely Dworkin's and Raz's objections to Incorporationism. In effect, Dworkin argues that Incorporationism is incompatible with the Conventionality Thesis, whereas Raz argues that it is incompatible with the Practical Difference Thesis.

Dworkin and Raz are both committed to exclusive positivism, but in different senses. Dworkin takes exclusive positivism to be the best and, indeed, only coherent version of legal positivism: a coherent but mistaken jurisprudence. For Raz, exclusive positivism is not only the correct interpretation of positivism, but also the correct jurisprudential view. Whereas both reject the possibility of positivism allowing contentful criteria of legal validity, they have very different reasons for doing so.

In Dworkin's case, contentful or moral criteria of legal validity create a problem for positivism because morality is inherently controversial. Controversy undermines law's conventionality. A controversial rule of recognition cannot be a social rule, and thus cannot be a rule of recognition in the positivist's sense. For Raz, the problem with morality as a condition of legality has nothing to do with morality's alleged controversiality. Instead, the problem is that an appeal to morality as a condition of legality undermines law's claim to authority. In Raz's view, the concept of authority precludes inquiring into a law's justifying reasons in order to determine its status or content—something which Incorporationism permits.[7]

It is possible to recast some of Dworkin's concerns as worries about Incorporationism's compatibility with the Practical Difference Thesis. In this formulation of the objection, it is part of our concept of law (for a positivist) that law effectively guides human conduct by offering reasons for action. A rule of recognition that is inherently controversial is incapable of offering effective guidance because individuals cannot reliably determine what the law requires of them. Even then, however, the concern is with the controversiality of moral criteria. In the end, Dworkin's worries about legal positivism invariably focus on what he takes to be its inability to offer a convincing account of the nature of

---

[7] These are very rough characterizations of the differences between Raz and me. For a detailed statement of the most important ones see nn. 49, 50, and 54 below as well as the accompanying text.

controversy and disagreement in law. Dworkin has consistently emphasized the importance of theoretical disagreement in law while worrying
about the extent of agreement necessary in order to understand its possibility.

I should make clear what may seem obvious to some readers, but
mysterious to others. In this essay, I focus on Dworkin's objections to legal
positivism, a view that must be distinguished from what Dworkin refers
to as 'conventionalism'. Conventionalism is his formulation of positivism
as an interpretive theory of law, a move he believes is necessary in order
to capture its insights.[8] No positivist with whom I am familiar, however,
accepts Dworkin's claim that conventionalism provides the best understanding of positivism, and all resist Dworkin's transformation of positivism into an interpretive theory of law.

Having expressed my reluctance to credit Dworkin's argument—that to
render it interesting positivism must be recast as an interpretive theory—I
should note that, were positivism understood as an interpretive theory of
law (which, I repeat, it is not, need not be, nor is best interpreted as),
conventionalism, in Dworkin's sense, would be a pretty good candidate for
the kind of theory it would be. But even then I would disagree with
Dworkin because the interpretive 'point' of law for the conventionalist/
interpretivist would not be the enforcement of settled expectations—as it is
in his construction—but the effective guidance of conduct. To be sure, effective guidance may often require enforcing settled expectations, but the
former, not the latter, would be, if anything had to be, the point of law
within the constructive interpretation conception of positivism.

Though positivism is not best understood as what Dworkin calls
'conventionalism', it *is* committed to explaining law as ultimately resting
on a social convention.[9] This is what I refer to as the Conventionality

---

[8] That is because Dworkin believes that as it is traditionally understood positivism is
subject to the dreaded semantic sting. To save the theory and to render it plausible, he
believes that positivism must be reformulated as an interpretive theory. That interpretive
theory is what he calls 'conventionalism'.

[9] Two tricky points that one has to keep in mind. First, conventionalism plays an enormously important role in positivism, but not the one Dworkin attributes to it. The role he
attributes to it is based on his view of it as an interpretive theory of law. He is welcome to
treat it that way. Positivists do not, however, and his semantic sting argument offers no
reason whatsoever for their having to do so. Second, in saying that conventionalism is
important to positivism, one usually has in mind the claim that the rule of recognition is a
social convention. This is tricky because Raz, as much a positivist as anyone, never actually
invokes the notion of a rule of recognition in developing his theory, though he does when
discussing Hart's. For Raz, there just are criteria or standards of legality. He does not believe
that it is necessary to introduce the idea of a rule of recognition as that which sets out these
criteria of legality. But he does appear to believe that these are the criteria of legal validity
just so long as there is a practice among officials of so regarding them. It is not a stretch to
think of that practice as constituting a convention among officials: that feature of law, its ultimate conventionality, is what I take to be common to all positivists.

Thesis. As I argue below, the point of insisting on law's conventionality has nothing to do with the conditions of effective guidance or the enforcement of settled expectations. Rather, the Conventionality Thesis is necessary to explain law's possibility, not its efficacy. Conventionality is a condition of law's existence, not of its effective guidance.

Finally, though I am unpersuaded by Dworkin's characterization of positivism as an interpretive theory, his general take on positivism and its failings is consistent and not without some plausibility. He is absolutely right to emphasize the importance of conventionality to positivism, though wrong to develop it in the way he does. He is also right to emphasize the importance to most positivists of law's role in guiding conduct by offering reasons.

It is not hard to understand why Dworkin emphasizes controversiality and disagreement, both of which are, in his view, difficult to accommodate within a conventionalist framework: both of which, moreover, are central features of existing legal practice. The obvious contrasting concepts to settled expectations, guidance, and conventions are fairness, principled adjudication, and controversy resolved through substantive argument—exactly the points emphasized within the Dworkinian conception of law.

As is well known, I argue that conventions can accommodate controversy and disagreement. Moreover, within positivism, the point of emphasizing law's conventionality has more to do with explaining the very possibility of legal authority than it has to do with ensuring effective guidance.

Controversy and disagreement pose no theoretical or conceptual problems for Raz. As I read him, that is because considerations of the extent to which law is controversial do not bear on what the law is, but on whether the law can be effective. A controversial or evaluative rule of recognition makes it difficult for individuals to determine the law or its content. For that reason, it is not likely to be an effective instrument of social coordination. If law fails to coordinate effectively, then it is less likely that individuals will do better acting on the basis of law's reason than they would do acting directly on the basis of the reasons they have. Ease of identification bears on the extent to which law serves as an *effective* authority.

In contrast, from a jurisprudential point of view, Raz's concern is with the possibility of guidance through law, not with its effectiveness. For him, only norms that have social sources or suitable pedigrees are compatible with law's potential for guiding conduct. The controversiality of norms without pedigrees limits their ability to guide effectively, which is a practical, not a conceptual or theoretical matter. Thus, unlike Dworkin, the controversiality of morality does not motivate Raz's rejection of inclusive positivism; their status as moral principles included in law in virtue of their content or merit does.[10]

Neither Dworkin's nor Raz's objections prevail, however. *Contra* Dworkin, Incorporationism is compatible with the Conventionality Thesis. The situation is very different with respect to the Practical Difference Thesis. Though Raz's particular concerns can, I believe, be met, other objections inspired by his and animated by the same kinds of worries are unanswerable. In particular, Scott Shapiro has developed a simple and powerful argument that demonstrates the incompatibility of Incorporationism and the Practical Difference Thesis.[11]

Whereas one can maintain the conjunction of either the Practical Difference Thesis and the Conventionality Thesis, or the Conventionality Thesis and Incorporationism, one cannot maintain the conjunction of Incorporationism and the Practical Difference Thesis. After characterizing and explaining Shapiro's argument, I offer here reasons for embracing Incorporationism at the expense of the Practical Difference Thesis.[12]

I. PROJECTS AND METHODS

Jurisprudence begins with the truism that law is a normative social practice. Whereas all legal theorists agree that a jurisprudential theory must explain central or important features of legal practice, it is controversial which features are important and why. This suggests that any theory of law is really a controversial conception of law: an account of what it takes to be law's most important or salient features. This process, what Stephen Perry calls (following Max Weber) 'concept formation', will necessarily be informed and regulated by norms reflecting potentially different theoretical and practical interests, including disparate and perhaps conflicting

[10] In 'Authority and Reason', I took part of Raz's argument from authority in support of the Sources Thesis to rest on the idea that if the law is an authority, it must be uncontroversially identifiable to ordinary citizens. How could law serve to affect the practical reasoning of ordinary citizens if they could not identify the law or determine, at least in general terms, what it required of them? Understood this way, controversial criteria of the sort envisioned by an Incorporationist Rule of Recognition would be ruled out a priori, since individuals could not easily or reliably identify which norms were law. I am certain that I there misunderstood the connection between Raz's view of authority and the Sources Thesis, and so I want to withdraw that objection. Jules L. Coleman, 'Authority and Reason', in *The Autonomy of Law*, ed. R. George (1997).

[11] Scott Shapiro, 'The Difference That Rules Make', in *New Essays in Legal Theory*, ed. B. Bix (1998).

[12] In upcoming essays I offer a reconfigured positivism, including an account of the place within it of the Separability Thesis, as well as an interpretation of the importance of that thesis to the ongoing debate between positivists and natural lawyers—a debate that has been unhelpfully characterized by both positivists and natural lawyers alike.

accounts of law's proper function or purpose.[13] Thus, some theorists, like Dworkin, see the function of law as expressing and controlling the coercive power of the state, or as requiring the principled adjudication of disputes, whereas others see the proper function of law as the guidance of human conduct by reasons.

The aim of jurisprudence is to shed light on actual legal practice. There are many ways of shedding light, but the distinctive philosophical method is to do so by analysing the concepts that figure prominently within it. In analysing the concept of law, the theorist specifies the features of law one deems especially important or central. A theory of law is a contestable conception of law, reflecting, as it must, an account of law's function or purpose. Disputes between or among conflicting legal theories are ultimately normative disputes, resolvable by substantive moral and political argument.

In evaluating a jurisprudence, one therefore has to assess not only the explanation it provides of the 'data'—the law—but also the plausibility of its conception of the person presupposed by the theory as well as its account of the purpose or function of law. Legal theory is thus a branch of normative philosophy in two senses: a jurisprudential theory is itself a normative theory; disputes between or among theories are resolvable by recourse to moral or political theory.

One need not accept the (perhaps too) strong claim that jurisprudence is ultimately a branch of political philosophy in order to accept the weaker claim that jurisprudence is a normative discipline. If true, either claim would appear to suffice to render impossible the project of general, descriptive jurisprudence of the sort Hart has advocated (his commitment to which he reiterates in the Postscript).[14]

This seductive and increasingly appealing line of argument (even to some positivists, including Gerald Postema[15]) explicitly embraced but obliquely defended by Dworkin,[16] explicitly articulated and the subject of a sustained argument by Stephen Perry,[17] is, I believe, both misleading

---

[13] Stephen Perry, 'Hesitation and Methodology in Legal Theory', in *Law and Interpretation*, ed. A. Marmor (1995), 112–21.

[14] Supra n. 1, at 240.

[15] 'Jurisprudence as Practical Philosophy', 4 Legal Theory (1998).

[16] *Law's Empire*, supra n. 5, at 45–86.

[17] In many ways, Perry's most important contribution to jurisprudence is his sustained development of the idea that the methodology of jurisprudence is an important subject in its own right. He is perhaps the leading Dworkinian currently working in jurisprudence. His efforts have been confined, however, to vindicating the interpretive or normative methodology, and he is careful to distinguish his endorsement of methodological interpretivism or normative jurisprudence from an endorsement of the substance of Dworkin's jurisprudence, namely law-as-integrity. Perry's other interesting claim is that Hart, the great substantive positivist, was himself a normative methodologist, his protests to the contrary: hence, Perry's claim that Hart was a pre-Dworkin Dworkinian. I do not find this claim persuasive,

and mistaken: misleading as an interpretation of Hart's position, and mistaken as a picture of the proper method of jurisprudence.

We can distinguish among different kinds of argument against a general, descriptive jurisprudence.[18] Some might argue that the projects of descriptive jurisprudence are uninteresting or that they are less interesting than those undertaken by normative jurisprudence. Or one could argue that descriptive jurisprudence is impossible. Or one could argue that the proponents of descriptive jurisprudence, especially Hart, were, contrary to their explicit denials, actually engaged in normative jurisprudence.

There are two standard arguments against descriptive, conceptual analysis in law—other than Dworkin's semantic sting argument, itself the subject of Joseph Raz's and Tim Endicott's contributions to this volume.[19] One rests on the empirical claim that people disagree about what falls within the category 'law', so that any attempt to get at the core of a legal concept by capturing what people take to be its essential features will ultimately, if not quickly, degenerate into an unresolvable battle of 'intuitions'.

There is always the possibility of disagreement about the extension of a concept. This is true in every domain of discourse, not only the law. Descriptive, conceptual analysis requires a core of agreement, not the absence of disagreement. It is the scope and breadth of disagreement, not its possibility that matters—in law as elsewhere. There is always disagreement because there are always potentially controversial cases. It does not follow from the existence of controversial cases that there is disagreement at the core, or that the core is empty. Those who embrace the possibility of descriptive, conceptual analysis do not claim on its behalf that it can fully

and part of my purpose in this section of the paper is to counter it. Perry, *supra* n. 13. See also Stephen Perry, 'Hart and Holmes: The Bad Man in Legal Theory', in *The Legacy of Oliver Wendell Holmes, Jr.: 'The Path of the Law' and its Influence*, ed. S. J. Burton (1998).

[18] In this essay, I will sometimes use descriptive and conceptual jurisprudence interchangeably for ease of exposition. They are importantly different, however. What Perry and others object to is descriptive jurisprudence, not conceptual analysis as such. In fact, the architecture of the categories is quite complex. The important differences among philosophers are between descriptive and normative analysis on the one hand and between a priori and a posteriori analysis on the other. Fundamentally, Hart, Raz, and I, for example, engage in descriptive, a priori conceptual analysis. Perry, Dworkin, and perhaps Postema embrace normative, a priori conceptual analysis. Others like Brian Leiter, so-called philosophical naturalists, reject or limit the role of a priori conceptual analysis of whatever sort, embracing instead a kind of a posteriori conceptual analysis. So Perry's real concerns are not with conceptual analysis as such, nor with the ability to engage in it a priori; his objections are to its claims to normative neutrality. See generally Brian Leiter, 'Naturalism and Naturalized Jurisprudence', in *New Essays in Legal Theory*, ed. B. Bix (1998).

[19] See Joseph Raz, 'Two Views of the Nature of the Theory of Law: A Partial Companion', 4 Legal Theory 249 (1998); Timothy A. O. Endicott, 'Herbert Hart and the Semantic Sting', 4 Legal Theory 283 (1998).

specify the content of a concept, nor do they deny that normative argument is appropriate to resolving disagreements at what Hart calls the 'penumbra'. It hardly follows from the appropriateness of normative argument at the 'frequency extremes' that there is no core, or that the core is unsettled, or that its content can be specified only by normative argument.[20]

The majority of arguments against descriptive jurisprudence are of the 'but they don't realize what they are up to' type. Many of Stephen Perry's most interesting arguments are designed to show that Hart himself had no option but to engage in normative, not descriptive, analysis. Of course, Hart presents himself as engaging in descriptive, conceptual analysis, but the arguments he offers—more importantly, if Perry is correct, the ones he needs to offer—are normative. There is a sense, therefore, in which one could see Hart as a pre-Dworkin Dworkinian.[21] I believe that Perry mischaracterizes Hart's argument and what can be said on its behalf.

Hart (and Shapiro, I, and others) believe that jurisprudence does not begin by trying to determine which features of law are important or interesting. It begins by asking whether there are features of law that are essential or, in an appropriate sense, necessary to law or to our concept of it: essential to our concept in the sense that a social practice that fails to have them could not qualify as law. If they exist, these features do not depend on a controversial theory of law's proper function, but on an understanding of what the law is.[22] Are there such features, and can we identify them without recourse to a contestable view of law's proper function?

Hart believed that there were such features and that we could identify them without recourse to a controversial, normative account of law's purpose. The following is a compressed version of his simple but elegant argument. He begins with an observation: while there may be many important similarities between commands backed by threats and law,

---

[20] A related but equally familiar mistake is to infer from the in-principle revisability of what, at any time, we take to be the core of a concept, the claim that the concept has no core. The difference between revisability and stability is often missed in jurisprudence. The core can change; it is subject to revision. That does not mean that it is always being revised or rethought or reconsidered: nor, of course, does it mean that it is empty. This is one of the most important tenets of pragmatism, a corollary, in many ways, of the belief/doubt principle. *See* Hart, *supra* n. 1, at 12, 123, 147–54.

[21] This view reminds me of one of my favourite graduate school stories. The late, great Wilfred Sellars was a Visiting Professor at Rockefeller University while I was a student there. He was co-teaching a course on Kant with Margaret Wilson. On the first day, he proclaimed his affection for Kant as an early and particularly talented Sellarsian. It took most of the students a week to figure out what he was saying, and a semester to appreciate the extent of the compliment he took himself to be conferring.

[22] No one denies that inquiry, conceptual or other, is regulated by norms. This is as true in the hard and social sciences as it is in law. In this sense, all inquiry is normative. The descriptive jurisprudent denies the much stronger claim that we cannot identify law's necessary features without also defending a particular normative conception of law's function.

there appear to be certain important differences as well. If we take a gunman as an example of the former, one thing to note is that the force of the gunman's command evaporates when the threat is withdrawn, whereas law can outlive those who create it; and the authority to create or adjudicate law is not conferred on a particular person, but on persons in virtue of their occupying an office. Hart refers to these features of law as its persistence and continuity. They distinguish law from commands and legal systems from gunmen.

Hart does not distinguish law from the gunman with the suggestion that the former, but not the latter, involves a legitimate use of power or force. He points instead to features of law which are independent of its legitimacy and which, though they serve functions within legal practice, do not depend on a controversial theory of those functions for their identification. This is important. Once the status of persistence and continuity as necessary features of our concept of law is established, a good deal more follows. Persistence and continuity imply that law must be an *institutional* social practice. Institutions create and revise laws and adjudicate disputes arising under them. Institutions, in turn, are constituted by rules. Famously, Hart refers to 'institution-creating' rules as 'secondary rules'. One can have a system of rules without secondary—or institution creating—rules, but one cannot have law without such rules.

Even more follows from these modest beginnings. Return to the distinction between law and the gunman. A critic might agree that the demands the gunman imposes evaporate when the threat is withdrawn, whereas the reasons the law creates persist over time, but object that this is because law is a gunman whose capacity to threaten is, in effect, never withdrawn—though particular threats can be and are. Of course, even were this correct or helpful, the law would not be the *same* gunman all the time; so we would have to invoke the idea of secondary rules that create the 'office' of gunman in order to explain this picture of it.

Our concept of law includes rules that make institutions possible: that create authority and responsibility—a power to act and a duty to do so according to certain other rules or guidelines. The power or authority to act is distinctive of secondary rules, as is the duty to act in accordance with the norms regulating the offices created by them.

Secondary rules are not reducible to primary rules. Even if primary legal rules were like the commands of the sovereign or the gunman, an elliptical way of issuing a threat, this could not be true of secondary rules for a variety of reasons. For one thing, such rules impose no sanctions for non-compliance; for another, they make sanctioning possible. They are the social facts that explain sanctioning, not the other way around.

Similarly, even if primary rules are understood, not as an elliptical way of threatening, but as a way of grounding or making a prediction about how officials will act, a similar objection applies. Even supposing that predictive theories provide a plausible account of primary rules of obligation—and of the way such rules figure in the deliberations of those to whom they apply—such theories cannot account for secondary rules that make primary rules possible. That is because secondary rules are not predictions about what officials will do, but instead create and authorize officials. The very possibility of analysing other legal rules as predictions of official behaviour presupposes secondary rules that cannot themselves be so analysed.

One important difference between primary rules of obligation and the secondary rule of recognition is that the latter is an existence condition of the former. There are no primary *legal* rules without criteria for legality On the other hand, primary rules of obligation are not part of the existence conditions of the rule of recognition. It is not just that secondary rules cannot be reduced to primary rules: their existence conditions differ.

According to Hart, the rule of recognition is a social rule. Its existence conditions include those that make social rules possible. Though Perry takes issue with Hart's claim to descriptive jurisprudence, he does not, I believe, take issue with Hart's account of social rules. Social rules exist only if there is a practice among participants that is accepted from the internal point of view by the majority of them. The internal point of view is thus an existence condition of secondary rules—in particular, the rule of recognition. It is not an existence condition of primary rules of obligation, which need not be or correspond to social rules.

The internal point of view is the committed point of view. It expresses the idea that sometimes a rule is action-guiding because it is viewed by those to whom it applies as reason-giving. Those who accept rules from an internal point of view see the rules as reason-giving in virtue of their being rules rather than in virtue of the sanction that might attend noncompliance with them. Thus, officials must be committed to secondary rules—especially the rule of recognition—whereas ordinary folk need not be committed to primary rules of obligation.[23]

---

[23] Stephen Perry accuses Hart of failing to countenance that there are many 'insider's' points of view. Perry argues that Hart privileges one kind of 'insider's point of view': the point of view of the person who accepts the law as legitimate, and reason-giving accordingly: in other words, his version of the 'internal point of view'. Perry argues that Hart must defend his privileging this particular insider's perspective. Perry then claims that such a defence presupposes both a particular conception of the person (a normative one) and a particular view of law's purpose (to guide conduct by offering reasons). Hence, Perry's claim that Hart is a pre-Dworkin Dworkinian.

Briefly, just as Hart does not deny that there are many possible motivations for compliance, he does not deny that there are many possible *insider's* perspectives. He does not identify the insider's perspective with the internal point of view, and then choose one of many such perspectives. The insider's perspective is the insider's perspective. The internal point of view is one kind of insider's perspective. It is the perspective of the person who sees the

Law is the union of primary rules of obligation and a secondary rule of recognition (these are minimal conditions). The existence of primary rules of obligation depends on a secondary rule of recognition. Hart does not really believe that primary rules can be reduced to sanctions or predictions, but even if they could be conceived of in this way—even if that is all there were to be said about the way in which such rules figure in the deliberative processes of those to whom they apply—the same could not be said of the secondary rule of recognition. It is a social rule. Its existence is made possible by a practice accepted from the internal point of view: the committed point of view.

The argument from persistence and continuity gets the ball rolling. A proper understanding of those features entails the idea of secondary rules. Secondary rules, in turn, entail the idea of the internal point of view. One could take issue with various steps in the argument. When they are understood in the way I have just outlined, I find Hart's arguments on these matters basically persuasive. The soundness of Hart's argument is not at issue, though. The kind of argument he conjures is. Nothing in it or in its component parts invokes a contestable conception of law's function. Its soundness does not hang in any way on whether Dworkin or the positivists are right about law's purpose in controlling coercion, providing the resources for principled adjudication, or guiding conduct. Nor does it rest on a normative argument for privileging the internal point of view.

There is no evidence to suggest that Perry would deny either law's institutionality or the related claim that secondary rules are essential to our concept of law. Nor does he appear to deny that the internal point of view—not the 'insider's' point of view, but the critical, reflective aspect of rules—is a necessary or existence condition of secondary or institution-creating rules. Nor does it appear that any of this depends on a particular contestable conception of law's function or point. Not only is descriptive jurisprudence possible, but it is hard to imagine jurisprudence without it. Frankly, I do not see that Hart ever claimed more than this; importantly,

---

law as reasoning, or legitimate in that sense. Hart never says that this is the preferred perspective or the only perspective insiders can adopt. What he says is this: that (as a conceptual not a normative matter) it is impossible to understand our court of law without attributing the internal point of view as the perspective of at least some individuals (i.e. officials) toward at least some rules (i.e. secondary rules, especially the rule of recognition). In other words, Hart does not privilege a particular conception of the internal point of view so much as he demonstrates the very different point that our concept of law presupposes the conception he offers of it.

Perry's extremely interesting, subtle, but, I believe, ultimately unconvincing argument is developed in Perry, 'Hart and Holmes', *supra* n. 17. For an artful and, by my lights, convincing response to Perry's arguments, see Scott Shapiro, 'Hart v. Holmes: The Bad Man in Legal Theory', in *The Legacy of Oliver Wendell Holmes Jr.*, ed. Burton.

and quite correctly, I believe, he never claimed less than this—nor could anyone.[24]

Beyond asking whether there are any conceptual truths about law, it is reasonable to look at law from different points of view reflecting different interests. Like photographs, all of which can illuminate interesting truths about an object, there may well be something to be said for seeing law from the point of view of its role in limiting the power of the state, just as there may be something to be said for seeing the law in terms of the ways in which it guides conduct. The possibility of descriptive jurisprudence does not preclude the possibility or desirability of various normative projects for jurisprudence.

Even so, it does not follow from the fact that some of the projects of jurisprudence are normative that they are informed and regulated by moral or political norms. In trying to determine law's interesting features, we may have in mind the project of exploring the ways in which law is similar to or different from various other social and normative systems. (Certainly, Hart had this project in mind, for he clearly believed that we could learn something about the nature of morality by understanding the nature of law.) This project is regulated by epistemic and theoretical norms, not moral or political ones.

We can put these points another way. No positivist, including Hart, denies that there are a number of plausible theories of law differing from one another both in terms of their theoretical and practical consequences and in their political or moral attractiveness. Hart believed that his positivism was attractive politically and that it brought to light important differences and similarities between law and other social institutions. A choice among such theories may rightly be influenced by—even made on—these kinds of normative grounds. On the other hand, Hart makes two fundamental claims: first, that common to every theory of law—if it is to include a conception of *our* concept—are certain essential features. These features can be roughly characterized as constituting law's 'institutionality'. They include institution-creating (secondary rules) and the internal point of view as a way of expressing their role in the deliberative processes of those to whom they apply. Second, one does not need a contestable view of law's function in order to determine law's essential features.

---

[24] Having emphasized the conceptual or descriptive projects of jurisprudence, several points should be noted. The descriptive project of jurisprudence is to identify the essential or necessary features of *our* concept of law. No serious analytic legal philosopher-positivist or interpretivist believes that the prevailing concept of law is in any sense necessary: that no other concept is logically or otherwise possible. Nor do we believe that our concept of law can never be subject to revision. Quite the contrary. Technology may some day require us to revise our concept in any number of ways. Still, there is a difference between the claim that a particular concept is necessary and the claim that there are necessary features of an admittedly contingent concept.

Nor is Hart engaged in an arid enterprise—expressing an interest in the concept of law tantamount to a scholastic interest in the concept of a 'chair' or a 'table'. Quite the contrary. The concept of law is important because law is, and law is important because it is a normative or practical institution. Law claims to make a difference in the lives of those living under it, in the quality and character of their deliberations and in the course of their conduct. The subject matter of the concept of law is, first and foremost, law's practicality—its normativity.

To understand law is in part to understand it as a normative or practical institution. But first one has to identify the features of law that characterize law's distinctive normativity, and the conditions of their possibility (i.e. their existence conditions). For Hart, this project turns out to imply the existence of a rule of recognition accepted from the internal point of view: the rule of recognition itself setting forth the existence conditions for subordinate legal rules. Thus, the project requires specifying the existence conditions of the rule of recognition. The second project is to make intelligible the ways in which legal practicality, or law's normativity, is capable of making a difference for those living under law: for those, in other words, who view it as a source of obligation, rights, privileges, and responsibility. How is law, so conceived, capable of functioning in the deliberations and actions of those to whom it applies.[25]

Hart never wavers from his commitment to the possibility of descriptive jurisprudence. The most accurate and plausible interpretation of his argument instantiates that commitment to descriptive conceptual analysis. Those who would argue otherwise misread him. More importantly, perhaps, I take my argument to have shown not only that Hart's execution of his project is true to the ambitions of descriptive jurisprudence, but that there is a way of executing the project of descriptive jurisprudence that is faithful to its requirements.

In other words, my argument makes a claim that is independent of its claim to being the best interpretation of Hart's view. Even if I am mistaken in ascribing this argument to Hart, I take it that I have presented an argument—whether Hart's and mine or mine only—that makes the case for descriptive jurisprudence. It is not enough to show that it is not Hart's argument, though of course my view is that it is.[26] What is needed is a

---

[25] Whereas I find Hart's descriptive jurisprudence basically convincing, I do not find his particular account of the kinds of reason the law creates plausible. Hart claims that the concepts of right and obligation in law have a different meaning or sense than they do in morality, and this line of argument runs into serious trouble. His introduction of content-independent reasons for action is extremely valuable and one of the great contributions to legal philosophy, but his particular use of it is not persuasive.

[26] Much of the argument against descriptive jurisprudence takes the form of purporting to show that Hart, contrary to his own reflections on the matter, did not engage in or faithfully execute a descriptivist methodology. Such arguments are extremely interesting and

more general argument that is not indexed to Hart: an argument that would demonstrate the fallacies in my argument, and others like it, not one that seeks to draw the implications of a certain interpretation of Hart's.

No such argument is forthcoming; and that is because it is impossible to deny law's institutionality. By law's institutionality, I mean the complex thought that part of the distinguishing feature of law's authority is the idea that legal rules are the result of institutional action of various kinds. It is supposed to matter to us, not just that something may be a good thing to do, but that it is the law to do it, and to say that it is the law is to say something about its being the result of institutional action of a certain kind. If we do not understand law as an institutional phenomenon, then we do not understand law. That claim does not, it seems to me, depend in any interesting or troubling way on a particular conception of law's purpose or function.

Once we identify the object of inquiry, two fundamental questions remain: (1) How is law possible?[27] What are its existence conditions? Can one explain law without assuming law? (2) How can we make intelligible law's claim to make a practical difference in the lives of those to whom it applies? How, in other words, is legal rule-governance possible? In what sense and in what ways is it practically significant? As I see it, the fundamental problems of jurisprudence are to explain law's *possibility* and its *normativity*. The Conventionality Thesis speaks to the first of these issues, the Practical Difference Thesis to the second.

II. THE CONVENTIONALITY THESIS

Can one explain the possibility of law without assuming the possibility of law? If so, how?[28] The distinctive feature of legal positivism is that it attempts to explain law in terms of *social facts*. Austin provides a good example. For Austin, law is explained in terms of power and habits of obedience: the defining elements of the sovereign-properly-so-called. The

genuinely important, whether ultimately sound or not. Even if they are sound, however, they fall short of undermining the very possibility of a descriptive jurisprudence, focusing so much, as they do, on Hart.

[27] In asking 'How is law possible?' I do not mean to invite a causal or historical answer. The question is conceptual. It asks: 'What are the existence conditions for law?'

[28] Part of what distinguishes positivism from natural law is the answer each provides. Very roughly, we might say that natural lawyers explain the possibility of law by deriving or embedding it in morality (political morality or natural law). So understood, law is the institutional embodiment of an important aspect of morality: namely political morality.

There are several problems with this kind of approach, not the least of which is that it assumes rather than explains law's most salient feature—that is, its institutionality. In an obvious sense, therefore, this line of argument does not really explain law without invoking law.

powerful thought in Hart, widely misunderstood and mistakenly criticized, and the one with which I am in complete agreement, is that law is made possible by an interdependent convergence of behaviour and attitude: what we may loosely think of as a kind of 'agreement'.

Hart expresses the relevant notion of agreement in terms of a social practice comprising two elements: convergent behaviour and a critical reflective attitude toward that behaviour—an acceptance of it. This reflective, critical attitude is the so-called internal point of view. The internal point of view, in turn, is expressible in behaviour (but not reducible to the behaviour that expresses it). Acceptance of a rule from the internal point of view is exemplified by appealing to it as a reason for acting and as a ground for criticizing non-compliance.

Law is made possible by the existence of a certain kind of social fact: the existence of a practice among officials of setting out criteria of legality or validity. This is the rule of recognition: the signature of a legal system. The rule of recognition is not a sufficient condition for law. It is a condition of its possibility: a necessary condition. In addition to the rule of recognition, Hart imposes various efficacy conditions (e.g. that a substantial proportion of the populace comply with the rules recognized under the rule of recognition).

Law exists (is actual) when there is a rule of recognition and rules valid under it that are generally followed by the majority of the population. Acceptance from the internal point of view by officials is a conceptual requirement of the possibility of law; acceptance from the internal point of view by a substantial proportion of the populace is neither a conceptual nor an efficacy requirement. Even if they characteristically do, these individuals, *as a conceptual matter,* need not accept the bulk of the other rules or the rule of recognition in a legal system from the internal point of view.[29] On the other hand, it may be desirable on efficiency grounds that a population treat law as legitimate or obligation-imposing in that fewer public resources might then be required to ensure compliance.

The organizing idea of legal positivism is that law's possibility must be

[29] Stephen Perry argues that Hart's confining the necessity of acceptance from the internal point of view to officials, and not extending it to the public at large, is an embarrassment to his position. Hart's point is that acceptance from the internal point of view by officials is necessary to explain the possibility of law, whereas acceptance by the bulk of the populace does not bear on any of the fundamental questions of jurisprudence. Hart may be wrong to think that acceptance from an internal point of view by the bulk of the population is unnecessary from the point of view of answering the fundamental questions of jurisprudence, but he was right to think that it was irrelevant to any of the fundamental questions in which he was interested. Frankly, I think he was right about the more general claim as well. In any case, he has good reason to focus on officials in his discussion of the internal point of view while ignoring the common folk. Thus, it is unfair to view his failure to do so as an embarrassment. See Perry, 'Hart and Holmes', *supra* n. 17. For an objection to this line of argument similar to mine, see Shapiro, *supra* n. 23.

explained in terms of social facts.[30] I call this the Social Fact Thesis, and nothing is more important to legal positivism. Positivists can and do differ from one another with respect to the underlying social facts that explain law.

There is another dimension of potential disagreement among positivists. Some positivists like Austin and the Scandinavian Realists are *reductionists*. For them, law is explained by social fact in the sense of being reducible to social fact. Austin reduces law to power and habits of obedience. The Scandinavian Realists reduce law to predictions of untoward consequences in the event of non-compliance. Hart explicitly rejects all reductive accounts because they define out of existence, in the sense of having no room for, an essential feature of law, namely the internal point of view. Because Hart rejects reductive accounts of law, perhaps we should read him as embracing the view that law *supervenes* on the relevant social facts, but is not reducible to them. To say that the rule supervenes on the practice is to say that whenever the practice exists so too does the rule, and that any change in the one entails a change in the other.

All positivists embrace the Social Fact Thesis, the claim that while law is a normative social practice it is made possible by some set of social facts. Positivists differ from one another with respect to (1) the relevant social facts and (2) the relationship between those facts and law. Austin advocates a reductive account in terms of power and habits: the Scandinavians are reductionists in terms of predictions. An alternative would be to understand law in terms of supervenience on practice and the internal point of *view*.

The Conventionality Thesis claims that the relevant social fact is a convention among officials.[31] In one sense the point of claiming that the rule of recognition is conventional is simply to draw a contrast between it and so-called normative rules. The difference is one of existence conditions. The existence of a conventional rule depends on behaviour and attitude, whereas the existence of a normative rule depends on substantive (moral) argument. Not all conventional rules are conventional in the same sense, however, and more needs to be said about the kind of conventional rule the rule of recognition is.

---

[30] This is *the* point of Coleman, 'Negative and Positive Positivism', *supra* n. 5.

[31] The Conventionality Thesis leaves open whether the relationship between rule and practice is reduction or supervenience, or some other kind of relationship which would need further explanation. One reason for thinking that Hart might have understood the relationship as supervenience is that supervenience in ethics was in the air at Oxford during the period in which *CL* was written. Ever since the publication of *CL* many philosophers, in both moral philosophy and the philosophy of mind, have offered reductive accounts. Hart rejects reductive accounts. That much is unarguable. I reject such accounts as well. I do not mean to suggest, however, that acceptance of the Conventionality Thesis entails rejection of reductionism. One could be a reductivist about the relationship between the rule of recognition and the relevant practices among officials. Neither Hart nor I are.

Andrei Marmor draws a distinction between two kinds of convention: coordination conventions and what he calls constitutive conventions.[32] Coordination conventions are familiar from game theory; they represent solutions to coordination games. Constitutive conventions are not solutions to problems that arise in virtue of structural features of human action, but instead help define, characterize, or create practices, institutions or 'games', while shaping the norms and values associated with them. The idea is familiar from ordinary games or sporting events, and Marmor extends it to activities as diverse as opera and law.

Marmor defends the constitutive convention view of the rule of recognition while arguing against the coordination convention view. Though Hart does not explicitly discuss the issue, I explicitly characterize the rule of recognition as a coordination convention. The rule of recognition solves the coordination problem of settling on a particular set of criteria of validity. If it is a good idea to have law at all, then it is clearly better that some set of criteria be agreed upon than that there be no agreement, even if individuals differ from one another as to their ranking of the options. The Conventionality Thesis allows a variety of possible interpretations of the kind of convention the rule of recognition is. Marmor adopts what he calls the constitutive convention view; I defend the coordination convention view.

Notwithstanding Marmor's objections to it, there is something important to be said on behalf of the coordination convention conception.[33] The

---

[32] Andrei Marmor, 'Legal Conventionalism', this volume.

[33] Marmor argues that coordination conventions are incapable of explaining the sense that many people in most communities have that their rule of recognition is correct, desirable, just, especially reasonable or sensible. No one develops any special attachment to the convention of driving on the right or the left. Coordination conventions do not seem to explain what we might think of as 'attachment' to the rule of recognition. It would seem just a bit perverse for Americans to feel a special pride about the practice of driving on the right in contrast to the British practice of driving on the left, whereas it would be surprising if Americans did not take pride in the rule of recognition.

Despite its superficial attractiveness, this argument is unpersuasive. Marmor's own position is also subject to precisely the same objection. First, people can and do develop attachments to arbitrary conventions. This implies the more fundamental point that there is no reason to suppose that the fact that a rule solves a coordination problem must provide the explanation of the attachment to it that might develop. The grounds of attachment may be completely different. The rule exists and survives because it solves a coordination problem, and represents a Nash equilibrium. Whether people develop an attachment to it or not depends on a range of other factors. It is simply naive to suppose that the explanation of attachment must have the same grounds as the explanation of its existence or stability. Marmor's objection is based on ignoring the distinction between the causal explanation of attachment to the rule and normative justification of it. The rule is justified because it solves a coordination problem. People get attached to it for all other sorts of reason if they get attached to it at all.

Were this a good objection to the coordination convention conception of the rule of recognition, it would be an equally powerful objection to the constitutive convention conception. After all; what is it about the fact that certain rules constitute or define games that explains the attachment people have to those rules? In the end, Marmor notes that the explanation of the attachment some feel to the rule of recognition needs some other explanation.

project of positivism is to show how a certain kind of rule-governed behaviour (law) can be explained by seeing how it is made possible by a rule that guides behaviour (namely a secondary rule of recognition).

Among other things, law consists in rules that purport to provide those subject to it with reasons for acting: reasons for acting, moreover, in virtue of their being law. The question is: how is this phenomenon possible? Part of the answer, according to Hart and other positivists who emphasize law's conventionality, is that there is a rule that picks out other rules as legal. The rule that performs that task, however, is different in kind from the rules that govern behaviour generally, for their claim to govern derives in part from the fact that they are validated by this rule. This rule—the rule of recognition—requires a different source for its claim to provide reasons for acting.

The key idea in the conventionalist picture is that this rule provides reasons because it is *adopted* by individuals in order that it guide their behaviour: guide their behaviour by directing them to apply certain criteria of validity determining the conditions of membership of other norms in the category 'law'—thus enabling those norms to claim a power to provide reasons for acting in virtue of their being law. The possibility of legal rules governing behaviour depends on a rule whose existence in turn depends on its being adopted. Adoption, in turn, requires a practice of applying certain standards within the group and an internal point of view toward the practice of doing so. In that sense, the rule is conventional. The rule of recognition guides behaviour in the sense that the rule is the reason for acting, and in acting the relevant parties intend to comply with its demands.

The conventional rule—the rule of recognition—must not merely be capable of recognizing or validating other rules. It must actually be the standard employed by the relevant officials. That is, it must provide them with reasons for applying the standards set forth in it. The rule exists for them only when they accept it from an internal point of view, which is to say that it exists only if they view it as providing them with reasons for acting.

Put it this way: individual rules subordinate to the rule of recognition need not be followed in order for them to be law or for them to govern (or purport to govern) the behaviour of ordinary folk. The possibility of their being law and purporting to govern as law, however, depends on a rule of recognition. The rule of recognition can be reason-giving only if it is treated by those to whom it applies (officials) as reason-giving: only if they act in accordance with it for the reason that they adopt it as a rule for them. Why would they do that? At this point, the idea of a coordination convention may prove illuminating, for there is a familiar way in which such conventions create reasons for acting[34]—that is, by creating a system of stable reciprocal expectations.[35]

Let me point out a problem with Hart's theory of the rule of recognition while further exploring the usefulness of the coordination convention view of the rule of recognition. Hart claims that reductive accounts of law omit the internal point of view and lack the resources, therefore, to explain law's normativity. This has led many critics to infer that Hart meant to claim that the internal point of view transforms a social fact—a mere convergence of behaviour—into a reason for acting. If other accounts fail to explain law's normativity because they leave out the internal point of view, then it must be the internal point of view that explains law's normativity.

Having read Hart this way, many then went on to criticize him for thinking that the internal point of view could transform a social fact into a normative or moral one. The criticism is the familiar one that a rule cannot impose an obligation just because people treat it as doing so. If Hart claims that the internal point of view explains law's normativity, he is saddled with a bad argument. If he does not claim that the internal point of view explains law's normativity, he appears to have no argument: no argument, that is, adequate to explain *how* the rule of recognition could guide the behaviour of officials.

The criticism is compelling, but on reflection I do not think that Hart ever meant to claim that the internal point of view grounds, creates, or explains a rule's capacity to provide reasons. The internal point of view is an existence condition of a social rule, and it marks the fact that people treat the rule as reason-giving. It does not explain why or how the rule does so. This means that Hart never really gives an account of how the rule of recognition in particular, or how social rules in general, create reasons for action or guide behaviour. My suggestion is that the coordination convention conception of the rule of recognition in conjunction with the internal point of view could be understood as providing the missing argument.

In my view, the rule of recognition is a coordination convention that

---

[34] I do not suppose that conventions provide reasons, only that they are capable of doing so. The question is: under what conditions are conventions capable of doing so?

[35] One of my objections to Marmor's argument is that he asks us to abandon the coordination convention conception of the rule of recognition in favour of the constitutive convention conception when the ways in which the former give rise to reasons for acting are well understood, whereas the ways in which constitutive conventions do is mysterious. To reduce the mystery, Marmor offers analogies. The conventions governing certain activities, like opera, create norms and values internal to the activity. There is no reason why this should not be true of law. The problem is that we need an account of the ways in which the conventions in opera and elsewhere actually create reasons or values; otherwise the analogy may prove unhelpful.

creates reasons for acting in the way in which coordination conventions generally do—when they do. This is by creating a system of reciprocal, legitimate expectations. The internal point of view, I suggest, is part of the causal explanation of how such a rule creates stable, reciprocal expectations. Acceptance from an internal point of view is exhibited in public behaviour. Someone who accepts a rule from the internal point of view offers the rule as a grounds to others for his or her conduct, and as the basis for one's criticism of non-compliant behaviour. People announce that they act in a certain way; they criticize failures to act in that way; and so on. This enables each person to develop a degree of confidence in the behaviour of others and to form expectations legitimated interdependently. The internal point of view, as expressed in public behaviour, creates and sustains a sense of reciprocity: that free riding or non-compliance is subject to public criticism, and so on. Stability, reciprocity, and mutuality of expectation are created and enhanced by the behaviour exhibited by those accepting a rule from the internal point of view.

I do not pretend that any of this is obvious or obviously correct. I note three things, however. First, the coordination convention account of the rule of recognition places it in a familiar domain of social rules that are reason-giving, whose capacity to create reasons is well understood. Second, this account explains the importance of the internal point of view to the rule of recognition's normativity as well as to its existence. Hart had the right instinct. The internal point of view is not only a normative point of view; it is part of the explanation of the rule of recognition's normativity. Hart just lacked a plausible argument about how the internal point of view figures in that explanation.

Finally, and most interestingly to a philosopher, the internal point of view contributes to the explanation of the rule of recognition's normativity in virtue of its *causal* role. This reverses the usual order of things. In the usual story, reasons can be causes, provided, in part, that they are seen as or believed to be reasons. (This commonplace is one of Donald Davidson's great insights.[36]) The suggestion here is that, in part, the rule of recognition is a reason for officials because an aspect of it—the internal point of view—is a cause for them.[37]

One problem remains. We need to consider the question with which this section begins. Does the Conventionality Thesis really explain law without assuming law? The rule of recognition exists when officials act in a certain way, but whether or not individuals are *officials* in the relevant

---

[36] Donald Davidson, 'Actions, Reasons and Causes', 60 J. Phil. 685 (1963), 690–700.

[37] I am indebted to Scott Shapiro for helping me formulate this argument and especially for bringing its possibility to light. Shapiro is also responsible for characterizing the project of legal positivism as showing how certain kinds of rule-governed behaviour (law) are made possible only by understanding the connection to rule-guided behaviour.

sense depends on the existence of a rule of recognition. The rule of recognition makes law possible, but the rule of recognition depends on the idea of an official. The idea of an official in turn depends on laws that create officials; and those laws in turn depend on a rule of recognition. So doesn't positivism explain law in terms of law?

There is a real worry here to which a positivist must respond. The positivist does not say that the individuals who decide to have their behaviour guided by the relevant practice are officials. They are individuals who choose to have their behaviour guided by a certain rule. If that rule takes hold in the sense of establishing membership criteria in a system of rules, and if those rules are complied with generally, and if institutions of certain types are then created, and so on, at some point it may be fair to say that a legal system exists. If a legal system exists, then that rule which guides the behaviour of a group of individuals is correctly described as the rule of recognition for that legal system. It is the test of validity for that system. It is part of the reason we think of the system of rules that emerges as constituting a *legal* system. And those individuals who guide their behaviour by that rule are thus appropriately conceived of as 'officials'. They are, in a sense, officials in virtue of that rule, but they are not officials prior to it (in either the factual or the logical sense). Their behaviour makes the rule possible; but it is the rule that makes them officials.

III. THE PRACTICAL DIFFERENCE THESIS

Among Joseph Raz's most significant contributions to legal theory is his account of authority. According to Raz, it is not necessary that law provide agents with reasons for acting; it is, however, necessary that law claim to provide agents with reasons for acting. The claim to authority may be false, and, on Raz's view, often it is.

Law's claim to authority is a conceptual truth: it is a truth about what it means for something to be law. The claim could be true, even if it is in fact false. This means the theorist must be able to make the claim intelligible consistent with the rest of the theory. What, in other words, must be true of law if its claim to authority is to be (or can be) true? The truth of the claim is less important for jurisprudence than is the possibility of its truth. The possibility of its truth imposes constraints on the kind of thing law can be: law must be the sort of thing whose claim to authority could be true.

Raz's view about law and authority is an instance of the more general Practical Difference Thesis (PDT). The basic claim of the PDT is that law *must in principle be capable of making a practical difference*. It must be capable of affecting deliberation and action. Like the Social Fact Thesis, the PDT purports either to assert a necessary truth about our concept of law or to express an essential truth about law. If the rules that constitute the law of a particular community are not in principle capable of making a practical difference, then it is impossible for them to do so. If it is impossible for them to make a practical difference, then the law of that community cannot coherently claim to guide human conduct. The PDT implies that wherever there is law, the standards that constitute the law must in principle be capable of making a practical difference. Otherwise those rules cannot be law in the relevant sense.

Just as important, the standards constituting a community's law must be capable of guiding human conduct *in virtue* of their being law. Imagine that the standards constituting a community's law are a proper subset of that community's moral standards. If we assume that each moral standard is capable of making a practical difference, then it is true of every legal standard that it too is capable of making a practical difference. But it remains an open question whether it is capable of making a practical difference in virtue of its legality. That depends on whether the fact of its legality contributes in any way to its impact on deliberation and action.

In short, the PDT asserts that legal rules must in principle be capable of making a practical difference, and that they must be capable of doing so in virtue of their being law. It is more general than Raz's view about law's claim to authority in part because Raz specifies a particular way in which law purports to make a difference: that is, by providing *reasons and by structuring reasoning*. The PDT allows that law might make a practical difference either *epistemically* (i.e. by providing information) or *motivationally* (i.e. by providing reasons).

Hart is committed to the PDT. On my reading, his position is complex and draws on two distinctions: the familiar one between the rule of recognition and rules subordinate to it, and the less well-noticed one between guidance by information and guidance by reason. For rules subordinate to the rule of recognition, the law's claim to guidance is best understood epistemically. The law need not claim to provide reasons; it is enough that it can claim to provide information. Thus, Hart emphasizes law's impact on the 'puzzled' as well as on the 'bad' man.[38] The rule of recognition, however, must guide the behaviour of officials by offering reasons. (My argument that the rule of recognition be thought of as expressing a coor-

---

[38] The person who looks to the law for reasons sees the law motivationally. The fact that something is the law motivates him: he does it because it is the law. The person who looks to the law for information corresponds to Hart's 'puzzled man'. The puzzled man needs no motivation; he just needs information. The law can guide his conduct not by offering him reasons different from what he already has but by offering him information about what those reasons actually require of him.

dination convention is designed to help us understand the way in which the rule of recognition creates reasons for action among officials.)

We now have in hand characterizations of both the Conventionality and the Practical Difference Theses, and Hart's views on both. It remains to characterize Incorporationism. Incorporationism is a response to Dworkin's original objection to Hart's apparent failure to countenance moral principles as potentially legally binding sources of law. So one way of understanding Incorporationism is via the dispute between positivists and Dworkin regarding the legal standing of certain moral principles.

IV. THE ORIGINAL PROBLEM AND THE INCORPORATIONIST SOLUTION

Ronald Dworkin's original objection to Hart is built around the conjunction of two premises. The first is that sometimes moral principles can be legally binding in virtue of their substantive merit. The second is that legal positivism requires pedigree or social-source criteria of legal validity. Therefore, legal positivism cannot account for the way in which moral principles figure (i.e. as binding legal sources and not as discretionary standards) in legal practice.

Countenancing moral principles as legally binding, Dworkin believes, undermines each of positivism's more fundamental claims. If moral principles are legally binding in virtue of their merits, then morality is a condition of legality (at least for some legally binding norms), and the separability thesis (the claim that morality cannot be a condition of legality)[39] has to be abandoned. The rule of recognition must be abandoned as well, because the claim that it specifies necessary and sufficient conditions of legal validity turns out to be false. The rule of recognition must set forth a pedigree test, and some moral standards are legally binding for non-pedigree reasons. Finally, the need and opportunity for discretion is reduced as the number of legally authoritative standards is increased; in the limiting case, it evaporates altogether.

A number of lines of response are available to the positivist. Appearances to the contrary, one might insist that moral principles are not

---

[39] There are several possible formulations of the separability thesis. Only under the formulation according to which morality could never be a condition of legality would Dworkin's argument, if sound, undermine the separability thesis. I have defended a different formulation of the separability thesis, according to which morality is not necessarily a condition of legality, in which case, even if Dworkin's argument were sound, it would not entail that the separability thesis is false. One of the more interesting disputes among legal positivists is the disagreement Raz and I have about where the modal operator should be placed in characterizing the separability thesis.

binding legal sources, and therefore that when judges appeal to them they are engaged in discretionary activity–sometimes legitimately, sometimes not. It is hard to see how such an approach does anything more than re-iterate the positivist's commitments.[40] It certainly does not defend them.

---

[40] Dworkin rightly notes that positivists do not understand discretion to be a privilege or power to resolve disputes by any standard or preference that strikes a judge's fancy. Discretion is a power to appeal to extralegal standards to resolve legal disputes. But the appeal must be regulated by norms of rationality and reasonableness and is subject to evaluation and criticism if it is not. Though regulated by norms and subject to criticism, Dworkin nevertheless conceives of discretion for positivists as being some kind of freedom from legal constraint. He is not alone in holding this view, but it does not strike me (as a positivist) as the correct characterization of discretion.

The positivist believes that even when and where law runs out, the judge is often *obligated* to appeal to certain moral principles and not to others. Discretion for many positivists is not primarily a power or privilege or freedom. It is not the absence of legal constraint. Rather, it is the legal duty to appeal to certain principles that are not law in order to resolve the issue at hand. Discretion is a claim about the *status* of the principles to which the judge must appeal.

We can distinguish two pictures of discretion: one focuses on the freedom of the judge, the other on the status of the standards to which the judge appeals. Dworkin paints a picture of the first sort. On his view, positivism is committed to seeing judges as having a kind of unavoidable, but regulated, freedom. In fact, most positivists view the judge as having no such freedom. Instead, the judge has a legal duty to appeal to certain principles and is bound by the conclusions drawn from them. It is just that these principles or standards are extralegal; they are not part of the community's law. *Contra* Dworkin, the positivist believes that in what he would call hard cases a judge is directed to appeal to appropriate moral principles: ones he has no freedom to ignore. He is bound by aspects of his role to appeal to such standards. The positivist's point is that even if those standards are binding on officials it is not because they are law. They are not the law of the relevant community, even if they are binding on the judge. Hence, the important distinction Raz has drawn between standards that are binding on judges and those that are part of the law of the community, and binding for that reason.

On the other hand, one could object on behalf of the Dworkinian that if this is what a positivist means by discretion, all the apparently interesting and important differences between positivists and Dworkin evaporate into semantic ones. Both believe that the judge is bound to appeal to moral standards in certain cases; the only difference is that the positivist believes that these standards are not law, though binding on officials, whereas Dworkin believes that the standards are binding because they are law. One might ask, why not just accept the Dworkinian characterization, which has the advantage of offering an elegant and simple explanation of why moral standards are binding on officials? They are binding because they are law.

This solution is plausible, but it misunderstands or under-appreciates the point of the positivist's refusal to treat these moral standards as binding law: binding, but not law. The reason is that positivists, especially Raz, are concerned primarily to vindicate law's claim to authority. For reasons I cannot delve into at this point, law's claim to authority—especially for Raz—is tied up with restricting the category 'law' to norms that have social sources. Moral principles that are not source-based cannot therefore count as part of the community's law. But that does not mean that such standards cannot be binding on officials.

This is one way in which my position differs from Raz's. I am not moved primarily by a desire to vindicate law's claim to practical authority. As a result, I have less trouble with Dworkin's characterization of these moral standards as binding on officials because they are law. For me, as will become clear, it is not important whether we treat the moral standards as binding on officials because they are law; what is extremely important is that if we treat them as binding *law,* we do so because they satisfy conditions set forth in a rule of recognition. Right here we have the differences separating inclusive and exclusive positivists and Dworkin, and some appreciation of the implicit motivations for each.

A better strategy relies on the distinction Joseph Raz emphasizes between legal validity and bindingness on officials. All legally valid norms are binding on officials, but not every standard that is binding on judges is legally valid, in the sense of being part of the community's law. The laws of foreign jurisdictions, the norms of social clubs as well as other normative systems generally can be binding on officials in certain adjudicatory contexts, though they are not part of the 'host' community's law. Judges may be authorized, even directed, by otherwise valid rules to appeal to such principles. They need not be part of a community's law in order for judges to be required to appeal to them in the context of a particular suit. Thus, it does not follow from the fact that judges may sometimes be bound by certain moral principles that those principles are themselves part of the law or are legally valid.

An alternative account advocated by Rolf Sartorious[41] and others allows that moral standards can sometimes be valid law, but argues that their status as law depends on their pedigree or history, not their content. All and only those moral principles identified as valid in virtue of their social source can count as part of a community's law. In pursuing this response, the positivist abandons the model of rules—the claim that legal standards are all rules—a position, moreover, that no positivist has ever actually endorsed. More important, the positivist can maintain each of the three remaining tenets. What makes something law is its satisfying the source test set out in the rule of recognition. Thus, both the rule of recognition and the separability thesis remain intact. Even though including moral principles within the domain of law increases available resources and narrows the scope of discretion accordingly, moral principles are often controversial and judges can disagree about their application in controversial cases. Gaps narrow, but the opportunities for discretion owing to conflicting and vague standards increase.[42]

---

[41] Rolf E. Sartorious, 'The Enforcement of Morality', 81 Yale LJ 891 (1972).

[42] Of course, even as discretion owing to the availability of legally binding resources decreases (as the set of available resources increases), the possibility of discretion owing to vagueness increases (as the set of controversial moral predicates legally binding on officials increases). The same predicates that reduce discretion on one front increase it on another: a consequence of Dworkin's own view that moral predicates are controversial and contestable. To defeat the positivist view of discretion Dworkin has to do more than show that the set of available legal resources on which a judge can draw is much greater than those open to the positivist, who limits the resources to a subset of rules has. Of course, no positivist really limits the set of resources binding on officials in the way Dworkin claims. The debate has to be resolved on grounds having more to do with the structure of argument and legal justification than with the set of binding legal sources.

Indeed, that is the line of argument Dworkin ultimately takes. His best argument is that positivists do not have a plausible account of the nature of adjudication (regardless of the size of the set of resources on which judges can draw). I think he is absolutely right about this, though the claim is a bit general, and does not apply to all positivists. I, for one, am a positivist with a view of the structure of adjudication and justification in law that is very

The social-source solution allows that moral principles can be legally binding, but it claims that the criterion of validity is social source, or what Dworkin calls pedigree. Incorporationism goes one step further. Incorporationism allows not only that moral principles can be legally valid, but also that some moral principles can be legally binding in virtue of their merits or value, not their pedigree. In this regard, the Incorporationist is prepared to accept more of Dworkin's suppositions than is the positivist, who insists that the legality of moral principles depends entirely on their source. Unlike Dworkin, however, the Incorporationist believes that this picture is compatible with positivism, in particular, with both the rule of recognition and the separability thesis.

We can neatly summarize Dworkin's objection and the possible solutions to it. Dworkin argues that the following two claims are inconsistent:

different from the one Hart presents in ch. 7 of *The Concept of Law*. I am a meaning holist whose views on the structure of legal discourse is very close to Dworkin's. Both of our views owe much to Quine. It is just that, in my view, there are a range of issues having to do with law's institutionality, possibility, and the individuation of legal systems that require the kind of conventionalist answer provided by the theory of the rule of recognition.

A theory of the structure of justification in legal discourse is not a theory of law: essential questions of the sort just mentioned are left unanswered by it. Like David Lewis in the philosophy of language, I believe that features of the relevant practice require a conventionalist answer. In philosophy of language, these issues include how terms get meanings (i.e. by conventions). Nevertheless, we have to draw a distinction between the question, how do bearers of semantic content get meanings? and the question, what meaning does a bearer of semantic content have? We answer the former question by invoking the idea of linguistic conventions. We do not (or need not) answer the second question in that way. Certainly a meaning holist would not. Lewis, well known for his possible-world semantics, does not either.

There is an important and overlooked analogy between the role of conventions in the philosophy of language and in jurisprudence. In my view, the convention (the rule of recognition) is necessary because it helps to explain how norms secure their status as law. But we do not continually refer back to the convention in order to determine the validity of particular legal claims. Unlike other positivists, I do not believe that we resolve disputes about what the law is on a particular matter by referring back to the conventions that make law possible. Such a view would be incompatible with the meaning holist picture to which I am drawn.

This is another aspect of Incorporationism as I develop it that is distinct from the traditional forms of legal positivism. I have no reason to think that other Incorporationists who accept the basic structure of the position I set out on the rule of recognition do or would accept the account of the structure of legal discourse that I do. It is clear from ch. 7 of *The Concept of Law* that Hart has something else in mind altogether. I have no reason to think that Dworkin has conceived of the issues in this way, separating questions of the structure of justification in law from questions about the nature of law. On my reading of the body of his work, I do not think that he does. Indeed, most people read Dworkin as identifying the theory of law with the theory of adjudication. At the very least, one can plausibly read him as deriving the theory of law from the theory of adjudication. In any case, I am inclined to separate the two. The debate between us ultimately is whether there are interesting and important questions in law or about law that need to be answered or which are left unanswered by a theory of the structure of justification in legal discourse. I think there are, and I think the best explanation of them is conventionalist. This is one of the main issues I take up in the third Clarendon Lecture.

sometimes moral principles are legally binding in virtue of their substantive merits; positivism is committed to a pedigree criterion of legal authority. A positivist could deny the first premiss, arguing that moral principles are not binding authority. Or he could argue that moral principles can be binding authority but in virtue of their source or pedigree, not their merit. In that way, he would accept the first part of the first premiss but not all of it. Or a positivist could reject the second premiss and accept the first in its entirety. That is the Incorporationist solution.

The rule of recognition expresses a social practice among officials to treat certain standards as criteria of legal validity. There is nothing in this conception of it that imposes any constraints on the conditions of validity. The Incorporationist sees no reason for assuming that these conditions cannot in principle include criteria making moral value or merit a condition of legality, at least for some norms. For the Incorporationist, what matters in the rule of recognition is not the criteria of validity set forth, but its existence conditions.

The rule of recognition must be a social rule; it expresses or represents a convention of a certain kind. Though we should likely find a great deal of overlap among them, the content of that convention may differ from one legal system to the next. The key move for the Incorporationist is the claim that positivism imposes no constraint on the criteria of validity. Whether a particular rule of recognition does so depends on the practice of officials. The separability thesis remains intact because it is not a necessary feature of our concept of law that the rule of recognition in every legal community require that morality be a condition of legality. Moreover, the rule of recognition exists if and only if certain facts obtain, not if some argument on its behalf can be sustained.

V. INCORPORATIONISM DETAILED

This is all somewhat compressed, as I have described and defended Incorporationism elsewhere.[43] Unfortunately, judging from what others have said about it—proponents and critics alike—some points that I have not previously emphasized require further elaboration.

Almost everybody gets right the initial premiss of Incorporationism— that one way of meeting Dworkin's objection is to reject the pedigree requirement. Understood in this way, most legal positivists—with notable

---

[43] See esp. Coleman, *supra* n. 5; Jules L. Coleman, 'Second Thoughts and Other First Impressions', in *New Essays in Legal Theory*, ed. Bix, 401–505; Jules L. Coleman and Brian Leiter, 'Legal Positivism', in *A Companion to Philosophy of Law and Legal Theory*, ed. Dennis Paterson (1996), 241–60.

exceptions, like Raz and Shapiro—turn out to be Incorporationists. Whereas most Incorporationists have understood its motivation and the fact that in order to be an Incorporationist one must reject or abandon the pedigree requirement, they have not really understood the problems that rejecting the pedigree requirement creates: the way in which it is in tension with other of positivism's commitments, notably the Conventionality and the Practical Difference Theses. To their credit, Shapiro and Raz—Incorporationism's strongest and best critics—have a better sense of the position's deep commitments than do many of Incorporationism's or inclusive positivism's strongest allies and staunchest supporters. Part of the problem is understanding precisely what Incorporationism does and does not claim.

The first mistake is to think that in rejecting the pedigree standard, Incorporationism embraces a substantive test of legality. Not so. Incorporationism is the claim that positivism *allows* or *permits* substantive or content tests; it is not the view that positivism advocates, endorses, or requires such tests. The second mistake is to think that when moral principles are binding law it must be in virtue of their merits. Not so. Incorporationism is the claim that positivism allows or permits such explanations of legal validity: not the view that positivism requires such explanations.

In short, Incorporationism is a theory of 'possible explanations' of the character of legality or legal validity. It says, in effect, that a positivist can accept not just that moral principles sometimes figure in legal argument, not just that these principles might even be binding on officials, but much more. A positivist can accept the much stronger claim that these principles figure in legal argument because they are binding on officials; that they are binding on officials because they are legally valid or part of the community's law; that they may be valid in virtue of their merits; and that they operate as conditions of legality by judging other norms on their substantive merits.[44]

---

[44] Even though Incorporationism makes clear both that morality can sometimes be a condition of validity and that it cannot necessarily be a condition of legality, some have associated Incorporationism with an altogether different claim, namely that law and morality must (at least in one possible legal system) diverge. This view doubly misunderstands Incorporationism. First, it confuses Incorporationism with Negative Positivism. Second, it misunderstands negative positivism. Let us begin with the latter confusion first.

Negative positivism is the view that there must be one logically possible legal system in which morality is not a condition of legality. This follows from the Separability Thesis, the claim that morality is not a necessary condition of legality. It hardly follows from this that there must be a possible legal system in which morality and legality diverge. The latter advocates a form of *extensional* divergence, whereas negative positivism advocates a form of *intensional* divergence. Negative positivism is not Incorporationism, as the former claims that there is no necessary connection between law and morality, whereas the latter claims that sometimes there can be a connection between them, but there need not be. The two are obviously consistent. They are not equivalent, of course, because the latter entails the former, but not vice versa.

Incorporationism makes no claim as to the underlying merits of Dworkin's 'observations'. It does not embrace their truth, nor does it defend one or another interpretation of them. It is a 'conditional' or 'hypothetical' thesis. It is a way of showing that even if Dworkin is right about the status of moral principles in adjudication, his insights can be accommodated within positivism. Incorporationism says, in effect, that Dworkin's observations, left unchallenged, do not provide a reason for abandoning or even modifying positivism. Positivism can allow all this without abandoning anything of importance just as long as the criteria of validity are criteria of membership in virtue of the practice among officials. This is the important connection between Incorporationism and the Conventionality Thesis. It is also the point at which Dworkin wants to exert pressure. His claim is that Incorporationism is not available to a positivist because it is incompatible with the Conventionality Thesis.[45]

---

[45] We need a theory of law that merges the idea of a rule of recognition with the view that moral principles can sometimes be binding on officials. Virtually everyone accepts the latter claim. Dworkin thinks that because moral principles, if binding, are so in virtue of their substantive merits, one has to abandon the former. Not only do I think he is mistaken; without the former, several key features of law are left inadequately explicated, if explained at all: in particular, law's possibility, its institutionality, and our capacity to individuate legal systems. Positivists who accept a rule of recognition offer a variety of different views about how to accommodate moral principles. Some treat them as not binding. Most treat them as binding, but not law. Some treat them as binding law but binding in virtue of their social source; and some, Incorporationists, treat them as binding in virtue of their merits. Which position one takes on this issue will depend, as I have suggested, on one's other motivations: in particular, on one's view about the importance of vindicating law's claim to authority, as well as what is required in order to do so.

Part of what distinguishes my Incorporationism from others is that I not only advance the view that moral principles can be legally binding in virtue of their merits, but also adopt something like a Dworkinian view about the way in which such principles and other binding sources figure in the legal practice of justification. On the other hand, I believe that a theory like Dworkin's, which has no place for a conventionalist rule of recognition, lacks the resources to provide a plausible account of law's possibility, institutionality, and individuation.

So when Dworkin argues that a non-pedigree criterion of legality cannot be a conventional rule, he is claiming that the particular kind of theory that I have been developing is impossible. My motivation in arguing that moral principles can be legally binding as law is that I am inclined to merge a general, holist view about justification with a conventionalist view about the conditions that make law possible. I want, in effect, to bolster, rather than to undermine, what I take to be the valuable and plausible parts of Dworkin's view.

There is a real question of a deep and philosophically interesting sort about whether, and in what ways, one can merge pragmatism and conventionalism. I think one can (in both philosophy of language and philosophy of law). Again, this is an issue I address in the third Clarendon Lecture.

It is not obvious that Dworkin appreciated my motivation for allowing moral principles to figure in legal practice when he argued against me. That doesn't matter. His arguments are not persuasive, and that is the issue I want to address in the next section.

VI. INCORPORATIONISM AND THE CONVENTIONALITY THESIS

Incorporationism shifts the burden of positivism from the criteria of legal validity to the existence conditions of the rule that specifies those criteria. It requires both that the rule of recognition be a social convention *and* that the rule be capable of imposing contentful criteria of validity. Dworkin argues that these two requirements are, in effect, incompatible. Whereas Dworkin's original objection to Hart was that the validity of moral principles is incompatible with the pedigree requirement, his objection to Incorporationism is that the kind of substantive criteria of legality that would account for the legality of moral norms is incompatible with law's conventionality.

The argument is this: moral principles are inherently controversial. Judges will disagree about which putative principles satisfy the demands of morality and what is required of the principles that do. In contrast, the rule of recognition is a social rule partially constituted by or supervenient on a convergent social practice. Thus, convergence is a condition of the rule of recognition. Convergence, however, is undermined by the disagreement that would attend any rule that makes morality a condition of legality. Thus, Incorporationism is incompatible with the Conventionality Thesis.

There are a number of problems with this line of argument. I have emphasized the point that Dworkin's argument misses the important difference between what the rule is and what falls under it. A rule, after all, cannot be defined by its extension. Judges may agree about what the rule is but disagree with one another over what the rule requires, especially in controversial cases. They could not disagree in every case or even in most cases, as such broad and widespread disagreement would render unintelligible their claim to be applying or following the same rule. Nevertheless, judges can and do disagree in some significant set of controversial cases. Thus, it hardly follows from the fact that judges disagree about some of the demands of morality that they disagree about whether the rule governing their behaviour requires that they resolve certain disputes by determining what morality demands. This difference between what the rule is and what it requires is logically independent of the kind of rule in question. Disagreement about the requirements of a rule and those about the rule itself arise whether the rule is a normative or a conventional one. Disagreement about its requirements is not incompatible with the conventionality of a rule. Indeed, there may even be a conventional understanding of the ways in which disagreements about what a conventional rule requires are to be resolved.[46]

---

[46] Dworkin offered a counter-response, but not to my mind a particularly persuasive one. A little chronology is in order. Long before 'Negative and Positive Positivism' other posi-

Dworkin's argument cuts no ice against the Conventionality Thesis. We might reformulate it so that it does not make a conceptual or theoretical point about the consistency of Incorporationism and the Conventionality Thesis, but a practical point about the value of a rule of recognition that incorporates morality into law's validity conditions. Arguably, law is of practical significance because it guides or purports to guide human conduct. The more controversial the rule of recognition, the

tivists noted that one way of responding to Dworkin's objections in 'The Model of Rules I' (in *Taking Rights Seriously*, 1977) would be to abandon the pedigree requirement. (I take no credit for discovering this way out, though I have been more worried than most about the implications for positivism of taking it.) Dworkin responded in 'The Model of Rules II' (in *Taking Rights Seriously*) that a rule of recognition that allowed morality to be a condition of legality could not be a social rule (or what I am calling a conventional rule). That is because reference to morality would lead to disagreement incompatible with the rule of recognition's being a social or conventional rule. Dworkin was the party offering the objections to positivism. The burden on positivism is not to show that controversy engendered by a rule of recognition is impossible or that Dworkin was mistaken in interpreting controversy in a way that made it compatible with his overall view. The burden on positivism was to show somehow that controversy engendered by the rule of recognition did not imply Dworkin's conclusion that the rule of recognition could not be a conventional or social rule. The burden was to show the compatibility of controversy and convention: no more, but no less.

This is where 'Negative and Positive Positivism' enters the picture. I advanced two main theses: first, and foremost, that for a positivist, the most important feature of law is that it rests on a social fact; that in Hart's and my versions of positivism, that fact is expressed in a rule that is itself a social fact—the social convention Hart refers to as a rule of recognition. Second, the rule of recognition could be conceived of as a conventional rule even in the face of controversy. My argument drew a distinction between disagreement about content and disagreement about application. My claim was that *many* controversies calling for or inviting controversial moral argument are understandable as disagreements about the application of the rule rather than as disagreements about the rule's content. Moral disagreement about the content of the rule would be incompatible with the claim that the rule is a conventional or social one. Disagreement about what the rule requires in a particular case is compatible with the rule of recognition being a social convention. That is because, as I argued, morality cannot settle what the convention is, but it can help us to determine what the convention requires in a particular case. This is a familiar and important distinction. Indeed, Raz draws on a similar distinction in his account of authority: for him, law's claim to authority precludes looking into a law's justifying reasons to determine its identity or content (what it is); but one can investigate the moral reasons that would justify the law in determining what the law requires in a particular case.

Though inclusive positivists rely on my argument, Dworkin was unpersuaded. What was surprising was that he began his counter-attack by labelling the distinction between content and application 'doubtful', but it is hard to understand what he could have meant: the distinction itself is so familiar. Sometimes you and I disagree about what the rule we are supposed to be following is. Other times we know full well what the rule is, but we disagree about what it requires of us. The only counter Dworkin offers to this obvious point is that we can always describe the same disagreement either way: as a disagreement of content or application. But even saying that affirms, rather than contests, the legitimacy of the distinction. Saying that either description is possible may be his way of saying that the distinction can do no work. But this too is false. Even if it did turn out to be logically possible to describe any disagreement about a rule as a disagreement about the rule's content or its application, it hardly follows that either description is equally apt all the time.

Sometimes the context will reveal to us which description is apt and why. Sometimes there may be no way of knowing independently of offering theoretical considerations on

less able it is to provide useful guidance. How can individuals conform
their behaviour to the law's demands when they cannot determine reliably what those demands are? If the rule of recognition invites dispute
and controversy, the motivation for insisting on its conventionality evaporates.

We can put the point somewhat differently. Suppose we accept, as
Dworkin sometimes does, that wherever there is law, there exists a test for
distinguishing the legal from the non-legal. The only question, then, is
whether this test is conventional or normative. If the point of insisting
upon its conventionality is that, when understood as a conventional rule,
the test provides more effective guidance, the controversiality of the
Incorporationist test undermines that claim. We are left with the more

behalf of one interpretation or the other. For my part, I nowhere claim that all disagreements
are best understood as disagreements in the application of the rule of recognition. I would
never say, and did not say, that the disagreement in the rule of recognition evidenced by
Marbury v. *Madison* was a disagreement in the application of the rule. It is a disagreement in
how the rule should be extended or developed. It is a disagreement in the rule's content.

Law's conventionality does not require that every disagreement be a disagreement in
application. Positivists do recognize discretion, and some disagreements, which are
disagreements in content, are best thought of as disagreements about how the law should be
extended. I know that in Dworkin's view they are always disagreements about what the law
is. But again, the choice between these two views has to be made on theoretical grounds.
Dworkin and I simply have conflicting but internally consistent characterizations of controversy. My burden was to show the consistency of a positivist's characterization; and, as far
as I can tell, Dworkin is the only legal theorist of note who thinks that the argument fails.

Ironically, faced with the same data and the same interpretive options, Dworkin invariably interprets the disagreements as disagreements of content. He does that because at the
time he was defending the view that the rule of recognition is a normative and not a social
rule. That thesis requires treating disagreements in the rule of recognition as normative
disagreements of content. So not only did Dworkin rely on a distinction he labelled 'doubtful', he chose the characterization favourable to his position without ever offering anything
like a theoretical reason for doing so. That would have been fine had he been in my position:
in the position of trying to show that an objection did not undermine his position. In other
words, if I had criticized his view by saying that disagreements of law are invariably
disagreements about the application of the rule of recognition, it would have been perfectly
fair for him to respond that the same disagreements could be characterized as disagreements
of content. If they are disagreements of content, then his view is not in jeopardy.

That would have been fair had his been the position under attack. But it wasn't. He was
on the offensive. Hart's position was the one under attack, and I defended it in a perfectly
plausible and sensible way by showing that the objection could be rendered harmless under
some plausible interpretation of it.

The dispute about how to understand controversy engendered by a rule of recognition
has to be resolved by appeal to theoretical considerations: elegance, simplicity, explanatory
power, and the like. For my part, I have tried to show how the explanation of law's possibility, institutionality, and individuation requires a conventionalist account of law; and
therefore that understanding disagreement in the rule of recognition in a way that is compatible with law's conventionality could be defended on theoretical grounds. Dworkin could
rightly argue that we need to understand controversy in a way that is true to the structure
of the practice of justification in legal discourse. I agree. My view is twofold: (1) such an
interpretation is not incompatible with a social convention at law's core; (2) the existence of
such a convention is necessary to explain law's possibility, institutionality, and individuation.

natural explanation of any test that makes morality a condition of legality: that a rule that imposes moral criteria is itself a normative or moral rule.

We need to distinguish between law's possibility and its efficacy. Positivists insist on law's conventionality as essential to our understanding its possibility. The claim that law is made possible by a rule of recognition that supervenes on a practice accepted from an internal point of view is a conceptual claim: it states possibility or existence conditions. It does not matter, for these purposes, whether the rule of recognition is controversial and, if so, how controversial it is.

On the other hand, a rule of recognition's efficiency varies with its controversiality. No positivist believes that it does not matter whether the rule of recognition is controversial. It is just that if controversy matters, it matters from the point of view of law's efficacy, not from the point of view of law's possibility.[47]

VII. THE RAZIAN OBJECTION

Like Dworkin, Joseph Raz believes that positivism cannot allow morality to be a condition of legality.[48] Unlike Dworkin, he does not believe that

---

[47] One might try to turn the practical objection to a controversial rule of recognition into a conceptual one in the following way. One might argue, as Stephen Perry does, that a conception of law's function is necessarily part of a theorist's conception of law. If a positivist is committed to the view that law's function is to guide conduct, then the function will constrain the rest of the theory. In order to be a rule of recognition in the positivist's sense, the rule must be capable at least in principle of satisfying the relevant function. A controversial rule of recognition, for example, one that embraces morality conditions of legality, would then be incompatible with positivism. The problem with this line of argument, I have suggested, is that the concept of law presupposes no controversial conception of law's function or purpose.

[48] I want to detail what I take to be the subtle but significant differences between Razians and me. As I mentioned earlier, Raz himself rarely talks about law in terms of a rule of recognition. Instead, he talks entirely in terms of criteria or conditions of legality. So instead of asking what the constraints are on the rule of recognition to which the exclusive positivist is committed, we should ask: what constraints, if any, does exclusive positivism impose on the conditions of legality? The answer depends on the theory of authority. On my reading, the theory of law for the exclusive positivist is driven by the theory of authority.

For the exclusive positivist all criteria of legality must operate through social sources. The legality of a norm depends on its social source. But this does not imply that moral principles cannot be conditions of legality. This is an important and subtle point. Moral principles can be conditions of legality provided the way in which they operate as conditions of legality is by directing officials to *social sources*. Let me explain.

Take the following moral principle: individual citizens ought to follow the enactments of duly elected legislatures only. Treat this as a principle of political morality. It might also constitute a condition of legality provided it operates by directing citizens and officials to social sources. Only those enactments passed by duly elected legislatures can be legally binding on citizens.

So here is a case of a moral principle that can be a condition of legality because it operates this is because such criteria are controversial. A rule that is an authority functions in practical reasoning by pre-empting or replacing the dependent reasons that would justify it. Authorities mediate between persons and the reasons that apply to them. If in order to identify the authority or its content, one must appeal to the dependent reasons that the authority replaces, the claim to authority is vitiated. Law's claim to authority entails, therefore, that one cannot determine the law's identity or content by appealing to the dependent reasons that would justify it. A rule of recognition that allows morality to serve as a condition of legality appears to require that one investigate the dependent reasons the law replaces or preempts in order to determine the law or its content, thus vitiating the claim to authority.

The claim to authority entails the possibility that the claim might be true. Law's claim to authority must be intelligible, so it must be the sort of claim that could be true, even if it turns out not to be. Thus, one's theory of the kind of thing law is or can be is constrained by this account of authority and the fact that law necessarily claims to have it. If legality cannot depend on morality, then (provided legality is not a natural fact) it must depend on social fact or source. Hence, the Sources Thesis. The possibility of authority entails the Sources Thesis. The Sources Thesis is incompatible with Incorporationism.

Incorporationism can withstand the argument from authority, however. First, not every morality condition of legality directs us to the law's underlying or justifying conditions. Thus, on the assumption that authority precludes identification by appealing to its justifying or dependent reasons, not every Incorporationist rule of recognition will be incompatible with the possibility of legal authority.

as a condition of legal authority by directing officials and citizens to social sources only. It operates through social sources.

In contrast, inclusive positivists do not require that in order to be a condition of legality a moral principle must operate through social sources. According to the inclusive positivist, the principles of morality can operate directly in the sense of requiring that a norm be evaluated on its substantive (moral) merits. Thus, the inclusive positivist can allow *morality* to be a condition of legality. Morality can only operate as a condition of legality by directing officials to the substantive moral merits of particular norms. That is an important difference between inclusive and exclusive positivists.

Inclusive positivists (Incorporationists in my sense) can allow morality to be a condition of legality provided the rule of recognition sets morality forth as a legality condition. Morality then operates by evaluating norms directly on the basis of their merits. Exclusive positivists can allow moral *principles* to operate as conditions of legality only if they direct officials to social sources.

An inclusive positivist can object to the exclusive positivist in either of two ways. The exclusive positivist account of the conditions of legality is animated by the theory of authority. Therefore, an inclusive positivist can reject the theory of authority or argue that the theory of authority does not require the constraints on the conditions of legality the exclusive positivist claims it does. In this section I adopt the second approach, arguing that the Sources Thesis as a constraint on legality is not required by the Razian theory of authority.

Second, the conjunction of the claim that law necessarily claims authority and the view of authority as precluding determination of content and identity by recourse to substantive moral argument imposes no constraints on the conditions of legality. This is not only a welcome outcome for the Incorporationist but one that even an exclusive positivist needs to accept if his position is to be plausible. I argue both points in order.

A rule of recognition specifying that 'only rules that treat individuals fairly can be legally valid' would express an evaluative test, but it does not direct us to the dependent reasons that would justify any particular legal rule. It would be a constraint on or a condition of legality for all rules, regardless of the reasons that justify any rule in particular. Certain reasons of fairness and equality (e.g. does the law offer fair opportunities for appeal? is it fairly administered?) are not part of the justification for laws prohibiting murder, for example—not part of the reasons why it would be morally good or desirable to have such a law. Nor, importantly, are they part of the dependent reasons that the law would replace. Thus, as conditions of the legality of norms, such criteria of legality do not direct officials or citizens to the justifying or dependent reasons the law purports to replace. This is just another way of saying that the evaluative considerations that go to the legality of a rule need not coincide with those that go to the merits of the rule.

An Incorporationist rule of recognition, therefore, need not pose a threat to law's authority because laws valid under the kind of rule described above can serve the requisite mediating role between reasons and persons.[49]

---

[49] In 'Second Thoughts and Other First Impressions', I consider possible responses to my argument. There I say the following.

'One might respond by claiming that all considerations of fairness are part of the underlying justification of any rule—including the prohibition against murder. All fairness considerations are part of the dependent reasons that are replaced by accepting the rule as binding authority. So, if I ask myself whether I ought to accept the rule against murdering others as authoritative, I have to ask whether the demands of right reason, including those of fairness, will be better satisfied by following it than by following the first-order reasons that counsel against murder anyway. And if the rule is unfairly administered, if it does not give individuals sufficient opportunity to appeal, etc., then the demands of right reason—including those of fairness—are not better served by accepting the rule as binding authority. I would do better by simply complying with the demands of right reason directly.

'This response appears to blur the distinction between the question of whether I will do better by accepting a rule as an authority over me and the very different question about whether it would be better in general to have such a rule. The two are merged only if we understand the demands of right reason applicable to me to be, in effect, to see to it that no rules are adopted that violate fairness: that, in other words, the kinds of consideration that ought to figure in the deliberations of others who have to face the question about whether to accept such a rule as binding on them *given that they will be administering it* are reasons that necessarily apply to me, that I have to consider, even though I do not administer it. The argument appears, in other words, to slip in a form of agent-generality or agent-neutrality that I had always taken to be absent from it.

The worry is that if one has to inquire into what the law should be in order to determine what the law is, the law would be incapable of being an authority. More generally, if one has to inquire into the dependent reasons the law purports to replace or pre-empt in order to determine what the law is, then the law cannot serve its mediating role. The Sources Thesis, which is incompatible with Incorporationism, ensures the possibility of law performing the requisite mediating role. But it is too strong in the sense that not every appeal to morality as a condition of legality directs us to considerations of what the law should be or to its justifying reasons. The Sources Thesis is sufficient to protect law's claim to authority, but it is not necessary. Not every appeal to morality as a condition of legality poses the threat to authority against which the Sources Thesis is designed to guard. That is because not every appeal to morality as a condition of legality directs one to the dependent reasons that law is meant to replace.

A true Incorporationist claims more than that the rule of recognition can impose moral constraints that do not go to a law's justifying or dependent reasons. The Incorporationist claims that a rule of recognition can, in principle, allow conditions of legality that go to the dependent reasons that would justify the law and which the law, if authoritative, would replace. This is a far more expansive rule of recognition. Is such a rule incompatible with law's claim to authority? This is the second issue I mean to address. Whereas the exclusive legal positivist believes that the expansive Incorporationist rule of recognition is incompatible with the theory of authority, I do not.

The theory of authority in conjunction with law's claim to authority does not, in my view, entail the Sources Thesis as a constraint on the conditions of legal validity. The claim to authority (and the theory of authority) entails a certain metaphysical claim about the nature of law: a constraint on the kind of thing law must be. It is important to state that constraint precisely. Law must be the sort of thing that in principle is capable of having its identity and content determined without recourse to

---

'In fact, I do not see how a Razian could advance this line of response. Raz claims that law can be an authority over me—or I can accept it as an authority—without having to accept all law as having authority over me. Similarly, one would think, the same law can be an authority over me, but not over everyone else. And that is just another way of saying that the relevant demands of right reason, and our capacity to satisfy them without relying on legal directives, can differ among us. There is, in other words, a kind of agent-specificity in the way the Razian account of authority is presented that appears inconsistent with the kind of agent-neutrality to which the response seems committed.'

My point is that at least some evaluative (substantive or moral) criteria of legality need not direct us to the underlying reasons that justify the law. So not every evaluative or substantive criterion of legality is inconsistent with the claim to authority. This is especially true where the evaluative or moral criteria are employed to *specify* necessary or validity-negating legality conditions.

moral argument that would undermine its claim to authority: that is, its capacity to mediate between persons and reasons.[50] If the identity and content of law could *only* be determined by recourse to moral argument, then law could not, even in principle, serve the mediating role between reasons and persons that the theory of authority claims law purports to perform. Failure to satisfy this conceptual constraint would vitiate law's claim to authority: a claim that might well be false, but which, if it is to make sense, must be capable of being true.

The Sources Thesis is a sufficient condition for law being the sort of thing whose identity and content is determinable without regard to moral argument of the unacceptable sort. If legal validity is a matter of social source, then law will be the sort of thing whose identity and content are determinable without recourse to moral argument. That is, one could determine the content of the law by appealing to the conditions of validity, which, because they are social sources, do not rely on substantive moral argument.

The Sources Thesis is not necessary, however, and that is the important point. The theory of authority requires that wherever there is law, there must be some way for individuals to identify it and its content without recourse to moral argument about what it should be, arguments about what would justify it. We might even say that this metaphysical or conceptual constraint requires something like a Sources Thesis. What it does not require is a Sources Thesis as a constraint on the conditions or criteria of legality. It requires it as a constraint on modes of identification. The criteria of validity may also be employed as modes of identification, but they need not be.

That is my point, and that is the point I have always emphasized in drawing distinctions among identification, validation, and existence conditions. The rule of recognition sets out validity or membership conditions. It may, but it need not, serve an epistemic role. It may, but it need not, provide the vehicle through which individuals identify the law and its content.

If law is to be capable of being an authority, there must be some way of identifying it and its content without recourse to morality, but there is no reason why that vehicle must be the rule of recognition, and no reason

[50] For ease of exposition, let us always mean by the phrase 'without recourse to moral argument' 'without recourse to moral argument about what the law should be'. Surely, if any kind of moral argument would vitiate law's claim to authority, it would be argument about what the law should be as a condition of determining what the law is. Notice that the Razian view of authority is spelled out in terms of mediation between persons and reasons. It may well turn out that the dispute between exclusive and inclusive legal positivists turns on this controversial conception of practical authority. See *infra* n. 53.

why, therefore, the rule of recognition should not be capable of imposing morality conditions on legality.[51]

One might object to my argument in the following way.[52] First, we need to draw a distinction between something having the property of being capable of being an authority and its having the property of being capable of being a successful authority. Law purports to be an authority. Because necessarily law claims to be an authority, it claims to be the sort of thing that has the property of being capable of being an authority. The claim to authority may or may not be true. In order for the claim to be true, law must be the sort of thing that is capable of being an authority.

Even when the law is an authority, it does not follow that it is successful with respect to all those over whom it has authority. The notion of successful authority is not mine, and I find it somewhat tricky. The idea, however, is that the law may be an authority but fail nevertheless in practice to perform the mediating role between reasons and persons that it is (because it is an authority) capable of playing. For the law to be a successful authority, it needs to operate in the deliberations of each person by replacing the dependent reasons that would otherwise apply. A rule that is an authority may not be a successful authority for someone if, in fact, it fails to operate in the appropriate way for that person. If someone learns what the law is by consulting the reasons that it purports to replace, then the law is not a successful authority for that person, even if the law is an authority for everyone. Presumably, law can be an authority over all those to whom it purports to apply without being successful with respect to all (indeed, over any) of them. There is a kind of agent-relativity in the idea of successful authority that is not part of the concept of authority itself.

The theory of authority is a claim about the property of being an authority, not the property of being a successful authority. Law's claim to authority presupposes the truth of the claim that law is the sort of thing that has the capacity to be an authority. Law's claim to authority is, moreover, a claim it has with regard to everyone it claims authority over. It is not relative to some and not to others. Let us now put these two points together and see what constraints on the conditions of legality, if any, follow.

---

[51] The argument from authority concerns the criteria by which citizens determine what the law is; it does not concern the criteria by which the law is made determinate. In other words, the argument from authority bears on matters of identification, not validation. The rule of recognition, in contrast, sets forth criteria of validity. This is just the difference between the criteria that make something *determinate* and those that bear on *determining* that something is of that sort: the difference between existence and epistemic conditions.

[52] I am not sure that this is the kind of argument that Raz would advance in response. It was suggested to me in a very illuminating, helpful, and fruitful exchange with Ruth Chang, and she believes that it is the kind of response Raz would make. I just do not know whether it is. It is, however, a particularly interesting argument, one worth pursuing on its own merits, and very revealing. I take it up for those reasons.

For law to be the sort of thing that is capable of being an authority, it must be the sort of thing that can, in principle, play the mediating role between persons and the reasons that apply to them. For law to play that mediating role, its identity and content must be capable of being determined without recourse to moral argument invoking the dependent reasons it purports to replace. For law to have authority it must be possible that the law be in principle identifiable without recourse to moral argument about what it should be. Because law's claim to authority covers all those to whom it is directed or applies, law must in principle be identifiable by each person (or an idealized version of each person) without recourse to moral argument about what it should be.

This condition cannot be met by an Incorporationist rule of recognition, however. Even if everybody learns the law by asking the 'legal/moral' expert, so that for each of them they determine the law in a suitable way, the expert cannot learn the law without engaging in the kind of moral argument about what the law should be. Therefore, it is not true for him that he can learn the law without recourse to moral argument about what the law should be. Thus, the rule of recognition is incompatible with the constraints imposed by the theory of authority. Only a rule of recognition in which the conditions of legality are social sources can satisfy the in-principle identifiability condition. Hence the Sources Thesis.

This is, as I said, an intriguing argument, but not, in the end, persuasive. Let us suppose I am the legal/moral expert who learns the law by investigating what the law should be. Strictly speaking, even for me, the law is something that is in principle determinable without recourse to moral argument about what it should be. The law is that sort of thing. It is just that, *in fact*, that is not how I determine what the law is. How I determine what the law is does not bear on the kind of thing law is. It may well be the kind of thing that is identifiable without recourse to moral argument, even if it is not the sort of thing that I identify in that way. Therefore, there is no reason why an Incorporationist rule of recognition cannot satisfy the in-principle identifiability condition.

It is certainly true that even if the law is in principle identifiable by each and every person over whom it claims authority without recourse to moral argument about what it should be, it does not appear to be the case that each and every person can in fact identify the law in that way. Someone will have to engage in the prohibited moral argument. Thus, even if the law is in principle capable of being identified without recourse to moral argument about what it should be, the law cannot in fact be identified by everyone in this way.

It is not obvious why that should matter if the constraint imposed by the theory of authority is that the law can in principle be identified without recourse to moral argument about what it should be. The law can in

principle be so identified by everyone, even if it cannot in fact be so identified. Without further argument, this fact seems uninteresting.

Here is one possible argument for making that fact interesting and
important. If someone has to identify the law by engaging in moral argument about what the law should be, then the law is incapable of being a
successful authority for that person. So one thing an exclusive positivist
could argue is that the law must in principle be capable of being a successful authority for everyone. The 'legal/moral' expert who identifies the
law by appealing to the moral considerations that would justify it or make
it as it should be precludes the law from performing a mediating role for
that person. Therefore, whenever there is an Incorporationist rule of
recognition, there will be at least one person for whom the law cannot,
even in principle, serve as a successful authority.

The exclusive positivist would then have to be understood as being
ultimately concerned with law's being the sort of thing that could be a
successful authority, not with its capacity to be an authority. On this refor-
mulation, the law must be the sort of thing that at least in principle should
be capable of being a successful authority for everyone to whom it is
directed. It seems that an Incorporationist rule of recognition cannot
satisfy this requirement. Indeed, only a rule of recognition that satisfies
the Sources Thesis can. Thus, properly understood, the theory of authority entails the Sources Thesis.

Even this argument will not do the trick of undermining Incorporationism. First, even if we accept that in order for law to be capable of
being an authority it must be capable of being a potentially successful
authority for everyone, there is no reason to think that this requirement
cannot be satisfied by an Incorporationist rule of recognition. Take an
Incorporationist rule of recognition for some political domain, say, the
United States. If the rule is Incorporationist, that means that at least one
person must identify its content by appeal to the moral considerations
about what law ought to be. But there is no reason to suppose that that
person must be someone over whom the law of the United States claims
authority. In deference to my friend Frances Kamm, let me suppose that
the person who engages in the required but prohibited (by the theory of
authority) line of moral argument is a Swede. The law could not serve the
mediating role for the Swede, but then again, it does not claim authority
over the Swede. Then every person over whom the law directs itself could
learn the law from the Swede. Thus, it would in fact be true that the law
is a potentially successful authority over all those to whom its authority is
directed.

One response to this objection is that it is not enough to learn the law
from the Swede, who is a social source. One must, in principle, be capable of learning the law from the law's source, that is, from the rule of

recognition. That response entirely begs the question and is unmotivated. It has the consequence of entailing the Sources Thesis; but why must it be the case that one must be able to learn what the law is from the rule of recognition? Almost no one ever does; and the authority of a rule does not depend on how one learns what the rule is or what its content is, but on how the rule affects one's deliberations. How one learns the law or its content matters only insofar as that bears on its capacity to mediate between persons and reasons. Any other constraint is unmotivated by the theory of authority.

The second problem with the requirement that the capacity to be an authority entails the capacity to be a successful authority for everyone is that it, too, is arbitrary and unmotivated. We are trying, after all, to make intelligible law's claim to authority. It should be enough to say that something can be an authority provided (1) its identity and its content are in principle determinable without recourse to moral argument about what it should be; and (2) it can in principle be a successful authority for at least one person. The law's claim to authority makes no sense if it could not serve as a successful authority even for one person; but if it could succeed as an authority for one person, then the claim is perfectly intelligible. There is no reason to suppose that it must be potentially successful for everyone in order for the claim to authority to be intelligible. In any case, as I argued above, there is no reason to think that an Incorporationist rule of recognition could not satisfy what I am, on independent grounds, suggesting might well be an unmotivated constraint. I see no reason to think that Incorporationism is incompatible with the Razian or Razian-like view about both law's claim to authority and his account of what authority consists in.

The exclusive positivist does not claim that the rule of recognition must be an epistemic rule any more than I do. What the exclusive positivist claims is that because the rule of recognition (on his understanding of it) sets out a sources test of legality, it is always possible for the law and its content to be identifiable without recourse to moral argument by consulting the rule of recognition. The debate between inclusive and exclusive legal positivists, on my reading of it, is not about whether the rule of recognition must serve an epistemic function; nor is it about the ways in which, as an empirical matter, ordinary folk come to learn the law of their community. Neither Raz nor I (I believe) think that the connection of ordinary folk is mediated by the rule of recognition. Instead, the disagreement concerns the constraints on the conditions of legality imposed by the theory of authority: in particular, by law's claim to authority. There is, I believe, no plausible interpretation of the argument from authority that imposes any constraints on a rule of recognition incompatible with Incorporationism. The Sources Thesis* as a constraint on identification remains. The Sources Thesis as a constraint on legality does not.[53]

VIII. INCORPORATIONISM AND THE PRACTICAL DIFFERENCE THESIS

Incorporationism survives the Razian challenge, but it cannot survive every kind of challenge animated by Razian concerns. A powerful and convincing objection to Incorporationism is developed in a recent paper by Scott Shapiro.[54] Shapiro does not explicitly argue against Incorporationism. Rather, he shows that, properly understood, Incorporationism is incompatible with the PDT.

The general form of a rule of recognition is: A rule (standard, principle, norm) is a legal rule (standard, principle or norm; i.e. valid law) provided

---

[53] Scott Shapiro has brought one final line of response to my attention. Take a rule like, 'The law is whatever is just'. My argument in this section is that, in the end, everyone to whom the law is directed can identify the rules validated by this rule of recognition without recourse to the dreaded form of moral argument by consulting the notorious Swede who is the moral/legal expert. The law is not directed toward the Swede, so the law is the sort of thing that is capable of being identified without recourse to moral argument about what it should be by every member of the community to whom the law is directed. A Razian could say that in the case as I have constructed it, the rule 'The law is whatever is just' does not perform the mediation function between reasons and persons that authorities do. For those of us who learn the law from the Swede, he is the authority. And it is not just because we learn the law from him. Rather, it is his judgment that mediates between reason and persons.

The same does not hold in the case of a source-based rule of recognition. Even if each of us learns what the law is from our lawyer, and not from the rule of recognition, it is the rule of recognition and the law valid under it that mediates for us. The lawyer just passes on that information. He does not mediate. He simply reports.

Someone drawn to exclusive positivism from a commitment to the Razian account of authority might claim that an incorporationist rule of recognition could not in principle play the requisite mediating role between persons and reasons that the theory of authority claims law purports to. Only source-based conditions of legality can.

I have not made up my mind about this response, but a couple of things come to mind. As I have always claimed, though others have disagreed, if this is what the argument against incorporationism comes to, its basis is an epistemic, not a metaphysical claim about the nature of law. Second, and more importantly, the argument rests on accepting the Razian account of authority as mediating between reasons and persons. This is a controversial view, and one with which I am not in agreement. Working out that difference must await another occasion. Still, it would be very interesting to know whether in the end the objection to Incorporationism that exclusive positivists have is based entirely on a theory of authority that sees law, and authority generally, as mediating between persons and reasons, something, it appears, an Incorporation first rule of recognition may preclude.

Note, however, that some exclusive positivists object to Incorporationism on other grounds. For example, Shapiro, like me, understands authority as mediating between (or among) option in his case, by making some infeasible; in my case, by making one salient. Nevertheless, he objects to Incorporationism on the grounds that it is incompatible with the PDT. I take up Shapiro's argument in the next section.

[54] *Supra* n. 11.

it satisfies conditions $x_1, x_2, \ldots, x_n$ This entails that all rules that satisfy x_1, $x_2, \ldots, x_n$ must in principle be capable of creating reasons for acting. When these two claims are conjoined, we can reformulate the rule of recognition as being of the general form: Guide your conduct by rules that satisfy conditions $x_1, x_2, \ldots, x_n$.

Now take an incorporationist rule of recognition: A rule is a legal rule provided it is a moral rule. Following the operations outlined above, this translates into the rule: 'Guide your conduct by moral rules' or simply, 'Act morally'.

Shapiro's point is that someone cannot have his conduct guided both by the rule of recognition *and* by the rules validated under it. The reason is simple: if one is guided by the rule of recognition, one will be moved to act morally. That is what the rule of recognition asserts, and if one is guided by the rule, one is moved to act in accordance with it for the reason that the rule requires it. If that is the case, 'legal' rules identified under the rule of recognition cannot add anything of practical significance. One is, after all, already moved to act morally by the rule of recognition. The rules identified as law under the rule of recognition are not capable of adding anything of practical significance.[55]

If such rules cannot in principle add anything of practical significance, they cannot be legal rules. Legal rules must in principle be capable of making a practical difference. These cannot. Thus, they cannot be legal rules. If they cannot be legal rules, then the rule of recognition that sets out the conditions that validate them cannot be a rule of recognition. Thus, the classic incorporationist 'rule of recognition' cannot, in the end, be a rule of recognition at all. The same argument holds for any clause, x_i, in the rule of recognition in which morality is made a condition of legality.[56]

The same considerations do not apply if the rule of recognition is source based. Consider the rule: 'Guide your conduct by whatever Dr John says.' In this case, one can be guided both by the rule of recognition and by those 'rules' that satisfy the relevant legality condition (that is, what Dr John says), because the latter can still make a practical difference even if one is guided by the rule of recognition. After all, what one will have reason to do will depend on what Dr John says. One can be guided by the rule of recognition and it can still be the case that what one actually does will depend on what Dr John actually says. If he says one thing, then someone who accepts the authority of the rule of recognition will

[55] Other legal rules could help specify more precisely the content of what the rule of recognition requires, but they would give no additional reasons for acting on their own. This is Shapiro's key point.

[56] For examples of how the argument can be generalized for any such 'incorporationist' clause, see Scott Shapiro, 'On Hart's Way Out' (this volume).

have reason to do one sort of thing; whereas if he says something else altogether, one will have reason to do something else. In both cases, one can be guided by the rule of recognition as well as by the rules satisfying the conditions set forth in it.

If the Shapiro objection is sound—as I am inclined to believe it is—then standards incorporated into law by criteria that make morality a condition of legality cannot provide reasons for acting. Thus, they cannot guide conduct in the motivational sense. Nor could such rules guide conduct by offering information, as their legal status adds no new information regarding what one is required to do. Incorporationism is incompatible with both the motivational and epistemic versions of the PDT.

The upshot is that Incorporationism and the Conventionality and Practical Difference Theses constitute an inconsistent set. The Conventionality Thesis is compatible with both the PDT and Incorporationism. The PDT is compatible with the Conventionality Thesis. The problem is that Incorporationism is not compatible with the PDT.

It may be helpful to contrast the Razian and Shapiro objections. Though both focus on the compatibility of incorporationism and the PDT, they approach the problem differently. Whereas the Razian argument is based on the idea that law must be the kind of thing identifiable without recourse to moral argument, Shapiro's objection has nothing to do with the conditions under which law or its content is or can be identified. Instead, Shapiro worries that if individuals are guided by an Incorporationist rule of recognition, there is nothing left for rules subordinate to the rule of recognition to do. Once one is guided by the rule of recognition, there is no practical work that can be done by legal rules validated under it. Thus, my distinction between identification and validation, which is relevant to my response to Raz, has no bearing on Shapiro's objection.[57]

If Shapiro is right, the PDT and the general form of Incorporationism—indeed, the one that is necessary in order to absorb Dworkin's insights about the variety of ways in which moral principles figure in legal argument—cannot, however, be maintained. That, of course, is the version that both Hart and I defend: the one, moreover, that must be true if a positivist is to absorb Dworkin's objections to it.

Put that way, it is fair to say that in embracing Incorporationism and the Conventionality and Practical Difference Theses, Hart is apparently

---

[57] Shapiro also has an objection to that distinction at least as it applies to officials. On his reading, for officials the rule of recognition typically serves both epistemic and validation functions. He has a neater way of putting the point, but I have not made my mind up about the merits of the argument just yet. His objection I do consider here is powerful enough. See Shapiro, *supra* n. 11.

committed to an inconsistent set of core beliefs, a commitment that he cannot maintain on pain of inconsistency: apparently not a worry for the postmodern crowd, but a serious problem for those of us who take argument and coherence seriously. Given his general commitments, as well as further textual evidence,[58] it seems that Hart would be led to abandon Incorporationism in a way that would bring his position much closer to Raz's. Like other Incorporationists, Hart never fully appreciates the implications of Incorporationism for other of positivism's basic commitments. That is why Hart would have been better served to have worried more about Razian objections than he did.

IX. POSITIVISM RECONFIGURED

That Incorporationism and the Conventionality and Practical Difference Theses form an inconsistent set is a problem not just for Hart but also for me. Something has to give, and it cannot be the Conventionality Thesis. That leaves either the PDT or Incorporationism.

One alternative is to abandon Incorporationism. Someone who abandons Incorporationism would then have to contest rather than absorb Dworkin's characterization of the ways in which morality figures in legal argument. I want to suggest that instead of holding onto the PD Thesis at the expense of Incorporationism, a positivist might be better served by maintaining the latter at the expense of the former. What does it mean to abandon the PDT, and what could justify doing so? We should choose between Incorporationism and the PDT based in part on whether, and in what ways, each helps us respond to the fundamental problems and questions of jurisprudence. What problem of jurisprudence does Incorporationism purport to answer? What problem is the PDT a response to?

Incorporationism responds to legal positivism's ambitions as a general, descriptive jurisprudence. It asserts that wherever there is law, there is a social rule (the rule of recognition) that sets out criteria of legal validity. The argument for Incorporationism rests on its motivation, and that is to render positivism compatible with what some take to be the most plausible characterization of the role of moral argument in legal practice. The only kind of rule of recognition that is capable of describing accurately and satisfactorily the criteria of legality in modern liberal democracies is one that allows for moral or substantive tests and not only pedigree or non-contentful ones.

---

[58] H. L. A. Hart, 'Commands and Authoritative Reasons', in *Essays on Bentham* (1982).

In contrast, the PDT gives expression to the claim that law is a normative social practice. The discourse of law is the discourse of obligations, rights, responsibilities, duties, and privileges. Law typically functions in people's lives as a guide to conduct: setting forth what must and cannot be done; and what one is free to do. We might say that part of what we mean to assert in saying that law is a normative social practice is that law matters practically—at least in principle. Law is an important social institution precisely because it claims to matter practically.

Even if law does not always make a practical difference, it must in principle be capable of making a difference. Something cannot make a difference unless it is in principle capable of making a difference. The PDT asserts at least two different but related propositions. (1) Necessarily, law claims to make a practical difference; (2) in order for that claim to be true, all law necessarily must in principle be capable of making a practical difference.

There is an important difference between these two modal claims. One can accept the second without accepting the first, but one cannot accept the first without accepting the second. In rejecting the PDT, I abandon the first, but not the second modal claim. In abandoning (1), I suggest that we explore other ways of giving expression to the idea that law is a normative social practice.

We can explain the sense in which law is a normative social practice, the sense in which it makes a practical difference, without committing ourselves to the claim that it is part of our concept of legality that nothing can count as law unless it purports to make such a difference. To be sure, laws generally affect deliberation and action. They do so by offering reasons or by providing information. Most law, most of the time, does either or both. Nevertheless, it is hard to see why a putative legal rule would fail to constitute law simply because it could make no practical difference.

There seems to be a difference between the status of the claim that persistence and continuity are necessary features of law and the claim that capacity to make a practical difference is. It is not possible to imagine law lacking persistence, continuity, and their implications: institutionality, secondary rules, an internal aspect. It is less clear that rules are incapable of being legally valid or binding simply because they are incapable of guiding behaviour. We might say, then, that the claim that law is a normative social practice implies that most law most of the time makes a practical difference. Law typically affects action by offering guidance and by structuring deliberation. Law's importance and interest both depend on its having these effects.

Understood in this way, it is just not part of our concept of law that capacity for practical difference is a condition of legality, though a general capacity to make a difference is a feature of law generally. This seems right, but not strong enough. For all I have said so far, a norm could count as law and make no difference at all: its status as law counting for nothing. Whereas it may not be part of our concept of law that the fact of legality must make a practical difference, it may be part of our concept of law that the fact of legality should add something. Legal status surely should make some sort of difference. What could that difference be?

In a sense, the difference must be practical, but not necessarily instrumental. In other words, the legality of a norm need not be connected directly to the interests, goals, and projects of agents whose deliberations about what to do are guided by norms generally and by law in particular. Instead, legal rules can be understood in terms of the role they play in *justifying* decisions, not in *causing* or *guiding* action. Certainly, Dworkin has sympathies with this general line of argument. The difference law makes can be understood justificatorily as well as instrumentally.[59]

---

[59] I need to develop this suggestion further, but not here. The general idea is that legality always must purport to imply the possibility of a practical difference. Positivists typically associate this difference with instrumental guidance: enabling individuals to pursue their interests or satisfy the requirements of right reason, or the like. Alternatively, legal rules need not be seen entirely in terms of the role they play in furthering interests and guiding action accordingly. A rule's legality allows it to play a role in the justification of a decision or the resolution of a dispute that, in the absence of its having that status, it could not play. I take it that there is a sense in which the Dworkinian project involves the generalization of this idea. That, in turn, marks the difference between seeing law as guiding action—as positivists typically see it—as adjudicating disputes according to accessible, defensible standard as Dworkin typically sees it. My claim is that neither conception of law expresses a conceptual truth about law. In a sense, that is why, at bottom, I do not see the PDT as asserting a conceptual truth about law.

5

On Hart's Way Out

SCOTT J. SHAPIRO

This guy goes to a psychiatrist and says 'Doc, uh, my brother's crazy. He thinks he's a chicken.' And, uh, the Doctor says, 'Well, why don't you turn him in?' And the guy says, 'I would but I need the eggs.'[1]

I. THE LAW'S CLAIM TO LEGAL AUTHORITY

A. Chicken or egg?

It is hard to think of a more banal statement one could make about the law than to say that it necessarily claims legal authority to govern conduct. What, after all, is a legal institution if not an entity that purports to have the legal power to create rules, confer rights, and impose obligations? Whether legal institutions necessarily claim the *moral* authority to exercise their legal powers is another question entirely. Some legal theorists have thought that they do—others have not been so sure.[2] But no one has ever

This paper is a slightly revised version of an article published under the same name in *Legal Theory*'s symposium on Hart's Postscript. The original article provoked several extensive responses, three of which were published together as: Kenneth Einar Himma, 'H. L. A. Hart and the Practical Difference Thesis', 6 Legal Theory 1; Wil Waluchow, 'Authority and the Practical Difference Thesis: A Defense of Inclusive Legal Positivism', 6 Legal Theory 45; Matthew Kramer, 'How Moral Principles Enter into the Law', 6 Legal Theory 83. See also Jules L. Coleman, *The Practice of Principle*, ch. 10. I responded in 'Law, Morality and the Guidance of Conduct', 6 Legal Theory 127.

For republication, I have opted to leave the presentation of the paper's main argument unchanged. This decision is certainly not based on any belief that the paper is without flaws: in my response article I point to several places in the argument where clarifications and emendations are in order (in particular those relating to the concepts of rule-conformity, rule-guidance, and practical difference). My reason for leaving the main text intact is rather based on my belief that to do otherwise would make it much more difficult for the reader to follow the debate that the original article engendered. However, I have revised several paragraphs at the end of Sections I (B) and IX (A), in part because the thoughts they expressed were confused and in part because no one seems to have noticed.

I would like to thank David Golove, Peter Hilal, Andrei Marmor, and the participants of the Legal Theory Workshop at Boalt Hall, University of California at Berkeley, for helpful comments on a previous draft. I would also like to thank Jules Coleman, whose guidance (both epistemic and motivational) was invaluable to me in writing this paper.

[1] Woody Allen, *Annie Hall*.
[2] Cf. H. L. A. Hart, 'Legal Duty and Obligation', in *Essays on Bentham* (1982), with Joseph Raz, 'Hart on Moral Rights and Legal Duties', 4 Oxford J. Legal Stud. 123 (1984).

Scott J. Shapiro

denied (how could they?) that the law holds itself out as having the *legal* authority to tell us what we may or may not do.

Philosophy, however, deals with the banal. Philosophical puzzles are designed to challenge our uncritical acceptance of accepted wisdom and to demonstrate that our common sense often makes no sense. The more banal the observation challenged, the better the puzzle.

In large part, the philosophical project of jurisprudence begins with the observation that the law's claim to legal authority is actually a deeply paradoxical assertion. The paradox arises as follows: any claim of legal authority presupposes the existence of some set of legal rules that confer it. Legal authority, after all, is a product of legal rules. However, for the authorizing rules to exist, some source invested with legal authority must exist to create them. Legal rules, after all, are the product of legal authority. Who, then, is this legal authority responsible for the existence of the authorizing rules? Surely, the source of the rules cannot be identical with the subject of the rules, because the subject does not have legal authority before the rules confer it. Conversely, if the source is different from the subject of the rules, then it must have secured its legal authority from some other set of legal rules. But then we are forced to ask the same question once again: Which legally authoritative source is responsible for the existence of these legal rules? It seems as if we can continue this questioning indefinitely and get no closer to an answer. The attempt to establish the law's claim to legal authority appears to lead either to a vicious circle or to an infinite regress.

Consider, in this regard, a US court that claims the legal authority to sentence an American citizen to prison for income tax evasion. Federal courts have the power to impose such sentences pursuant to Article III, Section 2 of the United States Constitution[3] and Title 26 USC 7201.[4] Congress, in turn, derives its legal authority to prohibit income tax evasion from the Sixteenth Amendment[5] and the Necessary and Proper Clause of Article I, Section 8.[6]

So far, so good. We might, however, take this exercise one step further: From where does the Constitution get its legal authority? A promising place to look for the answer is the provision that the Constitution itself

---

[3] 'The judicial Power shall extend to all Cases . . . arising under . . . the Laws of the United States.'

[4] 'Any person who willfully attempts in any manner to evade or defeat any tax imposed by this title or the payment thereof shall, in addition to other penalties provided by law, be guilty of a felony and, upon conviction thereof, shall be fined not more than $100,000 ($500,000 in the case of a corporation), or imprisoned not more than 5 years, or both, together with the costs of prosecution.'

[5] 'The Congress shall have power to lay and collect taxes on incomes.'

[6] 'Congress shall have power to make all Laws which shall be necessary and proper for carrying into Execution the foregoing Powers.'

claims to be the source of its legal authority, i.e. Article VII. Article VII provides that 'Ratification of the Conventions of the nine States shall be sufficient for the Establishment of this Constitution between the States so ratifying the Same'. This sounds like a good answer until one realizes that Article VII is itself *part* of the Constitution. To claim that the states have the legal authority to ratify the Constitution would already presuppose that the Constitution is valid law. It seems circular to assert that Article VII can confer authority, via the states, *on* the Constitution if it derives its legal authority *from* the Constitution.

On the other hand, if one assumes that Article VII derives its legal validity from some extra-Constitutional source, then that source must derive its legal authority from some other authorizing norm. But then one could claim that this more fundamental norm, and not Article VII, is ultimately responsible for conferring validity on the Constitution. To be sure, one might conclude that Article VII is useless from a legal perspective. On this view, the Constitution would derive its validity from this more fundamental norm, rather than from Article VII itself. However, such a concession breaks the circle only by starting a regress. For this more fundamental norm would have to issue from some source even more fundamental, which would then create the need to find some further legal norm to authorize this source of law. Using this argument, every authorizing norm could be shown to be useless by simply pointing to the need for some further authorizing legal norm to substantiate a source's claim to legal authority. The conclusion of this chain of argument would delight any anarchist: because every authorizing legal rule is useless, the US Constitution cannot be legally binding and, hence, no institution in the United States can rightly claim legal authority.[7]

The problem here is not that some legal institutions may not have the legal authority they claim to have. Such arrogations of power are commonplace and raise no paradoxes. The problem, rather, is that it appears that *no* legal institution has the legal authority it claims to have. Even the wisest and most benevolent democratically elected ruler

---

[7] Legal systems without written constitutions do not escape such problems. Consider e.g. the British Parliament's claimed right to enact legislation. According to the usual story, this right derives from custom. It would seem, therefore, that the British system must contain a legal norm that confers validity on rules which have been practised over a sufficient period of time. However, this custom-validating norm cannot itself be based on custom, for that would render this norm legally superfluous: whenever the conditions are met to validate custom-validating norms, these norms are no longer necessary. The source of this norm's authority cannot be legislative either—it is circular to claim that the custom-validating norm confers validity on Parliament when the custom-validating norm derives its authority from Parliament. If, however, the custom-validating norm derives its authority from some other source, say, from judicial practice, we would have to ask the same questions about the source of judicial authority in these matters. Again, we are forced to choose between vicious circles and infinite regresses.

would be precluded from coherently asserting his right to rule, for he cannot claim a right that, as a matter of simple logic, he cannot possibly have.

This paradox arises because of the self-reflexive nature of law. On the one hand, it seems that legal rules can only be generated by authoritative legal sources. Not anyone may make a legal rule—only those vested with legal authority may—yet it also appears that the authority of a legal source can only be generated by legal rules. Congress, the Supreme Court, the President, and Parliament are all themselves products of law. Hence, we find ourselves in a situation where we need law in order to make law. This leads to a classic 'chicken–egg' problem: if legal authority can only be created by rules, who makes the rules that creates the authority?

The history of analytical jurisprudence can usefully be told as a series of attempts to solve this chicken–egg problem. According to the classical natural law theorists, the buck stops with God. God has the inherent authority to create the natural law, and these rules, in turn, invest manmade law with authority. We might say that the classical natural law theorists rejected the notion that legal chickens (i.e. sources) must always come from legal eggs (i.e. rules). God is posited as the 'First Chicken', the unmoved normative mover who is able to set legal authority in motion through the agency of natural law.

John Austin also denied that legal authority is necessarily the product of legal rules, but positivism precluded his appealing to the natural law in order to stop the regress. Austin thus replaced God with the sovereign and analysed the concept of sovereignty reductively in terms of social facts: the authority of the sovereign did not depend on rules, divine or otherwise, but on power. The sovereign is the one whose threats are habitually obeyed and who habitually obeys no one else.[8] Some chickens, we might say, do not hatch from eggs but become chickens by successfully intimidating the other barnyard animals.

H. L. A. Hart showed, however, that positivists could not actually take this reductionistic route. In Chapter 4 of *The Concept of Law*, he argued that it was impossible to account even for the most basic properties of legal systems by resorting to the concept of a habit. For example, Hart demonstrated that Austin's theory could not explain the continuity of legal systems. When Rex I dies, his successor, Rex II, has the power to make new laws, despite the absence of a habit on the part of the population to obey his every command. Rex II is still the king even without a track record. In order to explain Rex II's sovereignty, Hart argued that we needed to invoke the concept of a 'rule' that bestows authority on the

---

[8] See John Austin, 'Province of Jurisprudence Determined', Lecture vi.

office of the king. Rex II has the power he does because the rules confer it on him, just as they did to his father before him.[9]

Hart's achievement in *The Concept of Law* consisted not only in showing that Austin's cure was worse than the disease. He offered a solution to the chicken–egg problem that was so promising that it gave theorists reason to abandon the reductive positivistic paradigm. Indeed, Hart's genius was to show how legal authority was dependent on rules without resorting to the natural law and without generating vicious circles or infinite regresses.

B. Norm-governance and norm-guidance

To understand Hart's solution, we must first introduce some definitions and distinctions. By a 'norm', I will mean any standard that purports to regulate conduct. A standard purports to 'regulate' conduct whenever it purports either to permit, forbid, require, or empower certain action. Some norms are merely 'possible', others 'actual'. Before Prohibition, for example, the 'no-drinking' norm was merely a possible legal norm. During Prohibition it became an actual legal norm and, with the passage of the Twenty-First Amendment, it reverted back to a merely possible one.

Let us distinguish between two different kinds of behaviour. 'Norm-governed' behaviour is behaviour that is subject to the regulation of an actual norm, whether or not the behaviour conforms to the norm. Many New Yorkers jaywalk despite the fact that there are legal rules which forbid it. Crossing the street in New York, therefore, is behaviour that is norm-governed. 'Norm-guided' behaviour, on the other hand, is behaviour that conforms to a norm for the reason that the norm regulates the action in question. Many drivers, including New Yorkers, stop at red lights not only because they don't want to get tickets, but also because the traffic laws require them to do so. Stopping at red lights, therefore, is both norm-governed and norm-guided behaviour.

Some behaviour can be norm-governed without being norm-guided. If I jaywalk, then I have not conformed to the 'no-jaywalking' rule and hence do not guide my conduct by it. Similarly, if I refrain from jaywalking, not because the law forbids it, but because I judge that it is unsafe, then I also have not guided my behaviour by the norm even though I conform to it. Conversely, some behaviour can be norm-guided but not norm-governed. To be guided by a norm does not require that the norm exists. If I refrain from drinking because I forgot that Prohibition ended, then I am guiding my conduct by a possible, but not an actual, norm. I

---

[9] H. L. A. Hart, *The Concept of Law* (2nd edn., ed. Penelope A. Bullock and Joseph Raz, 1994), 50–61.

have therefore guided my behaviour by a norm that does not govern my behaviour.

Given this terminology, the chicken–egg problem can be redescribed in the following way. How is legal norm-governed behaviour possible? For a legal norm r_n to govern a situation, it has to be created by someone who is engaging in norm-governed behaviour. We might then ask who created the legal norm r_{n-1} that is to govern the creation of r_n? Surely not someone who is governed by r_n because r_n does not exist before r_{n-1} does. The only possible candidate is someone whose activities are governed by a legal norm r_{n-2}. But who created r_{n-2}?

Hart's attempt to stop this infinite regression was as simple as it was brilliant. In essence, he denied that all norm-governed behaviour is dependent on other *norm-governed* behaviour, arguing, instead, that all legal norm-governed behaviour is dependent on *norm-guided* behaviour. Legal rules come into existence by virtue of the fact that certain people accept certain standards of conduct as norms and guide their conduct accordingly.

According to Hart's solution, the foundation of all legal authority is social practice. The norms that create legal authority are themselves created by the fact that certain members of the group are guided by a rule that treats these norms as authoritative. The Constitution has the authority it claims because certain members of the population of the United States are guided by a master rule that imposes a duty on them to take constitutional claims seriously. The master rule itself, which Hart termed the 'rule of recognition', comes into existence simply in virtue of its being practised. It governs behaviour in virtue of its guiding behaviour.

In primitive legal systems, the rule of recognition may be widely practised by the members of the population. Rex II is the king because the population considers the son of Rex I to be the rightful successor. It is their practice of recognition, not Rex II's whip, which invests Rex II with legal authority. In modern systems, however, rules of recognition can be quite complex and typically do not guide the conduct of non-officials. Most American citizens, for example, have no idea what is contained in the US Constitution or in the rule of recognition which validates it.[10] The rule of recognition governs conduct in such systems because it guides the behaviour of its courts, not its citizens.[11]

Unlike the secondary rule of recognition, the primary rules of the system need not guide in order to govern. These norms may come into

---

[10] For a very illuminating discussion about the relationship between the US Constitution and the rule of recognition, see Kent Greenawalt, 'The Rule of Recognition and the Constitution', 85 Mich. L. Rev. 621 (1987).

[11] *Id.* at 113–16.

existence simply by being validated by the rule of recognition. They may govern behaviour, in other words, simply in virtue of their relationship to a rule that guides behaviour. Indeed, it is a defining feature of mature legal systems, as opposed to primitive pre-legal systems, that the primary legal norms need not be social norms. Jaywalking, as we mentioned, is prohibited by law in New York City even though nearly everyone ignores the rule.[12] It is a law because it is valid, not because it is practised.

Although Hart chose to locate the normative origins of law in the courts, instead of the law-making sovereign, his positivistic solution to the chicken–egg problem shares the same basic structure as Austin's. Like Austin, Hart believed that legal authority could be created *ex nihilo*, that is, in the absence of rules conferring it. It is not necessary for courts to be pre-authorized by some legal or moral rule to generate the secondary rules of the legal system. The courts have the power they do as a conceptual matter: it is part of our concept of a social rule that these rules govern conduct in a group because, and only because, members of that group guide their conduct accordingly. Because rules of recognition are social rules, courts are able to create such rules simply by engaging in a certain practice with the appropriate critical attitude.[13]

Hart's solution differs most dramatically from Austin's in that Hart did not attempt to reduce authority to coercive power. Courts are able to generate rules of recognition not because they are stronger than everyone else or because others habitually obey them. Their capacity to create the master rules of a legal system emanates from their capacity to guide their behaviour by a rule. It is the power over themselves, rather than over others, that grounds their authority.

It might be objected that Hart's account does not really solve the chicken–egg problem because his view privileges the role of legal officials, and courts in particular, in the creation of law. In modern legal systems, according to Hart, it is the courts that have the legal authority to create the rule of recognition. This authority seems to presuppose that certain legal rules exist antecedent to the rule of recognition and that confer the exclusive authority on the courts to create it.

---

[12] Hart insisted, nevertheless, that most of the primary rules of the legal system would have to be obeyed by most of the population most of the time if we were to say that such a community had a legal system. Legal systems must be generally, although not universally, efficacious. *Id.* at 103–4.

[13] To be precise, courts are not able to create rules of recognition *all by themselves*. Rules of recognition exist only when legal systems exist and legal systems exist only when certain conditions are met, i.e. other legal officials generally take the internal point of view towards the secondary rules and the population generally obeys the primary rules. What courts are able to do is to generate a social rule that impose obligations on themselves to apply certain rules that bear certain characteristics. However, this social rule is not a rule of recognition until all of the existence conditions for legal systems are met.

This objection assumes, however, that bodies are courts of a certain legal system only when some rule singles them out as the sole determiners of the system's criteria of validity. On the contrary, bodies are courts of a certain legal system because they generate and sustain that system's rule of recognition. We should not, therefore, confuse Hart's claim that courts have the authority to generate the rules of legal systems with the false claim that they have this authority *by virtue of their being the courts of those systems*. Once we have determined that certain bodies have created and sustained the secondary rules of a legal system, we can claim that those bodies *are* the courts of that system, for courts belong to a certain legal system when they have been successful in creating and sustaining its normative infrastructure.

C.   A problem with the solution

The idea that norm-governance is dependent on norm-guidance constituted a major breakthrough in analytical jurisprudence. It vindicated the law's claim to legal authority on terms acceptable to the positivist but without reducing legal authority to power relations. Hart pulled off this trick by arguing that certain legal rules are best understood as social rules and that members of a group always have the ability to generate social rules by engaging in practices with a certain attitude.

Because Hart's solution depends so heavily on his theory of social rules, his critics have sought to challenge the former by assailing the latter. Ronald Dworkin, for example, attacked Hart's claim that the existence of duty-imposing rules is dependent on rule-guided behaviour. In particular, he pointed out the oddity of thinking that all moral rules practised by a community are generated by that practice. This gets matters backwards: moral rules *guide* conduct because it is believed that such rules already *govern* conduct. The oddity is made even more apparent in situations involving moral rules that are not generally practised in a community. If Sheila the vegetarian believes that no one should eat meat, she need not believe that everyone else is a vegetarian. The fact that there is very little vegetarian rule-guided behaviour need not change her opinion that meat eating is a rule-governed behaviour.[14]

Of course, Dworkin was not simply content to show that some *moral* norm-governed behaviour is not dependent on norm-guided behaviour. After all, Hart's claim that moral rules are a species of social rules is not essential to his theory of law, and he eventually abandoned it in the Postscript.[15] Rather, Dworkin was more interested in demonstrating that at

---

[14] Ronald Dworkin, 'The Model of Rules II', in *Taking Rights Seriously* (1977), 52–3.
[15] Hart, *Concept of Law, supra* n. 9, at 256.

least some *legal* norm-governed behavior is not dependent on norm-guided behaviour. In his seminal articles 'The Model of Rules I' and 'The Model of Rules II', Dworkin claimed that some legal principles are treated by judges as legally binding despite the fact that they are not validated by the master rule of recognition. Some of the most important legal principles are not, and could not be, dependent on the reflected glory from the social rule of recognition. They possess their own intrinsic authority, and this explains why judges treat them as authoritative.

By arguing that a class of legal norms govern behaviour but are not ontologically dependent on norm-guided behaviour, Dworkin attempted to undermine Hart's solution to the chicken–egg problem. For Dworkin, legal authority is not the product of law itself, but of political morality. Dworkin parts company, however, with older natural law views by denying that the existence of moral rules depends on the actions of some extralegal legislator, be she divine or secular. Returning to the 'chicken–egg' metaphor for one last time, we might say that whereas Aquinas thought that there can be legal chickens without legal eggs, Dworkin thought that there can be legal eggs without legal chickens.

The debate between the Dworkinian and Hartian camps on these issues has been the story of analytical jurisprudence for the last thirty years. Some positivists have argued that moral principles can indeed be validated by the rule of recognition.[16] The criteria of legal validity embedded in the rule of recognition can make reference to moral criteria and can, therefore, validate Dworkinian legal principles. Others have accepted Dworkin's claim that the rule of recognition cannot validate moral principles that lack a social pedigree but have not been bothered by this limitation.[17] They point out that most legal principles in fact do have pedigrees and those that don't may still be legally binding on courts even though they are not law.

In the Postscript, Hart broke his long silence on these matters, accepting the first response. He saw no reason why the rule of recognition could not specify moral worth as a condition on legal validity.[18] Legal norm-governance would still be dependent on legal norm-guidance because, in those legal systems where legal principles are valid, there would exist a practice among judges to treat morally worthy principles as law. All legal norms would still ultimately be grounded in social practice.

In this matter, however, Hart uncharacteristically made the wrong choice. As I will argue, this brand of positivism is, in fact, inconsistent

---

[16] See e.g. Jules Coleman, 'Negative and Positive Positivism', in *Markets, Morals and the Law* (1982, 1988); David Lyons, 'Moral Aspects of Legal Theory', 7 Midwest Stud. Phil. 223 (1982); Wilfred Waluchow, *Inclusive Legal Positivism* (1994).

[17] See e.g. Joseph Raz, 'Legal Positivism and the Sources of Law', in *The Authority of Law* (1979); 'Authority, Law and Morality', in *Ethics in the Public Domain* (1994).

[18] Hart, *supra* n. 9, at 250.

with Hart's other views about the relation between norm-governed and norm-guided behaviour. Specifically, this way out offends his view that the primary function of the law is to guide conduct. In Hart's theory of law, norm-guidance is not simply the *efficient* cause of the law; it is also its *final* cause. I intend to show that any principle that satisfies a social rule of recognition simply by virtue of its moral content cannot guide conduct as a legal norm. If norm-governed behaviour is to result *from* rule-guided behaviour, it cannot result *in* norm-guided behaviour. Hart, therefore, is in a bind: he must either give up the idea that all legal norm-governance is dependent on norm-guidance or that all legal norms must be capable of guiding conduct. The only way he can preserve both theses, I will conclude, is to accept the second, rather than the first, response to Dworkin's challenge, i.e. to accept the idea that moral principles can be binding on judges even without being law.

II. THE MODEL OF RULES

A. Dworkin's positivism

In 'The Model of Rules I', Dworkin challenged the positivist contention that legal norm-governed behaviour is ultimately dependent on rule-guided behaviour. His strategy was to show that such a position can only be held on the pain of ignoring an important class of legal norms (i.e. legal principles). Legal principles do indeed generate legal obligations even though they are not themselves generated by rule-guided behaviour.

Dworkin characterized the core commitments of legal positivism by the following three theses:

(1) Pedigree Thesis: The law of a community ... can be identified and distinguished by specific criteria, by tests having to do not with their content but with their pedigree or the manner in which they were adopted or developed.
(2) Discretion Thesis: The set of these valid legal rules is exhaustive of 'the law', so that if someone's case is not clearly covered by such a rule (because there is none that seem appropriate, or those that seem appropriate are vague, or for some other reason) then that case cannot be decided by 'applying the law'. It must be decided by some official, like a judge, 'exercising his discretion'.
(3) Obligation Thesis: To say that someone has a 'legal obligation' is to say that his case falls under a valid legal rule that requires him to do or to forbear from doing something.[19]

---

[19] Ronald Dworkin, 'The Model of Rules I', in *Taking Rights Seriously*, supra n. 14, at 17.

The Pedigree Thesis requires that every valid law pass a test of legal recognition whose criteria of validity refer only to the law's pedigree (i.e. its manner of enactment). This master test may, for example, validate all norms that are issued by some agency or practised by some group in a community. It may not, however, distinguish norms based on their moral content. A test that validated norms because they are just or fair, or only if they are just or fair, would fail to be a positivistic rule of recognition, even if such a rule were practised by legal officials.

The Discretion Thesis states that, in the absence of legal rules, judges must exercise discretion in looking beyond the law. Whenever there is no applicable legal rule or the rule contains vague or ambiguous terms, judges have no choice but to fashion a new legal solution for the novel situation. While it may, in general, be good policy for unelected judges to apply the law instead of making it, sometimes there is simply no law to apply and judges must, of necessity, don the legislator's mantle if a decision is to be rendered.

It might be wondered why Dworkin claimed that the Discretion Thesis is a distinctively positivistic thesis, given that it seems virtually tautological: if there are no applicable legal rules, then there would appear to be no law for the judge to apply. The Discretion Thesis is trivial, however, only if one assumes that all legal norms are legal rules. As the title of his article suggests, Dworkin criticized positivists for making this very assumption, and argued that there was a substantial difference between norms that are 'rules' and those that are 'principles'.[20] Rules are 'all or nothing' standards that give agents conclusive reasons for action. When a valid rule applies in a given case, then that fact is dispositive and no argument for a different conclusion can be successful. Dworkin's examples of legal rules include the rule that valid wills need to be signed before two witnesses and that no one may drive over 55 miles per hour.

Principles, on the other hand, have a dimension of weight and give agents non-conclusive reasons for action. Valid principles, as opposed to valid rules, may conflict and their resolution is based on the aggregate weight of the principles on either side of the argument. Famous examples of principles include 'no man may profit from his own wrong' and 'courts should respect freedom of contract'.

Given this understanding of legal rules as distinct from legal principles, the Discretion Thesis holds that when the legal *rules* run out, so do the legal norms. It denies, in other words, that principles can ever count as legal principles. The Obligation Thesis is essentially a corollary of the Discretion Thesis: it denies that principles can ever generate legal obligations.

[20] *Id.* at 22–8.

B. The problem with principles

Dworkin began his critique by chastising positivists for equating legal norms with legal rules. Positivism is the 'model of rules' and, given its overly narrow conception of legal norms, it has failed to appreciate the prevalent role that legal principles play in adjudication. By rehearsing the courts' reasoning in famous common law cases such as *Riggs* v. *Palmer* and *Henningsen* v. *Bloomfield Motors, Inc.,* Dworkin set out to show that judges often apply moral principles in situations when the legal rules have run out. In *Riggs,* for example, Palmer poisoned his grandfather so as to prevent him from changing his will, according to which Palmer was the chief beneficiary, and then had the chutzpah to demand his share of the estate from the probate court. Palmer had the plain language of the New York statute of wills on his side. The rules did not make explicit exceptions for beneficiary-murderers and, therefore, seemed to uphold the validity of the bequest. However, despite the statute's plain language the majority of the Court of Appeals denied that the law should be construed literally. The majority opinion claimed that the rule, when properly read, did not cover such an unusual case and cited the principle that no man should profit from his wrongs in order to deny Palmer his share of his grandfather's estate.

While *Riggs* was certainly an extraordinary case given its bizarre origin, it was not unusual in its invocation of legal principles in order to resolve a difficult legal question. 'Once we identify legal principles as separate sorts of standards, different from legal rules, we are suddenly aware of them all around us.'[21] According to Dworkin, the positivistic inattentiveness to legal principles was not harmless and constituted reversible error: once their considerable presence in the law is recognized, the Discretion Thesis has to be abandoned. Even when the legal rules run out, it seems that judges are not free to legislate as they see fit, but are constrained by a whole constellation of legal principles. Hard cases are governed by law just as easy cases are.

Dworkin suggested two ways in which positivists might respond to the challenge posed by the existence of legal principles.[22] They might claim that these principles are extralegal and that when the rules run out, judges are free to look to these moral principles in order to decide the case at hand. Courts that resort to the same principles, therefore, are not 'really' legally obligated to do so; they just happen to choose, on average, the same extralegal principles when plugging up gaps in the law.

Alternatively, positivists might admit that these principles are indeed part of the law but argue that they can be validated by a social rule of

---

[21] *Id*. at 28.   [22] *Id*. at 29.

recognition. According to this approach, the reason that judges give applicable moral principles due weight in their deliberations is the same reason that they apply applicable legal rules—because they are valid law.

Dworkin argued, however, that the leak in the positivist ship could not be patched so easily. The first alternative is unsatisfactory because it does seem that judges are bound to apply these principles when the rules run out. The majority in *Riggs*, for instance, did not think that they had discretion whether to invalidate the will. Their dispute with the dissent was a disagreement over their legal obligations, for each thought that a different set of legal principles compelled a different legal conclusion.[23] To be sure, both sides had to exercise a weak form of discretion in interpreting the legal principles involved. But, as Dworkin pointed out, that is different from having the discretion whether to apply the legal principle at all to the case at hand. That judges have the discretion to ignore legal principles, Dworkin thought, is absurd on its face.

Positivists, it would seem, would have to argue that principles can be binding on judges by virtue of their validation by the rule of recognition. However, as Dworkin argued, positivists cannot take this route without offending the Pedigree Thesis, given that many legal principles are 'valid' simply by virtue of their content, not manner of enactment.

The origin of [the *Riggs* and *Henningsen* principles] as legal principles lies not in a particular decision of some legislature or court, but in a sense of appropriateness developed in the profession and the public over time. Their continued power depends upon this sense being sustained. If it no longer seemed unfair to allow people to profit by their wrongs, or fair to place special burdens upon oligopolies that manufacture potentially dangerous machines, these principles would no longer play much role in new cases, even if they had never been overruled or repealed.[24]

If a principle is made part of the law because, and only because, it is deemed morally worthy, then the rule of recognition can no longer validate solely on the basis of pedigree.

Dworkin did admit that legal principles have social pedigrees, for example, they are used in judicial opinions, the preamble of statutes, etc., and that establishing a given principle as legally binding normally requires one to cite to these pedigrees. He denied, however, that legal principles are legal norms *in virtue of* having these social pedigrees. Although Dworkin provided no evidence for this claim, he did argue that the positivist has no option but to accept his intuitions. He doubted, for example, that any rule of recognition could be fashioned that would be sensitive enough to pick out those principles based on their social source.

---

[23] *Id.* at 35.   [24] *Id.* at 40.

Even if such a rule could be constructed, he thought that the resulting rule would be so ungainly that it would no longer count as a (usable? useful?) conventional rule.

> We argue for a particular principle by grappling with a whole set of shifting, developing and interacting standards (themselves principles rather than rules) about institutional responsibility, statutory interpretation, the persuasive force of various sorts of precedent, the relation of all these to contemporary moral practices, and hosts of the other standards. We could not bolt all of these together into a single 'rule,' even a complex one, and if we could the result would bear little resemblance to Hart's picture of a rule of recognition, which is the picture of a fairly stable master rule specifying 'some feature or features possession of which by a suggested rule is taken as a conclusive affirmative indication that it is a rule'.[25]

If the above arguments are correct, then it would seem that Dworkin has proved that at least some legal norm-governed behaviour is not dependent on rule-guided behaviour. Legal principles are legal norms and they impose obligations even though all of them cannot be validated by a social rule of recognition. As with moral rule-governed behaviour, Hart's analysis of governance and guidance with respect to legal norms has the relationship between the two concepts backwards: legal principles guide behaviour because they are recognized as norms that govern behaviour.

In 'The Model of Rules I', it was unclear whether Dworkin meant only to challenge the positivistic picture as it applied to legal principles, conceding its truth with respect to legal rules, or whether he intended to attack positivism's treatment of all legal norms. In later writings it became evident that he saw the problem posed by legal principles as threatening the entire conventionalist foundations of positivism. Having established that *some* legal norms are not generated by rule-guided behaviour, Dworkin suggested that, at least in Anglo-American legal systems, *no* legal norm is generated by rule-guided behaviour. While he did not prove the latter claim, Dworkin certainly thought he gave the jurisprude strong reasons to give natural law theories another look. If conventions are sometimes superfluous in order to explain the possibility of legal authority, then maybe they are always superfluous. And if morality is sometimes needed to explain the possibility of legal authority, then maybe it is always needed.

III. WAYS OUT

One of the most effective ways of defending one's theory is to show that the theory criticized is not, in fact, one's theory. In responding to

---

[25] *Id.* citing Hart, *The Concept of Law, supra* n. 9, at 94.

Dworkin's challenge, such a strategy seems promising, given the lack of textual evidence suggesting that Hart held the views attributed to him by Dworkin. On the contrary, Hart seemed explicitly to deny the Pedigree Thesis. For example, he claimed that the ultimate criteria of legal validity may make reference to moral criteria. 'In some systems, as in the United States, the ultimate criteria of legal validity explicitly incorporate principles of justice or substantive moral values.'[26] This would seem to contradict the idea that a rule of recognition must validate legal rules based solely on their pedigree, rather than their content.

The Discretion Thesis sounds much more like something Hart would support. According to Hart's theory of law, when a case falls outside the core of' a legal rule, a judge has to reach beyond the law and exercise discretion.[27] However, what Hart meant by a rule was not what Dworkin took him to mean. For Hart, a rule is any normative standard that is capable of guiding conduct. Dworkin, as we have seen, took rules to be a specific type of norm, i.e. those that give agents conclusive reasons for action. There is no textual reason, however, to suppose that Hart meant to limit his theory to legal rules in Dworkin's sense. If a case fell outside the core of a legal rule, but within the core of a legal principle, Hart would probably have said that judges should be guided by that principle in their deliberations.

More disturbing still is the way in which Dworkin interpreted the positivistic conception of 'discretion' set out in the second thesis. As Dworkin noted, saying that judges exercise 'discretion' in the absence of legal rules is ambiguous.[28] An official might be said to have discretion in a given case if, for example, he or she has the final authority to decide the disposition of the case according to a set of rules. This form of discretion is weak because the rules are issued by those of superior authority and purport to control the official's conduct. A second weak sense of discretion, mentioned before, concerns the exercise of authority that requires judgment in deciding cases according to the rules. An official exercising this weak discretion must decide whether the rules apply, not whether to apply the rules. An official is exercising 'strong' discretion when the judge is not even required to apply applicable rules. Such an official is free to choose which extra-authoritative standards he or she will apply in the cases arising before the official.

Dworkin claimed that the concept of discretion used in the second thesis is of the strong variety. For positivists to say that judges sometimes exercise weak discretion when deciding cases would be to make

[26] Hart, *supra* n. 9, at 204.
[27] *Id*. at 141–7.
[28] Dworkin, 'The Model of Rules', *supra* n. 19, at 31–3.

an unremarkable claim, given that it is equivalent to saying that judges sometimes have the final authority to interpret rules or sometimes must exercise judgment when interpreting the rules. According to Dworkin, the distinctive claim made by positivists is that when the rules run out, judges are free to choose whichever standards they think are appropriate, consistent with the requirement that they act fairly and reasonably.[29]

To be sure, Hart did think that judges often have to reach beyond the law and choose those standards not set out by the authorities. But he nowhere said that judges are free to choose *whichever* standards they believe reasonable. Whether judges are legally obligated to apply certain types of extralegal standard—for example, moral, economic, aesthetic, etc.—or are left unconstrained in that choice is not an issue on which Hart took a stand.

Given these possible misattributions, it seems that the best option for Hart's supporters is to claim that Hart did not, or should not, hold one of the theses involved. One might reject, for example, the Pedigree Thesis and maintain that positivism places no substantive restrictions on the criteria of validity set out by the rule of recognition. Rules of recognition, in other words, may set out non-pedigree criteria of validity. The bindingness of principles in adjudication would be explained by the existence of a judicial convention to treat principles of morality as binding law in certain circumstances.

Alternatively, one might reject the Discretion Thesis and claim that judges do not have strong discretion when the rules run out. Judges, according to this account, are legally obligated to apply the principles of political morality in adjudication whenever applicable legal standards are absent. These principles would be legally binding on judges even though they are not law.

As we will see, Hart's supporters have split along these very lines. 'Inclusive' legal positivists accept Dworkin's assessment that moral principles can be law even without the right pedigree and, therefore, place no restrictions on the criteria of legality. 'Exclusive' legal positivists, on the other hand, reject Dworkin's contention that moral principles can be incorporated into law without social pedigrees and thus require the rule of recognition to set out non-evaluative criteria of legality. They do not deny, however, that judges can be obligated to apply moral principles, only that their being obligated to do so does not entail that such principles are law.

In the next several sections, I will discuss the inclusive positivist counter to Dworkin's challenge. As it turns out, Hart eventually endorsed this basic manoeuvre in the Postscript to his book. I will attempt to show,

---

[29] *Id.* at 34.

however, that such a response is not available to Hart if he wishes to remain faithful to his other views about the nature of the law.

IV. SOCIAL RULES AND SOCIAL CRITERIA OF LEGALITY

At first glance, the simplest solution to Dworkin's challenge is for the positivist to reject the Pedigree Thesis. There is no reason, one might think, for the positivist to insist that the rule of recognition condition legality on the manner of a rule's enactment. As long as judges treat moral principles as law, they are law.[30]

The key distinction drawn by this response is between the existence conditions for the rule of recognition and the nature of the criteria of legality it sets out. The positivist idea that law is a product of social convention is expressed through its commitment to a 'social' rule of recognition. The rule of recognition comes into existence by virtue of a practice among legal officials to treat norms of a certain type as binding on them. The idea that the foundation of law is conventional, however, does not pose any constraints on the criteria of validity. Whether these criteria refer to a norm's pedigree or to its content is simply irrelevant to the positivist. All law can be considered positive law as long as the rule of recognition is a social rule.

While this response seems promising, it is seriously inadequate as it stands. As Dworkin argued in 'The Model of Rules II', positivists could not maintain that the rule of recognition requires judges to resolve hard cases by resorting to moral principles and still claim that the rule of recognition is a social rule.[31] Hard cases are hard precisely because no practice has developed for dealing with such cases. If such practices existed, these would be easy cases.

In *Riggs*, for example, the court was divided on whether to invalidate the will or let it stand. The dissent relied on the principle that the literal meaning of the statute should always control absent some clear legislative intention to the contrary, while the majority thought that literal interpretations should be avoided when absurd consequences follow. How, Dworkin wondered, could positivists point to a convention to treat certain principles as law in order to explain the bindingness of principles in cases like *Riggs*, when judges on that very court disagreed about which principles were appropriate to apply? Disputed conventions are simply

---

[30] For this type of response, see Philip Soper, 'Legal Theory and the Obligation of a Judge: The Hart/Dworkin Dispute', 75 Mich. L. Rev. 473 (1977); David Lyons, 'Principles, Positivism and Legal Theory', 87 Yale LJ 415 (1977); Coleman, 'Negative and Positive Positivism', *supra* n. 16.

[31] Dworkin, 'The Model of Rules II', *supra* n. 14.

not conventions. The rule of recognition could not require judges to look toward moral principles to resolve hard cases and still be a social rule.

In his 'Negative and Positive Positivism', Jules Coleman showed how positivists could get around this problem.[32] Coleman distinguished between two types of disagreement. The first type involves disputes over the content of the rule of recognition. Some courts might, for example, argue that the rule of recognition validates custom, while others might deny it. Let us call disagreements of this sort 'content disputes'. By contrast, certain disagreements presuppose consensus about the content of a rule, but involve disputes about its implementation. Courts might agree that custom is binding law, but disagree about whether some behaviour should count as the custom of the community. Let us call these types of disagreement 'application disputes'.

Coleman suggested that we see hard cases as involving application disputes. In situations where the legal rules have run out, there exists an accepted convention among judges to look toward the principles of morality to resolve legal disputes. When judges disagree about which principles to apply, they are disagreeing over the correct application of the rule of recognition. Hard cases are hard not because judges disagree about the content of the rule of recognition. For if these disagreements were about the nature of the fundamental law-making conventions, then resolving such controversies would not just be hard—they would be impossible. According to Coleman, hard cases are hard because questions about the correct application of the rule of recognition are hard questions. All judges agree, in other words, that the rule of recognition requires them to look toward moral principles in adjudication, thereby making those moral principles valid law. They simply disagree about what counts as a true moral principle.

Coleman's ingenious attempt to respond to Dworkin, however, does not go far enough. It does not show how, in controversial cases, a convention can exist requiring judges to apply moral principles. It merely shows that in controversial cases, judges can all be *committed* to the same rule, not that they can be *guided* by the same rule, given that guidance by a rule presupposes at least a high degree of conformity. In hard cases, it is not clear whether we can say that there has been conformity to the rule of recognition—and hence whether a convention has formed—only that there has been a concerted effort by all parties involved to try to conform to it.

What Coleman must say, therefore, is that in systems that have non-pedigree rules of recognition, most courts actually succeed in applying true moral principles when resolving hard cases. While it may be difficult to say in any hard case whether the court acted correctly, it must be true

---

[32] Coleman, 'Negative and Positive Positivism', *supra* n. 16, at 20.

that over the range of hard cases, courts generally have acted correctly. Substantial controversy about the correct application of the rule of recognition must be local, not global.

In his Postscript to *The Concept of Law,* Hart endorsed Coleman's position. First, Hart rejected Dworkin's contention that positivism is committed to the Pedigree Thesis. 'In addition to such pedigree matters the rule of recognition may supply tests relating not to the factual content of laws but to their conformity with substantive moral values or principles.'[33] Second, Hart dismissed Dworkin's inference that controversy entails the absence of a convention. 'Judges may be agreed on the relevance of such tests as something settled by established judicial practice even though they disagree as to what the tests require in particular cases.'[34]

V. THE COUNTER-COUNTER RESPONSE

Dworkin responded to Coleman by arguing that the distinction between the two types of disagreement is 'doubtful'.[35] If such a distinction were sound, then every judicial dispute could be described as a disagreement about application. Dworkin, for example, wondered whether constitutional controversies about the proper role of judges could be spun by a positivist as agreements 'on a more abstract convention to the effect that judges have all but only the powers given to them by the best interpretation of the constitution', but disagreements 'about whether it follows from that more abstract convention that they have the particular power in question'.[36] If so, then the positivistic commitment to the existence of a social rule of recognition would amount to nothing more than the claim that 'in every legal system officials accept the requirement that they must make their decisions about the law in the way such decisions ought to be made'.[37] Such conventions are trivial and unworthy of the pride of place positivists give to the rule of recognition.

Dworkin's response, however, is not persuasive. One cannot impugn a distinction between types of description simply because one could describe an object using either description. The question is not whether one *could,* but whether one *should.* One could, I suppose, characterize any rule-guided behaviour as a habit without doing extreme violence to the phenomenon, yet that would not mean that such a description would be apt. Likewise, the fact that a positivist may treat some judicial disagreements about moral principles as involving application disputes does not

---

[33] Hart, *supra* n. 9, at 258. [34] *Id.* at 258–9.
[35] Ronald Dworkin, 'A Reply by Ronald Dworkin', in *Ronald Dworkin and Contemporary Jurisprudence* (ed. Marshall Cohen, 1984), 252.
[36] *Id.* at 253. [37] *Id.*

mean that they believe every dispute should be viewed in this way. For example, it would be very difficult to interpret *Marbury* v. *Madison*[38] as an application dispute. In *Marbury*, Chief Justice Marshall held that the Constitution conferred upon the federal courts the right of judicial review. Because this was a case of first impression, there had been no practice established with respect to the foundational issue in question. As Hart famously argued, in many high-level controversies we must see judicial behaviour as extending the rule of recognition, not applying it. In these completely unregulated cases, 'all that succeeds is success'.[39]

There is another way to understand Dworkin's complaint. He may have been worried that utilizing the distinction between content disputes and application disputes would be non-falsifiable in adjudicative contexts. Because 'neither their judicial nor their linguistic behavior would force us to choose one way rather than another of these descriptions',[40] it is begging the question in favour of positivism to privilege certain descriptions over others. Positivism could never be refuted if positivists had free rein to characterize any alleged unconventional behaviour as involving innocuous disputes about application.

It is not clear, however, why it is legitimate for Dworkin to choose the type of description that paints positivism in its worst light, but illegitimate for Coleman to choose the type of description that portrays positivism in its best light. If there is truly no way to tell which description is appropriate, then why assume that the appropriate description precludes treating the rule of recognition as a social rule? The underdetermination would seem to cut both ways: if there is no evidence to support either description, this would imply that the phenomena of hard cases cannot be used as leverage against positivism. The only way to decide which description is most apt would be to resort to theoretical considerations— which is precisely what Coleman and Hart do.

We should remind ourselves what these theoretical considerations are. The inclusive legal positivist's claim that hard cases be understood as application disputes was made in response to Dworkin's challenge. Dworkin charged that legal norm-governed behaviour could not depend on norm-guided behaviour because some legal norms (i.e. legal principles) are valid in virtue of their content, not pedigree. They guide conduct because they are believed to govern conduct, rather than the other way round. When positivists responded by claiming that, in hard cases, rules of recognition can validate norms based on their content, Dworkin

---

[38] *Marbury* v. *Madison*, 1 Cranch 137, 2 L.Ed. 60 (1803).
[39] Hart, *supra* n. 9, at 153.
[40] Dworkin, *supra* n. 35.

countered that such rules of recognition would cease to be social rules. Hard cases involve controversy and controversy precludes conventionality. If legal norms governed behaviour in hard cases, it could not be in virtue of their relation to norm-guided behaviour.

By arguing that hard cases involve application disputes, Coleman was able to save Hart's idea that norm-governed behaviour is ultimately dependent on norm-guided behaviour. Controversy precludes conventionality, Coleman pointed out, only when the disputes involve the content of a social norm, not its applicability. Hard cases may indeed involve norm-guided behaviour, just in case the controversy involves the application of the social rule of recognition.

Unless Dworkin produces evidence tending to falsify Coleman's characterization of hard cases, it does not seem to me to be necessary for Coleman to produce evidence tending to substantiate it. What does matter in this debate is (1) whether Coleman has sufficient grounds for believing that Hart's solution is the correct one to the chicken–egg problem and (2) whether his proposed account of hard cases answers Dworkin's challenge in a theoretically satisfying manner—that is, it is simple, consistent, elegant, etc.

I will leave this defence to Coleman.[41] What I would like to discuss, however, is whether Hart can help himself to Coleman's way out. As I will argue, he cannot.

VI. GUIDANCE OF CONDUCT

Although I do not think that Dworkin's arguments against Coleman are persuasive, I do share his scepticism about inclusive rules of recognition. There is something a bit fishy about these social norms: they seem to satisfy positivistic requirements in a purely formalistic way. As I will argue, the critical problem with inclusive rules of recognition is not that their guidance is too *weak*; rather, their guidance is too *strong*. For I intend to show that if an agent is guided by an inclusive rule of recognition, then he cannot be guided by the moral principles supposedly validated by it.

This result is damaging for Hart because he has always claimed that the essence of law is the guidance of conduct. If moral principles that have no direct pedigree cannot guide conduct in the face of guidance by the rule of recognition, then these primary norms cannot serve their essential function. The problem with Dworkin's attack on inclusive positivism is that

---

[41] See Jules L. Coleman, 'Incorporationism, Conventionality, and the Practical Difference Thesis', this volume.

he focused on the *ontological*, and ignored the *functional*, dependence of norm-governance on norm-guidance. Norm-governed behaviour is not merely supposed to result *from* norm-guided behaviour but is supposed to result *in* norm-guided behaviour. The fatal flaw of inclusive legal positivism, I will argue, is that norms that lack pedigrees cannot guide conduct if they are the product of norms which themselves guide conduct.

A. The function of law

In later writings, Dworkin's attack on positivism took another form. In *Law's Empire*, Dworkin tested all jurisprudential theories by their ability to justify state coercion.[42] With respect to positivism, or as Dworkin called it 'conventionalism', past political acts justify state coercion because fair warning has been given by the relevant social conventions.[43] Laws are based on 'plain social facts' established by convention because, in so being, legal officials will not unfairly surprise individuals through the exercise of their power. Conventionalism is the 'ideal of protected expectations'.[44]

After having characterized positivism as an interpretive theory, Dworkin went on to complain that the conventionalist's exclusive concern with protecting expectations is unjustified. The only time it would be unfair to upset expectations is when legal officials encourage citizens to rely on certain social conventions and then thwart the expectations they themselves deliberately induce. As Dworkin pointed out, it begs the question to argue for the conventionality of law based on the unfairness of upsetting settled expectations: if the law were independent of social convention, then it would not be unfair to upset expectations based on those practices, because those expectations would not be justified.[45]

In his Postscript, Hart rejected the suggestion that conventionalism is a plausible construal of his theory. First, he denied ever having endorsed the interpretivist idea that law should be identified as the set of rules which would justify state coercion. Second, he thought that 'thick' concepts of law such as Dworkin's could not serve as a basis for a general jurisprudence: the only function that all law can be said to satisfy, according to Hart, is that it seeks to guide human conduct. 'I think it quite vain to seek any more specific purpose which law as such serves beyond providing guides to human conduct and standards of criticism of such conduct.'[46]

In this instance, Hart actually misread Dworkin. Dworkin offered

---

[42] See e.g. *Law's Empire* (1986), 96.   [43] *Id.*, ch. 4.
[44] *Id.* at 117.   [45] *Id.* at 140–2.
[46] Hart, *supra* n. 9, at 249.

conventionalism not as a construal of what positivism is, but what it ought to be. Conventionalism was supposed to capture the appeal of positivism—to show it in its best light—without suffering the dreaded 'semantic sting'.[47] It was, therefore, unfair of Hart to accuse Dworkin of misunderstanding his methodological commitments when Dworkin intentionally reconstructed positivism on grounds that he knew Hart rejected.

Hart's mistake, however, was not merely hermeneutical. According to Hart's response, a positivist did not have to show that his theory of law provides a moral justification for state coercion. He need only show that his theory is consistent with the guidance function that every legal system necessarily must serve. Hart clearly thought that his theory met this test. Indeed, *The Concept of Law* is replete with arguments showing why the accounts of his predecessors, such as Hans Kelsen and Alf Ross, failed to show that the law can guide conduct and that his theory could.[48]

Nevertheless, I would like to argue that Hart's version of positivism itself fails to satisfy this necessary condition. If a judge is guided by a rule of recognition that validates certain norms based on moral criteria, those norms that pass such a test will not be able to guide conduct. To demonstrate this, however, we need to have a much better understanding of what Hart meant by his claim that the function of law is the 'guidance of conduct'.

B. Two concepts of guidance

Despite the obviously important role that the notion of guidance plays in *The Concept of Law,* Hart never actually specified what he meant by it. We are, therefore, left to piece together his intentions from his various pronouncements on the subject of rules and guidance. A promising place to begin is with his seminal discussion of the 'internal point of view'.[49]

As already mentioned, Hart believed that social rules come into existence whenever members of the group conform to patterns of behaviour with a certain critical attitude. Hart dubbed this attitude 'the internal point of view'. Members take the internal point of view when they regard the rules as legitimate standards of public behaviour. These attitudes manifest themselves not only in conformity to the rules, but also in the criticism of those who deviate from the established pattern. To take the

---

[47] Dworkin, *supra* n. 42, at 45–6. See also Joseph Raz's contribution to the symposium.

[48] See e.g. Scott J. Shapiro, 'The Bad Man and the Internal Point of View', in *The Legacy of Oliver Wendell Holmes, Jr.: 'The Path of the Law' and Its Influence* (ed. Steven J. Burton, 2000).

[49] Hart, *supra* n. 9, at 55–7.

internal point of view toward a social rule is to judge that everyone has good reasons for following the rule, whatever those reasons may be.[50]

Hart deployed the concept of 'the internal point of view' for several different purposes. He used it, first, to define the existence conditions for social rules and, in turn, legal rules. He also used it to explicate the concept of 'rule acceptance'. People accept a social rule whenever they take the internal point of view toward that rule.

Accepting a rule, however, does not imply that one is guided by it. I am not now guided by the rule not to murder because I have no inclination to kill anyone. I do not murder *because* of the rule, although I think that the rule is a reason to refrain from so acting. One suggestion might be that Hart thought of 'rule-guidance' as rule-conformity which arises out of rule-acceptance: people are guided by a social rule whenever they take the internal point of view toward that rule and conform to the rule because they take the internal point of view. While I am not guided by the rule prohibiting murder, I am guided by the rule to pay my taxes because I accept that rule and my conformity is motivated by that acceptance.

If we interpret Hart's notion of guidance along the lines just suggested, however, we run into a major difficulty. We would have to take Hart to mean that the essential function of law is to ensure that ordinary citizens adopt the internal point of view toward its rules. But why should we think it essential that the law care about the motivations of its citizenry? To be sure, legal officials must be concerned about the reasons why their colleagues conform to the law, insofar as the rule of recognition can only arise when they take the internal point of view toward it. However, it seems entirely possible for these officials to be unconcerned with the reasons why citizens obey the law—as long as they obey the law. Even if one believes, as Aristotle did, that a good government should promote virtue, it surely is not a conceptual truth about all legal systems that the state must undertake such a task.

These difficulties arise, I believe, because the concept of 'rule-guidance' is ambiguous. To be guided by a rule is to conform to the rule for the reason that the rule regulates one's conduct. However, a rule can give someone a reason to act in at least one of two ways. The rule can motivate action simply in virtue of the fact that the rule regulates the action in question. Or it can inform the person of the existence of certain demands made by those in authority and, as a result, that conformity is advisable.

---

[50] It is a mistake, therefore, to interpret Hart as meaning that someone takes the internal point of view toward a rule whenever the person believes that the norm imposes a moral or social obligation to obey. See e.g. Fred Schauer, 'Critical Notice of Roger Shiner's Norm and Nature: The Movement of Legal Thought', 24 Canadian J. Phil. 495, 501–2. Hart is explicit that a person can accept the law and guide his conduct accordingly even if his allegiance is based on self-interested considerations. See e.g. Hart, *supra* n. 9, at 198.

The first alternative we might call 'motivational guidance'. Someone is motivationally guided by a legal rule when his or her conformity is motivated by the fact that the rule regulates the conduct in question. Our suggestion was that Hart characterized the relevant notion of motivation using the internal point of view. To be motivated to conform to a legal rule by the rule itself is to believe that the rule is a legitimate standard of conduct and to act on belief.

The second alternative we can call 'epistemic guidance'. A person is epistemically guided by a legal rule when he learns of his legal obligations from the rule provided by those in authority and conforms to the rule. Notice that it is not necessary that the agent be motivated to follow the rule *because* of the rule. A rule can epistemically guide conduct even though compliance is motivated by the threat of sanctions, just in case the person learns from the rule what he must do in order to avoid being punished.

Legal rules serve two important epistemic functions. As Hart explained, one of the distinctive features of law as a method of social control is that its demands are not communicated from legal official to citizen in a 'face-to-face' manner. Ordinary citizens are charged with learning what the law requires of them by using the rules provided and applying the rules themselves.

[T]he characteristic technique of the criminal law is to designate by rules certain types of behaviour as standards for the guidance either of members of society as a whole or of special classes within it: they are expected without the aid or intervention of officials (1) to understand the rules and to see that the rules apply to them and (2) to conform to them.[51]

Legal rules guide conduct, therefore, by serving as intermediaries between officials and non-officials. They allow legal officials to communicate their demands to many more people in many more situations than they would be able to do were officials restricted to direct face-to-face commands.

Legal rules not only obviate the need for officials to personalize their norms for each individual occasion but also eliminate the need for non-officials to solve every normative problem by themselves. Given the myriad of norms that might compete for our allegience, the law designates certain rules as those to which we are required to conform. Indeed, as Hart has explained, legal systems arose in order to remedy the deficiencies inherent to social systems that do not perform such 'designation' functions. In simple regimes of primary social norms, for example, there is no way of resolving societal controversies regarding obligatory behaviour. If

---

[51] Hart, *supra* n. 9, at 38–9 (numbers added).

no practice has formed regarding a certain standard, or it has begun to degenerate, then individuals have no way to determine whether such a practice should emerge or be maintained.

> It is plain that only a small community closely knit by ties of kinship, common sentiment, and belief, and placed in a stable environment, could live successfully by such a regime of unofficial rules. In any other conditions such a simple form of social control must prove defective. . . . Hence if doubts arise as to what the rules are or as to the precise scope of some given rule, there will be no procedure for settling this doubt.[52]

As groups expand and become more heterogeneous, they acquire the need to be able to distinguish between competing standards of conduct. Legal systems address this need by designating certain norms as 'authoritative'. These norms need not be practised in order to exist—they merely need to bear the mark set out by the system's rule of recognition. Legal rules, therefore, are able to inform people which actions have been designated as obligatory in virtue of their bearing the mark of authority.

   We might say that when legal norms epistemically guide, they mediate in two different senses. First, legal norms mediate between officials and non-officials. *Qua* rules, they eliminate the need for officials to issue particularized orders. Second, legal norms mediate between rival standards of conduct. *Qua* law, they eliminate the problems that arise when non-officials must answer all normative questions and resolve all social controversies by themselves.

   To be guided by a legal rule in an epistemic fashion, therefore, is to learn of one's legal obligations from the rule and to conform to the rule because of that knowledge. It does not imply that one is motivated because of the rule. As mentioned, it is perfectly consistent to claim that someone is epistemically guided by a legal rule but conformed because he or she wanted to avoid the sanctions that would follow from disobedience.

   If we take Hart's claims regarding the essential function of law to be about epistemic guidance, then the difficulty we encountered earlier disappears. According to the 'epistemic' reading, the primary function of the law is to provide rules so that citizens may determine which standards of conduct the law deems legitimate. It does not consist in convincing ordinary citizens to take the internal point of view. As long as its citizens learn what is expected of them and act accordingly, the law need not concern itself with the reasons why they act accordingly.

   While Hart thought that the primary function of the law is the epistemic guidance of ordinary citizens, this cannot be true for legal officials.

---

[52] *Id.* at 92.

The rule of recognition, after all, must motivationally guide the conduct of judges.

Individual courts of the system, though they may, on occasion, deviate from these rules must, in general, be critically concerned with such deviations as lapses from standards, which are essentially common or public. This is not merely a matter of the efficiency or health of the legal system, but is logically a necessary condition of our ability to speak of the existence of a single system. If only some judges acted 'for their part only' on the footing that what the Queen in parliament enacts is law, and made no criticisms of those who did not respect this rule of recognition, the characteristic unity and continuity of a legal system would disappear. For this depends on the acceptance, at this crucial point, of common standards of conduct.[53]

We see that Hart actually operated with two different concepts of guidance, one epistemic, the other motivational. His claim about the guidance function of the law, therefore, turns out to be a composite claim: the law's primary function is to epistemically guide the conduct of its ordinary citizens via its primary rules and to motivationally guide the conduct of judicial officials via its secondary rules.

C. Peremptory and content-independent reasons

In later writings, Hart substantially modified his account of motivational guidance. In his *Essays on Bentham*, he claimed that people are guided by legal rules whenever they treat these rules as 'content-independent' and 'peremptory' reasons for action.[54] A reason is content-independent if the validity of the reason is independent of the validity of its content. If, for example, Able asks Baker to help him with his homework, Able's request gives Baker a reason to act that is independent of whether Baker ought to help Able. It is the fact *that* Able asked, rather than *what* he asked, which gives Able a reason to act. Requests, therefore, are content-independent reasons for action. Likewise, rules are content-independent reasons in that agents who are committed to the rule try to conform simply because the rule regulates the action in question.

Requests and rules differ from one another, however, in that the content of a request is relevant to whether a request ought to be granted, whereas the content of a rule is strictly irrelevant to whether the rule ought to guide conduct. If Able is simply being lazy and is undeserving of help, Baker should not grant his request. Although his request is a reason, it is just not a very good reason. By contrast, someone who is

---

[53] *Id.* at 116.
[54] Hart, 'Commands and Authoritative Reasons', in Essays on Bentham, *supra* n. 23, at 253.

committed to a rule will try to follow that rule irrespective of whether he agrees with its recommendation. In Hart's terminology, rules are 'peremptory' reasons for action, i.e. reasons not to deliberate on the merits of the case at hand. When someone who is guided by a legal rule is confronted with a situation where the rule applies, that person does not deliberate about whether to follow the rule—he or she simply follows the rule.

This account of rule-guided behaviour solves a major problem of the previous analysis. That analysis did not distinguish between acting on a rule and acting on a generalized normative judgment. If a third baseman draws near when he suspects a bunt, he may think that he is acting as all third basemen should, and do, act in such a situation. In Hart's sense, he would be taking the internal point of view toward that practice. He might even infer from his belief that all third basemen should act this way to the belief that he should so act. However, in reasoning in this way, he would not necessarily be acting on a rule. He would be doing what he thinks he generally ought to do, which is not the same thing as being guided by a rule.

Rules differ from generalized normative judgments in two respects. First, rules are content-independent reasons, whereas generalized normative judgments are not. The validity of a generalized normative judgment is strictly a function of its content. If a third baseman had any reason to doubt whether he should draw near when a bunt is suspected, he would *ipso facto* have a reason to doubt whether his judgment should be followed.

Second, for rules to guide conduct, they must be capable of making 'practical differences', i.e. they must be capable of motivating agents to act differently from how they might have without their guidance. The general belief that all third basemen should draw near when a bunt is suspected does not make a practical difference. For even if the third baseman did not act on this general belief, he would still end up being motivated to draw near, given that he knows that he should draw near in this particular case. Indeed, Hart himself recognized that obedience to legal rules presupposes that such rules must be capable of making practical differences. He argued, for example, that Austin's reduction of obedience to habits ignored the fact that obedience is present in precisely those situations where habits are absent. 'What, for example, is the relevance of the fact, when it is a fact, that the person ordered would certainly have done the very same thing without any order? These difficulties are particularly acute in the case of laws, some of which prohibit people from doing things which many of them would never think of doing.'[55] Obedience only

---

[55] Hart, *supra* n. 9, at 51.

makes sense when the person obeying the rules might have acted differently if he did not think that he was obligated to comply.

When rules are seen as peremptory reasons, it follows that people can take them in these ways only when they believe the rules are capable of making practical differences. For if rules gave the same answers as deliberation on the merits, agents would never believe themselves to have reasons not to deliberate about a rule's recommendation. Hart's new account thereby ensures that a person can only be guided by a rule when he or she believes that the rule is capable of making a practical difference.

We might say that Hart's account of rules as content-independent and as peremptory reasons for action is a refinement on his earlier account of guidance as conformity motivated by the internal point of view. The critical attitude necessary for rule-guidance amounts to more than just accepting the rule as a legitimate standard of conduct. To be guided by a rule requires that the person treat the standard as a reason to conform (1) because the rule regulates the action in question and (2) as a reason not to deliberate. 'The judges not only follow [the rule of recognition] as each case arises, but are committed in advance in the sense that they have a settled disposition to do this without considering the merits of so doing in each case and indeed would regard it not open to them to act on their view of the merits.'[56]

VII. THE CENTRALITY OF RULE-GUIDANCE

A. The impossibility of inclusive guidance

Now that we have a better sense of what Hart meant by rule-guidance, we can revisit the question of whether Hart's embrace of inclusive legal positivism is consistent with his views about the essential guidance function of law. It should be immediately clear that the answer must be 'no' if we consider epistemic guidance. According to this conception of guidance, the primary function of the law is to designate certain standards of conduct as legitimate. It is hard to see, however, how the law can serve this function with respect to rules that are valid in virtue of their moral content. Telling people that they should act on the rules that they should act on is not telling them anything! Marks of authority are supposed to eliminate the problems associated with people distinguishing for themselves between legitimate and illegitimate norms. However, a mark that can be identified only by resolving the very question that the mark is supposed to resolve is useless. A norm that bears such a trivial mark,

---

[56] Hart, *Essays on Bentham, supra* n. 2, at 158–9.

therefore, is unable to discharge its epistemic duties.[57] In this respect, systems with inclusive rules of recognition are no advance over regimes of primary rules: people are left to discover which rules they ought to apply rather than being able to rely on the mediating role of authorities.

It is surely an unwelcome implication of Hart's theory that it admits of legal rules that are incapable of fulfilling their function with respect to ordinary citizens. Yet, such a result is not as bad as it may seem. It is still possible for moral rules that are valid in virtue of their content to guide judges in court even though they cannot guide ordinary citizens out of court. And to some extent, this possibility is more important to inclusive legal positivism, because Dworkin's challenge concerned the nature of *judicial* obligation. Dworkin claimed that the court in *Riggs* felt obligated to apply rules that were valid in virtue of their content. To answer this objection, Hart does not need to show that these rules must be capable of guiding Palmer—he must show how they can guide the court.

According to our first argument, however, we know that such rules cannot epistemically guide judges in adjudication. Inclusive rules of recognition[58] do not tell judges which moral rules they should apply— they simply tell judges to apply moral rules. These rules cannot give epistemic guidance because judges are left to figure out for themselves what these rules are. Vis-à-vis such rules, they are like ordinary citizens.

I am not sure, however, whether Hart need be concerned with this result either. When he claimed that rules of recognition must motivationally guide courts, I think he intended to claim that the primary rules must, at the very least, motivationally guide them as well. If a judge is motivated to act on a rule about a rule, then it would seem that the judge would be motivated to act on the underlying rule itself.

Accordingly, we should ask whether it is possible for judges to be motivationally guided by these moral rules in adjudication. Unfortunately for Hart, the answer is still 'no'. To see this we must recall that in order for a rule to be capable of guiding conduct, it must be capable of making a practical difference. To know whether a rule makes a practical difference, we must consider what would happen if the agent did not appeal to the rule. The rule makes a difference to one's practical reasoning only if, in this counterfactual circumstance, the agent might not conform to the rule. If, on the other hand, the agent were fated to conform to the rule even though he or she did not appeal to it, we would have to conclude that the

---

[57] This argument has much in common with Joseph Raz's critique of inclusive legal positivism. See e.g. Raz, *Ethics in the Public Domain, supra* n. 17. The arguments are not the same, however, insofar as they use different concepts of 'mediation'. For Raz, rules mediate between reasons and people, not between competing standards of conduct.

[58] To be precise, the problems associated with inclusive rules of recognition apply only to their inclusive parts. Inclusive rules can contain pedigree criteria of validity as well.

rule does not make a practical difference. What can be shown is that if a judge guided his or her conduct by the inclusive rule of recognition, then that judge would act in conformity to any valid rule even if he or she never appealed to such a rule.

Consider, therefore, the following inclusive rule of recognition: 'In hard cases, act according to the principles of morality.' In *Riggs*, judges guided by this inclusive rule of recognition would conform with the principles of morality when deciding whether to invalidate the will. Let us further assume that the only relevant principle of morality is that people should not profit from their own wrongs and that the majority in that case believed this to be so. A judge guided by the rule of recognition, therefore, would invalidate the will.

It follows, I think, that the principle that no man may profit from his wrong cannot itself make a practical difference as a legal norm. For if the judge were guided by the inclusive rule of recognition, but did not appeal to the moral principle, he or she would still end up invalidating the will. Let us imagine, for example, that in an effort to conform to the inclusive rule of recognition, the judge consults a very wise rabbi about what justice requires in this case. Because the rabbi will appeal to the principle that no person should profit from his own wrong, he will tell the judge that Palmer must lose. The moral principle, therefore, can make no practical difference once the rule of recognition makes a practical difference, because the judge will act in exactly the same way whether he or she personally consults the moral principle or not. Guidance by the inclusive rule of recognition by *itself* is always sufficient to give the judge the right legal answer.

This poses a serious problem for Hart: the rule of recognition is supposed to create the possibility of legally authoritative guidance. However, guidance by an inclusive rule of recognition actually has the opposite effect—it precludes the possibility that the primary rules can guide anyone's conduct. For once the judge is guided by an inclusive rule of recognition, the rules supposedly validated by it can no longer make a practical difference.

It should be said that there is a sense in which the moral principle that no person should profit from his or her own wrongdoing can guide the judge in adjudication. It can help him figure out what the *secondary* rule of recognition requires. It cannot guide conduct, however, as a *primary* legal norm. To guide as a primary legal norm it must guide either epistemically or motivationally. It cannot guide epistemically because, as we have seen, rules valid in virtue of their moral content cannot help anyone discriminate between legitimate and illegitimate standards of conduct. It does not guide motivationally because, by hypothesis, the judge is simply using it to figure out what the rule of recognition requires, not following it because it is required by the rule of recognition.

It would seem, therefore, that moral rules that are valid in virtue of their content cannot perform any of their essential functions. They can guide the conduct neither of ordinary citizens nor of judges.

B. The possibility of exclusive guidance

Exclusive legal positivists insist on pedigree, or source-based, criteria of legality. Unenacted or unpractised moral rules may never be regarded as legal rules in any legal system. This austere position should seem more understandable in light of the problems we have seen with inclusive legal positivism. Most obviously, legal rules that have social sources can epistemically guide conduct. Simply by identifying a legal norm's pedigree, ordinary citizens are able to discriminate which standards of conduct the law has designated as legitimate.

It is also the case that rules validated by an 'exclusive' rule of recognition can motivationally guide conduct at the same time that the rule of recognition motivationally guides conduct. For example, consider the following rule of recognition: 'Act according to all of the rules passed by Congress.' Let us say that the legislature passes a law requiring everyone to pay 30 per cent of income in taxes under the penalty of imprisonment. The income tax rule makes a practical difference because it now requires the judge to apply it in cases that come before him or her. The law, therefore, changes the satisfaction conditions of the rule of recognition. Should the rule be repealed, the judge would no longer be motivated to act accordingly.

In contrast with moral rules that are valid in virtue of their content, the income tax law may guide both as an aid in applying the secondary rule and as a primary legal rule. Given that the judge is committed to applying those rules that are passed by the legislature, knowing that the income tax rule is such a law will enable the judge to fulfil that meta-commitment. Moreover, if the judge is truly guided by the rule of recognition, he or she will be required by the rule of recognition to apply the income tax law. The income tax rule will thereby make a practical difference because appealing to it will have the appropriate motivational effect: it will motivate the judge to sentence tax-dodgers to prison, whereas it would not motivate if it is subsequently repealed. The income tax rule, therefore, can make a practical difference both because its conformity is required *by* the rule of recognition and by enabling conformity *to* the rule of recognition.

It is instructive to see why the problems with inclusive rules of recognition do not crop up here. Exclusive rules of recognition are, to coin a term, 'dynamic' secondary rules—the actions that the secondary rule is capable of motivating depends on which primary rules exist at the time of application. When the legislature passes the income tax rule, for example, the rule of recognition motivates committed judges to act in accordance with that new law. If the rule is repealed, the court's motivations change.

Because this rule of recognition is dynamic, its guidance does not necessarily entail that judges will act in the manner specified by any primary rule. It is this 'elbow room' carved out by dynamic rules of recognition that allows the primary legal rules to make practical differences. They guide conduct because it is always up to us to imagine that the norm no longer exists and hence the behaviour witnessed no longer results, even though the judge remains committed to the same rule of recognition. It is precisely the fact that the commitment to the legislature's will does not entail—in the absence of the income tax rule—that tax-dodgers will be sentenced to prison that allows the income tax rule to guide conduct when it is present.

In general, exclusive rules of recognition are dynamic because the extension of social-source terms like 'legislative enactments', 'judicial rulings', and 'customary norms' are determined by social facts and hence they expand or contract depending on the actions of legal officials or members of the community. This elasticity allows an agent to be guided both by an exclusive rule of recognition and by the subsidiary rules validated by it. Imagining that a subsidiary rule no longer motivates, owing either to its repeal or, in the case of custom, to its social demise, requires one to suppose that the extensions of the social-source terms in the rule of recognition have changed. Agents guided by the rule of recognition are therefore not fated to act in accordance with the rule no longer in force, thereby showing the practical difference made by the subsidiary rules when they are in force.

In contrast to the exclusive rule of recognition, the inclusive one is static. The set of possible motivated actions is fixed at its inception and never varies. The reason for this is simple: morality is a static system—it has no 'rule of change'. Morality differs dramatically from law in this respect. While legal rules routinely change over time, moral rules do not.[59] It is incoherent, for example, for someone to say that promises no longer need be kept. If promises must be honoured today, they must be honoured tomorrow.

But claiming that morality is a static system is not to deny the claims of moral relativists. The validity of moral rules might be relative to specific cultures or tastes, but given that relativity, their validity does not change over time. If female circumcision is morally acceptable in some African cultures, then those who hold this belief will think that these practices are

---

[59] This statement is a bit too strong. Moral rules do not change relative to a set of behaviours. Over time, new behaviours emerge and new rules may come into being because of the existence of these behaviours. But the old behaviours will be subject to the same rules.

always acceptable. To be sure, cultures do change their views about morality. Someday all cultures might ban female circumcisions. But this does not mean that, in those cultures, the people will think that the 'true' moral rules have changed; it would simply indicate that their views about which rules are the true moral rules have changed.

Because it is part of the concept of morality that morality is a static normative system, inclusive rules of recognition must be static secondary rules. By specifying that judges are to apply moral rules and principles in hard cases, the actions possibly motivated by this secondary rule are fixed at the outset. It is, therefore, conceptually impossible to imagine a situation in which a judge is motivated by such a static secondary rule but where the judge does not conform to the primary rules referred to by it. This means that these moral rules cannot make practical differences *qua* legal rules. The inclusive rule of recognition swallows the primary moral rules, precluding the possibility that they may have their own normative existence as primary legal norms.

If all rules of recognition were static, therefore, the law would be a trivial normative system. The only law that would exist would be the rule of recognition. Legal systems exist in the form that we are familiar with—that is, as hierarchical systems of norms—only because rules of recognition are dynamic.

VIII. WEAKER VERSIONS OF INCLUSIVE POSITIVISM

A. Derivation versions

Is it possible for Hart to avoid the previous objections by weakening his theory? We might distinguish between two versions of inclusive legal positivism.[60] The first permits moral principles to count as law simply because courts treat these norms as legally binding. We have seen that such a theory seems inconsistent with the action-guiding nature of legal norms. Another version denies that moral principles can be considered law in the absence of some social source, but would nevertheless permit them to play a role in fixing the contents of laws containing moral terms. For example, suppose Congress passes a law requiring every employer to pay employees a fair wage. Assume further that paying someone less than $6 an hour is morally unfair. According to this second version of inclusive positivism, it would follow that there is a law requiring employers to pay their employees at least $6 an hour, even before a court or agency has settled on this interpretation, just in case courts generally treat such inferences as law.

---

[60] I thank Brian Bix for suggesting this possible defence of Hart.

This second version is clearly weaker than the first because it does not permit moral rules to be law absent a social source. It concedes that an agent cannot be guided by an inclusive rule of recognition and a moral rule at the same time. In this variant, moral rules make themselves known not by guiding actions directly but by serving as premises in sound practical inferences involving other legal rules. The results of these inferences can be law even though some of the premises are themselves not law. Let us call an inclusive rule of recognition a 'derivation' rule if it validates rules that can be derived from pedigreed primary rules via sound principles of morality.

Despite its less ambitious claim, however, even this weaker version of inclusive positivism is vulnerable to the arguments of the previous sections.[61] For it can be shown that no agent can be guided by a derivation rule and a rule that can be inferred from a pedigreed rule via true moral premises. To see this, we must prove that such a derived rule can never make a practical difference. Consider, therefore, how a judge who believed it was morally unfair to pay employees less than $6 an hour would act in the absence of the derived rule requiring employers to pay their employees at least $6 an hour. Given the guidance of the derivation rule, the judge will be committed to ordering employers to pay their employees a fair wage, which for the judge means ordering them to pay employees at least $6 an hour. Hence, the judge will believe that he or she will act in exactly the same manner in the absence of the derived rule as the judge would have had he or she appealed to it directly. The commitment to the derivation rule, therefore, negates any impact that the derived rule might have had. The derived rule cannot be law if the rule of recognition provides guidance because the former cannot make a practical difference to the behaviour of judges if the latter does.

B. Necessity versions

So far we have discussed versions of inclusive legal positivism that allow morality to be a *sufficient* condition of legality.[62] We concentrated on these versions because we were investigating various ways of responding to Dworkin's challenge. If a positivist wants to show that moral principles can become legal principles without a direct social pedigree, he or she must argue that the rule of recognition may incorporate moral criteria as sufficient conditions on legality. Demonstrating that moral criteria may act, within the rule of recognition, as necessary conditions on legality does

---

[61] It is trivially true that derived rules cannot epistemically guide, for we have seen that contentful marks are useless as authoritative marks. The only interesting question is whether they can motivationally guide.

[62] This section was prompted by a challenge made to me by Ben Zipursky.

not get a positivist any closer to demonstrating that all legal norm-governed behaviour is, at bottom, dependent on norm-guided behaviour.

Although Hart says that he does not place any restrictions on the content of the rule of recognition, the only example he gives of an inclusive rule of recognition is the Fifth Amendment to the US Constitution, which is best construed as a necessary condition on legal validity.[63] Even his descriptions of inclusive legal positivism focus on the necessity version.

There is, for me, no logical restriction on the content of the rule of recognition: so far as 'logic' goes it could provide explicitly or implicitly that the criteria determining validity of subordinate laws should cease to be regarded as such if the laws identified in accordance with them proved to be morally objectionable. So a constitution could include in its restrictions on the legislative power even of its supreme legislature not only conformity with due process but a completely general provision that its legal power should lapse if its enactments ever conflicted with principles of morality and justice.[64]

Could Hart maintain a necessity version of inclusive legal positivism and reject the sufficiency version? If he were to do so, he would have to answer Dworkin by saying that moral principles can never become legal principles absent a direct social pedigree. Cases such as *Riggs* would have to be understood either as instances of judicial discretion or as the application of a moral principle that did in fact have a social pedigree by virtue of its practice by past courts.

While such manoeuvres would deprive inclusive legal positivism of much of its appeal, we might nevertheless wonder whether Hart could adopt such a position. In fact, he could not, and for much of the same reasons that felled the sufficiency version. If someone is guided by a rule of recognition that makes morality a necessary condition on legality, then that agent cannot be guided by a rule which passes such a test.

This assertion is remarkably easy to prove. Consider an employer who is guided by a rule of recognition requiring everyone to follow any rule passed by Congress, provided it is not 'grossly unfair'. Assume that Congress passes minimum-wage legislation mandating that employers pay their employees at least $6 an hour and that such rules are not grossly unfair. Can the employer be guided by the minimum-wage rule?

The answer is 'no' if we have in mind epistemic guidance. As we saw, a legal rule epistemically guides when the agent learns of his legal obligations from the rule. It follows that a rule cannot epistemically guide when

---

[63] See e.g. Hart, *supra* n. 9, at 72; Hart, 'Positivism and the Separation of Law and Morals', at 51.

[64] H. L. A. Hart, 'Lon L. Fuller: The Morality of Law', in Essays in Jurisprudence and Philosophy, 361.

the only way a person can figure out whether he or she should follow the rule is to deliberate about the merits of following the rule. For if someone is supposed to judge not only whether a rule is applicable but whether to apply the rule in the first place, then the rule cannot tell him whether he is obligated to apply it.

Can the minimum-wage rule at least motivationally guide a judge? The answer to this question is also 'no'. Recall that a rule motivationally guides conduct when it is taken as a peremptory reason for action; it follows that a rule cannot motivationally guide if the agent is required to deliberate about the merits of applying the rule. As the application of the minimum-wage rule depends, pursuant to the inclusive rule of recognition, on the employer first assessing whether the rule is grossly unfair, he cannot treat the rule as a peremptory reason for action and hence cannot be motivationally guided by it.

We should be careful about the argument. The claim is not that a rule cannot epistemically or motivationally guide if the rule itself conditions application on the fairness of its own recommendation. Indeed, to reject the necessity version of inclusive legal positivism is to accept that constitutional provisions such as the Equal Protection Clause are not part of the rule of recognition but are, in some sense, built into every law of the system. This way of individuating norms does not offend the idea that legal rules must be capable of guiding conduct because, in following such a rule, one would not be testing to see whether the entire rule (i.e. its recommendations plus its conditions of applicability) is grossly unfair. The problems arise only when the 'grossly unfair' provision is not seen as part of an *existing* legal rule but rather as part of the test of whether the legal rule *exists*. If a rule is not a legal rule because it is judged morally defective, then even a rule that passes the moral test cannot epistemically or motivationally guide the agent who engages in such deliberations.

Because someone who is guided by a rule of recognition that makes morality a necessary condition of legal validity can be neither epistemically nor motivationally guided by a rule supposedly validated by it, we must conclude that Hart cannot coherently embrace the necessity version of inclusive legal positivism. Notice that this argument is similar, but not identical, to the objection that was made against the sufficiency condition. The claim made here is not that a rule supposedly validated by an inclusive rule of recognition that made morality a necessary condition on legality cannot make a practical difference. The problem is that such a rule cannot make a practical difference *in the way that* rules are supposed to make practical differences: if the agent is required to determine whether the rule ought to be followed on the merits, then it can count neither as an epistemic tool for authoritative designation nor as a peremptory reason for action.

IX. THE ROAD NOT TAKEN

A. The functional conception of law

I began this essay by describing Hart's solution to the chicken–egg problem. Legal norm-governed behaviour is possible, according to Hart, because of norm-guided behaviour. The fundamental norms govern the operations of law creation and application because of a practice to recognize these operations as authoritative. Ordinary legal norms are generated, in turn, by virtue of their validation by this practised rule of recognition.

Dworkin's challenge took legal philosophy by storm because it threatened to upset this claimed dependence of norm-governance on norm-guidance. If certain norms were law even though they could not be validated by a rule of recognition, then this indicated that legal norm-governance is not necessarily, or even ever, dependent on norm-guidance. Once this relationship is abandoned, it is not clear how to solve the chicken–egg problem without resorting to the natural law.

As we saw, certain positivists responded to this challenge by attempting to show how moral principles can be validated by a rule of recognition. According to this account, positivism is only committed to the idea that the rule of recognition must be a social rule, not that this rule must set out conditions of legality which refer exclusively to a norm's social source. It is possible, and indeed is the case in Anglo-American legal systems, that judges are required by social practice to appeal to moral principles in order to resolve hard cases. Moral principles may not have a social source, but they are nonetheless validated by a social rule. In other words, unenacted or unpracticed moral principles can govern behaviour as law because they can be related in the appropriate way to norm-guided behaviour.

Although Hart did take this tack in his Postscript, we have seen that this choice is inconsistent with his understanding that the law is essentially action-guiding. For Hart, legal norms must not only result *from* norm-guided behaviour but must also possibly result *in* norm-guided behaviour and, as I argued, this cannot be the case for moral principles, which are valid solely in virtue of their content. No one can be epistemically guided by such norms, for contentful marks of authority cannot help anyone distinguish legitimate from illegitimate standards of conduct. Judges also cannot be motivationally guided by such principles if they are motivationally guided, as they must be, by the rule of recognition. For even if judges did not appeal to the principles themselves in adjudication, they would still conform to these principles given the guidance of an inclusive rule of recognition. It turns out, therefore, that Hart cannot save his solution to the chicken–egg problem without significantly changing his views about the essential nature of the law.

To be sure, he could avoid this inconsistency by giving up the claim that the essence of the law is to guide conduct. Jules Coleman, for example, has never argued that the law is essentially action-guiding, and therefore his version of inclusive legal positivism is untouched by these objections.[65] Whether one should subscribe to this view about the law's function or not, it seems clear that Hart cannot distance himself from it without radically changing his theory. In *The Concept of Law*, virtually every one of Hart's criticisms of his predecessors and peers depends, in some essential way, on the claim that the function of law is the guidance of conduct. For example, he famously ridiculed the legal realists by pointing out the absurdity of their theory of rules: if legal rules are merely predictions of judicial behaviour, then how is a court to decide any legal question—is a court supposed to use the rules to predict its own behaviour? Legal rules enable people to predict judicial behaviour because legal rules guide judicial behaviour, not vice versa. It is slightly ironic that Hart's embrace of inclusive legal positivism commits him to a form of legal realism: as we have seen, according to inclusive legal positivism, a judge can never be guided by the rules supposedly validated by the inclusive part of the rule of recognition.

The primacy of rule-guided behaviour in Hart's jurisprudence, I believe, is actually the product of an even deeper commitment to a *functionalist* conception of law. On this view, legal systems exist, and exist in the form that they do, because they serve certain functions. By having available institutions that create, modify, and apply rules, the law is able to secure benefits that it would not be able to secure, or secure as well, without them. The functionalist view does not imply that the functions served by the law are worthy ones. For a positivistic functionalist such as Hart, the benefits made possible by law need not be ones in which everyone shares: the ends may range from the maximization of human happiness to the enrichment of the ruling classes. The functionalist conception does, however, require that the proper way to evaluate the law is to assess whether legal institutions are serving worthwhile functions and whether they are serving them well.

In *The Concept of Law*, Hart mentioned many of the functions that legal systems typically serve, such as defining and protecting rights to life, limb, and property, enabling the voluntary creation and transfer of rights, and providing mechanisms for the resolution of disputes. What all of these functions have in common, Hart pointed out, is that they involve *rules*. The law secures its ends, whatever they may be, by affecting the

---

[65] See Coleman, *The Practice of Principle*, ch. 10.

practical reasoning of its subject in a rule-based manner. Legal institutions provide the rules and these rules, in turn, guide conduct. Hence, Hart's pronouncement that the essential function of law is the provision of rules for the guidance of conduct: whatever task the law seeks to accomplish, it does it through guidance by rules.

On a functionalist view, therefore, primary legal rules are tools of a certain sort. They exist in order to be used by legal officials to secure benefits that would not be possible without them. When these rules turn out to be ill-conceived or have outlived their uselessness, they tend to be replaced with new norms. Secondary legal rules, then, are tools that create and extinguish other tools.

Given this functionalism, we can thus see why it is so important that rules be capable of making practical differences: in order for an entity to have a function, there must be some event that it is supposed to bring about—some event that counts as the fulfilment of its function. In the case of a rule, in order for it to have the function of guiding conduct there must be some action that it is supposed to bring about—some action the performance of which counts as the guidance of conduct. A rule guides conduct only if conformity is secured by the rule making a difference to the practical reasoning of an agent. Hence, if a rule is to have the function of guiding conduct, then the action that it is supposed to bring about is one where the rule secures conformity by making a difference to the practical reasoning of an agent. However, if a rule is in principle incapable of securing conformity by making a difference to practical reasoning, then there can be no action where conformity is secured in this manner. Hence, if a rule is in principle incapable of making a practical difference, then there can be no action that the rule is supposed to bring about—no action that counts as the fulfilment of its guidance function. It follows that no rule that is in principle incapable of making a practical difference is one that has the function of guiding conduct. However, since, on a functionalist account, all legal rules have, as their function, the guidance of conduct, no rule that is in principle incapable of making a practical difference can be a legal rule.

Moreover, the functionality of law explains why legal norm-governed behaviour depends on norm-guided behaviour. On a functionalist account, to say that a legal rule exists is to say that a tool with a certain function or functions exists. As it turns out, the best explanation of how legal rules are able to serve their functions is that certain people treat them, or the rules which validate them, as guides to their conduct. The instrumentality of the rule of recognition, for example, consists in its ability to solve a type of coordination problem: given the plethora of rules that might claim allegiance, there is a need for a rule to select, from among these norms, a relatively stable subset as the correct standards of public behaviour. The best explanation for how the rule of recognition fulfils this function is through the establishment of a convention. By requiring judges to apply certain rules that have certain characteristics on a regular basis, the rule engenders the formation of expectations about future judicial conduct.[66] The rule of recognition fulfils its coordinative function, in other words, because it is a rule that guides conduct.

Likewise, the best explanation of how the primary legal rules are able to serve their functions is by being related to a rule that solves, at least to some degree, the relevant coordination problem. Again, given the multitude of standards available, there must be some rule by which people can determine which standards ought to guide their conduct. Primary legal rules are capable of fulfilling their functions, therefore, because they are designated as authoritative by the system's rule of recognition.

This is not to say, of course, that it is a good thing that any given rule of recognition, or rule validated by it, fulfils its function or that when it exists, it functions efficiently. The claim, rather, is that the best explanation for how legal rules manage to serve their functions, *even poorly*, is through their connection to rule-guided behaviour. That is why the existence of rule-guided behaviour is a condition on the existence conditions for rule-governed behaviour.[67]

B. Exclusive legal positivism

Having denied Hart his way out, I do not mean to suggest that Dworkin's challenge cannot be met within the general confines of Hart's theory.

---

[66] 'Rules are conventional social practices if the general conformity of a group to them is part of the reasons which its individual members have for acceptance.' Hart, *supra* n. 9, at 255.

[67] Contrast this picture with Dworkin's theory of law. Arguably, for Dworkin the point of legal practice is not functional. The law is not meant to secure benefits that would not be available without it. The benefits are secured by state coercion—the role of the law is to justify this coercion. In Dworkin's non-functionalist framework, it is a mistake to ask, 'For what purposes do these legal rules exist?' Like the rules of critical morality, there is no reason why any legal rule exists—they simply do. We would not say, for example, that the purpose of the moral rule against murder is to enable people to live up to their moral obligations not to murder. For Dworkin, the existence of the legal rule against murder does not depend on such functional considerations either. Legal rules do the same kind of normative work as do moral rules—both sets of rules are essentially justificatory. They may guide conduct when people recognize that they exist, but they do not exist in order to guide conduct.

As one might expect, therefore, the concept of rule-guidance does not play a prominent role in Dworkin's theory. Because legal rules do not exist in order to guide conduct, there is no requirement that they make practical differences. A legal rule exists if it justifies past political acts; it need not be capable of motivating agents to act in ways they might not have acted had they not appealed to these rules. Moreover, the mere fact that certain people guide their conduct according to a rule is not sufficient by itself to ensure that the behaviour gives people reasons to act. Legal rules can no more be grounded in actual practice than morality can. Rule-governed behaviour can never be made to depend on rule-guided behaviour because no one has the authority to change the moral law.

Instead of rejecting the Pedigree Thesis, he can disavow the Discretion Thesis, or at least Dworkin's interpretation of it. That is, Hart can agree with Dworkin that a positivistic rule of recognition must set out pedigree criteria of legality. He may also concede that, in Anglo-American systems, courts are never free to disregard moral standards when the pedigree standards run out. However, he need not say, with Dworkin, that the legal obligation to apply moral principles in such cases thereby converts them into *legal* norms. Hart can, in other words, embrace exclusive legal positivism.

Central to the exclusive legal positivist position is the distinction between *legal validity* and *legality*.[68] The criteria of legal validity mark off those norms that a court is required to apply in any given case. The criteria of legality, however, distinguish among the set of legally valid norms those norms which are part of the legal system in question. Any norm that is law in a given system is legally valid in that system, but a legally valid norm may not be a law of that system. In conflict-of-law cases, for example, judges are often required to apply the law of foreign jurisdictions. The law of the foreign jurisdiction is legally valid *in* the home jurisdiction, although it is clearly not the law of that jurisdiction.

It is the contention of the exclusive legal positivist that, although morality can be a condition of legal validity, it may never be a condition of legality. In *Riggs*, for example, the positivist can accept Dworkin's intuitions that the moral principle that no person should profit from wrongdoing is binding on the court (i.e. it is legally valid). However, what he denies is that this principle is a *legal* principle.[69] If such a position is sound, then it follows that all legal norms that govern behaviour are related in the appropriate way to rule-guided behaviour, for those norms that are not so related (i.e. moral principles that lack pedigrees) turn out not to be legal norms.

As far as I can tell, Dworkin has no response to this line of argument. Recall his attack on the Discretion Thesis in 'The Model of Rules I'. Dworkin argued that in situations where pedigree standards have run out, judges do not take themselves to have strong discretion. A judge has strong discretion whenever he or she is legally permitted to apply whichever standards the judge wishes—that is, as long as the judge does not do so in an arbitrary, biased, or silly way. As we have seen, however, Hart need not maintain, if he ever did, that when judges have discretion, they have strong discretion. A judge has discretion in these cases only in

---

[68] See Joseph Raz, 'The Identity of a Legal System and Legal Validity', in *The Authority of Law* (1979).

[69] According to the exclusive positivist, the 'legal obligation' operator is opaque to moral implication. If someone is legally obligated to p, and morally obligated to q if p, it does not follow that such a person is legally obligated to q.

the sense that, when pedigreed standards run out, it is not true that the judge is obligated to apply any legal rules. A judge's actions, therefore, are not governed by the rule of recognition. But it does not follow that in reaching beyond the law, he appeals to 'extra-legal principles he is *free* to apply if he *wishes*'.[70] The judge may be legally obligated to apply extra-legal principles in order to resolve legally unregulated disputes.

In his reply to Joseph Raz, Dworkin charged that exclusive legal positivism was an arbitrary position and did not accord with standard usage. 'I think Raz's use is arbitrary because it does not represent ordinary usage and is pointless as a stipulative definition. But he is entitled to use words as he wishes.'[71] In this essay, I have tried to show why Raz's use of the word 'law' is neither arbitrary nor stipulative. Exclusive legal positivism represents the idea that legal institutions have certain functions and those functions all involve the guidance of conduct through rules. As a result, exclusive legal positivism imposes certain constraints on the rule of recognition so as to ensure that it does not countenance legal rules that are constitutionally incapable of fulfilling their functions. As we have seen, when legal rules lack social sources, they are unable to guide conduct. They can neither inform people of their obligations nor motivate judges to comply.

Exclusive legal positivism, therefore, is forced on the legal positivist who is committed to a functionalist conception of law. To be sure, not every positivist embraces such a vision. But it is my contention that Hart was so committed and, as a result, it was a mistake for him to answer Dworkin in the way that he did.

[70] Dworkin, 'Model of Rules I', *supra* n. 14, at 29.
[71] Ronald Dworkin, 'Reply to Raz', in *Ronald Dworkin and Contemporary Jurisprudence*, 262.

6

Legal Conventionalism

ANDREI MARMOR

There are two questions I would like to address in this article. The first and main question is whether there are rules of recognition, along the lines suggested by H. L. A. Hart. The second question concerns the age-old issue of the autonomy of law. One of the main purposes of this article is to show how these two issues are closely related. The concept of a social convention is the thread holding these two points tightly knit in one coil. Basically, I will argue that a novel account of social conventions can be employed to re-establish Hart's thesis about the rules of recognition, and that this same account shows why, and to what extent, law is partly an autonomous practice.

I. RULES OF RECOGNITION

Hart's thesis about the existence of the rules of recognition has probably become one of the main dogmas that we have taught our jurisprudence students for decades. It is also, undoubtedly, one of the main theses of *The Concept of Law.*[1] Basically, it maintains that in each and every modern legal system there are 'social rules', as Hart called them, which are followed by the pertinent legal community (particularly judges), and which define the sources of law. That is, the rules identify those facts or events that are taken to yield established ways of the creation, modification, and annulment of legal standards in the relevant legal system.[2]

The idea that there are, as a matter of social fact, rules of recognition had not been the main worry of Hart's critics for quite some time. It was

I am grateful to Jules Coleman, Chaim Gans, Leslie Green, Alan Harel, Stephen Perry, Joseph Raz, Scott Shapiro, Martin Stone, and Ben Zipursky for their comments on drafts of this article. I am also indebted to the participants of York University Philosophy Department Colloquium, the Cardozo Law School Faculty Seminar, and the legal theory workshop of Duke University School of Law for their comments and suggestions.

[1] H. L. A. Hart, *The Concept of Law* (1961), esp. ch. 5.

[2] Hart further assumed that in each and every legal system, eventually one rule of recognition can be identified, which subsumes, in a hierarchical ordering, all the rest. This further assumption we need not share here, and I shall henceforth assume that nothing substantial is lost if we hold the more plausible assumption that the rules of recognition are not necessarily hierarchically structured.

the further, conceptual thesis of Hart and other legal positivists that engendered the main controversies, namely that the concept of legal validity is exhausted by the reference to the rules of recognition. According to this conceptual thesis, a norm is legally valid if and only if it derives its validity from one of the sources of law identified by the rules of recognition. Dworkin's main critical efforts in the 1970s, for instance, were aimed to show that this conceptual thesis is groundless, as the law comprises numerous norms whose legal validity cannot be traced back to the sources of law identified by the rules of recognition.[3] In other words, it is not the existence of the rules of recognition but their importance for the explication of the concept of legal validity that was the focus of most of the controversy at the time.

None of this, however, renders Hart's thesis about the existence of rules of recognition unproblematic. Ronald Dworkin, for one, seems to have changed his mind recently, and he now certainly claims that there are no rules of recognition at all. But even before this shift occurred, serious problems were noticed concerning Hart's thesis, by fellow positivist and non-positivist critics alike, and it is worth noting what those difficulties are.

In *The Concept of Law* Hart provided two main characteristic features that rules of recognition possess. First, rules of recognition are secondary, power-conferring rules. Second, they are 'social rules' whose validity consists in the fact of their 'acceptance' by the pertinent community. I will not be concerned here, however, with the first characteristic, though it is a contested issue whether or not the rules of recognition are power-conferring rules. It is the characterization of the rules of recognition as social rules that embodies the difficulties I will focus on. The idea of a social rule is actually a term of art in *The Concept of Law,* and it is based on Hart's *practice theory of rules,* to which we must turn for a moment.

II. THE PRACTICE THEORY OF SOCIAL RULES

There is an enormous variety of rules that we encounter in our lives. In a modern society people follow a great many kinds of rule that have been enacted by one institution or another, public or private. But there is also a great variety of rules that people follow (sometimes without being very much aware of it) which have no institutional origins. These are mostly social rules—that is, the rules we follow in numerous contexts that have no particular origin in the enactment of an individual or an institution. Although there is undoubtedly an enormous diversity of such social

---

[3] R. M. Dworkin, *Taking Rights Seriously* (1977).

rules, Hart's practice theory of rules was meant to capture the essence of them all, in the following definition. Hart maintained that a social rule, say *R*, exists in society *S* if and only if the following conditions obtain:

1. There is a regularity of behaviour according to *R*, in *S*: namely that most members of *S* regularly conform to *R*.
2. Most members of *S* manifest a normative attitude toward *R*, which Hart called 'acceptance'.

The idea of 'acceptance' consists of basically two components:

(a) For most members of *S*, the existence of *R* constitutes reasons for action in accordance with *R*.
(b) The existence of *R* is employed by members of *S* both as grounds for criticizing deviant behaviour and as a justificafion for exerting social pressure on other members of *S* to conform to *R*.

In *The Concept of Law* Hart presented this account of social rules as a general explication of the nature of social rules.[4] In this generalization he had been clearly wrong, as he himself came to admit years later. In the posthumously published Postcript to *The Concept of Law*,[5] he conceded some of the critical points raised against his account, both by Joseph Raz and by Ronald Dworkin, and he suggested a considerable modification of the practice theory of rules, to which I shall return in a moment. To understand these modifications, however, we must dwell, briefly, on the main reasons that have been provided for the inadequacy of Hart's original account. Two main points have been raised against the practice theory of rules, and though differently formulated, I believe that they are shared by Raz and Dworkin.[6]

First, it has been noted that Hart's account of social rules seems incapable of distinguishing between an instance of following a rule and that of following a generally accepted reason.[7] This is a crucially important

---

[4] Hart, *supra* n. 1.

[5] H. L. A. Hart, *The Concept of Law* (2nd edn., ed. J. Raz and P. A. Bulloch, 1994), Postscript.

[6] Dworkin, *supra* n. 3, and J. Raz, *Practical Reason and Norms* (1975). There is some lack of clarity about the question whether Hart thought that the practice theory of rules applies to morality as well. In any case, it is clear enough that it cannot apply to moral rules. Rules of morals and similar domains need not be practised in order to be valid. Hart's requirement for a regularity of behaviour as a basis for the rule's existence simply does not apply to such spheres as morality. We often hold moral rules to be valid despite the fact that they are not practised in the pertinent community, or anywhere.

[7] 'Following a reason' may sound rather awkward, and perhaps it is. I use this unusual term (instead of e.g. 'acting on a reason') not only to emphasize symmetry, but also because I intend to refer to those cases where people act according to a reason with some generality. Generality is actually twofold, referring both to the kind of reasons and to the occasions in which those reasons are taken to apply.

distinction, both for any reasonable account of the concept of a rule and particularly for the question whether there are any rules of recognition as Hart envisaged. As we shall shortly see, it is the upshot of Dworkin's recent criticism of the rules of recognition, namely that at best they are generally accepted reasons, but not rules at all.

Consider, for example, the distinction between the rules of a game—those rules which define what are the moves one is entitled to make, what is considered as winning or losing the game, etc.—and generally accepted strategies within the game.[8] Strategies are principles of action that are generally accepted as reliable guides of conduct, but they are not considered and acted upon as the rules of the game. Hart's account of social rules seems to hold about both rules and strategies. In both cases we would have a regularity of behaviour, and a normative attitude of 'acceptance' as the latter is defined by Hart.

The point that Hart's original account misses here is delicate but important. Hart thought that the normativity of a social rule consists in the fact that the rule is considered to constitute a reason for action. But, though this is clearly correct, it is not a sufficient characterization of a rule's normativity. Rules constitute reasons for action in a special way, in that they are taken to replace something which would have applied to the circumstances had there not been a rule governing it. It is, of course, extremely difficult to articulate what this 'something', which the rules are there to replace, really is. I tend to think that there are different elements of practical reasoning that different kinds of rule are there to replace, but we need not go into this complicated matter here.[9] Suffice it to say that Hart's practice theory of rules, even if basically correct, is in need of some crucial addition. It must be construed in such a way as to make allowance for the distinction between following a rule, and following a generally accepted reason. Otherwise, Hart's theory of the rules of recognition remains open to the charge that there are actually no such rules at all, but only generally accepted reasons for compliance with various institutions' decrees (which may or may not be good reasons), but they are not rules at all.

Second, and more importantly, both Raz and Dworkin have noted that

---

[8] The distinction, as well as the game example, was first suggested by G. J. Warnock, *The Object of Morality* (1971), 43–6.

[9] Raz, *supra* n. 6. In his famous analysis of mandatory rules in *Practical Reason and Norms*, Raz claimed that such rules are there to replace the balance of the first-order reasons, which would have applied to the circumstances. Mandatory rules, Raz claims, are a combination of first-order reasons for action and exclusionary reasons, namely reasons not to act on certain types or excluded reasons. Although I tend to agree with this analysis as far as mandatory rules are concerned, I do not think that this account is adequate to explain the uniqueness of other types of rule, such as 'rules of thumb' and, perhaps more importantly, constitutive rules. For a detailed account of the normativity of constitutive rules, see A. Marmor, *Positive Law and Objective Values* (Oxford, 2001), ch. 2.

Hart's original account of the normativity of social rules is largely vacuous. There is simply nothing in the practice theory of rules to explain what kind of reasons people have for following a social rule. Hart's account simply leaves one wondering what is it that justifies people in regarding a rule as a reason for action. Simply pointing to the fact that there *is* a regularity of behaviour, which seems to be suggested by Hart as part of the reason for following a social rule, is clearly the wrong answer. It is only in special and unique circumstances that the reason for following a rule partly consists in the fact that others follow it too: namely in those cases where the rule in question is a social convention. But not all the social rules are conventions, of course.

It is here, in this last point, that Hart found the anchor for his modified account. In the Postscript to *The Concept of Law,* he basically conceded these critical observations and inferred the obvious conclusion: the practice theory of rules, he claimed, is not a general account of social rules as such, but only of one subcategory of social rules, namely social conventions. Because it should have been clear from the start that the rules of recognition are conventions, this late concession would have no effect on Hart's main insights about the rules of recognition. As he put it in his own words: 'the theory remains as a faithful account of conventional social rules which include . . . the rule of recognition, which is in effect a norm of judicial customary rule existing only if it is accepted and practiced in the law-identifying and law-applying operations of the courts.'[10]

Thus, according to Hart's modified version, the rules of recognition are social conventions, and the original practice theory of rules is now presented as an account of the concept of a social convention. But, of course, there is a crucial element that is added to the original definitions, very succinctly, though, and this is the idea that a necessary *reason* for following a rule which is a social convention consists in the fact that others also follow it. The fact that there is a regularity of behaviour according to R provides a crucially important reason for members of S to regard R as a reason for action and follow it too.

This late modification did not convince Dworkin, however. He clearly rejects Hart's suggestions about the conventionality of the rules of recognition:

On my view, there is no fully shared rule of recognition at all: the supposed convention, that the American Constitution is the supreme law of the land or that Parliament is the supreme lawgiver in Britain, can only be described as conventionally accepted if we ignore the fact that what those abstract formulations mean to some lawyers, as guides to identifying true, concrete propositions of law, is very different from what they mean to others.

[10] Hart, Postscript, *supra* n. 5, at 256.

And in the sequel:

So Hart's picture of law, as fixed by a conventional rule of recognition, cannot be sustained even for Anglo-American legal systems, except by making the convention so abstract that it becomes: law must be identified by the right tests for identifying law. And then there is no longer any point to calling that a *convention*.[11]

It should be said that Dworkin's current position about the rules of recognition had been formulated long before Hart's Postscript became publicly known. At least as early as the mid-1980s, when *Law's Empire* was published, it was clear enough that Dworkin was no longer willing to assume that there are any conventions about the recognition of the law, even with respect to the most limited, standard, and humdrum instances that we would call 'easy cases'. There are instances of widespread agreement among an 'interpretative community' about what counts as law, and there are even paradigms of law, but none of this amounts to the existence of social conventions, as Hart would have it. According to Dworkin, such interpretative starting-points, or 'raw material', never amount to more than a local and tentative convergence of beliefs and attitudes, which may well be widely shared; but again, these never amount to more than that, namely widely shared beliefs and attitudes. Such beliefs do not constitute a conceptual framework for the understanding of law, and they are never secure from challenge by better interpretations that would rule them out of existence by the sheer power of interpretative reasoning.[12]

Dworkin's objection to the existence of rules of recognition, however, is seriously impeded by two recurrent mistakes underlying his conception of conventionalism. He has always assumed that conventions manifest a pattern of agreement, and that, as a consequence of this consensus basis of conventions, the existence of a social convention is basically incompatible with substantial controversies about its content. Both assumptions, however, are misguided. Conventions, as we shall see in detail below, have no such consensual basis. It is not anything like a tacit agreement, or an implicit consensus, that brings about the existence of a social convention. On the contrary: social conventions tend to emerge precisely in those cases where an agreement is difficult or impossible to reach.

The fallacy of Dworkin's second assumption is even clearer. A controversy over the content of a rule of recognition does not prove that there is no such rule. Even when there are several ways of understanding a rule (or anything else for that matter), there must be something there that people can understand differently and argue about. There are different ways of understanding the American Constitution, and there are different

[11] Ronald Dworkin, 'Hart's Posthumous Reply' (unpublished MS).
[12] Ronald Dworkin, *Law's Empire* (1986), 91.

ways of understanding its normative supremacy, but none of this controversy would have been intelligible in the first place if such conventions
were indeed 'so abstract that [they] become: law must be identified by the
right tests for identifying law'. The apparent plausibility of Dworkin's
argument stems, perhaps, from a confusion between the question
whether there is a rule, and the different question, whether we can agree
on the formulation of the rule. It may well be the case that there is no
general agreement on the appropriate formulation of a rule of recognition
(or any other rule for that matter), but this does not entail that there is no
rule there.[13]

In other words, it is not the controversial nature of the rules of recognition that render them problematic. It has been noted many times that
social conventions need not be non-controversial in order to exist and
fulfil their functions as conventional rules. Dworkin's recent position,
however, indicates that there is another criticism hidden there, and I
would like to suggest that it presents a much more serious challenge. The
'rules of recognition', Dworkin seems to be claiming, are at best generally
accepted reasons, but they are not rules, and hence they are not conventions either. Although Dworkin himself hardly provides any arguments to
support this claim, I believe that a closer look at the contemporary philosophical analyses of conventions may well reveal some reasons to side
with Dworkin on this question. These reasons, though, have nothing to do
with the controversial nature of the rules of recognition.

III. A FIRST LOOK AT SOCIAL CONVENTIONS

When Hart published *The Concept of Law* little philosophical attention had
been paid to the analysis of the concept of social convention. There were,
of course, important discussions about the conventionality of language,
but little attention had been paid to trying to understand what conventions are. This changed dramatically, however—and only about a decade
later—with the publication of David Lewis's pioneering book, *Convention:
A Philosophical Study*.[14] Lewis defined the purpose of his project as an
attempt to answer Quine's objection to the conventional basis of
language. Quine argued that the supposed conventions of language
cannot be much like the standard instances of conventions, because
conventions are agreements, and, of course, we have never agreed with
one another to abide by the conventions of language. Quine's assumption,
Lewis argued, was simply wrong: conventions are not agreements

---

[13] I am indebted to Ben Zipursky for mentioning this possibility to me.
[14] David Lewis, *Convention: A Philosophy Study* (1969).

because they are rules that emerge as practical solutions to recurrent co-ordination problems.

A typical coordination problem arises, according to Lewis, when several agents have a particular structure of preferences with respect to their mutual modes of conduct, namely that between several alternatives of conduct open to them in a given set of circumstances, each and every agent has a stronger preference to act as the other agents will, than his own preference for acting upon any one of the particular alternatives. Most coordination problems are easily solved by simple agreements between the agents to act upon one, arbitrarily chosen alternative, thus securing uniformity of action among them. However, when a particular coordination problem is recurrent, and agreement is difficult to obtain (mostly because of the large number of agents involved), a social rule is very likely to emerge, and this rule is a convention. Conventions, in other words, emerge as solutions to recurrent coordination problems, not as a consequence of an agreement, but as an alternative to such an agreement, precisely in those cases where agreements are difficult or impossible to obtain.[15]

Lewis's analysis of conventions in terms of solution to recurrent co-ordination problems embodies remarkable advantages: quite apart from the fact that it is capable of explaining the emergence of conventions without relying on the necessity of agreement, it is also apt to explain two important intuitions largely shared about the unique features of social conventions. First, there is an important sense in which we think about conventions as *arbitrary* rules. One of the most basic intuitions about conventions we have is that if a rule is a convention, there must be at least one other alternative rule that people could have followed instead, achieving the same purpose. Second, and with equal conviction, we seem to hold that our reasons for following a rule that is a convention are strongly tied to the fact that others follow it too. And hence, it is typically thought that there is no point in following a conventional rule if it is not actually practised by the pertinent community.

Now, both these two intuitive features of conventional rules are nicely explicable by Lewis's analysis. Beginning with the second, we can easily see that according to Lewis's analysis, the whole point of a conventional rule is to secure uniformity of action among a number of agents. After all, it is precisely the point of a coordination problem that each and every agent's dominant preference is to act just as the other agents will. Hence, the relevant agents would have no reason to abide by the conventional rule if they believed others would not abide by the same rule too. Thus,

---

[15] It is worth keeping in mind that the solution of a coordination problem—unlike other types of game-theory situation—does not call for a sanction-based solution.

the rationale of conventions as a solution to coordination problems easily explains why the reason to follow a convention is dependent on the fact that others also follow it.

Lewis's analysis can also explain why, and to what extent, conventional rules are rightly considered arbitrary. It is the basic structure of a coordination problem that there are at least two alternatives of conduct open to the agents in question, and that as between these alternatives, the agents have a stronger preference for uniformity of action as compared to their preference for any one of the particular alternatives open to them. Thus, from the agents' own perspective, the choice between any one of the relevant alternatives is pretty much arbitrary; they would like to abide by whichever option secures uniformity of action among them.

These, and some other advantages that I cannot mention here, quickly turned Lewis's analysis of conventions into the mainstream, almost textbook-like philosophical account of the concept of social convention. Several philosophers criticized Lewis on certain details of his definition, but the core idea, that conventions are solutions to recurrent coordination problems, has been widely shared ever since. Remarkably, however; with few notable exceptions,[16] legal philosophers have paid very little attention to this mainstream philosophical account of social conventions. This *is* remarkable, as it takes little effort to realize that Hart's account of the 'conventional' rules of recognition does not square easily with Lewis's analysis of the concept of social conventions. If Lewis is basically right about what conventions are, the rules of recognition would not seem to be conventions at all.

Two main problems come immediately to light: First, it would be very difficult to maintain that the rules of recognition are *arbitrary* rules. Some of them may be, but the *fundamental* rules of recognition of a legal system would certainly not be regarded by the members of that system arbitrary at all. For the American judges, jurists, and the public at large, the normative supremacy of the US Constitution is not just one arbitrarily chosen alternative among several other rules of recognition that are equally acceptable. And, of course, the same is true of the British rule of the supremacy of Parliament, and numerous similar examples. After all, the rules of recognition define what the law is in a given community, and this is clearly a matter of the utmost political importance. It matters a great deal to all of us who makes the law, and how it is to be enacted. Thinking of such rules of recognition in terms of arbitrariness would certainly strike most jurists and politically conscientious people as a crazy idea. There seems to be nothing arbitrary in the fact that the Americans opted for the

---

[16] G. J. Postema, 'Coordination and Convention at the Foundations of Law', 11 J. Legal Stud. 165 (1982). See also J. Raz, 'Facing Up: A Reply', 62 S. Cal. L. Rev. 1153 (1989).

kind of constitutional structure they have, and continuously maintain. The Americans obviously believe that their fundamental rules of recognition, embodying the supremacy of their Constitution, federalism, adherence to common law, and so forth, reflect political choices of great importance. How can this political dimension be squared with the conception of rules of recognition being arbitrary solutions to recurrent coordination problems?

And here we come to the second and main problem: the rules of recognition do not seem like solutions to recurrent coordination problems at all. Perhaps some of the more technical rules of recognition can be so regarded; but the fundamental rules of recognition of the legal system do not seem closely tied to the solution of coordination problems. The political choices they embody are far more complex and manifold than the basic structure of a coordination problem.[17] Consider, for instance, the basic idea of federalism in the United States. The federal structure of the American legal system is instantiated by a set of rules of recognition that American judges and lawyers follow. These rules have a purpose, a political rationale, which originated in the famous political compromise of the Independence, and was reshaped by subsequent political events, like the Civil War and the New Deal. But these reasons, and political solutions that underlie the rationale of the rules of recognition, which instantiate the idea of Federalism, have little to do with the idea of a coordination problem. It was not the need to coordinate the political power of the states and the federal government that was conceived of as the problem to be solved. It was the more pressing political question of whether the emerging states should yield their political independence to a central government at all which generated the famous federalist compromise. Federalism, and the rules of recognition it instantiates, is a delicate and subtle compromise between conflicting claims to authority, and not a solution to a coordination problem.

My guess is that these, or similar thoughts, may have led Dworkin (and, presumably, many others) to conclude that the alleged rules of recognition are not conventions at all, but, at best, generally accepted reasons. The supremacy of the American Constitution is a widely shared political conviction, Dworkin maintains, and not a conventional rule. Our discus-

---

[17] It should be admitted that the analysis of coordination problems has advanced considerably in the last few decades, and a great deal of complexity and richness has been added to Lewis's original account. Nor should we assume that coordination problems are typically simple or of one particular kind. Complexities notwithstanding, the basic idea of a coordination problem remains the same: securing some form of uniformity of action where such uniformity is in the best interest of the parties involved, and is recognized by them as such. For reasons to be clarified later on, I do not believe that this is the rationale of most of the rules of recognition.

sion so far seems to suggest that if Lewis is basically correct about what social conventions are, Dworkin may well be quite right about the alleged rules of recognition: they do not look like conventional rules at all. I want to suggest, however, that such a conclusion is premature. A closer look at the concept of social conventions is necessary at this point. Such an analysis would reveal that Lewis's conception is much more limited in scope than has been generally assumed. An additional alternative account of conventions can show why the rules of recognition are conventions after all.

IV. A CLOSER LOOK AT SOCIAL CONVENTIONS

Let us begin with a refinement of the notion of 'arbitrariness', which is characteristic of conventional rules. There is, indeed, an important sense in which rules that are conventional are arbitrary: we feel that if, say, R is a conventional rule, there must be at least one other rule, say R', that could have been followed instead, achieving the same purpose.[18] This is clearly manifest, for example, in those cases where we are familiar with different rules solving the same type of coordination problem. In most of the Commonwealth countries people drive on the left side of the road, and in most others, they drive on the right. The choice between these two options seems to be pretty much arbitrary; both rules solve the same kind of coordination problem. Hence, the rule is, in a sense, arbitrary. But it is crucially important to be precise about what 'arbitrariness' means here, mainly because some philosophers were quick to conclude that 'arbitrariness' is equivalent to indifference, and this is not so.[19] People need not be indifferent as to the choice between the conventional rule they actually follow and any other rule they could have followed instead. To show that 'arbitrariness' does not imply 'indifference', a formal definition of the arbitrariness of social conventions may prove useful. The following is the definition I propose:

Given that A is the main reason[s] for members of a population, P, for following a rule, P, in circumstances C, R is an arbitrary rule if and only if: there is at least one other rule, R', so that if most members of P were complying with R' in circumstances C, then for all members of P, A would be a sufficient reason to follow R' instead of R. The rules R and R' are such that it is normally impossible to comply with them concomitantly in circumstances C.[20]

---

[18] I am not assuming here that conventional rules necessarily serve a particular purpose. My doubts about such functionalist explanations of conventions will be spelled out in the sequel, mainly the last section. For the time being, however, Lewis's framework should suffice for the illustration of the arbitrariness of conventions.

[19] See e.g. M. Gilbert, *On Social Facts* (1989), 340–1.

[20] I have presented and defended this definition in my article 'On Convention', 107

Now consider the following example, which is a typical case of what David Lewis called an 'imperfect' coordination problem. Cellular phones are abundant in my country and most people use them regularly. These phones, however, tend to be rather capricious, and many conversations are cut off in the middle. So now we face a standard (recurrent and multiply) coordination problem: who should resume the call—the original caller, or the person called? For obvious reasons, it would be much preferable to have a social convention whereby the original caller is expected to resume the call if the conversation is prematurely cut off (at least we can be sure that he or she knows the number). Nonetheless, if for some obscure reason, a convention evolves whereby it is the receiver of the call who is expected to resume it in such cases, then despite the clear preference of the alternative rule, most of us would be better off complying with the convention that is actually practised. That is, of course, as long as the reasons for having a convention in the first place are more important for us than the reason for preferring an alternative course of action.

So we can see now that conventional rules are arbitrary, even if we are far from indifferent as to the choice between R and R'. Furthermore, we can also see that the notion of arbitrariness admits of degrees. Conventions can be more or less arbitrary. We could say that a conventional rule is completely arbitrary if it is true that the agents are indeed completely indifferent as to the choice between R and R'; and the rule would be less and less arbitrary as we move away from complete indifference, up to the point where the preference of uniform conformity is just slightly stronger than the preference of a particular option.

Thus far, my story goes pretty much along the lines suggested by David Lewis's original account.[21] There are two modifications, however; that need to be considered. The first is modest, but important. It concerns the question of whether people should be thought to be aware of the arbitrary nature of the rule they follow in order for that rule to be a social convention. Lewis believed that the answer is affirmative. He insisted on a condition of *common knowledge* of the arbitrariness of the rule in question.[22] Yet I think that Tyler Burge has convincingly demonstrated that Lewis erred here.[23] People can be mistaken about the conventional nature of the rules they follow. To mention just one of Burge's examples, imagine

---

Synthese 349 (1996). There is, however, one clarification that I should mention here: the reason(s), A, which motivates people to comply with the rule R in the first place, need not be independent of the conventions themselves. I may have no reason whatsoever to play chess if there is no such conventional game to play. If I do have a reason to play chess, surely it depends on the fact that there is such a game that I can actually play. The importance of this point (which goes against Lewis's definition) will only become apparent later on.

[21] See Lewis, *supra* n. 14, at 76–80, for an account of imperfect coordination problems.
[22] See *id*. at 75.
[23] 'On Knowledge and Convention', 84 Phil. Rev. 249 (1975).

a small, completely isolated linguistic community, none of whose members has ever heard of anyone else speaking a different language. Now suppose that the people in this community believe that the language they speak is the only possible language in the world. They think that there are no humanly possible alternatives to speaking their language. Nevertheless, we would have no inclination to deny that their language is conventional just as any other language is. As Burge put it, 'They are simply ignorant or wrong about the nature of their activities.'[24]

Now we come to the second modification of Lewis's account, which is much more radical. I do not wish to doubt that Lewis's account of conventions is at least partly correct, and in many cases illuminating. Undeniably, numerous conventions emerge as solutions to recurrent coordination problems and this explains their entire rationale. Doubts arise, however, with respect to the generality of this thesis, and now I would like to substantiate these doubts. I would like to argue that there is another type of conventional rules, arbitrary in the sense I have defined, which cannot be explicated by Lewis's account. These are the constitutive conventions of autonomous practices.[25]

When we claim that a conventional rule functions as a solution to a recurrent coordination problem, the following condition must obtain: it should be entirely possible for us to describe the precise nature of the coordination problem, and the relevant agents' preferences, antecedent to the existence of the conventional rule in question. In other words, there must be a coordination *problem* first, and then its solution, in the form of a conventional rule. Furthermore, if Lewis's analysis is not to be thought of as completely vacuous and unhelpful, the coordination problem we diagnose must be pretty well structured. 'Here we are, let's do something' is not a coordination problem in the relevant sense. Otherwise, just about anything *we* do could be described as a solution to a coordination problem.

Now the problem is that this obvious condition is not met by numerous conventional practices we are familiar with. Take the rules constituting the game of chess, for example (just about any structured game would do, of course). It seems rather awkward to claim that the rules constituting the game of chess are solutions to a recurrent coordination problem. Antecedent to the game of chess, there was simply no problem to solve. Of course, once the game is there to play, and it is played, it may give rise to certain coordination problems that might then get settled by additional conventions. But chess itself, as a game of a particular kind, is not a solution to a problem of coordination. 'Let's have a competitive intellectual

---

[24] *Id.* at 250.
[25] I have already presented the basic argument about constitutive conventions. *See supra* n. 2.

game' or something like this is not a coordination problem along the lines suggested by Lewis. If it were, then 'Let's have a just Constitution' would also be a coordination problem, and, of course, it is not. Thus, the problem is this: either we stick to the idea of a coordination problem as a fairly structured set of conditions and preferences, in which case numerous conventions could not be described as solutions to such problems, or else we think of a coordination problem as something rather loose, applying to any set of circumstances where some form of collective action is pertinent, in which case just about any rule we follow would be an instance of following a convention.

Have we not reached the point of a useless quarrel over definition? In order to dispel this impression, let me concede the following. Perhaps it is not so important whether the emergence of a game, like chess, can or cannot be described as a solution to some coordination problem or other. Even if it can be so described, namely even if chess is a solution to some loose form of coordination problem, I would argue that in the case of chess, this is not illuminating. The uniqueness of such conventional practices, like playing chess, would be completely missed if we analysed such practices along the lines suggested by Lewis. In the case of a coordination convention, such as the telephone call-resuming convention, the whole point of the rule consists in the solution of the coordination problem that engendered it. The reason for having this convention is the same reason people would have for following it in each particular instance.

On the other hand, it would be ridiculous to maintain that the whole point of playing chess consists in the solution of a coordination problem between the players. People who play chess follow the rules of the game because by doing so they can engage in an activity they regard as, say, intellectually rewarding. Whatever the reason for having the game might be, or whatever 'problem' it was invented to solve, would have little bearing on the reasons people have for playing it. Once the game is there to play, it establishes, as it were, its own point.

It is a typical feature of conventions constituting such practices as the game of chess that they partly constitute the point or value of the activity itself, and it is in this sense that we can talk about autonomous practices: namely that the point of engaging in them is not fully determined by any particular purpose or value that is external to the conventions constituting the practice. In such cases, it is the practice itself which provides its own point, as it were, and at least some of its own standards of evaluation. The purpose, point, or value of an autonomous practice is partially set by the conventions constituting the practice. This is true not only of games, such as chess, but of numerous other social practices constituted by social conventions, such as practices of etiquette, conventions of fashion, and artistic genres. The point of the conventions constituting, for example, the genre of opera is not to solve a coordination problem (whose problem would that be, anyway?), but it is precisely the point of constituting a distinct and partly autonomous genre. The conventions constituting the practice of operas themselves define, to a considerable extent, what is the point of operas, and what it makes sense to say about them.

All this is just a rough sketch, and a great deal more needs to be said about conventions constituting autonomous practices. I hope that the following observations, even if far from comprehensive, prove useful.

A. Constitutive conventions are systematic

One distinguishing mark of constitutive conventions, in contrast to the coordination conventions explained by Lewis, is that the former, but not necessarily the latter, typically come in systems. There must be a system of conventional rules to establish a social practice, that is, some cluster of rules intertwined in a more or less complex structure. This is a feature that stems from the constitutive function of such conventions, from the fact that they constitute a practice.[26]

Furthermore, it should be kept in mind that conventions, by themselves, do not constitute social practices. A social practice does not consist in a set of rules, although it is constituted by rules. It is the whole 'grammar' of the activity constituted by the conventions that makes it an activity of a certain kind.[27] If there is a social practice, then there are many things that it makes sense to say about that practice. And, of course, many things it does not make sense to say about it. As Wittgenstein famously remarked, 'Grammar tells what kind of object anything is'.[28] Consider, for instance, the genre of (contemporary) theatre. It is an artistic genre constituted by a set of conventions, distinguishing, among other things, theatre from other conventionally established genres of stage performances. Thus, a great many things that normally take place in a theatre performance are instantiations of recognized conventions. However, such conventions also establish a whole grammar that is appropriate for this particular genre. We know, for instance, that it makes perfect sense to praise (or to complain about) the dramatic aspects of a theatre show, but that it makes no sense to complain, for example, that theatre performance is not competitive enough, or that it is a bad show because it does not

---

[26] The systematic nature of constitutive rules was first observed by Searle. See J. Searle, *Speech Acts* (1969), 33–42. Although I certainly draw here quite heavily on Searle's distinction between constitutive and regulative rules, I am not sure that I want to subscribe to his basic idea that these are two separate types of rule. Others have claimed, and perhaps they are right about this, that all rules have both constitutive and regulative functions.

[27] On this particular point, see the very intriguing article of Hubert Schwyzer, 'Rules and Practices', 78 Phil. Rev. 451 (1969).

[28] L. Wittgenstein, *Philosophical Investigations* (1953), sec. 373.

manifest physical strength. Such values as competitiveness and physical strength are not associated with the intrinsic values of theatre. If they were, it would have been a different social practice.

B. Partial autonomy

More importantly, however, we should realize that the autonomy of social practices is always partial. All social practices are related to general human concerns of one kind or another. Even the game of chess, which is relatively one of the most autonomous practices we are familiar with, is nevertheless closely related to such general human concerns as competitiveness, intellectual superiority, being 'a sport', and the like. Its autonomy, however, consists in the fact that the conventions constituting the practice are *radically underdetermined* by those general values and human concerns that they instantiate. There is, after all, an indefinite number of potential practices that could instantiate those same general human concerns which are instantiated by chess. The latter is just one option, arbitrarily 'chosen', as it were.

Most social practices, however, are less autonomous than chess. Consider, once again, distinct artistic genres like opera. Operas instantiate general musical and dramatic values, which are themselves related to more general artistic human concerns. In this respect, the autonomy of operas is rather limited and partial. Nonetheless, there are certain values, standards of appraisal, and concerns that are distinctly operatic, so to speak. The conventions establishing the genre of opera also define, to some extent, opera's own intrinsic values, and a considerable extent of its grammar: they define a great deal of what it makes sense to say about operas.

Thus, in each social practice constituted by conventions, we have a mix of general concerns which these practices are there to serve or instantiate and values associated with the practice in ways that are constituted by the conventions constituting the practice itself. Different practices can be more or less autonomous, according to the specific mix of such values.

C. The dynamic aspect of constitutive conventions

Constitutive conventions are prone to change. In this they markedly differ from coordination conventions. The latter serve specific functions in a specific set of circumstances; hence, as long as the circumstances remain as they were, the convention is unlikely to change. As we have already noted, in the case of a coordination convention, the reasons for having the convention in the first place, and the reasons for following it in each particular instance, are basically the same. Hence the relative stability of such conventions.[29]

Conversely, conventions constituting autonomous practices constitute a whole grammar of, *inter alia*, evaluative concerns that might then affect the point, and consequently the content and shape, of the constitutive conventions themselves. In other words, constitutive conventions tend to be in a constant process of interpretation and reinterpretation, which is affected partly by external values and partly by those same values constituted by the conventional practice itself. The rapid changes that occurred in the conventions of the visual arts during the twentieth century provide a dramatic example of this process. Some of the pressure for change came from external influences of a rapidly changing world, such as mass industrialization and development of new techniques. However, some of the pressure for change derived from new interpretations of those old values that were thought to be constitutive of the genre. Artists have gradually realized, for instance, that the point of a painting need not be achieved by a figurative composition; once this dramatic shift occurred, in the form of cubist and mainly abstract paintings, the constitutive conventions of painting also underwent a considerable change. Thus, just as the constitutive conventions establish the values associated with the practice, so changes in those values tend to change the conventions that initially constituted them. We may safely assume that the more a given practice tends to be interpretative, the more likely it is that such changes will occur.

D. Division of labour

It is typical of constitutive conventions that we tend to have a very partial knowledge of them. Most of us, for example, are aware of the fact that there are conventions constituting the genre of opera, but I confess that my knowledge of the content of those conventions is very partial, and I suspect that a lot of people are in the same boat. We know, however, that others know what those conventions are. There are, in this field, as in many others, experts or, perhaps better, practitioners. But the dividing line between the practitioners, whose practice determines the conventions, and others, who are more or less aware of them, is not a sharp one. To the question, 'Whose convention is it?' there is rarely a simple answer. What we would normally see is a kind of division of labour: a core of practitioners whose practices and self-understandings determine, to the

---

[29] It is true, of course, that if the coordination convention does not instantiate the optimal solution to the relevant coordination problem, a certain pressure may build up to move toward the optimal solution. But once the optimal solution has been reached, there would be no further inherent pressure for change.

greatest extent, what the convention is, and further groups of people in outer circles, whose knowledge of the convention is much more partial, and whose influence on its content is relatively marginal. But again, these distinctions between the relevant populations is not a hard and fast one; a complex division of labour may obtain, whereby even those groups who are relatively further removed from the inner circle do affect, though in limited ways, the shape and content of the relevant conventions.

Perhaps the clearest example of this actually obtains in the case of the law. Most people are only faintly aware of the rules of recognition of their country, and most people rely on their lawyers to know what those conventions really are. But even within the legal circles, some groups are more important than others. Judges and, perhaps to a similar extent, legislatures play the crucial role. The rules of recognition, as has been noted by Hart himself, are, first and foremost, the conventions of judges, particularly in the higher courts. But in fact other legal officials can also play various roles in determining the content of the rules of recognition. The practices of police officers, accountants, tax-collectors, city councillors, etc., all contribute something, though to a lesser extent, to what the rules of recognition are. So once again, the image I suggest is a division of labour taking place in concentric circles: the closer one is to the centre, the greater effect one has on what the convention is—and vice versa, of course. Generally speaking, however, most of us are, most of the time, in the outer circles, and rely on others who know better, namely on those whose practice it is.

Note, by the way, that none of this is expected to obtain in the case of coordination conventions. Coordination conventions are there to solve a particular recurrent coordination problem. Such conventions cannot be expected to solve the coordination problem if people are largely ignorant about their content. To be sure, I am not trying to suggest that people must be aware of the existence and nature of the coordination problem that gave rise to the emergence of the convention. But they must be aware of the solution, otherwise the convention cannot fulfil its function as such a solution.

E. The condition of efficacy

A final clarification is needed before we return to the rules of recognition. We have already noted the widespread assumption that the reasons for following a social convention are strongly tied to the fact that others also follow the same rule. Consequently, it is typically the case that there is no point in following a conventional rule that is not actually followed by the pertinent community. Let us call this the *condition of efficacy*. We have also seen that this condition of efficacy is easily explicable by David Lewis's analysis: If it is the point of a convention to solve a recurrent coordination problem, then the assumption is that for each and every agent, uniformity of action is preferable to any other alternative course of action. Hence the dominant preference of each agent is simply to act as the other agents will act in the relevant circumstances. Once the condition of efficacy is not met, the alleged convention can no longer fulfil its original function, and hence there is no reason to follow it. Now the question arises of whether we have an alternative explanation of the condition of efficacy for those social conventions which are not coordination conventions. Or should we claim that the condition of efficacy does not hold with respect to constitutive conventions?

I believe that the former option should be pursued, since the explanation is clear enough: it consists in the idea of a social practice. Conventional rules can constitute a social practice only if the rules are actually followed. Conventions, unlike (for example) moral rules, do not exist in the abstract: 'it ought to be that it ought to be that p' normally entails that 'it ought to be that p'. Whereas 'it ought to be that it is a convention that p' does not entail that 'it is a convention that p'. Only practised conventions are conventions.

Does this mean that the reasons for following a set of constitutive conventions consist in the fact that others follow it too? Not necessarily. We cannot explain people's reasons for engaging in a conventional practice just by reference to a desirability for uniformity of action. (Some people go to the opera just because others go to it too; but they would normally try to conceal this embarrassing explanation for their action.) It is normally the values inherent in the practice that explain people's reasons for engaging in it. But of course, sometimes people engage in a conventional practice for no reason at all, or for various obscure reasons that have nothing to do with the point of the practice itself. This should come as no surprise: we have already seen that there is an important difference between constitutive conventions and coordination conventions in this respect. In the latter case, the reasons for following the convention in each particular instance are closely tied to the reasons for having the convention in the first place, viz. the solution of the pertinent coordination problem. In the case of constitutive conventions, no such close relationship necessarily exists.

Nevertheless, in both cases the condition of efficacy holds true. Conventional rules exist only if they are actually practised by the pertinent community. It is the practice of following the rule that makes it a convention in the first place.

To be sure, I am not trying to suggest that the idea of a social practice is very clear. Suppose my wife and I go to the cinema every Tuesday evening; is this a social practice? I guess not. But now suppose we just add more people to this habit of going to the cinema on Tuesday evenings, say, my neighbours; would it become a social practice just by getting the sufficient number of people? I am still inclined to say no. But what would be missing here? One is inclined to reply that what is missing is the idea that the Tuesday cinema habit is a social practice, and not just a happy coincidence of personal habits or reasons. Now, this may not be as silly or circular an answer as it sounds. Social practices exist when there is a custom of following a rule. The idea of a custom, however, is not to be confused with something like 'a lot of people doing the same thing'. There is no custom of drinking water, although most people drink water very often. The contrast here is not like the one between an aria and a chorus, but like the contrast between making noise and playing music: a lot of people making the same noise does not make it music. A social practice has a history, a set of values it instantiates, and a sense in which the fact that others follow the same rules is, in itself, crucially significant.

V. THE RULES OF RECOGNITION REVISITED

I think that by now we have most of the pieces of the puzzle at our disposal, and we just need to put them in place. The rules of recognition, I would like to show, are (by and large) constitutive conventions, establishing partly autonomous practices of identifying the sources of law. Now, some of the worries about the conventionality of the rules of recognition that we have mentioned, we can relieve rather quickly; others require more careful treatment.

First, however, let me give an illustration of the kind of recognition convention I have in mind. Consider the following example. Common law jurisdictions have a well-defined set of rules establishing the doctrine of precedent. Now, whereas precedent is a conventionally recognized source of law in common law jurisdictions, it is not such a recognized source of law in other jurisdictions (e.g. France and Germany). Even in France and Germany, however, one can observe certain patterns of legal arrangements and legal decisions that resemble precedent. The lack of a doctrine of precedent in French law does not entail, in practice, a total lack of deference to higher courts' decisions on part of the lower courts. The hierarchical structure of the court system and the possibility of appeals by themselves dictate a certain amount of precedent-like behaviour, so to speak, in the actual practice of the French and (mainly) German courts.

In other words, once we have a hierarchical structure of courts there is always some pressure toward a precedent-like behaviour. Nevertheless, despite this almost universal phenomenon, we witness the fact that in some jurisdictions a well-defined doctrine of precedent evolved, and in others it is not only lacking but doctrinally denied (particularly in France). Different rules of recognition are practised in similar circumstances in these two types of jurisdiction. Furthermore, the practices established by these rules of recognition embody a whole grammar of descriptive and evaluative judgments. The doctrine of precedent does not only consist in a set of rules that courts follow; it consists in a whole cluster of behavioural and argumentation patterns characteristic of them, and a great many things it makes sense to say, or doesn't make sense to say, within and about the various aspects of the practice.

Now this is, I think, a good illustration of the partial autonomy of conventional practices. On the one hand, there is a set of circumstances calling for some form of precedent-like practice; on the other, it is evident that these circumstances, and the needs emergent from them, are not definitive of the practices emergent from them. The conventional practice, in other words, is underdetermined by the external needs giving rise to its emergence. The constitutive conventions themselves constitute part of the practice's point, many aspects of its grammar, and some of the values associated with it.

What is it that explains the difference, then? One option would be to maintain that what we face here is a standard coordination problem, differently solved by these two different legal systems. But there is an obvious difficulty with this suggestion, because it would actually present the French and German legal systems with an unsolved coordination problem. If the pressure for precedent-like behaviour on part of the courts stems from coordination needs, and only the common law countries have a developed precedent practice, Continental systems would seem to be in a pathetic predicament: here there is an obvious problem of coordination, and the Germans or the French have declined to develop the conventions for solving it! Quite an unlikely scenario. The real difference lies, of course, in the respective histories of these different legal systems.[30]

There is a general lesson here, which most of Hart's commentators have crucially missed. Conventionalism in any social domain inevitably calls for historicism. In this respect, conventionalism is markedly at odds with traditional functionalist explanations of social practices. On this Functionalist v. Historicist dichotomy, conventionalism sides with the latter. In order to explain a conventionally established social practice—that is, in the case of constitutive conventions, as opposed to simple coordination conventions—one must always consult history. This is just another way of conveying the idea of the partial autonomy of social practices. Even if

[30] As every amateur legal historian knows, the roots of the Continental system's declining to follow the practice of precedent are in the French Revolution and the rigid doctrine of separation of powers it engendered.

there are relatively well definable needs that a social practice is there to solve, as in the case of legal precedent, the practice which is actually constituted by conventions is normally underdetermined by those external needs. The practice's development, and its emergent grammar, is largely determined by historical contingencies.

How far can we generalize the precedent example, that is, as a general model of the conventional rules of recognition? I think that we can do this pretty much all the way down. However, this requires us to take stock of previous sections, and dispel some of the worries we had initially encountered. First, there was the problem that the rules of recognition do not look like solutions to recurrent coordination problems. We have dealt with this problem at length. We have seen in detail that constitutive conventions do not emerge as solutions to coordination problems at all. One main worry remains, however, with respect to the arbitrariness of conventional rules. Can we reconcile the moral-political aspect of the rules of recognition with their arbitrary-conventional nature?

Two clarifications already mentioned bear on this point. First, we have noted that a given rule can be arbitrary, in the relevant sense, even if it is not recognized as such by the pertinent community. People need not be aware of the arbitrary nature of the rule they follow for that rule to be a convention, and arbitrary in the relevant sense. A legal community can be wrong, or ignorant, about the real character of the rules of recognition they follow.[31]

Second—and this is the crux of the matter—we have seen in detail that the condition of arbitrariness does not imply the idea of indifference. A rule can be arbitrary, in the sense we have defined, even if it reflects moral or political convictions. And the same is true in other areas, of course. Opera, theatre, and even the game of chess instantiate evaluative convictions, and this evaluative dimension does not impair the conventional foundation of such practices. The crucial question is not whether the rules of recognition reflect political convictions, but whether those same convictions provide sufficient reasons for acting in accordance with the rule, even if the rule in question is not followed by others. By saying that the rule is conventional, we suggest a negative answer only to this last question. Suppose that a German judge genuinely believes that the doctrine of precedent, for example, is superior to any other conceivable alternative, morally, politically, or otherwise. Would it not be rather absurd to maintain that one has to abide by this doctrine even if it is not practised by one's fellow judges in Germany?

---

[31] But not the content, of course. I am certainly not trying to suggest that a whole legal community can be wrong about the content of the rules of recognition. On the contrary: I have elsewhere argued at some length that the conventional foundations of law make it impossible for a whole community of lawyers to misidentify their law. See Andrei Marmor, *Interpretation and Legal Theory* (1992), ch. 5.

One could insist, of course, that the doctrine of precedent is not only a conventional set of rules of recognition in the common law systems, but also a political ideal worthy of respect in itself, regardless of practice. One would then have to say, among other things, that the French and German legal systems are morally or politically deficient in their lack of respect for this doctrine. Perhaps so; but then, of course, one is no longer talking about the rules of recognition.

To sum up so far: the condition of arbitrariness, essential to the idea of a social convention, is not at odds with the moral or political content of the rules of recognition. Rules of recognition do reflect, as they must, political convictions that have been shaped by the history of the relevant legal system. Their conventionality consists in the close link between the reasons for following the relevant rules and the fact that those are the rules which are actually practiced in the community. This is perfectly consistent with the definition of arbitrariness of conventions I have suggested in the previous section.

Another problem, however, seems to emerge here. Can conventional rules of recognition give rise to a judicial *obligation* to follow the rule? If the rule of recognition is only a social convention, why should a judge feel obliged to follow the rule if he or she could follow a different rule that the judge considers, for example, morally superior? As Leslie Green observed, Hart's 'view that the fundamental rules [of recognition] are "mere conventions" continues to sit uneasily with any notion of obligation,' and this Green finds troubling, because the rules of recognition point to the 'sources that judges are *legally* bound to apply'.[32]

I believe that this is a spurious worry. From a moral or political point of view, the rules of recognition, by themselves, cannot be regarded as sources of obligation. Whether judges or anybody else should or should not respect the rules of recognition of a legal system is purely a moral issue that can only be resolved by moral arguments (concerning the age-old issue of political obligation). And this is more generally so: the existence of a social practice, in itself, does not provide anyone with an obligation to engage in the practice. The rules of recognition only define what the practice is, and they can say nothing on the question of whether one should, or should not, engage in it. But of course, once one does engage in the practice, playing the judge, as it were, there are *legal* obligations defined by the rules of the game.

In other words, Green should not be worried by the notion of a *legal* obligation to follow the rules of recognition. The referee of a soccer game is equally obliged to follow the rules of his game, and the fact that the game is conventional poses no difficulty from this, let us say, 'internal

---

[32] 'The Concept of Law Revisited', 94 Mich. L. Rev., 1687 (1996), 1697.

player's' perspective. But again, the constitutive rules of soccer cannot settle for me the question whether I should play soccer or not. Similarly, the rules of recognition cannot settle for the judge, or anyone else for that matter, whether one should play by the rules of law or not. They only tell the judges what the law is.

In one important respect, however, the analogy between law and games that I have been using throughout this essay is potentially misleading. Unlike games, such as chess or soccer, which are relatively isolated from general human concerns, and hence autonomous to a very considerable extent, law is much more closely related to numerous practical concerns. Law's relative autonomy is much more limited and partial than are games and artistic genres. The dimension of partial autonomy is best seen as a continuous scale, whereby games like chess are on one extreme side, being perhaps one of the most autonomous social practices, and law on the other extreme side, as probably one of the least autonomous practices we are familiar with. (Artistic genres would be somewhere in the middle, closer to games than to law, I guess.) If I am right about this, a methodological question arises here. Why bother about this issue at all? Why should we care about the autonomy of law if we initially admit that it is very limited and partial?

The main answer to this question cannot be given here because it concerns the issue of the objectivity of law, which is complicated enough to deserve a separate essay.[33] But I can suggest three related observations here. First, as I have tried to show in some detail above, the autonomy of law (as of other social practices) is a consequence of its conventional foundations. Law is partly autonomous because it is conventional, and not the other way around. Second, we must keep it in mind that conventionalism is a significant doctrine only if it is not maintained across the board. It is significant precisely because not everything is a matter of social conventions. In our case, it is mainly the contrast between law, which is claimed to be conventional, and morality, which is not, that is of particular interest. Finally—and this is a point I have already mentioned—but I would like to re-emphasize: conventionalism, properly understood, strongly supports historicism as opposed to functionalism. There are a lot of 'isms' in this sentence, so let me be clear about what I mean.

David Lewis's account of social conventions is basically a functionalist explanation. It explains both the emergence of conventions and their rationale in terms of a specific function conventional rules are there to fulfil (viz. of solving a particular coordination problem). I have tried to argue here that this explanation is too impoverished; a great many conventions are not fully explicable in such functional terms. Historical

---

[33] See Marmor, *Positive Law and Objective Values*, ch. 7.

contingencies, and the emergent constitutive conventions, play a crucial role in determining the shape and content of the social practices we encounter. Functionalism without the history is like a novel's basic plot without the narrative. The narrative is written by history, and it shapes the plot much more than functionalists would like to admit. The partial autonomy of social practices is simply the consequence of this narrative-dependent plot.

Perhaps this connection between conventionalism and historicism that I attribute to the legal positivism espoused by Hart would surprise many of Hart's critics. (Not all of them—Leslie Green, for example, has made this point very convincingly, though I think that he failed to notice the conventionalist foundation.[34]) Perhaps it is not only the critics' fault. Hart, like Wittgenstein before him, was very much aware of the historicism entailed by conventionalism, but both of them paid too little attention to history to make this explicit enough.

Be this as it may, I hope I have said enough to show that Hart's theory about the rules of recognition still deserves to be considered very seriously. I have also tried to show that Hart's theory is basically correct, although between the original practice theory of rules and the explicit conventionalism of his Postscript, I have tried to substantiate the latter.

---

[34] Green, *supra* n. 32, at 1698 ff.

7

The Model of Social Facts

BENJAMIN C. ZIPURSKY

I. INTRODUCTION

Rules are central to *The Concept of Law*[1] in at least two respects—one pertaining to certain propositional or linguistic entities, the other, to certain kinds of practice within a community. While one vital theme of the book is that a legal system is a system of rules, a second, and equally important, theme is that for some norm to be a law is for the officials of the community to have a special kind of rule—a social rule—of treating certain norms as laws only if they comply with certain criteria, and for that norm to comply with those criteria. The notion of a *rule of recognition* fuses these two senses of 'rule', being both a fundamental secondary rule within a legal system and an important social rule within a legal community.

Dworkin's attack on *The Concept of Law* highlights the central role given to rules, particularly in the seminal articles, 'The Model of Rules I' and 'The Model of Rules II'.[2] Each of these articles focuses principally on one of the two rule themes referred to above. 'The Model of Rules I' argues that the model of legal systems as sets of rules is fatally flawed because it ignores the pervasive place of principles in the law. 'The Model of Rules II', by contrast, does not focus on rules and principles in legal systems. It takes aim at Hart's practice account of *social rules*, and at his effort to explain legality as a matter of fact about the conduct and attitudes of legal officials.[3]

I am grateful to Jules Coleman, Jill Fisch, John Goldberg, James Kainen, Charles Kelbley, Arthur Ripstein, Anthony Sebok, and Scott Shapiro for helpful discussions of the ideas put forward in this essay.

[1] H. L. A. Hart, *The Concept of Law* (2nd edn., ed. P. Bulloch and J. Raz, 1994) (hereinafter *CL*).

[2] Ronald Dworkin, 'The Model of Rules I', in *Taking Rights Seriously* (2nd edn., 1978), 14–45 (hereinafter *TRS*); 'The Model of Rules II', in *TRS*, at 46–80. 'The Model of Rules I' will be referred to in text and notes as MOR I and 'The Model of Rules II' will be referred to as MOR II; page references in the notes will be to *TRS*.

[3] Both MOR papers treat both issues; the question is one of focus. See esp. *TRS*, at 48–64 (sections of MOR II, criticizing Hart's theory of social rules). Indeed, MOR I obviously does not rest on a mischaracterization of Hart as believing that legal systems consist only of 'rule-like' norms, as opposed to principles. Nevertheless, it is fair to characterize the gestalt theme of MOR I as built upon Hart's inability to go beyond rules and accommodate principles in law, and the gestalt theme of MOR II as built upon the idea that social rules, in the Hartian sense, cannot be what makes valid law valid.

Hart responds to both of the lines of attack in the Postscript, and in each case defends his position against Dworkin, while conceding some ground. There is, however, a notable difference in the tenor of these two responses. This difference suggests a distinction both in Hart's estimate of the power of Dworkin's respective criticisms and in the comparative centrality of the two centres of *The Concept of Law*. On the topic of rules and principles, Hart openly concedes that it is a defect in the original edition of *The Concept of Law* that it paid insufficient attention to arguments from legal principles in the law.[4] And while he carefully argues that many of Dworkin's contrasts between rules and principles were overdrawn, he implicitly concedes that many legal provisions that would aptly be described as 'principles' are not adequately described as 'rules'.[5] Most importantly, Hart declares unambiguously in the *Postscript* that he accepts the intermediate position of soft positivism.[6] Soft positivism—or, as I will call it, 'inclusive positivism'—is a view advanced by Coleman,[7] Soper,[8] Waluchow,[9] and others, which asserts that in many legal systems—including American law—the so-called 'rule of recognition' actually incorporates moral criteria and considerations of principle. While these thinkers have offered powerful arguments that there is conceptual space for such a view, nevertheless, when one rereads chapter 5, 'Law as the Union of Primary and Secondary Rules', and sees the crystalline structure envisioned in the first edition, one is tempted to say that the inclusion of principles at both the primary and, through inclusive positivism, the secondary level constitutes a substantial alteration of Hart's original view.[10]

If Hart can be seen as meeting Dworkin half-way on the rules versus principles debate, the same cannot be said for their controversy over the connection between law and social rules. At first blush, Hart is perhaps even more conciliatory on this issue, admitting that '[s]ome of Dworkin's

---

[4] *CL*, at 259.   [5] *Id*. at 263.

[6] I do not mean to commit myself to the claim that, in endorsing soft positivism, Hart is altering his position. In the Postscript, Hart states his commitment to soft positivism by referring to passages in the 1st edn. of *CL*, and in 'Positivism and the Separation of Law and Morals', where he recognizes the possibility of a rule of recognition that includes moral criteria, as in the US Constitution. *CL*, at 250. On the other hand, given the debate between inclusive and exclusive positivism that has ensued since those works were first published, the relatively scant attention Hart paid the issue previously, and the substantial attention devoted to it here, Hart's declaration that he endorses soft positivism in the Postscript is in and of itself significant.

[7] Jules L. Coleman, 'Negative and Positive Positivism', 11 J. Leg. Stud. 139 (1982), repr. in *Ronald Dworkin and Contemporary Jurisprudence*, ed. M. Cohen (1984) (hereinafter *RDCJ*), 28–48; also repr in Jules L. Coleman, *Markets, Morals and the Law* (1988), 3–27.

[8] E. Philip Soper, 'Legal Theory and the Obligation of a Judge: The Hart/Dworkin Dispute', in *RDCJ*, at 3–27.

[9] W. J. Waluchow, *Inclusive Legal Positivism* (1994).

[10] But see *supra* n. 6, and sources referred to therein.

criticism of my original account of social rules is certainly sound and important for the understanding of law', and noting that the Postscript offers 'considerable modifications'.[11] However, the text reveals only two concessions to Dworkin on this issue, and neither is particularly significant to Hart's jurisprudence. Hart readily admits that the conventionality of a social practice is not simply a matter of the concurrent practices of members of a group for what may be independent reasons, but involves, in part, conformity with a rule because it is conventionally accepted. And he asserts that his prior account of social rules is only applicable to rules 'which are conventional in the sense I have now explained', and that his practice theory does not provide a 'sound explanation of morality, either individual or social'.[12] On the 'social rules' issue that is weightier in the Hart–Dworkin debate, however, Hart remains firm. He adheres to his original thesis that the social rule account captures the nature of rules of recognition in a legal system: 'But the theory remains as a faithful account of conventional social rules which include ... certain important legal rules *including the rule of recognition.*'[13] In a few dense pages of the Postscript, Hart offers a defence of his analysis of rules of recognition against Dworkin's 'Model of Rules II' critique.

The Postscript's response to the MOR II critique replies mainly to two Dworkinian arguments: the argument from rule-of-recognition normativity and the argument from disagreement. Dworkin's initial presentation of the rule-of-recognition normativity argument runs as follows:

We must therefore recognize a distinction between two sorts of statements each of which uses the concept of a rule. The sociologist, we might say, is asserting a *social rule*, but the churchgoer is asserting a *normative* rule. We might say that the sociologist's assertion of a social rule is true (or warranted) if a certain factual state of affairs occurs, that is, if the community behaves in the way Hart describes in his example. But we should want to say that the churchgoer's assertion of a normative rule is true (or warranted) only if a certain normative state of affairs exists, that is, only if individuals in fact do have the duty that they suppose they have in Hart's example. The judge trying a lawsuit is in the position of the churchgoer, not the sociologist. He does not mean to state, as a cold fact, simply that most judges believe that they have the duty to follow what the legislature has said; he means that they do in fact have such a duty and he cites that duty, not others' beliefs, as the justification for his own decision. If so, then the social rule cannot, without more, be the source of the duty he believes he has.[14]

In the Postscript, Hart comments that Dworkin's embrace of the idea of a 'normative state of affairs' strikes him as obscure, and that Dworkin appears to neglect the phenomena in which participants in social practices cite behaviour of other participants. At a broader level, however, Hart can be understood as saying that Dworkin appears to be adopting a form of moral foundationalism or moral reductionism about normative rules, and that this is implausible both in the legal case and with regard to other social rules. It is not simply that Dworkin rejects the social rules view for law or for social practices. It is that he insists that judges, in reaching conclusions about legal validity, must be operating from premises about what there is a moral duty to do. And there is no indication that, when Dworkin discusses normative rules or duty imposition or what there is a duty to do, he means anything other than fully-fledged moral duties of judges. Hence, it is not surprising that Hart finds Dworkin's suggestion not only perplexing but also totally implausible from a hermeneutical point of view. For whatever we do within conventional social practices, and whatever judges do in deciding the validity of laws, they seem to be doing something utterly different, and much more practice-bound, than the sort of normative argumentation that Dworkin seems to be advocating. Judges are not deliberating from or reasoning about what it is their moral duty to do. They are deliberating about and reasoning from premises about what conditions must be satisfied in order for there to be law.[15]

Dworkin's argument from disagreement runs as follows (according to Hart): there is not a rule of recognition that satisfies the conditions that Hart sets out for social rules, since there is often substantial controversy over what criteria ought to be used in assessing legal validity. The social rules model asserts that a rule of recognition is a social rule and a social rule is one that members of a community agree upon. Hart responds to this argument in the Postscript. He answers that Dworkin has excluded the possibility that a rule of recognition may be agreed upon even if its application is not agreed upon. All disagreements which Dworkin takes as evidence that there is no rule of recognition that is agreed upon are better interpreted as disagreements in application of an agreed upon rule.

In his confident rejection of Dworkin's principal MOR II critique, Hart signalled his continuing allegiance to the Social Rules Thesis. Juxtaposing this firm adherence against his equally open-minded embrace of Inclusive Positivism, we are led to a particular view of the sense in which Hart was a positivist, at least in his later years. Neither the Sources Thesis nor the Separation Thesis (in any particularly hard form) appears to have been central to Hart, nor does any particularly harsh thesis about the centrality

---

[15] This is not to deny that rules of recognition may be viewed by judges as providing the content of what it is their obligation, as judges, to do in deciding cases. Nor is to deny that, for Hart, the theory of rules of recognition as social rules explains the possibility of judges' having duties in applying the law. Neither of these is equivalent to the claim that reasoning from rule of recognition statements is reasoning about duties. See *infra* Part IV.

of rules, as opposed to principles. As Coleman's work suggests,[16] the centre of Hart's positivism might now appear to be the thesis that law is constituted by social facts. With this modification in mind, we might improvise upon Dworkin's work and select 'the model of social facts' as an appropriate catchphrase for a central theme of *The Concept of Law*, as seen through the Postscript.

Dworkin took Hart to be embracing a model of social facts in roughly the following sense: a view that social facts are what make rule-of-recognition statements true, and therefore social facts are what make it the case that the law is one way rather than another. As I shall argue in Part II, this was an understandable and probably correct interpretation of an aspect of the theory Hart intended to be offering. But for reasons I will set forth in Parts III–VI, that view of the relation between legal statements and social facts is untenable, and 'the model of social facts', so interpreted, must be rejected. Part VII argues that, despite evidence that Hart adhered to a 'model of social facts' view, Hart's central jurisprudential aims do not require adherence to a model of social facts. Notwithstanding the critique of Parts III–VI, I argue, an acceptable form of conventionalism is available to Hart. The possibility of a Hartian, conventionalist view of law *without the model of social facts* is the central point of this article.

The rejection of the model of social facts immediately invites another project, however, one which the remainder of the article commences. If rule-of-recognition statements are not made true by social facts, the question arises as to what sort of semantics is available for them. Part VIII offers a very sketchy beginning of a 'legal coherentist' account of the semantics of rule-of-recognition statements and of legal statements more generally, one which is intended to complement a conventionalistic account of law, not to replace it. Part IX transforms the Hartian critique undertaken in most of the article and suggests that, since conventionalism does not entail the model of social facts, a great deal of Hart's work about the conventional nature of law may also be available to Dworkin.

In brief, I aim to show that Dworkin's rejection of Hartian positivism as a theory of the subject matter and truth conditions of legal statements is consistent with Hart's adoption of conventionalism in descriptive jurisprudence. While inclusive positivism can be seen as a partial reconciliation of Hart and Dworkin on the rules/principles debate, *coherentist conventionalism* brings us closer to a reconciliation of Hart and Dworkin on the respects in which law depends for its existence on social practices. Understood as a semantic and metaphysical picture—as a model of legal facts resting upon social facts—Hart's conventionalism is seriously

---

[16] See e.g. Coleman, *supra* n. 7; Jules L. Coleman, 'Incorporationism, Conventionality, and the Practical Difference Thesis' (this volume).

misleading, but understood as a means of grasping the constructive nature of law and legal concepts, it is a startling philosophical achievement.

II. THE MODEL OF SOCIAL FACTS

Much of the debate over Dworkin's critique of Hart's 'model of rules' goes to the question of whether Hart in fact entertained the view that Dworkin labelled 'the model of rules' in anything like the manner Dworkin alleged. Without entering that controversy, one can at least take a lesson from it. This debate counsels caution in attributing yet another 'model' to Hart—the model of social facts—particularly since the phrase 'the model of social facts' (like 'the model of rules') is not Hart's (in this case, my own), and the attribution will set the stage for my critique of Hart. The reader should bear in mind not only that there is significant textual support for the following attribution, but also that I shall later in the essay conjecture a second interpretation of Hart's conventionalism that is immune from the objections I am offering. In this respect, the attribution of 'the model of social facts' view to Hart is in part an exegetical device.

If Hart's positivism is (as Coleman suggests[17]) characterized by a view of the centrality of social facts to the law, then he must be interpreted as holding quite a substantial thesis about the connection between law and social facts. An example of a thesis that is too weak is the thesis that law would not exist as an institution if people did not behave in certain ways —that certain facts about human conduct and attitudes are a necessary condition for the existence of human law. The model of social facts must say more than this, for Dworkin and perhaps even Aquinas and natural law theorists seem committed to this. It is therefore not enough to single out positivism. A slightly stronger claim is that social practices 'make law possible', but again, this claim is certainly held by thinkers such as Dworkin and Fuller, and therefore is not definitive of a positivistic conception of law.[18]

---

[17] One of Coleman's characterizations of the 'Social Facts Thesis' is 'the claim that while law is a normative social practice it is made possible by some set of social facts'. Coleman, *supra* n. 7, at 395. In fact, he suggests that this is 'the distinctive feature of legal positivism', and cites Austin, but it is clear that Coleman takes Hart and *CL* to represent an exceptionally good example of a form of positivism that recognizes the centrality of a social facts thesis.

[18] *Id*. at 397. The modal formulation quoted in the text is offered by Coleman subsequent to two slightly different formulations. 'The distinctive feature of legal positivism is that it attempts to explain law in terms of *social facts*.' *Id*. at 395. The emphasis on 'explanation' here is epistemic (or methodological), as opposed to modal. Between the epistemic formulation on 395 and the modal formulation on 397 is a hybrid epistemic/modal formulation: 'The

The Concept of Law suggests a deeper and broader sense in which Hart conceived of law in terms of a model of social facts. He appears to maintain that a statement about what the law is is made true by certain social facts—facts regarding the conduct and attitude of certain persons in the community, and relatedly, facts about what the law is consist in facts about the conduct and attitude of certain persons. When I refer to 'the model of social facts', that is what I shall be referring to.

Two prominent passages in *CL* , taken together, support attributing the model of social facts to Hart. In discussing the distinction between internal and external statements, Hart comments that a rule of recognition is unlike other rules in a system. 'The assertion that it exists can only be an external statement of fact',[19] by which he means facts about the acceptance of a rule of recognition. And in discussing the special role of a rule of recognition, Hart concurred with prior philosophers that statements about the legal validity of primary rules 'do indeed carry with them certain presuppositions'.[20] Crucially, he goes on to say of such a rule of recognition that it is not only accepted by the person who presupposes it 'but is the rule of recognition actually accepted and employed in the general operation of the system. If the truth of this presupposition were doubted, *it could be established by reference to actual practice: to the way in which courts identify what is to count as law, and to the general acceptance or acquiescence in these identifications.'*[21]

Of course, Hart believed that what made it true that a certain statute was valid was that it satisfied the criteria set forth in the rule of recognition in force in the legal community. It thus becomes pivotal to whether a statute is valid law whether a particular rule of recognition is in force. As the prior paragraph indicates, Hart thought: (i) there was no sense in which it could be the case that a rule of recognition was in force in a legal community, except that certain social facts existed (e.g. it was accepted); (ii) certain social facts existing did indeed make it true that a rule of recognition was

organizing idea of legal positivism is that law's possibility must be explained in terms of social facts. I call this the Social Facts Thesis, and nothing is more important to legal positivism.' *Id.* at 396–7. Coleman expressly rejects the idea that the social facts thesis requires reductionism about legal statements, and notes that Hart's insistence on capturing the internal point of view precluded reductionism. This leaves open the possibility of attributing to Hart the view I put forward in the text, that social facts made legal statements true (one need not concede that the force or meaning of such statements was 'reduced' to social facts). While Coleman mentions supervenience, the idea is not developed, and there is properly no attribution of a supervenience view to Hart himself.

A second interpretation of Hart's social facts thesis, which I offer in Pt. VII, resembles the epistemic and methodological aspect of Coleman's view, but (a) does not emphasize the modal aspect and (b) does not claim centrality in accounting for the authority of law. Moreover, I am much less confident than Coleman that a model of social facts thesis so construed is in and of itself a form of positivism, let alone the core of positivism.

[19] *CL*, at 110.   [20] *Id.* at 108.
[21] *Id.* (emphasis added)

in force. The upshot seems to be that social facts 'established' the truth of the presupposition used by those identifying the valid norms of a system. For this reason, facts about social practices appear to be what make statements about the validity of primary rules true, and the validity of primary rules appears to consist, in part, in the social facts existing in light of which the primary rules' possession of certain attributes makes them law. This is both the evidence that Hart endorsed the model of social facts and the defence he offered for it.[22]

The model of social facts so understood is appealing both as an effort to represent a broad strand of positivism and more generally. With regard to the former, the model of social facts replaces—but retains the same spirit as—the Austinian idea that whether a command is *law* turns on how that command is 'positioned', and how it is positioned is a matter of social and historical fact about the position and conduct of the issuer and audience of the command. While positivism's emphasis on separation is no doubt important to its significance and what some view as its essence, Austin can be interpreted as arguing for separation from this more basic point that the status of being law turned on actual position, and actual position was a matter of social and historical fact. Hart clearly took it to be a central part of his project in *The Concept of Law* to rescue this tradition of thinking about law from its own errors and limitations. Facts about patterns of obedience and actual issuance of command are replaced, in part, by facts about general obedience and official acceptance of a rule of recognition. But, arguably, it remains the case that what makes it true that a putative law is valid law is that certain social facts obtain; this is at least true of the rule of recognition and derivatively of all norms, for they get their validity from the rule of recognition.[23] The model of social facts so construed renders Hart's social rules theory a recognizable form of positivism in the spirit of Austin.

Dworkin's attack on Hart in MOR II is perhaps more easily understood as an attack on the model of social facts, so interpreted, than as an attack on a model of rules. For his fundamental complaint is that, for Hart, the 'existence of the social rule, and therefore the existence of the duty, is

---

[22] As one reader has correctly pointed out, this passage is far from conclusive evidence that Hart endorsed the model of social facts. What is needed is an argument that Hart did not simply mean that the existence of the rule of recognition could be demonstrated—that he additionally thought this could make true the social fact statement that was part of the discursive justification in question. The passage itself does not confirm this interpretation. Later in this essay, I offer further reasons for supposing Hart might have had this in mind. See *infra*, Pt. VII. However, as indicated above, the attribution of the model of social facts to Hart is tentative, and is ultimately complemented by a somewhat different view, consistent with the caveat offered at the beginning of this footnote.

[23] The effects of Hart's embrace of Soft Positivism on this view are discussed in VII, *infra*.

simply a matter of fact'.[24] As we shall see, it is far from clear whether it really matters to Dworkin whether there are social conventions, agreements, or social rules of the sort he denies. What is plainly vital to Dworkin's position, however, is his denial that the existence of legal rights and duties, or the validity of putative laws, is simply a matter of social fact.

III RULES OF RECOGNITION AND THE MODEL OF SOCIAL FACTS

This part has three aspects: interpretive, constructive, and critical. At an interpretive level, it aims to discern, through a sort of dialectical exegesis, what Hart meant by 'rule of recognition' and what roles were played by rules of recognition in his theory, as well as what is meant by 'internal statement' and 'external statement'. At a constructive level, it sketches a conventionalistic theory of rules of recognition along the lines endorsed by Hart in the Postscript and suggested in this volume by Andrei Marmor.[25] At a critical level, it launches the central argument of the article, that rule-of-recognition statements are not made true by social facts.

A. Ambiguities in the phrase 'rule of recognition'

In *The Concept of Law*, Hart uses the phrase 'rule of recognition' in three interrelated ways. First, he sometimes suggests that rules of recognition are linguistic entities that designate what the primary rules of the system are (famously, through designating the criteria for legal validity). Thus, Hart's first example of a rule of recognition is 'an authoritative list or text of the [primary] rules to be found in a written document or carved on some public monument'.[26] In the Postscript, and in 'Positivism and the Separation of Law and Morals',[27] Hart suggests that the United States Constitution may be a part of the rule of recognition in the American legal system, and this is certainly an example of a text.[28] The tendency to see the rule of recognition in this way is further supported by the fact that primary rules of a legal system are very plausibly identified with linguistic entities—with texts—and Hart appears to regard primary rules and secondary rules as different species of the same type of thing—rules.

---

[24] *TRS*, at 50.
[25] Marmor, 'Legal Conventionalism' (this volume). The view here is more consonant with Marmor's constitutive conventionalism than with Coleman's coordinative conventionalism.
[26] *CL*, at 94.
[27] 71 Harv. L. Rev. 593 (1958).
[28] *CL*, at 250.

Second, Hart often suggests that the rule of recognition is what certain linguistic entities (such as certain provisions within the United States Constitution) express. The rule of recognition, on this view, is the designation of standards or criteria that determine what the primary rules of the system are. But no particular verbal formulation *is* the rule of recognition. Such formulations merely *express* it. On this view, the rule of recognition is a proposition that sets forth the standards which determine what the primary rules of a legal system are. It is plain that the first, purely linguistic aspect is inadequate for interpreting *The Concept of Law*: 'In the day-to-day life of a legal system its rule of recognition is very seldom expressly formulated as a rule.'[29] 'The use of unstated rules of recognition, by courts and others, in identifying particular rules of the system is characteristic of the internal point of view.'[30] Moreover, Hart frequently speaks of acceptance of a rule, by which he means accepting *that certain criteria determine which putative norms are legally valid*, and accepting the latter is accepting something of a propositional order.

Third, and most famously, Hart frequently claims that a rule of recognition is a particular kind of social practice, which he calls a 'social rule'. This claim, and the analysis of social rules to which it is conjoined,[31] lie at the core of his account of law,[32] as recent scholarship suggests.[33] The conceptualization of a rule of recognition as a social rule of treating putative legal norms in a particular manner is seemingly confirmed by Hart himself in the Postscript:

My account of social rules is, as Dworkin has also rightly claimed, applicable only to rules which are conventional in the sense I have explained. This considerably narrows the scope of my practice theory and I do not now regard it is a sound explanation of morality, either individual or social. But the theory remains a faithful account of conventional social rules which include . . . certain important legal rules including the rule of recognition, which is in effect a form of judicial customary rule existing only if it is accepted and practised in the law-identifying and law-applying operations of the courts.[34]

Hart's three different uses of the phrase 'rule of recognition' unfortunately gives rise to a certain amount of confusion. To begin with, it would appear that several aspects of his theory hinge on certain attributes of rules of recognition, and yet if 'rule of recognition' simultaneously refers to things in different ontological orders, it is unclear whether all the asserted attributes could coexist. For example, it is vital to Hart's theory

---

[29] *Id*. at 101.   [30] *Id*. at 102.
[31] *Id*. at 55–6.   [32] *Id*. at 116–17.
[33] See e.g. Coleman, *supra* n. 7; Marmor, 'Legal Conventionalism'; Scott J. Shapiro, 'On Hart's Way Out' (this volume).
[34] *CL*, at 256.

that rules of recognition state criteria that primary legal rules satisfy or fail to satisfy. This feature seems to require the first or second version of 'rule of recognition' as something propositional. But it is similarly vital to Hart's rule of recognition that it is a social practice of judges. Yet a social practice is not something propositional, and a linguistic or propositional entity is not a practice of judges.

Beyond this basic concern about the different orders of propositions and practices, the demonstration of three uses illuminates Dworkin's central contention in MOR II, that Hart is mistaken in treating rule of recognition existence as merely a social fact. Hart presents this criticism in the Postscript as follows:

Dworkin's central criticism of the practice theory of rules is that it mistakenly takes a social rule to be constituted by its social practice and so treats the statement that such a rule exists merely as a statement of the external sociological fact that the practice conditions for the existence of the rule are satisfied. That account cannot, so Dworkin argues, explain the *normative* character possessed by even the simplest conventional rule. For these rules establish duties and reasons for action to which appeal is made when such rules are cited, as they commonly are, in criticism of conduct and in support of demands of action. This reason-giving and duty establishing feature of rules constitutes their distinctive normative character and shows that their existence cannot consist in a merely factual state of affairs as do the practices and attitudes which according to the practice theory constitute the existence of a social rule.[35]

Applied to the context of law, Dworkin's criticism can be put as follows: secondary legal rules articulating standards of validity for putative legal norms are put forward as reasons justifying the acceptance or rejection of putative legal norms, and justifying the [judicial] conduct that acceptance of such putative legal norms would entail. The secondary legal rules are in this important sense normative. Yet on Hart's theory, a rule of recognition is merely a social practice that exists. This is not of the right category to justify.

At a simplistic level, this argument is sound. For if a rule of recognition is simply a practice, then that entity will not justify any more than, for example, an automobile will. But the real question is whether the fact that such a practice exists (or the statement that such a practice exists) is capable of justifying the acceptance or rejection of a putative legal norm. Once we rephrase the position so that there is a propositional entity (proposition or sentence) alleged to be justifying the acceptance of legal norms, it is no longer obvious that it is categorically incapable of doing so.

A natural Dworkinian response would be that the assertion of a certain state of affairs could justify a putative legal norm only if there is a

---

[35]   *Id.* (citing *TRS*, at 48–58).

suppressed normative premiss such as: *a judge has a duty to accept a legal norm only if it satisfies the criteria that as a matter of fact are deemed necessary within the practice.* While the existence of a social practice will suffice to establish one of the premisses, it will not suffice to establish the other, plainly normative premiss, and the rule of recognition (taken as a practice) will function as a secondary legal norm only if it has both components.

The important thing to see about this version of Dworkin's critique is that it has virtually nothing to do with the relation between law and morality as that debate is traditionally conceived. Indeed, Hart would not necessarily face this objection (though he would face others) if he simply took the position that purely source-based criteria of legal validity ought to be used. Dworkin's objection, here, is not that Hart fails to interconnect criteria of legal validity with the moral fabric of the universe. Nor is it (as Hart explicitly conjectures) that a social rule does not exist unless there are good moral grounds for complying with it. It is that he fails to recognize that a rule of recognition cannot be merely a social practice if it is meant to function as a standard that justifies the assertion of legal norms, because such standards must by their very nature have the normative force of a secondary legal rule. While the fact of a social practice may be normatively significant, neither that fact nor a sentence expressing it itself has the propositional content of a secondary legal rule. The criticism, at root, is not an accusation of moral conventionalism; it is the specification of a category error in the assertion that a social practice (or a sentence describing it) could be something with the propositional content of a secondary legal rule. As the discussion above reveals, Hart's threefold ambiguity in the use of the phrase 'rule of recognition' renders him vulnerable to this objection.

B. Conventions and the uses of 'rule of recognition'

The ambiguity of 'rule of recognition' in *The Concept of Law* is not, I shall argue, an insoluble problem. I shall offer an interpretation of Hart's theory that explains how a rule of recognition can figure both as a secondary legal rule and as a social practice. I shall suggest that Hart himself held roughly the view I develop and, indeed, that the appearance of equivocation by Hart was illusory. Moreover, I shall argue, Hart is able to respond to Dworkin's normativity argument while retaining his practice conception of rules of recognition. Nevertheless, I conclude that a cogent account of conventionalism in law ultimately requires an abandonment of the model of social facts as many positivists—and possibly Hart himself—have understood it.

The view I offer borrows from and builds upon David Lewis's work in

Convention, A Philosophical Study[36] and, more particularly, his subsequent article 'Languages and Language'.[37] While both of these works were published after *The Concept of Law*, I agree with a number of commentators that Lewis's work sheds light on Hart.[38] Unlike Marmor and Postema, however, it is not Lewis's analysis of certain social practices as conventions that I shall draw upon. Rather, I shall focus on his demonstration of the *dual* nature of semantic theory, and argue that legal theory has a similar dual nature. The point of this interlude is, however, quite indirect, and quite unrelated to Lewis's views or to language. Displaying the dual nature of legal systems will lead to an analysis of rules of recognition as propositions and as social rules.

According to Lewis, one aspect of semantic theory is the specification and analysis of certain kinds of systems of semantic entities that fit together in certain ways and have certain important formal properties—specifically, that are functions from strings of symbols to meanings: languages.[39] A second aspect of semantic theory is an analysis of what the phenomenon of linguistic communication is as a rational social practice within a community; this is an inquiry into the nature of language. Lewis saw how these two aspects of semantic theory could be understood to pose a single, and third, challenge: what is it for a *language* (in the first sense of a system), to be the *language of a community* (in the second sense)? Lewis's well-known theory of conventions was used to answer this second question; for a community to have a language was for it to have a conventional pattern of behaviour and belief through which its members communicated with one another. But Lewis fused the first and second answers to produce an answer to the third: a language was *the language of a community* if the members of the community behave and think a certain way *with respect to certain features of that language (analysed as a certain kind of system)*.

The Concept of Law is best understood as containing (at least) two aspects of jurisprudential theory, just as Lewis addresses two aspects of semantic theory. Hart addresses the question: what is a legal system? His answer is that 'a legal system is a complex union of primary and secondary rules'.[40] This account is intended as a sophisticated alternative to Austin's deeply flawed command theory. A profoundly important aspect of this theory is of course that a legal system is internally self-sustaining because of the existence of rules of recognition, rules of change, and rules of adjudication.

---

[36] *Convention: A Philosophical Study* (1969).

[37] In *Minnesota Studies in the Philosophy of Science* 7, ed. Keith Gunderson (1975), 3–35; repr. in David Lewis, *Philosophical Papers* 1 (1983), 163–88.

[38] See Marmor, 'Legal Conventionalism'; G. J. Postema, 'Coordination and Convention in the Foundations of Law', 11 J. Leg. Stud. 165 (1982).

[39] 'Languages and Language', at 163. [40] *CL*, at 114.

Just as Lewis recognized the essentially social nature of language even as he offered a formal account of language as a system, Hart also recognized that to understand law is, in part, to understand how a legal system is connected to a community—that is, in significant part, what his theory of social rules is used for. Moreover, like Lewis, Hart explicitly recognized that an account was needed to connect the system to the community; he recognized that the account of law as a union of primary and secondary rules 'is not all that is needed to describe the relationships to law involved in the existence of a legal system'.[41] He supplemented this account with the following:

There are therefore two minimum conditions necessary and sufficient for the existence of a legal system. On the one hand, those rules of behaviour which are valid according to the system's ultimate criteria of validity must be generally obeyed, and, on the other, its rules of recognition specifying the criteria of legal validity and its rules of change and adjudication must be effectively accepted as common public standards of official behaviour by its officials.[42]

This passage is phrased as an analysis of 'the existence of a legal system', but that phrase is elliptical. More precisely, it is the analysis of what it is for a legal system to be the legal system *of a particular community*: the members of that community must generally obey rules of behaviour that are valid according to the system's ultimate criteria of validity, and the legal officials of that community must effectively accept the rules of recognition, change, and adjudication as common public standards.

With these aspects of Hart in mind, let me return to the topic of rules of recognition. What kind of thing is a rule of recognition? Clearly, Hart categorized rules of recognition as secondary rules within legal systems. As such they have propositional content and they are normative in nature. They specify that certain putative legal norms are valid and others are not. It is essential to the content of such a rule that it designate which norms are valid and which not. Whether or not rules of recognition are themselves members of legal systems (and Hart clearly believed they were), they are essential to characterizing each legal system, just as, in the linguistic example, a proposition or set of propositions stating the truth conditions of each sentence is essential to a language.

What, then, can we say about Hart's frequent and pivotally important statements that rules of recognition are social rules? I think this is merely an imprecise way of saying that for a rule of recognition of a legal system (considered as an abstract union of primary and secondary rules) to be the rule of recognition *of a community* is for there to be a certain kind of social

---

41 *Id.*   42 *Id.* at 116.

practice among the legal officials in that community of accepting that rule of recognition (considered as a propositional entity). Indeed, just as it is an attribute of the proposition that the earth is not flat that it is widely believed among educated persons today, and an attribute of the proposition that the sentence 'My coffee is hot' is true if and only if my coffee is hot that it is accepted by English speakers, it is an attribute of the proposition that a statute must not violate the United States Constitution to be valid, that it is accepted (and treated as a social rule) by American judges. Hence, according to Hart's view, it is true of rules of recognition of *extant* legal systems that they are *social rules for the legal officials of some community*. This is not, however, to say that a social practice is the very kind of thing a rule of recognition is. It is to describe an attribute of certain rules of recognition. Of course, if we are limiting our view (as we might) to rules of recognition of extant legal systems, then it is an attribute of all such rules, and, moreover, an attribute that is critical to the existence of those legal systems. It is therefore not surprising that Hart can be found suggesting that rules of recognition *are* social rules, as in the aforementioned passage from the Postscript.

My account of social rules is, as Dworkin has also rightly claimed, applicable only to rules which are conventional in the sense I have explained. This considerably narrows the scope of my practice theory and I do not now regard it is a sound explanation of morality, either individual or social. But the theory remains a faithful account of conventional social rules which include . . . certain important legal rules including the rule of recognition, which is in effect a form of judicial customary rule existing only if it is accepted and practised in the law-identifying and law-applying operations of the courts.[43]

I am suggesting that Hart should be interpreted as saying that the practice account of social rules is aimed to account *not for what a rule of recognition is,* but rather for *what it is for a rule of recognition to be the rule of recognition of a particular legal community.* This, in turn, (partially) explains what it is for a legal system to be the legal system of a community.

This interpretation of Hart leads me to offer quite a different response to Dworkin's critique from that offered by Hart himself in the Postscript. Dworkin is right that secondary rule discourse—including the articulation of rules of recognition—figures in the justification of legal claims, and of actions pursuant to those claims. But, for the reasons already articulated, this does not undercut the contention that it is an important attribute of certain rules of recognition—those which count as the rule of recognition of a legal community—that there is a particular kind of social practice of accepting the rule among legal officials.

---

[43] *Id.* at 256.

Let us now turn to the question of whether a rule of recognition, for Hart, is a proposition or a particular formulation. The overwhelming evidence is that Hart intended 'rule of recognition' to refer, in its primary sense, to that which particular verbal formulations *expressed*, and that he did not intend it to refer to the formulation itself. In addition to the passages cited above, Hart nowhere makes the implausible claim that there is a particular formulation in each legal community that all regard as the ultimate criterion. On the contrary, his contention that there is a widely accepted ultimate standard of law, notwithstanding apparent explicit controversy over standards, commits him to the view that there is an implicit acceptance of a norm, whose proper formulation remains problematic. Indicating agreement with several of his followers, Hart also recognizes that the application of this criterion may also be in dispute.

C. The distinction between secondary legal rule statements and social fact statements

This account leads us to a fundamental distinction between two types of sentence relating to secondary legal rules. One type of sentence expresses a secondary rule that states criteria for the validity of primary rules. For example, the sentence 'No putative law is valid unless it has been duly passed by Congress' expresses the proposition that no putative law is valid unless it has been duly passed by Congress. The latter proposition is a secondary legal rule: a proposition that is a standard of legal validity for primary legal norms. Relatedly, the sentence 'No putative law is valid unless it has been duly passed by Congress' *means that* no putative law is valid unless it has duly passed by Congress. A sentence that takes as its meaning a secondary legal rule will be termed a 'secondary legal rule statement'.

A rather different type of sentence asserts that some secondary legal rule has a particular status in a particular legal community, to wit, has the status of being accepted as a social rule in that community. For example, 'It is a criterion of validity in the American community that no putative law is valid unless it has been duly passed by Congress.' The proposition which this sentence expresses is the proposition that some other, normative, proposition (*no putative law is valid unless it has been duly passed by Congress*) is treated as providing a condition of legal validity in the American community. Plainly, a proposition about how a group of people treats a particular normative proposition is not itself a normative proposition (even though it could be normatively significant). It is a proposition of social fact. Likewise, the sentence that expresses the proposition asserts that a social fact exists. I shall therefore designate such a statement a 'social fact statement'.[44]

I have argued above that rules of recognition, for Hart, are propositional entities. They are the sorts of things that are expressed by sentences such as: 'No putative law is valid unless it is passed by Congress under a power that Congress enjoys.' While this is perhaps only a partial rule or recognition—and I am willing to leave open the possibility that there is a hierarchical structure with a single all-encompassing rule of recognition— a fuller one might include both a disjunction of possible sources or exceptions to source requirements, and either embedded or distributive necessary conditions that would defeat such authorizing conditions.[45] The important point on the model I have constructed is that rules of recognition are propositions about what features of putative norms make them valid law, propositions whose acceptance by legal officials is constitutive of a legal system being the legal system of a community. Because they are propositions, however, they are at least in principle the sort of things that could be expressed in language.

The question then arises as to how one would properly categorize a statement that asserted rule of recognition. There are two important preliminaries to answering this question. The first is that the question is not simply about speech act types. It is about sentence types. It is one thing to provide an analysis of the speech act of a judge uttering 'Statutes passed by a majority but vetoed, and then not overridden by at least two-thirds of each house, are law' in the course of declining to apply a particular statute. The act of the judging in uttering that statement can be viewed as the speech act of expressing acceptance of and allegiance to a particular social practice, that of applying the aforementioned rule. On the other hand, there is the question of what the sentence itself means, and relatedly, what would make it true.

The second and related point is that the question is not about a particular statement within each community—i.e. the one that expresses the rule of recognition of that community. Nor is it about an equivalence class of such sentences. The question is about the category of sentence that putatively expresses a rule of recognition of a linguistic community. A person—say, a law student—could presumably mis-state the rule of recognition of the community. The statement she or he uses to mis-state

---

[44] The distinction between secondary legal rule statements and social fact statements relates to, but is distinct from, both Hart's distinction between 'internal statements' and 'external statements' (see *infra* III (D)) and Dworkin's distinction between 'normative rules' and 'social rules'. See *infra*, IV.

[45] Cf. Neil MacCormick, *H. L. A. Hart* (1981), 110 (setting forth, as a rule of recognition, conjunction of universally quanitified propositions that designate putative norms as laws if they satisfy certain conditions).

the rule of recognition of the community presumably could have the same form as a statement that properly expressed the rule of recognition. Thus, for example, the statement 'Any law that the vice-president vetoes is not valid law' is a rule-of-recognition statement, in the sense that it purports to provide (part of) a rule-of-recognition. More particularly, a semantics of rule-of-recognition statements must be broad enough to cover inaccurate statements as well as accurate ones.

With these preliminaries in mind, recall that there are certain forms of statement that express complex propositions about what features of a putative legal norm make it valid law. These are secondary legal rule statements. A rule of recognition is a secondary legal rule, albeit a particularly important one. Statements expressing propositions appropriately complex and basic to be a rule of recognition are simply examples of secondary legal rule statements. By contrast, a statement that asserts that a certain rule of recognition (proposition) is accepted within a legal community as a social rule is a social fact statement about a rule of recognition. Both secondary legal rule statements of putative rules of recognition and social fact statements about rules of recognition are general types. Each is capable of being correct or mistaken.

D. Hart on internal and external statements

In several respects, it appears that the distinction I have drawn between secondary legal rule statements and social fact statements would have been congenial to Hart. Indeed, it might be deemed an application (to secondary legal rules) of a distinction that Hart is to be credited with having made—the distinction between internal statements and external statements.[46] What I have called a 'secondary legal rule statement' resembles a Hartian 'internal statement'; it is used by those involved in applying the law to justify assertions that particular legal norms are valid, and it is accepted as a sound criterion of validity; its utterance 'manifests the internal point of view and [it] is naturally used by one who, accepting the rule of recognition and without stating the fact that it is accepted, applies the rule in recognizing some particular rule of the system as valid'.[47] By contrast, what I have called a 'social fact statement' would appear to be an 'external statement': 'it is the natural language of an external observer of the system who, without himself accepting its rule of recognition, states the fact that others accept it.'[48] Moreover, the framework I have constructed is useful for making one of the principal negative points Hart intended to establish with this framework: that it is a category error to suppose (with Holmes) that to assert

---

[46] *CL*, at 102–3.   [47] *Id.*   [48] *Id.* at 103.

the validity of a legal norm was to make a prediction regarding officials' behaviour.[49]

Nevertheless, there are several notable differences between Hart's framework and that which I have put forward. First, the category of 'internal statement' is defined, by Hart, in terms of the point of view of those who utter it.[50] Second, the maker of an internal statement must, by definition, presuppose a rule of recognition. Neither of these is essential to my account of a secondary legal rule statement (as opposed to a social fact statement). Third, internal statements appear to be principally (and perhaps only) about the validity of putative legal norms—largely primary norms, one presumes. It is simply not clear how Hart intended it to apply to secondary legal norm assertions, if at all; my account is of course precisely about secondary legal norm assertions. Fourth, and working from my own account, the characterization of secondary legal statements is precisely in terms of their propositional content. Propositional content is not principally, if at all, what drives Hart's distinction; rather, it appears to be the pragmatic context of assertion.

The difference in the framework is most pronounced and important when it comes to rules of recognition themselves. With regard to other sorts of rule, Hart held the rather nuanced position that an internal statement might actually be viewed as presupposing a rule of recognition and asserting the validity of another rule under it. Insofar as he maintained this position, he was recognizing a possibly different propositional content. However, with regard to expressions of rules of recognition, he rejected the possibility entirely:

In this respect, however, as in others, a rule of recognition is unlike other rules of the system. The assertion that it exists can only be an external statement of fact. For whereas a subordinate rule of a system may be valid and in that sense 'exist' even if it is generally disregarded, the rule of recognition exists only as a complex, but normally concordant, practice of the courts, officials, and private persons in identifying the law by reference to certain criteria. Its existence is a matter of fact.[51]

This was not to deny that speakers could ever express rules of recognition, or could ever do so from the internal point of view.[52] It was to say that the propositional content of such an assertion must be the same as that of the external statement itself.

E. The nature of rule-of-recognition statements: the first argument against the model of social facts

As suggested in Part II, Hart's denial that there is any existence to a rule of recognition, apart from social fact, and the analysis of rule of recogni-

---

[49] *Id.* at 104–5. [50] *Id.* at 102. [51] *Id.* at 108. [52] *Id.* at 106–10.

tion statements upon which it rests, plays a foundational role in the structure of his theory. It is made in the context of a discussion in which he asserts the ultimacy of certain secondary legal rules. The question whether or not a putative legal norm is law for Hart ultimately turns on certain secondary legal rules. Yet whether those legal rules are applicable—whether they exist—is ultimately a matter of social fact.

Some writers, who have emphasized the legal ultimacy of the rule of recognition, have expressed this by saying that, whereas the legal validity of other rules of the system can be demonstrated by reference to it, its own validity cannot be demonstrated but is 'assumed' or 'postulated' or is a 'hypothesis'. This may, however, be seriously misleading. . . . First, a person who seriously asserts the validity of some given rule of law, say a particular statute, himself makes use of a rule of recognition which he accepts as appropriate for identifying the law. Secondly, it is the case that this rule of recognition, in terms of which he assesses the validity of a particular statute, is not only accepted by him but is the rule of recognition actually accepted and employed in the general operation of the system. If the truth of this presupposition were doubted, it could be established by reference to actual practice: to the way in which courts identify what is to count as law, and to the general acceptance of or acquiescence in these identifications.[53]

Together these two premises are intended to yield the conclusion that whether a putative legal norm is valid is ultimately a matter of social fact. Hart's insistence that rule-of-recognition statements can only be *external* statements is in this way basic to the model of social facts that has been attributed to him.

   The analysis thus far provides at least a prima facie argument that, in asserting that rule of recognition statements are made true only by social facts, Hart has made a mistake. While social facts pertaining to actual practice will confirm the truth or falsity of a statement that a certain rule of recognition (proposition) has the status of a social rule within a community of officials, that does not apply to statements of the rule of recognition. For example, it will confirm whether it is the case that American legal officials treat the proposition that *laws otherwise valid are not invalidated by a vice presidential veto* as law or whether they treat the proposition that *circuit court opinions expressly designating themselves as lacking precedential value are not precedent* as a social rule: whether they act in accordance with it and expect such action of others, and conform in part because of the mutual expectation of others. But such facts do not suffice to confirm or disconfirm the (putative) rule of recognition norm itself, e.g. the proposition that laws otherwise valid are not invalidated by a vice-presidential veto, or the proposition that circuit court opinions expressly designating themselves as lacking precedential value are not precedent.

[53] *Id.* at 108.

To think otherwise is to commit a category mistake. It is of some significance whether circuit court opinions designating themselves as lacking precedential value are precedent or not. This is a matter of law. It is also of siginficance whether a certain pattern of attitude and behaviour with respect to that proposition exists—a matter of social fact. But these two matters of significance are not the same.

Perhaps the simplest argument for the difference between these two matters is that one is embedded in the other. As argued above, what it is for a putative rule of recognition to be the rule of recognition in a particular legal community is for the legal officials of the community to accept that proposition, and act in accordance with it. It follows that the content of the putative rule of recognition must be a different proposition from the proposition that a particular rule of recognition is accepted by the group.

A difference between these two matters entails a difference between the two kinds of statement expressing the respective matters: social fact statements and secondary legal rule statements. A statement that members of a community treat a particular secondary legal rule as their rule of recognition is distinct from an assertion of that secondary legal rule. The former is an example of a social fact statement. It is made true by the proposition that a particular group of people behave a certain way, and confirmed or disconfirmed by evidence regarding the conduct of those persons. The latter is secondary legal rule statement. It is made true by a certain legal state of affairs obtaining—by it being the case that the legal proposition asserted does obtain (e.g. that laws otherwise valid *are not* invalidated by a vice-presidential veto, or that circuit court opinions expressly designating themselves as lacking precedential value *are not* precedent).

The foregoing argument against Hart, if sound, undercuts the model of social facts. Parts IV and V present arguments to supplement the basic argument from the distinction between statements that assert that there is a practice of accepting a certain proposition, and statements that assert the proposition. These supplementary arguments are suggested by Professor Dworkin's critique of Hart in MOR II.

IV. THE ARGUMENT FROM RULE-OF-RECOGNITION NORMA-TIVITY

The MOR II critique of the social rules theory of rules is put in terms of a distinction between a statement of a social rule and statement of a normative rule. A statement of a social rule, according to Dworkin, is an assertion that people behave in a particular way and take up certain critically reflective attitudes, and it is true (warranted) just in case the members of the community so described do in fact behave as described, and take up certain attitudes, etc. A statement of a normative rule, however, asserts not that people do in fact behave in some way (although they might, so far as the normative rule statement goes) but that they have a duty to behave in that manner, and it is true (or warranted) just in case they do have such a duty.[54] Dworkin's crucial point is that when a judge decides to apply a law because, for example, the legislature has enacted the law, his reason is that there is a duty to follow what the legislature has said. That is articulated by the statement of the normative rule. On Hart's model, however, the judge deploying a rule-of-recognition statement to justify his decision is deploying a statement of a social rule, not a normative rule. Hence, he is supporting his decision with a statement that others believe there is such a duty (or act in conformity with such belief), not a statement that there is such a duty, on Hart's model. But such an appeal surely does not justify a judge's decision that he does have a duty to follow the law on a particular occasion. That decision requires support from the normative premiss, not the sociological one: 'the social rule cannot, without more, be the source of the duty he believes he has.'[55]

The Dworkinian critique weaves together negative and positive strands of argument. From a critical point of view, Dworkin is arguing that Hart's analysis of rules of recognition in terms of social rules is unable to capture the nature of a judge's decisions applying the law, because those decisions have a normative aspect that Hart's theory omits. From a constructive point of view, he is offering the materials for building an account of that judicial decision—a framework according to which a judge is deliberating about what it is her or his duty to do. As indicated in the introduction to this article, Hart's reply to Dworkin's objection asserts the implausibility of supposing that moral reasons bearing upon the existence of a judge's duty are the only or principal sorts of reasons guiding her conduct. Even if we accept the forcefulness of this reply to Dworkin, it is evidently only a reply to the positive strand. It does not respond adequately to the charge that there is something in the nature of judicial decision-making that is not captured by the model of social facts.

A variation of this argument can be framed in terms of the distinction I have drawn in the preceding section between secondary legal rule statements and social fact statements.

Consider a judge who reasons as follows:

(1) 'Whatever the legislature has duly enacted by a majority vote is valid law.'
(2) 'Statute 44, stating that one is prohibited from fishing in the month of

May and setting a fine of $100 for violations of this prohibition, was
duly enacted by the legislature by a majority vote.'

(3) 'Fishing in the month of May is prohibited. Whoever violates this
statute shall be fined $100. Statute 44.'

(4) 'Jones fished in May of 1999.'

(5) 'Jones violated Statute 44.'

(6) 'Jones shall be fined $100.'

(7) 'Jones is hereby fined $100.'

The first statement in this justification, (1), is a (partial) rule-of-recognition
statement.[56] The question arises as to whether it is a secondary legal rule
statement or a social fact statement. However, when we look at the justificatory role it is required to play in this argument, we see that it cannot
be a social fact statement. Whatever (1) is, if we are to capture judicial
argumentation as offering genuine warrants for their conclusions, then (1)
must be something whose content conjoined with (2) will yield (3). But if
(1) is interpreted as a social fact statement, then it is equivalent in content
to: *the judges in the American legal community accept as a social rule the proposition that whatever the legislature has duly enacted by majority vote is valid law.*

What follows from its conjunction with (2) is

(3′) 'Under the rule judges in the American legal community accept as a
social rule, statute 44 is valid.'

(3′) does not mean the same as (3). (3′) does not, in conjunction with (4),
yield (5), (6), and (7).

Therefore, (1) cannot be interpreted as a social fact statement.

The argument obviously generalizes into an argument that *insofar as
rule-of-recognition statements* are part of what judges use to justify assertions that certain putative legal norms are valid law, and to warrant their
applications of this law, rule-of-recognition statements cannot be merely
social fact statements. Since, on Hart's own theory, rules of recognition are
secondary legal rules that provide the criteria of validity for putative
laws, and since on his theory judges at least implicitly do employ rules of
recognition in deciding what the law is, the analysis of rule-of-recognition
statements as social fact statements must be rejected.

Hart might have several replies to this criticism. First, note that his
distinction between internal statements and external statements does not
help him to avoid the problem I have identified. It would give him two
options. The first, which seems to match what Dworkin anticipates for
Hart, is that he would say (1) was an internal statement. As such, the

---

[56] It may be complained that (1) is really a rule of change statement. Nothing turns on
whether the example concerns a statute that was passed (seeming to indicate a rule of
change) or, e.g., a set of decisions by courts, not purporting to create new law.

judge who utters it is expressing her own acceptance of the norm, not simply asserting that it was accepted by members of her community. On this view, (3) is inferred from (2) *because* the judge accepts the rule of recognition described (semantically) and evinced (as a matter of speech act type) in (1).

This appeal to the role of the internal point of view in the utterance of (1) actually serves to make Hart's problem more evident, not to reduce it. The foregoing is an articulation, from a first-person perspective, of how it is that (3) is reached by someone who accepts (2); the person also accepts the proposition that she ascribed to members of her community in (1). But this narrative account is not a reconstruction of the argument used by judges. It is, in effect, an analysis according to which there is merely the appearance of a sound argument. It shows the putative argument to be a hybrid: while (3)–(7) may be sound, (1)–(3) is something of a description of the process of the judge, not a justification of (3). Some philosophers of law might embrace this quasi-justificatory account of judicial warrant, but I think Hart would not and should not be among them. Judges justify, according to Hart, and they also take themselves to be justifying. Moreover, a great contribution of Hart's entire theory is his account of how it is that rules of recognition do justify claims that certain primary norms are valid, even if they do not happen to be accepted from the internal point of view. If Hart's theory of rules of recognition requires an abandonment of the view that judges engage in genuine justification of their legal conclusions, then it would clearly be regarded by Hart himself as requiring repair.

Interestingly, I do not think that the response anticipated above best captures what Hart says in *The Concept of Law*. Indeed, he seemed to have resisted the suggestion (by Dworkin) that rule-of-recognition statements were internal statements. As discussed above, his prototypes of 'internal statements' were actually of primary legal rules, not secondary legal rules.[57] And he defined 'internal statements' as ones uttered, from the internal point of view, by speakers who tacitly accepted a rule of recognition.[58] This definition, while of course not eliminating the possibility that rule-of-recognition statements would be made by a person who accepted them, and made from the internal point of view, seems to exclude rule-of-recognition statements from possibly satisfying the definition of an 'internal statement'.

A more textually grounded response to the argument I have offered would deny that the argument is true to the nature of judicial (or lawyerly) justification. Hart suggests in *The Concept of Law* that express justification typically begins with recognition of primary legal norms, as

---

[57] *CL*, at 102–3.   [58] *Id.* at 102.

in (3); rules of recognition are not, on his view, a normal part of express legal justification by judges, lawyers, or citizens:

> In the day-to-day life of a legal system its rule of recognition is very seldom expressly formulated as a rule; though occasionally, courts in England may announce in general terms the relative place of one criterion of law in relation to another, as when they assert the supremacy of Acts of Parliament over other sources or suggested source of law. For the most part the rule of recognition is not stated, but its existence is *shown* in the way in which particular rules are identified, either by courts or other officials or private persons or their advisers. . . . *The use of unstated rules of recognition, by courts and others, in identifying particular rules of the system is characteristic of the internal point of view.*[59]

Hence, it might be replied by Hart, an account of legal justification need not render the inference from (1)–(3) sound, because such inferences are not part of legal justification, except on rare occasions.

There are two serious problems with this response. The first is that, at least in the American legal system, Hart's characterization of reference to the rule of recognition as 'rare' is inaccurate. Explicit use of rules governing validity of putative legal norms is common in the United States. This is not simply because our system involves an elaborate written federal constitution which both articulates conditions of legal validity and creates legal enigmas with regard to validity. The point goes beyond anything dependent on American constitutionalism. Courts are frequently called upon to decide the force and applicability of holdings from other courts, the interrelation between federal and state law, state and local law, international and national law, and between different branches of government. These requirements—many of which apply even to non-federalist, and non-constitutional systems—are quite pervasive. Even if the run-of-the-mill case does not expressly involve such issues—and I am inclined to agree with Hart that it does not—the characterization of such references as 'very seldom' is not tenable today. This point is elaborated in Part V(B).

The second problem is more fundamental than the first. Whether an adequate account of the role of rules of recognition in justification is necessary does not turn on whether the rule of recognition figures explicitly or implicitly in justification. If it figures in justification either way, then an account of its logical form that permits us to see why it can figure non-fallaciously in the justification is required. As the italicized passage above indicates, Hart himself asserts that rules of recognition figure implicitly in legal justification. He therefore needs an account that explains why they in fact license inferences such as the one from (1)–(3). The view that rule-of-recognition statements are social fact statements does not produce this.

---

[59] *Id.* at 101–2 (emphasis added).

It will not do to respond that Hart treated rules of recognition as tacit heuristic devices, not as implicit components of justification. In the first place, a 'mere heuristic device' view of rules of recognition is alien to the text of *The Concept of Law*. Second, as the passage above suggests, Hart believed that rule-of-recognition justifications could, as it were, be pressed for, and if so, could sometimes be produced. Such a view contemplates a foundational epistemic role for rules of recognition, which may be difficult to put into words; it plainly does not contemplate that they merely serve as heuristic devices. Third, it is part of the explanatory power that Hart fairly claims for his entire theory that he can account for why it is that some statements are valid and others are not; at least it is part of his enterprise to explain why those who occupy the internal point of view may rightly regard themselves as being justified in counting some norms as valid and others not. This goal clearly requires seeing rule-of-recognition statements as playing a genuine justificatory role, not merely a heuristic one.

A third Hartian response might be to reconstruct the argument so that the qualifier 'under the rule accepted as a social rule by judges in the American legal community' follows through, nearly to the end of the argument, e.g.:

(6') Under the rule accepted as a social rule by judges in the American legal community, Jones shall be fined $100.

Then, note that we would need a premise such as:

(6a) I shall adjudicate according to the rule accepted as a social rule by judges in the American legal community.

This would lead to the practical conclusion:

(7) Jones is hereby fined $100.

There are numerous reasons for rejecting this reconstruction. First, as a logical matter, the argument from (3'), (4) , and (5) to (6') is invalid, because it requires breaking into the logical operators in the embedded imperative of (3'). Second, the need for (6a) makes the argument unusually incomplete (even assuming, contrary to fact, its validity). Premiss (6a) is not true. It is simply the expression of a resolution to act a particular way. It is thus highly misleading to characterize (7) as the conclusion of a sound practical inference. More importantly, the adjudicative conduct of the judge is not justified, on this account. Of course, we might replace (6a) with:

(6b) An American judge ought to adjudicate according to the rule accepted as a social rule among American judges.

And

(6c) I am an American judge.

implying

(6d) I ought to adjudicate according to the rule accepted as a social rule among American judges.

implying (7).

But the problem with this account (in addition to the logical fallacy already mentioned) is that (6b), which is plainly a normative premiss, is quite implausible from a normative point of view. It is brute conventionalism as a normative matter. Moreover, it seems highly implausible that this premiss is part of the justification actually used, i.e. the reconstruction through (6b) fails to capture a plausible account of the sorts of justification actually deployed. Finally, the 'ought' in (6b) is of the wrong sort to capture Hart's view. For insofar as Hart thought judges were obligated to apply rules of recognition, it was critical to his view that the obligation was not a moral obligation to do what every other legal official did, but an obligation having a character potentially distinct from that of moral obligations, existing as part and parcel of the existence of the social rule. The prior argument, travelling through premiss (6b), utterly misses this, deploying a more general form of 'ought' that applies to the output of the rule of recognition as independently derived, rather than existing in virtue of the rule.

An apparently rather different means of responding to this critique might accept the justification of (1)–(7), but add to it at the front end, rather than in the middle or at the end. Thus, perhaps (1) is understood as a secondary legal rule statement, but (1) is justified by:

(0)   'Whatever the legislature has duly enacted by a majority vote is valid law' is a social rule in the American legal community.
(0a) This legal community is the American legal community.
(0b) 'Whatever the legislature has duly enacted by a majority vote is valid law' is a social rule of this legal community.

The statements (0) and (0a) are arguably empirical, and entail (0b), which appears to justify the judge's actual deployment of the rule of recognition as a rule of recognition in (1) through (3).

In fact, however, this argument only highlights the equivocation upon which what I have called the Hartian position seems to rely. For, unless (0b) is merely an emphatic way of announcing (1) *as* a rule of recognition, it is an empirical statement of social fact. If it is that, however, there is no reason to think that it entails a statement about the validity of putative norms, which statement could lead to practical decisions in applying those norms.

Finally, the Postscript itself includes a response to what I have called Dworkin's argument from normativity, and since the argument I have put forward in this section is in some ways modelled after Dworkin's, perhaps Hart's Postscript response to Dworkin will be instructive. Hart takes Dworkin to be asserting that judges deciding whether to apply a putative legal norm are deciding a normative question—to wit, whether it is their duty to apply the norm. Dworkin takes Hart's theory of social rules to commit him to the view that this normative question about duty is decided by whether or not officials have a social practice that covers the case. Dworkin rejects this view, arguing that the question is not whether, from a sociological point of view, there is such a practice, but whether, from a moral point of view, putative legal norms ought to be treated as law under such circumstances.

Hart appears, in the Postscript, to accept Dworkin's framing of the issue and to hold up the conventionalist side of the debate so framed. He does seem willing to assert that it is a sufficient reason to conclude that there is a judicial duty to apply putative norms with certain attributes as valid law and that there is a social rule of doing so. To this extent, Hart appears to endorse the argument that travels through (6b) above. For the reasons already articulated, that argument is unacceptable.

There is, however, a yet larger problem with the account Hart appeared to accept in the Postscript. That account appears to concede to Dworkin that rules of recognition impose duties. Indeed, this view might be thought to provide, in broad terms, the key to a critique based on the normativity of arguments from rules of recognition. In fact, the discussion of judicial duties does the opposite, for it diverts attention from a pivotally important insight of *The Concept of Law*: judges' decisions to apply certain putative norms as law are themselves applications of shared criteria of validity. This insight lies at the core of Hart's deep-seated conventionalism. Although Dworkin is correct that the model of social facts is incapable of capturing the normativity of legal justification, it is not the morally loaded or obligatory nature of adjudication which presents a problem. As I have argued, it is the *practicality* of adjudication. Dworkin appears to score an easy victory over Hart by drawing him into the view that rules of recognition impose duties, and then depicting the Hartian as holding an untenably conventionalistic account of duty.

Hart, and some Hart scholars, are attracted to the view that rules of recognition are duty-imposing rules. This may seem to follow from the fact that judges have obligations to apply the law and the rule of recognition is a rule that tells them the conditions under which they have such obligations.[60] If that is the source of the view, then it is fallacious. To take an analogy, a teacher examining her students on a state-wide writing examination may have an obligation to penalize students whose essays

---

[60] This is not necessarily the only motivation for this view. Coleman, for example, in his forthcoming *The Practice of Principle* (2001) adopts a view of rules of recognition as coordinative conventions that arguably provides a different basis for such obligations.

contain grammatical errors. The rule 'All sentences must contain at least one verb' plays a role in specifying which essays contain grammatical errors, and therefore which students there is an obligation to penalize. It would be wrong to infer that the preceding grammatical rule was a duty-imposing rule. Likewise, so far as the theory of rules of recognition as social rules goes, judges' general duty to apply the law may come from a variety of different sources. Rules of recognition play a substantial role in giving content to those duties, but they are not necessarily what imposes the duties in the first place.

The important point of this part does not concern duties or social facts. It concerns criteria of validity. When legal justifications push to the level of rules of recognition—as, for Hart, they may do explicitly—the discourse concerns criteria of validity. The statements of rules of recognition are therefore statements that assert criteria for validity. They are not statements about what legal officials believe or treat as the criteria of validity, but about what such criteria are. It is only because they are this that they are capable of yielding the practical conclusions of applying the law as valid law.

V. THE ARGUMENT FROM CONTESTABILITY

A. Dworkin's disjunctive argument

We are now in a position to see more clearly Dworkin's argument from disagreement, or, as I shall call it, his argument from contestability. As discussed above, Hart interprets Dworkin as casting doubt on the existence of a rule of recognition as a social rule, by pointing out the existence of important disagreements on criteria of validity. Hart responds by stating that it is possible to have an agreed upon rule of recognition, which is a social rule, but which is not determinate on every legal issue, and about which there is disagreement in application. This would, according to Hart, not undercut the existence of a rule or its status as a social rule.

Dworkin had anticipated this move in MOR II, and offered the following disjunctive argument against it.[61] If rules of recognition are treated as convergent social practices, which is what the social rules theory of rules of recognition seems to contend, then *as to aspects of the rule of recognition on which legal officials do not converge in conduct*, the rule of recognition does not exist.[62] The upshot is that the validity of a putative legal norm in a

---

[61] Dworkin's actual argument is not presented by this name, or in this form, and has components that are neglected here.
[62] *TRS*, at 54–5.

case that turns on a controversial issue of validity is not settled by the rule of recognition. Hence, wherever there is such a controversial issue as to validity, the rule of recognition of the legal community, if there is one, simply does not extend to it. The putative law is not really law under the rule of recognition. If Dworkin is right that such cases are not anomalous but legion—and I think he is—then his objection does substantial damage to the thesis that rules of recognition may be treated purely as convergent social practices.

On the other hand, Dworkin argues, rules of recognition might be treated as particular verbal formulations such as 'Whatever Parliament enacts is law'.[63] Then, while there might be agreement that this is the rule of recognition, there would nevertheless be disagreement over how to interpret this formulation. Yet Dworkin argues forcefully that it is not plausible that all the controversies over validity turn on the interpretation of particular words in a given formulation.[64] He therefore rejects Hart's thesis that it is central to a legal community's existence that it have a rule of recognition that is a social rule.

The disjunctive argument as so presented invites an obvious rejoinder, based upon my reconstruction of Hart's framework for thinking about rules of recognition, in Part III. Dworkin selects two disjuncts for what a rule of recognition is: a practice, or a verbal formulation. As I argued in Part II, there is a third possibility—that a rule of recognition is a proposition; moreover, this third possibility in fact provides the best account of Hart's view. As Hart's response in the Postscript confirms, he did regard rules of recognition as propositions. Hence, he thought there was an accepted proposition or set of propositions whose acceptance as a social rule constituted the legal system's existence in that community. But the acceptance of such a proposition leaves open the question of how it would be applied in a particular case. It is not prima facie implausible that the range of arguments over validity within a sophisticated legal community should be arguments over the application of such a proposition or propositions to various different kinds of issue, though it would be if the claim were that there was a privileged verbal formulation. Conversely, there can be an agreement *that* validity is determined by a particular set of criteria, even if there is not agreement in conduct. The convergence in conduct that constitutes the social rule, as argued in Part III, is *acceptance of a particular proposition or propositions*. The rule of recognition *is* the proposition; it is an important attribute of this proposition that it is a social rule. Once we have clarified that 'proposition' was the kind of thing a rule of recognition was intended to be, it is possible to explain more fully than Hart did in the *Postscript* why Dworkin's disjunctive argument is unsound.

[63] *Id.* at 62.   [64] *Id.* at 63.

B. Contesting rule-of-recognition statements

While Dworkin's disjunctive argument in MOR II is adequately met by the claim that rules of recognition are propositions which there is a social rule of accepting, this is only a temporary victory. The more interesting version of Dworkin's argument from disagreement, I suggest, applies precisely when we recognize that rules of recognition must be propositions on Hart's view. For then we are returned to our question of what is the status of statements that assert rules-of-recognition. Hart adhered to the view that rule-of-recognition statements could only be understood as external statements, or as utterances whose propositional content was equivalent to that of an external statement. But if rules of recognition are propositions, and moreover, it is possible to disagree about whether a particular case falls under the rule, then rule-of-recognition statements must, again, be secondary legal rule statements.

The argument from contestability goes one step further, however, for it provides another ground for rejecting the claim that rule-of-recognition statements have social facts as their truth conditions. We must broaden our view of Dworkin's critique of Hart to see why. The argument from disagreement, in MOR II, can be seen as an early, and in some ways less contentious, version of the semantic sting argument in *Law's Empire*.[65] It shares with that argument the premiss that legal officials commonly and appropriately engage in reasoned disagreement with one another over criteria of legal validity, and the conclusion that it is not the case that social facts provide the truth conditions for statements about legal validity. Unlike the semantic sting, it does not purport to criticize positivism as a theory of the meaning of the term 'law'—a contention that Hart has persuasively rebutted in the Postscript.[66] Both arguments are taken by Hart as an argument that the disagreement in question is inconsistent with there being a conventionally accepted rule of recognition.[67] For the reasons that Hart offers, that I have undergirded, and that Professors Coleman, Endicott, Raz, and Marmor have elaborated, the argument so construed is not persuasive.[68]

But the lack of actual agreement in practice, and the internal inconsistency of claiming that a social rule covers a certain issue even where agreement is lacking, is not the most important point in Dworkin's critique. What is important is the possibility of a certain kind of reasoned discourse about whether or not to accept a statement regarding the conditions of validity. In

---

[65] *Law's Empire*, at 31 ff.   [66] *CL*, at 244–8.

[67] *Id.* at 245–6 (although Hart interprets the semantic sting as putting this objection in semantic terms).

[68] Coleman (this volume); Timothy A. O. Endicott, 'Herbert Hart and the Semantic Sting' (this volume); Marmor, 'Legal Conventionalism'; Raz (this volume).

short, what is important is that disagreements about validity display the possibility of contesting, or arguing over whether particular rule-of-recognition statements are true, and engaging in such argument by providing reasoned legal discourse.[69] This is an argument that rule-of-recognition statements are not social fact statements. For if they were social fact statements, it would not be cogent (as it is) to contest them except by pointing out certain facts about legal officials' practices. Their contestability by appeal to reasons other than social facts demonstrates that the rule-of-recognition statements within judicial discourse are secondary legal rule statements, not social fact statements. More generally, it also shows that truth conditions for these rule-of-recognition statements are not simply social facts.

Hart has suggested, in response, that any reasoned disagreement that purports to be a disagreement about the proposition that is the rule of recognition is actually a disagreement about its application.[70] Indeed, Coleman has argued that the burden is on Dworkin to say why it is that disagreements should always be interpreted as disagreements over the content of the proposition accepted, rather than over its application.[71] As I will elaborate in the next section, and in Part VIII, this seems to me to mis-state the argumentative burden, at least given Dworkin and Coleman's shared holism, and given an epistemic environment in which foundationalism is generally frowned upon. Dworkin need not insist that all disagreements be cast as disagreements about the rule of recognition; he is permitted to maintain that some disagreements are over application, not content. He might simply reject the contention that no disagreements, even those that appear to be about criteria of validity, are really disagreements about which rule-of-recognition statements to accept, but are all disguised applications.[72]

Finally, it is noteworthy that the reconstructed argument from contestability is complementary to the argument from the normativity of rule-of-recognition statements. While the latter argument showed that rule-of-recognition statements must be secondary legal rule statements, because of *the inferences drawn from them*, the argument from contestability

---

[69] Cf. Arthur Ripstein, 'Law, Language and Interpretation', 46 U. Toronto L. Rev. 335 (1996) (reviewing Andrei Marmor, *Interpretation and Legal Theory* (1996)).

[70] Coleman put forward this position in 'Negative and Positive Positivism', and Dworkin replied to it in 'A Reply by Ronald Dworkin', in *RDCJ*, at 252–4.

[71] Coleman, *supra* n. 16, at 410–12, n. 46.

[72] In his response to Coleman, Dworkin seems to contest the idea of characterizing an apparent disagreement over the content of the Rule of Recognition as a disagreement in application. '[Coleman] says there is a difference between controversy about what the reigning convention, properly understood, really is, and controversy about what follows from the reigning convention, and he seems to think that controversy of the former sort poses a greater problem for law-as-convention. This is a doubtful distinction.' *RDCJ*, at 253.

shows that rule-of-recognition statements must be secondary legal rule statements because of *the reasons offered in their support*.

C. Illustrating the argument from contestability

A recent example will help solidify these conclusions. *Anastasoff* v. *United States*[73] concerns a taxpayer's claim that the United States Internal Revenue Service (IRS) wrongfully refused a claim for a tax refund on the ground that it was received late. The substantive issue was whether a 'savings' provision in the Tax Code, expressly permitting claims that were not timely received under a certain statute to be dated according to their postmark, would figure into the calculation of the time between the original overpayment and the filing of the refund claim. The District Court sided with the IRS, and the taxpayer appealed to the United States Court of Appeals for the Eighth Circuit.

On appeal, the Eighth Circuit Court of Appeals noted that it had already decided this precise issue in an unpublished opinion, *Christie* v. *United States*.[74] The plaintiff argued that, under Eighth Circuit Rule 28A(i), '[u]npublished opinions are not precedent'. The court held, however, that unpublished opinions are precedent, and followed *Christie*. It held that Rule 28A(i) exceeded the judiciary's power to depart from precedent, under Article III of the US Constitution.[75] In broad terms, the court reasoned that the doctrine of precedent was inherent in the power of federal courts as vested in them by Article III, and that therefore courts were not at liberty to depart from precedent in the manner that Rule 28(A) purports to license them to do. Judge Richard Arnold, the eminent Eighth Circuit judge deciding the case, drew upon important Supreme Court decisions and historical considerations regarding the framers' understanding of the federal courts, as well as broader concerns relating both to courts' power and to the importance of stability.

Anastasoff illustrates several important features of the argument from contestability. First, what was at issue in this case was whether to accept or reject a particular secondary legal rule statement: 'unpublished opinions of the Eighth Circuit are not precedent.' The judges in *Anastasoff* did not decide whether to accept this statement simply by looking at what other judges did. They began by looking at another legal norm, a rule that the Court had laid down itself. The deeper issue then became whether to reject or accept a closely related secondary legal rule statement: 'A federal court of appeals has the power to lay down a rule that has the effect of

---

[73] 223 F.3d 898 (8th Cir.), vacated on other grounds, 235 F.3d 1054 (8th Cir. 2000) (en banc).
[74] 91–2375MN (8th Cir. Mar. 20 1992) (per curiam) (unpublished decision).
[75] US Const. Art. III, § 1, cl. 1.

empowering itself, on occasion, to issue decisions that will not have precedential effect.'

The core of the argument from contestability is that statements like those above are contestable, and not simply by reference to social facts. It is not simply a matter of whether other judges or courts accept this statement. In fact, *Anastasoff* is quite a remarkable example of the contrary, for Eighth Circuit judges did in fact have a practice of treating unpublished opinions as lacking precedential force. More generally, federal judges across the nation have a similar practice, and have the related practice of applying Circuit Court Rules that designate unpublished opinions as lacking precedential force. Nevertheless, the judges' question in *Anastasoff*; 'do unpublished opinions have precedential force'?, and more specifically, 'do courts have the power to designate categories that lack precedential force?', are perfectly cogent questions for the court to ask. Moreover, there are arguments to be mustered on both sides of this issue, and these arguments are continuous with legal argument more generally. They involve the deployment of precedent, of constitutional provisions, of principles of law respected by the court, and also, perhaps, of considerations of practicality. All of these arguments are offered to support (or rebut) the rule-of-recognition statement that unpublished decisions are precedent. What this shows is that the rule-of-recognition statement does not take as its truth conditions simply social facts.

It is tempting to think that *Anastasoff* belongs to the class of American cases that present a peculiar strength for Dworkin and weakness for Hart—the constitutional cases. Indeed, the case is decided under Article III of the US Constitution. It might be argued that the real rule of recognition, here, is the US Constitution, and that it is only because there is a social fact of agreement that the Constitution (and in particular Article III) is the rule of recognition that certain other secondary legal rule statements are accepted or rejected. The disagreement, on this view, is simply a disagreement as to application of an agreed rule of recognition. As discussed above, this is the thrust of Hart's response to the argument from disagreement in the Postscript.

This argument is unpersuasive in *Anastasoff* and more generally. It is unpersuasive in *Anastasoff* because Article III does virtually no work in the court's decision. Article III, § 1, clause 1 states only: 'The judicial Power of the United States, shall be vested in one supreme Court, and in such inferior Courts as the Congress may from time to time ordain and establish.'[76] The Eighth Circuit used it as a shell into which its decision might be poured. It contains within it no standard whose application is the nub of the dispute. The reasons cited by the court are extrinsic to the

---

[76] *Id.*

pertinent text of Article III, and to the substance of the supposedly agreed rule. Hence, to treat *Anastasoff* as a case of an agreed rule with a disagreement in application would be to engage in the sort of dogmatism that the holist and pragmatist makes it a point to reject.

Returning to the earlier point, it would be a mistake to try to explain away *Anastasoff* as an exceptional case, merely illustrating the complexities that American constitutionalism introduces into our legal system. The case does not turn on the divisive questions of political morality that understandably tempt Dworkin's critics to wonder whether his points in constitutional interpretation genuinely carry over into jurisprudence more broadly. Indeed, similar questions can and do arise within state courts, concerning which decisions of which courts are to be regarded as precedents. These questions are asked and answered as difficult legal questions. They are debated and decided by reference to statutes, rules, precedents, principles, and a variety of other considerations, whether or not they nominally contain constitutional issues. They include, for example, questions about choice of law, the bindingness of federal appellate decisions in state courts, the precedential forces of decisions putatively vacated pursuant to settlement agreements, and the status of law that purports to be retroactive on certain issues. Such issues are, of course, the stuff of whole areas of law. The point is not that we do not have settled law on such questions. It is that statements of law as to these issues are at least in principle contestable by reference to matters other than social fact. Conversely, to the extent that such statements are true, it is not simply by virtue of social fact.

VI. REJECTING THE MODEL OF SOCIAL FACTS

The argument I have offered thus far has had five parts. First, I attributed to Hart a view labelled 'the model of social facts', according to which what makes a statement of law true is that the legal norm that it asserts satisfies the conditions set out by some rule of recognition, and social facts obtain in light of which that rule of recognition exists in the legal community in question. Under the model of social facts, the truth of legal statements is a matter of social facts. The model of social facts appears to flow smoothly out of Hart's conventionalism, and to provide a form of positivism in the spirit of Austin, without suffering from its shortcomings.

Second, by way of clarifying Hart's account, and simultaneously setting up my critical account, I argued that Hart's conventionalist view requires treating rules of recognition as propositions, which may or may not have the attribute of being a social rule among the legal officials in a given legal community. The latter determines, for Hart, whether a legal system with that rule of recognition is the legal system extant in a particular community.

Third, this analysis implied that a statement might, at least in principle, be related to a rule of recognition in at least two different ways. One sort of sentence would express a rule of recognition—this sort would be a subset of secondary legal rule statements. Another sort would assert that a certain proposition that has the form of a rule of recognition was treated in a certain manner by members of a legal community—this sort would be a social fact statement. The first argument against the model of social facts is simply that rule-of-recognition statements appear to be secondary legal rule statements, not social fact statements, yet Hart's model of social facts depends on rule-of-recognition statements having the same truth conditions as social fact statements.

Fourth, I sought to deepen the argument against the model of social facts by developing an argument in the spirit of MOR II. Rule-of-recognition statements are actually or potentially part of legal justifications that culminate in judicial decisions applying law as valid law. These statements could not play the role they do play (or could play) in legal justifications if their truth conditions were provided by social facts.

Fifth, I drew upon Dworkin's arguments in MOR II and elsewhere, pointing out the contestability of rule-of-recognition statements. In particular, judges commonly contest rule-of-recognition statements, but not necessarily simply by reference to social facts. I argue, from this, that rule-of-recognition statements do not simply take social facts as their truth conditions.

If these arguments are sound, then the model of social facts, as I have defined it, must be rejected. We should therefore abandon the view that it is facts about the conduct and attitudes of legal officials that determine whether or not, for example, a certain procedure is sufficient to confer validity on a putatively valid statute. We should therefore, also, abandon the view that whether particular statements about legal norms, rights, and duties are true depends upon the social facts. Whether these legal statements are true depends upon the status and validity of certain other legal norms, and this is not simply a matter of social fact.

Nothing I have said, however, is intended to undercut Hart's conventionalism in the form set out in Part III. None of it provides grounds for rejecting the claim that for a legal system to exist in a particular community is for legal officials to have certain social rules, or conventions, of accepting certain propositions about validity as controlling. Indeed, the correctness of this conventional view was part of the argument against the model of social facts. For when we see that the conditions of being extant require that legal officials *accept* certain secondary legal rules and act in accordance with them, and when we see that those secondary legal rules are themselves propositional entities, *we also see that* the statements of such rules assert propositions, rather than describing conduct.

VII. HART ON DESCRIPTIVE JURISPRUDENCE

In order to evaluate the effect of the foregoing arguments against the social facts thesis on Hart's overall jurisprudence, it is important to ascertain in what sense he genuinely adopted a social facts thesis. Doing so requires developing an understanding of what motivated Hart's adoption of such a thesis, how it fitted with the theoretical enterprise he took himself to be engaged in. Indeed, when we properly characterize Hart's own central project in *The Concept of Law*, we will see that the foregoing critique of the social facts thesis is consistent with that project.

One possible motivation for adopting a social facts thesis is political. Plainly, a broad strand of positivistic jurisprudence from Hobbes through to Bentham and Austin takes *law* to provide a solution to a global, as well as a series of local practical problems in societies of conflicting desires and opinions. Where both desire and moral discourse can lead to conflict, a legal system overseen by judges might be able to avoid some of that conflict. But it cannot do so if the existence and content of law is incapable of being discerned without the deployment of judgments that are themselves contentious in the same manner that moral discourse is.[77] A system in which what the law is is simply a matter of social and historical fact would avoid this problem, it might be argued, and retain public order. Hence, we have normative reasons, stemming from political theory, to embrace a social facts thesis. On this view, the social facts thesis is a broadening of an Austinian thesis about the provenance of legal norms. In MOR I (repeated in MOR II), Dworkin seems to intimate that Hart was motivated by Austinian concerns such as the foregoing, and he seemed to suggest that the notion of social facts constituting the law was linked to a concept of *pedigree*, which was Austinian in the sense mentioned.[78]

Second, and closely related, there is a conceptualistic as opposed to a political reason for adopting the social facts thesis, one which builds upon the problem of conflict noted above. On this view, it is not only a salutary feature of law that it can resolve such disputes. It is actually an essential feature of what makes the law *authoritative*, and what makes the law *law*, that it is capable of doing so. Hence, the existence of criteria for validity

[77] Cf. Jeremy Waldron, 'Kant's Legal Positivism', 109 Harv. L. Rev. 1535, 1538–41 (1996).

[78] *TRS*, at 17–19 (depicting Austin as explaining how law establishes public order with pedigree criterion, and portraying Hart as repairing defects in the Austinian model, while retaining a core of positivism).

that are discernible without recourse to moral judgment is not simply appealing or correct as a matter of political morality. It is built into the concept of law itself. This is, in rough form, Raz's view.[79]

A third sort of motivation might be called 'metaphysical'. On this view, law is like numbers and goodness and beauty and meaning and mind—it is a thorn in the side of the hard-headed twentieth-century philosopher. It is undeniable that there is some sense in which we have law, but there is no obvious way that law or legal validity fits into the fabric of the universe. To a naturalist or near-naturalist, divine law or Thomistic natural law are clearly unacceptable. Yet behaviouristic accounts are highly implausible. However, if the category of *social facts* is broadly enough construed, and a sufficiently rich practice theory is articulated, it might be possible to find a way of making law metaphysically modest and philosophically safe.[80]

Fourth, and related to the third, is a semantic problem about the term 'law'. One might find it puzzling that we have a practice of asserting that certain putative norms are 'law' (and accepting such assertions). Lawyers, judges, and others seem to grasp this practice. Yet it is arguably unclear what 'law' means. A social facts thesis promises to explain how the predicate 'is law' could be meaningful; there are certain social facts whose obtaining makes something law, we grasp the centripetal force of these criteria, and we are therefore able to retain command of the term. Because this command is shared, 'is law' is part of our shared language.

We have, then, at least four possible sorts of motivation for adopting a social facts thesis: political, conceptual, metaphysical, and semantic. Interestingly, the Postscript casts doubt on all four of these reasons. To begin with, Hart's embrace of inclusive legal positivism directly undercuts both the political and the conceptual motivations. Since he believes that a

---

[79] See e.g. Joseph Raz, 'Authority, Law and Morality', in *Ethics in the Public Domain* (1994). Note that, in presenting this argument and the prior one, I have not carefully distinguished between a social facts thesis and a sources thesis. Arguably, one might take a sources thesis motivated by either of these arguments to indicate a receptiveness to a similar argument for a social facts thesis. I think the distinction, in this context (and others), is considerably more important than this would indicate. Conversely, my rejection of the social facts thesis does not entail a rejection of a sources thesis. Nevertheless, as a historical matter, the foregoing arguments have motivated both a sources thesis and a social facts thesis, in some philosophers. Anthony Sebok is an example of a contemporary positivist whose primary concern is neither the separation thesis nor the social facts thesis but the sources thesis. See Anthony J. Sebok, *Legal Positivism in American Jurisprudence* (1998).

[80] I suggest in 'Legal Coherentism' 50 SMU L. Rev. 1679 (1997), 1689–94, that several twentieth-century movements in jurisprudence, including positivism, can fruitfully be understood as stemming from the same philosophical motivations that led to revisionist views in philosophy of mathematics, ethics, and aesthetics. Raz's comments on Hart's early aspirations for the potential of Austinian speech act theory to render the objectivity of law consistent with some form of naturalism are highly illuminating. See Raz, *supra* n. 68.

system with a rule of recognition that utilizes moral criteria could, in principle, have laws (and have laws by virtue of certain primary norms satisfying moral criteria), he plainly does not share Raz's belief in the
incompatibility of the concept of law and the contestability of the criteria
used to decide the validity of a putative law. As to the political argument,
it is defective as an interpretation of Hart for the same reason and others.
First, an inclusive positivistic system runs into the same difficulty as a
system would if its rule of recognition were not discernible as a matter of
social fact, for at the end of the day what the law is cannot be decided
without recourse to moral argumentation. Hence, if Hart had been
advancing a social facts thesis for political reasons, he would not have
supported inclusive legal positivism. Moreover, it is plain from *The
Concept of Law* that, however conscious Hart may sometimes have been
about the value of agreed rules and standards, he never elevated that
observation into a politically motivated criterion for law.[81]

Hart's embrace of inclusive legal positivism also diminishes the plausibility of the 'metaphysical motivation', although I shall later argue that
this account retains some force. The problem is that the metaphysical
status of law is no more secure than the weakest aspect of it. Therefore, if
validity turns on moral criteria, then even if it is social facts that make
validity turn on moral criteria, states of affairs concerning legal validity
are ultimately on no firmer footing than moral states of affairs (or 'normative states of affairs') more generally. While Hart tellingly besmirches
Dworkin's reference to 'normative states of affairs'[82]—suggesting a
considerable level of metaphysical discomfort of the sort hypothesized—
he does suggest that the central theory of the concept of law retains its
vitality even if conjoined with inclusivism. More generally, it is worth
noting that Hart says nothing in *The Concept of Law* limiting the content of
predicates that go into the rule of recognition, thereby not only letting in
inclusive legal positivism but undercutting the suggestions entertained
above that the social facts thesis is adopted out of a motivation to limit the
law to what is discernible, uncontestable, and metaphysically unproblematic. Finally, note that Hart's principal adversary in the Postscript is
Dworkin, yet Dworkin's metaphysical baggage would seem to be equal to
that of inclusive positivism: social practices and morality.

The fourth 'motivation' is not so quickly undercut by inclusive legal
positivism; it is more in tune with Hart's evident interest in language and
semantics in *The Concept of Law,* and is quite consistent with the prevailing winds of the ordinary language philosophy that dominated Oxford

[81] Liam Murphy, 'The Political Question of the Concept of Law' offers an entirely different 'political' reading of Hart's jurisprudential motivation (this volume).
[82] *CL*, at 256–7.

and Hart's environment when he wrote *The Concept of Law*. The hypothesis that this is what led Hart to the social facts thesis was attractive enough to lead Dworkin near it in his famous chapter on the 'semantic sting' in *Law's Empire*. Unfortunately, there is little in *The Concept of Law* or Hart's other writing to bear out this interpretive hypothesis. Indeed, as mentioned above, Hart's Postscript soundly and persuasively rejects the semantical motivation and position that Dworkin attributes to him, as do the articles by Endicott and Raz in this volume.[83]

Why, then, does Hart insist on saying that what the law is is constituted by social facts? Like Rick in *Casablanca*, Hart is 'saying it because it's true'. He does not begin with the aim of showing that law is *exclusively* a matter of social fact. Rather, he begins with the observation that law is a profoundly *institutional* matter to which social practices (and facts about those practices) are plainly of enormous importance. The goal in *The Concept of Law* is more constructive than defensive. It is to explain the sense in which social practices are constitutive of certain aspects of law. Connectedly, it is to demystify certain legal concepts by understanding the way they are enmeshed within these social practices. Above all, however, it is to begin to explain the variety and the complexity of legal concepts in a manner that is modest and illuminating. For Hart, this largely meant doing so in terms of social practices, and, relatedly, facts about social practices.

Hart is straightforward and forceful about the centrality of these aims in the first paragraphs of his substantive discussion in the Postscript, on the nature of legal theory:

My aim in this book was to provide a theory of what law is which is both general and descriptive. It is *general* in the sense that it is not tied to any particular legal system or legal culture, but seeks to give an explanatory and clarifying account of law as a complex social and political institution with a rule-governed (and in that sense 'normative') aspect. This institution, in spite of many variations in different cultures and in different times, has taken the same general form and structure, though many misunderstandings and obscuring myths, calling for clarification, have clustered round it. . . . My account is *descriptive* in that it is morally neutral and has no justificatory aims: it does not seek to justify or commend on moral or other grounds the forms and structures which appear in my general account of law, though a clear understanding of these is, I think, an important preliminary to any useful moral criticism of law.[84]

Hart goes on to recognize that Dworkin conceives legal theory as 'in part evaluative and justificatory and as "addressed to a particular legal culture" '.[85] He does not criticize legal theory as Dworkin has conceived

---

[83] *See supra* n. 68 and accompanying text.   [84] *CL*, at 239–40.
[85] *Id.* at 240 (quoting *Law's Empire*, at 102).

it; indeed, he recognizes the importance of this evaluative enterprise. However, he firmly asserts that the existence and importance of the evaluative enterprise in legal theory in no way undercuts the importance of the general and descriptive enterprise that he has sketched out, and within which he produced *The Concept of Law*. To think otherwise is to endorse what Dworkin himself has now described as a form of 'imperialist' claim.[86] It is particularly significant that Hart puts forward his *descriptive* picture of legal theory in explaining why it is that he has analysed concepts such as 'rules of recognition', 'acceptance of rules', 'internal and external points of view', 'internal and external statements', and 'legal validity'. Indeed, he characterizes his use of these concepts as 'a means of carrying out this descriptive enterprise'.[87]

It is misleading to suggest that Hart's aims are merely descriptive and constructive, and not defensive, metaphysical, semantic, or political. In at least one respect, it is all of these. For as Hart himself says, those who have preceded him—such as Holmes and Austin—have deployed their own characterizations of the nature of law and legal institutions in such a manner as to claim that certain metaphysical, semantical, moral, and political conclusions follow. In offering a constructive theory of law and of the concept of law, Hart is deliberately and explicitly warning us against reaching those conclusions on the basis of his predecessors' faulty accounts of law.[88] In this sense, *The Concept of Law* is of a piece with the work of J. L. Austin and the later Wittgenstein.[89] Its aim is to deal with conceptual and philosophical difficulties by offering more sensitive and nuanced accounts of the manner in which certain kinds of concepts are embedded in social practice. The effort is not to reduce or replace current concepts. Nor is the effort necessarily to establish a naturalistic framework. It is to remain methodologically modest, in terms of the kinds of ontological resource employed in an account, while nevertheless capturing as much of the conceptual and social phenomena as one can. The aspiration is to understand and explain these phenomena. On a more defensive front, it is to wash away the errors of those who have paid insufficient attention to the language, the concepts, and the practices, and who, in so doing, have generated metaphysically bloated or conceptually

---

[86] *CL*, at 243 (quoting R. M. Dworkin, 'Legal Theory and the Problem of Sense', in *Issues in Contemporary Legal Philosophy: the Influence of H. L. A. Hart*, ed. R. Gavison (1987), 19).

[87] *CL*, at 240.

[88] *Id*. at 239–40: 'This institution [law] . . . has taken the same general form and structure, though many misunderstandings and obscuring myths, calling for clarification, have clustered round it. . . . My account is *descriptive* in that it is morally neutral and has no justificatory aims; . . . though a clear understanding of these is, I think, an important preliminary to any useful moral criticism of law.'

[89] Cf. MacCormick, *supra* n. 45, at 12–19 (discussing effect of Austin, Ryle, and Wittgenstein on Hart); Raz, *supra* n. 68 (discussing effect of Austin on Hart).

impoverished accounts of central concepts in the relevant area of discourse.[90]

The obvious question, now, is whether the critique of the model of social facts that I have offered really undercuts the model of social facts as Hart himself intended it. I think the answer must be mixed. On the one hand, there is little question that Hart took the distinction between internal statements and external statements to be a highly significant aspect of his theory; he took rules of recognition to be ultimate; and he took it to be the case that the only sense in which a rule of recognition could be said to exist was that it was in fact accepted. This conjunction of positions left him in the position of contending that answers to questions about the validity of legal norms were a matter of social fact. I have argued that on this claim, Hart was mistaken. A rule-of-recognition statement is a secondary legal rule statement, and its truth or falsity is not simply a matter of whether certain social facts obtain, but rather a matter of whether legal validity does turn on what the statement asserts it turns on. The latter is determined in the context of the web of legal statements that justify it, as any other legal statement is evaluated. Hence, the semantics of rule-of-recognition statements to which Hart appears committed— insofar as he appears committed to any—is false. And the suggestion that a rule of recognition's being so can only be, ultimately, a social fact is also false. To this extent, Hart's model of social facts must be rejected.

On the other hand, the account I have offered of both the content of Hart's views and his aims in offering it suggest that the central features of his view can remain intact. Nothing I have said undercuts the view that, in a legal community, officials accept certain propositions about validity, and that it is by virtue of their doing so that those propositions are in force in that legal community. Nothing has undercut the idea of saying that for a legal system to be the legal system of a community is for such secondary legal rules to be accepted by legal officials in the community, in the conventional manner Hart suggests. Indeed, the framework I have offered for thinking about the relation between legal systems and law provides a systematic way to make those points, and to keep clear on the sense in which a rule of recognition is a social rule. Just as late twentieth-century philosophers of language have offered illuminating explanations of how members of a community are able to constitute *meaning* through a certain kind of shared practice,[91] so Hart has explained, through his social

---

[90] A particularly striking example of where Hart believed he had done this was in his refutation of Austin on obligation and Holmes on the predictive theory of what it means to say that a rule is valid. *CL*, at 104–5.

[91] Whether Hart's theory could be reconstructed along the lines of Lewis's conventions theory of language (and whether it would be desirable to do so) is a delicate issue, as the debate in this volume between Coleman and Marmor indirectly indicates. The more histor-

rules theory, how members of a legal community are able to constitute validity through a certain kind of shared practice. Insofar as Hart's model of social facts is a form of conventionalism—an account of how shared practice of treating a certain kind of rule in a certain manner permits a legal system to exist in a community—it remains a great, and viable, contribution to legal theory. As I have argued, nothing in this theory entails that the truth conditions of secondary legal norm statements are provided by social facts.

VIII. TOWARD COHERENTISM IN LAW

The critique of the model of social facts relied upon arguments against a certain picture of what made legal statements true.[92] A natural question that arises is therefore how to analyse secondary legal rule statements that are rule-of-recognition statements if (a) they are not merely external statements; (b) they are not utterances with the propositional content of external statements that express acceptance of the rule-of-recognition in question; (c) they are not Dworkinian statements of moral duty. I will not attempt to give a complete answer or defence of my answer to this question; however, at least a sketch of an alternate position is in order.

The approach I have elsewhere labelled 'legal coherentism'[93] analyses legal statements generally in a manner that follows a broader programme of coherentism and anti-foundationalism in epistemology, minimalism or at least anti-representationalism in the theory of truth, and holism in the theory of meaning.[94] It is easy to specify the truth condition of a rule-of-recognition statement such as 'a law is valid only if passed by a majority of the legislature'. It is true iff a law is valid only if passed by a majority of the legislature. The same is done for each legal sentence, including rule-of-recognition sentences. We can assert these truth sentences and say that they are true (or false) without needing any explanatory theory. Minimalists like Paul Horwich treat the words 'is true' and like phrases as simply

---

ically accurate and broader point is simply that there is a range of accounts of meaning that rely on social practices, and these are on a spectrum, from the unsystematic and perhaps anti-theoretical account in Wittgenstein's *Philosophical Investigations* to the game-theoretic account of Lewis in *Convention*. Hart's own account of law, like (e.g.) Searle's account of language, is not at either end of this spectrum, but lies between.

[92] Dennis Patterson has rightly called attention to the extent Dworkin's work displays a concern for providing an adequate semantics for legal statements. Dennis Patterson, *Law and Truth* (1996), 8 quoting Dworkin, Introduction to *Philosophy of Law*, ed. Dworkin (1977), 8–9: 'There can be no effective reply to the positivist's anti-realist theory of meaning in law, however, unless an alternative theory of propositions of law is produced.'

[93] Zipursky, *supra* n. 80.

[94] See *id.* 1695–1707.

devices for expressing the content of the underlying sentence itself.[95]

The minimalist about truth still, of course, faces many questions, and indeed Hart's own philosophical theory of law was not motivated by an attempt to capture the use of 'truth' or 'is true' as applied to legal statements. We will still need an account of how legal statements are justified and what they mean. Hart's answer on justification was clear, and a replacement bears a significant burden. Hart explained that primary rule claims (and, indeed, non-rule-of-recognition claims) were ultimately justified by a rule of recognition. The rule of recognition is the assumed starting point. The evaluation of any other legal claim was made, in part, by implicitly or explicitly applying a rule of recognition as a standard. The rule of recognition is simply assumed; it could not itself be justified. In this sense, Hart regarded the rule of recognition as 'ultimate'.[96]

The legal coherentist shares much with Hart's treatment of discourse over the validity of primary rules. An assertion that a primary rule exists as valid law is typically justified by appeal to statements that express the criteria of validity of such law. That is why, as Hart argued, the status of any particular norm as a law does not depend on its being taken to have the force of law by the members of the community. However, as I argued in Part V, Hart was mistaken in treating rule-of-recognition statements as incontestable. Indeed, Hart's argument contains a non sequitur. He explains that primary rule statements are justified by appeal to other statements that express criteria of validity, and that those statements may themselves be defended by appeal to more basic statements expressing validity. Even if we assume, with Hart, that there must therefore be statements expressing criteria of validity that are not less fundamental than any other statement (i.e. that there cannot be an infinite regress), it would not follow that such statements were not justifiable by appeal to any other statement. This confuses the epistemic order of justification with the legal order of validation. The argument for an ultimate criterion of validity, within a legal system, does not show that there is any statement that cannot itself be justified; it shows (at most) that there is some rule that cannot be validated.

These comments highlight what Dworkin claims is apparent from the nature of legal discourse, education, and practice, as well as adjudication. Legal arguments run in all directions. Frequently, lawyers and judges are called upon to justify claims about high-order rules of validity. In assessing these they bring to bear a variety of claims, of which the most important are often nearly incontrovertible claims about the validity of particular primary rules. The claims to validity of particular rules, or decisions, or other legal norms is often much more epistemically solid

---

[95] Paul Horwich, *Truth* (1990).   [96] *CL*, at 107.

than the claims to validity of broad propositions concerning the criteria of validity of norms. This is not to say that these primary rule statements are incontestable; they, too, are contestable, and can be justified, and must be capable of justification. As a contemporary coherentist like Robert Brandom might put it, to know the law, and to know how to justify claims of law, is to have the kind of mastery that enables one to justify claims at all these levels, and to evaluate such claims to assess whether they are justifiable.

In the decades leading up to Hart's publication of *The Concept of Law*, the suggestion that justification could run 'in all directions' would have met with considerable resistance, at least if the suggestion were intended to characterize some area as a genuine body of knowledge. Knowledge required a foundation, according to the prevailing view, and justifications proceeded from that foundation upwards. Just as logical positivists surmounted the lack of an apparent foundation in semantics or mathematics by selecting assumptions or postulates and constructed a system of justification upon them, so Hart (like Kelsen) constructed legal justifications upon an assumed ultimate criterion of law, a rule of recognition. In law, as in semantics, it also seemed possible to produce a descriptive analysis of the status of that criterion within a particular community.

This is not the place to recount the reasons put forward by Wittgenstein, Quine, Sellars, Rorty, and others for rejecting both positivism and foundationalism, nor is it my intention to evaluate any of these arguments.[97] What it is fair to say, however, is that coherentist approaches to epistemology, which eschew both postulated foundations and empirical ones, have now been well enough defended that, far from being intrinsically suspicious, there are well-recognized general philosophical reasons for thinking such approaches are, at the very least, promising and legitimate.[98] Moreover, coherentist approaches in epistemology have been applied to a variety of domains, which, in the philosophical culture out of which *The Concept of Law* was born, were deemed particularly suspicious; ethics, morality, and aesthetics being examples. Rawls's reflective equilibrium is a form of coherentism, and more generally Davidson, Putnam, and McDowell have embraced what can fairly be characterized as forms of coherentism across the board, specifically including ethics and morality.

Of course, a list of eminent philosophers in other areas who adopt views that loosely fall under an anti-representationalist, anti-foundationalist rubric of 'coherentism' hardly makes for a view in jurisprudence. The

[97] See Zipursky, *supra* n. 80, at 1695–1705.
[98] See e.g. Donald Davidson, 'A Coherence Theory of Truth and Knowledge', in *Truth and Interpretations: Perspectives on the Philosophy of Donald Davidson*, ed. Ernest Lepore (1986).

question arises what these sorts of view might look like applied to the
philosophy of law. Fortunately, one does not need to begin at square one
on this question, for Dworkin's own jurisprudential views bear a number
of strong affinities to the aforementioned views. Indeed, in light of this
backdrop of well-known intellectual history, it is somewhat surprising
that greater attention has not been directed towards Dworkin's coherentism, in evaluating his thought in relation to Hart. While the role of coherence in Dworkin's jurisprudence is by now a well-worn subject, this has
been treated almost entirely as a topic within the theory of law proper,
rather than within the semantics and epistemology of law.[99] Yet
Dworkin's work has displayed a marked attachment to coherentist thinking both in the theory of truth and in the theory of knowledge. He has
repeatedly displayed a similar penchant for deflationary attacks on metaphysical realism, in his arguments from the distinction between internal
and external scepticism (as applied to morality). The central thrust of the
argument in a his 1996 article 'Objectivity and Truth: You'd Better Believe
It!'[100] is that it is a mistake to infer that the statement that a metaphysical
or metalinguistic expression such as 'The statement "slavery is wrong"
captures reality' or 'The statement "slavery is wrong" is true' is actually
asserting anything different from the content of the first-order sentence
itself, i.e. that slavery is wrong. From this, Dworkin argues that there is no
cogent position for the external sceptic to be rejecting. The external sceptic is therefore nothing other than the internal sceptic, a figure with whom
Dworkin is prepared to argue at the first-order level.

The aforementioned argument, whether or not successful in its stated
aim of showing that no form of external scepticism can be articulated, is
interesting in what it reveals about Dworkin's view of the modesty of
truth claims. He evidently takes a deflationary approach toward what it
means to say that some statement 'is true'. More importantly, he is characteristically forceful in maintaining that this is the only cogent view to
take toward truth sentences in question, or the 'reality' sentences in question. While the article in question principally concerns moral and ethical
discourse, its structure and theme hark back implicitly and explicitly to
Dworkin's critique of external scepticism as to claims of legal interpretation, in *Law's Empire*.

There is obviously an argument to be made that Dworkin is a coherentist as to the justifiability of legal claims. This is not simply because the
arguments from internal and external scepticism are a thinly veiled
version of Neurath's boat. Indeed, *Law's Empire*, building upon 'Hard

---

[99] See e.g. Kenneth Kress, 'Legal Reasoning and Coherence Theories: Dworkin's Rights
Thesis, Retroactivity, and the Linear Order of Decisions', 72 Cal. L. Rev. 369 (1984).
[100] *Phil and Pub. Aff.* 25 (2) (Spring 1996), 87–139.

Cases', has as one its central theses that the justifiability of a claim about what the law is, in a particular case, *cannot in principle be decided except by taking it as part of a grand theory of all the law*. Dworkin's holism is closely connected to a form of coherentism, insofar as the former springs from a rejection of legal truth as correspondence between legal statement and identifiable (pedigreed) legal norm. Justifiability turns not on the quality of the established match between sentence and legal norms (though fit is obviously a constraint), but on the degree to which the statements within the entire legal theory cohere as a whole which best satisfies the relevant overall epistemic desiderata—for Dworkin, fit and justification.

If these observations have any merit, then there is reason for at least some optimism about the possibility of a coherentist theory in law. Let us return to the question which brought us here: the status of rule-of-recognition statements, if understood as secondary legal rule statements. What makes a rule of recognition statement such as 'A statute passed by a majority of Congress is valid law' true is that it is so—that a statute passed by a majority of Congress is valid law. Truth adds nothing, and cuts no ice. As to justifiability, the statement is justified by a variety of statements, the same statements that a person who had mastery of the law would use to justify it. Insofar as the statement is used to justify primary legal rule statements, nothing in the account needs to change from Hart's. It is simply that the justification can go in more than one direction.

IX. DWORKIN REVISITED

The critique offered in Parts II–VII was in some ways derived from Dworkin's critique of Hart in MOR II. Combining it with the suggestion in the preceding part that Dworkin's views display a form of coherentism provides a different (but by no means complete) picture of one of Dworkin's lines of attack on Hart. It is also significant, I hope, for what it shows about the possibilities of holding a position that in numerous important respects is Dworkinian.

First, the critique does not rely upon any premises regarding the central place of moral considerations in the law or legal discourse. To be sure, the account I have offered is committed to its being the case that secondary legal rule statements express propositions about the conditions of *validity* of putative legal norms, and license inferences that certain putative legal norms are valid. Moreover, these inferences are not just linguistic but practical, on the account I have constructed. Judges apply certain norms as valid law as inferences from secondary legal rule statements (and other premises). To this extent, rule-of-recognition statements are practical and conduct-guiding. It is appropriate, for these reasons, and

also because of the nature of the concept of *validity*, to describe secondary
legal rule statements on the account I have offered as 'normative'. To this
extent, it does not do violence to language to call them 'normative rules',
as Dworkin appears to do in MOR II. However, it does not follow that
secondary legal rule statements are statements about moral duties, or
even that they license inferences about moral duties. Indeed, to the extent
that they license inferences about what judges have duties to do, this may
well be because of the plausibility of a background principle that judges
have prima facie moral duties to apply the (valid) law.

Indeed, Dworkin's coherentism does not rely upon, but rather
supports, his arguments for the role of morality in law. For while it is not
the possibility of moral justification that drives the argument, the argument renders it coherent to offer a moral consideration as a reason for or
against a secondary legal rule statement. Legal justifications are put
forward as overall theories with a variety of statements within them. As
Dworkin forcefully argued in MOR I and subsequently in several articles
and books, moral statements are among those. In this sense, while the
observation that judges include such statements in their legal arguments
does not in any sense flow from the coherentism I have sketched, the
contention that it is permissible for judges to do so, and that the justifiability of a statement about the law will sometimes turn on a moral consideration—these are statements that flow from the capacity of the
coherentist model to absorb moral statements into the fabric of legal
discourse.

Third, the positive account (though not the critique, more narrowly
conceived) draws upon at least some aspects of coherentism in epistemology and the philosophy of language. It deploys a coherentist, as
opposed to a foundationalist, account of the justification of legal statements. A foundationalist would model the justification of primary legal
rule statements as proceeding from secondary legal rule statements,
which in turn rely for their justification on a rule-of-recognition statement.
The foundationalist take the justifiability of each of the higher-up steps to
depend on the rule-of-recognition statement. This means that the rule-of-
recognition statement must be privileged in some way, or else everything
falls through. It also means that the rule-of-recognition statement cannot
itself be justified from the less fundamental secondary legal rule statements or from the primary legal rule statements. As is well known,
Dworkin's model of legal justification is quite different from this. The
justifiability of primary legal rule statements may indeed involve
secondary legal rule statements and other sorts of statement, but it does
not follow that these must all come to rest on some foundation of legal
statements that is itself secure.

Fourth, the positive account so portrayed does also draw upon the availability of certain coherentist ideas in the theory of truth. At a minimum, a particular robust and metaphysical version of the correspondence theory of truth is rejected by Dworkin and by me, and this rejection plays a significant role in rendering plausible the positive account I have sketched. Part of what renders that plausible is that when we reject the statement that the truth condition for a rule-of-recognition statement is some social fact obtaining, we offer in its place another account of the truth condition of the rule of recognition. Yet this alternative account is quite minimalist, and does not itself purport to carry any heavy metaphysical baggage. In light of the spirit of Dworkin's arguments in MOR II, as well as his express statements in *Law's Empire* and subsequent work, I have argued that secondary legal rule statements and rule-of-recognition statements are capable of figuring in justifications and being true (or false), even if not rendered so by social facts as truth conditions

The prior two points—suggesting a relationship between forms of coherentism in metaphysics and epistemology on the one hand and the embrace of a Dworkinian view of jurisprudence on the other—should not be over-interpreted. I do not mean to suggest that the truth of epistemic anti-foundationalism, as a general view, is a necessary or sufficient condition for the truth of Dworkin's jurisprudential view. A similar qualification applies to coherentist or minimalist truth theories. The point is rather that, once one has come to see these coherentist positions as a cogent and promising way to understand a certain subject area, from an epistemic and semantic point of view, it suggests a cogent and philosophically promising direction in which to build an alternative to the model of social facts within jurisprudence. Given that Dworkin himself appears sympathetic to these epistemic and semantic positions, and has in fact offered an alternative to the model of social facts, the connection between the two ought to be noticed, and merits further attention.

Finally—and perhaps somewhat counterintuitively—I suggest that, once we have rejected the model of social facts, Hart's analysis of law in terms of conventions in a legal community is available not only to Hart but also to Dworkin. For the same reasons that it is wrong for Hart to adopt the model of social facts as a theory of what makes legal statements true, it is wrong for Dworkin to reject Hart's conventionalism as a descriptive analysis of the nature of legal systems. A central contention of this paper is that conventionalism in the analysis of the nature of legal systems does not entail the model of social facts. As to Hart, we used this to show that he should not adopt the model of social facts, even if he was a conventionalist. Dworkin clearly starts from the other end, in his certitude that the model of social facts is mistaken. But his rejection of the model of social facts appears to lead him to a rejection of conventionalism in the analysis of the nature of legal systems. This is simply the other side of the problem Hart faced: rather than incorrectly inferring the model of social facts from conventionalism, Dworkin is incorrectly inferring the falsity of conventionalism from the falsity of the model of social facts. What I have tried to do is display their separability. As Parts II–VII showed, the risk to be avoided is that, once one embarks on a form of conventionalism in descriptive jurisprudence, one will be tempted to transform this into an account of the truth conditions of legal statements. Dworkin seemed to have something similar in mind when he wrote, 'it is worth stressing how pervasive that question [of sense] is in the issues that general theories, like Hart's, have mainly discussed'.[101] Of course, in his discussion of the semantic sting, and to a lesser extent in the MOR papers, Dworkin seems to believe the very point of Hart's conventionalistic accounts is to provide a roughly naturalistic account of the meaning and truth conditions of legal discourse.

Hart's clarification in the Postscript of his own goals in legal theory is thus essential to understanding both why Hart and Dworkin often talked past each other and also why an opportunity for a greater convergence in their views was missed. As argued above, Hart was aiming to understand the sense in which legal practices were able to constitute law. It turned out, in his day of ordinary language philosophy, to be rather seductive to stretch such an account so that it looked as though legal facts rested upon social facts both metaphysically and semantically, and there is certainly a strain of such thinking in *The Concept of Law*. But that was neither his central aim nor his central point. The practice-based account of law, legality, and validity and several other concepts was the principal goal. There is nothing in Dworkin's coherentism that stops him from adopting such a conventionalism, so long as we stop short of reductive semantics. In this way, coherentist conventionalism is available as a reconciliation of Hart and Dworkin.

X. CONCLUSION

Hart's Postscript recognizes and responds to Dworkin's critique in MOR II. In vigorously defending his position on social rules while simultaneously embracing inclusive positivism, Hart invites us to see *The Concept of Law* as motivated less by a picture of rigid rules—as Dworkin suggested—and more by a 'model of social facts'. Yet, I argue, Hart's model of social facts is not adequately defended against the driving forces of Dworkin's MOR II critique. Dworkin was at root insisting that it was a conceptual confusion to treat rule-of-recognition statements as semantic-

---

[101] Dworkin, 'Legal Theory and the Problem of Sense', at 19.

ally equivalent to assertions that certain social facts obtain. In this insistence, he was right. We see the soundness of his critique *even within a Hartian framework* once we are able to develop a clear conventionalistic model
of law and rules of recognition, and can build a semantics of rule-of-
recognition statements upon that model. Rule-of-recognition statements
assert secondary legal rules about validity, and their truth depends on
whether what they assert about validity is so, not on whether certain
social facts obtain. Hart avoided this conclusion by adopting an analysis
of rule-of-recognition statements that made their truth turn on *whether* a
social rule existed—whether certain social facts obtained. Once we shift to
a coherentist framework in epistemology and semantics, however, we see
that there are stronger philosophical reasons for treating rule-of-recognition statements in a manner that does not assimilate them to social facts
statements, and for rejecting the model of social facts in the positivistic
form in which Hart characteristically presented it.

This article has diverged in an important respect from several other
commentaries on the Postscript which have displayed a great interest in
Hart's embrace of inclusive positivism. That interest is understandable.
As Jules Coleman presented it eighteen years ago, inclusive legal positivism promises to capture the best of both worlds.[102] For it offers an
account of the facts about legal validity that is as unmysterious as practices themselves; this is a great appeal of positivism. On the other hand, it
captures the appeal in Dworkin by making room for morality in law at the
ground floor, in the criteria for legal validity. While I have argued above
that a version of the model of social facts that treats legal statements as
true by virtue of social facts is both untenable and undesirable, the argument left open what might be called an 'inclusive' view that is Hartian
both in its analysis of legal systems and in its conventionalism. Such a
view might adopt the central Hartian tenets that a legal system is a union
of primary and secondary legal rules. And it might also contend that for
a legal system to exist in a given community is for its rule of recognition
to be treated as a social rule by legal officials. Its inclusivism would
consist in its permitting systems with rules of recognition whose expression includes moral predicates to count as legal systems. Whether an
inclusive positivism so modified is really a form of *positivism*, whether it
can be defended against the authority-based critiques of Raz, Shapiro,

[102] Coleman, 'Negative and Positive Positivism'. Coleman recognized in that paper that
'[I]t is well known that one can meet the objections to positivism Dworkin advances in
MOR-I by constructing a rule of recognition (in the semantic sense) that permits moral principles as well as rules to be binding legal standards'. *Id*. at 35. Nevertheless, one of the ideas
his paper is to be credited with is the recognition that a certain understanding of legal reality as constituted by social facts is consistent with Dworkin's emphasis on moralism, and
that, therefore, what are arguably principal virtues of each theory can be reconciled.

and others, and whether it is, all considered, a tenable position are questions I leave for another time.

Instead, I have suggested that coherentist conventionalism offers
another path to the reconciliation of Hart and Dworkin, another way to
get 'the best of both worlds'. However, it begins with different judgments
as to what the 'best' in each world is. The core strength of Hart is not his
ability to keep law a matter of social fact. It is his fundamental yet detailed
account of how it is that human practices make legal systems possible and
give legal concepts content. Likewise, the core strength of Dworkin is not
necessarily his ability to include morality in law, per se. It is his analysis
of the complex and irreducible nature of legal discourse and legal justification, and his ability to turn these features of legal justification into a
defence of the possibility of legal truth, rather than an abandonment of it.
If this is right—if the best of Dworkin is his coherentism and the best of
Hart is his conventionalism—then we can indeed have the best of both
worlds, not as inclusive positivists, but as coherentist conventionalists.

8

Law's Claim of Legitimate Authority
KENNETH EINAR HIMMA

In the Postscript, H. L. A. Hart reaffirms his commitment to the Incorporation Thesis, according to which 'a criterion of validity may be in part a moral test'.[1] On Hart's view, it is conceptually possible for a legal system to have a rule of recognition that incorporates moral norms. Satisfaction of moral criteria can hence be either a necessary or sufficient condition for legal validity. The Incorporation Thesis, then, denies that the 'criteria provided by the rule of recognition must be solely matters of pedigree' (CL 250).

Critics on both sides of the positivist/anti-positivist divide allege that the Incorporation Thesis is inconsistent with other core commitments of Hart's positivism. On the anti-positivist side, Ronald Dworkin argues that the Incorporation Thesis is inconsistent with the Separability Thesis.[2] On the positivist side, Joseph Raz argues that the Incorporation Thesis is inconsistent with the nature of legal authority. In this essay, I will examine the Razian critique and evaluate one of the theses on which it critically relies: the thesis that it is a conceptual truth that law claims legitimate authority.

I. RAZ'S ACCOUNT OF AUTHORITY

As Hart describes it, the Separability Thesis asserts that 'it is in no sense a necessary truth that laws reproduce or satisfy certain demands of morality' (CL 185–6). According to the Separability Thesis, then, it is conceptually possible for something that constitutes a legal system to exclude moral norms from the criteria that determine whether a standard is legally valid. In such a legal system, it is neither necessary nor sufficient

Thanks to Scott Shapiro, whose comments helped me greatly to improve this essay. I owe a special debt to Jules Coleman and Ronald Moore, who have taught me everything I know about legal philosophy. If there is anything of philosophical value in my work, they deserve the credit.

[1] H. L. A. Hart, *The Concept of Law*, 2nd edn. (Oxford: Clarendon Press, 1994), 253 (hereinafter *CL*).

[2] See Kenneth Einar Himma, 'Incorporationism and the Objectivity of Moral Norms', *Legal Theory*, 5(4) (1999), 415–34, for a discussion of Dworkin's views on this issue.

for the validity of a norm that it be logically related to some set of moral standards.

Put this way, the Separability Thesis purports to be agnostic on whether it is conceptually possible for something that constitutes a legal system to *have* moral criteria of validity. Hart was the first to think deeply about this issue, and he came out long ago in favour of the Incorporation Thesis. In responding to Lon Fuller's view that positivism precludes restrictions on legislative power, Hart writes:

There is, for me, no logical restriction on the content of the rule of recognition: . . . a constitution could include in its restrictions on the legislative power . . . a completely general provision that its legal power should lapse if its enactments ever conflicted with principles of morality.[3]

According to Hart's inclusive positivism, then, there are conceptually possible legal systems in which the criteria of validity include moral norms. In such legal systems, whether a norm is legally valid depends, in part, on its logical relation to the relevant moral norms.

Against Hart, exclusive positivists argue that the existence and content of law must be determinable by reference to sources without moral argument. But it is crucial to realize that this does not commit exclusive positivists to denying either that legal systems sometimes include moral language in constitutional norms or that judges often engage in moral argumentation in making validity decisions.[4] What exclusive positivists deny is that constitutional provisions containing moral language succeed in making moral requirements part of the validity criteria. Instead, they construe these provisions as requirements that courts consider moral norms in deciding certain legal issues.

Accordingly, exclusive positivists can acknowledge that the term 'cruel' contained in the Eighth Amendment has moral content, and that judges often engage in moral argument in deciding whether to allow a punishment under the Eighth Amendment. But, *contra* Hart, they must construe it as requiring that judges consider moral norms regarding cruelty in determining whether to allow a particular punishment. Complying with this directive, of course, will require precisely the sort of moral argument that is common in constitutional cases; however, exclusive positivists insist that judicial rulings on such matters create new law in the exercise of judicial discretion. Legal provisions using moral language succeed, at most, in incorporating into the law judicial holdings about morality.

---

[3] Book review of *The Morality of Law*, 78 Harvard Law Review 1281 (1965), in Hart, *Essays in Jurisprudence and Philosophy* (Oxford: Clarendon Press, 1983), 361.

[4] I will assume that provisions of a written constitution express validity criteria. Any claim I make using such provisions could be made, though less perspicuously, in terms of criteria of validity.

One might think, at first blush, that Hart has the better of the dispute, as his interpretation of laws using moral language seems easier to reconcile with the relevant legal practices. After all, the Eighth Amendment states that 'cruel and unusual punishment [shall not be] inflicted' and not 'judges should consult the moral notion of cruelty in deciding whether to allow a punishment'.

But while the plain language of constitutional provisions may seem to favour Hart, Raz argues that the Incorporation Thesis is inconsistent with the nature of authority. According to the Authority Thesis, it is a conceptual truth that law claims legitimate authority.[5] While this claim is often false, it is 'part of the nature of law' that it claims authority: 'though a legal system may not have legitimate authority, or though its legitimate authority may not be as extensive as it claims, every legal system claims that it possesses legitimate authority' (ALM 215). Insofar as 'the claim to authority is part of the nature of law' (215), it follows that a normative system that does not claim authority is conceptually disqualified from being a legal system.

Accordingly, the Authority Thesis implies an important constraint on the existence conditions for law: 'If the claim to authority is part of the nature of law, then whatever else the law is it must be capable of possessing authority' (215). In other words, every conceptually possible system of law must be *capable* of possessing authority. A system of norms incapable of bearing authority cannot sincerely claim legitimate authority, and is thus conceptually disqualified from being a legal system.

On Raz's view, a normative system is conceptually incapable of bearing authority unless it can perform authority's conceptual function of 'mediating between people and the right reasons that apply to them' (ALM 214). To discharge this function, a normative system must satisfy two conditions. First, it must be the source of directives that reflect the balance of reasons with respect to what subjects ought to do. Thus, according to the Dependence Thesis, 'authoritative directives should be based, among other factors, on reasons which apply to the subjects of those directives and which bear on the circumstances covered by the directives' (214).

Second, a normative system must, so to speak, stand between people and right reason in the following sense: the authority's decision must be able to replace (or preempt) the reasons that would otherwise be considered by the subject. As Raz puts it:

The [authority's] decision is . . . a reason for action. They ought to do as he says because he says so. . . . [But] it is not just another reason to be added to the others,

---

[5] Joseph Raz, 'Authority, Law, and Morality', in *Ethics in the Public Domain* (Oxford: Clarendon Press, 1994), (hereinafter *ALM*).

a reason to stand alongside the others when one reckons which way is better supported by reason. . . . The decision is also meant to replace the reasons on which it depends. (ALM 212–13)

According to the Preemption Thesis, 'the fact that an authority requires performance of an action is a reason for its performance which is not to be added to all other relevant reasons when assessing what to do, but should replace some of them' (ALM 214).[6]

Raz's so-called service conception of authority suggests a thesis regarding the justification of authority. According to the Normal Justification Thesis (NJT), authority is justified to the extent that the subject is more likely to do what right reason requires by following authoritative directives than by following her own judgment:

The normal and primary way to establish that a person should be acknowledged to have authority over another person involves showing that the alleged subject is likely better to comply with reasons which apply to him (other than the alleged authoritative directives) if he accepts the directives of the alleged authority as authoritatively binding, and tries to follow them, than if he tries to follow the reasons which apply to him directly. (ALM 214)

Though NJT is not implied by the service conception of authority, it coheres well with it: given the mediating function of authority, it is natural to suppose that authority will be justified only to the extent that it does a better job than its subjects of deciding what ought to be done according to right reason.

The service conception of authority, broadly construed to include NJT, affords Raz two arguments purporting to show that, as a conceptual matter, it must always be possible to identify an authoritative directive without recourse to its dependent moral justification. First, the Preemption Thesis implies that a directive cannot be authoritative unless it is capable of preempting the subject's evaluation of the balance of reasons. But a directive that cannot be identified without recourse to its dependent justification *is incapable* of preempting the subject's evaluation of the balance of reasons because the subject's evaluation *is necessary* to identify the directive. Such a directive is, thus, conceptually disqualified under the Preemption Thesis from being authoritative.

Second, NJT implies that a directive cannot be legitimate unless it is more likely that the subject comply with right reason by following the directive than by following her own judgment of the balance of reasons. But a directive that cannot be identified without recourse to the balance of reasons is *incapable* of satisfying this condition. In such circumstances, the subject is no more likely to comply with the demands of right reason by

---

[6] This distinguishes authority from other forms of normativity.

following the directive than by following her own judgment. For inasmuch as she uses her judgment to identify its existence or content, she is essentially following *her own* judgment about what right reason requires. Thus, if NJT is a conceptually necessary condition for legitimacy, it follows that a directive that cannot be identified without recourse to its dependent moral justification is conceptually disqualified under NJT from being *legitimately* authoritative.

Accordingly, Raz concludes that for law to be capable of legitimate authority, it must be possible to identify the existence and content of a legal norm without recourse to the dependent reasons justifying it. But if the validity criteria incorporate moral norms, then whether a norm is legally valid depends on its moral merits. Insofar as legal validity depends on moral merit, it is not possible to determine that a norm is legally valid without recourse to the moral reasons justifying that norm. Thus, if the validity criteria incorporate moral norms, it is not possible to identify the existence and content of law without recourse to the moral norms that form part of the dependent justification for the law.

We cannot, for example, determine that a punishment norm is valid under a validity criterion prohibiting morally cruel punishments without recourse to the moral standards of cruelty that ultimately justify that punishment norm. This implies that the content of such a moral principle cannot be incorporated into the Eighth Amendment because, *qua* authority, it is supposed to settle the issue of what punishments are permissible. As Raz might put it, a norm that tells us the state may impose morally permissible punishments tells us little about which punishments the state may impose. Thus, the Authority Thesis precludes construing the Eighth Amendment as incorporating moral norms regarding cruelty. Since the Authority Thesis is hence inconsistent with the Incorporation Thesis, Hart must give up the latter.

II. THE AUTHORITY THESIS: PRELIMINARY CONCERNS

Raz's critique of the Incorporation Thesis ultimately rests on the Authority Thesis, according to which it is a conceptual truth that 'every legal system claims that it possesses legitimate authority' (ALM 215). On this view, any institutional normative system that does not claim legitimate authority is conceptually disqualified from being a legal system. The claim to legitimate authority, then, is part of the very nature of law.

But what exactly does the conceptual claim of legitimate authority assert? In other words, what exactly is a legal system claiming when it asserts 'that it possesses legitimate authority'? To answer this question, it is crucial to note that Raz, like most theorists, regards the notion of legitimacy as a *moral* notion associated with the existence of a moral obligation to obey law:

[The claims made by law do not show] legal authorities have a right to rule, which implies an obligation to obey. But it reminds us of the familiar fact that they claim such a right, that is, they are *de facto* authorities because they claim a right to rule and because they succeed in establishing and maintaining their rule. They have legitimate authority only if and to the extent that their claim is justified and they are owed a duty of obedience.[7]

Thus, Raz concludes, 'No system is a system of law unless it includes a claim of legitimacy, or *moral* authority. That means that it claims that legal requirements are *morally* binding, that is, that legal obligations are real (moral) obligations arising out of the law.'[8]

And this moral obligation to which legitimate authority gives rise, on Raz's view, is content-independent in the following sense: the fact that a directive is legally valid implies a moral obligation to obey that directive regardless of its content. As Raz describes the notion of content-independence:

A reason is content-independent if there is no direct connection between the reason and the action for which it is a reason. The reason is in the apparently 'extraneous' fact that someone in authority has said so, and within certain limits his saying so would be reason for any number of actions.[9]

Of course, this should not be construed as denying that one can have content-independent and content-dependent reasons for performing the same act. Thus, for example, an authoritative directive might express both a content-independent obligation and a content-dependent obligation, as presumably occurs when a legitimate authority prohibits murder.

Law's essential claim to legitimate authority, then, amounts to this: law claims that its citizens have a moral obligation to obey legal directives precisely because they have the status of law. While, on Raz's view, there can be political authority that is not owed a moral duty of obedience, '[it is] a mistake to think that . . . there can also be one [that] does not claim that it is owed such a duty' (AJ 5). Thus, the Authority Thesis is logically equivalent to the claim that it is a conceptual truth that every legal system claims that its citizens have a content-independent moral obligation to obey law.

---

[7] 'Authority and Justification', *Philosophy and Public Affairs*, 14(1) (Winter 1985), 5 (hereinafter AJ). Insofar as Raz believes that 'a legal system may not have legitimate authority' (ALM 215), the relevant notion of obligation must be *moral*. The idea that citizens are *legally* obligated by laws is tautologously true; hence, if all Raz meant by a legal system's claim to authority is that laws give rise to *legal* obligations, a legal system's claim to authority could not possibly be false.

[8] 'Hart on Moral Rights and Legal Duties', *Oxford Journal of Legal Studies*, 4(1) (Spring 1984), 131 (emphasis added).

[9] *The Morality of Freedom* (Oxford: Clarendon Press, 1986), 35 (hereinafter MF).

A. How could law claim authority?

The proposition that citizens have a content-independent moral obligation to obey law is, at first blush, a peculiar claim to attribute conceptually
to law. After all, as Raz points out, 'it is all too plain that in many cases the
law's claim to legitimate authority cannot be supported' (ALM 216).
Indeed, there have been too many legal systems that lack legitimate
authority; the legal system in apartheid South Africa is but one depress-
ing example among many. Raz's case against inclusive positivism, then,
rests on attributing as a conceptual matter to legal systems a claim to
authority that is frequently false.

But the situation might be even worse than this: philosophical anarchists believe that law's claim to legitimate authority can never be true, in
part, because the failure to obey an authority's directive can never, *by
itself*, justify the application of force. For such theorists, there is *no* conceptually possible legal system in which citizens have a content-independent
moral obligation to obey law. These theorists do not deny that there are
often *content-dependent* moral obligations to obey law; they simply deny
that the mere status of a directive as law can give rise to a moral obligation to obey that directive. If such theorists are correct, then the claim to
legitimate authority is *necessarily* false.

This creates a minor problem for the Razian critique. Raz argues, as we
have seen, that 'if the claim to authority is part of the nature of law, then
whatever else the law is it must be capable of possessing authority' (ALM
215). But insofar as law's claim to authority is *necessarily* false, it could not
be 'capable of possessing authority'. While there is an intuitive sense in
which it makes more sense to attribute authority to law than to a milk
carton, this cannot rescue the Authority Thesis if philosophical anarchists
are correct. For if there is no conceptually possible legal system in which
law's claim to authority is true, then it is false that law is capable of legitimate authority.[10] Thus, the Razian critique of inclusive positivism
assumes that philosophical anarchism is false.

Of course, such a presupposition is not likely to bother many people;
anarchist theories are well away from the mainstream of contemporary
political thought. For this reason, resting a defence of inclusive positivism
against the Authority Thesis on the strength of a theory that asserts the
impossibility of legitimate authority will not convince mainstream legal
theorists.

A potentially more serious worry is that it is not immediately clear how

---

[10] Raz equates authority with legitimate authority; for this reason, I will follow Raz in
using the terms interchangeably. An entity that is falsely believed to have authority is a
merely de facto authority.

law can make claims. A legal system comprises many elements. Most obviously, a legal system consists of a set of first-order legal norms and a set of second-order validity criteria. But it also consists of various institutions that are defined by those validity criteria; these typically include judicial, legislative, and executive institutions. And each of these institutions is composed of officials who have duties defined by certain legal norms, which may include validity criteria and first-order norms, as well as by internal regulations that do not, strictly speaking, constitute law.

Considered individually, some of these elements are obviously capable of making claims. Officials, for example, are intentional agents and are hence capable of making claims in what I will call the *performative* sense: by performing various linguistic acts that bear truth value. As abstract propositional objects, legal norms cannot make claims in the performative sense because abstract objects cannot *perform* acts. Instead, legal norms make claims, if at all, in the *expressive* sense: by expressing propositions about what the law requires.

These straightforward observations, however, are of little help in making sense of the Authority Thesis because it is a thesis about what is claimed by a *legal system*, and no one of these elements constitutes a legal system. Indeed, to the extent that a legal system constitutes a unified institution, it must be characterized as a set containing all of these various elements—and a set is a *non*-propositional abstract object. This probably comes as no surprise; the thought that there is a single *physical* object that constitutes the legal system has likely tempted few legal theorists.

But the idea that a non-propositional abstract object can claim authority does come with a few metaphysical puzzles—minor perhaps, but certainly worth addressing before accepting a claim as potent as the Authority Thesis. To begin with, it seems clear that, unlike propositional objects, a non-propositional abstract object cannot make claims in the *expressive sense*. A sentence expresses claims in virtue of being an aggregate of various linguistic entities that bear meaning. While it might not be obvious *how* the meanings of the atomic parts combine to determine the meaning of the whole, it seems clear that the meaning of the sentence is fully determined by the meaning of those parts. But a set that consists of *sets* of norms and *sets* of individuals is not an aggregate of linguistic entities; sets of propositional objects are aggregated with sets of individuals to compose the set constituting a legal system. Though every entity contained in one of the sets making up a legal system can make claims in either the expressive sense or the performative sense, there is no way to aggregate those sets to *express* a proposition. For this reason, the Authority Thesis is *necessarily* false if construed as asserting that every legal system, in the literal sense, *expresses* a claim to legitimate authority.

Nor does the Authority Thesis fare any better if we construe it as asserting that every conceptually possible legal system, in the literal sense, *performatively* claims authority. Entities capable of making claims in the performative sense can do so only in virtue of possessing certain properties. What makes it possible for us to make claims is that we are rational, intentional agents who can use language to communicate the content of mental states to others. And each of these properties seems necessary for being able to make claims in the performative sense. It is, of course, tautologously true that the ability to make claims in the performative sense requires linguistic competence. Rationality is necessary because the ability to use language presupposes the ability to form concepts. Intentionality is necessary because claims typically express the content of mental states, which are always *about* something. It would seem, then, that the absence of any one of these properties is enough to render a being incapable of making claims. If so, then it is not conceptually possible for legal systems to make claims in the performative sense.[11] Thus, the Authority Thesis is *necessarily* false if construed as asserting that legal systems, in the literal sense, *performatively* claim legitimate authority.

Unfortunately, these considerations do little to help the inclusive positivist. Although non-propositional abstract objects like legal systems are not claim-making entities in *any* strict metaphysical sense, this does not pose an insurmountable obstacle to accepting the Authority Thesis. For we often attribute claims to entities that are not, strictly speaking, capable of making claims. Thus, for example, we can speak sensibly of a corporation making claims simply by attributing claims made by corporate officials to the corporation itself; in so doing, we treat the corporation as if it were an intentional agent. This metaphysical fiction is incorporated into legal doctrine because it is useful to do so—making it possible, for instance, to treat corporations as 'persons' that can sue and be sued. As long as we respect its intuitive boundaries, there is no decisive reason to reject the use of such a device.

And the same can be said for philosophical theorizing about the existence conditions for legal systems. As long as we are careful, there is nothing objectionable about incorporating into our theorizing a fiction that treats the legal system as an agent capable of making claims. Thus, the status of a legal system as a non-propositional abstract object cannot, in and of itself, ground a cogent objection to the Authority Thesis.

There is, however, a preliminary point we can now make about the

[11] This is a little too strong. Since there are no obvious examples of an animal that instantiates only two of these three properties, we are not in a position to verify the hypothesis that each of these properties is necessary. Indeed, one might reasonably think it is not conceptually possible for a being to instantiate any one of these properties without instantiating them all. Nevertheless, it is not necessary to resolve this issue; since legal systems lack *all* these properties, they cannot make claims in the performative sense.

Authority Thesis. Since a legal system is a non-propositional abstract object, any claims it makes will have to be explained, at least indirectly, in terms of the behaviours of intentional agents participating in legal practice.[12] Some of these behaviours are likely to be deliberately expressive but they need not be; there is no a priori reason to rule out inferences that might be made on the basis of non-expressive behaviour. But whatever behaviours are identified as forming the basis for such claims, they must be present in *every conceptually possible legal system*, since the Authority Thesis attributes such claims to law as a conceptual truth. Any system of norms in which these behaviours do not occur, then, is conceptually disqualified from being a legal system.

This is not obviously problematic. After all, positivism includes behavioural constraints in the existence conditions for a legal system. Positivists hold, for example, that it is a necessary condition for the existence of a legal system in S that people in S generally obey the norms validated by S's criteria of validity. Though an efficacy requirement is a behavioural constraint, it is a plausible one because a legal system is a relational object that obtains *in* some society. As such, it is partly defined by its relation to the people whose behaviour it governs. If people in S do not obey the norms validated by the validity criteria V, then it does not makes sense to say that V gives rise to a legal system in S because the institutions defined by V do not stand in the appropriate relation to people in S.

While it is clear, then, that there can be behavioural constraints in the existence conditions for a legal system, the foregoing illustrates that the Authority Thesis must meet a substantial burden. There must be a persuasive non-question-begging reason for denying the status of legal system to an institution that has an efficacious rule of recognition but lacks the requisite behavioural elements making up law's claim to legitimate authority. In other words, there must be a good reason for thinking that the relevant behaviours are absolutely essential to the existence of a legal system.

I argue below that the Authority Thesis fails to carry this burden. A word about the argument strategies I employ would be helpful here. Sometimes I will argue that the relevant behaviour elements do not warrant the attribution to the legal system of a claim of authority. Assuming that such elements, then, are present in every conceptually possible legal system, they do not support the Authority Thesis because they do not give rise to a claim of authority. Sometimes I will argue simply that the relevant behaviour elements are not conceptually necessary. Assuming that such elements warrant attributing to the legal system a claim to

---

[12] I mean this in a very broad sense. In this sense, for example, a legal norm would be an appropriate behavioural explanation.

authority, they do not support the Authority Thesis because this thesis is a claim about what is true in *every conceptually possible legal system*. The contingent occurrence of a behaviour in some, but not all, legal systems that makes a claim of authority does not provide any support for the thesis that every conceptually possible legal system claims authority.

B. A preliminary approach: do legal norms claim legitimate authority?

At first blush, one might attempt to attribute an authority claim to legal systems exclusively on the basis of what is asserted or entailed by legal norms. For example, one might argue that a system of law claims legitimate authority if and only if there is a legal norm that asserts there is a content-independent moral obligation on the part of subjects to obey norms validated by the criteria of validity.

By itself, this manoeuvre will not vindicate the Authority Thesis because, as an empirical matter, it is false that every legal system includes a law asserting the existence of a content-independent moral obligation to obey law. There is certainly nothing like that in the US. The closest one gets to such a norm, I think, is the statement in the Constitution that it is 'the supreme law of the land', but that merely asserts that constitutional norms win in conflicts with other legal norms.

One could, I suppose, argue that any normative system not containing such a norm is conceptually disqualified from being a legal system, but this is implausible for a number of reasons. First, it entails that many normative institutions regarded as paradigmatic legal systems are not really legal systems at all. As an empirical matter, the US is probably not the only paradigmatic legal system lacking a legal norm that asserts a content-independent moral obligation to obey. Second, a legal norm cannot create a content-independent moral obligation to obey law simply by asserting there is such an obligation. For this reason, the idea that it is a conceptual requirement that every legal system contain such an ineffectual norm seems very difficult to motivate. Finally, the claim that a system of law must contain a legal norm asserting a content-independent moral obligation to obey law is inconsistent with the Separability Thesis. For, thus construed, the Authority Thesis defines a necessary moral constraint on the content of law. Though such a constraint is, as we just noticed, oddly ineffectual, a necessary moral constraint on law's content runs afoul of the Separability Thesis—no matter how ineffectual that constraint might be.

One might try to avoid such problems by replacing 'asserts' with the weaker 'logically entails'. On this account, a legal system claims authority if and only if it includes a set of legal norms that logically entails the proposition that there is a content-independent moral obligation to obey

law. Thus construed, the Authority Thesis asserts that in every conceptually possible legal system S there is a set Λ_s of legal norms entailing the
claim that people in S have a content-independent moral obligation to
obey the law in S.

Indeed, one might think that Λ_s consists of the same norms in every
conceptually possible legal system, namely those expressing the minimum content of natural law. Hart argues convincingly that law *must*
conduce to the 'minimum purpose of survival which men have in associating with each other' (*CL* 193) and that, hence, there could not be a
society in which theft and violence are not prohibited:

> Reflection on some very obvious generalizations—indeed truisms—concerning
> human nature and the world in which men live, show that as long as these hold
> good, there are certain rules of conduct which any social organization must
> contain if it is to be viable. . . . Such universally recognized principles of conduct
> which have a basis in elementary truths concerning human beings, their natural
> environment, and aims, may be considered the *minimum content* of Natural Law.
> (*CL* 192–3)

Strictly speaking, of course, such norms are valid in virtue of a social
convention and not in virtue of their moral merit. But, given certain
nomological facts about human beings, there could not be a normative
system lacking such norms that is sufficiently efficacious to satisfy the
minimum conditions for a legal system.

Accordingly, one might think that the set Λ_{NL} of norms expressing the
minimum content of the natural law, which belongs to every conceptually
possible legal system, logically entails a content-independent moral obligation to obey law, but this is false. First, the only moral obligation to
which each norm in Λ_{NL} clearly gives rise is *content-dependent*. For, by
hypothesis, each norm in Λ_{NL} prohibits a behaviour, like theft or murder,
that is morally wrong because it threatens survival. Second, while there is
a moral obligation to comply with the norms in Λ_{NL}, Λ_{NL} does not *logically*
entail the existence of such a moral obligation—at least not without the
help of extralegal moral standards. The problem is that the norms in Λ_{NL}
express *legal* obligations; such norms *legally* prohibit those behaviours.
But, as we will see below, if the Separability Thesis is true, then a set of
norms expressing only legal obligations cannot logically entail any claims
about moral obligations—content-dependent or otherwise.[13]

This suggests that an approach attempting to extract a claim to authority exclusively on the strength of what legal norms assert and entail
cannot succeed. For the Separability Thesis, broadly construed as asserting a conceptual separation between law and morality, seems to imply

---

[13] See *infra*, section III D for a more detailed discussion of this point.

that it is not the case that every possible legal system contains a norm that asserts the existence of a moral obligation. If so, there will be at least one conceptually possible legal system containing only legal norms that assert *legal* obligations. In that system, the set of binding legal norms does not entail the claim that there is a content-independent moral obligation to obey law.[14] While legal norms may play a role in a claim of authority, there must be *other* elements of legal practice that express such a claim to vindicate the Authority Thesis. Accordingly, if we are warranted in attributing a claim of authority to law, it will be because a broader range of legal practices warrants the attribution.

III. THE RAZIAN VIEW

Raz describes a number of practices supporting his view that law claims it has 'the *moral* attributes required to endow it with legitimate authority' (ALM 215; emphasis added). Most important is that 'the law presents itself as a body of authoritative standards and requires all those to whom they apply to acknowledge their authority' by complying even when there are good reasons for non-compliance.[15] In addition, Raz argues that:

The claims the law makes for itself are evident from the language it adopts and from the opinions expressed by its spokesmen, i.e., by the institutions of the law. The law's claim to authority is manifested by the fact that legal institutions are officially designated as 'authorities', by the fact that they regard themselves as having the right to impose obligations on their subjects, by their claims that their subjects owe them allegiance, and that their subjects ought to obey the law as it requires to be obeyed (i.e., in all cases except those in which some legal doctrine justifies breach of duty). Even a bad law, is the inevitable official doctrine, should be obeyed for as long as it is in force, while lawful action is taken to try and bring about its amendment or repeal. (ALM 215–16)

Thus, there are five practices that Raz believes signal a claim of authority: (1) the enforcement of law as exclusionary; (2) the use in the law of such terms as 'right' and 'duty'; (3) the official designation of legal institutions as 'authorities'; (4) the claims of officials that subjects 'owe' allegiance and

---

[14] Treating legal norms as claims made by the legal system may be problematic for another reason. Legal directives are not obviously descriptive. Consider, e.g. the case of promising. The words 'I promise that X' do not make a descriptive assertion; rather, they *accomplish* the act of making a promise. Likewise, a legal directive stating that murder is prohibited does not claim murder is prohibited; rather, it accomplishes the act of *prohibiting* murder. For this reason, it is not clear that the legal system *claims* that murder is prohibited. If the legal norm, by itself, makes no such descriptive claim, then it cannot make a claim on behalf of the legal system.

[15] Joseph Raz, *The Authority of Law* (Oxford: Clarendon Press, 1979), 33 (hereinafter *AL*).

'ought to obey the law'; and (5) the beliefs of officials that they have legitimate authority.

In the next five subsections, I will argue that none of these practices, by itself, warrants attributing to law a claim of legitimate authority. In the final subsection, I will argue that not even the set of *all* these practices warrants attributing such a claim to law. These two claims, if correct, show that the Authority Thesis is false.

A. Officials' belief that the system is legitimate

On Raz's view, law's claim to authority 'is manifested [in part] by the fact that . . . [officials] regard themselves as having the right to impose obligations on their subjects' (ALM 215–16). The idea seems to be that we can attribute a claim of legitimate authority to the legal system partly on the strength of the *attitudes* officials take towards it. Here it is important to note there is no suggestion in this part of the passage that the relevant attitudes *must* be publicly expressed. Thus, on this reading, insofar as officials typically *believe* the legal system has legitimate authority and hence creates a content-independent moral obligation to obey law, we can reliably infer a claim to legitimate authority.

There are a couple of problems with the view that we can attribute a claim of legitimacy to the legal system on the strength of what officials believe—apart from the assumption that we can accurately identify their unstated beliefs. Beliefs, of course, are mental states that have propositional content; the content of my belief *B* that apples are red is the proposition that apples are red. Nonetheless, it would be incorrect to think of such mental states as, in any relevant public sense, *expressing* that content. While my belief *B is about* the proposition that apples are red, *B* does not *express* that proposition. Claim-making in the expressive sense requires some sort of public sign (usually in the form of a sequence of linguistic symbols) that can be interpreted by observers. If this is correct, then beliefs are not capable of making claims in the expressive sense on behalf of the legal system.[16]

A similar problem seems to rebut the idea that beliefs can make claims in the performative sense. Claim-making in the performative sense involves a behavioural event that is public in two ways. First, the making of a claim generally requires some outward, observable expressive act. An intentional agent can make claims by making the right combination of sounds, gestures, or written symbols, but some such outward behaviour

---

[16] As I argued above, the Authority Thesis need not be construed as claiming that legal systems make claims in any literal sense; thus, the exclusive positivist is entitled to some latitude here. But it seems reasonable to require that any claim that is ultimately attributed to the legal system should be rooted in some occurrence of (in a literal sense) claim-making.

is necessary to make a claim. Second, the outward behaviour must be observed and understood in order for an agent to succeed in making a claim. It seems odd to think that a person who utters a sentence that cannot be heard or understood by anyone has succeeded in making a claim in any relevant sense. While that person has certainly expressed meaning, claim-making seems to involve more than just expressing meaning; it seems to involve a successful act of *communication*. And the communication of a claim presupposes an audience that apprehends the claim.[17]

One might argue that a claim C can be attributed to law on the ground that officials behave in ways that reliably indicate that they believe C— even if such behaviours did not include public statements affirming C. On this line of argument, what matters is that there is a public act on the part of one agent that succeeds in imparting propositional content to another agent. Any public behaviour, then, by one agent that reliably indicates a belief to other agents is enough to succeed in making a claim.

This line of argument overlooks the fact that claims can be made only by behaviour *intended* to communicate propositional content. Consider the difference between my eating a sandwich and my signalling hunger by way of a gesture that resembles my eating a sandwich. Both behaviours reliably indicate that I believe I am hungry. But only the latter makes a claim to that effect because only the latter evinces a communicatory intent. By itself, my eating a sandwich *cannot* make a claim of any kind. Thus, the occurrence of behaviours that reliably indicate that officials believe the legal system is legitimate, by itself, does not warrant attributing to the relevant officials, much less to the legal system, a claim that the legal system is legitimate.

But even if such behaviours were sufficient to make claims, this would not be enough to vindicate Raz's view. It is one thing to attribute a claim C to law on the ground that officials behave in ways that reliably indicate that they believe C is true. It is another to attribute C to law on the ground that officials *believe* C is true. I can make a claim by asserting it or by saying something that implies it or perhaps even by behaving in a way that indicates *clearly* that I believe that claim. But my private attitudes alone, no matter how passionate, can never express or imply a claim in the performative sense. Thus, we cannot in any possible legal system attribute a *public* claim of authority to a legal system solely on the basis of *private* beliefs. The grounds for such an attribution must consist of public behavioural evidence.

There is a second problem with Raz's inference of a conceptual claim to authority from the claim that officials believe themselves to have moral

---

[17] Or, at the very least, it involves an act that is likely to be understood as a claim by a reasonably sophisticated audience.

authority. To see the issue, it is helpful to contrast Raz's claims here with Hart's views about the internal point of view. Hart explains the normativity of social rules partly in terms of an attitude on the part of participants in the practice to which the rules belong:

What is necessary is that there should be a critical reflective attitude to certain patterns of behaviour as a common standard, and that this should display itself in criticism (including self-criticism), demands for conformity, and in acknowledgements that such criticism and demands are justified, all of which find their characteristic expression in the normative terminology of 'ought', 'must', and 'should', and 'right' and 'wrong'. (*CL* 56)

According to Hart's practice theory of rules, then, the normativity of social rules can be explained, at least partly, in terms of the internal point of view.

The internal point of view plays a role in legal normativity as well. While legal normativity requires that officials take the internal point of view towards the rule of recognition, it does not require that citizens do so: 'the reality of the situation is that a great proportion of ordinary citizens . . . have no general conception of the . . . criteria of validity' (*CL* 114). All that is required of citizens is that they generally obey the rules validated by the rule of recognition. Thus, Hart defines two minimum conditions for the existence of a legal system: 'On the one hand those rules of behaviour which are valid according to the system's ultimate criteria of validity must be generally obeyed, and, on the other hand, its rules of recognition specifying the criteria of legal validity . . . must be effectively accepted . . . by its officials' (*CL* 116).

Hart's claim that officials must take the internal point of view towards the rule of recognition is obviously conceptual.[18] For the claim that the rule of recognition is a social convention is clearly a conceptual claim; indeed, it is the emphasis on law's conventionality that distinguishes positivism from other conceptual theories of law. Likewise, the claim that a social convention is partly constituted by a cognitive element is also a conceptual claim; for convergent behaviour alone cannot give rise to a social convention. Hart's views about the internal point of view are intended, in part, to describe the cognitive element that is conceptually necessary to ground a social convention. The claim that officials must take the internal point of view towards the rule of recognition is thus a constituent of Hart's conceptual thesis that the rule of recognition is a social convention.

---

[18] And Hart intends it as such: 'Individual courts of the system though they may, on occasion, deviate from these rules must, in general, be critically concerned with such deviation as lapses from standards, which are essentially common or public. This is not merely a matter of the efficiency or health of the legal system, but is logically a necessary condition of our ability to speak of the existence of a legal system' (*CL* 116).

But Hart would deny that the sentence 'Officials regard themselves as having a moral right to rule or to demand obedience' expresses a conceptual truth. Officials must, according to Hart, view deviation from the relevant behaviour as a ground for criticism, but they need not view deviation as a ground for *moral* criticism. Indeed, on his view, officials may accept the rule of recognition for any reason at all:

[B]ut it is not even true that those who do accept the system voluntarily must conceive of themselves as morally bound to do so. . . . [T]heir allegiance to the system may be based on many different considerations: calculations of long-term interest; disinterested interest in others; an unreflecting inherited or traditional attitude; or the mere wish to do as others do. There is indeed no reason why those who accept the authority of the system should not examine their conscience and decide that, morally, they ought not to accept it, yet for a variety of reasons continue to do so. (*CL* 203)

As long as officials regard the rule of recognition as a common standard of public behaviour, it does not matter to Hart why they do. Since whether an official believes she has a moral right to rule depends on whether she believes that the rule of recognition is morally justified, an official can, on Hart's view, take the internal point of view towards the rule of recognition without believing she has a moral right to rule.

And Hart's view here seems quite reasonable. Interpreted as a conceptual truth about law, the claim that officials 'regard themselves as having the right to impose obligations on their subjects' seems implausibly strong. Thus construed, the claim asserts that it is conceptually necessary that officials believe that they have a moral right to rule and that citizens have a content-independent moral duty of obedience. On this interpretation, then, there cannot be an official who does not believe she possesses legitimate authority in virtue of her position within the legal system. But this implies that it is conceptually impossible for, say, a communist who rejects the legitimacy of the US legal system to be a US official. While it is unlikely, given public sensibilities, that a communist could secure an official position by election or appointment, it is implausible to think that it is in *any* sense impossible.

Thus, the only reasonable construction of Raz's claim about what officials believe is as a contingent, empirical claim about what officials typically believe. The idea here is that officials typically regard the legal system as legitimate and hence as giving rise to a content-independent moral obligation to obey legally valid directives. This construction, of course, allows for the possibility that in any given legal system there are officials who do not believe the legal system is morally legitimate. But, in the absence of further argument, it also leaves open the possibility of a legal system in which *most*—and even *all*—officials do not believe the legal system is morally legitimate.[19]

This creates a problem for Raz. Even if a claim of authority can plausibly be attributed to a legal system solely on the strength of the claim that most officials believe it is legitimate, considerably more is needed to establish the Authority Thesis. To show that every conceptually possible legal system claims legitimate authority, Raz needs to identify features present in *every* conceptually possible legal system that warrant the inference of a claim of authority. The claim that officials typically regard themselves as having moral authority in many or most conceptually possible legal systems, by itself, provides no support for the Authority Thesis. For it allows for the conceptual possibility of a legal system in which officials do not believe they have such authority.

B. Officials claim a duty of obedience

Raz argues that law's claim to authority is evidenced by the claims on the part of officials that subjects have a duty to obey the law:

The law's claim to authority is manifested by . . . [officials'] claims that their subjects owe them allegiance, and that their subjects *ought* to obey the law as it requires to be obeyed. . . . Even a bad law, is the inevitable official doctrine, *should* be obeyed for as long as it is in force, while lawful action is taken to try and bring about its amendment or repeal. (ALM 215–16; emphasis added)

The idea here is that officials make public statements that subjects have an obligation to obey the law even when there are strong moral reasons for disobeying the law. Only when the law itself justifies disobedience, according to these official statements, is it permissible for a law-subject to disobey the law.

Unfortunately, the relevant normative concepts of 'ought' and 'should' are left ambiguous in the above passage. One can construe such statements, of course, as making claims about what law-subjects *legally* ought to do. Thus construed, Raz is arguing that officials claim that 'their subjects [legally] ought to obey the law as it requires to be obeyed' and that 'even a bad law . . . [legally] should be obeyed for as long as it is in force'. On this construction, then, officials claim that subjects owe a *legal* obligation to obey the law.

At first glance, this may seem highly plausible. As an empirical matter, officials often make public statements about what subjects are legally obligated to do. Thus, a judge might say in the course of rendering a deci-

---

[19] I will consider the issue of whether it is conceptually true that in every possible legal system most officials believe that the legal system is morally legitimate. See *infra*, Section III F.

sion that the subject was legally obligated to obey the law prohibiting theft no matter what her financial circumstances were. Given the frequency of such statements, it is tempting to think it is part of the nature of law that officials claim the existence of a legal obligation to obey law.

One problem with this line of reasoning is that the claim to authority asserts a *general* right to rule and a *general* duty of obedience; it does not assert piecemeal duties to obey and rights to rule. While judges often make statements about a defendant's legal obligations in the course of rendering decisions, these statements are about particular legal obligations and are not about a general legal obligation to obey the law.

Notice that the set of all such statements about particular legal obligations does not logically imply a statement that there is a general legal obligation to obey law. The latter statement asserts a legal obligation that is distinct from the legal obligations asserted by particular norms. The existence of a legal obligation not to commit theft entails one can be held legally liable for committing such an act. The existence of a general legal obligation to obey the law entails that one is liable for failing to obey the law—in addition to being liable for failing to obey, say, the law prohibiting theft.

But it is implausible to think, at least in the case of most paradigmatic legal systems, that there is any such general *legal* obligation. It is one thing to claim that every legal norm gives rise to a legal obligation. It is another to claim that law itself gives rise to a legal obligation. The former simply asserts the definitional truth that every legal norm defines a standard of behaviour that is legally obligatory. In contrast, the latter asserts that there is a legal meta-norm defining a general legal obligation to obey the law, so that any particular violation of some legal norm gives rise to a *distinct* violation under this meta-norm. While one might be tempted to assign this role to the rule of recognition, the rule of recognition is addressed only to officials and hence cannot give rise to a general legal obligation on the part of *subjects* to obey.

In any event, to establish the Authority Thesis, Raz needs to show something stronger than that officials claim there is a general *legal* obligation to obey the law; he needs to show, of course, that officials claim there is a content-independent *moral* obligation to obey law. The problem, however, is that the obligation-claims that officials typically make are clearly intended as claims about *legal* obligation. And if the Separability Thesis is correct, we are never warranted in inferring a claim of moral duty solely from claims of legal duty. Thus, at the very least, Raz would need to show, as an empirical matter, that officials sometimes make claims to the effect that subjects owe lawmakers a content-independent *moral* duty of obedience.

But how many such claims would be necessary to warrant attributing a claim of moral duty to the legal system? It would be implausible to attribute to the legal system a claim that is made by just one official on just one occasion for a number of reasons. First, the relevant official might be objectively mistaken, and it simply seems wrong to attribute to the legal system as a whole the objectively mistaken view of one official. Second, there might be a split among officials on the issue, and it is unreasonable to attribute inconsistent claims to the legal system. Finally, some restrictions on context are clearly necessary. Not every statement made by an official in the course of performing official duties should be attributed to the legal system. It is clear, for example, that judicial dicta should not be attributed to the legal system as a whole.

Thus, if we are to attribute a claim made by officials to the legal system, it should be a largely uncontroversial claim that is commonly made in an appropriate context in the course of performing official duties. Of course, not all controversy among officials about a claim should be enough to preclude attributing it to the legal system. While it is difficult to draw an exact line, it is clear that one dissenting opinion about a claim should not preclude attributing the claim to the legal system. But it is also clear that we should not attribute a claim to the legal system on the strength of what officials say in the relevant context unless there is a general consensus among officials about the truth of that claim.

Given these constraints, there is only one likely context from which we might infer an official claim of moral duty that can be attributed to the legal system—namely, the judicial practice of punishing criminal violations which the defendant justifies on moral or religious grounds. One possible justification for punishing conscientious offenders, of course, that would lend support to the Authority Thesis is the claim that there is a content-independent moral obligation to obey the law that, all things considered, trumps any countervailing moral or religious considerations. To the extent that courts justify punishment of conscientious offenders on such grounds, they are explicitly claiming the existence of a *moral* duty of obedience. To the extent that such a claim is explicitly incorporated in some well-established legal doctrine, it makes sense to attribute that claim to the legal system as a whole.

But this is not the sort of theory that courts typically cite to justify punishing conscientious offenders. For example, in the landmark case of *Reynolds* v. *United States*,[20] the defendant argued he was justified in violating the bigamy prohibition on the ground that it violated his religious beliefs and hence his First Amendment rights. The Supreme Court had little trouble rejecting such reasoning:

---

[20] 98 US 145, 25 L. Ed. 244 (1878).

Laws are made for the government of actions, and while they cannot interfere with mere religious belief and opinions, they may with practices. . . . Can a man excuse his practices to the contrary because of his religious belief? To permit this would be to make the professed doctrines of religious belief superior to the law of the land, and in effect to permit every citizen to become a law unto himself. Government could exist only in name under such circumstances.[21]

There are a couple of observations worth making about this case. First, the defendant did not argue that his conduct was *legally* justified since the bigamy law interfered with his *moral* right to religious freedom and was hence *morally unjust*. Rather, he argued that his conduct was *legally* justified since the law violated his *constitutional* right to religious freedom and was hence *legally invalid*. Instead of being grounded in a claim about the moral quality of the act, then, the defendant's justification for his conduct was grounded in *legal* doctrine. That the defendant sought to ground his defence in legal doctrine rather than moral doctrine suggests that the issue did not turn in any way on what the defendant's moral obligations were. In particular, the issue did not turn on whether the defendant's moral obligations as defined by his religion would outweigh any purported claim that there is a general moral obligation to obey the law— content-independent or otherwise.

Second, the Court's reasoning can be construed as a policy argument or as a conceptual argument, but it cannot plausibly be construed as an argument that subjects have a content-independent moral obligation to obey the law. The Court's worry was that allowing citizens to decide when to obey the law would make every citizen 'a law unto himself'. One can, of course, construe this as consequentialist reasoning: allowing citizens to make such decisions would lead to anarchy—and anarchy is a bad thing. Alternatively, one can construe this as conceptual reasoning: allowing citizens to make such decisions is inconsistent with the very notion of government by law. But there is nothing in the Court's reasoning that remotely suggests what is at issue here is a moral obligation to obey law. At the very least, there is nothing that would warrant attributing to the legal system a claim that there is a content-independent moral duty of obedience.

The Supreme Court relied on a different ground in *Walker* v. *Birmingham*.[22] In *Walker*, a state court enjoined petitioners from staging civil rights demonstrations without the permit required by a Birmingham ordinance. The petitioners subsequently violated the injunction, arguing that the injunction was 'an unjust, undemocratic and unconstitutional misuse of the legal process' and that it was 'raw tyranny under the guise of maintaining law and order'. The Court disagreed:

---

[21] *Reynolds*, 25 L. Ed. at 250.   [22] 388 US 307 (1966).

The rule of law that Alabama followed in this case reflects a belief that in the fair administration of justice no man can be judge in his own case, however exalted his station, however righteous his motives, and irrespective of his race, color, politics, or religion. This Court cannot hold that the petitioners were constitutionally free to ignore all the procedures of the law and carry their battle to the streets. One may sympathize with the petitioners' impatient commitment to their cause. But respect for judicial process is a small price to pay for the civilizing hand of law. . . .[23]

While the last sentence of the quoted passage expresses a consequentialist justification for affirming the conviction, the first sentence seems to express a very different justification. The idea is that it would be *unfair* to allow some persons, but not others, to decide that they do not need to obey a law on the ground that it is unjust. Unlike the other arguments we have seen here, the first sentence expresses a *moral* argument.

One might think that, construing this as purely moral argument,[24] the Court's reasoning involves the assertion of a content-independent moral obligation to obey the law, but this would be mistaken. Thus construed, the Court is basing its decision on a claim about the fairness of treating people differently under the law. The ideal seems to be one of formal justice: fair administration of the laws requires treating similarly situated people similarly. And, at first glance, this seems to have little to do with a claim that there is a moral duty of obedience.

One might, I suppose, interpret this ideal as asserting a content-independent moral obligation *on the part of the courts* to obey some legal norm requiring them to apply the law fairly. This is not an interpretation that strikes me as especially plausible; after all, the Court seems to be appealing to the ideal of fairness and not to some general moral obligation. But, in any event, such an interpretation would still fall short of a general claim to authority in two ways. First, the scope of the obligation would not be sufficiently general; it would assert the existence of a moral obligation that is expressly concerned only with the court's duty to apply the law. And there is no reason to think that *this* duty is content-independent: it is a content-based duty to *apply the law regardless of content*.[25] Second, and more importantly, the set of persons subject to the duty is not sufficiently general. It applies to the courts and not to citizens; for such a duty would be defined by the rule of recognition, which addresses only the duties of officials.

---

[23] *Walker*, 388 US, at 320–1.

[24] One could, of course, construe this as being grounded in e.g. the Due Process Clause of the Fourteenth Amendment, which is a *legal* doctrine.

[25] That is, the reason for the duty D to apply the law without regard to content is that the *content* of some legal norm defines (or creates) D. Thus, the duty defined by the norm is content-dependent even if the norm defines a duty to apply every legal norm without regard to the moral quality of *its* content.

Even if we assume that the Court's justification in *Walker* is logically equivalent to a claim that there is a content-independent moral obligation to obey law, these cases nonetheless call attention to a problem. As we have seen, different cases have expressed logically independent rationales for holding conscientious offenders liable. While *Walker* seems focused on the moral implications of treating conscientious offenders differently from other offenders, the earlier decisions focus on conceptual and policy implications. But the availability of different justifications for such actions suggests that *none is conceptually required*. Whether or not the US has a legal system clearly does not depend on whether there is a judicial decision holding conscientious offenders liable on the ground that there is a content-independent moral obligation to obey law. If every case on the issue decided it on policy or conceptual grounds, it would still be clear that the US has a legal system. And this is true even if there is no other legal doctrine in the US that claims the existence of a content-independent moral duty to obey law.[26]

C. Designation of officials as 'authorities'

To begin with, it is not clear that the mere designation of officials as 'authorities' is enough to support attributing a claim of authority to the legal system. The problem here is that the relevant persons may not understand the notion of authority as entailing a content-independent moral obligation to obey the law. If the term 'authority' is not commonly understood to have such implications, the formal designation of officials as 'authorities' does not clearly commit those persons responsible for the designation to the view that official acts give rise to a content-independent moral obligation to obey law. If this is correct, the fact of such a designation would not, by itself, warrant an inference that the legal system claims legitimate authority; in addition, we would need to know how this term is generally understood among the relevant class of persons.

Moreover, the claim that legal institutions are officially designated as 'authorities' does not appear to be true, even as a contingent matter, of the US legal system. Nowhere in the Constitution, for example, are executives, legislators, or judges officially designated as authorities. Likewise, it is rare in court decisions that Congress is referred to as a body of legislative authorities. Nor, for that matter, do most people make it a common practice to refer to courts and lawmakers as the 'authorities'. I have occasionally

---

[26] A WESTLAW search of the ALLFEDS and ALLSTATES databases using the phrase 'moral /S obligation /S obey /S law' disclosed only 6 cases. Only one of these asserted a moral duty to obey—and that assertion was dictum. See *Petition of Orphanidis*, 178 F. Supp. 872 (1959), at 874.

heard the police referred to as the 'authorities', but this has not been a common experience for me. In any event, there is certainly no official practice or convention in this legal system designating officials and institutions of the legal system as 'authorities'. For this reason, it is not clear that it is typically true of conceptually possible legal systems that legal institutions are officially designated as 'authorities'—much less that this is true in *every* conceptually possible legal system.

D. The use of the language of rights and duties

Raz clearly intends the use of the language of rights and duties, as well as the exclusionary enforcement of law, to be conceptually necessary for a legal system to exist:

[T]ry to imagine a situation in which the political authorities of a country do not claim that the inhabitants are bound to obey them, but in which the population does acquiesce in their rule. We are to imagine courts imprisoning people without finding them guilty of any offence; damages are ordered, but no one has a duty to pay them. The legislature never claims to impose duties of care or of contribution to common services. . . . [I]f such a society were to exist we would not regard it as being governed by authority. (*MF* 27)

As a conceptual matter, then, Raz believes that there *cannot* be a legal system that does not frame legal norms in terms of rights and duties and enforce them as exclusionary. For this reason, each of these claims has the appropriate modal qualities to provide support for a conceptual thesis.

Surprisingly, the use in law of the language of rights and duties does not support the Authority Thesis—even if we assume the conceptual naturalist is correct about the moral quality of such language. Consider the Natural Lawyer's Second Semantic Thesis (SST), which Raz describes as follows:

[L]egal statements are moral statements. For example, when one states 'It is John's legal duty to repay the debt' one is asserting that John has a (moral) duty to repay the debt arising out of the law. (*AL* 158)

If SST is true, then the use in law of the language of rights and duties clearly supports the idea that a legal system necessarily claims that law gives rise to moral obligations. For SST implies that part of what is conceptually asserted by a statement of legal duty is a statement of moral duty because the notion of duty *is* a moral notion.

But establishing that every conceptually possible legal system claims law gives rise to moral obligations is not, by itself, enough to establish the Authority Thesis. For the Authority Thesis asserts something stronger than this: that law claims a *content-independent* moral obligation to obey law. And SST is not strong enough to imply that the use in law of 'rights' and 'duties' entails a *content-independent* moral obligation to obey law. The reason SST falls short in this regard is that the obligations and rights to which morality gives rise are *content-dependent*. It makes little sense to claim that one has a content-independent moral obligation to obey moral norms; the reason we are obligated to comply, for example, with the moral norm prohibiting murder is because of its content.

Even with the help of a potent assumption like SST, then, the use of terms such as 'right', 'duty', and 'obligation' does not entail a claim to legitimate authority. As will be recalled, the claim that an authority is legitimate is logically equivalent, on most traditional accounts (including Raz's), to the claim that authoritative directives give rise to content-independent moral obligations to obey. While SST's claim that such terms have moral content entails that every legal obligation gives rise to a moral obligation, that moral obligation can be deduced from the conceptual overlap between legal and moral terms and is hence content-dependent. But nothing more than this follows from the use of 'right', 'duty', and 'obligation', even if we assume that such notions necessarily import moral content. In particular, it does not follow that law asserts a content-independent moral obligation to obey law.[27]

In response, one might argue it is sufficient for Raz's purposes that law claims to give rise to content-dependent moral obligations. While this weaker claim might suffice to accomplish most of Raz's purposes, it is too weak to falsify the Incorporation Thesis. Whether law's claim to authority entails that it must always be possible to identify law without evaluating its content seems to depend on what kind of moral obligation is asserted by the authority claim. If, on the one hand, the moral obligation to which law claims to give rise is content-independent, then one's moral, and hence legal, obligations under the law cannot depend on its moral merits. Moral considerations would hence seem *necessarily* irrelevant in identifying the existence and content of the law. If, on the other hand, the moral obligation to which law claims to give rise is *content-dependent*, then one's moral, and hence legal, obligations *necessarily* depend on the merits of law's content. Identification of the law would hence seem to *require* evaluation of its content. For this reason, if all that is meant by law's authority claim, assuming SST, is that law gives rise to content-dependent moral obligations to obey law, then the Authority Thesis cannot falsify the Incorporation Thesis.

Of course, SST is inconsistent with the Separability Thesis that law and

---

[27] For a fuller discussion of this point, see Kenneth Einar Himma, 'Positivism, Naturalism, and the Obligation to Obey Law', *Southern Journal of Philosophy*, 36(2) (Summer 1998), 145–62.

morality are conceptually distinct.[28] If, as a conceptual matter, the
sentence 'X has a legal duty to do *a*' asserts or entails 'X has a moral duty
to do *a*', then morality functions as a constraint on law's content. For SST
seems to imply, as a conceptual matter, the invalidity of a norm requiring
the performance of a morally impermissible act—which is clearly inconsistent with the Separability Thesis. As Raz puts it:

Even if the law is essentially moral—the cautious positivist would argue—it is
clear that establishing the moral merit of a law is a different process relying on
different considerations, from establishing its existence as a social fact. The question of its value is a further and separate question. Since one may know what the
law is without knowing if it is justified, there must be a possibility of making legal
statements not involving commitment to its justification. . . . Thus, the positivist is
bound to reject [SST]. (*AL* 158–9)

But if the use in law of 'right', 'duty', and 'obligation' does not assert
or entail a content-independent moral obligation to obey under the strong
assumption that such terms have moral content, then use of such terms
without that assumption cannot assert or entail such an obligation. For if
these terms lack moral content, their use in framing legal norms cannot
by itself assert or entail *any* claim of moral obligation—content-independent or otherwise. Assuming that the Separability Thesis is true, then, the
claim that it is conceptually necessary that legal systems use the language
of rights and duties, by itself, does not support the Authority Thesis.

E. The enforcement of laws as exclusionary

The claim that it is conceptually necessary that law is enforced, for the
most part, as exclusionary seems uncontroversial. It seems straightforwardly implausible to think that there are conceptually possible legal
systems in which a subject is free to disregard the law when it strikes her
as inconsistent with right reason. A system of law is, as a conceptual
matter, supposed to make some behaviours non-optional. An institutional
system of norms that always allows a subject to decide to disregard the
law on the basis of her evaluative judgments does not make *any* behaviours non-optional.

But the reasonable claim that it is conceptually true that law is enforced
as exclusionary warrants inferring only that it is conceptually true that

---

[28] Raz distinguishes this thesis from another one that he accepts: 'normative terms like "a
right", "a duty", "ought" are used in the same sense in legal, moral, and other normative
statements' (*AL* 158). Note that 'duty' can be used in the same sense in both 'legal duty' and
'moral duty' without violating the Separability Thesis. Thus, if the locution 'P has an X-duty
to do *a*' means e.g. 'there is an X-norm requiring P to do *a*', then legal duties have no necessary moral content even though 'duty' is used in the same sense in 'legal duty' as it is 'moral
duty'.

subjects are not permitted to disregard law even when there are good reasons for doing so; it does not warrant inferring that there is a general *moral* requirement to obey law. That is, while such practices entail that each law gives rise to a *legal* obligation, they do not entail that there is a content-independent *moral* obligation to obey law. Thus, such enforcement practices alone, even if conceptually necessary, fail to preclude the possibility of an autonomous system of law not supported by a content-independent moral duty to obey.

One might object that even if such practices are consistent with an autonomous system of obligations, there are nonetheless cogent grounds for inferring a claim to moral legitimacy from a policy of exclusionary enforcement. Philip Soper argues that 'to refer to what "the law" claims, is to refer to what any sensible individual, putting him or herself in the position of a representative of the legal system . . . *ought* to recognize as the implicit claim that accompanies such official action'.[29] According to Soper, people who enforce laws as exclusionary ought to believe they are morally justified in doing so:

The natural response to one who suggests that law makes no such claim [to authority] is simply to call attention to common features of social life: the kinds of things that law does when it imposes sanctions—taking a person's property, liberty, or life—are such serious invasions of another's interests that it is impossible to exempt them from the normal assumption that a morally conscientious agent will commit such acts only in the belief that they are justified. (LNC 219)

The emphasis has changed significantly: it has shifted from a descriptive claim about what can be inferred from the various elements of a legal system to a normative claim about what morally conscientious agents *should believe* given the quality of their acts. As we have seen, the thesis that we can attribute a claim C to law simply on the ground that officials *actually* believe C is problematic because claims, unlike beliefs, are public events. But this idea, at least, is consistent with the plausible view that we cannot attribute a claim to an intentional agent unless we can ground it in some mental state. Soper's view that we can attribute a claim C to law on the ground that officials *should* (but may not) believe C seems doubly problematic because the attribution is not grounded in *any* actual mental states. Accordingly, a policy of exclusionary enforcement of law, by itself, does not warrant attributing a claim of legitimacy to law.

F. The claims taken together

In response to this analysis, one might concede that none of the features

---

[29] 'Law's Normative Claims', in Robert P. George (ed.), *The Autonomy of Law* (Oxford: Clarendon Press, 1996), 215–48, at 218 (emphasis added) (hereinafter *LNC*).

discussed above, by itself, warrants attributing a claim of authority to law, but argue that the entire set of such features does. There are a couple of problems with such a response. To begin with, the Authority Thesis purports to be a conceptual truth about the nature of law. If, as I have argued, the claims pertaining to the beliefs of officials and the designation of institutions as authorities are contingent claims, they provide no support for the Authority Thesis. Accordingly, to make out the case for the Authority Thesis, Raz must show that the exclusionary enforcement of law and the use of the language of rights and duties, in and of themselves, warrant the attribution of a claim of moral authority to law.

More importantly, the idea that there could be legal systems lacking most of the characteristics Raz believes give rise to a claim of authority is considerably more plausible than may first appear. Suppose there is a society *S* that is as much like ours as is consistent with the following properties: all the lawmakers and subjects in *S* have seen the attempts to show law can be legitimate. None of these arguments conclusively establishes that conclusion—and there are enough counter-arguments available that the residents of this society, including the officials, are all sceptical that law can ever give rise to even a prima facie moral duty of obedience. As a result, officials and citizens refrain from using the potentially misleading terms 'authority', 'duty', 'obligation', and 'right', relying instead on terms like 'official', 'required', 'mandatory', 'non-optional', and 'permitted'. Despite such thoroughgoing scepticism about the possibility of moral legitimacy, the laws of *S* are just and justly administered.

Notice that the convergence and convention requirements for a rule of recognition are satisfied. The officials of *S* adopt the internal point of view towards the putative rule of recognition out of a sense that, as a practical matter, something must be done to regulate behaviour. And likewise *all* the subjects of *S* believe it is in everyone's interest to structure a system of rules around the conventions adopted by the officials—and, thus, also take the internal point of view towards the criteria of validity. And, recognizing the advantages of having a system of rules for regulating behaviour, the subjects generally obey the directives validated by the putative rule of recognition.

There are a number of observations worth making about this normative system. First, the terms 'duty', 'right', 'obligation', and 'authority' do not appear in the 'law' of *S* or in conversations about what it requires or permits.[30] But even if they did, no one would construe those terms as bearing any relation to the corresponding moral notions; for the example is constructed so that the citizens regard these legal notions as

---

[30] The quotation marks are there to indicate that 'law' is not being used here in a literal sense, as I do not wish to beg any questions.

autonomous. Second, subjects in *S* are often morally obligated to obey the law but the obligation arises because of the law's content. For example, there are content-dependent moral obligations to obey the prohibition of murder (because murder is wrong) and the requirement to drive on the right side of the road (because the requirement solves a dangerous coordination problem). Third, subjects refer to these rules as being 'law' because they are enforced by the police power of the state, and citizens use the term 'law' to distinguish standards backed by the state's police power from other standards.

What plausible, non-question-begging reason could there be to deny that this system of rules is a legal system? The only notable difference between the two systems of rules is that the officials in one system typically believe that their system is legitimate, while the officials in the other system clearly lack such a belief—a difference that seems irrelevant to the classification of the latter. All the major institutions are there: the rule of recognition defines institutions that create, modify, and adjudicate law. All the citizens of that society accept the determinations of the officials as reasons for action. The rules of that society are obeyed to precisely the same extent as they are in this society.[31] Given these observations, it makes sense to characterize that society as having a legal system because it has all the pieces necessary for efficacious state regulation of behaviour—even though there is nothing that could be construed as an institutional claim to legitimate authority. If this is correct, the Authority Thesis is false.[32]

IV. OBJECTIONS AND REPLIES

In the last subsection, I constructed an example of an institutional normative system *S* that I argued is plausibly characterized as a legal system despite making no claim to legitimate authority. In this section, I would like to consider a number of objections that might be raised to my analysis. I limit my discussion here to those objections involving *S* because any objection to my earlier arguments straightforwardly translates into an objection to my analysis of *S*.

[31] Other theorists have made this point. For example, Soper suggests that '[n]othing in the practice of law as we now know it would change if the state, convinced by arguments that there is no duty to obey law *qua* law, openly announced that it was abandoning any such claim' (LNC 233).

[32] At the very least, the inclusive positivist can reasonably characterize this as a legal system without having to compromise any important theoretical commitments. Thus, if it is not possible to resolve a disagreement between an inclusive positivist who characterizes *S* as a legal system and an exclusive positivist who does not, the availability of such an example provides the inclusive positivist with a sensible ground for denying that law necessarily claims authority.

A. *S* is empirically unlikely and hence unhelpful

The normative system of *S* is, of course, a counterexample to the Authority Thesis—and an empirically unlikely one at that.[33] Arguments relying on this kind of counter-example have recently been challenged in the literature. Jeffrey Goldsworthy, for example, finds such arguments of little theoretical value: 'To focus on very unusual and extreme borderline cases in analysing [the] inter-relationships [between law, coercion, and morality] must lead to distortion.'[34] The problem, then, is that insofar as the description of *S* involves qualities that are extremely unlikely in a legal system, an analysis based on *S* is likely to be unilluminating at best and misleading at worst.

It is, of course, indisputable that *S* is an 'extreme borderline case'. But the point in formulating *S* is not to identify some central feature of a legal system; if it were, then the analysis of *S* would be highly misleading. Rather, the point in formulating *S* is to challenge Raz's view that a claim to authority is a conceptually necessary condition for a legal system to exist. Otherwise put, *S* is presented as a challenge to Raz's view that a claim to authority is a central feature of a legal system. A possible legal system that makes no claim to authority, no matter how empirically improbable, falsifies this claim.

In this connection, it is crucial to understand that Raz's view that the concept of authority is inconsistent with Hart's Incorporation Thesis depends on a very strong claim:

AI: There is no conceptually possible legal system in which the criteria of validity incorporate moral norms.

AI is just the negation of the Incorporation Thesis. But inasmuch as it asserts the *conceptual impossibility* of moral criteria of legal validity, it makes a much stronger claim than the Incorporation Thesis (which claims that it is conceptually possible for a legal system to have moral criteria of validity). As a result, it requires the support of at least one other claim that is equally strong.

In essence, Raz offers two conceptual theses in support of AI. The first is, of course, the Authority Thesis, which denies there can be a conceptually possible legal system that does not claim legitimate authority. The second is the thesis that law's claim to legitimate authority is inconsistent with the existence of moral criteria of legal validity. Otherwise put, the thesis asserts that there is no conceptually possible legal system in which

---

[33] Raz anticipates the possibility of constructing a normative system like the one I have constructed and argues that 'it is unlikely that any such society ever existed' (*MF* 27).

[34] Jeffrey D. Goldsworthy, 'The Self-Destruction of Legal Positivism', *Oxford Journal of Legal Studies*, 10(4) (1990), 459.

it is true *both* that law claims legitimate authority *and* that there are moral criteria of validity. AI is, of course, a direct corollary of these two theses.

At the highest level of abstraction, then, the Razian argument can be summed up roughly as follows:

1. The Authority Thesis is true (i.e. in every conceptually possible legal system law claims legitimate authority).
2. The Authority Thesis is inconsistent with the Incorporation Thesis (i.e. there is no conceptually possible legal system in which it is true both that law claims authority and that the criteria of validity incorporate moral norms).
3. Therefore, the Incorporation Thesis is false (i.e. there is no conceptually possible legal system in which the criteria of validity incorporate moral content).[35]

To show that it is *conceptually impossible* for a legal system to incorporate moral criteria of validity, it is not enough to show it is atypical for a legal system not to claim authority. Raz must show that it is *conceptually impossible* for a legal system not to claim authority; in other words, that there is no conceptually possible legal system that does not claim legitimate authority. If *S* is a legal system, this strong claim is false.

B. It is sufficient to defeat Hart that *S* claims it provides preemptive reasons

This line of objection concedes that *S* is a legal system that does not claim the existence of a content-independent moral obligation to obey law, but argues that it is enough to falsify the Incorporation Thesis that *S* claims to provide preemptive reasons. The idea is as follows. A preemptive reason 'is a reason . . . which is not to be added to all other relevant reasons when assessing what to do, but should replace some of them' (ALM 214). Such reasons, then, *replace* the subject's evaluation of the balance of reasons in determining what ought to be done. For law, then, to claim sincerely that it provides preemptive reasons, it must be conceptually capable of providing preemptive reasons. But, as we have seen, a system that makes the identification of law turn on moral considerations is conceptually incapable of preempting the subject's evaluation of the balance of reasons because it *requires* the subject to evaluate the balance of reasons in order to determine what the law is. Thus, a conceptual claim to provide preemptive reasons is inconsistent with the Incorporation Thesis. Accordingly, if *S* claims to provide preemptive reasons, it does not matter that *S*

---

[35] Of course, there is a great deal of interesting work that Raz puts to the service of showing premiss 2 in this overly general representation of the argument.

is a legal system; *that* claim is inconsistent with there being moral criteria of validity.

There are a number of problems with this line of reasoning. To begin with, it is not clear that the notion of a preemptive reason can be separated in Raz's analysis from the notion of a moral obligation. Raz often states that a proposition *p* concerning what an agent *A* ought to do provides a content-independent preemptive reason for action if and only if *A* has a content-independent moral obligation to do what *p* requires. Consider, for example, the Razian analysis of commands:

Orders and commands are among the expressions typical of practical authority. Only those who claim authority can command. As we saw, in requesting and in commanding the speaker intends the addressee to recognize the utterance as a reason for action. The difference is that a valid command (i.e., one issued by a person in authority) is a [preemptive] reason. *We express this thought by saying that . . . valid authoritative requirements impose obligations.* (MF 37; emphasis added)

Moreover, this claim follows from three other basic Razian claims. First, Raz holds that '[the thesis that authoritative directives provide preemptive reasons] *is only about legitimate authority*' (MF 46; emphasis added). Second, he holds that the notion of legitimate authority is a *moral* concept: 'A legal system may lack legitimate authority. If it lacks the *moral* attributes required to endow it with legitimate authority, then it has none' (ALM 215; emphasis added). Third, Raz equates legitimate authority with the existence of a moral right to rule and a moral duty to obey: 'No system is a system of law unless it includes a claim of legitimacy, or *moral* authority. That means that it claims that legal requirements are *morally* binding, that is that legal obligations are real (moral) obligations arising out of the law.'[36] It follows that authoritative directives provide content-independent preemptive reasons if and only if they define content-independent moral obligations.

Also relevant in this connection is Raz's view that the concept of authority incorporates the notion of moral legitimacy. The directives of a merely de facto authority (i.e. one that is falsely believed by subjects to be legitimate) do not, objectively speaking,[37] give rise to content-independent reasons for action: 'since not every authority is legitimate not every authoritative directive is a reason for action' (MF 46). Insofar as only morally legitimate authorities can create content-independent reasons for

[36] Raz, 'Hart on Moral Rights and Legal Duties', 131 (emphasis added).
[37] Raz uses the notion of a reason in an objective sense. Whether *R* is a reason for action does not depend on the subject's subjective assessment of *R*. Similarly, right reasons are those reasons that *objectively* apply to a person regardless of whether she is subjectively aware of them. Likewise for the balance of right reason: what the balance of right reason requires does not depend on how the subject perceives that balance. There are, of course, subjective analogues of these ideas, but Raz intends the objective notions.

action and insofar as the concept of authority entails the ability to create such reasons, it follows that every genuine authority is morally legitimate. A merely de facto authority is not, strictly speaking, properly characterized as an authority on this view; thus, an illegitimate legal system is a merely de facto authority. Given that genuine authority is distinguished from merely de facto authority, on Raz's view, by its ability to create both content-independent preemptive reasons for action and content-independent moral obligations, it is natural to conclude that all and only content-independent preemptive reasons define content-independent moral obligations.

Nevertheless, it would be unwise to rest a defence of inclusive positivism on this response to the objection. For it might be possible to untangle the notions of legitimacy and authority in Raz's view without having to give up much of theoretical value. Arguably, any plausible view that separates the concept of legitimacy from the concept of authority would also create logical distance between the concept of a content-independent preemptive reason for action and the concept of a content-independent moral obligation to obey. Since there is no obvious reason to think that this cannot be done, it is important to consider the possibility that a claim to provide content-independent preemptive reasons for action can reasonably be inferred from legal practice in S.

One element of legal practice in S suggests such an inference. Like every other conceptually possible legal system, S contains norms that make some behaviours legally permissible and others legally impermissible. Thus, it is reasonable to conclude that norm-sentences express propositions of law that have the following formal structure:

PL: It is (not) legally permissible (or required) for a subject to do act A.

Every legal norm-sentence in S, then, expresses a PL-proposition that articulates the law's requirements.

The only straightforward implications of PL-propositions also express propositions about what is legally permissible or required of some set of law-subjects. For example, the proposition that it is not legally permissible to murder clearly entails the proposition that it is not legally permissible to commit a premeditated killing of another person. Accordingly, the only straightforward implications of PL-propositions *are also PL-propositions*. For this reason, if legal norms have any straightforward implications regarding preemptive reasons, it would have to be either the proposition

PL1: It is legally required that subjects treat legal norms as preemptive reasons

or the proposition

PL2: It is not legally required that subjects treat legal norms as preemptive reasons.

Clearly, PL2 provides no support for the Authority Thesis. The claim
that subjects are free, legally speaking, not to treat legal norms as preemptive reason provides no grounds whatsoever for thinking that the legal
system claims to provide preemptive reasons. Indeed, the reverse is true;
the truth of PL2 militates strongly *against* thinking that the legal system
claims to provide preemptive reasons.

PL1, in contrast, asserts that the law requires every subject to treat legal
norms as replacing her evaluation of the balance of reasons in deciding
what ought to be done. This, of course, is a highly implausible claim to
attribute to any legal system. First, it is not clear how mental states, which
are not generally subject to direct volitional control, *could* be regulated.
Second, it is not clear why any lawmaker would want to regulate mental
states; if behaviour is effectively regulated, that would be enough to
accomplish everything a lawmaker could reasonably want. As Raz puts it,
'what counts, from the point of view of the person in authority, is not
what the subject thinks but how he acts. I do all that the law requires of
me if my actions comply with it' (*MF* 39).

The idea, then, that PL1 can be attributed to S on the strength of PL-
propositions that are true in S comes at an unacceptable cost. For the legal
system in S was modelled after the paradigmatic legal system in the US.
If the set of PL-propositions true in S justify attributing to the legal system
in S the claim that subjects are legally obligated to treat laws as preemptive reasons, then the set of PL-propositions true in the US justify attributing to that legal system the very same implausible claim. Indeed, it would
seem to follow that every conceptually possible legal system claims that
subjects are legally obligated to treat laws as preemptive reasons—and
this counter-intuitive result is a *reductio* of any theory that entails it.

It is true, of course, that the legal norms in S are enforced in a manner
that is consistent with their providing preemptive reasons for action but
this modest fact about legal practice in S is not enough to warrant inferring that S claims to provide preemptive reasons. That most citizens
would probably not draw this conclusion is evidenced by the fact that it
took a theorist of Raz's preeminent stature to produce the theory of
preemptive reasons, and by the fact that this theory is still highly controversial among legal theorists. Since highly sophisticated theorists disagree
about whether law provides such reasons, it is not likely that the issue
would even occur to an ordinary citizen. If, as seems reasonable, we can
attribute only those claims to law that would reasonably be inferred from
legal practice by ordinary citizens, then we cannot attribute to S the claim
that law provides preemptive reasons for action.

What we *can* expect ordinary citizens to infer about legal practice in *S* is, I think, considerably more modest. Philosophers disagree about the conceptual function of law, but all such accounts involve the straightforward observation that the point of law is to govern *behaviour*: law tells people what to do. For this reason, an ordinary citizen is likely to infer from general legal practice in *S* that she is not permitted to disobey valid legal norms in *S*. In other words, an ordinary citizen is likely to infer that legal norms will be enforced against her subject only to exceptions explicitly described in the law. But it is unlikely that ordinary citizens—or, for that matter, ordinary lawmakers—would make any inferences about how law does or should function in practical deliberations. Even if ordinary citizens were likely to consider this issue, it is unlikely, given the controversy among legal theorists surrounding the theory of preemptive reasons, that they would infer from legal practice in *S* that *S* claims to provide preemptive reasons.

C. Citizens in *S* have a belief that implies a claim that *S* is legitimate

One might argue that although the citizens in *S* do not have a conscious belief that the legal system is legitimate, they have a conscious belief that entails the claim that the legal system is legitimate.[38] As I structured the example, everyone in *S* takes the internal point of view towards the rule of recognition out of a sense that it is in everyone's interest to have an institutional system of norms defined by that rule of recognition. One might think it follows that everyone believes that each person is more likely to do what right reason requires by following the norms validated by the rule of recognition than by following their own judgments about what right reason requires. In other words, one might think it follows that each subject believes that the conditions of the Normal Justification Thesis (NJT) are satisfied. Accordingly, each subject has a conscious belief that entails the claim that the legal system in *S* is morally legitimate.

There are several problems with this line of reasoning. First, it depends on the assumption that NJT is a correct account of the conditions of moral legitimacy. If NJT is not the correct account of moral legitimacy, then the claim that it is to everyone's advantage to have that legal system does not entail the claim that the legal system is morally legitimate.

Second, the fact that subjects believe something that logically entails the claim that the legal system is morally legitimate does not warrant attributing that claim to the legal system. As we have seen, beliefs, unlike claims, are purely private events, and hence cannot warrant the attribution of a public claim to the legal system as a whole. But notice that *S* is

---

[38] I am indebted to Brian Butler for this line of argument.

constructed so that the subjects are sceptics with respect to moral legitimacy. While they believe a claim that, at most, entails that the legal system
is morally legitimate, they do not actually believe that it is morally legitimate; each subject is an agnostic with respect to the legitimacy of the legal
system in S. If the claim that subjects have a conscious belief that p cannot
warrant attributing a claim of p to the legal system, then the even weaker
claim that the subjects have a conscious belief that logically implies p
cannot warrant the attribution of p to the legal system.

Finally, the claim that it is in everyone's best interest to structure a
normative system around the rule of recognition in S does not logically
imply the claim that the conditions of NJT are satisfied. These conditions
are satisfied for a particular subject l to the extent that l is 'better likely to
comply with reasons which apply to him (other than the alleged authoritative directives) if he accepts the directives of the alleged authority as
authoritatively binding, and tries to follow them, than if he tries to follow
the reasons which apply to him directly' (ALM 214). The appeal here is to
what right reason requires of l without necessary reference to l's particular prudential interests and without necessary reference to the prudential
interests of other persons.

But the relevant belief of S-subjects explicitly makes reference to
prudential interest: the belief is that it is in *everyone's* best interests to have
such a normative system and to abide by its laws. This, of course, does not
entail that, for each subject l in S, it is in l's best interest to abide by the
laws in S. Rather, it entails the weaker prudential claim that a subject l in
S is better off, prudentially speaking, if *everyone* accepts the legal system
in S and conforms to the requirements of first-order legal norms in S than
if no legal system is accepted. But this does not logically preclude that
persons in S are prudentially disadvantaged by doing what the law
requires; a subject who complies with laws prohibiting theft might lose a
great deal in the process. More to the point, this does not logically
preclude that persons in S are often required to act against what right
reason requires of them. The relevant belief simply entails that the law in
S is a system of principles that is, in some sense, prudentially advantageous to *all*. As David Gauthier would probably put the point, the law in
S 'is a system of principles such that it is advantageous for everyone if
everyone accepts and acts on it, yet acting on the system of principles
requires that some persons perform disadvantageous acts'.[39] Not only
does this weaker claim fall short of entailing that the conditions of NJT are
satisfied, it also falls short of being a plausible account of moral legitimacy.

---

[39] See David Gauthier, 'Morality and Advantage', *Philosophical Review* (Oct. 1967).

D. *S* cannot be a legal system because it is purely coercive

Alternatively, one might attempt to deny that the system of norms in *S* constitutes a legal system on the ground that a system of norms that makes no claim to legitimacy must be purely coercive—and law cannot be purely coercive. Nevertheless, there is little reason to think that the system of norms in *S* is any more purely coercive than, say, the legal system in the US. Indeed, the system in *S* enjoys a level of knowledgeable acceptance that the US system does not—so much so that it is more probably legitimate than the legal system of the US. If a purely coercive system of norms involves, as seems reasonable, imposing that system on the subjects against their wills, then it seems clear that the normative system in *S* cannot plausibly be characterized as purely coercive.

Further, it is not clear why there could not be a legal system in which *legal* obligation is purely a matter of enforcement by coercive force. Hart rejected Austin's view that legal obligation is *conceptually reducible* to the presence of a sanction for non-compliance on the ground that it assimilates legal norms to a gunman's demand for money. The subject of such a demand can plausibly be characterized as being 'obliged' to comply, but not as being 'duty-bound' or 'obligated' to do so. On Hart's view, the application of force alone can never give rise to an obligation—legal or otherwise.

Unfortunately for Hart, the situation is no different if the gunman takes the internal point of view towards his authority to make such a threat. Despite the gunman's belief he is entitled to make the threat, the victim is obliged, but not obligated, to comply with the gunman's orders. The gunman's behaviour is no less coercive because he believes he is entitled to make the threat. And likewise for a minimal legal system in which *only* the officials take the internal point of view towards the rule of recognition. A belief on the part of officials that they are entitled to make law can no more give rise to an obligation to comply with their enactments than a belief on the part of a gunman that he is entitled to demand money gives rise to an obligation to hand it over. If Hart's argument succeeds as an objection to Austin's theory, then it also seems to succeed as an objection to every positivist theory of law, including Hart's.[40]

While I cannot fully defend the intuition here, I think Hart's objection is partially flawed. Where Austin went wrong was in conceptually reducing the notion of legal obligation to being subject to sanction; on Austin's view, in every possible legal system, legal obligation is purely coercive.

---

[40] This is a variation on the Payne Problem: Michael A. Payne, 'Hart's Concept of a Legal System', 18 William and Mary Law Review 287 (1976). See also Roger Shiner, *Norm and Nature: The Movements of Legal Thought* (Oxford: Clarendon Press, 1992), 160–1.

Hart was certainly correct to reject this claim inasmuch as Austin's
account conceptually *precludes* the possibility of a legitimate legal system
in which there is more to legal obligation than just coercive force. But
notice that rejecting Austin's account commits us only to the following:

O1: It is not true that, in every conceptually possible legal system, legal
     obligation is purely coercive.

Hart, of course, went one step further; he not only embraced O1, but the
much stronger:

O2: It is true that, in every conceptually possible legal system, legal obli-
     gation is not purely coercive.

O1 claims only that it is not a necessary truth that legal obligation is
purely coercive; put otherwise, O1 claims it is not the case that legal obligation is essentially coercive. But O2 makes the stronger claim it *is* a necessary truth that legal obligation is not purely coercive; that is, O2 claims
that legal obligation is conceptually *non*-coercive.[41]

There is a trivial sense, of course, in which legal obligation in Hart's
minimal legal system is not *purely* coercive. If all that is meant by 'purely
coercive' is that *every* law is imposed against the subject's will by coercive
force, then the minimal legal system is not purely coercive because, on
Hart's view, the rule of recognition, which gives rise to legal obligations,
must be accepted by the officials. Thus, it would not make sense to say
that the rule of recognition is being forced on the officials against their
will. But the fact that the officials all take the internal point of view
towards the rule that empowers them to exercise coercive force against
the citizenry does not do anything to distinguish them from the gunman
who believes he is morally entitled to coerce the victim. What really
matters with respect to the question of law's coerciveness is the relation of
lawmaker to law-subject. Hart gets into trouble because his analysis of the
gunman case commits him to O2, which is inconsistent with his minimal
legal system.

O1, of course, leaves open the possibility of there being legal systems
that are purely coercive in roughly the sense that Austin believed all are—
and this strikes me as plausible.[42] Hart's minimal legal system might be
purely coercive with respect to law-subjects but it nonetheless seems to be
a fully functioning legal system. Here it is worth noting, as Matthew

---

[41] Matthew Kramer makes a similar point: 'To argue that legal norms can be stark imperatives (as opposed to prescriptions) is not to argue—in the manner of nineteenth-century
jurisprudential positivism—that legal norms are *always* stark imperatives': 'Requirements,
Reasons, and Raz', *Ethics*, 109 (Jan. 1999), 375–407, at 377.

[42] It strikes me as a conceptual truth that legal obligation involves coercive state enforcement. A society with a working normative system in which the norms are not coercively
enforced strikes me as a society that, as a Marxist might put it, has *transcended* law.

Kramer does, that Hart's minimal legal system is different from the gunman's situation in two respects: (1) the directives in Hart's minimal legal system are general with respect to the class of addressees and relevant behaviours; (2) the rule of recognition is accepted as providing *standards* governing official behaviour. (1) and (2) are not, of course, enough to justify characterizing the minimal legal system as non-coercive. But, as long as the term 'obligation' lacks moral content, (1) and (2) seem to create enough logical space between an Austinian legal system and the gunman example to permit characterizing the directives of only the former as (legally) *obligatory*.

And likewise for the legal system in *S*. The system of *S* is distinguishable from the Austinian sovereign on such grounds, but it is also distinguishable from Hart's minimal legal system in a way that suggests it is non-coercive. Both officials and citizens in *S* take the internal point of view towards the rule of recognition and consent to abide by the rules validated by it—though no one in *S* takes this view of the system because they believe it is *morally* legitimate. But if, despite these characteristics, the system of norms in *S* constitutes a coercive system of norms, it nonetheless seems to give rise to *legal* obligations and hence to warrant being characterized as a legal system.

In this essay, I have examined Joseph Raz's influential view that Hart's Incorporation Thesis is inconsistent with the Authority Thesis. According to the Authority Thesis, it is part of the very concept of law that law claims morally legitimate authority; thus, any institutional normative system that fails to make such a claim is conceptually disqualified from being a legal system. I have attempted to show that this widely accepted claim is false.

9

Hart's Methodological Positivism

STEPHEN R. PERRY

To understand H. L. A. Hart's general theory of law, it is helpful to distinguish between *substantive* and *methodological* legal positivism. Substantive
legal positivism is the view that there is no necessary connection between
morality and the content of law. Methodological legal positivism is the
view that legal theory can and should offer a normatively neutral description of a particular social phenomenon, namely law. Methodological positivism holds, we might say, not that there is no necessary connection
between morality and law, but rather that there is no connection, necessary or otherwise, between morality and legal theory. The respective
claims of substantive and methodological positivism are, at least on the
surface, logically independent. Hobbes and Bentham employed normative methodologies to defend versions of substantive positivism,[1] and in
modern times Michael Moore has developed what can be regarded as a
variant of methodological positivism to defend a theory of natural law.[2]

   In the first edition of *The Concept of Law*,[3] Hart offered an extended
defence of what has become an extremely influential version of substantive legal positivism. The core of the substantive theory is the fairly
straightforward idea that law consists of a union of two types of rule: (i)
secondary (meaning second-order) rules, which are rules that have been
accepted as binding by judges and other officials, and (ii) primary rules,
which are rules that have been identified as valid by a particular
secondary rule called the rule of recognition.[4] At a methodological level,

---

[1] On Bentham, see esp. Gerald Postema, *Bentham and the Common Law Tradition* (1986),
328–36.
[2] Michael S. Moore, 'Law as a Functional Kind', in *Natural Law Theory*, ed. (Robert P.
George (1992), 188. But see *infra*, n. 33.
[3] (1961). In this essay, all citations to this work are to the second edition, and are given
by parenthetical page references in the text. H. L. A. Hart, *The Concept of Law*, 2nd edn., ed.
P. Bulloch and J. Raz (1994).
[4] As other commentators have observed, Hart draws the distinction between primary
and secondary rules in at least two different ways. See P. M. S. Hacker, 'Hart's Philosophy of
Law', in *Law, Morality, and Society: Essays in Honour of H. L. A. Hart*, ed. P. M. S. Hacker and
J. Raz (1977), 1–21. At one point Hart draws the distinction in terms of the rules' supposed
normative function: primary rules are said to impose duties, whereas secondary rules are
said to confer powers (81). At another point he writes that secondary rules 'may all be said
to be on a different level from the primary rules, for they are all *about* such rules' (94). This
second distinction is a logical one: secondary rules are in effect characterized as second-

however, Hart's views are somewhat less easy to discern. In the Postscript to the second edition, responding in large part to the challenge of Ronald Dworkin's interpretivist approach to legal theory, Hart has made some of his methodological presuppositions more explicit.

In a section of the Postscript entitled 'The Nature of Legal Theory', Hart describes the type of theory that he had intended to provide in writing *The Concept of Law*. The theory is supposed to be both general and descriptive. 'It is *general* in the sense that it is not tied to any particular legal system or legal culture, but seeks to give an explanatory and clarifying account of law as a Complex social and political institution with a rule-governed (and in that sense "normative") aspect' (239). The theory is *descriptive* 'in that it is morally neutral and has no justificatory aims: it does not seek to justify or commend on moral or other grounds the forms and structures which appear in my general account of law' (240). Hart notes that legal theory thus conceived 'is a radically different enterprise' from Dworkin's conception, which is said to be in part evaluative and justificatory—that is, it is not purely descriptive—and also to be addressed to a particular legal culture—that is, it is not general. Hart goes on to observe: 'It is not obvious why there should be or indeed could be any significant conflict between enterprises so different as my own and Dworkin's conceptions of legal theory' (241).

Hart's claim in the Postscript that he had intended to provide in *The Concept of Law* a theory that is both general and descriptive is very good evidence that he meant to adopt a framework of methodological positivism. I shall argue that in developing his substantive theory Hart in fact combines elements of two distinct methodological approaches, which we can call the descriptive-explanatory method and the method of conceptual analysis. Of these, only the first can appropriately be said to involve a form of methodological positivism. The second, when understood and analysed in its own terms, turns out in all significant respects to be

---

order rules that in some way operate on, or permit operations with, primary rules; primary rules are then simply the rules at the first level in a logical hierarchy. It seems clear that the second of these distinctions, based on logical type, is the more appropriate way to understand the difference between primary and secondary rules. (Even so, it is necessary to regard the notion of one rule being 'about' another in a fairly loose sense.) The most important secondary rule, the rule of recognition, is duty-imposing rather than power-conferring, and the primary rules it identifies as valid could be either power-conferring or duty-imposing. A second ambiguity still remains, however. Hart sometimes uses the term 'primary rule' to refer to a rule that is, according to some rule of recognition, *valid*. A primary rule in this sense could, presumably, be either duty-imposing or power-conferring. But sometimes Hart uses the term 'primary rule' to refer to a duty-imposing *social* rule—meaning a customary rule—that either stands alone or forms part of a 'regime' of primary rules (92). 'Regime' here simply means a non-systematic set of duty-imposing social rules that exist together in a community that has no secondary rules. In this essay I will follow Hart in using the term 'primary rule' in both these senses; the context should always make clear which is intended.

Dworkin's interpretivism under a different name. The two different strains in Hart's methodological thought produce tensions in his substantive theory, and to resolve these it is necessary to opt for one or the other of the two methodologies. The descriptive-explanatory approach is appropriate if one intends to do science, but for jurisprudence, which is a branch of philosophy, the most appropriate procedure is conceptual analysis. When jurisprudence is understood in this way, and gives up trying to borrow inappropriate elements from the descriptive-explanatory approach, it can be seen that particular theories of law must be offered from the internal point of view and must be defended, in part, by resort to moral argument. The result is the complete abandonment of methodological positivism.

I. THE GENERALITY OF LEGAL THEORY

Hart maintains that his theory is general in the following sense. It is supposed to describe an institution that, 'in spite of many variations in different cultures and in different times, has taken the same general form and structure' (240). This immediately raises the question of how we know or could come to know that these manifold social practices are in fact manifestations of *the same* institution, namely law.[5] A related question—perhaps at bottom it is the same question—concerns the status of propositions asserting that law *necessarily* does (or does not) possess such-and-such an attribute. Consider, for example, the soft positivist claim—one element of Hart's substantive positivist theory—that the criteria for identifying the content of law can in some legal systems be partly moral in nature, but are not necessarily so in all legal systems. What kind of necessity is at issue here, and to what domain of actual or possible practices does it apply?

There seem to be two main possibilities concerning how we could come to know which (actual or possible) social practices are instances of law. The first supposes that what does and does not count as law is determined by applying the scientific method to come up with a so-called descriptive-explanatory theory.[6] The idea would be to study those social

---

[5] Cf. John Finnis, *Natural Law and Natural Rights* (1980), 1–6. My thinking about methodology in legal theory has greatly benefited from Finnis's general discussion of this topic, and in particular from his illuminating critique of Hart. See *id*. at 1–22.

[6] See e.g. W. J. Waluchow, *Inclusive Legal Positivism* (1994), 19–29. Waluchow clearly believes that Hart is a proponent of the descriptive-explanatory method. *Id*. at 1–15. In *The* 'Varieties of Legal Positivism', 9 Can. J.L. &. Juris. 361 (1996), I criticize Waluchow's application of the descriptive-explanatory approach to jurisprudence in general. In Section II of the present essay I argue that Hart cannot be understood as employing that approach, at least in anything like a pure form.

practices that we call law, but from an external perspective. Taking a certain kind of familiar social practice—for example, those practices Hart refers to as 'modern municipal legal systems'—as a tentative starting-point, a theory of this kind would develop its own internal descriptive categories. These categories would not necessarily correspond to what 'we'—participants, in some appropriately loose sense, in modern municipal legal systems—have in mind, either explicitly or implicitly, in speaking of 'law'. To the extent that a descriptive-explanatory theory used the term 'law', it would have to be regarded as a term of art. Its meaning and extension would be determined by the relative explanatory power of accepting one way of categorizing and describing social practices over another, where 'explanatory power' would in turn depend on such standard metatheoretical criteria as the following: predictive power, coherence, range of phenomena explained, degree of explanatory unity, and the theory's simplicity or elegance. It thus might turn out that the initial examples of law on which we tend to focus at a pre-theoretical stage— modern municipal legal systems, let's say—are, from the perspective of the best descriptive-explanatory theory, just a minor variant within a wider class of social practices. The theory might, for example, regard the difference between modern municipal legal systems and instances of so-called primitive law as theoretically insignificant because a taxonomy of the social world that ignored that distinction turned out to have greater explanatory power.

The second possibility concerning how we could come to know which actual or possible social practices constitute 'law' would require us to analyse our own concept of law. We would inquire into the manner in which we conceptualize our own social practices so as, presumably, to clarify the concept and to come to a better understanding of the practices themselves. The notion of 'necessity' involved in such statements as 'Law necessarily does (or does not) possess such and such a characteristic' would then be conceptual rather than scientific necessity.

There are a number of indications, in both the original text of *The Concept of Law* and the Postscript, that might be taken to suggest that Hart intended to adopt something like a descriptive-explanatory methodology. He says in the Preface, for example, that the book can be regarded as 'an exercise in descriptive sociology'. In the Postscript he speaks of a 'descriptive jurisprudence' in which an 'external observer' takes account of or describes the internal viewpoint of a participant without adopting or sharing that viewpoint (242–3). At many other points, however, Hart states, as the title of his book in fact suggests, that his primary methodology is conceptual analysis. In the Preface he writes: 'The lawyer will regard the book as an essay in analytical jurisprudence, for it is concerned with the clarification of the general framework of legal thought.' (He goes on to say that the book may *also* be regarded as an essay in descriptive sociology.) The main features of Hart's substantive theory of law are said to be 'the central elements in the concept of law and of prime importance in its elucidation' (17). And in the Postscript he formulates the main thesis of substantive legal positivism in terms of conceptual rather than scientific or empirical necessity: 'though there are many different contingent connections between law and morality there are no necessary conceptual connections between the content of law and morality' (268).

I will argue in subsequent sections that while it is possible to discern elements of the descriptive-explanatory method in Hart's approach to doing legal theory, there are good reasons for believing that he does not in fact employ that method, or at least that he does not employ it in anything like a pure form. The most important such reason is that Hart adopts the particular characterization of law that he does, expressed in terms of a union of two types of rule, on the basis of evaluative judgments that have nothing to do with the metatheoretical criteria for assessing theories that were discussed above. I will also argue that there are good reasons for believing that the most fundamental aspect of Hart's primary methodology is conceptual analysis. The type of conceptual analysis he advocates is meant to be based on an external rather than an internal perspective, and in that respect resembles the descriptive-explanatory method. For present purposes, however, the details of Hart's particular conception of conceptual analysis are not of paramount importance. Our concern is with Hart's claim that his theory of law is 'general'. It is clear enough what 'generality' would mean in a pure descriptive-explanatory theory: the theory would apply to whatever range of social practices that its own categories of description, derived on the basis of their explanatory power, picked out. But what does it mean to say that legal theory is general when your methodology is some form of conceptual analysis?

It is worth emphasizing that Hart's starting point in elucidating the concept of law is not an assumed pre-theoretical knowledge of criteria that are capable of picking out, from among the social practices that have existed somewhere, at some time, in the history of the world, those that constitute 'law'. As he says in the Postscript, 'The starting-point for this clarificatory task is the widespread common knowledge of a modern municipal legal system which on page 3 of this book I attribute to any educated man' (240). At the specified point in the text Hart lists as follows the 'salient features' of a legal system that an educated person might be expected to be able to identify:

They comprise (i) rules forbidding or enjoining certain types of behaviour under penalty; (ii) rules requiring people to compensate those whom they injure in certain ways; (iii) rules specifying what must be done to make wills, contracts or other arrangements which confer rights and create obligations; (iv) courts to determine what the rules are and when they have been broken, and to fix the punishment or compensation to be paid; (v) a legislature to make new rules and abolish old ones. (3)

Hart is clearly not saying that a social arrangement that failed to possess all these features could not be a legal system. In fact, according to his substantive positivist theory, which defines law in terms of a union of two types of rule, only features (i) and (iv) appear to be necessary for the existence of law. Rather, Hart's rationale for beginning with the salient features of a modern municipal legal system would seem to be this. He is pointing to these features as (possibly conceptually contingent) attributes of a certain type of social institution that is, *for us,* a clear central case of *our* concept of law. He will then focus on that type of institution as he undertakes the task of clarifying that concept. Once this task has been accomplished and we have a more satisfactory grasp of our own concept, we will be in a better position to say whether or not various other types of social practice—for example, so-called primitive legal systems, inter-national law, historical practices of one kind or another, contemporary foreign practices quite different from our own, etc.—are instances of law, that is, instances of law according to our own lights. As Joseph Raz puts the point, 'There is nothing wrong in interpreting the institutions of other societies in terms of our typologies. This is an inevitable part of any intel-ligent attempt to understand other cultures.'[7]

What the process of conceptual analysis involves will be examined in greater detail in subsequent sections. For the moment, I wish only to emphasize the following point. Although the clarified concept of law that is supposed to emerge from Hart's process of theorizing will in one sense be general—once we have the concept, we can use it to elucidate radically different foreign or historical practices and classify them as being, from our perspective, law, non-law, or perhaps something in between—there is nonetheless a clear sense in which the genesis of the enterprise is 'local'. Hart begins with the knowledge that he takes to be common to educated persons in modern societies of an institution that holds a central place within those societies. A modern municipal legal system, as described by Hart, is a relatively specific type of institution that is located within the framework of a fairly recent historical innovation, namely the state. Hart does not claim that all instances of what we would and should call law are in all respects like modern municipal legal systems, but even so his project of conceptual clarification takes this local manifestation of the concept as its starting point.

One might quarrel with the characterization of 'modern municipal

---

[7] *The Authority of Law* (1979), 50.

legal systems' in general as 'local', but Hart clearly begins with the institutions most familiar to his readers—in chapter 1 of *The Concept of Law* he
discusses the knowledge that English people will have of the English legal
system—and then assumes that in other countries 'there are legal systems
which are broadly similar in structure in spite of important differences'
(3). At a certain point, as we encounter foreign institutions that are more
and more different from our own, this assumption might come to beg the
question. But the concern here is with a question of judgment that arises
in the process of investigation rather than with a denial of the idea that
legal theory must begin locally: how much do the practices of foreign
societies or cultures have to differ from our own before we ought to
regard them as something other than mere variants on our own practices?

Once we see that the starting point of Hart's legal theory is local in the
way just described, the distance between his jurisprudential methodology
and Ronald Dworkin's begins to lose the appearance of an unbridgeable
gulf. Dworkin's theoretical point of departure is the 'collective' identification of 'the practices that count as legal practices in our own culture': 'We
have legislatures and courts and administrative agencies and bodies, and
the decisions these institutions make are reported in a canonical way.'[8]
This collective and rather rough-and-ready singling out of familiar institutions as the initial focus of jurisprudential inquiry is very much reminiscent of Hart's reliance on the knowledge that he says any educated
person will possess of his own legal system and of others that are plainly
similar to his own. The following description that Dworkin gives of this
process of identification also seems to be very much in the spirit of Hart's
enterprise, at least if we replace the phrase 'the interpretive problem' by
'the task of conceptual clarification':

It would be a mistake . . . to think that we identify these institutions through some
shared and intellectually satisfying definition of what a legal system necessarily is
and what institutions necessarily make it up. Our culture presents us with legal
institutions and with the idea that they form a system. The question which
features they have, in virtue of which they combine as a distinctly legal system, is
part of the interpretive problem.[9]

In Sections VI and VIII I shall argue that, if we press hard enough on
the notion of conceptual analysis, the result is not far removed from what
Dworkin means by interpretation. For the moment, however, my concern
is with the related issues of where legal theory starts and how general it
is. Dworkin's starting point is a set of institutions that he says is presented
to us as a system by our culture; at other points in *Law's Empire* he speaks
of interpretmg our *legal* culture. While Dworkin clearly does not associate

---

[8] *Law's Empire* (1986), 91.   [9] *Id.*

'our' legal culture with the legal system of any single country, Hart is probably right when he asserts in the Postscript that the initial scope of Dworkin's theorizing is limited to something like Anglo-American law (240). Even so, as I hope the preceding discussion makes clear, all that really seems to be at stake here is a difference of opinion about the following question: to what extent should we assume, on the basis of superficial resemblance alone and in advance of actually formulating a theory of law, that foreign institutions really are similar, in every respect that might turn out to be theoretically relevant, to those institutions that in our own societies we call 'law'?

Dworkin is more cautious than Hart in the implicit answer that he gives to this question, but that by itself is hardly indicative of a deep methodological divide between the two. Both theorists begin locally; they just have different views on what should count as local. Where Dworkin begins with common law systems, Hart's point of departure is the broader notion of a modern municipal legal system. Perhaps Hart can be understood as bracketing the common law with the civil law and then treating this single category of system as his starting point, since most clear instances of a modern municipal legal system either derive directly from, or were significantly influenced by, one or the other of these two traditions. But the common law and civil law have the same historical roots: they are two strands within a larger historical tradition. Whether one begins one's theorizing with the common law or with the broader tradition of which it is a part might conceivably have an influence on the content of one's substantive theory, but regarded strictly from the point of view of methodology this does not seem to be a matter of great significance. The underlying issue is, in Dworkin's words, '[w]hich [historical] changes are great enough to cut the thread of continuity'.[10] This question is undoubtedly an important one, but it arises *within* a methodological approach in which the need to begin locally is already a given.

Both Hart and Dworkin go on to suggest that we can make use of the theories of law that each will develop from his respective starting point to make sense of social practices that truly are different from our own. Naturally, a difference of opinion about the scope of the starting point also represents a difference of opinion about which foreign practices should be treated as truly different from our own. Dworkin initially excludes Nazi Germany from the scope of his theorizing, for example, but holds that we can use the theory of law he ultimately develops to see that there is a sense in which the Nazis had law as well as a sense in which they did not. Hart, on the other hand, assumes from the outset, apparently as a pre-theoretical matter, that the Nazis really did, by our lights, have law. For

---

[10] *Id*. at 69–70.

the reasons already given, however, that difference should not, without more, be taken as an indication that Hart's theoretical project is radically different from Dworkin's. Of course I have not shown that their projects are not in the end radically different because I have only addressed the issues of starting point and generality. I have said nothing about Hart's claim that his theory of law, unlike Dworkin's, is 'descriptive', and it is to that issue that we must now turn.

II. THE DESCRIPTIVENESS OF LEGAL THEORY

Hart says in the Postscript that his theory of law is meant to be descriptive in the following sense: '[The theory] is morally neutral and has non-justificatory aims: it does not seek to justify or commend on moral or other grounds the forms and structures which appear in my general account of law' (240). To assess this set of claims it will be helpful to look at the substantive content of Hart's theory in somewhat greater detail than we have so far done. The two minimum conditions that he specifies as necessary and sufficient for the existence of a legal system are (i) the acceptance of certain types of secondary social rule by officials, the most important of which is a rule of recognition laying down criteria of validity for so-called primary rules, and (ii) general compliance on the part of the population at large with the primary rules these criteria identify as valid (116–17). Of these two conditions, it is the first that lies at the core of Hart's theoretical account of law. Law, he says, 'may most illuminatingly be characterized' as the union of primary and secondary rules (94), a union that, borrowing a phrase from Austin, he further describes as 'the key to the science of jurisprudence' (81). Occasionally Hart puts his point in terms of the rule of recognition in particular, rather than in terms of secondary rules generally: '[It is] the . . . complex social situation where a secondary rule of recognition is accepted and used for the identification of primary rules of obligation . . . which deserves, if anything does, to be called the foundations of a legal system' (100).

The rule of recognition is said by Hart to be a social (or customary) rule. Such rules are constituted both by a regular pattern of conduct and by 'a distinctive normative attitude' that he refers to variously as the phenomenon of 'acceptance' (255) and as the rule's 'internal aspect' (56). The internal aspect concerns the fact that 'if a social rule is to exist, some at least must look upon the behaviour in question as a general standard to be followed by the group as a whole' (56). The point of view of such persons is referred to by Hart as the 'internal' point of view; it is the point of view of one who accepts the rule as a guide to conduct and as a standard of criticism both for himself and for others in the group (89). It is important to note that those who take up the internal point of view adopt an attitude of *shared* acceptance (102), and they look upon the rules as standards that are 'essentially common or public' (116). Their acceptance takes the form of 'a reflective critical attitude' to the relevant pattern of conduct, and is given characteristic expression through the use of normative terminology such as 'ought', 'must', and 'should' (56–7). In the case of certain social rules, including in particular the rule of recognition, the terminology of 'obligation' takes hold: 'Rules are conceived and spoken of as imposing obligations when the general demand for conformity is insistent and the social pressure brought to bear upon those who deviate or threaten to deviate is great' (86).

The notion of a rule of recognition is the cornerstone of Hart's theory of law. In a given legal system this rule exists simply because it is accepted by officials (in the sense of 'acceptance' that emerges from Hart's characterization of social rules in general), so that its existence is said to be 'a matter of fact' (110). The theory thus characterizes law in purely factual, non-normative terms. Clearly this aspect of the theory is part of what Hart has in mind when he writes in the Postscript that he had intended to provide a theory of law that is descriptive. Hart also seems to be suggesting, however, that it is not just his particular theory that possesses this attribute but the general enterprise in which he is engaged. Legal theory, or at least the type of legal theory that Hart has opted to pursue, is itself descriptive in character. In other words, he appears to be claiming to be a methodological as well as a substantive legal positivist.

The most straightforward understanding of methodological positivism would look to what I earlier called the descriptive-explanatory method. Legal theory is, on this view, a form of scientific enterprise the point of which is to advance, from an external viewpoint, descriptive, morally neutral theories of the social world. A particular theory adopts the characterization of empirical phenomena that it does because the theory's proponents believe that characterization has explanatory power. As was noted in the preceding section, explanatory power is most plausibly understood as referring to metatheoretical criteria for assessing scientific theories: predictive power, theoretical simplicity, and so on. On the descriptive-explanatory interpretation of Hart's methodology, the reason for equating 'law' (understood now as a term of art internal to the theory) with social systems based on a rule of recognition would be that one has grounds for believing that such a characterization has explanatory power in the sense just described.

There is something to be said for the descriptive-explanatory interpretation of Hart's methodology. For one thing, it is consistent with his avowedly external theoretical perspective; as he says repeatedly, his theory is intended to take account of the internal point of view, but not to be offered from that point of view. For another, this interpretation offers a sensible understanding of the *sort* of claim Hart seems to be making when he places the notion of a rule of recognition at the centre of his theory of law. His assertion that all instances of the type of institution that he initially sets out to study—viz. modern municipal legal systems—contain a rule of recognition is, on the face of it, an empirical rather than a conceptual claim. Empirical claims are exactly what one would expect to find in a descriptive-explanatory theory. Moreover, Hart appears to treat this particular empirical claim as *novel*. Seen in that light, the claim does not seem to be plausibly regarded as an analysis of the concept of law (i.e. it does not seem to be plausibly regarded as figuring in our shared conceptualization of the practices that *we* call law). On a descriptive-explanatory approach, however, there is no necessary reason why the theory's categories should track the concepts of the participants in the social practices under study.

There are, however, serious problems with the descriptive-explanatory reading of Hart's methodology. As we have seen, the substantive theory he advances characterizes the phenomenon of 'law' in terms of the notion of a rule of recognition. On a descriptive-explanatory approach the reason for adopting such a characterization would be its explanatory power in a scientific sense. But Hart does not give us any reason to believe that his theory of law is superior, in terms of explanatory power thus understood, to what he calls radically external theories. He does not argue that theories of the latter kind, which look at social phenomena in purely behaviouristic terms and treat the internal point of view as epiphenomenal at best, must necessarily be deficient in predictive power, for example. Nor does he make such an argument about the possible class of theories that take Hart's own notion of acceptance as their basic explanatory category and treat the distinction between primary and secondary rules as theoretically unimportant. Hart does invoke the notion of explanatory power, but not in the ordinary scientific sense. He is interested, rather, in the power of a theory to elucidate concepts: 'We accord this union of elements [i.e. primary and secondary rules] a central place because of their explanatory power in elucidating the concepts that constitute the framework of legal thought' (81). Because the social practices under study are our own, the apparent claim is that Hart's theory will clarify our understanding of our own conceptual framework.

Hart offers, in effect, two answers to the question of why secondary rules generally, and the rule of recognition in particular, are of key importance in legal theory. The first is an elaboration of the idea just discussed—namely that at least one goal of legal theory is conceptual clarification. Hart argues that both the idea of a social rule and the associated notion of the internal point of view are required to analyse the basic concepts of obligation and duty. But there is, he says, a range of other legal concepts, such as authority, state, official, legislation, jurisdiction, validity, and legal power, that must be analysed by reference to the internal point of view of a particular type of social rule, namely secondary rules that have been accepted by a certain subgroup within society ('officials') (98–9). Hart's critique of Austin's theory of law as orders backed by threats is, in essence, that it does not have the internal resources to elucidate these concepts. However, the concepts of authority, state, legislation, etc., are *our* concepts, where 'we' must be understood as referring to participants in—or at least the subjects of—modern municipal legal systems. These are, in other words, the notions that we use to conceptualize certain of our own practices. This lends support to the suggestion that, when he speaks of conceptual analysis, Hart has in mind the clarification of the conceptual framework that we apply to certain aspects of our own social behaviour. This is not, however, a standard goal of descriptive-explanatory theory. A radically external theory that transcended or ignored the participants' conceptualization of their own practice might well have greater explanatory power in the usual scientific sense. Degree of conceptual clarification appears, in fact, to be the sole basis by which Hart would judge the success of particular theories of law. Conceptual analysis is apparently an end in itself, and not just an extra criterion of adequacy that has been conjoined with explanatory power as ordinarily understood.

The second answer that Hart gives to the question of why the rule of recognition should have a key role to play in legal theory concerns certain defects that he says are associated with a simple regime of primary rules. Such a regime is said to be, as compared to a system containing secondary rules, uncertain, static, and inefficient (91–4). This list of defects is best understood as a reference back to an earlier statement by Hart that '[t]he principal functions of the law as a means of social control are . . . to be seen in the diverse ways in which the law is used to control, to guide, and to plan life out of court' (40). As Hart puts the point in the Postscript, the 'primary function of the law [is] guiding the conduct of its subjects' (249). While a regime of primary rules guides conduct, it does not do so *well*. A system containing secondary rules (of recognition, change, and adjudication) is better at this task because it is more certain, the content of the rules can be deliberately changed, and the rules can be more efficiently enforced (94–9). Thus, secondary rules, according to Hart, remedy the defects of a simple regime of primary rules.

This second argument for the centrality in legal theory of secondary rules is not coterminous in scope with the first argument. The first argument is that the notion of a secondary rule is necessary for the analysis of certain specific legal concepts, such as authority, legislation, and legal power. The second argument is that the notion of a secondary rule is necessary for the proper analysis of the more general concept of *law*. Thus, even if the first argument is correct in its claim about the concepts of authority, legislation, and so forth, it leaves open the possibility that the overarching category of 'law' should abstract from the distinction between primary and secondary rules. As was suggested earlier, it is at least conceivable that the primary theoretical indicator of 'law' might be the general phenomenon that Hart describes as the acceptance of social rules. The significant feature of those systems of rules that counted as law might then be, not whether they contained secondary rules, but rather whether they were backed by serious rather than trivial social pressure. On an understanding of law along those lines, social systems based on the union of primary and secondary rules would count as law, but so would certain systems consisting of primary rules alone.[11] Hart's second argument is intended to show that systems of the former type are in fact the paradigm of law, and not just a special case.

The statement that a regime of primary rules has defects, like the statement that these defects are remedied by the introduction of a rule of recognition and other secondary rules, is an evaluative claim. The values in question relate, as I have said, to the guidance of conduct, which means that they have a normative dimension. The descriptive-explanatory method assesses theories by means of criteria that are properly called evaluative, such as predictive power and simplicity, but the values in question are applicable to all scientific theories, and they are not normative in character. Moreover, Hart is making evaluative claims not about theories but about the very social practices he is studying. It does not, however, seem consonant with the descriptive-explanatory method (i.e. with the scientific method) that the descriptive categories adopted by a particular theory should be based on evaluative judgments of this kind. Hart's theoretical enterprise thus cannot plausibly be regarded as grounded in that method, or at any rate in a pure version of it.

The nature of the two arguments that Hart advances for the centrality in legal theory of the notion of a secondary rule—that this notion is required for the analysis of specific legal concepts such as authority and legislation, and that it is required for the analysis of the general concept of law—enable us to reach the following two conclusions about his methodology in legal theory. First, he has not adopted anything like a

---

[11] In speaking of regimes of primary social rules that are backed by physical sanctions administered by the community at large rather than by officials, Hart says 'we shall be inclined to classify [such] rules as a primitive or rudimentary form of law' (86). The characterization of such a regime as 'primitive' is pre-theoretical and potentially question-begging. By itself, it cannot bear the weight of a fundamental theoretical demarcation between the simpler social arrangement and systems based on a union of primary and secondary rules. It is for that reason that Hart requires the argument that a regime of primary rules is in certain respects defective.

pure descriptive-explanatory approach; he is not doing science in the usual sense. Second, his main methodological technique is conceptual analysis, by which he means the clarification or elucidation of our manner of conceptualizing our own social practices. We must, of course, inquire more closely into what this technique involves, and one way to do this is to return to Hart's claim in the Postscript that his intent was to provide a theory of law that is 'descriptive'. What does this term mean when it is applied to conceptual analysis?

One thing the term 'descriptive' might mean in the context of conceptual analysis is that the concept of law—either the concept that emerges from Hart's theorizing or, to the extent that this turns out to be different, our general, shared concept—has a certain type of content: it picks out social practices as 'law' on the basis of purely factual, non-normative criteria. As was noted earlier, this is clearly a claim that Hart does wish to make, at least so far as his own theory is concerned. The particular conceptualization of law that he defends characterizes law in terms of two types of rule, which are in turn characterized by reference to various kinds of social fact.[12] Understood in that way, however, the claim that legal theory is descriptive is not methodological in nature. It is simply a claim about the content of the concept of law. It is a claim, in effect, that that concept is not thick; it picks out social practices on the basis of purely factual criteria, rather than, say, mixed moral and factual criteria. It is, in effect, just a way of stating the main thesis of substantive legal positivism.

But when Hart writes in the Postscript that his aim was to provide a 'descriptive' theory of law, he seems to be making a claim about methodology and not just about the content of his own theory; he is, in effect, holding himself out to be both a methodological and a substantive legal positivist. The methodological claim is not, presumably, that the concept of law is *necessarily* non-thick—that we could not have a concept of law that included normative or moral considerations among its identifying criteria—because there is no good reason to think that such a claim is true. The more plausible way to understand the methodological claim is that

---

[12] The point here is that Hart claims that law *as a general type of institution* is identifiable solely by reference to various kinds of social fact; thus, the general concept of law is non-thick. But, as Hart makes clear in the Postscript, he does not think that each valid law within a legal system must be identifiable solely in social terms: the rule of recognition can adopt moral as well as social criteria of validity. This soft or incorporationist version of positivism is to be contrasted with the sources thesis defended by Raz, which holds that all laws must be identifiable as such solely by reference to social facts and without resort to moral argument. It will not be necessary, for purposes of this essay, to decide between these two versions of positivism. For the best recent discussion of incorporationism, see Jules L. Coleman, 'Reason and Authority', in *The Autonomy of Law: Essays on Legal Positivism*, ed. R. George (1995), 287. On the sources thesis, see Joseph Raz, 'Authority, Law and Morality', 68 The Monist 295 (1985).

Hart is simply setting out to *describe* the conceptual scheme that we apply to certain of our own social practices (those that can be identified on a pre-theoretical basis as 'modern municipal legal systems'). Such a project can presumably be carried out in a morally neutral manner whether the relevant concepts turn out to be thick or non-thick. On this view, Hart is simply describing the content of the relevant concepts and the relationships between them, whatever that content and those relationships turn out to be. This interpretation of Hart's methodological positivism is also consistent with the external perspective from which the theory is clearly meant to be offered. The idea is to describe and elucidate our conceptual scheme from the outside, as it were. In that way the theorist can remain neutral with respect to such questions as whether the social practice in question is justified, valuable, in need of reform, and so forth. He or she can simply describe what is there.

I believe that the interpretation of Hart's methodology that was sketched in the preceding paragraph captures fairly accurately his own understanding of what is involved in doing legal theory. He intends to engage in conceptual analysis, but from the outside rather than the inside. It is important to emphasize that this is not just an application of the descriptive-explanatory method of ordinary science. The starting point of inquiry is the participants' own conceptualization of their practice, and from the perspective of the descriptive-explanatory approach that is an arbitrary limitation. Beyond that, Hart seems not to be particularly interested in the predictive power of his theory, or in other aspects of explanatory power in the usual scientific sense. Most importantly, his characterization of the general concept of law relies on evaluative judgments that simply have no place in the descriptive-explanatory methodology. He is engaged in a particular type of conceptual analysis that can appropriately be described as descriptive, but which is nonetheless distinct from the standard methodology of science. At this point it becomes necessary to inquire more closely into the nature of external conceptual analysis, as we might call this approach. That is the task we undertake in the following four sections.

III. DESCRIPTION VERSUS ELUCIDATION: THE PROBLEM OF NORMATIVITY

In work published subsequent to *The Concept of Law*, Hart has written as follows: 'For the understanding of [not only law but any other form of normative social structure] the methodology of the empirical sciences is useless; what is needed is a "hermeneutic" method which involves portraying rule-governed behaviour as it appears to its participants, who see it as conforming or failing to conform to certain shared standards.'[13] Hart's rejection of the 'methodology of the empirical sciences' might be read narrowly, as a rejection of behaviourist or radically empiricist methods of inquiry that forbid the theorist to take account of mental states and attitudes.

In light of the discussion in the preceding section, however, I believe the better view is that Hart is simply not employing the scientific method at all, at least in anything like the usual sense. He has not set out to offer a descriptive-explanatory theory, the adequacy of which is to be judged by standard metatheoretical criteria such as predictive power. Instead, he has deliberately invoked the notion of *verstehen* from the hermeneutic tradition in the philosophy of social science, which suggests that his theoretical goal is to understand how the participants in a social practice regard their own behaviour. But Hart does not want to go as far as those hermeneuts who, like Peter Winch, think that the theorist has no choice but to 'join the practice' and theorize about it from the participants' point of view.[14] Hart's project involves 'clarifying' or 'elucidating' the participants' conceptual framework, but from an external perspective. This can, perhaps, be viewed as a hybrid methodology. As in the hermeneutic tradition, Hart aims to understand how the participants regard their own behaviour, but he hopes to achieve this understanding by taking up an external, observational stance reminiscent of that adopted by pure descriptive-explanatory theories.

That this is the best interpretation of Hart's claim to be doing descriptive legal theory, and hence the best way to make sense of his methodological positivism, is suggested by the following passage from the Postscript. The passage is long, but worth quoting in full:

[Dworkin's] central objection [to descriptive legal theory] seems to be that legal theory must take account of an internal perspective on the law which is the viewpoint of an insider or participant in a legal system, and no adequate account of this internal perspective can be provided by a descriptive theory whose viewpoint is not that of a participant but that of an external observer. But there is in fact nothing in the project of a descriptive jurisprudence as exemplified in my book to preclude a non-participant external observer from describing the ways in which participants view the law from such an internal point of view. So I explained in this book at some length that participants manifest their internal point of view in accepting the law as providing guides to their conduct and standards of criticism. Of course a descriptive legal theorist does not as such himself share the participants' acceptance of the law in these ways, but he can and should describe such acceptance, as indeed I have attempted to do in this book. It is true that for this

---

[13] *Essays in Jurisprudence and Philosophy* (1983), 13.
[14] *The Idea of a Social Science* (1958). Hart cites Winch as holding a similar view to Hart's on the internal aspect of rules (289).

purpose the descriptive legal theorist must *understand* what it is to adopt the internal point of view and in that limited sense he must be able to put himself in the place of an insider; but this is not to accept the law or endorse the insider's internal point of view or in any other way to surrender his descriptive stance. (242)

In this passage Hart emphasizes the theorist's role in describing such facts as that participants accept rules as guides to conduct and standards for criticism. It is, of course, quite possible to describe social phenomena in a more or less value-neutral fashion, as Hart wishes to do. But it is worth bearing in mind that any given social phenomenon can be accurately described in an indefinitely large number of ways. Descriptions will differ from one another, for example, in the level of generality at which the practice is described (e.g. descriptions of individuals one by one versus generalizations about all individuals in the relevant group). Different descriptions will individuate practices and sub-practices in different ways. There will also be differences in degree of selectivity, as every description inevitably fails to include some attributes of the object being described. Descriptions thus differ from one another with respect to what and how much they leave out, or, to put the point more positively, they differ insofar as they focus on or highlight different aspects of what is being observed. Thus, in observing one and the same social practice one onlooker—call him Oliver—might call attention to the existence and motivating force of punitive sanctions, while another—call him Herbert— might emphasize that at least some people are moved to act because they accept the practice, internalize it, and treat it as a guide to proper conduct. Some descriptions, taking what Hart calls an extreme external point of view (89), will characterize a social practice behaviouristically, without reference to anyone's mental states. Other descriptions, like Hart's, will bring in the participants' attitudes and reasons for action. And so on.

Most of these possible descriptions will be of absolutely no interest to us, scientifically, philosophically, or otherwise. A set of descriptive statements is not, by itself, a *theory* of any kind, and that is so even if the statements are in certain respects general (i.e. apply to more than one occasion, or to more than one person). In ordinary science, a set of statements becomes a theory by making (preferably testable) predictions and/or by conceptualizing the world in a novel or abstract way. Hart, however, is not apparently interested in predictive power, and the whole point of his approach is to describe existing conceptualizations rather than to create new ones. To find a set of descriptive statements that constitutes the basis of a meaningful (non-scientific) theory, it is first of all clear that we must be observing the practice with a particular purpose in mind. Hart's purpose is, as I have said, to offer an external analysis of the participants' conceptualization of their practice, which means looking at that conceptualization from the outside.[15] Thus, Hart's particular descriptive account of law, focusing as it does on the phenomenon of acceptance, presumably becomes transformed into a theory because, as he emphasizes at a number of points throughout *The Concept of Law*, the account is supposed to 'elucidate' or 'clarify' the concepts that participants use: 'We accord this union of elements a central place because of their explanatory power in elucidating the concepts that constitute the framework of legal thought' (81).

It bears emphasis yet again that this notion of elucidation cannot simply be another term for explanatory power in the scientific sense. If that were the case, then Hart's theory would have to compete in the forum of predictive power with, for example, theories of social behaviour that abstracted from the participants' own conceptualization of what they were doing and used different categories of description altogether. Of course, one of Hart's claims is that behaviourists and radical empiricists are wrong to insist that mental states and attitudes should as a matter of methodological principle be excluded from theories of social behaviour, but it does not follow that there cannot be behaviourist theories, let alone that a behaviourist theory could not have greater explanatory power in the scientific sense than Hart's theory. Hart, however, does not even address this issue, and that must be because he understands 'elucidation' in a very different way. At this point we must therefore inquire more closely into what Hart means by this notion, asking in particular whether the goal of conceptual elucidation is consistent with a background methodological framework that insists on accurate external description.

Scientific theories are capable of transforming the way that we look at the world; they can lead us to reject old conceptual schemes and to adopt new ones. But Hart does not purport to be offering a scientific theory, at least not in the usual sense, and in any event the object of his descriptive efforts is itself an existing conceptual scheme. Because a primary goal of description is presumably accuracy, one would have thought that the external observer should simply describe what is there, confusions, obscurities, and all. The description should, so to speak, be passive, mirroring whatever the observer finds; the aim should not be to transform, even in so apparently an innocuous way as by 'clarification', that which is being observed. Thus, if, as Hart claims, participants in modern municipal legal systems, or at least some of those participants, are unclear what they mean when they speak of rules, obligations, authority, sovereignty, and so on, an accurate external description should surely just report that fact. If different people have different understandings of the

---

[15] 'For the observer may, without accepting the rules himself, assert that the group accepts the rules, and thus may from the outside refer to the way in which *they* are concerned with them from the internal point of view' (89).

relevant concepts, that fact too should simply be reported. Naturally, I do not mean to deny that an observer's external description of even a very familiar social practice like law could not give rise to new knowledge. For example, Hart would claim that the statement that all modern municipal legal systems possess a rule of recognition is an empirical observation.[16] If it is an empirical observation it is a novel one, and if it is true we have learned something. But producing new empirical knowledge is not the same thing as analysing, elucidating, or clarifying a concept. The latter terms all suggest that Hart is employing a methodological technique that goes beyond, and perhaps is in some tension with, the passive external description of an existing conceptual scheme.

Let us suppose Hart is right in thinking that the statement 'All modern municipal legal systems possess a rule of recognition' is a straightforward empirical observation. Even if that is so, Hart's theoretical claim that all instances of *law* possess a rule of recognition is not empirical in character, or at least it is not merely empirical. It is a conceptual claim of some kind that has, presumably, been produced by Hart's technique of conceptual analysis. Because this conceptual claim is, like its empirical counterpart, also novel, it is natural to ask whether the technique that produced it is consistent with the goal of accurate external description. Has the theory, through 'clarification', in some way transformed the concept that it was supposed to be describing from the outside? A rule of recognition is not, after all, one of those 'salient features' of a modern municipal legal system that Hart says would be known to any educated person. Indeed, the originality of Hart's substantive theory of law might be said to consist in part in the claim to have brought to light a previously unnoticed empirical fact about modern municipal legal systems, namely that they all contain a rule of recognition. But that means, among other things, that Hart cannot respond to the concern that he has, in clarifying our concept of law, effectively transformed it by maintaining that he is simply picking out a known feature of modern legal systems that is, as it were, particularly salient. Pushing this point a bit further, it is not immediately clear how drawing attention to a hitherto unnoticed empirical fact could even figure in a piece of conceptual analysis, external or otherwise.

[16] Hart would claim this because he holds (i) that the term 'modern municipal legal system' has a generally agreed pre-theoretical meaning and extension and (ii) that statements about the existence of a rule of recognition are simply statements of fact. I shall suggest in Section V, however, that to support the claim that even a particular legal system possesses a rule of recognition requires normative argument; a fortiori, the same would be true of the claim that all modern municipal legal systems possess such a rule. A less controversial example of how external observation could produce new knowledge might be the empirical demonstration or refutation of the claim that, say, all modern municipal legal systems permit greater penalties to be imposed for completed crimes, as opposed to attempts.

It will be helpful at this point if we ask just why Hart thinks that external conceptual analysis is a theoretically fruitful enterprise in the first
place. Put slightly differently, in what respect does he believe that the
concept of law stands in need of clarification or elucidation? Hart's
response to this question begins to take shape early on in *The Concept of
Law*, when he discusses the suggestion that nothing more is required by
way of an answer to the question 'What is law?' than an enumeration of
those features of a modern municipal legal system that are, according to
Hart, already known to most educated persons. (Such an enumeration is,
of course, a good example of passive external description.) This suggestion
will not do, he says, because it fails to throw any light on what it is about
law that has always puzzled legal theorists (5). As to what the sources of
puzzlement are, Hart points to 'three recurrent issues': 'How does law
differ from and how is it related to orders backed by threats? How does
legal obligation differ from, and how is it related to, moral obligation?
What are rules, and to what extent is law an affair of rules?' (13).

The point to notice here is that all three of these issues are aspects of, or
involve possible solutions to, a more general problem, which we might
label the problem of the normativity of law. By this I mean to refer to two
facts: first, legal discourse is pervaded by such normative terms as 'obligation', 'right', and 'duty'; and second, legal authorities and officials—
metaphorically speaking, the law itself—purport by their actions of
legislation, adjudication, and so on to place us under obligations that we
would not otherwise have. Hart, possibly speaking loosely, expresses this
latter point in terms not of purported but of actual obligation: 'The most
prominent general feature of law at all times and places is that its existence
means that certain kinds of human conduct are no longer optional, but in
some sense obligatory' (6; cf. 82). In speaking of the *problem* of the normativity of law, I mean to refer to a congeries of questions of the following
kind. How is the concept of legal obligation to be analysed? How is the
concept of legal obligation related to that of moral obligation? What does it
mean to claim authority over someone? Can law in fact give rise to obligations, either moral or of some other type, that people would not otherwise
have? Clearly, Hart's 'three recurrent issues' belong to this congeries.[17]

It is plausible to think that the provision of an account of the normativity of law is a central task of jurisprudence, if not the central task. In
speaking of an 'account' of the normativity of law I am being deliberately
vague, so as to subsume such disparate views as, on the one hand, the
natural law thesis that every law properly so called is morally binding

---

[17] This point is obvious in the case of the last two issues. It holds true of the first issue as
well because Hart's concern there is with Austin's reductive analysis of the concept of legal
obligation (i.e. with the analysis of legal obligation in terms of orders backed by threats).

and, on the other hand, the Holmesian thesis that legal obligation is an empty concept. Whatever the nature of the particular account that a theorist offers, however, the central questions he or she must confront are these. Does law affect persons reasons for action in the way that it claims to, namely by giving them obligations that they would not otherwise have? If law does so affect persons' reasons, what is the philosophical character of the resulting obligations and under what circumstances do they arise? It is because of this focus on the (apparent) reason-givingness of law that jurisprudence can plausibly be thought to be a *philosophical* discipline: it is, in effect, a branch of practical philosophy (i.e. the philosophy of practical reason). Hart is thus on strong ground in apparently placing the problem of the normativity of law at the heart of his own theoretical project. It is, moreover, very plausible to think that an inquiry into the normativity of law is, at least in part, a *conceptual* inquiry. Most people subject to modern municipal legal systems would probably identify as central to their experience of law the law's claim to authority—its claim, that is, to place us, through the actions of officials, under obligations that we would not otherwise have. (Many persons, but by no means all, would go on to add that the law succeeds in this endeavour.) The idea that the law purports to bind us by exercising authority over us is thus very plausibly regarded as an element of the concept of law. Hart implicitly makes this claim, and here, too, he is on very strong ground.

Viewed in methodological terms, then, Hart's project appears to be to clarify, from an external perspective, our shared concept of law, focusing in particular on the idea that law purports to bind us through authoritative acts. The substantive theory itself falls into three related parts. First, there is the general account of obligation, which Hart analyses in terms of social rules. Second, there is the account of the family of legal concepts like authority, state, legislation, validity, and legal power, which Hart analyses in terms of a particular type of social rule, namely secondary rules accepted by officials. Third, there is the analysis of the concept of law itself. Here Hart's account is that law is the union of secondary rules, and in particular the rule of recognition, with those primary rules that the rule of recognition identifies as valid. To arrive at a better understanding of what Hart has in mind when he speaks in general of analysing or elucidating concepts, it will be helpful to examine in turn each of these three specific instances of analysis.

IV. EXTERNAL CONCEPTUAL ANALYSIS: OBLIGATION

As already mentioned, Hart analyses obligation, including legal obligation, in terms of social rules. A social rule exists when (some appropriate but unspecified proportion of) the members of a group accept a general pattern of behaviour as a common standard of conduct for all members of the group. Deviations from the pattern are regarded as justifying demands for conformity and warranting criticism that is typically expressed in the normative language of 'right', 'ought', 'should', etc. (55–7). In the Post-script, Hart has made clear that his account is meant to apply only to *conventional* rules—that is, rules for which the general conformity of the group constitutes at least part of the reason for individuals' acceptance of the relevant pattern as a common standard of conduct (255–6).

A social rule is spoken of as giving rise to an *obligation* when the social pressure underlying the rule is particularly serious or insistent (86). Hart mentions two other characteristics of obligation that he says 'go naturally together with this one'. First, '[t]he rules supported by this serious pres-sure are thought important because they are believed to be necessary to the maintenance of social life or some highly prized feature of it' (87). Hart gives the examples of rules that restrict the free use of violence, require honesty, and enforce promises. 'Secondly, it is generally recog-nized that the conduct required by these rules may, while benefiting others, conflict with what the person who owes the duty may wish to do' (87). He goes on to observe that obligations are thus commonly thought of as involving sacrifice or renunciation. Even so, those who accept an obligation-imposing rule need not do so because they regard it as morally binding. Acceptance can also be based on 'calculations of long-term inter-est; disinterested interest in others; an unreflecting inherited or traditional attitude; or the mere wish to do as others do' (203; cf. 257).

The essence of Hart's response to the problem of the normativity of law is thus to point to the phenomenon of acceptance, where acceptance need not be grounded in moral reasons. The majority (or some other appropri-ate minimal proportion) of a group's members regard a general pattern of conduct from the internal point of view, meaning they regard the conduct as a general standard that is binding or obligatory for everyone in the group. It is in these terms that Hart wishes to account for the normativity of social rules, and law involves a special case of a social rule, namely the rule of recognition. It is, however, not entirely clear whether Hart believes that acceptance of a social rule gives rise to an *actual* obligation for the relevant group's members. He plainly does not think that acceptance creates a moral obligation, but at various points he can be understood as suggesting that it gives rise to what might be called a social obligation. The basis and character of such an obligation would be rather mysterious, however,[18] and in any event the focus of Hart's theory is clearly on the

---

[18] See Ronald Dworkin, 'The Model of Rules II', in *Taking Rights Seriously*, rev. edn. (1977), 46. In a previous article I interpreted Hart as making the claim in *The Concept of Law* that

external descriptive statement that people *regard themselves* as obligated by the rule.

We must now ask the following question: to what extent can this external descriptive account of obligation be conceived as an analysis or elucidation of our common concept? Typically, the philosophical analysis of a concept attempts to make explicit what the theorist claims is in some sense already implicit in our common understanding. This can take the form of drawing attention to propositions that the theorist argues are either implicitly presupposed or necessarily entailed by the concept's having the content that it has. It can also take the form of an attempt to show that, properly understood, the concept is equivalent in either meaning or use to some other concept or concepts. Sometimes such an analysis will be explicitly and trivially semantic—for example, the statement that the concept 'bachelor' comprehends the concept 'unmarried'—but in interesting cases it will amount to a more ambitious philosophical attempt to *reduce* one concept to a logical configuration of others. Austin, for example, famously advanced a reductive analysis of obligation that Hart, in an equally famous critique, thoroughly demolished. The precise nature of a reduction is controversial, but perhaps we can say that it consists in an attempt to make explicit an alleged implicit equivalence in meaning

social rules do create a special form of non-moral obligation, but Jeremy Waldron has convinced me in conversation that this reading is probably mistaken. See Stephen R. Perry, 'Interpretation and Methodology in Legal Theory', in *Law and Interpretation*, ed. Andrei Marmor (1995), 97, 105, 115–16, 122. It is, however, true that in later work Hart speaks of the rule of recognition as giving judges what he calls 'an authoritative legal reason'. H. L. A. Hart, *Essays on Bentham: Studies in Jurisprudence and Political Theory* (1982), 160. The general tenor of the discussion in that work suggests that Hart thinks that judges really do have such a reason and not simply that they regard themselves as having one. If Hart did believe that social rules give rise to actual (non-moral) reasons for action, that would be, for reasons that will become clearer below, the first step toward a theory of law advanced from the internal point of view. But until normative argument were offered to support the otherwise mysterious claim that actual reasons for action are created, the theory would remain incomplete.

It is worth remarking that the claim that social rules necessarily give rise to actual (non-moral) reasons for action would yield a very strong form of internal theory. A weaker internal theory would argue that the concept of law, properly analysed, sets out the *conditions* under which law is in principle capable of giving rise to new reasons for action, but without claiming that such reasons are necessarily always (or even ever) created in fact. See further the discussion in Section VII below. As I note later in the text of the present section, Hart begins in the Postscript to offer a conventionalist account of law that can plausibly be interpreted as an internal theory in this weaker sense. In other work Hart has, of course, offered an account of political obligation that centres on the so-called principle of fair play. See H. L. A. Hart, 'Are There Any Natural Rights?', in *Theories of Rights*, ed. J. Waldron (1984), 77. If that account were correct, it would show that certain kinds of joint enterprise give rise to obligations that people would not otherwise have. But, as Waldron has recently emphasized, Hart does not think that instances of law are necessarily joint enterprises in the requisite sense. See Jeremy Waldron, 'All We Like Sheep', 12 Can. J.L. & Juris. 169 (1999). Going beyond this empirical point, it is clear that Hart also rejects the idea that our *concept* of law implicates the principle of fair play. This rules out the possibility of an internal theory—even a weak internal theory—that takes that principle as its starting point.

between the concept being analysed and the concepts to which it is ostensibly being reduced.

Finally, conceptual analysis can take the form of argument, within an established intellectual and cultural tradition, about the meaning and significance of the concept and its relationship to other concepts.[19] Sometimes such argument will be normative in character. But this does not involve us in any confusion because, as Joseph Raz points out, in the case of certain concepts 'there is an interdependence between conceptual and normative argument'.[20] Raz's example is authority, but the point is equally true of obligation. In fact, in the legal context the two concepts are closely intertwined, as it is by means of the exercise of authority that the law claims to create new obligations. I will have something to say in the following section about the nature of legal authority. For now, it will suffice to point out that an analysis of the concept of obligation might well take the form of normative argument attempting to establish the conditions under which obligations are not just claimed to exist but really do exist (focusing, perhaps, on obligations of a particular sort, such as conventional obligations, or obligations ostensibly created by authority). An alternative analysis might be similarly normative but with a sceptical outcome, arguing that there are no obligations of the kind in question.

Hart's externally oriented, descriptive account of obligation cannot be said to offer an analysis of that concept in any of the senses discussed in the preceding two paragraphs. It does not offer a normative argument as to when, if ever, social rules really do create obligations, as opposed to the perception of obligations. Certainly the descriptive statement that people *regard* themselves and others as obligated by a general practice cannot, without more, tell us if and when they are in fact so obligated. If, on the other hand, we try to interpret Hart as offering either a semantic or a reductive analysis of obligation, the account is plainly deficient. If the members of the relevant group regard themselves as obligated in the sense of obligation that is supposedly being analysed, then the account is circular. If they regard themselves as obligated in some different sense then, as Hart does not specify what that different sense is, the account is incomplete. In any event the only plausible candidate for that different sense would be moral obligation, and Hart is clear that those who adopt the internal point of view do not, or at least do not have to, regard themselves as obligated morally.

As it happens, Hart's account of obligation does not suffer from circularity or incompleteness, but that is because it cannot be regarded as a proper analysis. At its core it is simply a descriptive statement that (a

[19] Cf. Joseph Raz, *The Morality of Freedom* (1986), 63–4.
[20] *Id.* at 63.

certain proportion of) members of the relevant group regard themselves and all others in the group as obligated to conform to some general practice. This statement uses rather than analyses the concept of obligation. In the original text of *The Concept of Law* Hart in effect maintains that officials regard themselves and all other officials as obligated, in that unanalysed sense, by the general practice that constitutes the rule of recognition. To those who so regard themselves, this presumably does not come as news. If they or others want to know whether they are in fact under such an obligation, and if so why, enlightenment is not forthcoming. Precisely because Hart's account of obligation is descriptive and external, it cannot be said to have succeeded in clarifying or elucidating the concept in any significant way.

In the Postscript, Hart specifies that social rules must be understood as conventional practices. This means that members of the group (have reason to) regard themselves as obligated, at least in part, precisely because there is general conformity to the pattern of conduct that constitutes the social rule. We have here the beginning, but only the beginning, of one possible philosophical analysis of the concept of legal obligation. A complete analysis would need to tell us why and under what conditions the mere fact of general conformity to a pattern of conduct can help to create a reason for action, amounting to an obligation, for individuals to conform their own conduct to the pattern. While there are well-known philosophical accounts of conventionalism that attempt to answer these questions,[21] the thesis that law is underpinned by a conventional rule is nonetheless a controversial one. Dworkin famously disputed it in 'The Model of Rules II', for example.[22] This particular debate between Hart and Dworkin is philosophical in nature, not empirical. As I will argue more fully in the following sections, normative argument, probably of a moral and political nature, will be required to settle it. For now, I simply wish to draw attention to two points. First, the thought that such a debate might be required to settle an important question in legal theory suggests that more is at issue here than the neutral description of a social practice. Second and relatedly, such a debate seems best construed as taking place not between two outside observers but rather between two insiders, participants in the practice who disagree, on philosophical rather than on empirical grounds, about the practice's fundamental nature.

Recall that Hart was originally motivated to produce his theories of obligation, authority, and law by puzzles concerning the normativity of law. The essence of the problem of the normativity of law is philosophical: does law in fact obligate us in the way that it purports to do? This is

---

[21] Some of these are discussed very briefly in the following section.
[22] Dworkin, *supra* n. 18, at 53–4, 59–61.

an issue that arises within the philosophy of practical reason, and it would seem inevitable that its resolution will require normative and probably moral argument. An external description of the practice, to the effect that people *regard* themselves and others as obligated, is not likely to succeed in elucidating either the general concept of obligation or the specific claim that the law creates new obligations that would not otherwise exist.

V. EXTERNAL CONCEPTUAL ANALYSIS: AUTHORITY

The second part of Hart's substantive theory of law is the account he gives of such concepts as authority, legislation, and validity. These concepts must be understood, Hart argues, by reference to secondary social rules. The basic idea is that officials accept, and thereby regard themselves as obligated by, the rule of recognition and certain other secondary rules that Hart calls 'rules of change' and 'rules of adjudication' (91–9). All of these are second-order rules—that is, they are rules about (primary) rules.[23] Rules of change confer authority on legislatures and perhaps courts to create new primary rules and repeal or amend old ones. Rules of adjudication confer authority on courts to determine whether a primary rule has been broken. The rule of recognition provides authoritative criteria for identifying primary rules as valid, and imposes a duty on courts and perhaps other officials to apply those rules. Hart notes that close connections exist among these various types of secondary rule. The rule of recognition will necessarily make reference to any rules of change, and a rule of adjudication, conferring jurisdiction on courts, will in effect be a primitive form of a rule of recognition. Hart clearly regards the rule of recognition as the most fundamental secondary rule in a legal system.

As in the case of Hart's account of obligation, it is not clear that his account of the concepts of authority, validity, and so on is in any significant sense properly designated an *analysis*. This is so, at least, as long as he insists on sticking with an external, purely descriptive theoretical perspective. To see this, notice first that Hart maintains that statements *about* rules of recognition, to the effect either that they exist or that they possess or fail to possess value of some kind, are necessarily external in character (107–10). But there is no reason why participants in a social practice should have to hold a particular external view of their practice, or indeed any external view of it at all. As Hart notes, 'For the most part the rule of recognition is not stated, but its existence is *shown* in the way in which particular rules are identified, either by courts or other officials

---

[23] *See supra*, n. 4.

or private persons and their advisers' (101). All that needs necessarily be the case, apparently, is that a certain subgroup within the larger society—the so-called officials—regard themselves as bound by a rule that the externally observing theorist, but not necessarily the officials themselves, can characterize both as a social rule and as a rule of recognition. Neither officials nor others within the larger group require the general concept of either type of rule, which consequently need not enter—indeed, given Hart's insistence that statements about rules of recognition are necessarily external, perhaps cannot enter—into whatever conceptualization of their practice that they hold. The *idea* of a rule of recognition appears to be an external theoretical notion, an instance of which has, from outside the practice, been observed within it. But simply to make such an observation does not, without more, constitute a clarification or elucidation of the participants' own conceptual scheme.

This is not to deny that participants, upon being told by the friendly neighbourhood legal theorist that their practice contains a rule of recognition, would not learn something about themselves. But they would come by that knowledge, and in the process master the new concept of a rule of recognition, *qua* external observers of their own practice. Their new knowledge could therefore not be said to elucidate or clarify—to offer an analysis of—their internal conceptual scheme. Of course, the natural response at this point is to argue that, even though the participants did not previously possess the concept of a rule of recognition, that concept was implicitly presupposed by their internal concepts of authority, validity, legal power, etc. Even though the participants might not have realized it, their internal conceptual scheme had already committed them to the idea of a rule of recognition. When this commitment is made explicit, the conceptual scheme is thereby clarified or elucidated. This is a perfectly reasonable characterization of how conceptual clarification might take place. The difficulty, however, is that the claim that the participants' existing conceptual scheme implicitly presupposes the idea of a rule of recognition looks more like an internal than an external statement. It is not a passive description offered from without, but rather an active clarification offered from within. As for the possible suggestion that statements about rules of recognition can be both external descriptions and internal clarifications, that might well be true. But if, as Hart states, the primary purpose of his theorizing is conceptual clarification, then for theoretical purposes it is the internal statement that matters, not the external one. If Hart's theory is to succeed in achieving this purpose, then it must be an internal rather than an external theory.

Consider once again the debate between Dworkin and Hart that was mentioned briefly in the preceding section. Hart argues that law is underpinned by a conventional social rule, whereas Dworkin maintains that the foundation of law might be a concurrent rather than a conventional normative practice. A concurrent normative practice is one in which the members of a group 'are agreed in asserting the same, or much the same, normative rule, but they do not count the fact of agreement as an essential part of their grounds for asserting that rule'.[24] In the case of convention, the fact of agreement does count as an essential part of the case for accepting the rule. How would the debate to settle the question of whether law is a conventional or a concurrent normative practice proceed? One might begin by looking to the reasons that officials and others actually give, or would be prepared to give, for accepting the authority of law. This would be an empirical and a descriptive enterprise, and one that could be carried on from an external perspective. Moreover, it is at least conceivable that the members of the community under study might be in substantial and explicit agreement that theirs was a conventional practice in the sense just defined. If so, Hart could claim at least a limited victory in the debate. He would have succeeded in giving an external, purely descriptive account of a social practice that was, as advertised, conventional in character. At least in the special circumstances envisaged, the suggestion of the preceding paragraph that Hart must 'go internal' seems to be mistaken.

Notice, however, that Hart could only claim this limited victory in the unlikely event that there existed substantial explicit agreement among participants that theirs was, in fact, a conventional social practice. In that case, the idea of a rule of recognition—understood explicitly to be a conventional, second-order social rule—would already figure in their conceptualization of that practice. They would already possess, internally, the concept of a rule of recognition, although probably not under that name. Their conceptual scheme would therefore not stand in need of clarification or elucidation.

If, however, we assume with Hart that there *is* a need for clarification, and in particular a need to make people aware of a previously unacknowledged conceptual commitment to a rule of recognition, then by hypothesis there is no substantial explicit agreement that the practice is a conventional one. The empirical data underdetermine the theory. Not only does this appear to be the situation that Hart is implicitly assuming to be the case, but it represents by far the most plausible supposition about the way things actually are. Some people will simply not accept the authority of law. Others will do so because they believe that law is a conventional normative practice in something like Hart's sense. Yet others will believe, with Dworkin, that law is a concurrent normative practice. Many, perhaps the vast majority, will accept the authority of the law with-

---

[24] Dworkin, *supra* n. 18, at 53.

out any very clear sense of why they are doing so. And all of this will typically be as true of officials as it is of citizens in general. In light of these facts, Hart's limited victory seems out of reach.

Hart is undoubtedly correct that an important task of legal theory is making clear our implicit conceptual commitments and presuppositions. But the need for clarification only exists if there is confusion, uncertainty, or disagreement of some kind within the internal conceptualization of the practice. Clarification cannot be achieved by an external description, which if it is to be accurate must either mirror the facts of confusion, uncertainty, and disagreement or—and this would be to give up the game altogether—simply avoid the issue by omitting any reference to these facts. (Recall that all descriptions are to a greater or lesser degree selective.) Conceptual clarification is, unavoidably, an internal enterprise. At this point it might perhaps be argued that it does not really matter whether Hart's theory is offered from an internal or an external perspective. What matters is that the theory is *descriptive* in Hart's specific sense of being 'morally neutral and [without] justificatory aims' (240). The suggestion is, in other words, that Hart is just making clear our conceptual commitments without either commending or condemning them, in a manner that does not involve moral or normative argument.

If the suggestion of the preceding paragraph were correct, then elucidation of the relevant concepts would have to be essentially uncontroversial. If an instance of conceptual analysis were to be characterizable as simply descriptive and without a normative aspect, it would have to be, once offered, more or less incontestable; it would simply point out what was there to be seen but had not, for some reason, been previously noticed. The analysis in question would presumably have to take the form of a demonstration that the concepts of authority, validity, legislation, and so on all contain (no doubt implicitly) the notion of a rule of recognition as part of their meaning, or, perhaps, that the use of any of these concepts normally presupposes the existence of a rule of recognition. But both of these claims seem false on their face.

What is *perhaps* true is that the majority of the concepts with which Hart is concerned here, such as legislation, validity, and sovereignty, are all analysable, in some fairly straightforward and uncontroversial sense, in terms of the concept of *authority*. Authority, in fact, appears to be both the linchpin in this family of concepts and the one whose analysis is key to arriving at a satisfactory philosophical theory of law. This is because, as Hart implicitly recognizes in allowing the problem of the normativity of law to shape his initial theoretical inquiry, it appears to be a core aspect of our concept of law that law claims authority over us. It is part of our concept of law, in other words, that those 'in authority' claim to be able by their actions to create obligations for us that we would not otherwise

have. But the concept of (political or legal) authority is *not* straightforwardly and uncontroversially analysable in terms of the notion of a Hartian rule of recognition (i.e. in terms of a social or conventional rule). For
one thing, an account of authority that appeals to a concurrent rather than
to a conventional normative practice is, at the very least, arguable. In this
context, then, it seems inevitable that conceptual analysis will involve
more than just semantic or reductive analysis, or the making explicit of
normatively neutral presuppositions.

Dworkin maintains that in order to show that law is a concurrent
normative practice rather than a conventional one, he would need to
appeal to 'controversial principles of political morality'.[25] He would have
to argue, in other words, that law's claim to authority must be understood
by reference to some independent moral principle rather than by reference to a convention, where the argument to that effect would itself be
moral in nature. This seems basically correct. Authority is in fact Joseph
Raz's prime example of a concept whose analysis properly involves
normative argument, although he would probably not go so far as
Dworkin in saying that such argument must be a matter of political
morality. I will have something to say about Raz's own analysis of the
concept of authority in Section VII. For now I wish only to point out that
our main philosophical reason for wishing to analyse this concept must
surely be our interest in knowing what kinds of reason for action the law
claims systematically to create, as well as our associated interest in knowing whether or not it in fact creates them. This is the heart of the philosophical problem of the normativity of law, which as we have seen is one
of Hart's points of departure in formulating his theory.

Nonetheless, in the first edition of *The Concept of Law*, Hart ultimately
ignores both these questions by simply *describing*, from an external
perspective, the phenomenon of acceptance. He says that people could
accept a rule for any of a number of reasons, including moral belief and
self-interest, but implies that these reasons are irrelevant to legal theory.
He thereby refuses to look behind the brute social fact of acceptance in
order to ask whether and under what circumstances that acceptance is
justified. It is, however, only by means of such an inquiry that a solution
to the problem of the normativity of law will be found.[26] As was noted in

---

[25] *Id.* at 60–1.

[26] Jules Coleman recognizes that a jurisprudential theory must address the problem of the
normativity of law, and that doing so requires, among other things, that the theory furnish
an account of the concept of authority. He further recognizes that such an account must
show whether and under what circumstances the law's claim to authority is justified, meaning it must show whether and under what circumstances the law creates the reasons for
action it claims to create. Coleman, supra n. 12, at 296–305. Coleman holds that Hart's social
rule theory 'claims that the internal point of view transforms what would otherwise be a
non-normative description of a convergent practice . . . into a reasoning practice'. *Id.* at 299.

the preceding section, the descriptive statement that people *regard* themselves as obligated by a general practice cannot, by itself, tell us whether or not the practice really does obligate them.

In the Postscript, Hart in effect begins to offer the outline of an internal account of authority when he says that part of the reason for accepting the rule of recognition is the very fact of its general acceptance. For the reasons given earlier, this cannot be a simple empirical observation about the reasons that either officials or other people might say they have for accepting the authority of law. It must be, at least in part, a philosophical theory about the reasons they really do (or at least might in principle) have, whether they acknowledge it at present or not. The process of conceptual clarification consists precisely in making clear what these reasons are, and that is why Raz is right to say that normative argument is involved. As it happens Hart's theory is incomplete, because he does not say why general conformity could be part of a reason for accepting a rule. There are, of course, well-known answers to this question. General conformity to some practice can solve a coordination problem or serve as a guide to what ought independently to be done.[27] General conformity can also make a type of activity that would otherwise be futile—that would be futile, in other words, if undertaken by one person or a few individuals only—morally worthwhile.[28]

The larger problem with Hart's inchoate internal theory is not its incompleteness in this sense, but rather that it cannot offer an account of the law's claim to authority over *everyone*.[29] Hart says that the rule of recognition is a practice defined by the attitudes of officials and no one else; although others in society might also share the internal point of view, it is possible to imagine extreme cases where the rule of recognition is accepted only by officials (117). But a social rule cannot in general give convention-based reasons for action to anyone other than those who

---

Athough I once thought this view of Hart's intent was correct (see *supra* n. 18), I now have my doubts. It seems to me that Hart is primarily concerned with describing the practice of law from the outside, and that in consequence he simply sets aside the problem of the normativity of law with which he begins. In any event, Coleman correctly argues that even for officials a rule of recognition cannot be authoritative simply in virtue of being a social rule, because acceptance from the internal point of view does not by itself give anyone a reason for action. He does suggest, however, that such acceptance might be a *reliable indicator* that the practice has independent normative force. This is compatible with its being a concurrent normative practice in Dworkin's sense. Coleman also suggests, as Hart eventually came to accept in the Postscript, that the rule of recognition might be the basis of a conventional social practice. Coleman, *supra* n. 12, at 300–2.

[27] See *id.* at 300–2.

[28] Cf. *Raz, supra* n. 7, at 247–8. Of course, in this type of case general conformity is only a necessary condition for the existence of a reason for action, and not a sufficient condition; the activity must also be morally worthwhile for independent reasons.

[29] Cf. Coleman, *supra* n. 12, at 298, 302. See also Jules L. Coleman and Brian Leiter, 'Legal Positivism', in *A Companion to Philosophy and Legal Theory*, ed. D. Patterson (1996), 241, 247–8.

belong to the conforming group. The upshot is that the rule of recognition, understood as a conventional practice among officials, can in general give only officials conventional reasons. The general citizenry over whom the law claims authority, or at least those who do not personally accept the rule of recognition as a convention applicable to them, have no such reasons. (Of course, they might have other reasons to obey the law, such as self-interest or independent principles of morality, but these reasons are not claimed to be systematically generated by the rule of recognition.) It is part of our concept of law, however, that law claims authority over everyone, thereby ostensibly obligating them in ways in which they would not otherwise be obligated, whether they accept the institutions of the law or not. The theory of the rule of recognition, far from being the sole possible basis for analysing the concept of authority, thus turns out to be incapable, at least in the form presented by Hart, of providing any viable analysis of that concept. Beyond purporting to impose a duty of enforcement on officials, all the rule of recognition does is set out formal criteria of validity for other rules. As Jules Coleman points out, 'validity is truth preserving [but] it is not authority preserving'.[30]

VI. EXTERNAL CONCEPTUAL ANALYSIS: LAW

The third part of Hart's substantive theory of law is the account he gives of the nature of law itself. The basic claim of that account is, as we have seen, that every legal system contains secondary rules and, in particular, a rule of recognition. Hart argues that the notion of a rule of recognition lies at the core of the concept of law, presumably meaning by this our concept. I noted in Section II that even if the argument discussed in the preceding section were correct, to the effect that the concepts of authority, validity, etc., must be analysed in terms of the notion of a rule of recognition, it would not, without more, entail that that notion is central to the concept of law.

To establish this latter proposition Hart therefore offers the following argument (91–9). He claims that a regime of primary rules is, as compared to a system containing a rule of recognition and other secondary rules, defective in certain respects: more particularly, such a regime is uncertain, static, and inefficient in the application of social pressure. Primary rules might be capable of guiding conduct—this being, according to Hart, the central function of law (39–40, 249)—but they do not do so well. The defects of a regime of primary rules are, however, remedied by the introduction of secondary rules. The status and content of primary rules—

---

[30] Coleman, *supra* n. 12, at 298.

meaning now rules that are identified by the rule of recognition as valid—can be more readily determined, and the rules can be changed deliberately and enforced by centrally imposed sanctions. Hart states that consideration of these remedies 'show[s] why law may most illuminatingly be characterized as a union of primary rules of obligation with . . . secondary rules' (94).

As was noted in Section II, this defence of the thesis that the concept of law must be understood by reference to the notion of a secondary rule appeals to evaluative judgments. A regime of primary rules is said to be defective, and its defects are said to be remedied by the introduction of secondary rules. Because these judgments are concerned with the guidance of conduct, they are not just evaluative but normative. It is, moreover, the very social practices under study that are being evaluated. By contrast, the metatheoretical criteria that figure in the descriptive-explanatory method are non-normative, and they are used to evaluate only theories, not the subject matter of theories. The fact that Hart appeals to normative judgments does not mean, of course, that the concept of law which rests on those judgments ceases to be descriptive. Hart's concept has the content that it has quite independently of the character of the theorizing he employs to defend it, and, as we saw in Section II, his concept identifies social practices as instances of law on the basis of purely factual, non-normative criteria.

For similar reasons, Hart's reliance on normative judgments at the level of methodology does not call into question the status of his theory as a version of substantive legal positivism. What does seem to be called into question, however, is his claim to be a methodological positivist. Insofar as he defends a particular theoretical characterization of law by appealing to the idea that secondary rules remedy the defects of regimes of primary rules, he cannot plausibly maintain that he is simply describing an existing conceptual scheme. He is opting for one conceptualization of social practices over others on the basis of normative argument.

The discussion in the preceding two sections suggests that Hart fails to achieve his goal of elucidating the concepts of obligation and authority, and thus fails to come to grips with the problem of the normativity of law, because he insists on simply describing the phenomenon of acceptance rather than inquiring into the conditions under which acceptance might be justified. That insistence on Hart's part is rooted in his commitment to methodological positivism. It might therefore be thought that, by implicitly abandoning methodological positivism in the development of his general theory of law, Hart has positioned himself to offer an account of the concept of law that is philosophically more satisfactory than those he offers of obligation and authority. That turns out not to be the case, however. The problem is that a satisfactory account of the concept of law must rest on a satisfactory account of the law's claim to authority (i.e. the claim that actions by those possessing authority give us obligations we would not otherwise have). Although Hart appears to abandon methodological positivism in the final stages of constructing his general theory of law, the accounts of obligation and authority upon which the theory builds are themselves developed, as we have seen, in accordance with the precepts of methodological positivism. The ultimate theory cannot transcend this starting point.

As I shall argue more fully in the following section, a philosophically satisfactory analysis of the concept of legal authority, and hence a philosophically satisfactory analysis of the concept of law that takes the law's claim to authority seriously (as Hart's theory at least purports to do), must be offered from the internal point of view. Such a theory will try to make sense of law to *us*—that is, to those who engage in or are subject to law—by offering an account of whether and how the law's claim to authority over us might be justified. It will do this by attributing a point or function to law and showing how law's serving that function either does give us, or could under certain conditions give us, reasons for action of a specified type. In specifying one type of reason for action over another the theory will attempt to refine our initial, rough, and partially unclear conceptualization of our own practice. In Hart's terms, 'the framework of legal thought' will thereby be clarified or elucidated. It is only in this way—looking at the practice from the participants' point of view, and employing normative argument—that conceptual clarification can take place.

This is not to deny that our conceptual scheme, as it exists at any given time, can be neutrally described from the outside. But such a description must faithfully mirror all confusions and disagreements. It does not clarify anything, and it is not a philosophical theory. A philosophical theory has the capability of clarifying, but it can only do so from the inside. Substantive legal positivism is one such clarifying theory—more precisely, it is a family of related theories—but there are others, such as Dworkin's theory of law as integrity. Sceptical theories, which argue that law has no point or function and is incapable of giving us reasons for action that we would not otherwise have, are also possible. The philosophy of law consists of a debate among proponents of different such accounts which takes place, in effect, within the social practice of law itself.

Now it might seem that, by attributing the function of guiding conduct to certain social practices and then offering an account of law that is based on judgments about how well various of those practices serve this function, Hart has, despite his claim to be offering an external theory, effectively joined the internal debate. The difficulty with this suggestion is that

Hart makes no attempt, at least in the main text of *The Concept of Law,* to show how law's serving the function of guiding conduct could give anyone a reason for action.[31] The explanation for why he makes no such attempt is, presumably, that he insists on describing the phenomenon of acceptance from an external point of view, without considering whether and under what conditions such acceptance might be justified. And the reason that he insists on limiting his theory in this way is his initial commitment to methodological positivism. Thus, even if he implicitly abandons methodological positivism in the later stages of his theory, his commitment to it at the earlier stages prevents him from offering a theory of law of the kind discussed in the two preceding paragraphs.

Because Hart makes no attempt to show how law's having the function of guiding conduct could give anyone a reason for action, his attribution of this particular function to law, together with the associated judgments about the remedying effects of secondary rules, are best understood as being offered from an external rather than an internal perspective. Hart construes the guidance of conduct as a form of 'social control' (40). The theorist, looking at the practice from the outside, is in a position to assess the (moral) value of social control, to determine which social practices are best able to achieve such control, and to make the judgment that control is only possible if a sufficient number of people internalize legal rules by adopting the internal point of view. But this is to look at the phenomenon of acceptance in a completely instrumental fashion. From the theory's external perspective, it does not matter why people accept the rule of recognition and/or the legal system generally, nor does it matter whether it is possible to justify such acceptance *to them* (i.e. as individuals). All that matters is that they accept it. It is to look at the social practice in question as a kind of invisible hand. The benefits of social control, if any, will be achieved as long as there is sufficient acceptance. The actual reasons for acceptance, and the possibility or impossibility of justifying that accep- tance to individuals, are irrelevant. At one point Hart writes that to mention the fact that members of a group look upon a general pattern of conduct from the internal point of view 'is to bring into account the way in which the group regards its own behaviour' (90). But to bring into

---

[31] As was noted in Sections IV and V, Hart begins in the Postscript to offer the outline of an internal theory, based on the idea that the rule of recognition creates convention-based reasons for action. This theory is incomplete and, for the reasons noted at the end of Section V, it is also problematic in its own terms. The important point for present purposes, however, is that this is a theoretical undertaking quite different from Hart's stated aim of simply describing, from the outside, the acceptance of social rules and other, related, social phenom- ena. The aim now is not simply to describe people's beliefs that law gives them reasons for action, but to show how and why it *in fact* gives them reasons for action. This new theoreti- cal undertaking involves a complete abandonment of methodological positivism and would, if carried to completion, yield an internal theory of law.

account the way in which the group regards its own behaviour it is not enough simply to describe their adoption of the internal point of view. We must inquire into their reasons, actual or possible, for adopting that point of view, and this is precisely what Hart refuses to do.

The argument supporting Hart's general theory of law, on the interpretation of the theory that was advanced in the preceding paragraph, has normative elements. This interpretation supposes that he has implicitly abandoned methodological positivism, or at least has abandoned the goal of offering a description of social practices that in no way depends on normative argument, but that he has nonetheless retained methodological positivism's external stance. A theory of law that takes this form is perfectly possible, and is indeed properly characterized as a philosophical theory. Let me call theories like this, which attribute a point or function to social practices from the outside, *external theories*. External philosophical theories can coexist with internal theories, which attribute a point or function to social practices from the participants' point of view. (There is no reason why a point cannot be ascribed to a social practice both internally and externally.) What an external theory cannot do, however, is claim to offer an analysis or elucidation of the participants' own conceptualization of their practice, which, in the case of law, means an elucidation of our shared concept of law. Only internal theories can do that. If a concept of law can appropriately be said to emerge from Hart's theory, it must be regarded as Hart's concept, not ours.

Moreover, an external theory like Hart's must compete with other external theories, which will conceptualize and perhaps individuate social practices in yet different ways. These theories will either attribute a different point or function to those practices (but always from an external perspective) or else will advance a different view of how social control, say, is best achieved. Holmes's theory of law, for example, can be regarded as an external theory which holds that social control is most readily maintained, not by the internalization of norms, but rather by coercion and the threat of punishment.[32] Holmes thus rejects the law's internal conceptual scheme, based on the notions of authority, obligation, and so on, as empty and a sham. As this is an external, normative critique of law, it is not touched by Hart's demolition of Austin's attempt to offer a reductive analysis of these concepts. A different kind of external theory, this time based on a natural law view, would argue that the point or function of law is, when viewed from the outside, to achieve justice, and thus only those social practices (of such-and-such an institutional character) that are in

---

[32] Cf. Stephen R. Perry, 'Holmes versus Hart: The Bad Man in Legal Theory', in *The Legacy of Oliver Wendell Holmes: The Path of the Law and Its Influence*, ed. S. J. Burton (Cambridge, Cambridge University Press, 2000), 158, 161–76.

fact just are properly called law. The nature of the philosophical debate among proponents of different external theories is not entirely clear.[33] Perhaps it is a form of pure political theory. At any rate, what it cannot be is a debate about how our shared concept of law should be clarified or elucidated.

VII. INTERNAL CONCEPTUAL ANALYSIS

If we take seriously Hart's apparent goal of analysing *our* framework of legal thought and *our* concept of law, then we must give up methodological positivism completely. This means abandoning not only the aspirations of methodological positivism to normatively untainted description but also its external perspective. A philosophical theory that has the goal of clarifying the way we conceptualize our social practices must attempt, from our own point of view, to make those practices transparent to us. In the case of law, this means showing that the law's claim to authority over us is always justified, showing that it is justified only under certain conditions (which might not always hold), or showing that it is never justified. In this section I offer a brief overview of this approach to doing legal theory.

A philosophical analysis of the concept of law can be regarded as an attempt to understand the nature of the social practice of law because the concept is very much bound up with our understanding of the practice, and in particular with our understanding of the way in which we take that practice to affect our reasons for action. As Raz has observed, 'The concept of law . . . plays a role in the way in which ordinary people as well as the legal profession understand their own and other people's actions'.[34] He goes on to note that 'the culture and tradition of which the concept is a part provide it with neither sharply defined contours nor with a clearly identifiable focus'; it is thus the task of legal theory to identify, from among various and

---

[33] I noted at the beginning of this essay that Michael Moore has adopted what could be regarded as a variant of methodological positivism. See Moore, *supra* n. 2. Moore says that the task of jurisprudence is 'descriptive', but he clearly includes moral facts about a social practice among the attributes that can figure in a description. Moreover, he sees the task of legal theory as showing law to be a 'functional kind', i.e. a type of institution which necessarily, in a metaphysical and not just a conceptual sense, uniquely serves some good. It might be better, therefore, to see Moore as a theorist who is seeking an external theory of the kind described in the text, rather than as a methodological positivist. His characterization of the debate among proponents of external theories would then be that each is putting forward a different understanding of the metaphysical essence of law. This is a coherent methodological view, but, as I have argued elsewhere, there does not seem to be any good reason to regard law as a functional kind in the way that gold and water are claimed by some philosophers to be natural kinds; there is no reason, that is, to view law as a type of entity having an essential nature. See Perry, *supra* n. 18, at 124 n. 62.

[34] *See* Raz, *supra* n. 12, at 321.

sometimes conflicting ideas, 'those which are central and significant to the way the concept plays its role in people's understanding of society'.[35] Raz elaborates on some of the methodological implications of this conception of legal theory in the following passage:

[I]t would be wrong to conclude . . . that one judges the success of an analysis of the concept of law by its theoretical sociological fruitfulness. To do so is to miss the point that, unlike concepts like 'mass' or 'electron', 'the law' is a concept used by people to understand themselves. We are not free to pick any fruitful concepts. It is a major task of legal theory to advance our understanding of society by helping us understand how people understand themselves.[36]

All this seems correct, and it helps to explain why legal theory does not involve an application of the descriptive-explanatory method of science. But it does not show the precise sense in which philosophical theories that set out to clarify the concept of law are properly called internal. The claim I wish to make is that the 'internality' of such a theory derives from the fact that it attempts to clarify the conceptual framework of the law by, among other things, addressing the problem of law's normativity. Such a theory either argues that law does not and cannot give rise to obligations that we would not otherwise have, in which case it is a sceptical theory, or else it attempts to make clear the conditions under which the law's claim to authority could be justified. A theory of the former kind argues, in effect, that law does not have any point or function, at least when viewed from an internal perspective. A theory of the latter kind attributes a function to law and then attempts to show how that function's being served could give those subject to law reasons for action they would not otherwise have. In specifying a particular type of reason for action, it proposes a clarifying refinement of the law's conceptual framework. Typically, this will take the form of a normative analysis of the concept of legal obligation. Generally speaking, a conception of the person as a practical reasoner will be at least implicit in such a theory, as it must claim that those subject to law are capable of acting upon reasons of the specified type.[37] A sceptical theory attempts to show, in effect, that law could never be justified. A non-sceptical theory attempts to show the opposite. In both cases the concern is with justification from the point of view of those who are subject to law: the question is whether law could give *them* (moral)

---

[35] *Id.*   [36] *Id. at* 321–2.

[37] For example, a Hobbesian theory of law, under an internal rather than an external interpretation, will adopt a conception of the person as a rational utility maximizer. By contrast, theories that argue that law gives rise or is capable of giving rise to moral reasons for action must suppose that people are capable of acting upon such reasons. See further Perry, *supra* n. 32, at 168–76.

obligations they would not otherwise have. It is in that sense that these theories are internal.[38]

As I have argued elsewhere, the methodology for legal theory that is outlined in the previous paragraph is, in all essential respects, Dworkin's interpretivism.[39] Space precludes an extended discussion, but let me go over some of the main points. Dworkin is, in the first instance, concerned with social practices that manifest a special 'interpretive attitude'. This attitude has two components:

> The first is the assumption that the practice . . . does not simply exist but has value, that it serves some interest or purpose or enforces some principle—in short, that it has some point—that can be stated independently of just describing the rules that make up the practice. The second is the further assumption that the requirements of [the practice]—the behavior it calls for or judgments it warrants— are not necessarily or exclusively what they have always been taken to be but are instead sensitive to its point.[40]

In cases where the interpretive attitude holds, participants conceptualize their practice in a certain way. They assume that the practice at least potentially has *requirements,* meaning that it gives rise, or could give rise, to reasons for action for them. It thus makes sense that Dworkin speaks of 'interpretive concepts' as well as of the interpretation of practices. He is concerned with practices whose associated concepts are, as was suggested earlier to be the case with law, intimately bound up with the way participants understand their own actions. The interpretive attitude is constituted by the following assumptions: first, the relevant social practice has a point or value; and second, the manner in which the practice affects reasons for action depends on what that point or value is taken to be. These are also the assumptions that underpin a non-sceptical internal theory of law.

Different 'justifications' or 'interpretations' of a social practice are, according to Dworkin, associated with different attributions of a point or value to it; in the case of law, these amount to different theories of law. The term 'justification' is somewhat ambiguous, but let me suggest that in the present context it refers to a proposal concerning how to make the best possible moral sense of a practice, from the participants' point of view. In Dworkin's terminology, one tries to put the practice in the best possible moral light. This involves showing how the practice, construed in terms

---

[38] Cf. Finnis, *supra* n. 5, at 14–15: 'If there is a point of view in which legal obligation is treated as at least presumptively a moral obligation . . . a viewpoint in which the establishment and maintenance of legal as distinct from discretionary or statically customary order is regarded as a moral ideal if not a compelling demand of justice, then such a viewpoint will constitute the central case of the legal viewpoint.'

[39] *See* Perry, *supra* n. 18, at 121–35.

[40] Dworkin, *supra* n. 8, at 47.

of a certain point or function that might plausibly be attributed to it, could under specified conditions give rise to moral obligations for participants that they would not otherwise have. The idea is to make moral sense of the practice by showing people why and under what circumstances they might have reason to comply with it. A sceptical theory will argue that they could never have such reason, but, as Dworkin quite rightly insists, sceptical theories must establish their conclusions by means of moral argument.

It should be noted that offering an internal justification for a practice does not commit a theorist to saying the practice is 'justified' in any absolute sense, so that it should not be changed or abolished. A non-sceptical justification tries to make the best moral case that can be made for a social practice. But the fact that such a case can be made, and that the practice should in consequence be regarded as reason-creating, does not mean that it should not be replaced by an even better reason-creating practice. Thus, it does not follow from the fact that an internal justification can be offered for tort law that tort law should not be replaced by, say, a social compensation scheme.[41]

I am suggesting, then, that a 'justification' in Dworkin's sense is concerned with illuminating the *conditions* under which an existing type of institution could give rise to obligations. It is not *directly* concerned with showing that such obligations do in fact arise, although the more unlikely it is that the posited conditions can exist—or rather, the more difficult it is to bring those conditions into existence—the less morally plausible the proposed justification will be. Thus, Dworkin's own substantive theory of law as integrity does not claim that law necessarily gives rise to what he calls associative obligations. Rather, the claim is that law's point or function is to justify state coercion by creating a certain kind of community, namely one that is based on the political ideal of integrity. This is best understood as a claim about our *concept* of law. Associative political obligations are said to arise in fact only when the conditions of integrity are met. These are, roughly, that members of the community reciprocally accept that they have special responsibilities toward one another, and that they plausibly suppose that their community's practices manifest an equal concern toward all members.[42]

---

[41] Cf. Jules L. Coleman, *Risks and Wrongs* (1992), 401–5.

[42] Dworkin, *supra* n. 8, at 197–202. The theory of law as integrity is meant to address what Dworkin calls 'the puzzle of legitimacy'. *Id.* at 190–5. It is possible to imagine 'external' accounts of law's legitimacy, which could well be associated with the kind of external philosophical theory that was discussed in the preceding section. These would argue for the moral legitimacy of state coercion without supposing that those subject to coercion have an obligation to comply. See e.g. Robert Ladenson, 'In Defence of a Hobbesian Conception of Law', 9 Phil. & Pub. Aff. 134 (1980). But for Dworkin legitimacy is intimately concerned with the question, 'Do citizens have genuine moral obligations just in virtue of Law?' Dworkin,

It is worth noting that nothing in Dworkin's interpretivism, understood strictly as a philosophical methodology for studying social practices, turns on the use of the word 'interpretation' or on the meaning the word bears in other contexts. Thus, nothing turns on whether legal practice can be treated as a 'text' in the sense of some more general theory of interpretation. It is possible to make all the methodological claims about legal theory that Dworkin wishes to make without bringing in the idea of interpretation at all, as I showed earlier in my characterization of internal theories. It is true that Dworkin himself maintains that there are connections between interpretivism, understood in the narrow methodological sense, and the interpretation of works of art. But those claims are severable from the case that can be made for the use of the interpretivist methodology in legal theory. It has thus been suggested, plausibly enough, that the goal of artistic interpretation is not to put objects of art in the best possible aesthetic light,[43] but it does not follow that the goal of a certain kind of legal theory is not to put the practices of law in the best possible moral light.

Raz's theory of law is an internal theory in the sense I have outlined here.[44] It is worth briefly elaborating on this point, because as a version of substantive legal positivism the theory bears some resemblance to Hart's, yet it rests on quite different methodological premises. Raz characterizes the function of law, in terms reminiscent of Hart, as the guidance of conduct by means of publicly ascertainable rules.[45] But Raz, unlike Hart, offers normative argument to show how law's serving this function could give people reasons for action. This argument is initially offered as an analysis of the concept of authority. However, because Raz recognizes that it is part of the concept of law that the law claims legitimate authority for itself—meaning that courts, legislatures, and other legal institutions claim to create, through the issuing of directives, obligations that people would not otherwise have—the normative argument he advances ultimately figures in his analysis of the concept of law itself.

supra n. 8, at 191. Dworkin's substantive theory of law can thus be interpreted as an attempt to outline the conditions under which the law's conceptual claim to authority is justified. For Dworkin, however, that claim must be construed in a broader sense than I have construed it elsewhere in this essay. Essentially following Raz, I have supposed that the law's claim to authority is a claim that citizens are obligated by (and only by) the specific acts of those *in authority*. But Dworkin must suppose that law's claim to obligate is broader than this, as his substantive theory argues that citizens are obligated not only by the specific acts of authorities but by the best justification of the settled law. Indeed, it is precisely because Dworkin maintains that the *concept* of law involves the moral idea of 'best justification' that his substantive theory is not a positivist one. (He does not become a positivist simply because, recognizing that the conditions of integrity might not be met in practice, he accepts that actual legal systems do not necessarily obligate.)

[43] Andrei Marmor, *Interpretation and Legal Theory* (1992), 52–3.
[44] Cf. Perry, *supra* n. 18, at 125–31.   [45] *Raz, supra* n. 7, at 50–2.

Raz offers what he characterizes as a normative-explanatory account of the concept of authority.[46] According to this account, which he labels the 'service conception', the law's conceptual claim to possess legitimate authority must be understood in terms of the following thesis. The normal way to establish that one person has authority over another involves showing that the latter is likely better to comply with the reasons for action that apply to him if he follows the former's directives than if he acts on his own judgment (the normal justification thesis). Let me call the reasons that apply to a person 'underlying reasons'. To the extent that the underlying reasons are moral in nature, the law's claim to have legitimate authority will be a moral claim. If the law has legitimate authority in the sense explained, then its directives will be reasons for action in their own right, excluding direct reliance on the underlying reasons. According to Raz, the directives of a legitimate authority *replace* the underlying reasons, and hence are what he calls exclusionary or pre-emptive reasons for action. This is why the law claims to create obligations or duties, and not just reasons to be weighed in the balance against other reasons. On the question of whether political authority ever is legitimate, Raz concludes that 'while [this] argument does confer qualified and partial authority on just governments it invariably fails to justify the claims to authority which these governments make for themselves'.[47]

Raz's argument for the service conception of authority is moral in nature. If it is right, then the anarchist thesis that the state could never have the moral authority it claims is wrong. The theory sets out moral conditions of legitimacy which Raz holds are implicit in the concept of law and which must be met if the law is to give rise to obligations that people would not otherwise have. Raz's theory of law is thus also a political philosophy that is in direct competition with, among others, Dworkin's integrity theory (itself both a theory of law and a political philosophy). I am not concerned here to mediate this dispute, but simply to point it out and say something about its nature. The two theories yield rival normative analyses of the concept of legal obligation; in consequence, they also yield rival accounts of how our concept of law should be elucidated and further refined. Raz argues that the law claims to create, in accordance with the normal justification thesis, exclusionary reasons; Dworkin, that it claims to create associative obligations. There is controversy about the appropriate normative and conceptual analysis of legal obligation even among positivists. Thus, Bentham's normatively defended version of positivism makes the conceptual claim that legal directives add to, rather than replace, the reasons for action people

---

[46] See Raz, *supra* n. 12, at 295–305; Raz, *supra* n. 19, at 38–105.
[47] *Id.* at 78.

already have.[48] Deciding among these various theories is not just a matter of determining which succeeds in better describing a pre-existing but partially implicit conceptualization of a social practice. There is no such conceptualization that, as Hart would apparently have it, can simply be described. This is philosophically contested ground, and the disagreement must ultimately be settled by moral and political argument intended to show which theory makes the best moral sense of the social practice we call law. In this way legal theory inevitably incorporates political philosophy.

VIII. CONCLUSION

Hart makes two very important methodological points in *The Concept of Law*. The first is that a philosophical theory of law involves conceptual analysis, meaning the clarification or elucidation of the concept of law and of 'the general framework of legal thought'. The second is that a philosophical theory should attempt to come to grips with certain puzzling issues concerning the normativity of law (5–13). I take this second point to mean that a philosophical theory of law should address the problem of the normativity of law. But Hart's own substantive theory does not offer a satisfactory conceptual analysis, nor does it truly come to grips with law's normativity. The reason for this, I have argued, is that Hart is also committed to methodological positivism, which holds that a theory of law should offer external descriptions of legal practice that are 'morally neutral [and] without justificatory aims' (240). Hart's own theory of law, being external, is admittedly without justificatory aims: it does not try to show participants how the social practice of law might be justified to them. But the theory is not, I have argued, morally neutral. Even so it does not offer a solution to the problem of the normativity of law in the way that, say, Raz's theory does. One reason for this is precisely that the theory is external; another is that it rests on a purely descriptive account of the concepts of obligation and authority. As far as these latter concepts are concerned, Hart is content simply to make the observation that officials and perhaps others accept the rule of recognition, meaning they *regard* it as obligation-imposing. This is to describe the problem of the normativity of law rather than to offer a solution.

The substantive difficulties faced by Hart's theory thus have methodological roots. The related philosophical goals of analysing the concept of law and addressing the problem of the normativity of law are plausible and appropriate ones for legal theory, but they cannot be accomplished by

[48] See Postema, *supra* n. 1, at 323–7.

taking an external, purely descriptive approach. Hart seems to have borrowed the idea of a purely descriptive theory from the methodology of science, which is a very different kind of theoretical enterprise from philosophy. The result, from a methodological perspective, is an unsatisfactory hybrid. Of course, I do not mean to deny that it is possible to describe a social practice in a more or less neutral fashion and from an external point of view. As was noted in Section III, there are indefinitely many descriptions that can be offered of any given practice, although most of them are entirely lacking in interest or theoretical significance. If there is conceptual confusion, lack of clarity, or disagreement within the practice, an accurate external description must simply report that fact; it cannot offer clarification.

Descriptions that are offered in accordance with the descriptive-explanatory method are potentially of scientific interest, but they will not necessarily track the participants' own conceptualization of their practice, nor will they offer an elucidation of that conceptualization that speaks to them as participants. Descriptive-explanatory theories are not philosophical in nature, and in particular they do not address the problem of the normativity of law. External philosophical theories are possible, as we saw in Section VI, and Hart's general account of law can be understood in these terms. But such theories, although grounded in normative argument, also do not come to grips with the normativity of law. The predominant tradition in Anglo-American legal theory, from Hobbes and Bentham to Coleman, Dworkin, Finnis, Postema, and Raz (but excluding Austin and Waluchow along the way), has always supposed that the provision of an account of law's normativity has been a central task of jurisprudence. Hart professes to take that task seriously, but his commitment to methodological positivism prevents him from following through.

10

Legal Realism, Hard Positivism, and the Limits of Conceptual Analysis

BRIAN LEITER

I. INTRODUCTION

The American Legal Realists, as I read them, are *tacit* legal positivists: they presuppose views about the criteria of legality that have affinities with positivist accounts of law in the sense that they employ primarily pedigree tests of legal validity.[1] Since Dworkin's well-known critique of Hart's positivism a generation ago, however, it has been hotly contested whether there is anything about positivism as a legal theory that requires that tests of legal validity be pedigree tests. So-called 'Soft' or 'Inclusive' versions of positivism are willing to relax the restrictions on the content of a rule of recognition to admit non-pedigree criteria of legal validity; 'Hard' or 'Exclusive' versons of positivism deny that such a move is compatible with the central commitments of positivism. Hard Positivism, of which Raz has been the leading proponent,[2] thus competes with various Soft Positivisms,[3] defended by, among others, Coleman, Lyons, Soper, Waluchow and now, explicitly, Hart himself in the 'Postscript'.[4] If the Realists

I am grateful to the students in my Fall 1997 seminar at UT Austin on 'Legal Positivism' for help in thinking about these issues, and to Brian Bix, Jules Coleman, John Gardner, Neil MacCormick, Joseph Raz, Scott Shapiro, and Stephen A. Smith for useful comments on earlier drafts. This is a revised version of an essay that originally appeared at 4 Legal Theory 533 (1998).

[1] For the arguments to this effect, see Brian Leiter, 'Legal Realism', in *A Companion to the Philosophy of Law and Legal Theory*, ed. Dennis Patterson (1996), 261, 268–9, and 'Legal Realism and Legal Positivism Reconsidered', 111 Ethics (2001).

[2] See e.g. Joseph Raz, 'Legal Positivism and the Sources of Law', in *The Authority of Law* (1979) (hereafter LPSL) and 'Authority, Law and Morality', 68 The Monist 295 (1985) (hereafter ALM).

[3] Some writers call the view 'Inclusive Positivism' or 'Incorporationism'. I follow Hart's terminology in the text, even though 'Soft' runs the risk of a pejorative connotation.

[4] Jules Coleman, 'Negative and Positive Positivism', repr. in *Ronald Dworkin and Contemporary Jurisprudence*, ed. Marshall Cohen (1983) (hereafter NPP); Jules Coleman, 'Incorporationism, Conventionality and the Practical Difference Thesis', 4 Legal Theory 381 (1998) (hereafter 'Incorporationism'); David Lyons, 'Principles, Positivism and Legal Theory', 87 Yale Law Journal 415 (1977); E. Philip Soper, 'Legal Theory and the Obligation of a Judge: The Hart/Dworkin Dispute', 75 Michigan Law Review 473 (1977); W. J. Waluchow, *Inclusive Legal Positivism* (1994); H. L. A. Hart, 'Postscript', in *The Concept of Law*, 2nd edn., ed. P. Bulloch and J. Raz (1994) (hereafter Postscript). Leslie Green argues, plausibly, that *The*

are positivists, as I claim, then it cannot be the case that Soft Positivism is a genuinely positivistic doctrine. But there is more at stake here than just labels. Realist arguments for the indeterminacy of law—arguments central to the whole Realist enterprise—depend crucially on their tacit Hard Positivism.[5] If, in fact, positivism has a more relaxed view of the criteria of legality than Hard Positivism supposes, then Realist arguments depend on unsound tacit premises about legal validity. What is at stake, then, is not whether Realists should be called (tacit) 'Positivists' or merely (tacit) 'Hard Positivists', but whether their underlying view of the criteria of legality is sound. It can only be so if the best arguments favour Hard Positivism.

II. POSITIVISM

Let us try to say now, more precisely, what is at stake in the dispute between Hard and Soft positivists. All positivists accept what we may call the Separation Thesis (what the law *is* and what the law *ought* to be are separate questions) and the Social Thesis (what counts as law in any society is fundamentally a matter of social fact).[6] They differ over the proper interpretation of these theses.

Soft Positivists interpret the Separation Thesis as involving only a modal, existential generalization of the following form: it is (conceptually) *possible* that there exists *at least one* rule of recognition, and thus one legal system, in which morality is not a criterion of legal validity.[7] Hard

---

Concept of Law by itself does not support attributing Soft Positivism to Hart. See Leslie Green, 'The Concept of Law Revisited', 94 Michigan Law Review 1687, (1996), 1705–7.

[5] See Brian Leiter, 'Legal Indeterminacy', 1 Legal Theory 481 (1995), and 'Legal Realism', 268–9.

[6] This differs slightly from the characterization offered in Jules Coleman and Brian Leiter, 'Legal Positivism', in Patterson, *Companion*, 241, a characterization which now seems to me too narrow to do justice to the full panoply of positivist doctrines.

[7] See Coleman, NPP. Coleman arrives at this doctrine by characterizing the Separation Thesis with a modal operator, i.e. there is no 'necessary' relationship between law and morality. (In fact, Hart's classic 1958 paper does not use the modal operator. See H. L. A. Hart, 'Positivism and the Separation of Law and Morals', 71 Harvard Law Review 593 (1958).) The resulting 'Negative Positivism' (as Coleman calls it) would be a weak enough doctrine if it claimed only that there exists at least one system in which the rule of recognition does not make morality a criterion of legality. But Coleman makes the doctrine even weaker by introducing yet a *further* modal element. He says that for Negative Positivism there need only be 'at least one *conceivable* rule of recognition . . . that does not specify truth as a moral principle among the truth conditions for any proposition of law', and that it is enough that 'we can *imagine* a legal system in which being a principle of morality is not a condition of legality for any norm' (*id.* at 30, 31; emphasis added). As Coleman has noted, even Dworkin need not deny Negative Positivism in this sense. Indeed, a natural law theorist could accept Coleman's modal interpretation of Negative Positivism as well, as long as the natural law claim that morality is a criterion of legality is taken to state a contingent, not

Positivists, by contrast, interpret the Separation Thesis as requiring a universal generalization of the form: for all rules of recognition, hence for all legal systems, it is not the case that morality is a criterion of legality, *unless* some content-neutral criterion makes it so.[8] Soft Positivists interpret the Social Thesis as saying only that a society's rule of recognition is constituted by the social facts about how officials actually decide disputes; thus, for example, if it is the 'practice' or 'convention' of officials to decide disputes by reference to morality, then morality, in that society, is a criterion of legality. Hard Positivists, by contrast, interpret the Social Thesis as a constraint on the *content* of the Rule of Recognition, not simply on its existence conditions. Thus, for Hard Positivists the Social Thesis says not only that a rule of recognition is constituted by social facts (e.g. facts about the conventional practice among officials in resolving disputes) but also that the criteria of legal validity set out by any society's rule of recognition must *consist* in social facts (e.g. facts about pedigree or sources).

III. CONCEPTUAL ARGUMENTS

All important arguments for Hard Positivism to date have been *conceptual* arguments: i.e. they defend Hard Positivism on the grounds that it provides a better explanation for various features of the concept of law. But what exactly is the 'concept' of law? The nature of conceptual analysis in legal theory is rarely discussed explicitly or at great length,[9] though it is widely acknowledged to be the dominant modus operandi of jurisprudents. We may start by asking: what is a 'concept'? A cynic might say that a 'concept' is just what philosophers used to call 'meaning' back when their job was the analysis of meanings. But ever since Quine embarrassed philosophers into admitting they didn't know what 'meanings' were, they have started analysing 'concepts' instead. The cynical view enjoys, I think a modicum of truth, but it is hardly the whole story.

necessary, truth about the concept of law, i.e. a truth that holds in this world, but not in all possible worlds. Of course, natural lawyers typically want to make a stronger claim than this.

Coleman does note elsewhere, 'Some might take the separability thesis to mean that law and morality are distinct in that no moral principles can count as part of a community's law.' 'Authority and Reason', in *The Autonomy of Law: Essays on Legal Positivism*, ed. R. George 1996, 287, 315 n. 5. I think it a desideratum in a characterization of the separability thesis that it allow for this possible reading, especially since Coleman's preferred 'modal' interpretation renders the thesis trivial, as Coleman himself acknowledges.

[8] Even in this latter scenario, Hard Positivists may want to deny that morality is an actual *standard* that *constrains* judicial decision.

[9] One recent exception is Brian Bix, 'Conceptual Questions and Jurisprudence', 1 Legal Theory 465 (1995), 470–5. Judging from recent work circulating in manuscript, it now appears the subject is attracting more attention from legal philosophers.

To start, there is the obvious point that the philosophical interest in 'concepts' (or 'meanings') is not like the lexicographer's interest in 'meaning': the philosophical aim is not to track and then regulate linguistic practice and usage. As Raz puts it, 'we do not want to be slaves of words' (LPSL, 41). At the same time we cannot ignore words, because words and concepts stand in a close (partly evidentiary, partly constitutive) relationship. Yet one important difference between words and concepts is that it is concepts, and not words, that are the objects of propositional attitudes. 'You can't do that, it's against the law' and 'You can't do that, the legislature has prohibited it' both express the same concept—that of illegality—though one speaks of 'the law' and the other of the actions of a legislature. So when jurisprudents appeal to the concept of law they are appealing to the object of a diverse set of propositional attitudes held by those who engage in 'law-talk': the law-talk has as its object the concept of law, and the various types of law-talk in which different people (lawyers, judges, legal scholars, ordinary citizens) engage has both evidentiary and sometimes constitutive value as to the contours of the concept. The objects of propositional attitudes, though, are abstract objects, and this invariably presents epistemic difficulties: the objects are not there to be picked up, weighed, measured, and scrutinized. We may sometimes wonder whether the object of all propositional attitudes concerning law is really the same 'thing'. Such a worry can prove fatal to the project of conceptual analysis. One reason ethical non-cognitivists think there is no fruitful analysis of 'good' in the offing is because they think the objects of propositional attitudes about goodness are, in fact, different. A similar worry could arise about law.

The concept 'law' seems, of course, to have referential content—it represents some feature of the real world—and it must be this point that Raz is making when he says that the argument for Hard Positivism 'is not an argument from the ordinary sense of "law" or any other term. It relies on fundamental features of our understanding of a certain social institution, the primary examples of which are contemporary municipal legal systems' (LPSL, 50). An 'understanding' of a social institution is, I take it, just our 'concept' of that institution—precisely what all our law-related propositional attitudes have as their common object, even though they are couched in differently worded sentences-in-the-head. But if the referent of the concept is the ultimate object of inquiry, are we still 'slaves' to words, at least at an evidential level? Not necessarily. Hart, it will be recalled, accepted J. L. Austin's (perhaps mistaken) rationale for 'looking at words', namely that we 'are using a sharpened awareness of words to sharpen our perception of phenomena' (CL, 14, quoting Austin). But if we are sceptical about the Hart/Austin view, then the rationale for 'looking at words' is less clear. Analysing law-talk *may* be instrumental to the goal of understanding the real world. There is no particular reason, though, to think it is the only or even the best instrument. Yet it is the one legal philosophers, at least, continue to claim, distinctively, as their own.

Legal philosophers, then, who defend Hard Positivism typically appeal to specific features of the *concept* of law—the concept manifest in all kinds of law-talk, the concept that is the *real* object of all the many propositional attitudes people have when they engage in law-talk—for which Hard Positivism alone provides the best explanation. To date, the major conceptual arguments for Hard Positivism have been *functional* arguments, i.e. arguments that appeal to some aspect of our concept of the *function* of law. We may distinguish two main types of Functional Argument: arguments from Public Guidance and from Authority.[10] Sections IV and V examine these arguments in detail, considering and, in some cases, responding to certain now familiar objections. In the end, I argue that only the argument from Authority succeeds, at least as a conceptual argument. Section VI concludes, however, by revisiting some of the worries about this whole style of argument. Satisfactory resolution of these debates, I suggest, requires that jurisprudence move beyond mere conceptual analysis.

IV. PUBLIC GUIDANCE

Dworkin ascribes to Positivism (and Raz, among others, accepts) the claim that the function of law is to 'provide a settled public and dependable set of standards for private and official conduct, standards whose force cannot be called into question by some individual official's conception of policy or morality'.[11] Against Soft Positivism, then, it is argued that if morality can be a criterion of legality, then law cannot discharge this function, since the inherently controversial nature of moral claims and arguments will leave the law unsettled and the boundary between settled law and an 'individual official's conception of . . . morality' vague.

Put this way, however, the argument claims too much: a claim about function may, indeed, be part of our concept of law, but it cannot plausibly

---

[10] Yet a third genre, which appeals to our concept of what it means to be guided by a rule, has recently been developed by Scott Shapiro. See 'The Difference That Rules Make', in *Analyzing Law: New Essays in Legal Theory*, ed. Brian Bix (1998), and 'On Hart's Way Out', (this volume). I do not discuss these interesting new arguments here.

[11] Ronald Dworkin, *Taking Rights Seriously* (1977), 347. Raz accepts this as a commitment of Positivism in ALM, 320. Raz does not, however, invoke this as an argument *for* Hard Positivism; only Dworkin does that. Hart, in the Postscript, seems to acquiesce in this move, as discussed *infra* n. 13.

be part of the *concept* that law functions *well* or *successfully*.[12] For this latter claim would then render a conceptual impossibility what seems, manifestly, to be an actuality: namely, that some legal systems function poorly. Thus, a successful functional argument against Soft Positivism must take the form of a pure *impossibility* argument: it must show that it is impossible for law to fulfil its function given the Soft Positivist theory of law. We can try to do this by recasting the argument in explicitly epistemic terms.[13]

On the epistemic version of the argument, the claim is that it is a distinctive feature of the rule of recognition (hence of law) that it fulfil an *epistemic* function, i.e. empowering (at least) officials to recognize what the law is, if not with absolute certainty all the time, then at least with some reasonably high degree of certainty most of the time.[14] The conceptual claim, then, is that we do not have a legal system when officials can not recognize law with a high degree of certainty most of the time. The argument is that Soft Positivism is not compatible, in principle, with this possibility, i.e. with the rule of recognition discharging this essential epistemic function.

---

[12] I am indebted to Scott Shapiro for clarification on this issue.

[13] Dworkin's argument for Hard Positivism based on the 'ideal of protected expectations' is really a variation on the *epistemic* version of the Public Guidance argument. See Dworkin, *Law's Empire*, 117 ff. According to Dworkin, the Positivist theory of law must answer the fundamental question of political philosophy: how can the exercise of coercive power be justified? It can only be justified, for Dworkin's Positivist, if the law 'give[s] fair warning by making the occasions of coercion depend on plain facts available [i.e. epistemically accessible] to all rather than on fresh judgments of political morality, which different judges might make differently'. *Id.* at 117. As an argument for Hard Positivism, this is vulnerable to the objection that it builds too much into the concept of law, insofar as it assumes (as Hart puts it) 'that the point or purpose of law and legal practice is to justify coercion'. Postscript, 248. Even if we do not go as far as Hart in claiming that 'positivism . . . makes no claim to identify the point or purpose of law and legal practices as such', we can agree with Hart's (not obviously consistent) claim that it is 'quite vain to seek any more specific purpose which law as such serves beyond providing guides to human conduct and standards of criticism of such conduct'. *Id.* at 249. In other words, Dworkin's more particularized version of the Public Guidance argument attributes to our *concept* of the function of law more than might uncontroversially be found there. For further discussion, however, of the problem with appeals to our 'concept' of law, see the final section of this paper.

[14] Thus, I reject Coleman's view that the *semantic* sense of the Rule of Recognition is primary. Coleman, NPP, 30–1. Treating the semantic interpretation as primary seems contrary both to what Hart actually says (e.g. Postscript, 251) and to the label he chose: it is, after all, a rule of '*recognition*', and recognition is an epistemic capacity.

In recent work, Coleman has recast his earlier distinction between *semantic* and *epistemic* versions of the rule of recognition in terms of the difference between the rule of recognition fulfilling a 'validation' function and an 'identification' function. While the rule always fulfils a validation (or semantic) function, it does not, says Coleman, fulfil an identification (or epistemic) function for ordinary citizens. See Coleman, 'Authority and Reason', 307 ff., and 'Incorporationism', 416 ff. While this distinction seems, initially, to have some force against Raz's authority argument (see the discussion in the text below), it has no force against the argument from epistemic function considered in the text, since the rule of recognition must still serve an epistemic function for officials if no one else.

According to Soft Positivism, the only constraint on a rule of recognition is that its existence-conditions are constituted by social facts, e.g. facts about how officials actually decide disputes. This means Soft Positivism is compatible, in principle, with what we may call the 'Extreme Scenario', that is, the scenario in which it is the practice or convention of officials to decide all disputes by reference to natural law.[15] Such a rule of recognition could not discharge its epistemic function, unless (a) there are moral truths and (b) we can have reliable knowledge of these truths most of the time. There is little reason to think that Soft Positivism could carry the heavy metaphysical and epistemological burden demanded by the prospect of the Extreme Scenario which Soft Positivism itself licenses. Since Soft Positivism is compatible, in principle, with the Extreme Scenario, Soft Positivism is incompatible, in principle, with the rule of recognition fulfilling its epistemic function.

Notice that it does not help the Soft Positivist to respond, as Waluchow does, that even a rule of recognition that satisfies Raz's Sources Thesis can still involve uncertainty.[16] This, of course, is true. But the only relevant question is one of degree, since Positivists do not maintain that the Rule of Recognition must eliminate all uncertainty.[17] Hard Positivism does require that there be truths about social facts and that we can have reliable knowledge of these truths. When comparing the ability of Hard and Soft Positivism to explain how a rule of recognition can fulfil its epistemic function, the crucial issue is whether we have reason to think that uncertainty will be compounded by the need to carry the metaphysical and epistemological burdens for both social facts *and* moral facts. But how could it not? How could ontological promiscuity and the resulting epistemological complexity such promiscuity entails *not* increase the burdens, hence increase uncertainty?

Of course, it remains possible that even though Soft Positivism necessarily increases uncertainty, it does not (in principle) increase it beyond the threshold that renders the fulfilment of the rule of recognition's epistemic function impossible. I do not see any way to rule out conclusively this latter possibility. In that event, the argument from Public Guidance can only make us sceptical about Soft Positivism, but cannot show it to be incompatible with law's function so conceived.

Interestingly, Hart acknowledges a related difficulty posed by permitting morality to be a criterion of legality, and it is worth looking at what he (as a defender of Soft Positivism) says about it. Hart writes:

---

[15] This would still be a weaker doctrine than traditional natural law theory, since natural law is a criterion of legality in the Extreme Scenario only because of a contingent fact, i.e. this is how officials actually decide disputes.

[16] Waluchow, *supra* n. 4, at 122.

[17] See e.g. Hart's Postscript, 251.

[A] moral test can be a test for pre-existing law only if there are objective moral facts in virtue of which moral judgments are true. . . . [I]f there are no such facts, a judge, told to apply a moral test, can only treat this as a call for the exercise by him of a law-making discretion in accordance with his best understanding of morality and its requirements and subject to whatever constraints on this are imposed by the legal system. . . . [I]f the question of the objective standing of moral judgments is left open by legal theory, as I claim it should be, then soft positivism cannot be simply characterized as the theory that moral principles or values may be among the criteria of legal validity, since if it is an open question whether moral principles and values have objective standing, it must also be an open question whether 'soft positivist' provisions purporting to include conformity with them among the tests for existing law can have that effect or instead, can only constitute directions to courts to *make* law in accordance with morality. (Postscript, 253–4)

Law, in short, fails to provide public guidance if moral criteria of legality are tantamount to a licence for judicial discretion, which is what they will be in the absence of an objectivist meta-ethic.

Note that nothing of importance in this passage turns on Hart's particular conception of what is required for the objectivity of morals, i.e. 'objective moral facts in virtue of which moral judgments are true'. What is important is Hart's concession that Soft Positivism requires the objectivity of morality *in some sense*. Yet he adopts a rather casual posture towards this meta-ethical issue because he thinks that 'the judge's duty will be the same' regardless of our meta-ethical stance: 'It will not matter for any practical purpose whether in so deciding cases the judge is *making* law in accordance with morality (subject to whatever constraints are imposed by law) or alternatively is guided by his moral judgment as to what already *existing* law is revealed by a moral test for law' (Postscript, 254). This response seems unsatisfactory on a couple of scores.

First, it is not clear why *making a practical difference* is a relevant consideration in this context. We are seeking a sound theoretical understanding of the social phenomenon of law. It suffices to defeat a candidate theory if it generates an intractable theoretical dilemma, like being unable to account for how law could possibly fulfil its 'public guidance' function or how the rule of recognition could possibly fulfil its epistemic function. Second, the issue at stake may, in any case, make a *practical* difference, in two different ways. Insofar as we view any incorporation of moral criteria of legal validity in to a rule of recognition as tantamount to a licence for the exercise of judicial discretion, then judges who are adverse to exercising discretion at the first level of deciding a case on the merits[18] may 'avoid the substance of the [moral] test and appeal instead to more familiar considerations like framers' intention, community consensus, or plain

---

[18] As distinct from the meta-level of deciding which rule of interpretation to employ.

meaning'.[19] Moreover, if an objectivist meta-ethic is correct, then it seems that would *necessarily* make a practical difference to how judges *ought* to decide cases that involve appeal to moral criteria of legality.

If these two points are correct, and if Hart were also correct in his meta-jurisprudential claim that 'legal theory should avoid commitment to controversial philosophical theories of the general status of moral judgments' (Postscript, 243–4),[20] then it would follow that Soft Positivism is untenable. For Soft Positivism requires taking a stand on controversial meta-ethical questions, and thus would violate the meta-jurisprudential scruples Hart endorses. But it seems unfair to rest an argument against Soft Positivism solely on Hart's particular, and perhaps idiosyncratic, meta-jurisprudential scruples.

V. AUTHORITY

The most important functional argument in favour of Hard Positivism is Raz's argument from authority. According to this argument, it is essential to law's function that it be able to issue in *authoritative* directives—even if it fails to do so in actuality. Raz claims that only his Sources Thesis is compatible with the possibility of law possessing authority. According to Raz, a legal system can only claim authority if it is possible to identify its directives without reference to the underlying ('dependent') reasons for that directive. This is a 'prerequisite' for authority because what distinguishes a (practical) authority in the first place is that its directives preempt consideration of the underlying reasons (including e.g. moral reasons) for what we ought to do, and in so doing actually makes it more likely that we will do what we really ought to do. But Soft Positivism makes the identification of law depend on the very reasons that authoritative directives are supposed to preempt, and thus makes it impossible for law to fulfil its function of providing authoritative guidance.

Soft Positivists have ventured three kinds of rejoinder to Raz's argument from authority. First, they might contest whether identifying laws

---

[19] W. J. Waluchow, 'Hart's "Postscript" ', 96 APA Newsletter 52 (Fall 1996), 54.

[20] Curiously, Hart does not avail himself of what would seem the easiest line of response, which would allow him to avoid meta-ethics and simply rely on the tacit semantics that informs his argument about the 'open texture' of language. For presumably moral predicates can have core and penumbral instances just like other predicates (e.g. 'vehicle'): the core of a moral predicate is just the extension to which most competent speakers of the language would readily assent. Now while the core meaning of moral predicates would generally be smaller, and the penumbral instances larger, it would still be the case that where the facts of the case fall within the core of the moral predicate, Soft Positivism would not simply license discretion, and for exactly the same reason it does not license discretion in the case of a rule like 'No vehicles in the park'.

by reference to moral considerations necessarily requires taking into account the dependent reasons on which those laws are based. 'The set of all moral reasons', Waluchow notes, may 'not [be] identical with the set of dependent reasons under dispute'.[21] Even if this were right, it would not prove enough. For it suffices to defeat Soft Positivism as a theory compatible with the law's authority if there exists *any* case in which the dependent reasons are the same as the moral reasons which are required to identify what the law is; that there remain some cases where these reasons 'may' be different is irrelevant.[22] Moreover, if moral reasons are always overriding in practical reasoning—a view accepted, in fact, by most moral theorists[23]—then moral reasons will always be among the dependent reasons for any authoritative directive. Therefore, if identifying that directive requires recourse to moral reasons, the preconditions for authority will fail to obtain.

Second, Coleman has argued that Soft Positivism is compatible with the law's claim to authority because the Rule of Recognition is not the rule by which ordinary people (those subject to the law's authority) *identify* what the law is.[24] Recasting his earlier, well-known distinction between the 'semantic' and 'epistemic' senses of the Rule of Recognition in terms of 'validation' versus 'identification' functions, Coleman argues as follows:

For there to be law there must be a validation rule—one that is as broad as incorporationism [i.e. Soft Positivism] allows. For law to be authoritative, however, there must be an identification rule—one that may not be so broad. There is a problem for incorporationism only if those two rules must be identical. They need not be, however, and often they are not. The Sources Thesis ... imposes a constraint [only] on whatever rule ordinary citizens employ to identify the law that binds them. Since most ordinary citizens are able to determine the law that binds them, whereas few, if any, are able to formulate or state the prevailing rule of recognition, it is unlikely that the rule of identification [i.e. the *epistemic* guise of the rule of recognition] is the [*semantic*] rule of recognition.[25]

---

[21] Waluchow, *supra* n. 4 at 139. For a similar objection, see Coleman, 'Incorporationism', 414–15.

[22] Waluchow has responded to this objection by claiming that 'the preconditions of the authority of *some* directives does not require the authority of *all* directives'. W. J. Waluchow, 'Authority and the Practical Difference Thesis', 6 Legal Theory 45 (2000), 71. But this misses the point that the authority argument is a *possibility* argument, i.e. an argument showing that the authority of law is *impossible* if one allows content-based criteria of legality. Thus, while it is surely true that *in actuality* some directives may prove to be authoritative and some not, what matters for the possibility argument is that it is even *possible* that some might fail to be authoritative, which is precisely the upshot of the Soft Positivist view of legality.

[23] Philippa Foot and Bernard Williams come to mind as exceptions. See the discussion in Brian Leiter, 'Nietzsche and the Morality Critics', 107 Ethics 250 (1997), 258–60.

[24] 'Authority and Reason', 307–8; 'Incorporationism', 416 ff.

[25] 'Authority and Reason', 308.

Coleman's argument calls attention to an important point: the in-principle authority of law is only impugned if the rule used to identify the law requires recourse to dependent reasons. The difficulty is that the rule of recognition must still perform an epistemic function for officials, and so Soft Positivism would still undermine the rule's authority vis-à-vis those individuals. Since Coleman has abandoned the claim about ordinary people in more recent work,[26] and since nothing turns on it, I refer the interested reader to an earlier version of this paper for a detailed (but now moot) refutation of that claim.[27]

Finally, some Soft Positivists have wanted to deny that *authority* involves *exclusionary* reasons, i.e. excluding from consideration the dependent reasons on which the authority bases his directive. 'There is no reason', says Waluchow, 'to think that authority is an all or nothing exclusionary matter.'[28] Waluchow endorses Perry's view that an authoritative directive provides only 'a second-order reason [which is] a reason for treating a first-order reason as having a greater or lesser weight than it would ordinarily receive, so that an exclusionary reason is simply the special case where one or more first-order reasons are treated as having zero weight'.[29]

If authoritative directives are *not* exclusionary reasons, then the fact that one might need to consider dependent reasons in order to identify law—a consequence of Soft Positivism—would not be fatal to law's claimed authority. The crucial question then is whether it is central to the concept of authority that an authoritative directive *exclude* from consideration all dependent reasons. Let us take the example of precedent, on which both Perry and Waluchow rely. If a court overrules a precedent, surely the natural thing to say is that the overruling court did not treat the precedent as authoritative. It is natural to say this precisely for Razian reasons: the overruling court went back and struck the balance among the dependent reasons differently from the overruled court. That is, it did not treat the prior court's decision as constituting an exclusionary reason for deciding the instant case a particular way, and in failing to do so, it did not treat the precedent as authoritative.

But on the Perry/Waluchow view, an overruled precedent may still be spoken of as authoritative insofar as the overruling court was required to 'weigh [it] . . . more heavily than normal, i.e. more heavily than in other contexts in which authority is not present and reasons compete equally on

---

[26] Coleman now denies that the issue is 'about the ways in which, as an empirical matter, ordinary folk come to learn the law of their community'. 'Incorporationism', 420.

[27] 'Realism, Hard Positivism, and Conceptual Analysis', 542–3.

[28] *Supra* n. 4, at 136.

[29] Stephen R. Perry, 'Judicial Obligation, Precedent, and the Common Law', 7 Oxford Journal of Legal Studies 221 (1987), 223.

their respective merits alone'.[30] Yet this way of looking at the matter entails the bizarre conclusion that an overruled precedent may be described as 'authoritative', when that is precisely what it seems not to be in virtue of having been overruled! Should we really say that an overruled precedent is 'authoritative' just because the overruling court says, 'We accord this precedent considerable weight in our decision, but in the end we decide the same issue the opposite way'?[31] The crucial idea behind the Razian analysis of the concept is precisely that what distinguishes authority is not simply that its pronouncements get taken 'seriously' (whatever that means[32]) but that they are taken so seriously that they exclude further consideration of the reasons pertaining to the matter at hand. That the Razian analysis coincides with our intuitive way of thinking about the status of overruled precedents suggests that it captures something essential about the concept of authority.

VI. THE LIMITS OF CONCEPTUAL ANALYSIS

We have seen that the leading arguments for Hard Positivism all depend upon claims about the concept of law, in particular about our concept of the function of law. Stephen Perry has argued in a number of papers[33] that such arguments are incompatible with what he calls 'methodological positivism', which 'maintain[s] that legal theory is a purely descriptive, nonnormative enterprise that sets out, in the manner of ordinary science, to tell us what one particular corner of the world we inhabit is like'.[34] His argument, in a nutshell, runs as follows: (1) we always require a background

---

[30] Waluchow, *supra* n. 4 at 137.

[31] Waluchow does not share my intuitions about how the rhetorical question should be answered. See 'Authority and the Practical Difference Thesis', *supra* n. 22, at 69–70. Waluchow thinks it equally 'natural . . . to say that [the later court] deemed the precedent's authority to be *outweighed* by *especially strong reasons*'. *Id.* at 70. Saying a precedent's authority is 'outweighed' is just a roundabout way of saying—to my ear at least—that it is not authoritative. But given my doubts about this mode of philosophical argumentation (see Section VI below), I will not labour the point here.

[32] Part of the difficulty here attaches to the critically ambiguous notion of 'weight' on which Perry relies. How much weight must we assign to a particular directive before it constitutes an authoritative directive? If the Supreme Court were to treat *Roe* v. *Wade* as a serious constraint on deciding whether a woman has a constitutional right to choose an abortion, but in the end decides that a woman has no such right, does it make any sense in this context to speak of *Roe* as 'authoritative' because the court 'weighed' it seriously before ignoring it?

[33] See esp. Stephen R. Perry, 'Interpretation and Methodology in Legal Theory', in *Law and Interpretation: Essays in Legal Philosophy*, ed. A. Marmor (1995), and 'The Varieties of Legal Positivism', 9 Canadian Journal of Law & Jurisprudence 361 (1996).

[34] *Id.* at 361. For a related line of argument against (what Perry calls) 'methodological positivism', see John Finnis, *Natural Law and Natural Justice* (1980), 3–22, esp. 3, 16.

conceptual framework that demarcates the data that our theory aims to describe and explain; we do not, for example, think that an adequate theory of adjudication must account for decision-making by judges who accept bribes, or that an adequate theory of American politics must account for the technology of voting booths, or that an adequate theory of history must account for the evolution of human language, even though this too transpires in real historical time; (2) part of the background conceptual framework essential for jurisprudence is a view about the *function* of law, a view which allows us to see which features of law the jurisprudential theory must capture; but (3) we cannot specify the function of law without engaging in normative argument, i.e. argument about what the function of law *ought* to be. Thus, we cannot do jurisprudence and be methodological positivists (as Hart, Waluchow, and others claim to be).

(1) is, or should be, an uncontroversial thesis in the general philosophy of science (including social science). (2) should be an equally uncontroversial observation about jurisprudence as one type of social scientific inquiry. (3) is the important claim for our purposes since it supposes that conceptual analysis—appeal to the *concept* of law (or to a *concept* of law's function)—cannot suffice in jurisprudence. For conceptual analysis *would* be a method consistent with methodological positivism, yet Perry's point is precisely that we cannot remain methodological positivists and still have access to the crucial notion of law's 'function' (or 'purpose' or 'point'). Why does Perry think this?

At bottom, Perry must think that our concept of the 'function' of law does not hang together sufficiently well to admit of analysis: there are too many incompatible understandings of the concept for the jurisprudent simply to fall back upon appeal to 'our' concept. Perry thinks, for example, that both the Dworkinian idea that 'the fundamental function of the common law is not the guidance of conduct but rather principled adjudication, i.e., the settlement of disputes in accordance with applicable moral principles'[35] and the Holmesian idea that the central concept is that of 'sanctions' which 'create . . . [prudential] reasons for action which are truly central to an accurate understanding of law'[36] have equal claims to being 'concepts of law' along with the Positivist idea of law as providing public guidance. (He also contests, of course, the Razian analysis of the concept of authority.) Conceptual analysis, by itself, gives us no reason to prefer one concept to the other; only a further, normative argument can do that—or so Perry argues.[37]

---

[35] *Id.* at 377.

[36] 'Interpretation and Methodology in Legal Theory', 113.

[37] For some doubts about Perry's argument, see Coleman, 'Incorporationism', esp. 392 n. 23. Even Coleman claims, however, that '*our* concept' of law has 'certain essential features';

Now even the arguments for Hard Positivism reviewed above presupposed somewhat different concepts of the function of law (e.g. providing
public guidance, or providing authoritative directives). That there should
be different concepts of the function is not per se worrisome, as long as a
single theory of law (e.g. Hard Positivism) provides the best account of all
the genuine features that have a claim to being part of the concept. What
is worrisome, however, is if the differing conceptual claims are in tension
such that no one theory can account for the viable concepts. That is the
position we find ourselves in if Perry's analysis of the situation is correct.

Is it correct? We might still fall back on the claim that certain intuitions
about the concept of law really are more fundamental than others, e.g.
that there is no 'more specific purpose which law as such serves beyond
providing guides to human conduct and standards of criticism of such
conduct' (Postscript, 249); or that authority really does demand exclusionary reasons. Can the Dworkinian or Holmesian conceptions plausibly
claim to capture as fundamental a feature of law as the one Hart identifies? Can the Perry/Waluchow view of authority claim to be as plausible
and intuitive as Raz's?

Philosophy becomes unsatisfying, though, when it turns into intuition-
mongering and armchair sociology about what is really fundamental to
'our' concepts.[38] One way to avoid the hopeless morass of warring
conceptual intuitions is to take Perry's route, and abandon methodological positivism as a constraint on jurisprudence.[39] There is, however,
another option consistent with methodological positivism, but which
requires heeding a more general lesson of modern philosophy of
language. Although Quine's seminal attack on the analytic-synthetic
distinction occasionally gets a polite nod from contemporary philosophers, it is less often that theorists take seriously its upshot: that the
claims of conceptual analysis are *always* vulnerable to the demands of a

---

he just denies that we need recourse to law's function to say what these features are (and
thus denies (2), above, in the text). *Id.* at 393–4. We can identify these 'essential features', says
Coleman, by recognizing 'law's institutionality', i.e. 'the complex thought that part of the
distinguishing feature of law's authority is the idea that legal rules are the result of institutional action of various kinds'. *Id.* at 395. Pitched at such a level of abstraction, however, it is
unclear how this is responsive to Perry's worry: what concept of law *exactly* flows from the
'institutionality' of law?

[38] Is it not this feature that makes most normative ethics so tiresome and pointless? Note
that I can agree with Coleman that 'It does not follow from the existence of controversial
cases that there is disagreement at the core, or that the core is empty.' *Id.* at 389. The worry,
however, is precisely that the intuitions conflict *at the core*.

[39] Another possibility is to contest Perry's slide from the claim that the concept of law
does not hang together sufficiently well to admit of analysis to the claim that we need *moral
and political norms* in order to individuate the subject matter of jurisprudence. But perhaps
epistemic norms will suffice, e.g. simplicity, consilience, and minimum mutilation of existing
theoretical claims. Perry needs to motivate the turn to moral and political philosophy as the
only normative solution.

posteriori theory construction.[40] It is in many ways a strange state of affairs that philosophers continue blithely with conceptual analysis, considering the disastrous record of pseudo-truths delivered by this method. As Gilbert Harman has recently written:

When problems were raised about particular conceptual claims, they were problems about the examples that had been offered as seemingly clear cases of a priori truth—the principles of Euclidean geometry, the law of excluded middle, 'cats are animals,' 'unmarried adult male humans are bachelors,' 'women are female,' and 'red is a color.' Physics leads to the rejection of Euclidean geometry and at least considers rejecting the law of the excluded middle. We can imagine discovering that cats are not animals but are radio controlled robots from Mars. Speakers do not consider the Pope a bachelor. People will not apply the term 'bachelor' to a man who lives with the same woman over a long enough period of time even if they are not married. Society pages in newspapers will identify as eligible 'bachelors' men who are in the process of being divorced but are still married. The Olympic Committee may have rejected certain women as insufficiently female on the basis of their chromosomes. Just as a certain flavor is really detected by smell rather than taste, we can imagine that the color red might be detected aurally rather than by sight.[41]

But if these 'classics' of conceptual analysis all failed for a posteriori reasons (or other a priori reasons), why in the world think conceptual analysis in jurisprudence will fare any better? If a proposed conceptual analysis is to be preferred to others, it must be because it earns its place by facilitating successful a posteriori theories of law and legal institutions. Such is, I take it, the final ambition of general jurisprudence, as Hart conceives it. And from this perspective, what is objectionable, say, about the Dworkinian take on the 'concept of law' is that it is excessively parochial, frustrating the ambitions of general jurisprudence. In other words, what would ultimately vindicate the conceptual arguments for Hard Positivism is not simply the assertion that they best account for the 'real' concept of law, but that the concept of law they best explicate is the one that figures in the most fruitful a posteriori research programmes, i.e. the ones that give us the best going account of how the world works. That would require jurisprudence to get up from the armchair and find out what anthropologists, sociologists, psychologists, and others can tell us about the social practices in and around law. The Realists, in fact, undertook such inquiries, and they did so, as noted at the beginning, employing a (tacit) Hard Positivist view of legality. That is surely defeasible evidence in favour of Hard Positivism—though perhaps too easily defeasible given

---

[40] Note that this is true even when everyone's intuitions about a concept coincide!

[41] Gilbert Harman, 'Doubts About Conceptual Analysis', in *Philosophy in Mind*, ed. M. Michael and J. O'Leary-Hawthorne (1994), 43, 45. Harman's citations of supporting secondary literature are omitted.

the mixed success of the Realist research programme.[42] But more recent research programmes in the spirit of Realism have often fared better.[43] These programmes, which try to understand the operation of courts in terms of the economic and social demographics that explain their behaviour, typically assume that law-based explanations of behaviour are confined to explanations in terms of pedigreed norms. At the same time, these social scientific approaches give us a picture of courts which fits them in to a broader naturalistic conception of the world in which deterministic causes rule, and in which volitional agency plays little or no explanatory role. Thus, what commends these accounts is that they effect an explanatory unification of legal phenomena with the other phenomena constituting the natural world which science has already mastered. And since these research programmes rely (implicitly) on the Hard Positivist 'concept' of law, Hard Positivism would be vindicated by its implicit role in our best a posteriori theories of law and its place in the causal order of nature.

[42] See Brian Leiter, 'Rethinking Legal Realism: Toward a Naturalized Jurisprudence', 76 Texas Law Review 267 (1997), 311–14.

[43] See e.g. Frank B. Cross, 'Political Science and the New Legal Realism', 92 Northwestern University Law Review 251 (1997), for a useful survey of the literature.

11

The Political Question of the Concept of Law

LIAM MURPHY

I. INTRODUCTION

In his Postscript to the second edition of *The Concept of Law*, Hart writes that 'it is not obvious why there should be or indeed could be any significant conflict between enterprises so different as my own and Dworkin's conceptions of legal theory'.[1] Whereas Dworkin's legal theory is justificatory in that it aims to show law in its best light—a light in which it can be seen to provide a justification for the force used in its name—Hart characterizes his own legal theory, by contrast, as descriptive 'in that it is morally neutral and has no justificatory aims'.[2]

Hart's theory of law certainly is not justificatory: it does not aim to show law in its best light. But it is somewhat misleading of Hart to say that his account is morally neutral. For the very decision not to aim to show law in its best light is one partly made, at least in his early work, on explicitly political grounds. Thus there is a substantive political disagreement between Hart and Dworkin. It is, moreover, an important disagreement, and it is regrettable that Hart chose not to pursue it in the Postscript.

The political disagreement between Hart and Dworkin relates to a certain question about the concept of law. It may seem that any such question must by its very nature be practically inconsequential, but this is not

Very many people have given me criticisms and comments on this paper, including members of an audience at the Analytic Legal Philosophy Conference at Columbia Law School in April 2000. I would like to thank in particular Ruth Chang, Jules Coleman, Julie Dickson, Christopher Eisgruber, John Goldberg, Leslie Green, Frances Kamm, Jody Kraus, Christopher Kutz, Thomas Nagel, James Nickel, Stephen Perry, Carlos Rosenkrantz, Lawrence Sager, Anthony Sebok, Scott Shapiro, Martin Stone, Jeremy Waldron, Wil Waluchow, Benjamin Zipursky, and, most especially, Ronald Dworkin, Sibylle Fischer, Lewis Kornhauser, and Joseph Raz. I have scarcely been able to begin to respond to all these critics. I would also like to thank the members of my legal philosophy classes over the past five years at NYU School of Law: more than anything else, it has been through discussion with these students that I have been able to come to an understanding, right or wrong, of this perplexing field. Finally, I am grateful for the support of the Filomen D'Agostino and Max E. Greenberg Research Fund of New York University School of Law.

[1] H. L. A. Hart, *The Concept of Law*, 2nd edn. (Oxford: Clarendon Press, 1994 [1st edn. 1961]), 241.

[2] Ibid. 240.

so. The question in issue is generated by people's disagreement about the role played by moral or political considerations in determining what the law is (as opposed to what it ought to be). This is not a disagreement that can be resolved just by looking at what lawyers do. It is clear to any honest investigator that lawyers appeal to moral and political considerations in their advocacy and that judges sometimes reach decisions in part on moral or political grounds.[3] The disagreement is over whether this appeal to political considerations by lawyers and judges is *properly understood* as part of an argument about what the law (already) is. Thus we have a genuine conceptual question, a question about a concept: does, or should, our concept of law allow that legal questions are answered in part by reference to political considerations?[4] Hart accepts a positivist answer to this traditional question: moral or political considerations play a role in determining what the law is only to the extent that there is some social or institutional warrant for this; a constitutional provision declaring a right to freedom of speech would be one such institutional warrant. Dworkin disagrees: on his view, moral considerations play a role in determining what the law is independently of social incorporation.

As I said, people in general disagree about the conceptual question just raised. This disagreement will survive, I believe, abstract reflection about the very idea of law. If this is right, then Hart and Dworkin's disagreement about the concept of law cannot be adjudicated by any philosophical investigation into what we already share by way of a concept of law.[5] How then should it be settled? And does it, after all, need to be settled? These two questions are related.

The conceptual disagreement between Hart and Dworkin needs to be settled because it matters, politically. The disagreement is not simply a result of varying conceptual intuitions; rather, it reflects substantive disagreement about the best—the politically best—way to conceive of law and its boundaries. Hart and Dworkin both believe that the way we conceive of the legal domain affects the nature of our political culture. Where they differ is that Dworkin believes, but Hart does not, that our political culture is better served if we understand law such that moral considerations play a role in its determination independently of social facts—Dworkin believes, but Hart does not, that it is politically for the best to understand law in such a way that shows it in its best light.

---

[3] Though it is true that this is often denied for the case of judges. The political implications of an institutional structure that encourages or allows judges to appeal to political considerations while denying that this is what they are doing are explored in Duncan Kennedy, *A Critique of Adjudication* (Cambridge, Mass.: Harvard University Press, 1997).

[4] On this conceptual question as the main concern of positivist jurisprudence, see Joseph Raz, *The Authority of Law* (Oxford: Clarendon Press, 1979), 37–8.

[5] See further pp. 380–2 below.

The way to resolve the conceptual disagreement between Hart and Dworkin must therefore be to evaluate the practical and political reasons that they offer for their respective positions. We must approach the traditional question about the concept of law as a practical aspect of political theory. Though for some time Neil MacCormick was almost alone in defending this methodology explicitly,[6] it was, as I have said, one strand of Hart's own methodology in his early work; it also plays an important role in Dworkin's work, embedded though it is in his more complex interpretive approach.

My aim in this paper is to develop and defend these points about Hart and Dworkin's conceptual and political disagreements, and to defend my own view that it is not for the best to conceive of law so as to show it in its best light. But before turning to that, we need to see that there is a sense in which Hart was perfectly right to say that his project in *The Concept of Law* was purely descriptive, and not political at all.

II. HART'S DESCRIPTIVE PROJECT

As I have said, the traditional question about the concept of law cannot be solved by way of description.[7] The reason why it is nevertheless appropriate for Hart to describe his project in *The Concept of Law* as descriptive is simply that the conceptual question is not, for the most part, what the book is about. Rather, the book largely takes for granted that law should be conceived of in a positivist manner, and then proceeds to describe the complex structure of law, so understood.[8] Hart defends his positivist

---

[6] See *H. L. A. Hart* (Stanford, Calif.: Stanford University Press, 1981), 158–60; 'A Moralistic Case for A-Moralistic Law?', *Valparaiso University Law Review* 20 (1985), 8–11. More recently, MacCormick has been joined by Frederick Schauer; see 'Positivism as Pariah', in Robert P. George (ed.), *The Autonomy of Law* (Oxford: Clarendon Press, 1996), 31–55; 'Positivism Through Thick and Thin', in Brian Bix (ed.), *Analysing Law* (Oxford: Clarendon Press, 1998), 65–78. Other legal philosophers who do not officially embrace the methodology on occasion express apparent sympathy with it; see e.g. the opening paragraph of Joseph Raz, 'Authority, Law, and Morality' (1985), in *Ethics in the Public Domain* (Oxford: Clarendon Press, 1994), 194; David Lyons, *Moral Aspects of Legal Theory* (Cambridge and New York: Cambridge University Press, 1993), pp. ix, 90–6. For criticism of MacCormick and the general approach I defend in this article, see Philip Soper, 'Choosing a Legal Theory on Moral Grounds', *Social Philosophy and Policy* 4 (1986), 31–48; W. J. Waluchow, *Inclusive Legal Positivism* (Oxford: Clarendon Press, 1994), 86–98.

[7] For more on this issue, see Ronald Dworkin, 'A Reply', in Marshall Cohen (ed.), *Ronald Dworkin and Contemporary Jurisprudence* (London: Duckworth, 1984), 250–2; Brian Bix, 'Conceptual Questions and Jurisprudence', *Legal Theory* 1 (1995), 465–79.

[8] I do not take a stand on the appropriateness of characterizing this description as in itself a detailed account of a concept of law, thus making more sense of the book's title. (For relevant discussion, see Joseph Raz, 'Two Views of the Nature of the Theory of Law'(this volume), 1–37.) The important point for me is that the description can only be an account of a positivist's concept of law, not an account of 'the' concept of law, and that the disagreement

conceptual stance only briefly, towards the end of the book; a much fuller defence was offered in his earlier classic article, 'Positivism and the Separation of Law and Morals'.[9] It is quite clear, then, that Hart's primary aim in *The Concept of Law* was to provide a better descriptive account of law than his positivist predecessors had done. His unqualified success in this enterprise, so rare in philosophy, may tempt contemporary readers to look for some other aim, one that continues to seem philosophically challenging.[10]

Once we leave to one side Hart's positivist conceptual presupposition, we can see that the major elements of his theory of law are indeed purely descriptive, and not motivated by further moral or political commitments. Thus, to take an important example, Hart's decision to focus on 'modern municipal legal systems' does not reflect a moral or political choice.[11] This decision is of course based on an evaluation of which kind of legal system it is most important to describe. In any descriptive account of a practice a prior decision must be made about what is to count as the clear case of the practice, with the effect that practices that do not exactly fit the description of the clear case will be regarded as marginal, or perhaps in some sense deficient.[12] In treating modern municipal systems as the standard case or ideal type, thus dooming other forms of law to the margins, Hart appears to have been motivated primarily by the nature of his own expertise and the nature of his expected audience, who were, of course, subjects of modern municipal legal systems. It is true that Hart describes the advantages that secondary rules, the key element of his new description of modern municipal legal systems, bring to a system of law—those of greater certainty, changeability, and efficiency.[13] However, in saying that these are advantages Hart's point is not that law has a

between positivists and non-positivists cannot be resolved by comparing the accuracy of their descriptions.

[9] See *The Concept of Law*, 200–12; 'Positivism and the Separation of Law and Morals' (1959), in *Essays in Jurisprudence and Philosophy* (Oxford: Clarendon Press, 1983), 49–87.

[10] Thus Stephen Perry's statement ('Interpretation and Methodology', in Andrei Marmor (ed.), *Law and Interpretation* (Oxford: Clarendon Press, 1995), 122) that 'Hart's theory of law does not, in the end, accomplish what it sets out to do' is based in large part on attributing to Hart an aim that, it seems to me, he did not have, viz. to explain how law can (or cannot) give rise to binding obligations (see also pp. 378 below). No doubt the explanation for Perry's attributing this aim to Hart is Perry's belief that without this aim jurisprudence would not qualify as a philosophical discipline; see 'Hart's Methodological Positivism' (this volume), 311–54. I believe, to the contrary, that while the question of whether law affects 'persons' reasons for action in the way that it claims to' (ibid.) is, of course, an important question of political or legal philosophy (it doesn't matter which), Hart's work shows that it is not the only worthwhile philosophical question that can be raised about the nature of law.

[11] See *The Concept of Law*, 17, 240.

[12] On this point as it arises for legal theory, see John Finnis, *Natural Law and Natural Rights* (Oxford: Clarendon Press, 1980), 3–19.

[13] See *The Concept of Law*, 91–9.

proper function and that secondary rules allow a legal system to perform that function well. Read in this way, he is open to the objection that his account of the proper function of law would need justification, no doubt from the domain of political theory.[14] But his point was surely the more mundane one that taking for granted, and by no means morally evaluating, the fact that law is a means of social control—'providing guides for human conduct and standards of criticism of such conduct'[15]—we can see that states with large populations cannot make do with 'primitive law', law that lacks secondary rules.[16]

To bring out the political neutrality of Hart's praise of secondary rules, consider Althusser, who holds that the whole point of law is to help the ruling class subject the working class to the process of surplus-value extortion, but who could agree that law is a more effective means of repression if it contains secondary rules, and thus also agree that the most important kind of legal system to describe comprehensively is the kind that makes use of secondary rules.[17] Or consider Finnis, for whom the correct focal case for description is law which generates at least presumptive moral obligations, but who can nevertheless make use of Hart's account as an illuminating characterization of law in the non-idealized, lawyer's technical sense. Finnis rejects Hart's account of law as being incomplete or ill-focused in a morally relevant way, but once that has been acknowledged there need be no further moral objection to Hart's focus on modern municipal legal systems.[18]

Though Hart's main project in *The Concept of Law* is descriptive, he was a philosopher and a lawyer—not a sociologist. It is natural, then, that he would focus on municipal legal systems as normative systems, rather than as concrete institutional social practices. Using Lewis Kornhauser's distinction, we can say that Hart offers a rather full description of the legal order, but almost no description of the legal regime.[19] By contrast, a sociologist would be more inclined to describe the legal regime—the legislative and

[14] See Dworkin, 'A Reply', 255; Perry, 'Hart's Methodological Positivism', 311–54. Michael Moore pursues 'functionalist jurisprudence'; see 'Law as a Functional Kind', in Robert P. George (ed.), *Natural Law Theory* (Oxford: Clarendon Press, 1992), 188–242, but holds that Hart practised a different and fully compatible kind of jurisprudence that was, indeed, wholly descriptive; see 'Hart's Concluding Scientific Postscript', *Legal Theory* 4 (1998), 301–27.

[15] *The Concept of Law*, 249.

[16] See the excellent discussion in Leslie Green, 'The Concept of Law Revisited', *Michigan Law Review* 94 (1996), 1698–1700, 1709–11.

[17] See Louis Althusser, 'Ideology and Ideological State Apparatuses', in *Lenin and Philosophy and Other Essays*, trans. Ben Brewster (New York: Monthly Review Press, 1971), 137.

[18] See Finnis, *Natural Law and Natural Rights*, 3–19, 25–9, 276–81; 'The Truth in Legal Positivism', in George, *The Autonomy of Law*, 195–214.

[19] See 'Three Roles for a Theory of Behavior in a Theory of Law', *Rechtstheorie* (forthcoming).

administrative processes, the selection and tenure of judges, the demo-graphics of imprisonment, the social and economic standing of lawyers, the means of the enforcement of judgments, etc. Insofar as any ideologi-cal force of law would be found in the content of the legal order, a reader whose main concern is to understand the way law operates as a means of repression would find Hart's description important; though such a reader would also want to know about the concrete workings of the legal regime.[20] But Hart's description of law is not less valuable for being partial—a description of the legal order only and not also a description of the legal regime; as I suggested, there is a natural division of descriptive labour here that tracks expertise. Moreover, Hart is of course aware that the legal order is not all there is to modern municipal legal systems and one of his main concerns is to tie his account of the legal order to obvious facts about the legal regime.

The most important part of any adequate description of the legal order will be what Dworkin calls a theory of the grounds of law, of what makes legal propositions true,[21] for this explains the operation of law as a system of norms. This is not to say that the theory of the grounds of law exhausts what is worth saying about the legal order. Thus Hart's point that some legal rules, such as those of contract law, are enabling rather than duty-imposing—enabling people to do what they would without law be unable to do—is enormously informative about the role of law in social life.[22] He also makes the point that in order for law to exist over time there must be more than the mere habit of obedience to a particular legal regime: the rules of the legal order, especially those governing the legal standing of the various elements of the legal regime, must be accepted by the 'officials and experts of the system', though not, significantly, by everyone.[23] But the core of Hart's description of the legal order clearly is his explanation of how valid legal rules are identified by a hierarchy of criteria of validity that ends in the supreme criteria of validity as identified by the rule of recognition.[24]

Despite its familiarity, I still find this theory of the grounds of law excit-ing. Hart's solution to the problem of a potentially infinite hierarchy of criteria of validity, viz. that the supreme criteria of validity are found in

---

[20] What Althusser calls 'the Repressive State Apparatus' contains 'the Government, the Administration, the Army, the Police, the Courts, the Prisons, etc.'. What he calls the 'Ideo-logical State Apparatuses' include 'the legal ISA'; he therefore notes that the ' "Law" belongs both to the (Repressive) State Apparatus and to the system of ISAs'; see 'Ideology and Ideo-logical State Apparatuses', 142–3. To mix Kornhauser's terminology with Althusser's, we can say that Althusser is interested in the legal regime as part of the repressive state appa-ratus and the legal order as one of the ideological state apparatuses.

[21] See *Law's Empire* (Cambridge, Mass.: Harvard University Press, 1986), 4, 11.

[22] See *The Concept of Law*, 26–33.   [23] See ibid. 60–1.

[24] Ibid. ch. 6, 'The Foundations of A Legal System'.

a rule that is neither valid nor invalid, but simply accepted, is both ingenious and deeply revealing about the nature of the legal order.[25] Hart showed that the obvious fact that the legal order of a modern municipal legal system is a very complex normative structure is fully compatible with the conviction that the foundations of that structure are contingent matters of social fact. His discussion of the implication of the social contingency of the foundations of the grounds of law—that where changes in the rule of recognition are concerned, 'all that succeeds is success'—is especially revealing and challenging. This is particularly so when the point is applied, as Hart himself applies it, to various kinds of radical change in the legal order; for in thinking about radical change we learn a lot about the nature of law in our own quieter times and places.[26]

Of course, as Hart accepts in the Postscript, his theory of the grounds of law needs to be improved in various ways in response to Dworkin's early criticisms.[27] Thus the focus on rules at the expense of broader, looser legal standards—'principles', in Dworkin's terminology—was misleading. He might have added that his original account paid insufficient attention to the role of standards governing interpretation. Thus if, in the case of *Riggs* v. *Palmer*,[28] Hart is to allow for the possibility that the law of New York all along did not entitle a murdering heir to inherit, his account of the legal order must have room for accepted canons of statutory interpretation that would explain this result. It is very important to note, however, that Hart did not purport to offer a complete theory of adjudication in *The Concept of Law*, neither as a normative theory of what the best approach to adjudication would be nor as an account of the standards governing adjudication actually found in any particular legal order.[29] So if New York law did entitle a murdering heir to inherit prior to *Riggs*, the correctness of that decision, disallowing the inheritance, is simply an open question for Hart. Of course, a complete account of the content of the legal order of any particular legal system would include an account of that system's standards governing adjudication. But Hart was not offering a complete account of any particular legal system's legal order. He was offering a structural account of the legal order that he believed would capture what

[25] Scott Shapiro says that, in 'large part, the philosophical project of jurisprudence begins' with the recognition of this problem; see 'On Hart's Way Out' (this volume), 149–91. Whether or not this is so, Shapiro is surely right to emphasize the centrality of the problem to Hart's project.

[26] See *The Concept of Law*, 117–23, 147–54.

[27] See ibid. 259; the main criticisms can be found in Dworkin, 'The Model of Rules I' (1967), in *Taking Rights Seriously* (London: Duckworth, 1978), 14–45.

[28] 115 NY 506, 22 NE 188 (1889); discussed in Dworkin, 'The Model of Rules I', 23 ff., and *Law's Empire*, 15–20.

[29] See Waluchow, *Inclusive Legal Positivism*, 33–42, 65–6. Waluchow rightly complains about the tendency among commentators to attribute an especially crude theory of adjudication to Hart. For a recent egregious example, see Kennedy, *A Critique of Adjudication*, 31–8, 177–9.

was common to all modern municipal systems. Still, as he also acknowledges, he might have said more about adjudication; there are, after all, various general or structural points that can be made on the topic.[30] Most importantly, he could have paid more attention to the fact that in a common-law legal order there needs to be a standard governing the legitimate overruling or ignoring of precedent or plain statutory meaning.[31]

To conclude this summary of the main features of Hart's descriptive project, we must refer to his explanation of 'the fact that where there is law, there human conduct is made in some sense non-optional or obligatory'.[32] Here he has been interpreted to have strayed from the descriptive path, since the presence or absence of obligation is not a matter to be described.[33] But though the text does contain some ambiguity, it seems fairly clear that Hart's discussion of law's normativity is offered not as an account of the moral obligation law does or could ground, nor as an account of law as generating some distinct kind of categorical obligation, but rather as a description of the deliberative role legal rules do play in at least some people's practical lives and as a philosophical account of what would need to be the case before something worth calling legal obligation could exist.[34] He remains fully neutral on what for him is the separate moral or political question of whether legal obligation, so understood, really does generate categorical obligations of some kind. It is true that in applying his account of social rules to moral as well as legal obligation Hart encouraged a different interpretation of his discussion of legal obligation; but he has explicitly abandoned his account of morality as a set of social rules, and so we need no longer be in any doubt about the best way to understand his discussion of legal obligation.[35]

---

[30] See Hart, *The Concept of Law*, 259; for a positivist account of adjudication, see Raz, *The Authority of Law*, ch. 10; *Ethics in the Public Domain*, ch. 10.

[31] See Dworkin, 'The Model of Rules I', 37.

[32] *The Concept of Law*, 51–61, 82–91; the quoted words are on p. 82.

[33] See Perry, 'Interpretation and Methodology'; Gerald Postema, 'Norms, Reasons, and Law', *Current Legal Problems* 51 (1998), 149–79; 'Jurisprudence as Practical Philosophy', *Legal Theory* 4, 329–57.

[34] As Green notes, Hart's 'main dispute was with two forms of reductionism: the coercion-based theories of classical positivism, which conceived of rules as orders backed by threats, and the behaviorist accounts influential among legal realists, which conceived of rules as predictions of official action. Against these, Hart's arguments are decisive' ('The Concept of Law Revisited', 1694).

[35] See *The Concept of Law*, 167–84; Dworkin, 'The Model of Rules II', in *Taking Rights Seriously*, 48–58; Hart, *The Concept of Law*, 254–9; *Essays on Bentham* (Oxford: Clarendon Press, 1982), 127–61, 264–7.

III. THE CONCEPT OF LAW

We have been able to summarize Hart's main claims in *The Concept of Law* without departing from the descriptive methodology. But as already indicated, the reason for this is that pretty much everything Hart says by way of describing of the legal order presupposes a particular stance on a disputed question about the concept of law.[36] Hart's description takes for granted that the legal order rests ultimately on social facts alone, and that moral considerations can become part of the legal order only if socially incorporated in some way.[37] Adopting a term of Raz, we can refer to this commitment as the 'social thesis'.[38] At some points Hart seems to have had in mind a stronger thesis, viz. Raz's 'sources thesis', which holds all law to be source-based in the sense that 'its existence and content can be identified by reference to social fact alone, without resort to any evaluative argument'.[39] The difference between these two conceptual commitments can be brought out by noting that the first allows that the correct account of the law of equal protection in the United States could turn on moral argument, since the text of the 14th Amendment to the US Constitution can be read as incorporating a moral principle, while the second insists that interpretation of the Constitutional text and subsequent Supreme Court decisions, insofar as this is a matter of declaring what the law of equal protection already is, must not invoke moral considerations.[40] We can follow Hart in labelling the view that accepts the social thesis but not the sources thesis 'soft positivism', and the view that also accepts the sources thesis 'hard positivism'. We can also take Hart at his word when he says, in the Postscript, that soft positivism was what he had in mind.[41]

[36] See also Raz, 'Two Views on the Nature of the Theory of Law', 1–37.

[37] Thus , though Jules Coleman's account of Hart's main arguments in *The Concept of Law*, in 'Incorporationism, Conventionality, and the Practical Difference Thesis' (this volume), strikes me as basically right, I disagree with his claim (p. 109) that this argument can be descriptive all the way down. However, as indicated above, pp. 374–5, I do agree with Coleman that Hart's project need take no stand on law's proper function; see ibid. 393.

[38] See *The Authority of Law*, 37: 'In the most general terms the positivist social thesis is that what is law and what is not is a matter of social fact.' As I use the label, the social thesis includes the more specific commitment that moral or political considerations can become part of the legal order only if socially incorporated in some way. This is a stronger thesis than the one Raz introduces as the 'weak social thesis', ibid. 41–5.

[39] Raz, 'Authority, Law, and Morality', 195.

[40] As Raz emphasizes, legal interpretation in accordance with the sources thesis could be controversial; see ibid. 218.

[41] *The Concept of Law*, p. 250. Though Green ('The Concept of Law Revisited', 1706) is right, I think, that the text of *The Concept of Law* is indeterminate on this issue. Note that in identifying the social and sources theses with versions of positivism, we assume that there are only two possible kinds of grounds of law—the moral/political and the social—and that law cannot somehow ground itself, in the manner of Hans Kelsen's 'pure' theory of law; see

I will return to the difference between hard and soft positivism below. For now, our question is this: how does Hart defend the social thesis? It is clear enough that a defence is needed. After all, Dworkin's main project in *Law's Empire* is also to offer a theory of the grounds of law, and he rejects the idea that moral and political considerations become part of the legal order only if socially incorporated in some way.[42] Moreover, if the social thesis must be rejected, Hart's description of the legal order is of rather little importance, for its most interesting aspects, summarized above, concern precisely the complexity of law's social foundations; it is in this respect that Hart's account is so great an improvement over that of his predecessors.

As I have indicated, though Hart did not devote much space to this conceptual issue in *The Concept of Law*, he did not ignore it either. Despite his avowal of a purely descriptive methodology in the Postscript, the argument he offered for the social thesis supports Dworkin's statement that 'any theory of law, including positivism, is based in the end on some particular normative political theory'.[43] At least, as I would prefer to put it, (part of) Hart's approach to the conceptual question is based in the end on some particular normative political claims—claims that might find support in a number of different, fully worked out political theories. But before discussing Hart's and Dworkin's methodologies further, we need to consider whether there is some plausible way of arguing for or against the social thesis that does not require appeal to moral or political argument.

The natural alternative, popular among contemporary defenders of positivism, is some form of politically neutral conceptual analysis. Perhaps our question about the concept of law can be approached in the way it was once popular to approach questions about the concept of knowledge. The philosophical task for analysis of the concept of knowledge was to reflect on the pattern of intuitions about when a person knew something and when she did not in order to develop a set of criteria that explained the application of the concept; knowledge turned out to be true justified belief. It later turned out that the justification criterion was hard to pin down; and later still the entire project fell somewhat out of favour.[44]

Pure Theory of Law, 2nd edn., trans. Max Knight (Berkeley and Los Angeles, Calif.: University of California Press, 1967; repr. Gloucester, Mass.: Peter Smith, 1989). On this point, see Green, 'The Concept of Law Revisited', 1691–2.

[42] See *Law's Empire*, 11; given the foundational nature of this disagreement, it is not surprising that Dworkin has, as Hart put it in the Postscript (*The Concept of Law*, 239), 'argued that nearly all the distinctive theses of [*The Concept of Law*] are radically mistaken'.

[43] See Dworkin, 'A Reply', 254. Dworkin's own methodology is discussed in Section V below.

[44] In its traditional form, at any rate. There is great contemporary philosophical interest in questions concerning the nature of concepts. Does possession of a concept amount to a

But the method was clear enough: undisputed examples of knowledge or its lack were used as the data around which to construct an account of the deep structure of our concept of knowledge. This kind of conceptual analysis was not, of course, merely a matter of setting out the meaning of the word 'knowledge'; competent speakers of English who had fully mastered the meaning of the word 'knowledge' and its cognates were not supposed to be able to produce the philosopher's criteria.

The concept of law cannot be analysed in the same way as the concept of knowledge, I believe, for the simple reason that there is no initial agreement about the data for the analysis. Undisputed examples of what is law exist, but there are also very many disputed examples of legal propositions. Most significantly, the most intense disagreement concerns precisely those cases that are in dispute between positivists and their opponents: reflection on 'our' concept of law is not going to determine whether moral considerations can be part of law without social incorporation because there is no agreement on the key examples that would need to be the basis of the reflection.[45] Nor is there agreement on any general characteristic of law that would immediately settle the dispute. Thus, though no one would disagree that law is in some sense an institutional phenomenon, the interpretation of what this amounts to is controversial; the social thesis cannot be derived from this uncontroversial but vague premiss.

A much more promising strategy can be found in the work of Raz.[46] Raz seeks the deep structure of the concept of law by exploring the implications of what can uncontroversially be asserted about it. There is no claim that these implications can be simply demonstrated, let alone that they are already evident to all possessors of the concept; rather, Raz believes that sophisticated philosophical argument, drawing inter alia on

certain capacity, or is it, rather, a matter of having certain mental representations? See e.g. Christopher Peacocke, *A Study of Concepts* (Cambridge, Mass.: MIT Press, 1992); Jerry Fodor, *Concepts: Where Cognitive Science Went Wrong* (New York: Oxford University Press, 1998). Armed with a philosophical theory of concepts construed as capacities, Peacocke proceeds to offer a theory of a particular concept, the concept of belief; such a theory answers this question: 'What is it to possess the concept of belief, to be capable of ascribing beliefs to oneself and to others?' (p. 147). My scepticism about the possibility of a theory of 'the' concept of law is entirely independent of the issues concerning the nature of concepts discussed by Peacocke, Fodor, and others, and is consistent with the possibility of illuminating philosophical theories of concepts, such as belief, for which the basic data are uncontroversial.

[45] See Dworkin, *Law's Empire*, e.g. 41–3. To give an example, Dworkin holds that the principles appealed to by the court in *Henningsen* v. *Bloomfield Motors, Inc.*, 32 NJ 358, 161 A.2d 69 (1960), were legal principles; but soft positivists hold that their status as legal principles turns on whether they were socially incorporated in some way; see 'The Model of Rules I', 23–4.

[46] See esp. 'Authority, Law, and Morality'; 'Two Views on the Nature of the Theory of Law'.

moral and political philosophy, is required to bring them out. Once this is
done, however, we will see that the existing concept of law did all along
provide an answer to our question whether moral and political considerations are or could be part of the grounds of law.

The apparently uncontroversial starting point for Raz's account is that
it is implicit in the concept of law that 'every legal system claims that it
possesses legitimate authority'.[47] I am not sure that Raz is entitled to this
first step, since a despotic regime that makes no attempt to claim that its
repression of some group is legitimate may nevertheless effect that repression by enforcing what we (many of us) would be willing to count as the
legal duties of that group. Such a repressive regime would, in Althusser's
terminology, make use of law only as part of the Repressive State Apparatus, and not as one of its Ideological State Apparatuses.[48] In any case,
whether or not I am right about this, Raz's account of the implications of
this weak initial conceptual claim proceeds by way of an account of the
concept of authority—leading eventually back to the conclusion that the
sources thesis is implicit in the concept of law. I cannot go into the details
of the argument here, but it seems rather clear to me that the existing
concept of authority is not robust enough to yield Raz's account of what
legal authority, properly understood, consists in—nor, for that matter,
does it seem robust enough to yield any other single account of the nature
of authority that is concrete enough to be of much help with our question
about the grounds of law.[49]

These brief remarks rather obviously do not do justice to the method of
politically neutral conceptual analysis. Perhaps I am wrong about the
plausibility of Raz's argument; and perhaps some other argument making
use of his methodology can yield an answer to our question about the
grounds of law.[50] As my main aim is to explore and illustrate a different
methodology, however, I will move on.

I have claimed that our existing concept of law does not provide an
answer to the question whether the grounds of law do or can include
moral and political considerations. But it is obvious that any attempt to
answer that question is constrained by the existing concept of law insofar

---

[47] 'Authority, Law, and Morality', 199. Raz himself does not claim that this assertion is
uncontroversial. I present his argument as if he did because I cannot see what would justify
this starting point other than the fact that no one can plausibly disagree with it and still be
taken, by the rest of us, to have a grasp of the concept of law.

[48] See n. 20 above.

[49] See Raz, 'Authority, Law, and Morality', 204: 'All I am assuming is that the service
conception is sound, i.e. that it correctly represents our concept of authority.' In disputing
this assumption, I am not taking a stand on whether Raz has offered a compelling political
theory of the conditions of legitimate authority; the fullest account of Raz's views about
authority is found in chs. 2–5 of *The Morality of Freedom* (Oxford: Clarendon Press, 1986).

[50] For one such argument, see Shapiro (this volume).

as it does have determinate content. If our question about the boundaries of law is important it is because law, the social phenomenon identified by the equivocal concept we already have, is important. Thus there is obviously no point answering the question by proposing a brand new concept of law that does not overlap with the existing one; what matters is where the boundaries of what we all now understand to be law are drawn.

To proceed from here, the natural course is to ask *why* the dispute about the boundaries of law matters, and choose our methodology accordingly. In addition to his political arguments, Hart suggests that the dispute matters in part because of its impact on theoretical inquiry.[51] The methodological upshot of this idea would be that we should let our theoretical practice develop the concept that suits it best: the 'best' concept of law will be the one that emerges in the process of developing the best social science of law. On this account, the concept that emerges will reflect its practical convenience as well as the theoretical interests of the inquirer (which may change or develop as she learns more about her subject matter).[52] As a general matter, this may well be the best way to think about concept formation in the natural and social sciences. Be that as it may, it is clear that in the specific case of the dispute over the concept of law, restricting ourselves to this approach would obscure what is most importantly at stake. Our existing equivocal concept of law has a central place in political practice and argument.[53] To the extent that acceptance or rejection of the social thesis affects political practice and argument, it matters, and this effect matters more, rather obviously, than any advance in the 'science' of law might matter. Thus suppose, what seems possible, that rejection of the social thesis severely limits social scientific inquiry into law; if law is tied up with morality, then truth in this domain will no longer be purely social scientific, and truth claims about the nature of law will become even more controversial. But one does not need to be sceptical about either social scientific or moral knowledge to deny that the pursuit of truth is always our most important goal.[54]

The political dimension of the dispute over the place of moral and political considerations in the grounds of law matters more than any

[51] See *The Concept of Law*, 209: 'If we are to make a reasoned choice between these concepts, it must be because one is superior to the other in the way in which it will assist our theoretical inquiries, or advance or clarify our moral deliberations, or both.' See also 'Positivism and the Separation of Law and Morals', e.g. 71–2, 78, where Hart writes that the positivist position has 'a moral as well as an intellectual value'. See also David Lyons, *Ethics and the Rule of Law* (Cambridge: Cambridge University Press, 1984), 57–9; Brian Leiter, 'Realism, Hard Positivism, and Conceptual Analysis', (this volume), 355–70.

[52] See pp. 374–5 and the work of Finnis cited in n. 12 above.

[53] See Dworkin, *Law's Empire*, e.g. 11; Raz, 'Authority, Law, and Morality', 221.

[54] See Nietzsche's discussion of the 'will to truth' in the Third Essay of *On The Genealogy of Morals*.

purely intellectual concerns we might have; and I cannot think of a third reason why the dispute might matter.[55] We must therefore approach our question about the concept of law as a practical aspect of political theory. The dispute about the concept of law is a political argument for control over a concept that has great ideological significance, where different sides in the dispute propose different ways of regimenting the existing equivocal concept. The dispute comprises the practical question of the social conse- quences of accepting one rather than another regimentation as well as the political question of which consequences we should be aiming at. Many different kinds of claim could be made within this general framework, but the gist of the disagreement between Hart and Dworkin can, as we have already seen, be put simply—it is the question of whether or not it is for the best always to endeavour to present existing law in its best light.

I will try to make good on this general characterization of the debate about the conceptual foundations of the grounds of law by illustrating it: I will present the practical-political case for the social thesis, followed by the practical-political case for the most important theory of the grounds of law that rejects the social thesis, Dworkin's theory of law as integrity. The arguments for the social thesis seem to me compelling; as we will see, however, they must in fact carry us further, all the way to the sources thesis and hard positivism.[56]

IV. THE POLITICAL CASE FOR THE SOCIAL AND SOURCES THESES

In presenting the consequentialist political reasons supporting the social thesis, it is important to have some concrete alternative views in mind.

---

[55] Gerald Postema and Stephen Perry argue that the right methodology in legal philoso- phy is that necessary to investigate the reason-giving force of law. See the works cited in nn. 10 and 33 above. As noted above, n. 10, the question of whether and how law could ever give rise to categorical obligations of some kind is obviously important. I doubt that it is appro- priate to characterize answers to it as elucidations of the concept of law, as Perry, in par- ticular, does (see 'Hart's Methodological Positivism'), but we can leave that aside (though see n. 98 below). Our question is different: Hart needed to resolve the conceptual dispute about the social and sources theses before he could proceed with his project of describing the legal order of modern municipal legal systems. Unlike both Dworkin (see n. 111 below) and Raz (see p. 382 above), Perry and Postema do not argue that the issue of law's authority is important *because* of its bearing on the social or sources theses or the theory of the grounds of law generally. Rather, they have, from Hart's perspective, changed the subject.

[56] The approach defended here should not be confused with the very different line of thought pursued in Tom D. Campbell, *The Legal Theory of Ethical Positivism* (Aldershot: Dart- mouth, 1996). Campbell assumes the social thesis and then presents an ethical or political argument in favour of rule-based legal orders where the application of the rules requires no appeal to moral or political considerations. The question of whether more or less formalistic (in this sense) legal orders are preferable is quite distinct from the conceptual question about the grounds of law pursued in this paper; see further pp. 392–3 below.

The caricature of the natural lawyer's view according to which law and justice or morality are more or less the same thing is of no interest, since it is incompatible with what is uncontroversial in the general understanding of law: the legal order and the legal regime are *in some way* connected.[57] In other words, no theory of the grounds of law will be plausible if it denies any role to institutional facts in the determination of the law. There thus seem to be two plausible non-positivist views to consider. I postpone discussion of the more important of these, Dworkin's theory of law as integrity, to the next section. In this section we can use as our non-positivist foil the view that Hart himself has in mind in his brief defence of the social thesis in *The Concept of Law*—the view that, while being just or morally good is not in general a criterion of legal validity, no outrageously unjust apparent laws are valid. We can think of this as positivism with a natural-law filter: all valid laws are socially grounded, but formally valid rules that fail to pass the minimal threshold for moral acceptability are not true law. Hart focused on the context in which this view most clearly emerges as a serious competitor to positivism, that of a radical regime change; in such circumstances even judges may be inclined to insist that, for example, uncontroversially formally valid legislation from the displaced regime was not law at all. Germany provided excellent illustrations of this kind of situation twice in the twentieth century. Indeed, Gustav Radbruch's version of the natural-law filter, the so-called 'Radbruch formula' first proposed in 1946, has recently been revived in the wake of the fall of the GDR: it has been applied by some German courts (though not the Federal Constitutional Court) in upholding the homicide convictions of East German border guards, and has been defended by at least one prominent German legal philosopher, Robert Alexy.[58]

[57] See Finnis, *Natural Law and Natural Rights*, 23–9.

[58] See 'A Defence of Radbruch's Formula', in David Dyzenhaus (ed.), *Recrafting the Rule of Law* (Oxford: Hart, 1999), 15–39; for details about the recent German cases, see also Julian Rivers, 'The Interpretation and Invalidity of Unjust Laws', pp. 40–65 in the same volume. Radbruch's own statement of his formula can be found in 'Gesetzliches Unrecht und übergesetzliches Recht' (1946), in *Gesamtausgabe*, ed. A. Kaufman (Heidelberg: C. F. Müller, 1990), iii. 89.

The Radbruch formula has been applied in decisions of the German Federal Court of Justice (Criminal Division); the leading case is BGHSt 39, 1 (1992); the gist of the argument is that the GDR law permitting shooting at persons fleeing over the Berlin Wall fails to pass through Radbruch's filter, and thus the homicide convictions in the trial court were correct. The German Federal Constitutional Court has not itself made use of the Radbruch formula in cases concerning the GDR, though it has upheld the constitutionality of the approach adopted by the Federal Court of Justice. See BVerfGE 95, 96, at 135. The Constitutional Court's own approach in this leading case (which involved one border guard and several officials of the GDR) is, in sum, to interpret the constitutional ban on retroactive punishment such that it does not apply to otherwise criminal acts that are made permissible by grossly unjust laws; see BVerfGE 95, 96, at 130–4. In other words, the court holds that not all retro-

The precise issue Hart discusses is whether, in the post-Nazi era, German courts should have treated some Nazi-era apparent laws as invalid because too unjust. Hart makes two practical-political arguments against the idea of the natural-law filter. The second of these arguments, said to provide the 'stronger reason', seems unfortunately to be question-begging. He says that embracing the natural-law filter would over-simplify the nature of the moral issues involved in a case such as that of a German who informed on another for offences against a Nazi statute and is in the post-Nazi era prosecuted for the crime of 'unlawful depriva-tion of liberty'. The question for the postwar court is, 'Are we to punish those who did evil things when they were permitted by evil rules then in force?' This is a different question from those of whether to obey or submit to punishment for breach of an iniquitous law. Hart writes that a 'concept of law which allows the invalidity of law to be distinguished from its immorality, enables us to see the complexity and variety of these separate issues; whereas a narrow concept of law which denies legal validity to iniquitous rules may blind us to them'.[59] This seems question-begging because the positivist concept of law will only be necessary for a full and accurate account of the moral issues involved if it is, indeed, the appropriate concept of law to employ.[60]

Perhaps we can interpret Hart such that he did not beg the question. In the relevant passages he writes about valid but evil 'rules', rather than valid but evil law. Even the natural lawyer under discussion must admit that the 'evil rules' existed in some sense. Moreover, these rules were of great relevance to anyone trying to predict how the Nazi officials would behave. Let us call such rules 'predictively useful rules'. Thus Hart could be read as saying that one of the issues raised by the case of the informer is that of the moral relevance of those predictively useful rules; and since we already have a way of talking about good law—it is what the law ought to be—we should make sure that we do not employ a concept of law that duplicates the concept we already have and at the same time makes it impossible to discuss the moral relevance of the predictively useful rules. Now it does seem clear that any discussion of the informer's case that fails to consider the moral relevance of the predictively useful rules is incomplete. For example, the existence of the predictively useful 'evil' rule could lead a potential informer to believe that if she did not turn a certain person in, both of them would face trouble; whatever its ultimate weight, this would be a relevant factor in any evaluation of her conduct.

active punishment is prohibited. This is essentially the route Hart preferred; see *The Concept of Law*, 208–12; 'Positivism and the Separation of Law and Morals', 76–8.

[59] See *The Concept of Law*, 208–11, 303 n.; the quotations are from p. 211.
[60] See Raz, *The Authority of Law*, 41–2; Waluchow, *Inclusive Legal Positivism*, 98–103.

But though the relevance of the predictively useful rules in this and other cases is an important point of political morality, it is still not an argument for the social thesis. For the natural lawyer could agree that the case is morally complex in just this way, and thus accept the need for consideration of predictively useful rules in any full discussion of the case of the informer, but still deny that this is relevant to our conceptual question of whether evil rules can be part of German law.[61] And to this Hart could not respond that it matters not just that there were predictively useful rules in force but also that those rules were, indeed, German law. For though it may be morally relevant whether these rules were part of German law, whether or not they were is precisely what we are trying to determine.

We can conclude that the moral complexity of the informer's case counts neither for nor against the social thesis. Nevertheless, at the end of his presentation of this argument, Hart does make a remark which points us in the right direction—back to arguments made earlier in *The Concept of Law* and also in 'Positivism and the Separation of Law and Morals'. Hart writes that a 'case of retroactive punishment should not be made to look like an ordinary case of punishment for an act illegal at the time'.[62] Of course, this again could be read as question-begging. But I prefer to read it as a reaffirmation of the earlier claim that it is not for the best to adopt a concept of law that helps us to believe that 'our law' has been, all along, both consistent and at least not terribly unjust. As Hart writes:

What surely is most needed in order to make men clear-sighted in confronting the official abuse of power, is that they should preserve the sense that the certification of something as legally valid is not conclusive of the question of obedience, and that, however great the aura of majesty or authority which the official system may have, its demands must in the end be submitted to a moral scrutiny.[63]

This is a straightforward consequentialist claim about the political advantages of the social thesis. In making it, Hart follows Bentham. Bentham attacked Blackstone for 'that spirit of obsequious *quietism* that seems constitutional in our Author' that 'will scarce ever let him recognize a difference between what is and what ought to be'.[64] The exact claim being made here, as I interpret it, is that if people think that bad law is not really law, they will be less inclined to subject what the legal regime

[61] See the related discussion in MacCormick, 'A Moralistic Case for A-Moralistic Law?', 9.
[62] *The Concept of Law*, 211–12.
[63] Ibid. 210; see also MacCormick, references given in n. 6 above. The Benthamite theme of law's aura of majesty and the consequent need to demystify it is pursued in Hart, 'The Demystification of the Law', *Essays on Bentham*, 21–39.
[64] Bentham, *A Fragment on Government*, in *Works*, ed. John Bowring (Edinburgh, W. Tait, 1838–43), i. 221, 294, as quoted in Hart, 'Positivism and the Separation of Law and Morals', 53–4; see also Gerald Postema, *Bentham and the Common Law Tradition* (Oxford: Clarendon Press, 1986), 304–5.

presents as law—apparent law—to critical appraisal. The implicit sociological premiss is that people for the most part rely on legal experts: if all
the experts are saying that the apparent law limiting suffrage to men is
valid law, well, it probably is morally all right too, since the experts know
as well as we do that if it were not morally all right it would not be law,
and they have thought about the whole thing more than we have.[65]

Kelsen had the same concern. A 'terminological identification of law
and justice', he wrote,

has the effect that any positive law . . . is to be considered at first sight as just, since
it presents itself as law and is generally called law. It may be doubtful whether it
deserves to be termed law, but it has the benefit of the doubt. . . . Hence the real
effect of the terminological identification of law and justice is an illicit justification
of any positive law.[66]

Elsewhere, Kelsen better expresses the bad effect of the natural law view
in these terms: 'it tends towards an uncritical legitimisation of the political coercive order.'[67] This is a better way of putting the point because the
bad effect of adopting one rather than another concept of law is not well
expressed as an effect on *law* (even 'positive law'). What law is, exactly,
obviously depends on which concept is being used, and so we cannot in
any simple way compare the effects on law of different possible concepts
of, precisely, law. In particular, if nothing is law unless it passes a moral
test, then law, so conceived, *is* to that extent justified. But it is clear enough
even in the first passage that Kelsen's concern is with the legitimization of
the state and its coercive institutional structure—what we have referred to
as the legal regime as opposed to the legal order. It is also clear that this is
what Hart was concerned about—writing, as he does, of the demands of
the 'official system'.

It should next be noted that the argument comparing the political
effects of embracing the positivist as opposed to the natural-law-filter
concept of law requires a fixed understanding of what it is for a rule to
'present itself as law'—we assume that under both conceptual options the
legal regime (construed broadly to include the authors of legal treatises)

---

[65] '[I]n the eyes of lawyers—not to speak of their dupes—that is to say, as yet, the generality of non-lawyers—the *is* and the *ought to be* . . . were one and indivisible.' Bentham, *A
Commentary on Humphrey's Real Property Code*, in *Works*, vol. v, 389, as quoted in Hart, 'Positivism and the Separation of Law and Morals', 54.

[66] Hans Kelsen, 'Law, State and Justice in the Pure Theory of Law', *Yale Law Journal* 57
(1948), 383–4. See also Schauer, 'Positivism as Pariah', 40–4.

[67] The passage continues: 'For it is presupposed as self-evident that one's own political
coercive order is an order of law.' 'Law and Morality', in Hans Kelsen, *Essays in Legal and
Moral Philosophy*, ed. O. Weinberger, trans. Peter Heath (Dordrecht: Reidel, 1974), 92. I am
grateful to Leslie Green for bringing this passage to my attention.

retains prima facie authority in respect of the content of the legal order.[68] If people employing the natural-law-filter concept would never regard a directive of the regime to be 'presented as law' absent a certification of sufficient justice from the National Conference of Catholic Bishops, for example, then there would be no direct threat of quietism about the legal regime (as distinct from the Catholic Church). My argument assumes that this possibility is ruled out by what is fixed in our equivocal concept of law. The more general point to make here is that the practical-political methodology of concept regimentation is only possible when there is sufficient content to the existing concept to allow us to frame the practical arguments in terms that are common to both the possible regimented concepts we are evaluating. Where that is not so, the argument can have no purchase; an argument about the practical effects of adopting one concept rather than another that employs conceptual resources available only if we adopt the preferred concept would obviously be empty.[69] We need to be convinced, using the notions we now have, that it makes sense to modify some of them. But there is sufficient content to the existing concept of law to allow us to frame the practical-political argument. As I have said, it is because this existing equivocal concept of law matters politically that the dispute over different possible ways of refining or regimenting it deserves our interest.

The two parts of the practical-political argument for the social thesis are the practical claim that convergence on a concept of law that rejects the social thesis brings the threat of quietism, and the political claim that this effect is undesirable.[70] The need to back up the political claim with political theory is clear enough, though as we will see in the next section

[68] In this paragraph I attempt to respond to criticism of the practical-political argument put to me by Joseph Raz.

[69] Several people have explained to me their rejection of the practical-political argument along roughly these lines: any regimentation leaves you with a different concept—so how *can* there be the conceptual common ground necessary to make this argument? This line of thought seems to depend on the assumption that even the slightest conceptual change produces radical incommensurability as between the old and the new concepts; a decision to include Tasmanian tigers in the category of wolf would mean that there were thenceforth no wolves. But that seems to be an entirely unwarranted fear; so long as the original equivocal concept and any proposed regimented concepts overlap as explained in this paragraph, we know what we are talking about. Instructive here is Dworkin's discussion of the 'semantic sting', in *Law's Empire*, 43–6.

[70] See also Waluchow, *Inclusive Legal Positivism*, 86–98. Waluchow rejects the validity of practical-political argument about the concept of law on the ground that it confuses what is the case with what we would like to be the case, see pp. 88–95. The trouble with this claim is that there is no fact of the matter here that we might be ignoring as we indulge in wishful thinking. Waluchow's own view (pp. 90–1) seems to be that the social thesis is established by way of more or less traditional conceptual analysis, as discussed above, pp. 380–1. Similar objections to the practical-political approach are made by Soper in 'Choosing a Legal Theory on Moral Grounds'.

the idea that a critical attitude towards law is desirable is compatible with a variety of political views. For the rest of this section we can simply take this idea for granted. The more immediate problem is the apparently speculative nature of the practical claim on which the argument also depends.[71] Why should we believe it—why not, indeed, believe the contrary claim that the denial of the social thesis leads not to quietism but rather to excessive *disrespect* for the legal regime? If people believe that apparent law is really law only if it passes a moral test, may they not believe themselves entitled to disobey any directive from the legal regime they disapprove of, with destabilizing or anarchic results? Indeed, Bentham himself made just this argument, without, apparently, being troubled that the two practical claims have opposite implications and may seem to cancel each other out.[72] Not surprisingly, Hart downplayed this aspect of Bentham's argument for the social thesis.[73]

It is clear that a full defence of the practical-political argument for the social thesis is not something a philosopher will be able to offer without help from other disciplines. This fact does not, however, count against the Benthamite methodology; it is, indeed, a straightforward implication of our conclusion in the previous section that the importance of the debate over the concept of law lies in the significance of the effects of general acceptance of one concept of law rather than another. Nor is this a dismal result, professionally speaking, for the legal philosopher, since his main role in the debate, that of untangling the values at stake, is indispensable too. (Not to mention the fact that once the debate about the concept is settled, it is the lawyer-philosopher who is in the best position to offer a description of law as a normative system—this, we recall, was Hart's main project in *The Concept of Law*.) Furthermore, it is not as if there is nothing useful that can be said from the armchair about the practical side of the practical-political argument.

Indeed, we can show that Bentham's anarchy concern lacks force. In the first place, this argument supposes that people's decisions whether or not to obey apparent law are based solely on their determination of whether an apparent law is, indeed, law. But Bentham himself would hope, as Hart certainly does, that we all understand the moral issue of obedience to be more complicated than that. There could be good reason to obey bad official directives even if we do not call them law, and good reason not to comply with a rule that truly is law. Hart raises exactly this point in reply to Radbruch, who had concluded that a positivistic understanding of law was partly to blame for the lack of German resistance to

---

[71] See Julius Stone, *Human Law and Human Justice* (Stanford, Calif.: Stanford University Press, 1965), 253–4.

[72] See Hart, 'Positivism and the Separation of Law and Morals', 53.

[73] See *The Concept of Law*, 211.

the Nazis. Hart pointed out that this could only be a plausible explanation if the German people *also* had a false understanding of the moral force of law, thus understood.[74] Bentham's concern that denial of the social thesis could lead to anarchy is based on the same kind of assumption.

In any case, it seems that the most important concern in the practical-political argument for the social thesis is not the effect on compliance.[75] Here several other forces, most notably the coercive power of the state, come to law's assistance.[76] The important concern, to my mind at least, is rather that of the overall political climate created by a view of law that merges law with morality. It seems, indeed, that if we focus on this question, the kind of thinking that Bentham thought might be destabilizing—'this unjust directive is not really law'—may in fact have the opposite effect. Suppose that we accept a concept of law with a natural-law filter and that this leads us to conclude that any apparent law providing for the execution of convicted criminals is not valid law. What then do we say about a country, such as the United States, where such executions happen in fact? There is little danger that any rational person will make the mistake of trusting to the truth about the legal order as opposed to what he knows the legal regime will do. As Austin put it in a famous passage, 'the Court of Justice will demonstrate the inconclusiveness of my reasoning by hanging me up, in pursuance of the law of which I have impugned the validity'.[77] But there is a danger here nonetheless, and it is again the danger of quietism.

The threat of quietism from the line of thought, 'Since this is presented as law, it probably is law, and therefore just', is intuitive enough; that the same threat is associated with the line of thought, 'This apparent law is unjust and therefore not really law', is less easy to see. For, to the contrary, this second line of thought would seem to add an additional basis for resistance to the legal regime; not only are all these executions wrong, they are, in fact, contrary to our law. But in part just for the reason that regime-threatening civil disobedience (Bentham's anarchy fear) is a rare event, the overall effect of this second line of thought may indeed be conservative. The opponent of the death penalty can actually rest somewhat more content because of her belief that, though the legal regime is imperfect (issuing as it does unlawful official directives), the overall legal system is not so bad since, after all, the death penalty is no part of the legal

---

[74] 'Positivism and the Separation of Law and Morals', 72–5. See also Schauer, 'Positivism as Pariah', 35–40.

[75] Much of Soper's critique, in 'Choosing a Legal Theory on Moral Grounds', is directed to the issue of compliance.

[76] See Stone, *Human Law and Human Justice*, 255.

[77] John Austin, *The Province of Jurisprudence Determined*, ed. Wilfrid E. Rumble (Cambridge: Cambridge University Press, 1995 [1832]), 158.

order. Moreover, it is not just the overall legal system, the legal order along with the legal regime, that looks better; the legal regime is itself shown in a better light by this line of thought. For, as we have noted, on no plausible account of the legal order is it entirely disconnected from the institutional facts of the legal regime. The legal order is, in some sense, at least in part a creature of the legal regime. Likewise, the legal regime is determined, at least in part, by the legal order; if there are no norms governing the operations of the relevant institutions, we uncontroversially refuse to describe them collectively as legal institutions. The legal order and the legal regime can be distinguished for the purposes of better understanding, but neither can exist without the other.[78] This complex and confusing interconnection between legal norm and institutional fact is, as has often been noted, what makes the study of the nature of law both difficult and interesting. But my present point is just to reiterate that part of what is uncontroversial about the concept of law is that the legal order is what it is at least in part because of facts about the legal regime. So when we employ a concept of law according to which the legal order of necessity passes some moral test, we inevitably show the legal regime in a better light as well. And a crucial element of this legitimizing effect is the impact such a concept of law has on the kind of criticism that will be directed at what are regarded as unjust directives from the legal regime. When we characterize unjust actions of the regime as mistakes about the legal order we actually show the legal regime in a positive light, since what we are saying, in effect, is that the legal regime is being false to its true (just) nature. To allow for the possibility of this kind of criticism, the criticism that says not just that the regime acts wrongly when it executes people but that the regime in some sense fails itself when it does so, is to encourage quietism. The more we infuse our concept of law with a moral ideal, such that we can regard unjust actions by the legal regime as *mistakes*—mistakes about a normative order that the regime is itself partly responsible for—the more accepting we will be of unjust directives from the legal regime.[79]

It is important to emphasize that the political argument I have offered concerns the concept of law that should underlie our theory of the grounds of law. It is not an argument about the best theory of adjudication; nor is it an argument about the optimal nature of the legal order—whether it

---

[78] See Kornhauser, 'Three Roles for a Theory of Behavior in a Theory of Law'.

[79] Positivist theories of the grounds of law of course acknowledge that the legal regime (e.g. a court) will make mistakes about the legal order. A theory of the grounds of law that does not allow for this is, in effect, a theory that denies the independent existence of the legal order, one that reduces the legal order to the legal regime; see ibid. The point in the text has to do with the specific issue of whether the regime's deviations from justice are treated as mistakes about the legal order.

should be more or less formalistic, for example.[80] Of course, these other questions, which must be addressed as a pair, raise political issues of their own. Thus, for example, one might be politically opposed to judges appealing to moral considerations when deciding cases, and if so one would be in favour of a theory of adjudication that disallows this; judges might be directed to resolve hard cases by, for example, appealing to their sense of 'community morality' (Cardozo's method of sociology).[81] One would also be in favour of a legal order that is as formalistic as possible, leaving minimal scope for illicit judicial moralizing.[82] In this paper I simply take for granted that there is no possible legal order that could make adjudication mechanistic, and thus eliminate the need, in hard cases, for judges to appeal to broader principles of political morality, some of which may not have been socially incorporated into the legal order. I also assume that on the best theory of adjudication judicial appeal to principles of political morality that are not incorporated into the legal order should be based on judges' own best judgment, rather than on some speculation about what the community believes; moreover, these appeals to political morality should not be hidden in a sophistical pretence of formalistic argument.[83] These are points on which more or less all sides in the debate over the theory of the grounds of law, including Hobbes, Bentham, Austin, Holmes, legal realists such as Felix Cohen, Hart, Raz, Dworkin, and Finnis, agree.[84] Of course, each of these theorists would offer very different accounts of the optimal legal order and the best theory

[80] I have in mind the use of the word 'formalism' that has to do with formal legal rules which require minimal substantive judgement for their application.

[81] See Benjamin Cardozo, *The Nature of the Judicial Process* (New Haven, Conn.: Yale University Press, 1921).

[82] See Campbell, *The Legal Theory of Ethical Positivism*.

[83] Note that in saying that it would be best if judges were to follow their own best views about what political morality requires I do not mean that judicial legislation should ignore the existing political and legal circumstances judges are confronted with. See, on this point, Raz, 'Authority, Law, and Morality', 219: Judges 'must bear in mind that their decisions will take effect in society as it is, and the moral and economic reasons they resort to should establish which is the best or the just decision given things as they are rather than as they would be in an ideal world.' See also n. 86 below.

[84] Kennedy (*A Critique of Adjudication*, 84–5) asserts that there is a 'dramatic historical moment' marking the first formulation of the critical strategy that claims (roughly) that judges inevitably must draw on their own ideological agendas to reach some decisions, since the common law is indeterminate, but they typically disguise this fact in their opinions: the publication of an article by Holmes in 1894. Kennedy is here discussing, specifically, 'American Critical Legalism'; nonetheless, and with all due respect to Holmes, it seems unlikely that he was the first American to take on board a line of thought that dates back at least as far as Francis Bacon. This, for example, is how Bacon begins his essay 'Of Judicature' (1625): 'Judges ought to remember that their office is *jus dicere*, and not *jus dare*: to interpret law, and not to make law or give law. Else will it be like the authority claimed by the Church of Rome, which under pretext of exposition of Scripture doth not stick to add and alter; and to pronounce that which they do not find, and by show of antiquity to introduce novelty.' See *The Essays*, ed. John Pitcher (Harmondsworth: Penguin, 1985), 222. See also Thomas Hobbes,

of adjudication, and in doing so appeal to different judgments, both about institutional competence and about background political values. But those complex and extremely important topics must not be confused with our topic, which is specifically the theory of the grounds of law and the conceptual foundations thereof.[85] Indeed, the reasons I have advanced for accepting the social thesis do not at all count against judges appealing to political considerations in hard cases; for so long as any appeal to political considerations not socially incorporated is well understood to be a legislative act, there is no encouragement of quietism.[86] The danger of quietism comes rather from the belief that in appealing to those moral considerations the judge is simply applying the law, which is thus shown to have been *already* rather good.[87]

There are of course some connections between the theory of the grounds of law and the two other issues just mentioned. Thus if judicial lawmaking is one's worst fear ('whatever the law is, I don't want it made by judges'), positivism will be easier to accept the more formalistic and complete the legal order. In general, it is fair to say that positivism has been more popular in the UK and in its more recently independent former colonies than in the US;[88] it is no coincidence, I think, that the legal order in the US is in general the least formalistic.[89] Similarly, there is this

A Dialogue Between a Philosopher and a Student of the Common Laws, ed. Joseph Cropsey (Chicago: University of Chicago Press, 1971 [166?]); for discussion, see Postema, *Bentham and the Common Law Tradition*, 46–60.

Indeed, no less an American than Thomas Jefferson seems to have shared this general perspective on the common law judge, writing in 1776 of the 'the eccentric impulses of whimsical, capricious designing man'; see letter to Edmund Pendleton in Julian P. Boyd et al. (eds.), *Papers of Thomas Jefferson* (Princeton, NJ: Princeton University Press, 1950–), i. 505, quoted in Gordon S. Wood, 'Comment', in Antonin Scalia, *A Matter of Interpretation* (Princeton, NJ Princeton University Press, 1997), 50. Wood (ibid.) notes the influence of Beccaria on Jefferson and like-minded contemporaries. On Beccaria's influence on Bentham, see Hart, *Essays on Bentham*, 40–52.

[85] As Dworkin recently reiterated, it is a mistake to object to law as integrity on the ground that it allows judges to appeal to moral considerations when deciding cases; see 'In Praise of Theory', *Arizona State Law Journal* 29 (1997), 360.

[86] This addresses the point made by Soper, 'Choosing a Legal Theory on Moral Grounds', 36–7. Note that the claim that judges legislate just means that part of their adjudicative role consists in making, rather than applying, the law. It does not imply that when judges make law they do so, or ought to do so, in just the same way that members of legislatures do—a view that Kennedy (*A Critique of Adjudication*, 31) wrongly associates with Hart. Kennedy is surely right to say that no one 'interested in the political analysis of the content of legal systems would adopt' this view.

[87] 'To the *Expositor* it belongs to shew what the *Legislator* and his underworkman the *Judge* have done *already*; to the *Censor* it belongs to suggest what the Legislator *ought* to do *in future*.' Bentham, *A Fragment on Government*, as quoted in Postema, *Bentham and the Common Law Tradition*, 304.

[88] See Hart, 'American Jurisprudence through English Eyes: The Nightmare and the Noble Dream', in *Essays in Jurisprudence and Philosophy*, 123–44.

[89] See P. S. Atiyah and Robert S. Summers, *Form and Substance in Anglo-American Law* (Oxford: Clarendon Press, 1987). For general comparative discussions of American legal

connection between the theory of the grounds of law and the theory of adjudication. If one's main concern is to limit judicial appeal to moral and political considerations as much as possible, then (hard) positivism will seem preferable to any other view because it marks the clearest boundary between the materials that constrain the judge, on the one hand, and moral reasoning, on the other; the clearer this boundary is marked the less likely it is that judges will stray over it. Furthermore, the clearer the boundary, the more clearly the critic can separate out technical from ethical judicial error.[90] And there are no doubt further connections that could be drawn between these different issues. The important point to remember, however, is that the quietism argument is about the effects on the general political culture of different theories of the grounds of law; in particular, it makes no claims about the effect of different theories of the grounds of law on the quality of judicial decision-making.[91]

Having presented the quietism argument in defence of the social thesis, it not hard to see that the argument cannot stop there: the reasons I have offered for the social thesis carry us all the way to the sources thesis.[92] For imagine that a moral filter is simply written into the constitution of some state: 'Parliament shall make no grossly unjust law', for example. The threat of quietism seems actually to be made worse, even if the social thesis is accepted. Citizens of this country can say, not just, 'Since this is presented as law, it probably is law, and therefore reasonably just—since it is part of the very concept of law that law is not grossly unjust.' They can say something less abstract and thus apparently less controversial— 'Since this is presented as law, it probably is law, and therefore just, since our constitution ensures that none of our laws are grossly unjust.'

Whether or not the problem of quietism is made worse by the incorporation of the moral filter, the important point is that both aspects of the

---

theory, see Hart, 'American Jurisprudence Through English Eyes'; Kennedy, *A Critique of Adjudication*, 73–96.

[90] See e.g. Felix Cohen, 'Transcendental Nonsense and the Functional Approach', *Columbia Law Review* 35 (1935), 841.

[91] David Dyzenhaus argues that positivism led certain judges in apartheid South Africa to make worse decisions than they otherwise might have. See *Hard Cases in Wicked Legal Systems* (Oxford: Clarendon Press, 1991). The argument depends on a rather bizarre claim about the effect of adopting a positivistic theory of the grounds of law on a judge's theory of adjudication; for criticism, see Anton Fagan, 'Delivering Positivism from Evil', in Dyzenhaus, *Recrafting the Rule of Law*, 81–112. For a subtle discussion of these issues, see Mark Osiel, 'Dialogue with Dictators: Judicial Resistance in Argentina and Brazil', *Law and Social Inquiry* 20 (1995); 481–560. It seems likely that no particular theory of the grounds of law can claim to do best overall, taking into account the entire range of types of political situation (wicked regime, progressive judges; progressive regime, wicked judges; stable regime, ordinary judges, etc.), in terms of its effect on judicial outcomes.

[92] For a different way in which the argument might be extended, see Waluchow, *Inclusive Legal Positivism*, 87.

problem of quietism remain unless we move all the way to the sources thesis. So long as a moral test is thought to play a role in the determination of what the law already is, there will be the danger that apparent laws will be given the benefit of the doubt, assumed to be true law, and thus assumed to have satisfied the moral test. And there is the second danger too, that when official directives are regarded as unjust, this will be characterized as a kind of internal malfunction on the part of the legal regime, not in itself cause for great alarm, certainly not cause to subject the legal system as a whole to searching criticism. The danger of quietism stems from the presence of the moral test in the grounds of law; it is immaterial whether or not that moral test becomes part of the grounds of law through social incorporation.

We can also see that if the presence of moral considerations in the grounds of law did not have regrettable effects, there would be no particular reason to insist that only socially incorporated moral considerations could be part of the grounds of law. I thus agree with Dworkin, though for different reasons, that soft positivism has little to recommend it.[93]

It should once again be emphasized what acceptance of the sources thesis does *not* imply. It does not imply that it is unwise to include substantive moral provisions in a constitution. It is better to illustrate this point with a more realistic example than the one I have used so far. The hard positivist account of a constitutional provision invalidating all law that violates 'the right to freedom of expression' could go as follows. To the extent that there is a plain meaning to 'the right to freedom of expression', or an agreed way of interpreting that phrase, as found in the constitution, which does not in itself depend upon moral argument, the protection of freedom of expression, thus understood, is part of the law from the moment the provision is adopted. But to the extent that purely legal interpretation leaves the matter open, the provision must be seen, in the first instance, as a directive to the legislature to pay close heed to the impact its proposed legislation would have on freedom of expression. If we now add in judicial review in respect of this provision, it can be seen as giving power to a court to make its own determinations, based on its own best account of the moral issue of freedom of expression, whether

---

[93] See *Law's Empire*, 124–30. The only ground I can think of for embracing soft positivism would be that traditional conceptual analysis yields the social thesis but not the sources thesis. That soft positivism is nevertheless a *coherent* position has been amply demonstrated; see e.g. the following influential articles: Jules Coleman, 'Negative and Positive Positivism', *Journal of Legal Studies* 11 (1982), 139–64, repr. *Markets, Morals and the Law* (Cambridge: Cambridge University Press, 1988), 3–27; Lyons, 'Moral Aspects of Legal Theory', in *Moral Aspects of Legal Theory*, 64–101; E. Philip Soper, 'Legal Theory and the Obligation of a Judge: The Hart/Dworkin Dispute', *Michigan Law Review* 75 (1977), 473–519; and the excellent book-length treatment in Waluchow, *Inclusive Legal Positivism*.

particular legislation violates the right to freedom of expression and is therefore invalid.[94] Adding finally a doctrine of *stare decisis*, the court's decisions legislate a more determinate constitutional law of freedom of expression for the future (to the extent that the holdings of those decisions can be interpreted without moral argument). As Raz puts it, 'the courts may be made custodians of freedom of expression, a supervisory body in charge both of laying down standards for the protection of free expression and adjudicating in disputes arising out of their application'.[95] When they perform their legislative role badly, from the point of view of the best account of the political morality of freedom of expression, we say just that; we do not say that they make mistakes about the law as it all along has been.

Having concluded this practical-political argument for the sources thesis, it must be remembered that Hart himself never explicitly defended the sources thesis as opposed to the social thesis, and indeed explicitly embraces soft positivism in the Postscript. Moreover, and more importantly, the Postscript fails to reaffirm Hart's earlier practical-political methodology for the dispute over the concept of law.[96] The Benthamite methodology I am defending, then, can be attributed to the early Hart only.

V. THE POLITICAL CASE FOR LAW AS INTEGRITY

It is time to turn to the most sophisticated non-positivist theory of the grounds of law, Dworkin's theory of law as integrity. Dworkin offers a political case for the rejection of the sources thesis that must be taken very seriously by positivists. After all, the quietism argument can hardly be considered irresistible; both the practical and the political sides to the argument will seem much more plausible to some than to others. It seems likely that one reason Hart was nevertheless so sure of the merits of the social thesis was that he was unaware of any powerful arguments *against* it.[97] Dworkin has advanced such arguments, and it is disappointing that in the Postscript Hart treats them as irrelevant to his project. Indeed,

[94] On the difference between the question of the existence of a constitutional norm, and the question of the appropriate institution to enforce it, see Lawrence Gene Sager, 'Fair Measure: The Legal Status of Underenforced Constitutional Norms', *Harvard Law Review* 91 (1978), 1212–64.

[95] 'Authority, Law, and Morality', 217.

[96] Waluchow (*Inclusive Legal Positivism*, 98 n.) cites personal correspondence in which Hart explicitly rejects this methodology; this means that for the late Hart the merits of positivism were no longer both 'moral and intellectual', but intellectual only.

[97] See, e.g. 'Positivism and the Separation of Law and Morals', 71–2, where Hart considers and rejects what is in effect a very crude version of law as integrity; what emerges most strongly from this discussion, for me at least, is that Hart simply cannot see any plausible reason to move in that direction.

pending new practical-political arguments, the case for or against positivism turns, I believe, on the relative plausibility of the quietism argument as compared to Dworkin's argument for law as integrity.[98]

Law as integrity is an interpretive theory of the grounds of law: 'propositions of law are true if they figure in or follow from the principles of
justice, fairness, and procedural due process that provide the best
constructive interpretation of the community's legal practice.'[99] Crudely
then, the idea is that the law is what follows from the morally best interpretation of the prior directives of the legal regime.[100] Construed as a
theory of adjudication, law as integrity has a great deal of plausibility,
both as a descriptive account of actual practice, especially in the constitutional and private common law domains,[101] and as a normative theory of
adjudication. But as a theory of the grounds of law, the Benthamite objection to it is obvious: it would be redundant to illustrate how the two
quietism-inducing lines of thought arise under law as integrity, as viewing the directives of the legal regime in their morally best light is this
theory's basic aim.[102] And it goes about this in an exceptionally sophisticated way: we are not asked to believe in some crude moral filter, but
rather that every decision about what the law is turns inevitably in part
on moral considerations. I will not here try to do justice to the complex
structure of this theory of the grounds of law. Rather, my concern is to
evaluate Dworkin's political case for this view; for that political case
stands in direct contradiction to the political claim that underlies the
quietism argument for the sources thesis.

The positivist's political claim is that an alert and critical attitude
toward the legal system is desirable because a legal and political culture
where this sceptical attitude prevails is more likely to progress towards
substantive justice (away from injustice) and less likely to regress from
justice already achieved. The political conclusion that quietism is bad
need not be based on some claim about the inherently repressive or other-

---

[98] One other important practical-political argument might be made against the social and
sources theses. Perhaps it could be shown that it is politically desirable that it be plausible
to believe that law, as law, is always prima facie morally binding or in some other sense a
source of categorical obligations. If so, there would be reason to regiment the concept of law
accordingly, which would presumably mean the rejection of the social thesis. I am indebted
here to Carlos Rosenkrantz; neither he nor, so far as I am aware, anyone else has developed
this argument in print.

[99] *Law's Empire*, 225.

[100] These prior directives are law in the 'preinterpretive' sense; see ibid. 65–7, 90–1. Note,
however, that the directives are not, on Dworkin's account, themselves necessarily part of
the legal order; the process of interpretation may require the interpreter to come to treat
parts of pre-interpretive law as mistakes.

[101] See Stephen Perry, 'Judicial Obligation, Precedent and the Common Law', *Oxford Journal of Legal Studies* 7 (1987), 215–57.

[102] It is evident that each of the examples used to illustrate the quietism argument in the
previous section could arise under law as integrity.

wise morally unacceptable nature of law in general; nor need it be based on a sense that since law's repressive potential is ever-present but its realization easily disguised, we should always be inclined to see a legal system as repressive or otherwise bad unless convinced to the contrary. Thus, though the sceptical attitude amounts to a refusal to view law in its best light, it is not an attitude of convinced condemnation, nor one that views law in its worst light.[103]

The sceptical attitude is compatible with a wide range of political outlooks. One does not need to share Bentham's utilitarianism to believe that a healthy legal culture is best promoted by a sceptical attitude towards the status quo. Indeed, it is initially rather hard to understand how any plausible political outlook could yield a different conclusion. To see this, it is important to emphasize the contribution the sceptical attitude makes to the maintenance of just arrangements already achieved. As Mill pointed out in his discussion of the virtues of freedom of speech in 'On Liberty', a critical perspective is beneficial even if (as it might turn out) what we already have *is* the very best. For criticism is necessary to keep alive any deep understanding of why what we have is indeed worth preserving.[104]

In the face of these plausible and catholic political thoughts, why might one conclude that it is, to the contrary, best always to view law in its best light? One possibility would be that a particular legal system is thought to have achieved enormous progress towards justice, but is subject to a persistent line of misguided criticism that threatens to undo its achievements; in that special context, it might be thought, the best strategy is to show what has been achieved in its best light. The constitutional jurisprudence of the United States since the New Deal may come to mind in this connection, and this is certainly a central concern for Dworkin.[105] But Dworkin's defence of law as integrity is more general than this; he does

---

[103] Dworkin appears to use the term 'sceptical' to denote one or other of these latter two attitudes. See *Law's Empire*, 95, 105, 160, 271–5. I prefer my usage, naturally, but the more important point is that Dworkin pays little attention to the attitude I call sceptical, and writes rather as if the alternatives to viewing law in its best light are to view it in its worst light or else to condemn it outright.

[104] For similar points, though restricted to the context of US constitutional law, see Robin West, 'Constitutional Scepticism', *Boston University Law Review* 72 (1992), 790–92.

[105] See *Freedom's Law* (Cambridge, Mass.: Harvard University Press, 1996). See also the discussion of Dworkin in Kennedy, *A Critique of Adjudication*, 113–30. Though Kennedy makes a plausible claim when he says that 'the liberal legal project has been to defend the legality of the liberal judicial law making of the past fifty years' (p. 129), he mis-characterizes Dworkin as attempting to give an account of adjudication that shows it to be ideologically neutral (see e.g. p. 125). He thus misses what is most bold and interesting, I believe, in Dworkin's work: the idea that adjudication can be deeply controversial as a matter of political conviction (the disagreement between Kennedy's liberals and conservatives is of this kind) and still count as law application rather than legislation. Insofar as Dworkin *is* carrying out the 'liberal legal

not argue that law as integrity is strategically desirable given a certain specific political environment.

Having said this, however, we must note the limits to the generality of application that law as integrity can claim. As Dworkin acknowledges, if the prior directives of a legal regime have been bad enough, it will not be possible to construct an interpretation that shows those directives in their morally best light. If a legal system or part of it is clearly based on a fundamentally abhorrent principle, such as racial supremacy, there is no morally best light to put it in; such a legal system, as Dworkin puts it, yields 'to no interpretation that can have, in any acceptable political morality, any justifying power at all'.[106] This is not troubling for Dworkin, however, for the reason that our language is flexible enough to accommodate different senses in which a regime's directives can count as law. For example, we could say that Nazi Germany certainly produced official directives that, in Dworkin's terms, were law in the pre-interpretive sense, even if we refuse to say that the regime produced law in the same sense as contemporary Germany does—law in the sense that is captured by the theory of law as integrity. Though Dworkin is surely right that the point of legal philosophy is not to provide some rigid univocal definition of law, this appeal to the flexibility of legal language does not in itself address the essentially practical problem raised by the fact that the integrity theory of the grounds of law does not apply to 'evil' regimes.[107] For law as integrity is not akin to Finnis's natural-law theory of law—an idealized account of law that is compatible with and is not designed to replace a separate, perhaps positivistic, account of law in the lawyer's technical sense.[108] A theory of the grounds of law just is a theory of law in the lawyer's technical sense; it is an account of what makes legal propositions, as used by lawyers, judges, and officials of government agencies, true. But since that is so, the inapplicability of the integrity theory of the grounds of law to the

---

project' as described, he is doing it by offering *both* a theory of adjudication and a theory of the grounds of law.

I should add that I find Kennedy's discussion of the legitimation effect of a practice of adjudication that denies the role of political ideology largely compelling (see pp. 236–96). My own claims about the quite different issue of the political consequences of different theories of the grounds of law are in roughly the same vein.

[106] See *Law's Empire*, 101–8; the quotation is from p. 102. See also Hart, *Essays on Bentham*, 147–53, and Dworkin, 'A Reply', 256–60; for Hart's rejoinder, see 'Legal Theory and the Problem of Sense', in Ruth Gavison (ed.), *Issues in Contemporary Legal Philosophy* (Oxford: Clarendon Press, 1987), 40–2. It should be remembered that Dworkin does not equate the possibility of providing an interpretation of a legal practice that has justificatory force in some acceptable political morality—the possibility of applying his theory of the grounds of law—with the political conclusion that people should obey, or officials apply, law so identified; he refers to this second set of issues as those of the 'force' of law; see *Law's Empire*, 108–13.

[107] See also Waluchow, *Inclusive Legal Positivism*, 62–4.

[108] See Finnis, *Natural Law and Natural Rights*, 276–81.

official directives of some regimes does seem to be a disadvantage of the theory. Consider a contract between a French oil company and an agency of the government of Burma, or between an Australian mining company and an Indonesian agency overseeing development in the Timor Sea. If, at a particular time, Burma's treatment of ethnic minorities in the region of the oil extraction, or Indonesia's military occupation of East Timor, are thought to render the relevant law of Burma or Indonesia incapable of yielding a morally best interpretation, then a choice of law dispute arising under one of these contracts would have to be treated as a dispute about two very different kinds of normative order. It would seem, however, that private international law in general, and the theory of international choice of law in particular, depends rather heavily on there being a single concept of law in the lawyer's technical sense. Of course, the correct response to this point might be to make international choice of law theory more sophisticated; but the proliferation of concepts of law for use by lawyers does seem to amount to a prima facie count against the integrity theory of the grounds of law, even in those jurisdictions where it is fully applicable to domestic law.

The case for law as integrity must be strong enough to overcome both this practical objection to parochial theories of the grounds of law and, much more importantly, the plausible and catholic political case for the sources thesis. As we will see, the benefits Dworkin claims for law as integrity are certainly weighty enough to sustain this burden. Before turning to the benefits of law as integrity, however, we must return briefly to the issue of methodology. For Dworkin's stated methodology for the development of a theory of the grounds of law is not the practical-political methodology I have defended. Instead, his methodology for resolving the dispute about the concept of law emerges from a more general theory of interpretation.

Law, Dworkin says, is an interpretive concept. This means, in the first place, that there is considerable disagreement about the conceptual foundations of the theory of the grounds of law; I have followed Dworkin on this point. The idea that law is an interpretive concept also entails, however, that the way to resolve that disagreement, the right way to approach what Dworkin calls theoretical disagreement in law, is to offer a constructive interpretation of legal practice. A constructive interpretation, in turn, is one that attributes a point to the practice and in so doing shows the practice in its best light.[109] Law as integrity, the theory of the grounds of law according to which law is what follows from showing the directives of the legal regime in their morally best light, is justified, in Dworkin's methodology, by the fact that this theory of the grounds of law shows legal practice in its best light.

---

[109] See *Law's Empire*, chs. 2 and 3.

Now, to resolve the disagreement about the concept of law by show-ing the associated practice in its best light is obviously not to practise the method I have defended, which directs us to resolve the disagree-ment in the way that is best for us.[110] The defence of the practical-polit-ical method is simple: how else to resolve the disagreement than in the way that is best in respect of the very issues that make the disagreement important? The attraction of the method of constructive interpretation is less clear to me. The early chapters of *Law's Empire* argue that the approach of constructive interpretation is appropriate for the concept of law because constructive interpretation is quite generally the best method of interpretation. This defence seems problematic precisely because it depends on such a general claim. It would be rather sur-prising, indeed, if there were a single best account of interpretation that applied equally to all cultural, political, and scientific practices. Furthermore, it is not clear how interpretation of legal practice, which on any account involves both applying and making law, could resolve conceptual disagreement about the role of moral considerations in determining what the law (already) is.[111] But I think we can leave Dworkin's general interpretive methodology to one side. For his constructive interpretation of the concept of law *includes* a consequen-tialist argument about the benefits of the integrity theory of the grounds of law.[112] This argument, if persuasive, would on its own amount to a sufficient reply to the positivist within the terms of the practical-political methodology.

The heart of Dworkin's argument is found in chapters 5 and 6 of *Law's Empire*, where the political value of integrity is explained and defended, and linked with the notion of a community of principle. The value of integrity is the value of coherent and principled governance; as such, it

[110] See also Waluchow, *Inclusive Legal Positivism*, 15–29.

[111] That disagreement could potentially be resolved, by contrast, by an interpretation of a certain shared account of what law is. Dworkin in fact approaches the conceptual question in just this way, characterizing different theories of the grounds of law as different concep-tions of the concept of law; see *Law's Empire*, 90–6. (Though he says that nothing in his succeeding argument depends upon prior agreement to this account of the concept of law; see ibid. 93.) Dworkin's suggestion is that the core of the concept of law, the elaboration of which is the aim of competing conceptions of law, is that 'the most abstract and fundamen-tal point of legal practice is to guide and constrain the power of government in the follow-ing way. Law insists that force not be used or withheld, no matter how useful that would be to ends in view, no matter how beneficial or noble these ends, except as licensed or required by individual rights and responsibilities flowing from past political decisions about when collective force is justified' (ibid. 93). I agree with Hart, *The Concept of Law*, 249, that this is too controversial to count as a neutral starting point for the resolution of the dispute about the concept of law.

[112] Dworkin, 'In Praise of Theory', 364, describes his approach as 'consequential in its overall aim: it aims at a structure of law and community that is egalitarian in the sense I tried to describe in *Law's Empire*'.

'would not be needed as a distinct political virtue in a utopian state'.[113] In a utopian state, Dworkin believes, there would be no disagreement about justice, and thus also no need for what he calls a principle of fairness, which is a principle that sets out the proper way for a community to reach political decisions in the face of such disagreement; majority decision is one example. But in actual states, there is disagreement about both justice and fairness. The commitment to integrity as a value, in these circumstances, amounts to the insistence 'that the state act on a single, coherent set of principles even when its citizens are divided about what the right principles of justice and fairness really are'.[114] This insistence breaks down into two more specific commitments: the principle of integrity in legislation, 'which ask those who create law by legislation to keep that law coherent in principle', and the principle of integrity in adjudication, which 'asks those responsible for deciding what the law is to see and enforce it as coherent in that way'.[115] Note that this second principle equates adjudication with the determination of what the law is—innocuously enough, for Dworkin, since the integrity theory of the grounds of law always provides an answer to legal questions and thus leaves no room for judicial lawmaking.[116] But as between the integrity theory and the sources thesis, this is a disputed matter. So it will be preferable for our purposes to call Dworkin's second principle the principle of integrity in the grounds of law.

Dworkin's argument for the political value of integrity turns on the issue of the conditions of the legitimacy of the state: 'a political society that accepts integrity as a political virtue thereby becomes a special form of community, special in a way that promotes its moral authority to assume and deploy a monopoly of coercive force.'[117] Indeed, Dworkin argues, the value of integrity figures in the theory of legitimacy that has the highest degree of plausibility—relative to competing accounts of legitimacy that have been offered by Locke, Rawls, and others.[118] On Dworkin's account, a legitimate state is one where its members have a general duty to obey its law; his crucial idea is that this duty to obey should be understood as an associative obligation, an obligation of the same general type as obtains between family members. The argument then proceeds by setting out the conditions for genuine associative obli-gations among the members of a political community and showing that only within a community that accepts the value of integrity—what Dworkin calls a community or association of principle—are those conditions met. The

---

[113] *Law's Empire*, 176. In what follows I have benefited from reading Jeremy Waldron's illuminating 'The Circumstances of Integrity', ch. 9 in *Law and Disagreement* (Oxford: Clarendon Press, 1999).

[114] *Law's Empire*, 166.   [115] Ibid. 167.   [116] Ibid. 260–2.

[117] Ibid. 188.   [118] Ibid. 192–5.

upshot is that acceptance of the value of integrity is a precondition for the legitimacy of the state.[119]

It is obviously not possible to offer a critique of this argument here—there is not even space for an adequate summary. But for our purposes we can simply accept the argument's conclusion about the value of integrity. The relevant question for us is whether this provides support for the integrity theory of the grounds of law. Integrity demands, Dworkin writes, 'that the public standards of the community be both made and seen, so far as this is possible, to express a single, coherent scheme of justice and fairness in the right relation'.[120] Among those public standards, of course, is law. But it is not obvious that the legitimacy argument actually establishes this conclusion. We may accept that the legitimacy of the state depends on the existence of a community of principle, a community that sees itself as bound together by a coherent set of political principles. But what reason does that give any community to see its *law* as (already) expressing such a set of coherent principles? On the face of it, the argument for legitimacy establishes only the principle of integrity in legislation: the principles that lawmakers appeal to in their deliberations should as far as possible be drawn from a coherent set of principles shared by the community (as opposed to the principles found in lawmakers' preferred theories of justice or fairness). In this way, the political life of a community of principle can be faithful to its shared set of principles, and a community that is not yet a community of principle will be moved in that direction by the lawmakers' efforts at uncovering a shared set of principles. But the principle of integrity in the grounds of law instructs us to conceive of our law as already flowing from such a coherent set of principles. Why should we do this?

One reason would be this: it is best to show law in its best light, as being the law a community of principle would want to have. But this is no reason, for the question under debate is precisely whether and why it would be best to show law in its best light. The legitimacy argument tells us that it is politically desirable that a community be a community of principle; but how does determining the answers to legal questions so as to show our law as already the law of a community of principle help us either to maintain or to achieve our status as a community of principle? Why should a community of principle not cast a critical eye on its law, noting the extent to which it fails to express the coherent principles that nevertheless do ideally find expression in political argument and the legislative activity of legislators and judges? And if the community is *not* a community of principle there would seem to be especially strong grounds for such sceptical vigilance. It does not seem sufficient to claim

---

[119] Ibid. 206–15.   [120] Ibid. 219.

that it is necessary to construe law as expressing one coherent set of principles in order that litigants can be treated equally, that is, all treated as required by some one coherent set of principles.[121] For again, this amounts to the claim that we should see our law such that it already is what we would like it to be. Why should we do that?

Dworkin's answer to the question I have been raising is, I believe, that if we look to law as expressing principles that bind us together as a community of principle, then we are more likely to be bound together, indeed, as a community of principle. To become or remain a community of principle, a community's members must in fact acknowledge a common set of principles. But where can such principles be presented? What is the means of their social expression that makes it possible for them to be identified by each person as the principles of her community? Dworkin's answer, at least in part, is that law provides that means. The point is clearest, I believe, in passages where he describes his account of legitimacy and his theory of law as protestant.

Political obligation is . . . not just a matter of obeying the discrete political decisions of the community one by one. . . . It becomes a more protestant idea: fidelity to a scheme of principle each citizen has a responsibility to identify, ultimately for himself, as his community's scheme.[122]

Membership in a community of principle is not a passive affair. One must seek out the principles that are the basis of that community. Where should one look? The last paragraph of *Law's Empire* is instructive:

Law's empire is defined by attitude, not territory or power or process. We studied that attitude mainly in appellate courts, where it is dressed up for inspection, but it must be pervasive in our ordinary lives if it is to serve us well even in court. It is an interpretive, self-reflective attitude addressed to politics in the broadest sense. It is a protestant attitude that makes each citizen responsible for imagining what his society's public commitments to principle are, and what these commitments require in new circumstances. . . . Law's attitude is constructive: it aims, in the interpretive spirit, to lay principle over practice to show the best route to a better future, keeping the right faith with the past. It is, finally, a fraternal attitude, an expression of how we are united in community though divided in project, interest, and conviction.[123]

What is so striking here is the tight link between each citizen's responsibility for imagining what his society's public commitments to principle are—and *law*. My own sense, to the contrary, is that if we try to discharge this responsibility by reflecting on law, we are likely to be led astray.

---

[121] Ibid. 165; see also 'The Model of Rules I', 30.   [122] *Law's Empire*, 190.
[123] Ibid. 413. See also, on the role of courts in particular, 'A Reply to Critics', in *Taking Rights Seriously*, 338; 'The Forum of Principle', in *A Matter of Principle* (Cambridge, Mass.: Harvard University Press, 1985), 70–1; *Freedom's Law*, 30–1, 344–6.

The reason is that law does not, for the most part, display its principled political rationale on its face. This is so even if we accept the integrity theory of the grounds of law. Even if it were right that the law is what figures in or follows from the principles of justice, fairness, and procedural due process that show the past directives of the legal regime in their best light, identification of law by this means would, as Dworkin notes, often require little principled reflection.[124] Thus it is easy enough to tell that there is no criminal-law duty to rescue strangers in peril in New York. The reason this is easy is that the principles of fairness and procedural due process that underlie the criminal law of New York dictate that, absent explicit statutory provision of such a duty, there is none; and that there is no such statutory provision is easy to see. But now the person looking to law for expression of his community's public commitments to principle may also be badly misled, in respect of the community's principles of justice especially, by the absence of any such duty in the criminal law. He may think it reflects a lack of commitment on the part of his community to a principle of responsibility for the welfare of its members. But this would not follow at all; there could be sound practical reasons why even a community of utilitarians would conclude that there should be no criminal duty to rescue.[125]

To take another example, it is easy enough to tell that gratuitous promises that have not been relied on by the promisee are unenforceable under contract law in the United States. One need not have an entire theory of contract law to know this: the contrary view would be disqualified by any competent interpreter's criterion of adequate fit with past directives from the legal regime.[126] But it would once again be a bad mistake to think that the community's conception of promissory obligation, in private or public matters, could be fully explained via the ideas of bargain and reliance.[127]

Or suppose that the best principled rationale for tort law turns, as Dworkin argues, on his theory of distributive justice as equality of resources.[128] This may be so, but it seems extremely unlikely that anyone other than a sophisticated political philosopher would be inclined to interpret tort law that way; tort law may be instinct with the theory of equality of resources, but the instinct has been rather seriously repressed

---

[124] See *Law's Empire*, 266.

[125] See Liam Murphy, 'Beneficence, Law, and Liberty: The Case of Required Rescue', *Georgetown Law Journal*, forthcoming.

[126] On the operation of the criterion of fit in the integrity theory of the grounds of law, see *Law's Empire*, ch. 7.

[127] For criticism of P. S. Atiyah's attempt, in *Promises, Morals, and Law* (Oxford: Clarendon Press, 1981), to derive a theory of promise from the law of contract, see Joseph Raz, 'Promises in Morality and Law', *Harvard Law Review* 95 (1982), 919–20.

[128] See *Law's Empire*, ch. 8.

in judicial opinions. The theory of equality of resources would be difficult to unearth from the law even in a society that embraced it in its full generality. An implication of equality of resources is that the community ought in effect to equalize the social consequences of natural talent on the ground that a person is not responsible for his genetic make-up; Dworkin argues that the best way to implement this idea may be through some scheme of taxation designed to mimic a hypothetical insurance market for shortfalls in skill.[129] It is clear enough that the route from the surface of the ideal tax code back to the underlying principle of equality of resources would be an arduous one.

Even a constitution setting out substantive individual rights can mislead. For suppose that positive economic rights to welfare are best not constitutionalized, for reasons having to do with institutional competency. Once again, this conclusion on the level of institutional design is obviously compatible with commitment to positive economic rights; but a person looking to a constitution that lists only negative rights of various kinds may be misled. Constitutional statements of principle could mislead in another way. Christopher Eisgruber convincingly argues that constitutional interpretation requires a theory of constitutionalism, of what good constitution-makers would do. In particular, where a constitution is hard to amend, as is the case in the United States, constitutional interpretation must employ an account of why it would be a good idea to make a constitution like that and interpret specific provisions accordingly.[130] That a particular principle of justice is shared in the community is not in itself sufficient ground to entrench it into the constitution. The community's principles of justice cannot, therefore, be read directly off the surface of the constitutional text.

The general concern here is that if law is taken to be a primary means for the expression of the principles of justice that play a part in constituting a community of principle, we are very likely to misidentify those principles.[131] I am obviously not saying that a judge in a hard case could not engage in the kind of institutional reasoning that shows the unenforceability of gratuitous unrelied-on promises to be fully compatible with the

---

[129] See Dworkin, 'What is Equality? Part II: Equality of Resources', *Philosophy & Public Affairs* 10 (1981), 304–34.

[130] See *Constitutional Self-Government* (Cambridge, Mass.: Harvard University Press, forthcoming).

[131] I should say that my claim that law can mislead us about political morality is not limited to the specific context of Dworkin's legitimacy argument. Even if we reject the political value of integrity, it seems clear that we do better in our political lives if we understand that the law does not wear its political justification on its face. See Mary Ann Glendon, *Rights Talk* (New York: Free Press, 1991), 89–108, and Mark Kelman's discussion of 'conflating legal solubility with the existence of a problem', in *A Guide to Critical Legal Studies* (Cambridge, Mass.: Harvard University Press, 1987), 275–9.

community's commitment to an unqualified principle of promissory obligation. Judges, other legal experts, and, indeed, pretty much all of us are clearly *capable* of extracting principled rationales of justice, fairness, and due process from any department of the law. That is not in dispute; the question is rather that of the value of law as a mode of public display of the community's principles. And my claim is that, since the principles of justice that in part justify and explain much of what is (on any view) law cannot be read off the surface of that law, but rather require sophisticated technical institutional knowledge for their unearthing, law is not where most people should be looking as they try to discharge their protestant responsibilities as members of a community of principle.

Now of course this doubt about law as a mode of display for a community's principles would not carry much weight if it were the only possibility. But it clearly is not. The obviously most suitable mode of display for such principles is public political discourse—the discourse of political argument as it takes place in political campaigns and public political discussion generally. If it is thought that public political discourse, in any particular place, is defective and unable to perform its role as the means of display of a community's principles, the appropriate response is to endeavour to improve it, not to transfer our hopes to another domain that we know is structurally unsuited for the purpose.

I conclude, then, that Dworkin's argument for the political value of integrity in making possible a community of principle and thus a legitimate state does not provide support for the integrity theory of the grounds of law. That theory shows law to be, so far as possible, what a community of principle would want it to be. But the only practical-political reason I can think of for wanting to do this is that law is an important means of expression of the community's principles; I believe, to the contrary, that law is an opaque and misleading means of expression of the community's principles. So we lack a positive practical-political reason, I think, for adopting the integrity theory of the grounds of law. And since that theory, which is all about showing law in its best light, rather obviously raises the problem of quietism, as well as practical problems in the domain of private international law, it seems to me that we have good reasons to reject it in favour of hard positivism.

Of course, even if I am right that the practical-political argument for the integrity theory of the grounds of law fails, this does not mean that Dworkin's case for that theory fails. What it does mean, however, is that the case must turn wholly on his defence of constructive interpretation as the appropriate methodology for the development of a theory of the grounds of law. If the right way to resolve disagreement about the conceptual foundations of the theory of the grounds of law just is to show legal practice in its best light, then we should adopt law as integrity, since that theory of the grounds of law shows law as being, so far as possible, what we would like it to be—the law of a community of principle. As noted above, I am sceptical about Dworkin's claim that the method of constructive interpretation is quite generally the appropriate method of interpretation, regardless of subject matter, but I have not had space to pursue the matter. My main purpose in this section has been to bring out that strand in Dworkin's work that amounts to a practical-political argument directly contrary to the one I have defended.

VI. CONCLUSION

My main aim in this paper has been to illustrate and defend what I take to be the appropriate methodology for the debate over the conceptual foundations of the theory of the grounds of law, a methodology that Hart once eloquently espoused. In doing this I hope to have shown that, contrary to what Hart writes in the Postscript, his theory of law and Dworkin's really are competitors. Underlying their different accounts is a fundamental disagreement about the politically most desirable way to conceive of law's domain. This, it seems to me, is a dispute well worth pursuing. But let me end by repeating that it is by no means the only legal theoretic debate worth pursuing. The theory and practice of adjudication and the issue of the nature of the optimal legal order both have more obvious practical political significance, as does an issue I have scarcely mentioned, that of the duty to obey the law. It may be, indeed, that compared to these other issues, the dispute over the concept of law, considered on its own, really does not matter all that much. Quietism is bad, but the rejection of the sources thesis may not produce so very much of it. Even so, it is worth thinking about exactly what is at stake in the long-standing philosophical dispute over the concept of law.

12

Normative (or Ethical) Positivism

JEREMY WALDRON

I

In recent years, philosophers of law have paid increasing attention to the possibility that legal positivism might be recast as a *normative* thesis about law. Legal positivism is commonly held to consist in a purely conceptual thesis—viz. that there is no necessary connection between law and morality or, more precisely, that there is no necessary connection between the grounds of legal judgment and the grounds of moral judgment.[1] (This is sometimes referred to as the 'separability thesis'.) But what I want to consider in the present paper is the thesis that this separability of law and morality, or this separability of legal judgment and moral judgment, is a good thing, perhaps even indispensable (from a moral, social, or political point of view), and certainly something to be valued and encouraged.

My title indicates that I would like to call this position 'normative positivism', but that there is some reason also to label it 'ethical positivism'. The former term is supposed to capture the point that legal positivism is being presented as a normative rather than a descriptive or conceptual thesis.[2] Unfortunately, however, that term has also been used in recent years to describe a different thesis—namely, the version of legal positivism that identifies law with norms (as opposed to brute facts about power, commands, and sanctions). On this account, the theories of H. L. A. Hart and Hans Kelsen qualify as versions of normative positivism even if they are not in themselves normative positions.[3] For this reason, Tom Campbell rejects the label 'normative positivism' in favour of 'ethical posi-

---

[1] But see also the other versions of legal positivism, set out (as 'Menu A') at the end of this paper (pp. 432–3 below).

[2] This connects also with the title of a section ('Normative Dimensions of Jurisprudence') in Gerald A. Postema, *Bentham and the Common Law Tradition* (Oxford: Clarendon Press, 1986), 328 ff., which is one of the more important presentations of the position I want to consider.

[3] See D. Beyleveld and R. Brownsword, 'Normative Positivism: The Mirage of the Middle Way', *Oxford Journal of Legal Studies* 9 (1989), 462. See also R. Tur, 'Paternalism and the Criminal Law', *Journal of Applied Philosophy* 2 (1985), 173. In the Postscript to the 2nd edn. of *The Concept of Law*, H. L. A. Hart uses 'normative' in this way, to characterize what he calls a purely 'explanatory and clarifying account of law as a complex social and political institution' (*The Concept of Law*, 2nd edn., ed. J. Raz and P. Bullock (Oxford: Clarendon Press, 1994), 239).

tivism'.[4] The term 'ethical' seems unsatisfactory to me, connoting as it does normative standards for personal behaviour, as opposed to normative standards for evaluating institutions. (Campbell, however, does not see it that way.)[5] In this paper I shall mostly use the label 'normative positivism', despite the possibility of confusion with the position that Beyleveld and Brownsword take themselves to be attacking.[6] The reader is hereby put on notice that when I use the term 'normative positivism' it is intended to convey something more than the idea of law being a system of norms; it is intended to refer to the propounding of legal positivism (whether normative in the Beyleveld and Brownsword sense or not) *as a normative thesis.*

In modern jurisprudence, the best-known proponents of the view that positivism should be understood as a normative position are Gerald Postema, Tom Campbell, Neil MacCormick, Stephen Perry, and perhaps Joseph Raz.[7] But it is evident, particularly from Postema's work, that this characterization is not put forward as a novel recasting of legal positivism. Postema argues that (what I am calling) 'normative positivism' is faithful to the early positivist tradition of Thomas Hobbes and Jeremy Bentham—jurists who gave great prominence in their philosophy to the

---

[4] *The Legal Theory of Ethical Positivism* (Aldershot: Dartmouth, 1996), 79.

[5] Campbell says (ibid. 3): 'The term "ethical" is preferred to "moral" because it better connotes a system of second order moral reasons which have bearing on the design of institutionalized practices and the ways in which those entrusted with institutional roles conduct themselves. Somewhat arbitrarily, I take the term "ethical" to point us towards the appraisal of complex institutional patterns and roles, which have to be seen largely in terms of their instrumentality for a range of morally significant human objectives, in contrast to the "morality" of more direct one to one social interactions. The term "Ethical Positivism" indicates that law is to be valued as an institutionalized way of doing things which serve important societal purposes. Further, it is part of the theory that the effective accomplishment of these purposes calls for ethical conduct on the part of participants in their various roles, as judge, as lawyer, as policeman and as citizen, a matter of role morality as distinct from personal morality.'

[6] See n. 3 above.

[7] Campbell, *Legal Theory*; Postema, *Bentham*; and Neil MacCormick, 'A Moralistic Case for A-moralistic Law', *Valparaiso Law Review* 20 (1985), 1. For Perry, see nn. 24 and 37 below.

Later I consider the extent to which Joseph Raz's legal positivism also falls into this category. Let me anticipate briefly. In a paper entitled 'The Problem about the Nature of Law', *University of Western Ontario Law Review* 21 (1983) at 217–18, Raz observes: 'The [positivist] doctrine of the nature of law yields a test for identifying law the use of which requires no resort to moral or any other evaluative argument. But it does not follow that one can defend the doctrine of the nature of law itself without using evaluative . . . arguments.' (This is quoted in Postema, *Bentham*, 332 n.) It certainly sounds like a version of what I am calling normative positivism. Consider also Raz's comment in 'Two Views of the Nature of the Theory of Law: A Partial Comparison', *Legal Theory* 4 (1998), at 267–8, where he says that Hart is wrong to think that identifying criteria for the correct use of concepts is a purely descriptive enterprise: 'For reasons explained by John Finnis and others, I believe that Hart is mistaken here, and Dworkin is right in holding that the explanation of the nature of law involves evaluative considerations.' (See also nn. 11, 45, 47, and 66 below, with accompanying text. In particular, n. 66 registers the hesitation I have about this ascription.)

evils that might be expected to afflict societies whose members were unable to disentangle their judgments about what was required or permitted by the law of their society from their individual judgements about justice and morality. In their respective versions of the separation thesis, Hobbes and Bentham showed no particular interest in the analysis of purely conceptual differences between law and morality. Instead, they were interested in the conditions necessary for coordination, for conflict resolution, and for the general stability of expectations in people's dealings with one another. Those were the normative interests that informed and shaped their positivist account of the nature and function of law.

II

Against this suggestion—that legal positivism might be understood as a normative thesis—Jules Coleman has said the following:

> Legal positivism makes a conceptual or analytic claim about law, and that claim should not be confused with programmatic or normative interests certain positivists, especially Bentham, might have had.[8]

Coleman's point deserves to be taken seriously, for it amounts to a claim that what I am calling 'normative positivism' puts the cart before the horse. Coleman does not deny that early positivists like Hobbes and Bentham might have had the practical interests and made the normative claims that I alluded to in the previous section. But I think Coleman is claiming that the best that can be said for those normative positions is that they already depend on the truth of legal positivism as a conceptual thesis. For consider: if legal positivism in the form of the separability thesis is false as a conceptual matter, then normative positivism is fatuous: it values or commends a state of affairs that cannot possibly obtain. (I mean that if legal judgment necessarily implicates moral judgment, then the hopes entertained by Hobbes and Bentham and their latter-day interpreters are forlorn: conflict cannot be reduced, nor coordination facilitated, nor expectations stabilized if what that takes is for law to be separated altogether from morality.) If, on the other hand, a robust version of legal positivism as a conceptual thesis is true, then normative positivism is equally fatuous. For if law cannot but be separate from morality—if it is not possible to grasp the concept of law without committing oneself to that separability— then normative positivism amounts to little more than opposition to anarchism. The normative positivist is simply in favour of law (as law can be shown, analytically, to be). And who isn't?

---

[8] 'Negative and Positive Positivism', in *Markets, Morals and the Law* (Cambridge: Cambridge University Press, 1988), 11.

Now, actually, there *is* a little bit of in-between. I mean: there is logical space between the proposition that law does not necessarily implicate morality and the proposition that law necessarily does not implicate morality. For it may be that, in a particular legal system, legal judgments (of a certain sort) do depend on the truth of moral judgements (of a certain sort), even though it is not the case in general that legal judgments necessarily depend on moral judgments. This possibility is sometimes referred to as *inclusive* positivism;[9] and the weak version of legal positivism that does not forbid it (on conceptual grounds) is known as *negative* positivism.[10] The version of positivism in which I am interested for the purposes of this paper may make its normative moves in the logical space that is left open by negative positivism Normative positivism might therefore be read as a position that condemns the inclusive possibility that negative positivism leaves space for.

Another way of putting this is that what I am calling normative positivism *assumes* what Coleman calls negative positivism (i.e. assumes it as a matter of normative pragmatics—there being no point to commending something that is impossible or conceptually incoherent) but *prescribes* something like exclusive positivism. It does not exactly follow that exclusive positivism is necessarily a normative position. But I think it often is. And the fact that someone holds exclusive positivism certainly raises the question of whether his positivism in jurisprudence has a normative tinge to it.[11]

But even if this possibility is granted (i.e. that normative positivism assumes negative positivism and prescribes exclusive positivism), *still* normative positivism seems to be what Jules Coleman suggested it is—a normative thesis *about* legal positivism, rather than the essence or basis of legal positivism itself. It still requires the analytic legal philosopher to do his work first, to establish the conceptual possibility of that which the normative theorist represents as desirable.[12]

---

[9] See Will Waluchow, *Inclusive Legal Positivism* (Oxford: Clarendon Press, 1994).

[10] See Coleman, 'Negative and Positive Positivism', 7.

[11] Hence the issue about Raz that I mentioned in n. 7 above.

[12] Campbell seems to concede the point. He says (*Legal Theory*, p. 71): 'Assuming, in accordance with the separability thesis, that law does not *need* to be identified through moral spectacles, this opens the way for saying that what legal Positivists in fact wish us to accept is that it is *undesirable* if there are such morally overt legal validity criteria. For such Positivists, the motivation behind the analytic point is to prepare the conceptual ground for the view that no legal system ought to permit morally explicit or other controversial stand-ards being used to establish the existence of law or determine its implications. We may label this the 'prescriptive separation thesis'.
'The "prescriptive separation thesis"—the view that law and morals ought to be separate at the point of application—is not of course established by conceptual analysis. . . . It is, however, made possible by such analysis, for the separability thesis supplies a semantic scheme within which to state the prescriptive separation thesis.'

III

Before I respond to that suggestion, I want to consider a second element in Jules Coleman's critique. After the passage already quoted, he went on to suggest that if normative positivism tries to build 'into the conceptual account of law a particular normative theory of law', then it commits 'the very mistake positivism is so intent on drawing attention to and rectifying'.[13] His suggestion seems to be that legal positivists are determined to separate our understanding of law from our commitment (or anyone's commitment) to particular controversial moral and political ideals—they are determined that the debate about the nature of law should not be held hostage to political, moral, and ideological controversy—and he seems to be suggesting that so-called normative positivism represents an explicit (and, Coleman must think, an oddly self-defeating) assault on this determination.

This criticism seems misconceived. Coleman says that to adopt a normative version of legal positivism is 'to infuse morality—the way law ought to be—into the concept of law—or the account of the way law is'.[14] But the phrase 'the account of what law is' is ambiguous. It could mean the *wholesale* account of what law, the institution, is (as opposed to other methods of governance); or it could mean the *retail* account of what the law on some particular subject is in a particular jurisdiction. Legal positivists are certainly interested in ways of identifying what the law is (of any given jurisdiction on any given subject) that are not contaminated by the exercise of moral judgement. But this interest at the retail level may not be undermined by a general or wholesale account of what law, the institution, is, or by a wholesale account of why in general it is important to be able to identify what the law is (of any given jurisdiction on any given subject) without exercising moral judgement. Even if that wholesale account is a moral account, it need not infiltrate moral considerations into the business of answering specific legal questions. So long as the retail account can be insulated from the moral account given at the wholesale level, normative positivism is not self-defeating.

As a response to this line of argument, Coleman might invite us to consider the discussions of positive law that one finds in natural law jurisprudence. We all accept that natural law theories are not *opposed* to positive law; they do not believe that natural law can do the work of positive law.[15] Instead, they offer a normative account of the functions of

---

[13] 'Negative and Positive Positivism', 11.   [14] Ibid.
[15] Natural law theories need not hold (as Kelsen appears to have thought they held) that positive law is 'superfluous' and that 'the activity of positive-law makers is tantamount to a foolish effort to supply artificial illumination in bright sunshine'. See Hans Kelsen, 'The

positive law.[16] Now what is noticeable about such accounts—Coleman might say—is precisely that they do not (indeed, they claim they *cannot*) insulate their account of the criteria for determining what the law is (on a given subject in a given jurisdiction) from their normative account of the point or the function or the tasks of law in general. Natural lawyers typically subscribe to some version of Augustine's proposition '*lex iniusta non est lex*', and their application of it at the retail level is informed by their general account of the function of law. Accordingly, if a natural lawyer is asked what the law of a given jurisdiction is on some topic, and the only thing he can find that looks anything like a law laid down in that area is egregiously unjust, he may have to say something like 'In this jurisdiction, there is no law governing this subject, but only at best something which is a perversion of law'. This—Coleman might say—should be a lesson to us: once we incorporate a normative account of the function of law into our jurisprudence, we necessarily undermine the distinctively positivist position that it must be possible to say what the law is without making moral judgments.

I think the point is a fair one; but it may have less force in the present argument than the version I have just set out suggests. For in fact modern natural law theorists are quite cautious about the application of '*lex iniusta non est lex*', and quite sophisticated in their treatment of the implied paradox '*lex . . . non est lex*'.[17]

Elsewhere I have argued in favour of even greater caution than Finnis seems willing to concede.[18] I have argued against any easy inference from a natural law account of the function of law to an application of the '*lex iniusta*' maxim. The argument, briefly, is as follows.

Suppose that the goods that can be secured by law are in the set G =

Natural-Law Doctrine Before the Tribunal of Science', in *What Is Justice? Justice, Law, and Politics in the Mirror of Science* (Berkeley, Calif.: University of California Press, 1957), at 142. I am obliged to Robert George's paper 'Kelsen and Aquinas on "the Natural-Law Doctrine" ', presented at Columbia Legal Theory Workshop, 29 Nov. 1999, for this citation.

[16] Along the lines of qu. 95 in the first part of the second part of Aquinas's *Summa Theologica* or more recently chs. 9 and 10 of John Finnis's *Natural Law and Natural Rights* (Oxford: Clarendon Press, 1980). See also John Finnis, 'The Truth in Legal Positivism', in Robert George (ed.), *The Autonomy of Law: Essays on Legal Positivism* (Oxford: Clarendon Press, 1996).

[17] See e.g. Finnis, *Natural Law and Natural Rights*, 364–6. Finnis reminds us that the central tradition of natural law theory did not formulate its thesis about the relation between law and justice by saying things like 'an unjust *edict* cannot be law' or 'a morally iniquitous *command* cannot be law'. Instead, says Finnis, 'the tradition . . . has affirmed that unjust LAWS are not law' (p. 364; emphasis original). He offers several elaborate (and convincing) explanations of why this paradox is not a contradiction. His explanations appeal to the distinction between normative, descriptive, and detached uses of terms like 'law', as well as to the further distinction, central to his jurisprudence, between the focal meaning and the secondary meanings of such terms (pp. 365–6).

[18] Jeremy Waldron, '*Lex Satis Iusta*', *Notre Dame Law Review*, 75 (2000), 1829 (special issue, honouring John Finnis).

$\{g_1, g_2, \ldots, g_n\}$ and that among the distinctive contributions that law offers in this regard is (as Finnis suggests) the *coordination* of the pursuit of G in a community whose members have a variety of bright ideas about how those goods should be pursued.[19] Then the fact that a given rule R_1 secures the goods in G in a way that is better than the way they are secured by an alternative rule R_2 cannot itself be a reason for regarding R_2, if it is laid down, as *less of a law* or as *law in a lesser sense* than R_1 would be. For the task of law in such a situation is precisely to coordinate the pursuit of G among people who disagree about whether R_1 is superior to R_2 in this regard. Unless R_2 promises to makes things worse than they would be without any coordination whatsoever, the positing of R_2 does indeed represent a solution to the coordination problem. But that solution cannot fully be realized if the participation of a large number of citizens in this coordinative solution is affected, offset, or undermined (or whatever other practical consequence '... *non est lex*' is held to have) by their conviction that the inferiority of R_2 to R_1 diminishes the claim that the imposition of R_2 has upon them.[20]

---

[19] Authority, Finnis argues, is needed in human communities not only on account of people's weakness or wickedness. It is also needed even among people of great intelligence and dedication so far as the demands of practical reasonableness and the common good are concerned (ibid. 231). A person dedicated to the common good 'will always be looking out for new and better ways of attaining the common good, of coordinating the action of members, of playing his own role. And the intelligent member will find such new and better ways, and perhaps not just one but many possible and reasonable ways. Intelligence and dedication, skill and commitment thus multiply the problems of coordination, by giving the group more possible orientations, commitments, projects, "priorities", and procedures to choose from. And until a particular choice is made, nothing will in fact be done' (ibid. 231–2).

So we face what Finnis calls 'coordination problems'—i.e. problems to which there are 'two or more available, reasonable, and appropriate solutions, none of which, however, would amount to a solution unless adopted to the exclusion of the other solutions available, reasonable, and appropriate for that problem' (ibid. 232). The function of legal authority, he says, is to resolve such problems, to enable the intelligent and imaginative creatures we are to focus our cooperation, in relation to each set of competing alternatives, on just one of the schemes that offers us a way to promote the common good.

[20] In *'Lex Satis Iusta'*, I add: 'The work that legal authority has to do, on Finnis's general conception, is to facilitate conscious coordination in situations where coordination is practically necessary in pursuit of the common good. The reference to *conscious* coordination is important. Neither authority nor legal validity can do their work silently, that is, irrespective of what people think about the work they are doing. To vary the metaphor slightly, law is not like an invisible hand. It cannot do its work unless people are aware of its doing its work (or, frankly, unless they are doing its work for it). Law certainly cannot do its work of coordination if some among those whose pursuit of the good is to be coordinated do not believe that law is making a proper contribution to the solution of a coordination problem. Cases in which the community is divided as to whether law is acting appropriately or not (so far as coordination is concerned) cannot be central cases of law. A standard of legal validity (and the account of what law is doing, which backs up that standard) must be a *shared* standard of validity. That means that a central case of the existence of a law—or, if you like, a central case of legal authority—cannot be a case in which the parties

If anything like this is correct, then retail judgments about what the law is *can* be insulated from wholesale judgments about the point of law, at least to a certain extent. They may not be wholly insulated: there may be practices or political arrangements which, from the normative point of view (the point of view that describes the function of law) are worse than no law at all; and for those cases, the normative account at the wholesale level *may* affect the retail account of whether (or in what sense) these practices or arrangements are to be regarded as laws. But these will be extreme cases: indeed, they will be exactly those cases for which it is most difficult anyway to defend the hard-line positivist insistence that it must be possible to determine whether something is a law without making a judgment about its justice or its moral character. But Coleman is right: normative positivism will not leave the retail level entirely untouched. And now the question is whether that is to be regarded as a point against it (or perhaps as a point in its favour).

Before we go on, here is an academic question. Does it count against normative positivism that, as a jurisprudental position, it can now no longer easily be distinguished from modern natural law theory? In general I think the answer is 'No'. The 'positivism versus natural law' antithesis has become, in all sorts of other ways, so hoary and threadbare that its evaporation should not be counted as a loss, but as (at most) an interesting consequence of the acceptance of normative positivism. Certainly its preservation is not to be regarded as a methodological imperative. If the dichotomy between positivism and natural law goes out the window, so be it.[21] As a matter of fact, however, there might still be room for some distinction. For consider the version of normative positivism that looks most like a natural law theory, so far as its account of positive law is concerned. An enduring difference between them might be the following. Normative positivism need not commit itself to any particular meta-ethics, nor to any particular account of how we arrive at an understanding of the goods or values that law serves.[22] By contrast, the natural law theory that most resembles it (in its jurisprudential account of positive law) is likely to differ from it in this regard. Natural law jurisprudence is usually packaged with a distinctive meta-ethic (cognitivist and objectivist), and often also with a very strong commitment to a rationalist account of moral and ethical understanding.

disagree about its centrality. Because of the commonality or shared-ness central to law, a case which is such that the parties disagree about its centrality must be less central than a case in which they do not.'

[21] Here I follow the lead of Neil MacCormick, 'Natural Law and the Separation of Law and Morals', in Robert George (ed.), *Natural Law Theory: Contemporary Essays* (Oxford: Clarendon Press, 1992).

[22] See Jeremy Waldron, 'The Irrelevance of Moral Objectivity' in George, *Natural Law Theory*; repr. as ch. 8 of Jeremy Waldron, *Law and Disagreement* (Oxford: Clarendon Press, 1999).

IV

I want to return now to the issue left hanging at the end of Section II—the suggestion, implicit in Jules Coleman's critique, that normative positivism is a thesis *about* legal positivism, not a version *of* legal positivism. Since normative positivism presupposes legal positivism as a conceptual thesis, it can hardly be thought to replace the latter in jurisprudential understanding. What one needs first—according to Coleman—is a demonstration that the propositions and judgments required for the operation of a modern legal system *can* be arrived at without making moral judgments. Coleman can afford to concede that it is up to the normative theorist what he wants to make of this possibility.

In fact, I think it is doubtful that the issues can be addressed in the order Coleman is suggesting. For suppose two theorists disagree about what (kinds of) propositions and judgments are required for the operation of a modern legal system. Suppose it is common ground between them that the truth conditions of a certain proposition P include a moral proposition (say, a proposition about justice), but that it is a matter of dispute whether P is to be regarded as a proposition of *law*, in the relevant sense. How is the issue between them to be determined? Presumably, the issue is to be settled by an analysis of the concepts 'law' or 'legal system', to see whether such analysis requires that propositions such as P be regarded as propositions of law. Then the question—whether positivism can be construed (or presupposed) as a purely descriptive thesis—will turn on whether the concepts under analysis are in fact given to us in a form that is (a) capable of resolving the dispute and (b) uncontaminated by normative considerations.

The issue may be illustrated by considering the debate between Ronald Dworkin and his opponents about whether there are 'right answers' to legal questions in hard cases. Dworkin argues that in a hard case where the interpretation of a statutory provision is contested or where the precedents appear indeterminate, a judge will properly ask himself the question, 'Which interpretation (of the statute or the precedents) will show the existing law of this community in its best light?' In answering this question, the judge's 'own moral and political convictions are . . . directly engaged';[23] but that does not mean, he says, that the question is not a question of law. If P is the right answer to the question, in the circumstances envisaged, then P *is* the law on the matter, says Dworkin. His opponents, of course, deny this inference. P might be the right answer to Dworkin's question; and the question might be the appropriate question

[23] Ronald Dworkin, *Law's Empire* (Cambridge, Mass.: Harvard University Press, 1986), 256.

for the judge to ask himself in these circumstances. But it does not follow, they say, that the question is a question of law, or that its right answer is a true proposition about what the law is in this case.

When a dispute like this erupts, how is it to be settled? Is P law simply by virtue of being the right answer to the question that the judge ought to be asking? Both parties can cite 'common usage' among lawyers and judges—as H. L. A. Hart, one of Dworkin's opponents in this regard, concedes.[24] Each of them can construct what looks like a coherent conceptual apparatus for the jurisprudence that his approach suggests. Which of them has got law right? I am not sure that there is any prospect of answering that question without testing the respective theories against our sense of why it is important whether something counts as the law or not.[25]

Or consider this: it is common ground that not all aspects of governance in a modern state are governance through law. Some involve legal governance; others involve non-legal governance (e.g. governance by direct command or managerial decree). Theories of 'the rule of law' attribute tremendous importance to this distinction. But even short of that, most jurists believe that a distinction along these lines has some degree of importance for a normative theory of statecraft. Unless our jurisprudence is a complete mess, we should expect what we say about *what law is* to have some sort of connection to *why law is seen as an importantly distinct mode or aspect of governance*. And to the extent that it does have some such connection, it cannot be entirely non-normative.[26]

Consider again Jules Coleman's position. Coleman argues that, at best, what I call normative positivism presupposes something quite independent of it—namely, legal positivism as a descriptive or conceptual thesis. That is, it presupposes the non-normative truth of negative positivism in order to establish the 'can', without which the 'ought' of normative positivism is fatuous. But in order to establish that there *can* be a legal system which does not involve the making of moral judgments in the recognition of legal propositions, one must have a sense of what it is that one is trying to exhibit in this light (and why). Suppose Coleman purported to establish negative positivism by pointing to an armed organization in which

---

[24] *The Concept of Law*, 274.

[25] For a more extensive and sophisticated version of this argument, see Stephen Perry, 'Interpretation and Methodology in Legal Theory', in Andrei Marmor (ed.), *Law and Interpretation: Essays in Legal Philosophy* (Oxford: Clarendon Press, 1997), 129–31.

[26] Perry makes a similar point, ibid. 123: '[T]he data can plausibly be conceptualized in more than one way, and choosing among conceptualizations seems to require the attribution to law of a point or function.' See also Michael Moore, 'Hart's Concluding Unscientific Postscript', *Legal Theory* 4 (1998). Moore asks (at p. 312) how a purely descriptive jurisprudence can distinguish between social conventions that are legal and others. 'A normative jurisprudent such as Bentham can answer in terms of the value he sees law as serving,' says Moore. But a descriptive jurisprudence is 'bereft of those resources'.

commands were barked out by a strongman and by and large followed, and by showing us that members of this organization were able to identify, remember, and obey commands without ever exercising their moral judgment. Would this be enough to refute what the opponents of negative positivism affirm? The opponents of negative positivism (who deny the separability of law and morality) might respond:

Look, we never denied that an armed organization could work in this way, without its members ever making or purporting to make moral judgments. What we denied was that any such organization could ever properly be dignified with the term '*law*'. There are, after all, all sorts of ways of running a society which do not involve law in any interesting sense. To refute our position, it is not enough to point us to one of those.

Being a 'soft' or 'inclusive' positivist, Coleman might say that he felt their pain, and that he too believed that any system of governance worth *dignifying* with the appellation 'law' would have to involve the exercise of moral judgment in its normal operation. He was just trying to show—he would say—that this was not conceptually or analytically necessary in any strict sense. Well, at that point, I suspect his opponents would start asking hard questions about what the point of this so-called conceptual analysis was, if it could not—without more—distinguish the pure command-based system as a non-legal mode of administration. More important, the normative positivists—who Coleman imagines to be awaiting his purely analytic demonstration that law *can* be conceived in a way that does not require the exercise of moral judgment—would deny that he has given them what they want or what their normative account presupposes. For theirs is not the claim that societies ought to be governed by systems like our imagined command-based arrangement— systems which are barely recognizable as legal systems in the way that term is ordinarily used. The claim of the normative positivists is that the values associated with law, legality, and the rule of law—in a fairly rich sense—can best be achieved if the ordinary operation of such a system does not require people to exercise moral judgment in order to find out what the law is. The testing of *this* claim—even on the basis that 'ought' implies 'can'—does not really presuppose any purely descriptive, conceptual, or non-normative phase at all. The argument is going to have to be normative all the way down, even beginning with the way we specify the field of contestation.

Notice that this argument is not just about disagreement at the margins.[27] (It is not even clear what would count as 'margins' in a

---

[27] Cf. Jules Coleman's characterization of the issue in 'Incorporationism, Conventionality, and the Practical Difference Thesis', *Legal Theory* 4 (1998), 381, at 389: 'Those who embrace the possibility of descriptive, conceptual analysis . . . do not deny that normative argument

genuinely negative positivism of the kind Coleman envisages: since negative positivism offers no more than to come up with *one* case of a legal system whose workings do not involve the exercise of moral judgment, there is no real room in its extension for a core/margin distinction.) The question is simply: 'Has the negative positivist illuminated something which is definitely a legal system?' And that phrase 'definitely a legal system' can hardly be parsed without some attention to the reasons people have thought it important to make definite distinctions in this area.

V

In the Postscript to the second edition of *The Concept of Law*, Hart writes that even if the theories that I label normative positivism are 'of great interest and importance as contributions to an evaluative justificatory jurisprudence',[28] that does not show that there cannot be a purely descriptive legal positivism or that such a purely descriptive positivism is not worthwhile. (He makes this point in opposition to what he takes to be Ronald Dworkin's claim in *Law's Empire* that legal positivism must be presented either as an interpretive theory—in Dworkin's sense of 'interpretive'—or else as a sterile semantic thesis.)[29] Whether or not there is something called normative positivism that presupposes the truth of negative positivism (as a descriptive or conceptual thesis), Hart is defending here the legitimacy and the worth of a purely descriptive legal positivism. He thinks it performs an important 'clarificatory task' in general jurisprudence.[30] And I know that Coleman thinks the same.[31] Hart says:

is appropriate to resolving disagreements at what Hart calls the "penumbra". It hardly follows from the appropriateness of normative argument at the "frequency extremes" that there is no core, or that the core is unsettled, or that its content can be specified only by normative argument.'

[28] p. 241.

[29] Cf. *Law's Empire*, 33–44, 431 n. 2. Hart says (*The Concept of Law*, 241, 242): 'It is not obvious why there should be or indeed could be any significant conflict between enterprises so different as my own and Dworkin's conceptions of legal theory. ... But in his books Dworkin appears to rule out general and descriptive legal theory as misguided or at best simply useless ... and he had earlier written that "the flat distinction between description and evaluation" has "enfeebled legal theory".' (See also Hart's comments at 271–2.)

[30] Ibid. 240.

[31] In 'Incorporationism, Conventionality, and the Practical Difference Thesis', 389, Coleman insists that 'jurisprudence does not begin by trying to determine which features of law are important or interesting'. He is opposed, he says, to argument 'of the "descriptive jurisprudents-are-themselves-really-normative-jurisprudents-but-they-don't-realize-what they-are-up-to" type'.

The starting point for this clarificatory task is the widespread common knowledge of the salient features of a modern municipal legal system which on p. 3 of [*The Concept of Law*] I attribute to any educated man. My account is descriptive in that it is morally neutral and has no justificatory aims: it does not seek to justify or commend on moral or other grounds the forms and structures which appear in my general account of law.[32]

Though it was published before Hart's Postscript, the section of Gerald Postema's book on Bentham entitled 'Normative Dimensions of Jurisprudence' may be read as a response to a position such as Hart's in the passage I have just quoted. Hart takes as his starting point 'widespread common knowledge of the salient features of a modern municipal legal system'. But Postema believes that an understanding of language points us in a different methodological direction:

Analytical Jurisprudence rests on a problematical philosophy of language. It mistakenly assumes that the concepts we use can be divorced from the language of everyday life in which they function. But language shapes thought, and language emerges from shared practices and patterns of meaningful human activity. . . . Conceptual analysis is not sharply distinct from the enterprise of gaining an understanding of the practices and forms of life in which the concepts have their life.[33]

Now, to a careless ear this might not sound so very different from Hart's view that descriptive jurisprudence begins with the understanding of law that can be ascribed to the ordinary educated man.[34] But an ordinary man can be 'educated' about law in two ways: he can be educated as a spectator or he can be educated as a citizen. Compare the ordinary educated man's knowledge of something like the Roman Catholic Church. Most people know about the Catholic Church, and have an idea of how to recognize its buildings, its functionaries, and even its doctrines; one's education would be lacking if one could not do this. Still, such ordinary knowledge on the part of a person who had had no insider contact with the Church (had never been a Catholic or been on intimate terms with anyone who was) would be a dubious starting point for a reliable account of what the Catholic Church *is*. To begin constructing a good account, one would need to grasp the point of things like church, worship, and sacrament in a deeper and more participant sense than (say) something like the following: 'Well, they have these priests and the Pope and they believe there is this God who threatens them with all sorts of stuff if they use

---

[32] *The Concept of Law*, 240. The passage continues in the vein of the argument we dealt with in Section IV, arguing that the clarification that his descriptive jurisprudence offers 'is, I think, an important preliminary to any useful moral criticism of law'.

[33] *Bentham*, 332–3.

[34] *The Concept of Law*, 3.

contraceptives, etc.' And something similar may be true of law. As Postema puts it,

Jurisprudential theory, . . . even when it appears to be engaged in conceptual analysis, is focused on the task of giving an account of legal institutions, and the practice and 'sensibility' that breathe life into them. . . . For these practices are not mere and mindless habits, or behavioural routines with no intrinsic significance to those who execute them. They are intelligible social enterprises with a certain, perhaps very complex *meaning* or *point*.[35]

How much of this is taken care of by Hart's own insistence on a jurisprudence that takes seriously 'the internal point of view'?[36] Well, it depends. As it is usually understood, Hart's jurisprudence requires that rules be grasped as though from the point of view of one who orients his conduct to them. On Hart's account, one would not adequately understand the idea of a legal system unless one had a sense of what it was to accept and follow both primary rules and secondary rules in the governance of one's own actions. He hastens to add that this does not mean that one must actually accept or follow any particular primary rules or secondary rules:

Of course a descriptive legal theorist does not as such himself share the participants' acceptance of the law in these ways, but he can and should describe such acceptance. . . . It is true that for this purpose the descriptive legal theorist must understand what it is to adopt the internal point of view and in that limited sense he must be able to put himself in the place of an insider; but this is not to accept the law or share or endorse the insider's internal point of view or in any other way to surrender his descriptive stance.[37]

Some commentators (for all I know, Postema too) may have difficulty with this as a matter of hermeneutics.[38] For present purposes, however, the trouble with Hart's descriptive theorist's grasp of the internal point of view is that it is inserted into jurisprudence at the wrong point to do justice to the concerns of the normative positivist. Hart believes (rightly) that a grasp of the internal point of view is indispensable for a proper theoretical grasp of rules: since rules are normative, one who seeks to

---

[35] *Bentham*, 334.

[36] *The Concept of Law*, 56–7, 89–91, *Bentham*, 242 ff. (This is the aspect of Hart's positivism that makes it 'normative' in the sense that Beyleveld and Brownsword used 'normative positivism'. See n. 3 above.)

[37] Ibid. 242.

[38] But I am going to leave aside specific questions about the success of Hart's account of the relation between his descriptive methodology and the internal point of view, so far as an account of the normativity of terms like 'duty', 'right', 'ought', 'obligation', etc. in the language of the law, is concerned. I am not wholly convinced by Stephen Perry's arguments against Hart on this point in ss. III–V of his essay 'Hart's Methodological Positivism', *Legal Theory* 4 (1998), 427, at 440–56, and in Perry, 'Interpretation and Methodology', 122.

understand them must know what it is like to orient oneself to a norm. But in this paper we are concerned with the import for legal philosophy of a more general proposition—viz. that since *law* and *legal system* are normative concepts, one who seeks a jurisprudential understanding must also have some grasp of what is at stake when a distinction is drawn between (say) legal rules and other sorts of rules, or between law and some other sort of 'norm-ish' enterprise (like cricket or corporate administration). To return to our Catholicism example, the analogy would be the gap between someone's understanding of what it was to follow a commandment (and a fortiori—but only a fortiori—what it was to follow God's commandments) and someone's deeper, theological understanding of the role played by *commandment* in God's dealings with mankind. This, I take it, is what Postema means when he says that an adequate jurisprudential theory cannot 'be divorced from consideration of the aim, point, or function of the institutions of law'.[39]

Now here's the rub. It is not open to Hart to simply *extend* his concession to 'the internal point of view' (and his characterization of its role in descriptive jurisprudence) to cover this aspect as well. (I am imagining that a supporter of Hart might say that just as the descriptive legal philosopher must understand (1) what it is to accept and follow a norm, so also he must understand (2) what is generally taken to be the point of law and legal practice among those who are committed to the enterprise, and what it would be like to take that as the point, etc.)[40] This won't do, because at the stage of grasping, understanding, and reporting what this point of view was (while not necessarily endorsing it), the Hartian legal theorist would turn out not to be doing jurisprudence at all, in his own voice. Instead, he would be doing something like the history or sociology of jurisprudence. The real first-order jurisprudents would be those whose point of view he was trying to grasp.

Here I differ somewhat from Gerald Postema. Postema says that the sort of normative approach he urges

does not imply that a theory of the nature of law must show that the beliefs and attitudes of self-identified participants in the legal practice are in fact justified. . . . It only requires that legal theorists frame their accounts of the nature of law in terms that take such participant beliefs into account and make them intelligible.[41]

---

[39] *Bentham*, 335. The passage continues: 'And thus no account of the nature of law can hope to advance our understanding of law and legal practice without relying at important points on normative considerations.'

[40] Hart comes close to this in the following passage (*The Concept of Law*, 243): 'Even if . . . the participant's internal perspective manifested in the acceptance of law as providing guides to conduct and standards of criticism necessarily also included a belief that there are moral reasons for conforming to the law's requirements and moral justification of its use of coercion, this would also be something for a morally neutral descriptive jurisprudence to record but not to endorse or share.'   [41] *Bentham*, 335.

But if the legal theorist is not presenting those beliefs and attitudes in his own voice, then he is doing legal theory in *oratio obliqua*. He is, in effect, grasping what it is like to do legal theory, but he is not doing it himself. I think there is an important asymmetry here between (1) the role of the jurist's grasp of the internal point of view in regard to following a rule and (2) the role of the jurist's grasp of the internal point of view in relation to the point or function of a legal system. In Hart's theory, (1) is an indispensable *component* of the legal theorist's understanding, but that which is grasped (someone's actual orientation to a norm) is not. (One must understand what it is like to orient oneself to a norm, but one need not actually do so.) In (2), that which is grasped just *is* a theoretical understanding of law, which the theorist who grasps it either subscribes to or rejects *as a legal theorist*. I am not saying that the legal theorist has to be subservient to the understanding of the point or function of law held among those who participate in a given legal/political culture. But by rejecting it, he competes with them; he should not think of himself as working at a different theoretical level.

Why is this? It is not because laws themselves are normative: that would be germane only to (1). And so Postema is wrong if he means to suggest that all this is true because 'the law by design concerns itself with individual and social interests, values rights, and goals'.[42] Instead, it is true because the very concept of law is normative, and one cannot use or understand that concept apart from participation in a form of life that sorts political practices in various ways—for example, finding some point in distinguishing (as I said earlier) between rule by law and other forms of governance.

VI

A wrinkle. The formulation with which I ended Section V can be understood in two ways. When we talk about a form of life that sorts political practices in various ways, and finds some point in distinguishing between rule by law and other forms of governance, we might have in mind (A) a form of life confined to scholars and theorists and oriented normatively to the pragmatics of theory-building, or we might have in mind (B) a form of life that attributes moral, social and political importance to the distinction. If what we have in mind is (A) only, then normative positivism becomes a rather trivial thesis. For, of course, every community of scholars has a sense that the concepts and categories they use are theoretically useful; otherwise they would choose different

---

[42] *Bentham*, 335.

concepts and categories.[43] That does not mean that the specific values and concerns in (A) are themselves trivial.[44] It means only that, as Joseph Raz has pointed out, the role of values in legal philosophy cannot be confined to (A):

> [I]t would be wrong to conclude . . . that one judges the success of an analysis of the concept of law by its theoretical sociological fruitfulness. To do so is to miss the point that, unlike concepts like 'mass'; and 'electron', 'the law' is a concept used by people to understand themselves. . . . It is a major task of legal theory to advance our understanding of society by helping us understand how people understand themselves.[45]

Normative positivism is interested, then, in *law* as a concept whose deployment in jurisprudential analysis is connected with the values that are engaged when citizens deploy it; we are not simply interested in the concept of law because of its connection with the technical or intra-theoretic values of jurisprudence.[46]

Once that is granted, what I have tried to emphasize in this paper (particularly the last section or two) is that citizens use the concept *law* not just to grasp particular obligations that they might have or the rules of particular juridical processes in which they may be involved. They use it also to grasp the desirability of being governed in certain ways (e.g. by law) rather than other ways (e.g. by decree or managerial direction). And they draw these distinctions not just as political scientists (interested in fruitful taxonomy) but as active citizens and politicians interested practically in the implications for their lives of various modes of governance.

So: we are trying to understand how people understand themselves. However, in his discussion of these issues, Raz makes the further point that the theorist's task is not simply to echo or endorse the use to which ordinary citizens put *law* as a normative concept.

> The concept of law is part of our culture and of our cultural traditions. It plays a role in the way in which ordinary people as well as the legal profession understand their own and other people's actions. It is part of the way they 'conceptualize'

---

[43] For Hart's acknowledgment of (A), see 'Comment', in Ruth Gavison (ed.), *Issues in Contemporary Legal Philosophy* (Oxford: Clarendon Press, 1987), 39. There is a good discussion of this acknowledgment in Perry, 'Interpretation and Methodology', 118.

[44] Theoretical values are very important. And, as Coleman has emphasized to me in conversation, they include values and principles that are highly normative: norms of logic, cogent argument, theoretical interest, etc. All that is trivial is the proposition that even *soi-disant* descriptive theory must be informed by such values.

[45] 'Authority, Law and Morality', in *Ethics in the Public Domain: Essays in the Morality of Law and Politics* (Oxford: Clarendon Press, 1994), 221.

[46] But perhaps we should also note the possible overlap between (A) and (B). Gerald Postema points out, in 'Jurisprudence as Practical Philosophy', *Legal Theory* 4 (1998), at 332, that there might be intimate connections between moral and meta-theoretical values. See also Perry, 'Hart's Methodological Positivism', 461 ff.

social reality. But the culture and tradition of which the concept is a part provide it with neither sharply defined contours nor clearly identifiable focus. Various, sometimes conflicting, ideas are displayed in them. It falls to legal theory to pick on those which are central and significant to the way the concept plays its role in people's understanding of society, to elaborate and explain them.[47]

Someone might count Raz's own 1977 discussion of 'the rule of law' as an instance of this: taking an embedded cultural understanding of an important set of social values associated with the idea of law, and tidying it up—reconstructing it—to make it more useful, not just for the theorist, but for the citizens and statesmen who use it to critique various events and practices in the governance of their society.[48] That would not be quite accurate, because Raz seems to indicate in that essay that he thinks 'the rule of law' is best understood as a label for certain distinctive virtues that law may or may not have, rather than as an idea informing our understanding of the concept of law itself.[49] But if he were to address moral and political ideas that he thought imbue our understanding of the concept of law itself, it would not be surprising if they turned out to need very similar reconstruction, tidying up, and disaggregation.

VII

I am sure there are many flaws in the argument I have presented. The one that is most striking to me is the implicit suggestion that in order to do positivist jurisprudence in the normative mode, one has to view law as *a good thing*. I seem to have argued myself into the position of saying that, even if a legal positivist wants to deny the justice or virtue of particular laws, he has to organize his jurisprudence around the idea that law as such is a desirable institution; otherwise (I seem to be saying) his jurisprudential methodology is sterile and merely semantic. Can that be right? Is it not possible to combine legal positivism and, say, anarchist hostility to law?[50]

   There are several points to be cleared up here. First, the force of the methodological arguments set out in the preceding sections would actually be appeased if 'law' were taken to be a negatively loaded concept

---

[47] 'Authority, Law and Morality', 221.

[48] See Joseph Raz, 'The Rule of Law and Its Virtue', in *The Authority of Law: Essays on Law and Morality* (Oxford: Clarendon Press, 1979), 210 ff.

[49] Evidently Lon Fuller thinks that something like the idea of the rule of law imbues the concept of law itself. And I have suggested something similar at various points in this essay.

[50] I hope that the discussion in the rest of this section will help allay some of the concerns about 'wishful thinking [and] sweet coating of moral rationalization' in connection with Dworkin's charitable approach to the interpretive functions of jurisprudence—concerns expressed e.g. in Waluchow, *Inclusive Legal Positivism*, 17 ff.

(like the concept 'totalitarianism') so far as its normative valence was concerned. Even though few people support totalitarianism, it is implausible to think there could be a purely descriptive analysis of the concept, because the proper use of the word 'totalitarianism' is to mark a politically and morally important distinction between types of regime: 'totalitarian' is supposed to pick out a distinctive form of evil. And one who thought that law was bad (and that the proper use of 'law' was to warn other anarchists or people wavering on the cusp of anarchism that a certain distinctively bad thing was in the offing) might say something similar. His jurisprudence, then, would still be normative, though its normativity would not be expressed in terms of function.[51] Its normative valence would be cautionary.

Secondly, even on the affirmative side, the normative positivist need not be committed to the thesis that law is, in E. P. Thompson's words, 'an *unqualified* human good'.[52] In a recent paper,[53] I have drawn attention to passages in *The Concept of Law* where observations about the advantages of legal over pre-legal arrangements are balanced by Hart's awareness of the costs of that transition and various dangers (including moral dangers) associated with law as a mode of governance. Now, as Stephen Perry has rightly pointed out,[54] the former account—i.e. *The Concept of Law*'s account of 'the defects' of a pre-legal society and the way in which the establishment of law remedies those defects[55]—gives the lie to Hart's claim to be engaged in a purely descriptive jurisprudence.[56] In a footnote, Jules Coleman acknowledges the interest and importance of arguments to the effect 'that Hart, contrary to his own reflections on the matter, did not engage in or faithfully execute a descriptivist methodology',[57] but he says that this does not show that there cannot be a descriptive positivism, only at most that Hart failed to produce one. That is fair enough. The question I want to ask, however, is this: is Perry's point undermined by Hart's acknowledgement in *The Concept of Law* of the following 'sobering truth'?

the step from the simple form of society, where primary rules of obligation are the only means of social control, into the legal world with its centrally organized

---

[51] And he would *definitely* need the benefit of my distinction, in Section V above, between (1) the role of the jurist's grasp of the internal point of view in regard to following a legal rule and (2) the role of the jurist's grasp of the internal point of view in relation to an account of the value of a legal system!

[52] *Whigs and Hunters: The Origin of the Black Act* (Harmondsworth: Penguin, 1975), 266.

[53] 'All We Like Sheep', *Canadian Journal of Law and Jurisprudence* 12 (1999), 169–86.

[54] 'Hart's Methodological Positivism', 437 ff.

[55] pp. 91–9.

[56] Perry writes ('Hart's Methodological Positivism', 438): 'The statement that a regime of primary rules has defects, like the statement that these defects are remedied by the introduction of a rule of recognition and other secondary rules, is an evaluative claim.'

[57] 'Incorporationism, Conventionality, and the Practical Difference Thesis', 395, n. 26.

legislature, courts, officials, and sanctions brings its solid gains at a certain cost. The gains are those of adaptability to change, certainty, and efficiency, and these are immense; the cost is the risk that the centrally organized power may well be used for the oppression of numbers with whose support it can dispense, in a way that the simpler regime of primary rules could not.[58]

Hart's account of law's institutional character leads him to see that those who make and can recognize enacted law may use that capacity and that specialist knowledge for their own benefit, and to the detriment of the rest, who find they know less and less about the detailed basis on which their society is organized. He sees that the specialization of normative authority may thus exacerbate whatever exploitation and hierarchy exist in a given society apart from its legalization, and that it may well make possible certain forms of oppression and injustice that were simply unthinkable without it.[59] Does this acknowledgement cancel out (so to speak) the affirmatively evaluative aspect of Hart's claim that law remedies certain defects in pre-legal society (the claim whose methodological significance Perry emphasized), leaving us with an account of law that is evaluatively neutral all things considered? The answer surely is 'No': an evaluative account does not become non-evaluative simply because it includes negative as well as affirmative evaluative elements.[60]

But it does mean that the normatively positivist aspect of this theory has to be understood quite carefully. Hart claims that the emergence of law (1) brings with it certain dangers and at the same time (2) helps secure certain benefits for a society. Unless he is the anarchist we entertained a page or two back,[61] the normative positivist is likely to focus on claim (2)—leaving (1) aside, not because he necessarily doubts its truth or importance, but because he is not promising at this stage to produce an all-things-considered account of law. Focusing on (2)—the benefits that law may secure—his claim is that law cannot secure these benefits unless it is set up in a way that enables people, by and large, to determine what the law is on a given subject without having to exercise moral judgment. Even if (2) does not ultimately outweigh (1), or even if the balance between them varies precariously from situation to situation, still this normatively positivist view of (2) is important. For now, the suggestion is

---

[58] p. 202.

[59] See ibid. 117, 200 ff. See also Waldron, 'All We Like Sheep', 174–81.

[60] However, I do stand by the claim, made at the beginning and the end of 'All We Like Sheep', that this recognition of costs as well as benefits and the issue of the balance between them, does also provide the basis for a *substantive* version of the separability thesis that has little to do with concerns about jurisprudential methodology. So: the separability thesis performs a number of important functions, some of them methodological, some of them substantial.

[61] See n. 51 above and accompanying text.

that law cannot provide any benefits to balance against the costs that accompany its introduction unless it is set up in a positivist way.[62]

VIII

I have mostly resisted the temptation to associate the discussion in this paper with Ronald Dworkin's thesis in *Law's Empire* that the agenda for legal theory is best understood in terms of the interpretation of a particular claim about the conditions under which the use of collective force in society is justified.[63] It seemed to me worth considering the methodological implications of presenting positivism as a normative thesis at a slightly more abstract level than that. But I want to end with a word or two about the approach taken in *Law's Empire*, for Dworkin's thesis is evidently intended as a general account of jurisprudence, under which the methodology of what I have called normative positivism would be a special case.[64]

Dworkin believes that legal positivism is best understood as a particular set of claims about the relation between (a) social norms that can be identified without the exercise of moral judgment and (b) the moral importance of constraining the use of collective force in certain ways.[65] Now, he argues in chapter 4 of *Law's Empire* that the relation Bentham and others have desired between (a) and (b) cannot in fact be established; and that is to be expected, for although Dworkin identifies what he sees as the normative agenda for positivist jurisprudence, he himself is not a positivist. But maybe actual real-life normative positivists feel they have been sold short here. For it is possible that they do not accept Dworkin's (b), or the account he attributes to them of the specific relation between (a) and

---

[62] I hope it is not necessary at this stage to re-emphasize that we are talking here not about a balance of retail costs and benefits—e.g. in the sense of an overall likelihood that a particular law will be just—but rather about a balance of wholesale costs and benefits associated with the operation of law as such, considered in abstraction from its contents.

[63] Dworkin, *Law's Empire*, 94: 'Governments have goals: they aim to make the nations they govern prosperous or powerful or religious or eminent.... They use the collective force they monopolize to these and other ends.... Law insists that force not be used or withheld, no matter how useful that would be to ends in view, no matter how beneficial or noble these ends, except as licensed or required by individual rights and responsibilities flowing from past political decisions about when collective force is justified.... Conceptions of law refine [that idea]. Each conception furnishes connected answers to three questions posed by the concept. First, is the supposed link between law and coercion justified at all? Is there any point to requiring public force to be used only in ways conforming to rights and responsibilities that "flow from" past political decisions? Second, if there is such a point, what is it? Third, what reading of "flow from"—what notion of consistency with past decisions best serves it?'

[64] Hart, of course, notices this; his Postscript is written largely as a response to Dworkin.

[65] See *Law's Empire*, 114 ff.

(b). They may think about the function or value of law in a way that does not involve this strong emphasis on political legitimacy. Perhaps they understand it, instead, in terms of the need for social coordination or in terms of the pragmatic usefulness of authority.[66] Or perhaps they understand the relation between (a) and whatever *they* think of as the function or value of law in a way that does not involve the strong claims concerning conventionalism that Dworkin attributes to them. I am not one of those who thinks that Ronald Dworkin's characterization of opposing theories is unerringly caricatural, or that there could not be a positivist who held the view that is criticized in chapter 4 of *Law's Empire*. (As a matter of fact, I think Jeremy Bentham probably did hold it, and that Dworkin has done his positivist opponents a service by insisting that this interpretation be discussed, even if it is alongside whatever 'semantic' or purely 'conceptual' thesis the modern positivists say they want to maintain.) Still, it may not have been helpful for Dworkin to insist that legal positivists face a stark choice between the particular interpretive position ('conventionalism') which he sets up in chapter 4 and some sterile semantic or conceptual thesis. That is why I think it is good that, for the most part, Hart's Postscript prescinded from these particular differences and concentrated its discussion on the more general methodological issue that evidently underlies Dworkin's particular account.

For it is surely worth discussing the general shape or character of a positivist jurisprudence, quite apart from the particular content that fills that shape. After all, legal positivism is a label associated with a very broad cluster of theories. At the level of the 'positivity' of law that interests legal positivists: some are interested in the separation of law and morality at the retail level;[67] some are interested in the textual and/or rule-like qualities of law, for reasons that go beyond or stand apart from the separability thesis;[68] some are interested in law as a distinctive insti-

---

[66] To the extent that Joseph Raz is a normative positivist, it is the law's aspiration to authoritativeness that drives his account of why (a) is important: see 'Authority, Law, and Morality'. By the way, the only reason I hesitate about labelling Raz a normative positivist is that it is not clear from his recent work whether the premiss of his account is (1) Law claims authority (which is a premiss that may be deduced simply by analysing the concept *law*), or whether it is (2) It is a good thing to organize a society with norms that can claim to be authoritative. I suspect that Raz's premiss is (2). But he seems quite careful in places not to be seen to be going beyond (1). His overall position remains unclear to me.

[67] And even just focusing on the separation thesis by itself: some may be interested in it for reasons that have to do with moral scepticism (e.g. Hans Kelsen, in *The Pure Theory of Law*, trans. by Max Knight (Berkeley, Calif.: University of California Press, 1970), 59–69); some may be interested in it for reasons that have to do with the political significance of disagreement (see Waldron, *Law and Disagreement*); some may be interested in it because of its relation to authority (Raz, 'Authority, Law and Morality'); some may be even interested in it for reasons that have to do with liberal neutrality or the exigencies of political liberalism.

[68] See e.g. Frederick Schauer, *Playing by the Rules* (Oxford: Clarendon Press, 1991), chs. 7 and 8. See also Frederick Schauer, 'Positivism as Pariah', in George, *The Autonomy of Law*.

tution and its institutional characteristics;[69] and some are interested in the ethical autonomy of various legal-professional roles, such as judging.[70] (We will call this 'Menu A'.) And at the level of what they see as the affirmative value or function of law (or legality or the rule of law), some normative theorists are interested in peace,[71] some are interested in predictability (and other values connected with predictability, such as utilitarian prosperity or Hayekian autonomy),[72] some are interested in the control of power, some are interested in democracy, some are interested in political obligation and/or legitimacy, and some are interested in the conditions of social coordination. (We will call this 'Menu B'.)

Those who resist the general jurisprudential methodology associated with normative positivism may do so because they fear that a particular one of these interests from Menu B is being foisted on legal positivists— as though they must all have the programmatic interests that, say, Bentham or Hobbes had, or not count as real positivists at all.[73] But the fear is groundless. Those like Campbell, Perry, and Postema who emphasize the normative dimension of positivist jurisprudence are not trying to foist their particular normative programme onto positivists in general (though no doubt they have their own views on the normative issues). They are simply saying that the selection of something from Menu A as the aspect of positivity to focus on in one's jurisprudence is not intelligible on its own, and cannot credibly be presented as a matter of pure 'analysis'. To be intelligible, it must be motivated. Accordingly, they are saying, we do not fully understand a positivist theory of law until we can map a choice from Menu A onto a choice from Menu B. Thus whether or not one accepts the pair of choices that Dworkin foists on positivists in chapter 4 of *Law's Empire*, in his attempt to reconstruct their jurisprudence as an interpretive position, one can see the point of such a reconstruction, and envisage a number of ways, not just one, in which it may be expressive of the positivist agenda.

---

[69] e.g. N. MacCormick and O. Weinberger, *An Institutional Theory of Law: New Approaches to Legal Positivism* (Dordrecht: Reidel, 1986), and Raz in *The Authority of Law*.

[70] e.g. Campbell, *Legal Theory*.

[71] e.g. Hobbes in *Leviathan*.

[72] In rather different ways, Bentham and Hayek (in *The Constitution of Liberty*).

[73] This seems to be true of W. J. Waluchow in his essay 'The Weak Social Thesis', *Oxford Journal of Legal Studies* 9 (1989), 38.

Index